T0234922

Building a Data Warehouse

With Examples in SQL Server

Vincent Rainardi

Apress®

Building a Data Warehouse: With Examples in SQL Server

Copyright © 2008 by Vincent Rainardi

ISBN-13 : 978-1-4302-1196-9

ISBN-10 : 1-4302-1196-2

ISBN-13 (electronic): 978-1-4302-0527-2

ISBN-10 (electronic): 1-4302-0527-X

Lead Editor: Jeffrey Pepper
Technical Reviewers: Bill Hamilton and Asif Sayed
Editorial Board: Steve Anglin, Ewan Buckingham, Tony Campbell, Gary Cornell, Jonathan Gennick, Jason Gilmore, Kevin Goff, Jonathan Hassell, Matthew Moodie, Joseph Ottinger, Jeffrey Pepper, Ben Renow-Clarke, Dominic Shakeshaft, Matt Wade, Tom Welsh
Senior Project Manager: Tracy Brown Collins
Copy Editor: Kim Wimpsett
Associate Production Director: Kari Brooks-Copony
Production Editor: Kelly Winquist
Compositor: Linda Weidemann, Wolf Creek Press
Proofreader: Linda Marousek
Indexer: Ron Strauss
Artist: April Milne
Cover Designer: Kurt Krames
Manufacturing Director: Tom Debolski

For information on translations, please contact Apress directly at 2855 Telegraph Avenue, Suite 600, Berkeley, CA 94705. Phone 510-549-5930, fax 510-549-5939, e-mail info@apress.com, or visit http://www.apress.com.

The source code for this book is available to readers at http://www.apress.com.

For my lovely wife, Ivana.

Contents at a Glance

Contents

About the Author

VINCENT RAINARDI is a data warehouse architect and developer with more than 12 years of experience in IT. He started working with data warehousing in 1996 when he was working for Accenture. He has been working with Microsoft SQL Server since 2000. He worked for Lastminute.com (part of the Travelocity group) until October 2007. He now works as a data warehousing consultant in London specializing in SQL Server. He is a member of The Data Warehousing Institute (TDWI) and regularly writes data warehousing articles for SQLServerCentral.com.

Preface

Friends and colleagues who want to start learning data warehousing sometimes ask me to recommend a practical book about the subject matter. They are not new to the database world; most of them are either DBAs or developers/consultants, but they have never built a data warehouse. They want a book that is practical and aimed at beginners, one that contains all the basic essentials. There are many data warehousing books on the market, but they usually cover a specialized topic such as clickstream, ETL, dimensional modeling, data mining, OLAP, or project management and therefore a beginner would need to buy five to six books to understand the complete spectrum of data warehousing. Other books cover multiple aspects, but they are not as practical as they need to be, targeting executives and project managers instead of DBAs and developers.

Because of that void, I took a pen (well, a laptop really) and spent a whole year writing in order to provide a practical, down-to-earth book containing all the essential subjects of building a data warehouse, with many examples and illustrations from projects that are easy to understand. The book can be used to build your first data warehouse straightaway; it covers all aspects of data warehousing, including approach, architecture, data modeling, ETL, data quality, and OLAP. I also describe some practical issues that I have encountered in my experience—issues that you'll also likely encounter in your first data warehousing project—along with the solutions.

It is not possible to show examples, code, and illustrations for all the different database platforms, so I had to choose a specific platform. Oracle and SQL Server provide complete end-to-end solutions including the database, ETL, reporting, and OLAP, and after discussions with my editor, we decided to base the examples on SQL Server 2005, while also making them applicable to future versions of SQL Server such as 2008. I apologize in advance that the examples do not run on SQL Server 2000; there is just too big a gap in terms of data warehousing facilities, such as SSIS, between 2000 and 2005.

Throughout this book, together we will be designing and building a data warehouse for a case study called Amadeus Entertainment. A data warehouse consist of many parts, such as the data model, physical databases, ETL, data quality, metadata, cube, application, and so on. In each chapter, I will cover each part one by one. I will cover the theory related to that part, and then I will show how to build that part for the case study. Specifically, Chapter 1 introduces what a data warehouse is and what the benefits are. In Chapters 2–6, we will design the architecture, define the requirements, and create the data model and physical databases, including the SQL Server configuration. In Chapters 7–10 we will populate the data stores using SSIS, as well as discuss data quality and metadata. Chapters 11–12 are about getting the data out by using Reporting Services and Analysis Services cubes. In Chapters 13–15, I'll discuss the application of data warehouse for BI and CRM as well as CDI, unstructured data, and search. I close the book with testing and administering a data warehouse in Chapters 16–17.

The supplementary material (available on the book's download page on the Apress web site, http://www.apress.com) provides all the necessary material to build the data warehouse for the case study. Specifically, it contains the following folders:

Scripts: Contains the scripts to build the source system and the data warehouse, as explained in Chapters 5 and 6.

Source system: Contains the source system databases required to build the data warehouse for the case study in Chapters 7 and 8.

ETL: Contains the SSIS packages to import data into the data warehouse. Chapters 7 and 8 explain how to build these packages.

Report: Contains the SSRS reports explained in Chapter 11.

Cubes: Contains the SSAS projects explained in Chapter 12.

Data: Contains the backup of data warehouse database (the DDS) and Analysis Services cube, which are used for reporting, OLAP, BI, and data mining in Chapters 11, 12, and 13.

CHAPTER 1

■ ■ ■

Introduction to Data Warehousing

In this chapter, I will discuss what a data warehouse is, how data warehouses are used today, and the future trends of data warehousing.

I will begin by defining what a data warehouse is. Then I'll walk you through a diagram of a typical data warehouse system, discussing its components and how the data flows through those components. I will also discuss the simplest possible form of a data warehouse. After you have an idea about what a data warehouse is, I will discuss the definition in more detail. I will go through each bit of the definition individually, exploring that bit in depth. I will also talk about other people's definitions.

Then, I will move on to how data warehouses are used today. I will discuss business intelligence, customer relationship management, and data mining as the popular applications of data warehousing. I will also talk about the role of master data management and customer data integration in data warehousing.

Finally, I will talk about the future trends of data warehousing, such as unstructured data, search, real-time data warehouses, and service-oriented architecture. By the end of this chapter, you will have a general understanding of data warehousing.

What Is a Data Warehouse?

Let's begin by defining what a data warehouse is. A data warehouse is a system that *retrieves* and *consolidates* data *periodically* from the source systems into a *dimensional* or *normalized data store*. It usually keeps years of *history* and is *queried* for *business intelligence* or other *analytical activities*. It is typically updated in *batches*, not every time a transaction happens in the source system.

In the next few pages, I will discuss each of the italicized terms in the previous paragraph one by one. But for now, I'll walk you through a diagram of a data warehouse system, discussing it component by component and how the data flows through those components. After this short walk-through, I will discuss each term in the previous definition, including the differences between dimensional and normalized data stores, why you store the data in the data store, and why data warehouses are updated in batches. Figure 1-1 shows a diagram of a data warehouse system, including the applications.

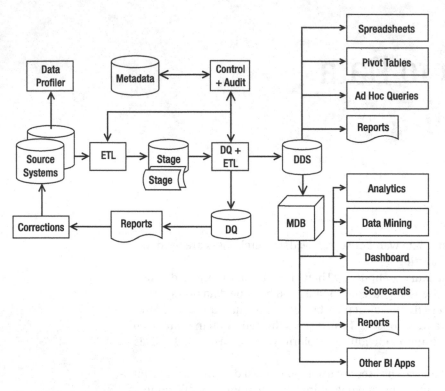

Figure 1-1. *A diagram of a data warehouse system*

Let's go through the diagram in Figure 1-1, component by component, from left to right. The source systems are the OLTP systems that contain the data you want to load into the data warehouse. Online Transaction Processing (OLTP) is a system whose main purpose is to capture and store the business transactions. The source systems' data is examined using a data profiler to understand the characteristics of the data. A data profiler is a tool that has the capability to analyze data, such as finding out how many rows are in each table, how many rows contain NULL values, and so on.

The extract, transform, and load (ETL) system then brings data from various source systems into a staging area. ETL is a system that has the capability to connect to the source systems, read the data, transform the data, and load it into a target system (the target system doesn't have to be a data warehouse). The ETL system then integrates, transforms, and loads the data into a dimensional data store (DDS). A DDS is a database that stores the data warehouse data in a different format than OLTP. The reason for getting the data from the source system into the DDS and then querying the DDS instead of querying the source system directly is that in a DDS the data is arranged in a dimensional format that is more suitable for analysis. The second reason is because a DDS contains integrated data from several source systems.

When the ETL system loads the data into the DDS, the data quality rules do various data quality checks. Bad data is put into the data quality (DQ) database to be reported and then corrected in the source systems. Bad data can also be automatically corrected or tolerated if it is within a certain limit. The ETL system is managed and orchestrated by the control system, based on the sequence, rules, and logic stored in the metadata. The metadata is a database containing information about the data structure, the data meaning, the data usage, the data quality rules, and other information about the data.

The audit system logs the system operations and usage into the metadata database. The audit system is part of the ETL system that monitors the operational activities of the ETL processes and logs their operational statistics. It is used for understanding what happened during the ETL process.

Users use various front-end tools such as spreadsheets, pivot tables, reporting tools, and SQL query tools to retrieve and analyze the data in a DDS. Some applications operate on a multidimensional database format. For these applications, the data in the DDS is loaded into multidimensional databases (MDBs), which are also known as *cubes*. A multidimensional database is a form of database where the data is stored in cells and the position of each cell is defined by a number of variables called *dimensions*. Each cell represents a business event, and the values of the dimensions show when and where this event happened.

Figure 1-2 shows a cube with three dimensions, or axes: Time, Store, and Customer. Assume that each dimension, or axis, has 100 segments, so there are $100 \times 100 \times 100 = 1$ million cells in that cube. Each cell represents an event where a customer is buying something from a store at a particular time. Imagine that in each cell there are three numbers: Sales Value (the total value of the products that the customer purchased), Cost (the cost of goods sold + proportioned overheads), and Profit (the difference between the sales value and cost). This cube is an example of a multidimensional database.

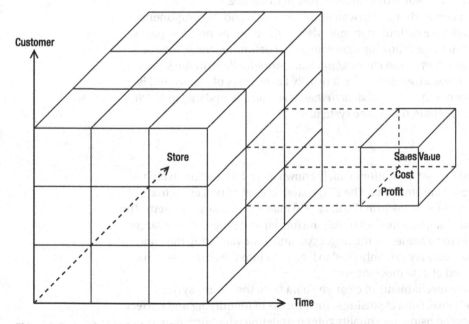

Figure 1-2. *A cube with three dimensions*

Tools such as analytics applications, data mining, scorecards, dashboards, multidimensional reporting tools, and other BI tools can retrieve data interactively from multidimensional databases. They retrieve the data to produce various features and results on the front-end screens that enable the users to get a deeper understanding about their businesses. An example of an analytic application is to analyze the sales by time, customer, and product. The users can analyze the revenue and cost for a certain month, region, and product type.

Not all data warehouse systems have all the components pictured previously. Even if a data warehouse system does not have a data quality mechanism, a multidimensional database, any analytics applications, a front-end application, a control system or audit system, metadata, or a stage, you can still call it a data warehouse system. In its simplest form, it is similar to Figure 1-3.

Figure 1-3. *Simplest form of a data warehouse system*

In this case, the data warehouse system contains only an ETL system and a dimensional data store. The source system is not part of the data warehouse system. This is pretty much the minimum. If you take out just one more component, you cannot call it a data warehouse system anymore. In Figure 1-3, even though there is no front-end application such as reports or analytic applications, users can still query the data in the DDS by issuing direct SQL select statements using generic database query tools such as the one hosted in SQL Server Management Studio. I will be discussing data warehouse architecture in Chapter 2.

Now that you have an idea about what a data warehouse system is and its components, let's take a look at the data warehouse definition in more detail. Again, in the next few pages, I will discuss each italicized term in the following data warehouse definition one by one: a data warehouse is a system that *retrieves* and *consolidates* data *periodically* from the source systems into a *dimensional* or *normalized data store*. It usually keeps years of *history* and is *queried* for *business intelligence* or other *analytical activities*. It is typically updated in *batches*, not every time a transaction happens in the source system.

Retrieves Data

The data retrieval is performed by a set of routines widely known as an ETL system, which is an abbreviation for extract, transform, and load. The ETL system is a set of processes that retrieve data from the source systems, transform the data, and load it into a target system. The transformation can be used for changing the data to suit the format and criteria of the target system, for deriving new values to be loaded to the target system, or for validating the data from the source system. ETL systems are not only used to load data into the data warehouse. They are widely used for any kind of data movements.

Most ETL systems also have mechanisms to clean the data from the source system before putting it into the warehouse. Data cleansing is the process of identifying and correcting dirty data. This is implemented using data quality rules that define what dirty data is. After the data is extracted from the source system but before the data is loaded into the warehouse, the data is examined using these rules. If the rule determines that the data is correct, then it is loaded into the warehouse. If the rule determines that the data is incorrect, then there are three options: it can be rejected, corrected, or allowed to be loaded into the warehouse. Which action is appropriate for a particular piece of data depends on the situation, the risk level, the rule type (error or warning), and so on. I will go through data cleansing and data quality in more detail in Chapter 9.

There is another alternative approach to ETL, known as extract, load, and transform (ELT). In this approach, the data is loaded into the data warehouse first in its raw format. The transformations, lookups, deduplications, and so on, are performed inside the data warehouse. Unlike the ETL approach, the ELT approach does not need an ETL server. This approach is usually implemented to take advantage of powerful data warehouse database engines such as massively parallel processing (MPP) systems. I will be discussing more about the ELT approach in Chapter 7.

Consolidates Data

A company can have many transactional systems. For example, a bank may use 15 different applications for its services, one for loan processing, one for customer service, one for tellers/cashiers, one for ATMs, one for bonds, one for ISA, one for savings, one for private banking, one for the trading floor, one for life insurance, one for home insurance, one for mortgages, one for the call center, one for internal accounts, and one for fraud detection. Performing (for example) customer profitability analysis across these different applications would be very difficult.

A data warehouse consolidates many transactional systems. The key difference between a data warehouse and a front-office transactional system is that the data in the data warehouse is integrated. This consolidation or integration should take into account the data availability (some data is available in several systems but not in others), time ranges (data in different systems has different validity periods), different definitions (the term *total weekly revenue* in one system may have a different meaning from *total weekly revenue* in other systems), conversion (different systems may have a different unit of measure or currency), and matching (merging data based on common identifiers between different systems).

Let's go through the previous concepts one by one:

Data availability: When consolidating data from different source systems, it is possible that a piece of data is available in one system but is not in the other system. For example, system A may have seven address fields (address1, address2, address3, city, county, ZIP, and country), but system B does not have the address3 field and the country field. In system A, an order may have two levels—order header and order line. However, in system B, an order has four levels—order header, order bundle, order line item, and financial components. So when consolidating data across different transaction systems, you need to be aware of unavailable columns and missing levels in the hierarchy. In the previous examples, you can leave address3 blank in the target and set the country to a default value. In the order hierarchy example, you can consolidate into two levels, order header and order line.

Time ranges: The same piece of data exists in different systems, but they have different time periods. So, you need to be careful when consolidating them. You always need to examine what time period is applicable to which data before you consolidate the data. Otherwise, you are at risk of having inaccurate data in the warehouse because you mixed different time periods. For example, say in system A the average supplier overhead cost is calculated weekly, but in system B it is calculated monthly. You can't just consolidate them. In this example, you need to go back upstream to get the individual components that make up the average supplier overhead cost in both systems and add them up first.

Definitions: Sometimes the same data may contain different things. In system A, a column called "Total Order Value" may contain taxes, discounts, credit card charges, and delivery charges, whereas in system B it does not contain delivery charges. In system A, the term *weekly traffic* may refer to unique web site visitors, whereas in system B it means nonunique web site visitors. In this matter, you always need to examine the *meaning* of each piece of data. Just because they have the same name doesn't mean they are the same. This is important because you could have inaccurate data or meaningless data in the data warehouse if you consolidate data with different meanings.

Conversion: When consolidating data across different source systems, sometimes you need to do conversion because the data in the source system is in different units of measure. If you add them up without converting them first, then you will have incorrect data in the warehouse. In some cases, the conversion rate is fixed (always the same value), but in other cases the conversion rate changes from time to time. If it changes from time to time, you need to know what time period to use when converting. For example, the conversion between the time in one country to another country is affected by daylight savings time, so you need to know the date to be able to do the conversion. In addition, the conversion rate between one currency and another currency fluctuates every day, so when converting, you need to know when the transaction happened.

Matching: Matching is a process of determining whether a piece of data in one system is the same as the data in another system. Matching is important because if you match the wrong data, you will have inaccurate data in the data warehouse. For example, say you want to consolidate the data for customer 1 in system A with the data for customer 1 in system B. In this case, you need to determine first whether those two are the same customer. If you match the wrong customers, the transaction from one customer could be mixed up with the data from another customer. The matching criteria are different from company to company. Sometimes criteria are simple, such as using user IDs, customer IDs, or account IDs. But sometimes it is quite complex, such as name + e-mail address + address. The logic of determining a match can be simply based on the equation sign (=) to identify an exact match. It can also be based on fuzzy logic or matching rules. (I will talk more about data matching in Chapter 9.)

When building the data warehouse, you have to deal with all these data integration issues.

Periodically

The data retrieval and the consolidation do not happen only once; they happen many times and usually at regular intervals, such as daily or a few times a day. If the data retrieval happens only once, then the data will become obsolete, and after some time it will not be useful.

You can determine the period of data retrieval and consolation based on the business requirements and the frequency of data updates in the source systems. The data retrieval interval needs to be the same as the source system's data update frequency. If the source system is updated once a day, you need to set the data retrieval once a day. There is no point extracting the data from that source system several times a day.

On the other hand, you need to make sure the data retrieval interval satisfies the business requirements. For example, if the business needs the product profitability report once a week, then the data from various source systems needs to be consolidated at least once a week. Another example is when a company states to its customer that it will take 24 hours to cancel the marketing subscriptions. Then the data in the CRM data warehouse needs to be updated a few times a day; otherwise, you risk sending marketing campaigns to customers who have already canceled their subscriptions.

Dimensional Data Store

A data warehouse is a system that retrieves data from source systems and puts it into a dimensional data store or a normalized data store. Yes, some data warehouses are in dimensional format, but some data warehouses are in normalized format. Let's go through both formats and the differences between them.

A DDS is one or several databases containing a collection of dimensional data marts. A dimensional data mart is a group of related fact tables and their corresponding dimension tables containing the measurements of business events categorized by their dimensions.

A dimensional data store is denormalized, and the dimensions are conformed. Conformed dimensions mean either they are exactly the same dimension table or one is the subset of the other. Dimension A is said to be a subset of dimension B when all columns of dimension A exist in dimension B and all rows of dimension A exist in dimension B.

A dimensional data store can be implemented physically in the form of several different schemas. Examples of dimensional data store schemas are a star schema (shown in Figure 1-4), a snowflake schema, and a galaxy schema. In a star schema, a dimension does not have a subtable (a subdimension). In a snowflake schema, a dimension can have a subdimension. The purpose of having a subdimension is to minimize redundant data. A galaxy schema is also known as a *fact constellation schema*. In a galaxy schema, you have two or more related fact tables surrounded by common dimensions. The benefit of having a star schema is that it is simpler than snowflake and galaxy schemas, making it easier for the ETL processes to load the data into DDS. The benefit of a snowflake schema is that some analytics applications work better with a snowflake schema compared to a star schema or galaxy schema. The other benefit of a snowflake schema is less data redundancy, so less disk space is required. The benefit of galaxy schema is the ability to model the business events more accurately by using several fact tables.

Note A data store can be physically implemented as more than one database, in other words, two databases, three databases, and so on. The contrary is also true: two or more data stores can be physically implemented as one database. When designing the physical layer of the data store, usually you tend to implement each data store as one database. But you need to consider physical database design factors such as the physical data model, database platform, storage requirement, relational integrity, and backup requirements when determining whether you will put several data stores in one database or split a data store into several databases. Putting one data store in one database is not always the best solution. (I will discuss physical database design in Chapter 6.)

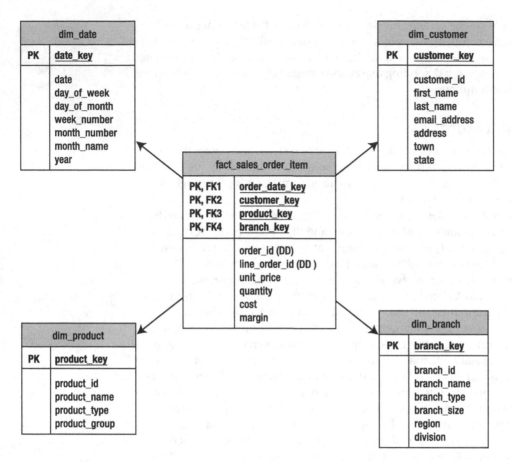

Figure 1-4. *Star schema dimensional data store*

Normalized Data Store

Other types of data warehouses put the data not in a dimensional data store but in a normalized data store. A normalized data store is one or more relational databases with little or no data redundancy. A relational database is a database that consists of entity tables with parent-child relationships between them.

Normalization is a process of removing data redundancy by implementing normalization rules. There are five degrees of normal forms, from the first normal form to the fifth normal form. A normalized data store is usually in third normal form or higher, such as fourth or fifth normal form. I will discuss the normalization process and normalization rules in Chapter 5.

Figure 1-5 shows an example of a normalized data store. It is the normalized version of the same data as displayed in Figure 1-4.

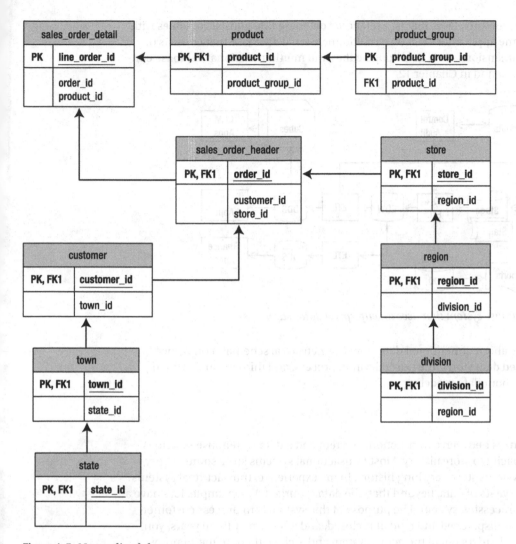

Figure 1-5. *Normalized data store*

A dimensional data store is a better format to store data in the warehouse for the purpose of querying and analyzing data than a normalized data store. This is because it is simpler (one level deep in all directions in star schema) and gives better query performance. A normalized data store is a better format to integrate data from various source systems, especially in third normal form and higher. This is because there is only one place to update without data redundancy like in a dimensional data store.

The normalized data store is usually used for an enterprise data warehouse; from there the data is then loaded into dimensional data stores for query and analysis purposes. Figure 1-6 shows a data warehouse system with a normalized data store used for an enterprise data warehouse (labeled as "EDW" in the figure).

Some applications run on a DDS, that is, a relational database that consists of tables with rows and columns. Some applications run on a multidimensional database that consists of cubes with cells and dimensions. I will go through cubes and multidimensional database concepts later in this chapter and in Chapter 12.

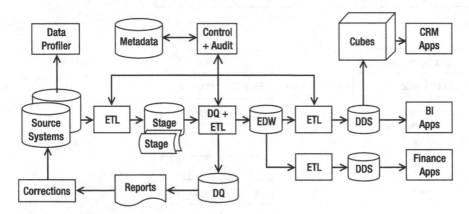

Figure 1-6. *A data warehouse system that uses an enterprise data warehouse*

I will discuss more about dimensional data stores, dimensional schemas, conformed dimensions, normalized data stores, the normalization process, and third normal form in Chapter 5 when I talk about data modeling.

History

One of the key differences between a transactional system and a data warehouse system is the capability and capacity to store history. Most transactional systems store some history, but data warehouse systems store very long history. In my experience, transactional systems store only one to three years of data; beyond that, the data is purged. For example, let's have a look at a sales order–processing system. The purpose of this system is to process customer orders. Once an order is dispatched and paid, it is closed, and after two or three years, you want to purge the closed orders out of the active system and archive them to maintain system performance.

You may want to keep the records for, say, two years, in case the customer queries their orders, but you don't want to keep ten years worth of data on the active system, because that slows the system down. Some regulations (which differ from country to country) require you to keep data for up to five or seven years, such as for tax purposes or to adhere to stock exchange regulations. But this does not mean you must keep the data on the active system. You can archive it to offline media. That's what a typical transaction system does: it keeps only two to three years of data in the active system and archives the rest either to an offline media or to a secondary read-only system/database.

A data warehouse, on the other hand, stores years and years of history in the active system. I have seen ten years of historical data in a data warehouse. The amount of historical data to store in the data warehouse depends on the business requirements. Data warehouse tables can become very large. Imagine a supermarket chain that has 100 stores. Each store welcomes 1,000 customers a day, each purchasing 10 items. This means $100 \times 1000 \times 10 = 1$ million sales order item records every day. In a year, you will have 365 million records. If you store 10 years of data, you will have 3.65 billion records. A high volume like this also happens in the telecommunications industry and in online retail, especially when you store the web page visits in the data warehouse. Therefore, it is important for a data warehouse system to be able to update a huge table bit by bit, query it bit by bit, and back it up bit by bit. Database features such as table partitioning and parallel query would be useful for a data warehouse system. Table partitioning is a method to split a table by rows into several parts and store each part in a different file to increase data loading and query performance. Parallel query is a process where a single query is split into smaller parts and each part is given to an independent query-processing module. The query result from each module is then combined and sent back to the front-end application. I will go through parallel database features such as table partitioning in Chapter 6, when I discuss physical database design.

Most transaction systems store the history of the transactions but not the history of the master data such as products, customers, branches, and vehicles. When you change the product description, for example, in my experience most of the transaction systems update the old description with the new one; they do not store the old description. There are some exceptions, however; for example, some specialized applications such as medical and customer service applications store historical master data such as old customer attributes.

In a data warehouse, on the other hand, storing the history of the master data is one of the key features. This is known as a slowly changing dimension (SCD). A slowly changing dimension is a technique used in dimensional modeling for preserving historical information about dimensional data. In SCD type 2, you keep the historical information in rows; while in SCD type 3, you keep the historical information in columns. In SCD type 1, you don't keep the historical information. Please refer to Chapter 5 for more information about SCD.

Also related to history, a data warehouse stores a periodic snapshot of operational source systems. A *snapshot* is a copy of one or more master tables taken at a certain time. A periodic snapshot is a snapshot that is taken at a regular interval; for example, the banking industry takes snapshots of customer account tables every day. The data warehouse applications then compare the daily snapshots to analyze customer churns, account balances, and unusual conditions. If the size of a source system is, say, 100MB, then in a year you would have accumulated 37GB. Storing source system daily snapshots could have a serious impact on data warehouse storage, so you need to be careful.

Query

Querying is the process of getting data from a data store, which satisfies certain criteria. Here is an example of a simple query: "How many customers do you have now?"[1] Here is an example of a complex query: "Show me the names and revenue of all product lines that had a 10 percent loss or greater in Q3 FY 2006, categorized by outlet."

A data warehouse is built to be queried. That is the number-one purpose of its existence. Users are not allowed to update the data warehouse. Users can only query the data warehouse. Only the ETL system is allowed to update the data warehouse. This is one of the key differences between a data warehouse and a transaction system.

---

1. Note: "How many customers do you have now?" is a simple question if you have only one application, but if you have 15 applications, it could be quite daunting.

If you refer once again to Figure 1-1, you can ask yourself this question: "Why do I need to get the data from the source system into the DDS and then query the DDS? Why don't I query the source system directly?"

For the purpose of simple querying and reporting, you usually query the source system directly. But for conducting heavy analysis such as customer profitability, predictive analysis, "what if?" scenarios, slice and dice analytical exercises, and so on, it is difficult to do it on the source system.

Here's why: the source system is usually a transactional system, used by many users. One important feature of a transactional system is the ability to allow many users to update and select from the system at the same time. To do so, it must be able to perform a lot of database transactions (update, insert, delete, and select) in a relatively short period of time. In other words, it should be able to perform database transactions very quickly. If you stored the same piece of data—say, unit price—in many different places in the system, it would take a long time to update the data and to maintain data consistency. If you stored it in only one place, it would be quicker to update the data, and you wouldn't have to worry about maintaining data consistency between different places. Also, it would be easier to maintain the concurrency and locking mechanism to enable many people to work together in the same database. Hence, one of the fundamental principles of a transaction system is to remove data redundancy.

Performing a complex query on a normalized database (such as transactional systems) is slower than performing a complex query on a denormalized database (such as a data warehouse), because in a normalized database, you need to join many tables. A normalized database is not suitable to be used to load data into a multidimensional database for the purpose of slicing-and-dicing analysis. Unlike a relational database that contains tables with two dimensions (rows and columns), a multidimensional database consists of cubes containing cells with more than two dimensions. Then each cell is mapped to a member in each dimension. To load a multidimensional database from a normalized database, you need to do a multijoin query to transform the data to dimensional format. It can be done, but it is slower. I will go through normalization in more detail in Chapter 5 and data loading in Chapter 8.

The second reason why you don't query the source systems directly is because a company can have many source systems or front-office transactional systems. So, by querying a source system, you get only partial data. A data warehouse, on the other hand, consolidates the data from many source systems, so by querying the data warehouse, you get integrated data.

Business Intelligence

Business intelligence is a collection of activities to understand business situations by performing various types of analysis on the company data as well as on external data from third parties to help make strategic, tactical, and operational business decisions and take necessary actions for improving business performance. This includes gathering, analyzing, understanding, and managing data about operation performance, customer and supplier activities, financial performance, market movements, competition, regulatory compliance, and quality controls.

Examples of business intelligence are the following:

- Business performance management, including producing key performance indicators such as daily sales, resource utilization, and main operational costs for each region, product line, and time period, as well as their aggregates, to enable people to take tactical actions to get operational performance on the desired tracks.

- Customer profitability analysis, that is, to understand which customers are profitable and worth keeping and which are losing money and therefore need to be acted upon. The key to this exercise is allocating the costs as accurately as possible to the smallest unit of business transaction, which is similar to activity-based costing.

- Statistical analysis such as purchase likelihood or basket analysis. Basket analysis is a process of analyzing sales data to determine which products are likely to be purchased or ordered together. This likelihood is expressed in terms of statistical measures such as support and confidence level. It is mainly applicable for the retail and manufacturing industries but also to a certain degree for the financial services industry.

- Predictive analysis such as forecasting the sales, revenue, and cost figures for the purpose of planning for next year's budgets and taking into account other factors such as organic growth, economic situations, and the company's future direction.

According to the depth of analysis and level of complexity, in my opinion you can group business intelligence activities into three categories:

- Reporting, such as key performance indicators, global sales figures by business unit and service codes, worldwide customer accounts, consolidated delivery status, and resource utilization rates across different branches in many countries

- OLAP, such as aggregation, drill down, slice and dice, and drill across

- Data mining, such as data characterization, data discrimination, association analysis, classification, clustering, prediction, trend analysis, deviation analysis, and similarity analysis

Now let's discuss each of these three categories in detail.

Reporting

In a data warehousing context, a *report* is a program that retrieves data from the data warehouse and presents it to the users on the screen or on paper. Users also can subscribe to these reports so that they can be sent to the users automatically by e-mail at certain times (daily or weekly, for example) or in response to events.

The reports are built according to the functional specifications. They display the DDS data required by the business user to analyze and understand business situations. The most common form of report is a tabular form containing simple columns. There is another form of report known as *cross tab* or *matrix*. These reports are like Excel pivot tables, where one data attribute becomes the rows, another data attribute becomes the columns, and each cell on the report contains the value corresponding to the row and column attributes.

Data warehouse reports are used to present the business data to users, but they are also used for data warehouse administration purposes. They are used to monitor data quality, to monitor the usage of data warehouse applications, and to monitor ETL activities.

Online Analytical Processing (OLAP)

OLAP is the activity of interactively analyzing business transaction data stored in the dimensional data warehouse to make tactical and strategic business decisions. Typical people who do OLAP work are business analysts, business managers, and executives. Typical functionality in OLAP includes aggregating (totaling), drilling down (getting the details), and slicing and dicing (cutting the cube and summing the values in the cells). OLAP functionality can be delivered using a relational database or using a multidimensional database. OLAP that uses a relational database is known as *relational online analytical processing* (ROLAP). OLAP that uses a multidimensional database is known as *multidimensional online analytical processing* (MOLAP).

An example of OLAP is analyzing the effectiveness of a marketing campaign initiative on certain products by measuring sales growth over a certain period. Another example is to analyze the impact of a price increase to the product sales in different regions and product groups at the same period of time.

Data Mining

Data mining is a process to explore data to find the patterns and relationships that describe the data and to predict the unknown or future values of the data. The key value in data mining is the ability to understand why some things happened in the past and to predict what will happen in the future. When data mining is used to explain the current or past situation, it is called *descriptive analytics*. When data mining is used to predict the future, it is called *predictive analytics*.

In business intelligence, popular applications of data mining are for fraud detection (credit card industry), forecasting and budgeting (finance), developing cellular/mobile packages by analyzing call patterns (telecommunication industry), market basket analysis (retail industry), customer risk profiling (insurance industry), usage monitoring (energy and utilities), and machine service times (manufacturing industry).

I will discuss the implementation of data warehousing for business intelligence in Chapter 13.

Other Analytical Activities

Other than for business intelligence, data warehouses are also used for analytical activities in nonbusiness purposes, such as scientific research, government departments (statistics office, weather office, economic analysis, and predictions), military intelligence, emergency and disaster management, charity organizations, server performance monitoring, and network traffic analysis.

Data warehouses are also used for customer relationship management (CRM). CRM is a set of activities performed by an organization (business and nonbusiness) to manage and conduct analysis about their customers, to keep in contact and communicate with their customers, to attract and win new customers, to market product and services to their customers, to conduct transactions with their customers (both business and nonbusiness transactions), to service and support their customers, and to create new ideas and new products or services for their customers. I will discuss the implementation of data warehouses for CRM later in this chapter and in Chapter 14.

Data warehouses are also used in *web analytics*. Web analytics is the activity of understanding the behavior and characteristics of web site traffic. This includes finding out the number of visits, visitors, and unique visitors on each page for each day/week/month; referrer sites; typical routes that visitors take within the site; technical characteristics of the visitors' browsers; domain and geographical analysis; what kind of robots are visiting; the exit rate of each page; and the conversion rate on the checkout process. Web analytics are especially important for online businesses.

Updated in Batches

A data warehouse is usually a read-only system; that is, users are not able to update or delete data in the data warehouse. Data warehouse data is updated using a standard mechanism called ETL at certain times by bringing data from the operational source system. This is different from a transactional system or OLTP where users are able to update the system at any time.

The reason for not allowing users to update or delete data in the data warehouse is to maintain data consistency so you can guarantee that the data in the data warehouse will be consistent with the operational source systems, such as if the data warehouse is taking data from two source systems, A and B. System A contains 11 million customers, system B contains 8 million customers, and there are 2 million customers who exist in both systems. The data warehouse will contain 17 million customers. If the users update the data in the data warehouse (say, delete 1 million customers), then it will not be consistent with the source systems. Also, when the next update comes in from the ETL, the changes that the users made in the warehouse will be gone and overwritten.

The reason why data warehouses are updated in batches rather than in real time is to create data stability in the data warehouse. You need to keep in mind that the operational source systems are changing all the time. Some of them change every minute, and some of them change every second. If you allow the source system to update the data warehouse in real time or you allow the users to update the data warehouse all the time, then it would be difficult to do some analysis because the data changes every time. For example, say you are doing a drilling-down exercise on a multidimensional cube containing crime data. At 10:07 you notice that the total of crime in a particular region for Q1 2007 is 100. So at 10:09, you drill down by city (say that region consists of three cities: A, B, and C), and the system displays that the crime for city A was 40, B was 30, and C was 31. That is because at 10:08 a user or an ETL added one crime that happened in city C to the data warehouse. The drilling-down/summing-up exercise will give inconsistent results because the data keeps changing.

The second reason for updating the data warehouse in batches rather than in real time is the performance of the source system. Updating the data warehouse in real time means that the moment there is an update in the source systems, you update the data warehouse immediately, that is, within a few seconds. To do this, you need to either

- install database triggers on every table in the source system or

- modify the source system application to write into the data warehouse immediately after it writes to the source system database.

If the source system is a large application and you need to extract from many tables (say 100 or 1,000 tables), then either approach will significantly impact the performance of the source system application. One pragmatic approach is to do real-time updates only from a few key tables, say five tables, whilst other tables are updated in a normal daily batch. It is possible to update the data warehouse in real time or in near real time, but only for a few selected tables.

In the past few years, real-time data warehousing has become the trend and even the norm. Data warehouse ETL batches that in the old days ran once a day now run every hour, some of them every five minutes (this is called a *mini-batch*). Some of them are using the push approach; that is, rather than pulling the data into the warehouse, the source system pushes the data into the warehouse. In a push approach, the data warehouse is updated immediately when the data in the source system changes. Changes in the source system are detected using database triggers. In a pull approach, the data warehouse is updated at certain intervals. Changes in the source system are detected for extraction using a timestamp or identity column. (I will go through data extraction in Chapter 7.)

Some approaches use messaging and message queuing technology to transport the data asynchronously from various source systems into the data warehouse. Messaging is a data transport mechanism where the data is wrapped in an envelope containing control bits and sent over the network into a message queue. A message queue (MQ) is a system where messages are queued to be processed systematically in order. An application sends messages containing data into the MQ, and another application reads and removes the messages from the MQ. There are some considerations you need to be careful of when using asynchronous ETL, because different pieces of data are arriving at different times without knowing each other's status of arrival. The benefit of using MQ for ETL is the ability for the source system to send out the data without the data warehouse being online to receive it. The other benefit is that the source system needs to send out the data only once to an MQ so the data consistency is guaranteed; several recipients can then read the same message from the MQ. You will learn more about real-time data warehousing in Chapter 8 when I discuss ETL.

Other Definitions

I will close this section with data warehouse definitions from Bill Inmon and from Ralph Kimball, the fathers of data warehousing:

- According to Bill Inmon, a data warehouse is a subject-oriented, integrated, non-volatile, and time-variant collection of data in support of management's decisions.[2]

- According to Ralph Kimball, a data warehouse is a system that extracts, cleans, conforms, and delivers source data into a dimensional data store and then supports and implements querying and analysis for the purpose of decision making.[3]

Both of them agree that a data warehouse integrates data from various operational source systems. In Inmon's approach, the data warehouse is physically implemented as a normalized data store. In Kimball's approach, the data warehouse is physically implemented in a dimensional data store.

In my opinion, if you store the data in a normalized data store, you still need to load the data into a dimensional data store for query and analysis. A dimensional data store is a better

---

2. See *Building the Data Warehouse, Fourth Edition* (John Wiley, 2005) for more information.

3. See *The Data Warehouse ETL Toolkit* (John Wiley, 2004) for more information.

format to store data in the warehouse for the purpose of querying and analyzing the data, compared to a normalized data store. A normalized data store is a better format to integrate data from various source systems.

The previous definitions are amazingly still valid and used worldwide, even after 16 years. I just want to add a little note. It is true that in the early days data warehouses were used mainly for making strategic management decisions, but in recent years, especially with real-time data warehousing, data warehouses have been used for operational purposes too. These days, data warehouses are also used outside decision making, including for understanding certain situations, for reporting purposes, for data integration, and for CRM operations.

Another interesting definition is from Alan Simon: the coordinated, architected, and periodic copying of data from various sources into an environment optimized for analytical and informational processing.[4]

Data Warehousing Today

Today most data warehouses are used for business intelligence to enhance CRM and for data mining. Some are also used for reporting, and some are used for data integration. These usages are all interrelated; for example, business intelligence and CRM use data mining, business intelligence uses reporting, and BI and CRM also use data integration. In the following sections, I will describe the main usages, including business intelligence, CRM, and data mining. In Chapters 13 to 15, I will go through them again in more detail.

Business Intelligence

It seems that many vendors prefer to use the term *business intelligence* rather than *data warehousing*. In other words, they are more focused on what a data warehouse can do for a business. As I explained previously, many data warehouses today are used for BI. That is, the purpose of a data warehouse is to help business users understand their business better; to help them make better operational, tactical, and strategic business decisions; and to help them improve business performance.

Many companies have built business intelligence systems to help these processes, such as understanding business processes, making better decisions (through better use of information and through data-based decision making), and improving business performance (that is, managing business more scientifically and with more information). These systems help the business users get the information from the huge amount of business data. These systems also help business users understand the pattern of the business data and predict future behavior using data mining. Data mining enables the business to find certain patterns in the data and forecast the future values of the data.

Almost every single aspect of business operations now is touched by business intelligence: call center, supply chain, customer analytics, finance, and workforce. Almost every function is covered too: analysis, reporting, alert, querying, dashboard, and data integration. A lot of business leaders these days make decisions based on data. And a business intelligence tool running and operating on top of a data warehouse could be an invaluable support tool for

---

4. See http://www.datahabitat.com/datawarehouse.html for more information.

that purpose. This is achieved using reports and OLAP. Data warehouse reports are used to present the integrated business data in the data warehouse to the business users. OLAP enables the business to interactively analyze business transaction data stored in the dimensional data warehouse. I will discuss the data warehouse usage for business intelligence in Chapter 13.

Customer Relationship Management

I defined CRM earlier in this chapter. A *customer* is a person or organization that consumes your products or services. In nonbusiness organizations, such as universities and government agencies, a customer is the person who the organization serves.

A CRM system consists of applications that support CRM activities (please refer to the definition earlier where these activities were mentioned). In a CRM system, the following functionality is ideally done in a dimensional data warehouse:

Single customer view: The ability to unify or consolidate several definitions or meanings of a customer, such as subscribers, purchasers, bookers, and registered users, through the use of customer matching

Permission management: Storing and managing declarations or statements from customers so you can send campaigns to them or communicate with them including subscription-based, tactical campaigns, ISP feedback loops, and communication preferences

Campaign segmentation: Attributes or elements you can use to segregate the customers into groups, such as order data, demographic data, campaign delivery, campaign response, and customer loyalty score

Customer services/support: Helping customers before they use the service or product (preconsumption support), when they are using the service or product, and after they used the service/product; handling customer complaints; and helping them in emergencies such as by contacting them

Customer analysis: Various kinds of analysis including purchase patterns, price sensitivity analysis, shopping behavior, customer attrition analysis, customer profitability analysis, and fraud detection

Personalization: Tailoring your web site, products, services, campaigns, and offers for a particular customer or a group of customers, such as price and product alerts, personalized offers and recommendations, and site personalization

Customer loyalty scheme: Various ways to reward highly valued customers and build loyalty among customer bases, including calculating the customer scores/point-based system, customer classification, satisfaction survey analysis, and the scheme administration

Other functionality such as customer support and order-processing support are better served by an operational data store (ODS) or OLTP applications. An ODS is a relational, normalized data store containing the transaction data and current values of master data from the OLTP system. An ODS does not store the history of master data such as the customer, store, and product. When the value of the master data in the OLTP system changes, the ODS is updated accordingly. An ODS integrates data from several OLTP systems. Unlike a data warehouse, an ODS is updatable.

Because an ODS contains integrated data from several OLTP systems, it is an ideal place to be used for customer support. Customer service agents can view the integrated data of a customer in the ODS. They can also update the data if necessary to complement the data from the OLTP systems. For example, invoice data from a finance system, order data from an ERP system, and subscription data from a campaign management system can be consolidated in the ODS.

I will discuss the implementation of data warehousing for customer relationship management in Chapter 14.

Data Mining

Data mining is a field that has been growing fast in the past few years. It is also known as *knowledge discovery*, because it includes trying to find meaningful and useful information from a large amount of data. It is an interactive or automated process to find patterns describing the data and to predict the future behavior of the data based on these patterns.

Data mining systems can work with many types of data formats: various types of databases (relational databases, hierarchical databases, dimensional databases, object-oriented databases, and multidimensional databases), files (spreadsheet files, XML files, and structured text files), unstructured or semistructured data (documents, e-mails, and XML files), stream data (plant measurements, temperatures and pressures, network traffic, and telecommunication traffic), multimedia files (audio, video, images, and speeches), web sites/pages, and web logs.

Of these various types of data, data mining applications work best with a data warehouse because the data is already cleaned, it is structured, it has metadata that describes the data (useful for navigating around the data), it is integrated, it is nonvolatile (that is, quite static), and most important it is usually arranged in dimensional format that is suitable for various data mining tasks such as classification, exploration, description, and prediction. In data mining projects, data from the various sources mentioned in the previous paragraph are arranged in a dimensional database. The data mining applications retrieve data from this database to apply various data mining algorithms and logic to the data. The application then presents the result to the end users.

You can use data mining for various business and nonbusiness applications including the following:

- Finding out which products are likely to be purchased together, either by analyzing the shopping data and taking into account the purchase probability or by analyzing order data. Shopping (browsing) data is specific to the online industry, whilst order data is generic to all industries.

- In the railway or telecommunications area, predicting which tracks or networks of cables and switches are likely to have problems this year, so you can allocate resources (technician, monitoring, and alert systems, and so on) on those areas of the network.

- Finding out the pattern between crime and location and between crime rate and various factors, in an effort to reduce crime.

- Customer scoring in CRM in terms of loyalty and purchase power, based on their orders, geographic, and demographic attributes.

- Credit scoring in the credit card industry to tag customers according to attitudes about risk exposure, according to borrowing behaviors, and according to their abilities to pay their debts.

- Investigating the relationship between types of customers and the services/products they would likely subscribe to/purchase in an effort to create future services/products and to devise a marketing strategy and effort for existing services/products.

- Creating a call pattern in the telecommunication industry, in terms of time slices and geographical area (daily, weekly, monthly, and seasonal patterns) in order to manage the network resources (bandwidth, scheduled maintenance, and customer support) accordingly.

To implement data mining in SQL Server Analysis Services (SSAS), you build a mining model using the data from relational sources or from OLAP cubes containing certain mining algorithms such as decision trees and clustering. You then process the model and test how it performs. You can then use the model to create predictions. A prediction is a forecast about the future value of a certain variable. You can also create reports that query the mining models. I will discuss data mining in Chapter 13 when I cover the implementation of data warehousing for business intelligence.

Master Data Management (MDM)

To understand what master data management is, we need to understand what master data is first. In OLTP systems, there are two categories of data: transaction data and master data. Transaction data consists of business entities in OLTP systems that record business transactions consisting of identity, value, and attribute columns. Master data consists of the business entities in the OLTP systems that describe business transactions consisting of identity and attribute columns. Transaction data is linked to master data so that master data describes the business transaction.

Let's take the classic example of sales order–processing first and then look at another example in public transport.

An online music shop with three brands has about 80,000 songs. Each brand has its own web store: Energize is aimed at young people, Ranch is aimed at men, and Essence is aimed at women. Every day, thousands of customers purchase and download thousands of different songs. Every time a customer purchases a song, a transaction happens. All the entities in this event are master data.

To understand which entities are the transaction data and which entities are the master data, you need to model the business process. The business event is the transaction data. In the online music shop example, the business event is that a customer purchases a song. Master data consists of the entities that describe the business event. Master data consists of the answers of who, what, and where questions about a business transaction. In the previous example, the master data is customer, product, and brand.

Here's the second example: 1,000 bus drivers from 10 different transport companies are driving 500 buses around 50 different routes in a town. Each route is served 20 times a day, which is called a *trip*. The business process here is driving one trip. That is the transaction.

You have $50 \times 20 = 1000$ transactions a day. The master data consists of the business entities in this transaction: the driver, the bus, and the route. How about the companies? No, the company is not directly involved in the trip, so the company is not master data in this process. The company is involved in a trip through the buses and the drivers; each driver and each bus belong to a company. The company, however, may be a master data in another business process.

In the previous examples, you learned that to identify the transaction data and the master data in a business process, you need to identify what the business event is in the process first. Then, you identify the business entities that describe the business event.

Examples of master data are the supplier, branch, office, employee, citizen, taxpayer, assets, inventory, store, salespeople, property, equipment, time, product, tools, roads, customer, server, switch, account, service code, destination, contract, plants (as in manufacturing or oil refineries), machines, vehicles, and so on.

Now you are ready to learn about MDM, which is the ongoing process of retrieving, cleaning, storing, updating, and distributing master data. An MDM system retrieves the master data from OLTP systems. The MDM system consolidates the master data and processes the data through predefined data quality rules. The master data is then uploaded to a master data store. Any changes on master data in the OLTP systems are sent to the MDM system, and the master data store is updated to reflect those changes. The MDM system then publishes the master data to other systems.

There are two kinds of master data that you may not want to include when implementing an MDM system:

- You may want to exclude date and time. A date explains a business event, so by definition it is master data. A date has attributes such as month name, but the attributes are static. The month name of 01/11/2007 is November and will always be November. It is static. It does not need to be maintained, updated, and published. The attributes of a customer such as address, on the other hand, keep changing and need to be maintained. But the attributes of a date are static.

- You may want to exclude master data with a small number of members. For example, if your business is e-commerce and you have only one online store, then it may not be worth it to maintain store data using MDM. The considerations whether to exclude or include a small business entity as master data or not are the number of members and frequency of change. If the number of members is less than ten and the frequency of change is less than once a year, you want to consider excluding it from your MDM system.

Now let's have a look at one of the most widely used types of master data: products. You may have five different systems in the organization and all of them have a product table, and you need to make sure that all of them are in agreement and in sync. If in the purchase order system you have a wireless router with part number WAR3311N but in the sales order system you have a different part number, then you risk ordering the incorrect product from your supplier and replenishing a different product. There is also a risk of inaccuracy of the sales report and inventory control. It's the same thing with the speed, protocol, color, specification, and other product attributes; they also expose you to certain risk if you don't get them synchronized and corrected. So, say you have five different systems and 200,000 part numbers. How do you make sure the data is accurate across all systems all the time? That's where MDM comes into play.

An MDM system retrieves data from various OLTP systems and gets the product data. If there are duplicate products, the MDM system integrates the two records. The MDM system integrates the two records by comparing the common attributes to identify whether the two records are a match. If they are a match, survivorship rules dictate which record wins and which record loses. The winning record is kept, and the losing record is discarded and archived. For example, you may have two different suppliers supplying the same product but they have different supplier part numbers. MDM can match product records based on different product attributes depending on product category and product group. For example, for digital cameras, possible matching criteria are brand, model, resolution, optical zoom, memory card type, max and min focal length, max and min shutter speed, max and min ISO, and sensor type. For books, the matching is based on totally different attributes. MDM can merge two duplicate records into one automatically, depending on the matching rule and survivorship rules that you set up. It keeps the old data so that if you uncover that the merge was not correct (that is, they are really two different products), then MDM can unmerge that one record back into two records.

Once the MDM has the correct single version of data, it publishes this data to other systems. These systems use this service to update the product data that they store. If there is any update on any of these applications to product data, the master store will be updated, and changes will be replicated to all other systems.

The master data is located within OLTP systems. There are changes to this master data in the OLTP systems from time to time. These master data changes flow from OLTP systems to the master data store in the MDM system. There are two possible ways this data flow happens. The OLTP system sends the changes to the MDM system and the MDM system stores the changes in the master data store, or the MDM system retrieves the master data in OLTP systems periodically to identify whether there are any changes. The first approach where the OLTP system sends the master data changes to the MDM system is called a *push approach*. The second approach where the MDM system retrieves the master data from the OLTP systems periodically is called a *pull approach*. Some MDM systems use the push approach, and some MDM systems use the pull approach.

MDM systems have metadata storage. Metadata storage is a database that stores the rules, the structure, and the meaning of the data. The purpose of having metadata storage in an MDM system is to help the users understand the meaning and structure of the master data stored in the MDM system. Two types of rules are stored in the metadata storage: survivorship rules and matching rules. Survivorship rules determine which of the duplicate master data records from the OLTP system will be kept as the master data in the MDM system. Matching rules determine what attributes are used to identify duplicate records from OLTP systems. The data structure stored in metadata storage explains the attributes of the master data and the data types of these attributes.

MDM systems have a reporting facility that displays the data structure, the survivorship rules, the matching rules, and the duplicate records from OLTP systems along with which rule was applied and which record was kept as the master data. The reporting facility also shows which rules were executed and when they were executed.

The master data management system for managing product data such as this is known as *product information management* (PIM). PIM is an MDM system that retrieves product data from OLTP systems, cleans the product data, and stores the product data in a master data store. PIM maintains all product attributes and the product hierarchy in the master data store and keeps it up-to-date by getting the product data changes from OLTP systems. PIM publishes the product data to other systems.

It is important to remember that the master data in the MDM system's master data store needs to be continuously updated. There is no point in synchronizing all the systems today when next week they will be out of sync again.

Now that you understand what MDM is, how does it relate to data warehousing? It relates for two reasons:

- If all the master data is clean, then it would make the tasks of creating and maintaining a data warehouse much easier. The data is already integrated and cleaned. All the data warehouse has to do is connect to this MDM store and synchronize all its dimensions with it. Of course, you would still have to maintain the surrogate key and SCD,[5] and so on, but the task is easier.

- You could use a data warehouse to store the master data. If you already have a data warehouse in place that pulls data from many different systems, cleans them, and integrates them in one place, then why don't you set up a service to publish this data and get those systems to subscribe or consume this service?

There is one more point that I need to discuss: *hierarchy*. Hierarchy is a structure where the master data is grouped into several categories, and the categories are classified into related levels. The top-level category has one or more second-level categories. Each of these second-level categories has one or more third-level categories. The same applies for further lower levels. The lowest-level categories have the individual master data as their members. Hierarchy is used to determine which attributes are applicable to which data. Hierarchy is also used when moving an item from one category to another.

For example, a product such as Canon EOS 400D belongs to a product category, such as SLR Digital Camera. A product category belongs to a product group, such as Digital Camera. A product group belongs to a product family, such as Camera. A product family belongs to a product type, such as Electronics. If you want to change the Camera product family to Video and Photo Camera and move the Video Camera product group under it, then you can do it in one place: the MDM hub. The MDM will then distribute this new hierarchy to other systems.

It is important that an MDM system is capable of maintaining hierarchy; otherwise, the product data in different applications would not be in sync, and you are exposed to those risks. And it is not an easy task; application A can have only three levels of product hierarchy, whereas application B has four levels.

Customer Data Integration

Customer data integration (CDI) is the MDM for customer data. CDI is the process of retrieving, cleaning, storing, maintaining, and distributing customer data. A CDI system retrieves customer data from OLTP systems, cleans it, stores it in a customer master data store, maintains the customer data, keeps it up-to-date, and distributes the customer data to other systems.

---

5. I will discuss surrogate keys and SCD in Chapter 5.

A CDI system enables you to have a cleaner, single, reliable version of customer data that other applications in the enterprise can use. This in turn can deliver business benefits such as increased customer satisfaction and better business analysis, and it reduces the complexity of the processes that use customer data. Of all the various kinds of master data management, CDI is the most widely used because every organization has customers. CDI provides clean integrated data for customer relationship management.

The importance of having a single accurate source of customer data is illustrated in the following examples. If in the customer service system you have Carol Goodman's date of birth as May 12, 1953, but in the policy management system it is May 12, 1973, then you are risking underwriting her life policy incorrectly. It's the same thing with the address and phone number, which also expose you to certain risks if you don't get them synchronized and corrected, just like the case with the product data discussed previously. CDI has different matching criteria compared to products, of course; for example, it can match customer records based on name, date of birth, Social Security number, telephone number, address, credit card number, and many other attributes. This time the criteria are not different from product group to product group, but rather universal. A human being is a human being, not like products that have different attributes for each product type.

Future Trends in Data Warehousing

Several future trends in data warehousing today are unstructured data, search, service-oriented architecture, and real-time data warehousing.

Unstructured Data

Data that is in databases is structured; it is organized in rows and columns. I have talked in great length in previous sections about data warehousing using structured data; that is, the source system is a database. It can be a relational database (tables, rows, and columns), and it may be an object-oriented database (classes and types) or a hierarchical database (a tree-like structure). However, they all have data structure.

Unstructured data, on the other hand, does not have a data structure such as rows and columns, a tree-like structure, or classes and types. Examples of unstructured data are documents, images (photos, diagrams, and pictures), audio (songs, speeches, and sounds), video (films, animations), streaming data, text, e-mails, and Internet web sites. Arguably, some people say this kind of data is semistructured data, with the argument that there is some structure, so it has attributes. For example, an e-mail has attributes such as from, to, date sent, date created, date received, subject, and body; a document has attributes such as title, subject, author, number of pages, number of words, creation date, and last-modified date.

How do you store unstructured data in the data warehouse? And, after you store it, how do you get the information that you need out of this data? Well, the answer to the first question is for each unstructured data item you define the attributes and then organize these items according to the attributes. You can store the unstructured data items in a relational database as a binary object column, with the attributes as other columns. Or you can store the unstructured data items in the file systems and just store the pointer to the file in the database.

Each type of unstructured data has different physical and content attributes. These attributes can be stored in a relational or multidimensional database to enable the users to easily find a particular piece of unstructured data. The content of the unstructured data itself can be analyzed, extracted, categorized, and stored to assist information retrieval.

For example, let's say you have 1 million e-mails as your unstructured data. They have attributes, such as from, to, cc, bcc, subject, date created, date sent, attachments, number of words in the body, host address, originator address, recipient address, and so on. You then store these attributes in a relational table, and the e-mails are stored as files with the file name and location stored in the table.

In addition to the physical attribute of the e-mail, you can also uncover the content attributes of the e-mail body. First, you do some text cleansing on the e-mail body to remove noises such as numbers and adjectives; convert past-tense verbs into present; correct plurals into singulars; eliminate meaningless words such as *ah, the, in* (well, they are not really meaningless, but what you are looking for are verbs and nouns); convert synonyms using a dictionary; and so on. Then you can count how many times each word occurs, giving a score depending on how far a word is located from another word and categorizing the items to a certain hierarchy that you have created based on the words, the statistical properties of these words, and the score for these words. Then you can put these categories and properties in those attribute columns to assist information retrieval.

It is probably not fair if we say that unstructured data is new. Text analytics have been around for a long time. It's just that recently people have started realizing that most of their data is stored in unstructured data, especially text such as documents and e-mails, and only a little bit of their data is structured data. So why do we spend a lot of effort storing and analyzing structured data (such as numbers) and only a little effort on unstructured data? Hence, structured data has become one of the current trends in data warehousing.

Search

This section answers the second question, how do you get the information out? The answer is by searching. To get the information out of structured data, provided that you know the structure, you can do a select query, whether using a static report or manual interactive ad hoc queries. If you use a BI application, the application can go through the metadata and display the structure of the data and then assist you in navigating through the data to retrieve the information you need.

To get the information out of unstructured data, especially text data such as documents, e-mails, and web pages, you do a search. Like on the Internet, the search engine has already crawled the data warehouse and indexed the unstructured data. The search engine has categorized the unstructured data based on their types and their properties and, in the case of web pages, their links.

You can now type what you want to find in a search box, and the search engine will go through its index, find the locations of the information, and display the results. It can also offer predefined searches, wrapped in a nice hierarchical structure for you to navigate and choose. It can also memorize user searches that could assist you in defining what to type when searching.

If the unstructured data contains links to other data—for example, hypertext documents such as XML or HTML—the search engine can utilize what it knows best in the Internet world, which is to use the links to score the relevance of the information when displaying the search results to the users. For searching images, the search engine could use the words around or near the image to verify the title or tag of the image. This is also applicable for other multimedia types, such as video and music.

Search in the Internet world has been around for quite a while (10 to 15) years, but in data warehousing it is relatively new (2 to 3 years). If the information in the data warehouse is huge, often it is easier to search than to browse. For example, a top international organization with 100 branches located in 50 countries could have 100 data marts totaling 100 terabytes for sales, purchases, finance, inventory, human resources, and a huge amount of documents. This is especially true for new users who have not learned the structure of the data warehouse, what reports are available, and how to navigate around the data using the OLAP interface. With search, you have only one box, and you can type whatever you want. What user interface could be simpler than that?

That is why currently search has become a trend in business intelligence and data warehousing—first, because people collect their unstructured data in a huge amount, and second, because search is easier to use, even for structured data.

Service-Oriented Architecture (SOA)

SOA is a method of building an application using a number of smaller, independent components that talk to each other by offering and consuming their services. These components can be distributed; in fact, they can be located on different sides of the world.

Almost every large application can benefit from an SOA approach. You don't build one giant application anymore. Instead, you build many smaller pieces that talk to each other. It is the nature of the IT industry that applications will need to be replaced every several years (I'd say every four to eight years). It could be because of obsolete technology or because of the functionality. Bankruptcy, mergers, and takeovers are also the other drivers to this.

If you make one giant application, it would be costly to replace it. If you make it from a number of smaller, independent components, it is easier to replace it. SOA gives us more flexibility to replace the components. In other words, you can do it in stages piece by piece without affecting the functionality. This is because the components are independent; that is, they don't care how the other components work internally as long as externally they get the responses they require. This enables you to rebuild one component with newer technology without affecting the others.

How does this SOA relate to data warehousing? If you refer to Figure 1-1, a data warehouse system consists of many components: source systems, ETL systems, a data quality mechanism, a metadata system, audit and control systems, a BI portal, a reporting application, OLAP/analytic applications, data mining applications, and the database system itself. You can build it as one giant application with all the components tightly coupled; that is, you cannot replace one component without affecting the other components. Or you can build it in service-oriented architecture—you build it as a number of smaller, independent components that talk to each other by offering and consuming their services.

Let's take a look at an example: ETL. During a recent project I was involved with, the project team built the ETL system as a service. It had various data retrieval services (for example, getService, getAccount, and getTransaction), which retrieved the data from the source system, wrapped it around XML messages, and sent it to a message queue. It had a scheduler service that acted as a mini-batch system; it invoked various data retrieval services at a certain frequency that we set, such as every 5 or 30 minutes. It had a queue management service that controlled the message queue. It had data transformation and data loading services that transformed and loaded the data into the data warehouse.

More and more data warehousing applications on all fronts are built using SOA: ETL, reporting, analytics, BI applications, data mining, metadata, data quality, and data cleansing. In the future, it would be easier to update one component without impacting the others and to connect different components that are made using different technologies.

Real-Time Data Warehouse

A data warehouse, a few years ago, was usually updated every day or every week. In the past two to three years, there has been more and more demand to increase the frequency of updates. The users want to see the data in the data warehouse updated every two minutes or even in real time. A real-time data warehouse is a data warehouse that is updated (by the ETL) the moment the transaction happens in the source system.

For example, you can put triggers on the sales transaction table in the source system so that whenever there is a transaction inserted into the database, the trigger fires and sends the new record to the data warehouse as a message. The data warehouse has an active listener that captures the message the moment it arrives, cleanses it, DQs it, transforms it, and inserts it into the fact table immediately. I'm talking about a two-second time difference here, between the moment a customer purchased a product on the web site and the moment data is available in the fact table.

The other approach of implementing a real-time data warehouse is to modify the operational source application to write to the data warehouse staging area, immediately after it writes the data in its internal database. In the staging database, you place triggers that would be invoked every time there is a new record inserted, and these triggers update the data warehouse.

Near real-time approaches can be implemented by using a mini-batch with two- to five-minute frequency, which pulls the data from the stage area instead of using triggers. This mini-batch also does the normal ETL job—transforming the data and loading it into the data warehouse dimensional database. The mini-batch can also pull the data directly from the source system, eliminating the need of modifying the source system to update the staging area.

Summary

This chapter introduced data warehousing. I showed many examples, with the hope that they would make the concepts easier to understand and would enrich your experience. I discussed a bit of today's situation so you know how it is now, and a bit of the future trends so you know what is coming. In the next chapter, I will discuss the architecture.

CHAPTER 2

■■■

Data Warehouse Architecture

A data warehouse system has two main architectures: the data flow architecture and the system architecture. The *data flow architecture* is about how the data stores are arranged within a data warehouse and how the data flows from the source systems to the users through these data stores. The *system architecture* is about the physical configuration of the servers, network, software, storage, and clients. In this chapter, I will discuss the data flow architecture first and then the system architecture.

Specifically, I will start this chapter by going through what the data flow architecture is, what its purpose is, and what its components are. Then I will discuss four data flow architectures: single DDS, NDS + DDS, ODS + DDS, and federated data warehouse. The first three use a dimensional model as their back-end data stores, but they are different in the middle-tier data store. The federated data warehouse architecture consists of several data warehouses integrated by a data retrieval layer.

I will then discuss the system architecture, which needs to be designed to suit the data flow architecture. So, the data flow architecture is determined first before you design the system architecture. The system architecture affects the actual performance of a data warehouse system delivered to the end users.

Toward the end of this chapter, I will introduce a case study that we will be using throughout the book. In subsequent chapters, I will show how to build a data warehouse for the company in the case study, Amadeus Entertainment Group. You can use this case study to learn all the data warehousing aspects covered in this book: architecture, methodology, requirements, data modeling, physical database design, ETL, data quality, metadata, reporting, multidimensional databases, BI, CRM, testing, and administration.

Data Flow Architecture

In data warehousing, the data flow architecture is a configuration of data stores within a data warehouse system, along with the arrangement of how the data flows from the source systems through these data stores to the applications used by the end users. This includes how the data flows are controlled, logged, and monitored, as well as the mechanism to ensure the quality of the data in the data stores. I discussed the data flow architecture briefly in Chapter 1, but in this chapter I will discuss it in more detail, along with four data flow architectures: single DDS, NDS + DDS, ODS + DDS, and federated data warehouse.

The data flow architecture is different from *data architecture*. Data architecture is about how the data is arranged in each data store and how a data store is designed to reflect the business processes. The activity to produce data architecture is known as *data modeling*. I will not discuss data architecture and data modeling in this chapter. I will discuss those topics in Chapter 5.

Data stores are important components of data flow architecture. I'll begin the discussion about the data flow architecture by explaining what a data store is. A *data store* is one or more databases or files containing data warehouse data, arranged in a particular format and involved in data warehouse processes. Based on the user accessibility, you can classify data warehouse data stores into three types:

- A *user-facing* data store is a data store that is available to end users and is queried by the end users and end-user applications.

- An *internal* data store is a data store that is used internally by data warehouse components for the purpose of integrating, cleansing, logging, and preparing data, and it is not open for query by the end users and end-user applications.

- A *hybrid* data store is used for both internal data warehouse mechanisms and for query by the end users and end-user applications.

A master data store is a user-facing or hybrid data store containing a complete set of data in a data warehouse, including all versions and all historical data.

Based on the data format, you can classify data warehouse data stores into four types:

- A *stage* is an internal data store used for transforming and preparing the data obtained from the source systems, before the data is loaded to other data stores in a data warehouse.

- A *normalized data store* (NDS) is an internal master data store in the form of one or more normalized relational databases for the purpose of integrating data from various source systems captured in a stage, before the data is loaded to a user-facing data store.

- An *operational data store* (ODS) is a hybrid data store in the form of one or more normalized relational databases, containing the transaction data and the most recent version of master data, for the purpose of supporting operational applications.

- A *dimensional data store* (DDS) is a user-facing data store, in the form of one or more relational databases, where the data is arranged in dimensional format for the purpose of supporting analytical queries.

I discussed the terms *relational, normalized, denormalized,* and *dimensional* in Chapter 1, but I'll repeat the definitions here briefly:

- A *relational* database is a database that consists of entity tables with parent-child relationships between them.

- A *normalized* database is a database with little or no data redundancy in third normal form or higher.

- A *denormalized* database is a database with some data redundancy that has not gone through a normalization process.

- A *dimensional* database is a denormalized database consisting of fact tables and common dimension tables containing the measurements of business events, categorized by their dimensions.

Some applications require the data to be in the form of a multidimensional database (MDB) rather than a relational database. An MDB is a form of database where the data is stored in cells and the position of each cell is defined by a number of variables called *dimensions*. Each cell represents a business event, and the value of the dimensions shows when and where this event happened. MDB is populated from DDS.

Extract, transform, and load (ETL) is a system that has the capability to read the data from one data store, transform the data, and load it into another data store. The data store where the ETL reads the data from is called a *source*, and the data store that the ETL loads the data into is called a *target*.

Figure 2-1 shows a data flow architecture with four data stores: stage, ODS, DDS, and MDB.

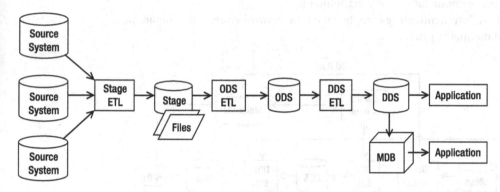

Figure 2-1. *A data flow architecture with a stage, ODS, DDS, and MDB*

The arrows in Figure 2-1 show the flows of data. The data flows from the source systems to a stage, to ODS, to DDS, and then to the applications used by the users. In Figure 2-1 there are three ETL packages between the four data stores. A stage ETL retrieves data from the source systems and loads it into a stage. ODS ETL retrieves data from a stage and loads it into ODS. DDS ETL retrieves data from ODS and loads it into DDS.

An ETL package consists of several ETL processes. An ETL process is a program that is part of an ETL package that retrieves data from one or several sources and populates one target table. An ETL process consists of several steps. A step is a component of an ETL process that does a specific task. An example of a step is extracting particular data from a source data store or performing certain data transformations. The ETL packages in the data warehouse are managed by a *control system*, which is a system that manages the time each ETL package runs, governs the sequence of execution of processes within an ETL package, and provides the capability to restart the ETL packages from the point of failure. The mechanism to log the result of each step of an ETL process is called *ETL audit*. Examples of the results logged by ETL audits are how many records are transformed or loaded in that step, the time the step started and finished, and the step identifier so you can trace it down when debugging or for auditing purposes. I will discuss more about ETL in Chapters 7 and 8.

The description of each ETL process is stored in metadata. This includes the source it extracts the data from, the target it loads the data into, the transformation applied, the parent process, and the schedule each ETL process is supposed to run. In data warehousing, *metadata* is a data store containing the description of the structure, data, and processes within the data warehouse. This includes the data definitions and mapping, the data structure of each data store, the data structure of the source systems, the descriptions of each ETL process, the description of data quality rules, and a log of all processes and activities in the data warehouse. I will discuss more about metadata in Chapter 10.

Data quality processes are the activities and mechanism to make sure the data in the data warehouse is correct and complete. This is usually done by checking the data on its way into the data warehouse. Data quality processes also cover the mechanism to report the bad data and to correct it. A data firewall is a program that checks whether the incoming data complies with the data quality rules. A data quality rule is the criteria that verify the data from the source systems are within the expected range and in the correct format. A data quality database is a database containing incoming data that fails data quality rules. Data quality reports read the data quality violations from the data quality (DQ) database and display them on paper or on the screen. I will discuss more about data quality in Chapter 9.

Figure 2-2 shows a data flow architecture complete with the control system, the metadata, and the components of data quality processes.

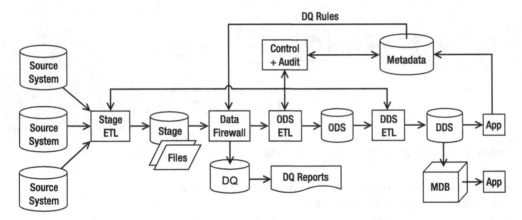

Figure 2-2. *A data flow architecture with control system, metadata, and data quality process*

A data flow architecture is one of the first things you need to decide when building a data warehouse system because the data flow architecture determines what components need to be built and therefore affects the project plan and costs. The data flow architecture shows how the data flows through the data stores within a data warehouse.

The data flow architecture is designed based on the data requirements from the applications, including the data quality requirements. Data warehouse applications require data in different formats. These formats dictate the data stores you need to have. If the applications require dimensional format, then you need to build a DDS. If the applications require a normalized format for operational purposes, then you need to build an ODS. If the application requires multidimensional format, then you need to build an MDB. Once you determine the data stores you need to build, you can design the ETL to populate those data stores. Then you build a data quality mechanism to make sure the data in the data warehouse is correct and complete.

In the following four sections, I will discuss four data flow architectures with their advantages and disadvantages:

- The single DDS architecture has stage and DDS data stores.

- The NDS + DDS architecture has stage, NDS, and DDS data stores.

- The ODS + DDS architecture has stage, ODS, and DDS data stores.

- The federated data warehouse (FDW) architecture consists of several data warehouses integrated by a data retrieval layer.

These four data flow architectures are just examples. When building a data warehouse, you need to design the data flow architecture to suit the data requirements and data quality requirements of the project. These four architectures are by no means exhaustive; you should design your own data flow architecture. For example, is it possible to have a data flow architecture without a stage? Yes, it is possible, if you can do the transformation on the fly in the ETL server's memory, especially if you have a low data volume. Can you have a data flow architecture without a DDS? Yes, you can have stage + NDS data stores only if you want to have a normalized data warehouse rather than a dimensional one. Is it possible to have two DDSs? Yes, of course you can have multiple DDSs—you can have as many as you need.

Now I'll go through these four data flow architectures one by one.

Single DDS

In this section, you will learn about a simple data flow architecture that consists of only two data stores: stage and DDS. In this architecture, the core data warehouse store is in dimensional format.

In single DDS architecture, you have a one dimensional data store. The DDS consists of one or several dimensional data marts. A dimensional data mart is a group of related fact tables and their corresponding dimension tables containing the measurements of business events, categorized by their dimensions. An ETL package extracts the data from different source systems and puts them on the stage.

A *stage* is a place where you store the data you extracted from the store system temporarily, before processing it further. A stage is necessary when the transformation is complex (in other words, cannot be done on the fly in a single step in memory), when the data volume is large (in other words, not enough to be put in memory), or when data from several source systems arrives at different times (in other words, not extracted by a single ETL). A stage is also necessary if you need to minimize the time to extract the data from the source system. In other words, the ETL processes dump the extracted data on disk and disconnect from the source system as soon as possible, and then at their own time they can process the data.

The physical form of a stage can be a database or files. The ETL that extracts data from the source system inserts the data into a database or writes them as files. A second ETL package picks up the data from the stage, integrates the data from different source system, applies some data quality rules, and puts the consolidated data into the DDS. Figure 2-3 describes a general model of this architecture.

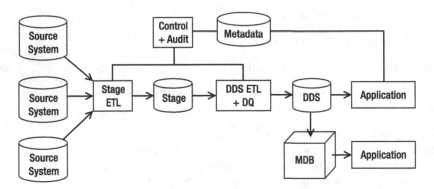

Figure 2-3. *Single DDS data warehouse architecture*

In Figure 2-3, the "Control + Audit" box contains the ETL control system and audit, as I discussed earlier. They manage the ETL processes and log the ETL execution results. The metadata database contains the description of the structure, data, and processes within the data warehouse.

The data warehouse applications, such as business intelligence (BI) reports, read the data in the DDS and bring the data to the users. The data in the DDS can also be uploaded into multidimensional databases, such as SQL Server Analysis Services, and then accessed by the users via OLAP and data mining applications.

Some ETL architects prefer to combine the two ETL packages surrounding the stage in Figure 2-3 into one package, as pictured in Figure 2-4. In Figure 2-4, the stage ETL, the DDS ETL, and the data quality processes are combined into one ETL. The advantage of combining them into one package is to have more control over the timing of when the data is written to and retrieved from the stage. In particular, you can load the data directly into the DDS without putting it to disk first. The disadvantage is that the ETL package becomes more complicated.

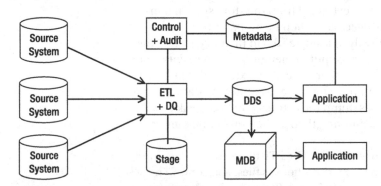

Figure 2-4. *Data architecture where the stage ETL and DDS ETL are combined*

An advantage of a single DDS architecture is that it is simpler than the next three architectures. It is simpler because the data from the stage is loaded straight into the dimensional data store, without going to any kind of normalized store first. The main disadvantage is that it is more difficult, in this architecture, to create a second DDS. The DDS in the single DDS architecture is the master data store. It contains a complete set of data in a data warehouse, including all versions and all historical data. Sometimes you need to create a smaller DDS containing a subset of the data in the master DDS for the purpose of specific analysis where you want to be able to change the data or you want the data to be static. To create this smaller DDS, you would need to create a new ETL package that retrieves data from the master DDS and populates the smaller DDS. You need to build this ETL package from scratch. You cannot reuse the existing ETL package because the existing ETL package retrieves data from the stage and populates the master DDS. It's a totally different data flow altogether.

For example, the users may require a static smaller DDS containing only order data for the purpose of analyzing the impact of a price increase across different customer accounts. They want the BI tool (Business Objects, Cognos, or Analysis Services, for example) to run on this smaller DDS so they can analyze the price increase. To create this smaller DDS, you need to write a new ETL package.

You would use a single DDS architecture when you need only a one dimensional store and you don't need a normalized data store. It is used for a simple, quick, and straightforward analytical BI solution where the data is used only to feed a dimensional data warehouse. A single DDS solution is particularly applicable when you have only one source system because you don't need additional NDS or ODS to integrate the data from different source systems. Compared to the NDS + DDS or ODS + DDS architecture, the single DDS architecture is the simplest to build and has the quickest ETL run time because the data is loaded straight into DDS without going into the NDS or ODS data store first.

NDS + DDS

In NDS + DDS data flow architecture, there are three data stores: stage, NDS, and DDS. This architecture is similar to the single DDS architecture, but it has a normalized data store in front of the DDS. The NDS is in third normal relational form or higher. The purpose of having NDS is twofold. First, it integrates data from several source systems. Second, it is able to load data into several DDSs. Unlike the single DDS architecture, in the NDS + DDS architecture you can have several DDSs. Figure 2-5 shows the NDS + DDS data flow architecture.

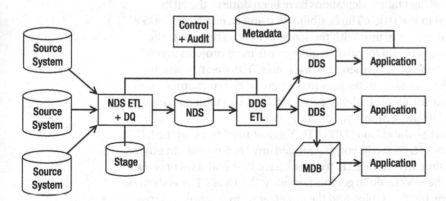

Figure 2-5. *NDS + DDS data flow architecture*

In the NDS + DDS architecture, NDS is the master data store, meaning NDS contains the complete data sets, including all historical transaction data and all historical versions of master data. Historical transaction data means the business transactions that happened in the past. Data from every single year is stored in the NDS. The DDS, on the other hand, is not the master data store. It may not contain all transaction data for every single year. NDS contains all historical versions of master data. If there is a change in master data, the attributes are not overwritten by new values. The new values are inserted as a new record, and the old version (the old row) is kept in the same table.

Similar to an OLTP source system, there are two types of tables in the NDS: transaction tables and master tables. A *transaction* table is a table that contains a business transaction or business event. A *master* table is a table that contains the people or objects involved in the business event. A sales order table is an example of a transaction table. A product table is an example of a master table. The NDS transaction tables are the source of data for the DDS fact table. In other words, the fact tables in the DDS are populated from the transaction tables in the NDS. The NDS master tables are the source of data for DDS dimension tables. That is, the dimension tables in the DDS are populated from the master tables in the NDS. I will discuss more about NDS in Chapter 5 when I talk about dimensional modeling.

NDS is an internal data store, meaning it is not accessible by the end user or the end-user applications. Data from NDS is loaded into DDSs in dimensional format, and the end users access these DDSs. The only application that is able to update NDS is the NDS ETL. No other application should be able to update NDS.

The principles about the stage, control, audit, and metadata discussed earlier are also applicable here. Some entities can fly through directly to NDS without being staged to disk first. In that case, the data integration/transformation is performed online in the memory of the ETL server. The ETL reads the data from the source system, transforms or integrates the data in memory, and writes the data to NDS directly without writing anything to the stage. Data transformation is converting, calculating, or modifying the data to suit the target database. Data integration is combining the same record from several different source systems into one record or combining different attributes of master data or transaction data.

In the NDS + DDS architecture, the DDS ETL that loads data into the DDS is simpler than the one in the single DDS architecture because the data in the NDS is already integrated and cleaned. In some cases, the DDS ETL needs to feed the data only incrementally to the DDS without any transformation. Most, if not all, fact table calculations have been done in the NDS.

The data in the NDS is uploaded to the DDSs. The flexibility of using a centralized NDS is that you can build a DDS that you need at any time with the scope of data as required. The ability to build a new DDS at any time is useful to satisfy requirements from projects involving data analysis. The ability to set the scope of data when building a new DDS means you can pick which tables, columns, and rows you want to transfer to the new DDS. For example, you can build a DDS containing only a customer profitability data mart (one fact table and all its dimensions) that contains only the last three months of data.

To populate a new DDS, you can use the existing DDS ETL. You just need to point the ETL to the new DDS. If you build the DDS ETL correctly, you can rebuild any DDS quickly, in other words, the only time we need is the time to run the ETL. You don't have to spend days or weeks to build a new ETL package to load the new DDS. To get this flexibility, the DDS ETL needs to be parameterized; that is, the date range, the fact tables, and the dimensions to be copied across are all set as parameters that can easily be changed to point to a new DDS. The database connection details are also written as parameters. This enables you to point the ETL to another database.

In NDS + ODS architecture, you can have several DDSs. But there is one DDS you have to build and maintain: the one that contains all the fact tables and all the dimensions. This one is sort of obligatory; all other DDSs are optional—you build them as you need them. You need to have this one obligatory DDS because it contains a complete set of data warehouse data and is used by all BI applications that require dimensional data stores.

The NDS tables use surrogate keys and natural keys. A surrogate key is the identifier of the master data row within the data warehouse. In the DDS, the surrogate key is used as the primary key of dimension tables. The surrogate key is a sequential integer, starting from 0. So, it is 0, 1, 2, 3, …, and so on. Using the surrogate key, you can identify a unique record on a dimension table. Surrogate keys also exist in the fact tables to identify the dimension attributes for a particular business transaction. Surrogate keys are used to link a fact table and the dimension tables. For example, using surrogate keys, you can find out the details of the customer for a particular order. In the NDS + DDS architecture, the surrogate keys are maintained in the NDS, not in the DDS.

A *natural key* is the identifier of the master data row in the source system. When loading data from the stage to NDS, you need to translate the natural key from the source system to a data warehouse surrogate key. You can do this by looking up the surrogate key in the NDS for each natural key value from the source system. If the natural key exists in the NDS, it means the record already exists in NDS and needs to be updated. If the natural key doesn't exist in the NDS, it means the record does not exist in the NDS and needs to be created.

Only internal administrative applications access the NDS directly. These are usually applications that verify the data loaded into NDS, such as data quality routines that check NDS data against certain firewall rules. End user applications, such as BI reports, access the DDS (dimensional model) and some applications, such as OLAP applications, access the multidimensional databases that are built from the DDSs. You need to understand what kind of data store is required by each application to be able to define the data flow architecture correctly.

The main advantage of this architecture is that you can easily rebuild the main DDS; in addition, you can easily build a new, smaller DDS. This is because the NDS is the master data store, containing a complete set of data, and because the DDS ETL is parameterized. This enables you to create a separate static data store for the purpose of specific analysis. The second advantage is that it is easier to maintain master data in a normalized store like the NDS and publish it from there because it contains little or no data redundancy and so you need to update only one place within the data store.

The main disadvantage is that it requires more effort compared to the single DDS architecture because the data from the stage needs to be put into the NDS first before it is uploaded into the DDS. The effort to build ETL becomes practically double because you need to build two ETL sets, while in single DDS it is only one. The effort for data modeling would be about 50 percent more because you need to design three data stores, whereas in single DDS you have two data stores.

The NDS + DDS architecture offers good flexibility for creating and maintaining data stores, especially when creating a DDS. The NDS is a good candidate for an enterprise data warehouse. It contains a complete set of data, including all versions of master data, and it is normalized, with nearly no data redundancy, so data updates are more easily and quickly compared to the dimensional master data store. It also contains both source systems' natural keys and data warehouse surrogate keys, enabling you to map and trace data between the source systems and data warehouse.

You would use an NDS + DDS architecture when you need to make several DDSs for different purposes containing a different set of data and when you need to integrate data in a normalized form and use the integrated data outside of the dimensional data warehouse.

ODS + DDS

This architecture is similar to an NDS + DDS architecture, but it has an ODS in the place of the NDS. Like NDS, ODS is in third normal form or higher. Unlike the NDS, the ODS contains only the current version of master data; it has no historical master data. The structure of its entities is like an OLTP database. The ODS has no surrogate keys. The surrogate keys are maintained in the DDS ETL. The ODS integrates the data from various source systems. The data in the ODS is cleaned and integrated. The data flowing into the ODS has already passed the DQ screening. Figure 2-6 shows ODS + DDS data flow architecture.

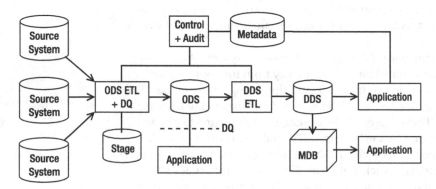

Figure 2-6. *ODS + DDS data flow architecture*

Like NDS, ODS contains transaction tables and master tables. The transaction tables contain business events, and the master tables contain the people or objects involved in the business events. The fact tables in the DDS are populated from the transaction tables in the ODS. The dimension tables in the DDS are populated from the master tables in the ODS. Unlike NDS, ODS's master tables contain only the current version of master data. ODS does not contain the historical versions of master data.

Unlike NDS, which is an internal data store, ODS is a hybrid data store. This means ODS is accessible by the end users and end-user applications. In NDS + DDS applications, NDS is not accessible by the end users and end-user applications. Unlike NDS, ODS is updatable. End-user applications can retrieve data from the ODS, but they can also update the ODS. To ensure the quality of the data in the ODS, data quality rules are also applied to these updates. The end-user application must not update the data coming from the source systems; it can update only the data that itself generates to complement the source systems' data. If the ODS is used to support a CRM customer support application, data such as status and comments can be written on ODS directly, but all the customer data is still from the source systems.

In the ODS + DDS architecture, the DDS is the master data store. Unlike an NDS + DDS architecture, in an ODS + DDS architecture you have only one DDS. The DDS contains a complete set of fact tables and the dimension tables. The DDS contains both the current version and all historical versions of master data.

The principles about the stage, control, audit, and metadata discussed in regard to the single DDS architecture are also applicable here. Some entities can fly through directly to the ODS without being staged first. Integration and transformation happen in the memory of the ETL server. The DDS ETL is simpler than the one in the single DDS architecture because the data in the ODS is already integrated and cleaned. In many cases, it is literally feeding DDS incrementally without any transformation. Most, if not all, fact table calculations have been done in the ODS.

In the ODS + DDS architecture, applications can access the data warehouse in three places in three different formats: those that need the data in normalized form can access the ODS, those that need the data in relational dimensional format can access the DDS, and those that need the data in multidimensional format can access the MDBs.

This architecture has these advantages:

- The third normal form is slimmer than the NDS because it contains only current values. This makes the performance of both ODS ETL and DDS ETL better than the ones in the NDS + DDS architecture.

- Like the NDS + DDS architecture, in the ODS + DDS architecture you have a central place to integrate, maintain, and publish master data.

- The normalized relational store is updatable by the end-user application, making it capable of supporting operational applications at the transaction level.

The disadvantage of this architecture is that to build a new, small DDS (say, 2007 Q4 sales data), you need to get it from the main DDS and cannot utilize the existing DDS ETL to do that. You need either to write custom queries (in other words, create table from select), which is not preferred because of standardization and consistency reasons, or to build a new ETL, which is not preferred either because of the effort, especially if it is a one-off, throwaway thing.

You would use an ODS + DDS architecture when you need only a one dimensional data store and you need a centralized, normalized data store to be used for operational purposes such as CRM. The ODS contains detailed, current-valued, integrated data that is useful for transactional queries.

Federated Data Warehouse

A federated data warehouse consists of several data warehouses with a data retrieval layer on top of them. A federated data warehouse retrieves data from existing data warehouses using an ETL and loads the data into a new dimensional data store. For example, because of merger and acquisition activities, you could have three data warehouses. Perhaps the first one is a dimensional data warehouse, the second one is a third normal form normalized data warehouse, and the third one is a relational data warehouse with a few big transaction tables referencing many reference tables. Figure 2-7 shows a federated data warehouse.

The granularity of the FDW data is the same as the highest of the granularities of source data warehouses. If the granularities of the source data warehouses are G1, G2, and G3, then the granularity of the FDW data is the highest of (G1, G2, G3). This is because you can consolidate data only on the same granularity and because you can transform data only from lower granularity to higher granularity, not the reverse direction. For example, if G1 is daily, G2 is weekly, and G3 is monthly, then the granularity of FDW is monthly. This is because you can transform G1 and G2 to monthly, but you cannot transform G3 to daily or weekly.

The ETL that extracts data from the source data warehouses needs to be aware of the timing of the data. The data in the source data warehouses may not arrive at the same frequency. The FDW ETL needs to match the frequency of the source DWs. If the source DWs have different update frequencies, the FDW ETL needs to run several times to match the frequency of each source DW.

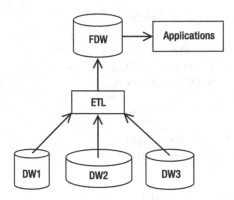

Figure 2-7. *A federated data warehouse from several data warehouses*

The FDW ETL needs to integrate the data from source DWs based on business rules. The ETL needs to identify whether records from one source data warehouse are duplicates of records from the other source data warehouses. Duplicate records need to be merged. The business rules need to be applied to determine which record should survive and which attributes need to be updated. In addition, the FDW ETL needs to transform the data from different source DWs into a common structure and common format.

You also need to bear in mind that the number of subject areas in the FDW is probably narrower than the number of subject areas in the source DWs. This is because the FDW is at a higher level than the source DWs, and at this level, not all subject areas are applicable and useful for the business users. For example, in the global data warehouse, you may be interested in sales and employees and leave inventory and campaigns in the regional data warehouses.

When you have several data warehouses like this, it is possible to implement enterprise information integration (EII) rather than ETL, as described in Figure 2-8, especially if the source data warehouses are similar. EII is a method to integrate data by accessing different source systems online and aggregating the outputs on the fly before bringing the end result to the user. Everything is done the moment a user requests the information. There is no storage of any form that stores the aggregated or integrated data. The main advantage of using EII is the data freshness; in other words, the result is truly real time. In Figure 2-8, even if data warehouse DW3 was changed a second ago, the end result will still include that last second change. Even though there is no integrated data warehouse, sometimes this architecture is also called federated data warehouse. For example, if the organization consists of three geographical regions, such as Asia Pacific, America, and EMEA, then each region has a different ERP system and different IT organizations; hence, they have three data warehousing projects. But they all agreed to standardize on the same structure: dimensional data warehousing with fact and dimension tables.

Instead of integrating several data warehouses, federated data warehouse can also be implemented when there are several nonintegrated data marts in the organization, as shown in Figure 2-9.

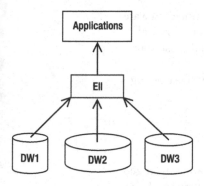

Figure 2-8. *Federated data warehouse using enterprise information integration*

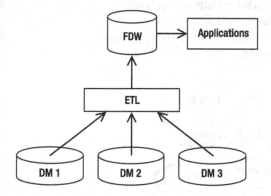

Figure 2-9. *A federated data warehouse from several data marts*

The source data marts in Figure 2-9 can be in many different forms. They can be dimensional, normalized, or neither. These marts could be two conformed fact tables surrounded by four to eight conformed dimensions in star schema format, properly designed using the Kimball dimensional modeling approach. They could be in a snowflake format where the dimensions are normalized. They could be in third normal form (or higher). And in many cases, they might not be data marts at all; in other words, they don't follow any formal data warehousing design approach and instead are just a collection of tables with good data inside them, and the users call these tables *data marts*. You can use FDW to integrate these data marts.

The same principles described previously when integrating data warehouses are still applicable, specifically, level of granularity, matching/deduplicating, reformatting, dealing with timing issues, and platform diversity. In some cases, you may want to consider bypassing some marts and accessing the source systems directly, especially if the same source system is supplying the same data to different data marts.

You can also still use the EII approach here when integrating the data marts. That is, you don't have a permanent data store at the federated level but can access the source data marts on the fly when users issue their requests.

The main advantage of this architecture is that you can accommodate existing data warehouses, and therefore the development time will be shorter. The main disadvantage is that, practically speaking, it is difficult to build a good-quality warehouse from such diverse standards found in the source data marts or data warehouses.

You would use federated data warehouse architecture when you want to utilize existing data warehouses or where you want to integrate data from several data marts.

System Architecture

The previous sections covered data flow architecture. They showed how the data is arranged in the data stores and how the data flows within the data warehouse system. Once you have chosen a certain data flow architecture, you then need to design the system architecture, which is the physical arrangement and connections between the servers, network, software, storage system, and clients. Designing a system architecture requires knowledge about hardware (especially servers), networking (especially with regard to security and performance and in the last few years also fiber networks), and storage (especially storage area networks [SANs], redundant array of inexpensive disks [RAID], and automated tape backup solutions). Figure 2-10 shows an example of a system architecture.

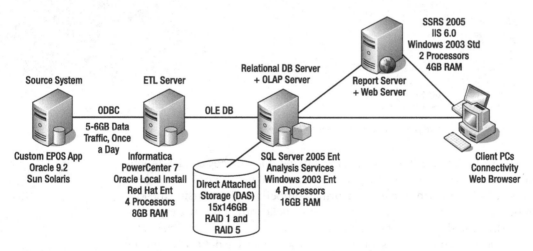

Figure 2-10. *Example of a system architecture for data warehouse*

In this example, the system architecture consists of three servers: one ETL server, one database server, and one reporting server. The source system is an electronic point-of-sale system that records retail sales in the stores running on Oracle 9.2 on Sun Solaris. The ETL server is Informatica PowerCenter 7 installed on Red Hat Enterprise Linux. The data warehouse data stores (stage, DDS, and MDB) are hosted in the SQL Server relational database engine and Analysis Services, running on Windows Server 2003. The data is physically stored in a DAS consisting of fifteen 146GB disks, making the raw capacity 2TB. The disks are configured in RAID 1 and RAID 5 for data resilience. (I will discuss RAID in Chapter 6 when I cover physical database design.) The reports are created and managed using SSRS installed on Windows Server 2003.

I chose this example because it represents a typical architecture for a medium system. We have a dedicated ETL server, separated from the database server. It's a medium size of data; the raw capacity of 2TB is about 400GB to 500GB final usable database space, assuming we have both development and production environments. The platform is a bit of a mixture, as typically found in organizations: the source system and ETL are not Microsoft. The Informatica was probably already there when the data warehouse project started, so they have to use what they already have. Therefore, you can create a system architecture with different platforms.

A data warehouse architect does not usually design the system architecture of a data warehouse infrastructure, but in my opinion, it is helpful if they know these subjects—perhaps not at a very detailed level, but they need to know at a high level. For example, they don't need to understand how to build a four-node cluster using Windows 2003 servers, but they need to know what kind of high availability can be achieved using clustering technology.

To design a data warehouse system architecture, you first establish the technology stack you want to use for ETL, the database, and BI, such as Microsoft SQL Server (SSIS, SSAS, SSIS), Informatica + Oracle 9i + Cognos, and so on. This is determined based on product capability and based on the company standard. After you determine the technology stack, you do a high-level design on the servers, network configuration, and storage configuration that supports the chosen technology, including high-availability design. Then you determine the detailed technical specification of the servers, network, and storage. This is done based on capacity and system performance requirements. You then order the hardware and software and build the system in the data center together with the hardware and network vendor. You then install and configure the software. Designing and building the environment is fundamental and critical to the performance and stability of the data warehouse system that you are going to build on top of it.

The other factor that greatly affects the system architecture is the choice of software in building the data warehouse, such as specific versions of SQL Server, Oracle, or Teradata. The system architectures required to run this software are different. For example, Teradata runs on massively parallel processing hardware. It does not share the storage between the nodes. On the other hand, a SQL Server cluster uses central storage. It shares the storage between the nodes.

In terms of software, there are two different types of database software: symmetric multiprocessing (SMP) and massively parallel processing (MPP). An SMP database system is a database system that runs on one or more machines with several identical processors sharing the same disk storage. When an SMP database system runs on more than one machine, it is called a *clustered configuration*. The database is physically located in a single disk storage system. Examples of SMP database systems are SQL Server, Oracle, DB/2, Informix, and Sybase. An MPP database system is a database system that runs on more than one machine where each machine has its own disk storage. The database is physically located in several disk storage systems that are interconnected to each other. An MPP database system is also known as a *parallel database system*. Examples of MPP database systems are Teradata, Neoview, Netezza, and DATAllegro.

The machines in SMP and MPP database systems are called *nodes*. An MPP database system is faster and more scalable than an SMP database system. In an MPP database system, a table is physically located in several nodes, each with its own storage. When you retrieve data from this table, all nodes simultaneously read the data from their own storage, so the process of reading the data from disk is quicker. Similarly, when you load data into this table, all nodes simultaneously load a bit of the data into their disks. In SMP database systems, there is a bottleneck on the disk storage. SMP database systems, on the other hand, are simpler, are easier to maintain, and have lower costs.

In this book, I'll show how to use SQL Server 2005 to build a data warehouse, but it also runs on SQL Server 2008. I will use SSIS for the ETL tool, I will build the NDS and DDS on SQL Server 2005 databases, and I will use SSRS for reporting and SSAS for OLAP and data mining.

Case Study

I will be using the following case study throughout this book. In this chapter, you will be studying the data warehouse architecture using this case study. In all further chapters, you will be using this case study to learn the subjects discussed in those chapters in a real project situation. For example, in Chapter 5, I will show how to create the data model; in Chapter 6, I will show how to design the database; in Chapters 7 and 8, I will show how to build the ETL, and so on.

This case study needs to cover all the aspects you want to learn in this book: architecture, methodology, requirements, data modeling, database design, ETL, data quality, metadata, data stores, report, multidimensional databases, BI, CRM, testing, and data warehouse administration. Ideally, I want the case study to be simple enough to understand and to deliver as a project, but I don't want it to be too simple because it will not cover some areas mentioned previously. So, it needs to simple but not too simple.

Some industries are "data warehousing friendly," meaning the nature of the data is ideal for data warehousing. Retail, utilities, telecommunication, health care, and financial services are some of them. In this case study, I chose the retail sector because the business operations are easier to understand since we experience them in our daily lives.

Amadeus Entertainment is an entertainment retailer specializing in music, films, and audio books. It has eight online stores operating in the United States, Germany, France, the United Kingdom, Spain, Australia, Japan, and India. It has 96 offline stores operating in those countries as well.

Customers can buy individual products such as a song, an audio book, or a film, or they can subscribe to a certain package, which enables them to download a certain quantity of products in a certain period. For example, with the Primer package, you can download 100 songs, 50 books, and 50 films a month for $50. Customers can also listen or watch a song, a book, or a film once for $\frac{1}{10}$ the cost of purchasing it. So if a film is $5, to watch it once it's only 50 cents. Customers use online streaming for this, so a good Internet connection is required.

Amadeus Entertainment has four main delivery channels: Internet, mobile phone, cable TV, and post. There are several payment models for customer subscriptions, such as annual, in advance, and monthly direct debit. The company purchases the products in bulk, such as any 10,000 songs from a record company, of any title, for a certain cost. For online streaming, the company pays a central provider (Geo Broadcasting Ltd.) based on usage (monthly invoice).

The company uses WebTower9, a custom-developed .NET-based system for dynamic web sites, multimedia trading, broadcasting, sales order processing, and subscription management, all running on an Oracle database. The back-end enterprise resource planning (ERP) system is Jupiter, an off-the-shelf AS/400-based business system running on DB2. This is where the inventory, products, and finances are managed. The Jupiter database size is about 800GB with about 250 tables and views.

Business activities in the offline stores are managed in Jade, which is a custom Java-based system running on Informix. This includes sales, customer service, and subscriptions. WebTower9 and Jade interface with Jupiter products and finances on a daily basis, but sales and customer data (including subscriptions) are kept on WebTower9 and Jade.

The company uses the SupplyNet system for interfacing with suppliers. It is a web services–based industry-standard supplier network in the online entertainment industry including music and film. WebTower9 and Jupiter are hosted in Amadeus Entertainment's head office. Jade is hosted in an outsourced company in Bangalore, India. The Jupiter overnight batch starts at 11 p.m. Eastern standard time (EST) for three to four hours. An offline backup job kicks off immediately after the overnight batch and runs for one to two hours. The Jade tape backup starts at 3 a.m. EST for two to three hours.

The IT architecture team decided to standardize the database platform on Microsoft SQL Server and use web-based services for its application platform. Hence, in this case study, I will show how to build a data warehouse system for Amadeus Entertainment using Microsoft SQL Server 2005. You can also use SQL Server 2008 to build it. I will be using NDS + DDS data warehouse architecture outlined earlier in this chapter. Figure 2-11 shows the system architecture for the production environment.

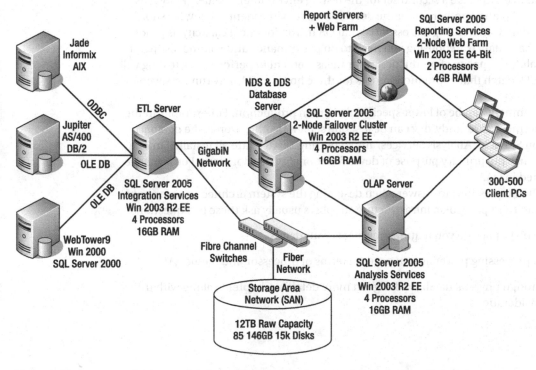

Figure 2-11. *System architecture for the production environment for Amadeus Entertainment data warehouse*

In Figure 2-11, Integration Services, Reporting Services, and Analysis Services will be installed on separate machines. We will be using SAN with a raw capacity of 12TB. The final storage capacity could be much less than the raw capacity. When I cover physical database design in Chapter 6, I will be using this system architecture as the basis of the design.

This is only a tentative architecture as an illustration of how it could be implemented. The server specifications in Figure 2-11 are high, probably too high for this project. When we get the requirements, we can further detail the design. For example:

- High-availability requirements (how many hours can they tolerate the data warehouse to be down) affect the clustering decision of the database servers.

- The volume of the data from the source systems affects the number of processors and the memory of the ETL server and whether we need to put SSIS on a separate machine.

- The volume of the data in the data warehouse affects the storage size and backup requirements. The SAN raw disk size may be less or more than 12TB depending on the actual requirements.

- The number and sizes of the OLAP cubes affect the memory and processors of the OLAP server and whether you need to put Analysis Services on a separate server.

You need to bear in mind, especially when budgeting for infrastructure (hardware and software), that you need to make a second set for the testing environment (widely known as quality assurance [QA]) and another set for the development environment (or dev, for short). Unlike in OLTP, in data warehousing it is essential that QA has an identical capacity as production. This is because in data warehousing you need to do performance and volume testing. If your QA is only half the capacity of production, your measurement in performance testing will be incorrect. An ETL batch that in production runs for three hours in QA may run for seven hours.

The dev environment can be of lower specifications than production. For example, in the Amadeus Entertainment case study, dev can be just one server; in other words, the database engine, Integration Services, Analysis Services, and Reporting Services are all installed in one server. This is because the primary purpose of dev is functionality development. Performance testing is conducted in QA.

The most difficult questions to answer when designing the system architecture are about sizing and/or capacity. In particular, infrastructure suppliers usually ask these two questions:

- How much disk space do you require (how big is your data)?

- How much processing power do you need (in terms of processor and memory)?

We will go through physical database design in more detail in Chapter 6, along with the infrastructure considerations.

Summary

In this chapter, I discussed several data warehouse architectures. The single DDS, NDS + DDS, and ODS + DDS architectures have dimensional data warehouse. The single DDS does not have a normalized store, while the others have a normalized store. The federated data warehouse architecture consists of several data warehouses integrated by a data retrieval layer. I also discussed the system architecture in particular for implementation using SQL Server 2005.

You'll use the case study introduced in this chapter to help you understand the subjects in later chapters. In Chapter 5, when I discuss dimensional modeling and entity relationship modeling, I will go through the data warehouse design in more detail. In Chapter 6, when I discuss physical database design, I will go through the elements of system architecture in more detail.

■ ■ ■

CHAPTER 3

Data Warehouse Development Methodology

Some people believe they do not need to define the business requirements when building a data warehouse because a data warehouse is built to suit the nature of the data in the organization, not to suit the people. I believe that all IT systems of any kind need to be built to suit the users. A system must be usable. If the system is not used, there is no point in building it. This usability concept is fundamental to this chapter, so keep that in mind.

In this chapter, I will explain the process, or *methodology*, of building a data warehouse. In software engineering, the discipline that studies the process people use to develop an information system is called the *system development life cycle* (SDLC) or the *system development methodology*. There are two main variants: waterfall and iterative. The waterfall methodology is also known as the *sequential methodology*. The *iterative methodology* is also known as the *spiral* or *incremental methodology*.

The waterfall methodology is one of the oldest methodologies (it has been around for about 30 years) and is widely used by many organizations to build their systems, including their data warehouse systems. The iterative methodology is very different from waterfall. It is not as widely used as waterfall, but it gives good benefits if used correctly. Some people prefer waterfall and some people prefer iterative, so I will compare the two and describe their advantages and disadvantages, along with some personal experience in implementing them in data warehousing projects, from which I hope we can all learn.

Waterfall Methodology

In a waterfall system, you have certain steps that need to be accomplished one way after the other, in a particular sequence, like going down the stairs or like a multistep waterfall (which is where it gets its name from). There are many variations of the steps' names, but in general they are feasibility study, requirements, architecture, design, development, testing, deployment, and operation. Figure 3-1 describes these steps in order.

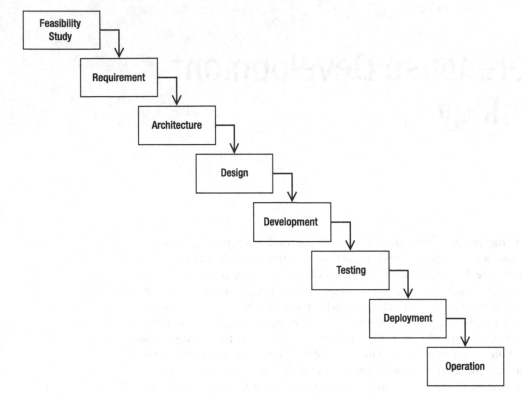

Figure 3-1. *Waterfall methodology*

Some variations of the step names are proposal, analysis, business requirement definition, technical architecture, functional design, technical design, unit testing, system testing, integration testing, user acceptance testing, rollout, implementation, maintenance, and support. Some variations turn bigger steps into smaller ones; for example, design is split into functional design and technical design, and testing is split into system testing, performance testing, integration testing, and user acceptance testing. Some of the names are synonyms; for example, instead of calling it *deployment*, some people call it *rollout* or *go live*.

Next, I will explain what needs to be done during each of these steps. But before I do that, I'll add two more boxes (labeled "Infrastructure Setup" and "Project Management") and rearrange all the boxes horizontally, as shown in Figure 3-2.

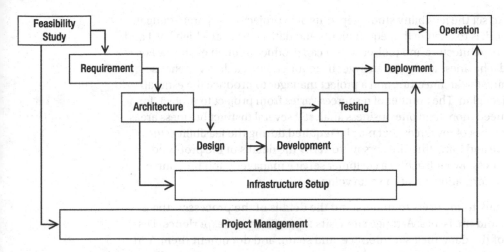

Figure 3-2. *Waterfall methodology with infrastructure setup and project management*

I'll now discuss the boxes in the figures one by one, detailing what you need to do when building a data warehouse:

Feasibility study. You gather the requirements at a high level (for example, determining why you need a data warehouse and whether data warehousing is the right solution), you have a quick look at the source systems to find out whether it is possible to get the data you need, you get sample data to assess the data quality, and you write a proposal (some people prefer to call this document the *business case*). The important things to mention in the proposal are the benefits, how long it will take, how much it will cost, and the business justifications. Other things that you probably need to put in the proposal are the requirements (just the summary), the project organization (including external resources such as consultants and contractors), and the project plan (it's very important to know who will be doing what when).

As you can see, in order to produce a decent proposal, you have to know everything in advance: the requirements, the solution, the architecture, the design, the infrastructure, the data quality, what tasks are required, and how you would resource it (external or internal). All these are required to find out how long it will take to build the data warehouse and how much will it cost. This step requires experience. It can really be done only by those people who have built data warehouse systems several times. For example, at this early stage, how would you know the specification of the servers and how long it would take to build the ETL system?

I find that it is best to set the feasibility study step as its own project on separate budget. In this phase, the work is to analyze the requirements and data volume at a high level and determine a suitable architecture and toolset so you can produce a rough estimate. For this work, you need a business analyst to analyze the requirements, a data warehouse architect to determine the architecture, and a project manager to produce the estimate and high-level project plan. The number of resources varies from project to project; for example, you may need more than one business analyst if several distinct business areas are involved. Other types of resources that may be required during the feasibility study phase are a hardware and infrastructure person (to verify the details of the proposed architecture), a business owner (such as a customer service manager), and the source system DBA (to get information about the data volume).

Requirements: You talk to the users to understand the details of the processes, the business, the data, and the issues. Arrange site visits to get firsthand experience. Discuss the meaning of the data, the user interface, and so on, and document them. You also list the nonfunctional requirements such as performance and security. I will go through the requirements in more detail in the next chapter.

Architecture: I discussed this in the previous chapter. Basically, you need to determine which data flow architecture you are going to use and what system architecture you are going to use, in detail, including the specification for database servers, the type of network, the storage solution, and so on. It is important to have somebody who has done this many times; if you don't have anybody in the organization with these skills, then hire from outside. It is not common to find data warehousing and infrastructure skills in one person. This is a critical step, meaning that if the architecture is wrong, you may have to redesign everything from scratch or restart the project from the beginning.

Design: You need to design three main parts of the data warehouse system: the data stores, the ETL system, and the front-end applications. These require different skill sets so potentially it could require different people. I will go through the data stores in Chapters 5 and 6, the ETL system in Chapters 7 and 8, and the front-end applications in Chapters 11 to 15. In addition, you need to design two other parts: data quality systems and metadata, which I will discuss in Chapters 9 and 10. Some people consider data quality and metadata as part of the ETL system.

Development: You need to build the three parts that you design: the data stores, the ETL system (including data quality system and metadata), and the front-end application. I'll discuss these topics in the relevant chapters mentioned in the previous paragraph. With some caution and consideration, these three parts can be built in parallel. The most important consideration when building in parallel is to define accurate interfaces between the parts.

Testing: Basically, you need to test the data stores, the ETL, and the front-end applications. This is potentially the weakest point in the whole project. In many projects I've worked on that used the waterfall approach, testing has always been the problematic part. Everything is quiet until the development finishes and testing begins. Why? Well, this is the first time all the components are put together and the first time the whole architecture runs as a system. This is the first time the users see the data warehouse. This is the first time the test environment and the production environment are used. This is the first time you try to run the system at maximum capacity (for performance testing). The go-live date is approaching fast, and you cannot risk any errors in the production environment. There are so many "first-time" happenings at the time of testing, it's no wonder there are many surprises. As a result, you spend a lot of time and money fixing the problems. (I will discuss data warehouse testing in Chapter 16.) You can mitigate these problems by putting together these components and running the whole architecture several times during development. Another way to mitigate these problems is by doing prototyping to discover problems early.

Deployment: Once the system is ready, you put all the components in the production boxes: the ETL system, the data stores, and the front-end applications. You do the initial load; that is, you load the data from the source system for the first time. You do a few tests in the production environment to make sure the data warehouse is populated correctly and the front-end applications are producing the correct figures. You produce the user guide, the operation guide, and the troubleshooting guide for the operations team. You train the users and the operations team. You support the system, the users, and the operations team for a few weeks. You hand over the system to the operations team, and you close the project. I will discuss deployment in Chapter 16 when I discuss testing.

Operation: The users continue to use the data warehouse and the application. The operations team continues to administer the data warehouse and to support the users. There are basically three types of support: solving errors or problems that happen when using the system, administering new users and their access rights (and of existing users), and helping new and existing users using the system (kind of "how do I...?" questions). Users will also have enhancement requests: to add more data to the data warehouse (or change existing data), to add a feature to the front-end applications, or to create a new report or a new cube. The operations team will then pass these requests to you in the development team. You prioritize the requests, and then either you reject them or you do them and include them in the next release.

Infrastructure setup: One of the biggest tasks when you build an application is to prepare the production environment where you are going to run the application and to build the development and testing environment. This task consists of creating system architecture, doing technical design, procuring goods (buying the hardware and software), installing hardware, installing and configuring software, connecting networks (including firewall changes), testing the infrastructure, producing infrastructure documentation, and handing it all over to the operations team. It is a project in itself and needs to be managed as such. At the very least it should be managed as a subproject. In my experience, many people underestimate the scale of this task, which usually results in the data warehouse project being delayed because the infrastructure is not ready.

Project management: This is when you maintain the project plan (that means at any time you have to know the status of each task and who will be doing what and when), maintain good communication with all stakeholders (project sponsors, users, and developers) including status reports and meetings, and attack the risks aggressively (rather than resolving them when they become issues).

Iterative Methodology

The basic principle of the iterative methodology is to release bigger and bigger portions of the complete project to discover problems early and make necessary adjustments when the requirements cannot be adequately defined by users. In the waterfall methodology, you go live once, and prior to that you have a period of testing when you try to fix errors. In the iterative methodology, you release a version of the system several times into production to be used by selected users. For example, say it will take eight months to build a data warehouse system; using the waterfall methodology, it is going live in month 8. If you use the iterative methodology, you will be releasing a version in months 3, 6, and 8 (three times) into production.

You build the data warehouse in pieces horizontally. In each iteration, you build a piece from end to end. In other words, in each iteration you do the requirements, design, build, test, put it into production, and have the users use it. And you build all the necessary components to support that piece in production. For example, if you want to deliver a data mart, you build the ETL, the data stores, and the front-end application. Figure 3-3 shows this concept.

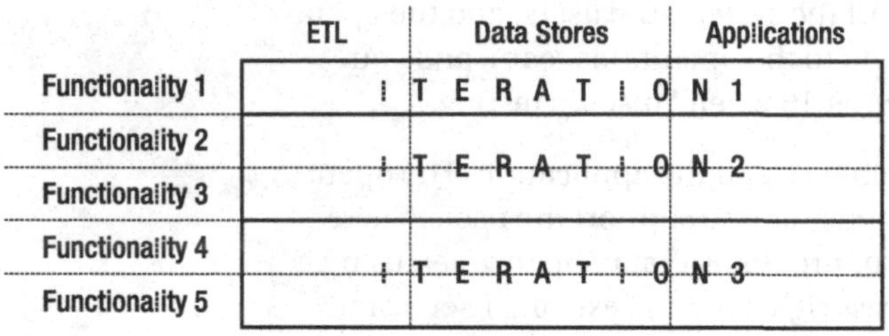

	ETL	Data Stores	Applications
Functionality 1		I T E R A T I O N 1	
Functionality 2		I T E R A T I O N 2	
Functionality 3			
Functionality 4		I T E R A T I O N 3	
Functionality 5			

Figure 3-3. *Building a data warehouse in multiple iterations*

You can also picture the iterative methodology as a circle or spiral where each cycle consists of design, development, testing, and deployment. The architecture needs to be done only in the first iteration. Figure 3-4 describes this.

When working on the sections labeled as "Design" in Figure 3-4, you need to define the requirements too. Also, you need to do a feasibility study before the section labeled as "Arch" in Figure 3-4. To be completely thorough, after the last "Deploy" section, you can add the "Operation" segment too.

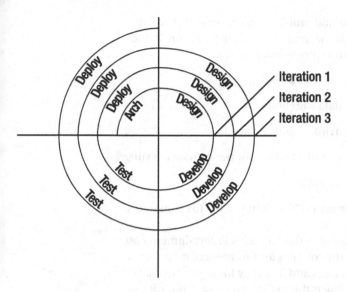

Figure 3-4. *Iterative cycles*

The main reason for doing the project this way is to minimize the risks. One of the bottle-necks in a waterfall methodology, as I explained previously, is the testing period. The testing period is the riskiest time in a waterfall methodology because of the following reasons:

- This is the first time all the components are put together and the first time the whole architecture runs as a system.

- This is the first time the users see and use the data warehouse.

- This is the first time the test environment and the production environment are used.

- This is the first time you try to run the system at maximum capacity (for performance testing).

- The go-live date is approaching fast, and you cannot risk any errors in the production environment. There are many "first-time" happening at the time of testing.

■**Note** To be fair, there are ways to mitigate these risks in the waterfall methodology. For example, you can build a prototype where you put all the components together and run them as a whole architecture to detect potential issues early. Also, by building a prototype, the business users are able to see the user interface early.

The iterative methodology eliminates all five risks and problems mentioned earlier! All five of them have been done since iteration 1 so that at the final go-live date (iteration 3), the system will run a lot more smoothly. Let's go through this process step by step:

1. In the first iteration, you run the whole architecture as a system.

2. In the first iteration, the users see and use the data warehouse.

3. In the first iteration, the test and production environments are used.

4. In the first iteration, you run the system at maximum capacity for performance testing.

5. In the first iteration, you deploy to production (go live).

And by the time you reach the last iteration, there are no "first times" left! This eliminates those risks and problems.

Perhaps it is easier to explain with an example. Let's use the Amadeus Entertainment case study that I described in Chapter 2. Say, for example, the solution for this particular project is to build four data marts: sales, purchasing, inventory, and CRM. Let's say for argument's sake that CRM is the most complex data mart and purchasing is the easiest data mart. You will see the detailed design of these data marts in Chapter 5 when I discuss dimensional modeling, but for now let's concentrate on how to use the iterative methodology. Let's also say that the system architecture that you are going to use is similar to Figure 2-11. You will be using the NDS + DDS data architecture (please refer to Chapter 2). There will be five full-time people working on the project: a project manager (PM), a data warehouse architect (DWA), a business analyst (BA), and two developers.

In this particular project, you will go live three times. The focus of the first iteration is the architecture. This doesn't mean you don't deliver any functionality. You do deliver functionality by building the easiest data mart (purchasing). In fact, you are building the entire system, from ETL to data stores to reports to cubes. But the focus in the first iteration is on architecture, which is why you don't want to take the most difficult data mart to build during the first iteration. In the Rational Unified Process (RUP) methodology, this type of iteration is called *elaboration*, where you focus on the architecture. RUP is one of the methodologies that uses an iterative approach.

The focus of the second iteration is the functionality. Therefore, in the second iteration, you pick the most complex data mart (CRM). Because it is the most difficult data mart, if you can do this mart, all other marts should not be a problem. In RUP, the type of iteration where you focus on functionality is also an *elaboration* phase.

Now that you have made sure the architecture works and that you can build the most demanding functionality, in the third iteration you just need to work like a factory to produce code as efficiently as possible. In RUP, this type of iteration is called *construction*, where you do mass production to complete the system. In RUP, there is one more type of iteration called *inception* (which is the first iteration), where you focus on getting the stakeholders to agree on the objectives, the rough architecture, and the high-level schedule.

In the Amadeus Entertainment case study, iteration 1 will run for three months, producing a live system in the production environment. The system is not necessarily ready for use by all users, because not all functionality is built yet. The main goal of this iteration is to prove that the system architecture and data architecture work. You do this by getting the easiest data mart (purchasing) up and running in the production system. The DWA will specify the system architecture technically (as in Figure 3-5), and the PM will coordinate with infrastructure people to get it purchased, installed, and set up, including the necessary connectivity to and from different parts of the network to build the architecture. The DWA will supervise the installation technically, for example, the disk carving of the SAN and the configuration of SQL Server. The infrastructure team (internal or external contractors) will get production, quality assurance (QA), and development environment set up and ready. The result is an up-and-running system architecture and infrastructure, as shown in Figure 3-5.

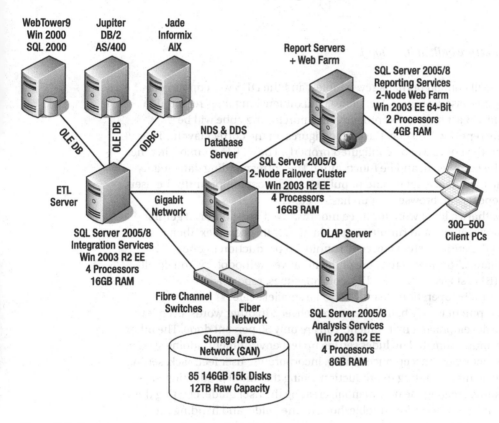

Figure 3-5. *System architecture built in iteration 1*

The BA and DWA will work together to design and create part of the NDS and DDS databases required by the purchasing data mart, as shown in Figure 3-6. They will also specify the front-end application for three reports and one OLAP cube. The two developers will build the ETL and the report and set up the OLAP cube. The system will extract the purchase order table from the Jupiter, Jade, and WebTower9 systems every day and load the data into the NDS database. The DDS ETL will get the data into the DDS database, as shown in Figure 3-6.

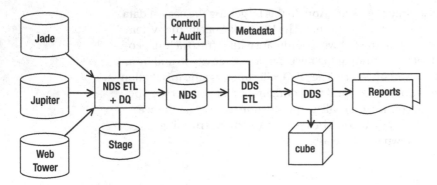

Figure 3-6. *Data flow architecture built in iteration 1*

At this time, the NDS will contain perhaps seven tables, and the DDS will contain perhaps five tables—only the necessary entities, fact tables, and dimension tables required to support the purchasing data mart to function properly. The purchasing cube will be refreshed periodically. The report will display the correct figures, in the correct layout. The security in the reports and the cubes will be configured properly. The ETL for purchasing the data mart will be tested, be completed, and be functioning. The corresponding data quality routines are built, and the metadata is set up and populated. And most importantly, the users will use the purchasing reports and browse the purchasing cube.

You might say, "Wow, that's a lot of work for three months." Well, the point is if getting just the easiest part of the system up and running in production is this complex, then what are the chances of getting the entire system correctly running in production in one go? I think the answer is "no chance." So, that is the core of the iterative methodology. You do all the system components (ETL, stage, NDS, DDS, DQ, control, cubes, reports)—including the training and the handover to the operations team—but on a smaller scale.

My point is that development is only half of the entire delivery. In other words, even if you get everything built in the development environment, you are only 50 percent done. The other 50 percent that is usually underestimated includes setting up test environments, doing system testing, fixing errors, conducting user acceptance testing, incorporating user feedback, setting up the production infrastructure, migrating to production, doing the initial production loading, doing production testing, creating the user manual, creating the user guide, creating the usability guide, creating the operation guide, troubleshooting the guide, and handing everything over to the operations team.

In contrast to the waterfall methodology, in the first iteration you already experience all those remaining 50 percent activities, and you deliver a production system that is used by the users. This enables immediate user feedback, which could be incorporated in the following iterations. This approach also eliminates the five eminent risks mentioned earlier that usually appear in the testing period. In return for that benefit, the iterative methodology requires the production environment up front, which is needed for deploying the system into production.

The second iteration will focus on delivering the functionality. In this iteration, you will build the most difficult data mart, that is, the CRM data mart. You will do the same activities as the first iteration, from defining the requirements to handing everything over to the operations team. This iteration will take approximately three months. During this period, you will build all the components required to support the CRM mart: the ETL, the data stores, the application, the data quality, and the metadata. This second iteration is usually easier than the first iteration because the people now have the experience to develop, test, and deploy to production. In addition, the development, quality assurance (QA), and production environments are already set up and configured properly, and the users know what to expect, so there are no surprises there.

The last iteration will deliver the remaining functionality, the sales and inventory data marts. In this iteration, you can accommodate change requests based on the user feedback on the first two iterations. You will do the same activities as the previous two iterations: from gathering the requirement to handing everything over to the production team. You will build the same components: the ETL system, metadata system, data quality system, data stores, and front-end applications.

The advantage of using this iteration methodology is obvious: it minimizes the risks. In other words, the project has more of a chance to be successful, and the delivered system will have a better quality. The main disadvantage is that the infrastructure needs to be delivered up front.

Summary

The waterfall methodology is commonly used in software development including in data warehousing. There are three main streams of work: ETL, data stores, and front-end applications. In the waterfall methodology, you go live once, while in the iterative methodology you go live many times. With waterfall, the riskiest period is during testing. This is because it is the first time the whole architecture runs as a system, the first time the users see the data warehouse, and the first time the production environment is used. It's also risky because the go-live date is approaching fast, and you cannot risk any errors in the production environment.

The iterative methodology overcomes those problems by bringing deployment to production up front. By doing this, you do all the critical things in the first iteration. You minimize the risks because you go live with only one piece of the system.

■ ■ ■

CHAPTER 4

Functional and Nonfunctional Requirements

It is important to define functional and nonfunctional requirements when building a data warehouse system to make sure that the system we build will help users achieve the business objectives. *Functional requirements* define what the system does. They contain the features that the data warehouse system should have. *Nonfunctional requirements* guide and constrain the architecture.

Sometimes the best way to learn something is by doing it. In this chapter, I will use the Amadeus Entertainment case study described in Chapter 2 to show how to gather functional and nonfunctional requirements. First, we will find out about Amadeus Entertainment's business issues and challenges. Then we will identify the business areas that would benefit from a data warehouse system. We will then dive into each of these areas and learn about the business operations within that area. By that I mean the purpose, the processes, the roles, the exceptions, and the issues. We will need this understanding later when we do data modeling in the next chapter.

After we understand the business operations, we will define the functional requirements, that is, the things that define what the data warehouse system does, such as the questions or issues that a data warehouse system will be able to answer, the data that will be stored in the data warehouse, and the analysis the users will be performing. We will also define the nonfunctional requirements, such as security, availability, and performance. An example of a nonfunctional requirement (in this case, availability) is that the data warehouse is expected to be up and running with downtime of less than one hour a month.

We will then investigate the operational systems (Jupiter, WebTower9, and Jade) and conduct a data feasibility study to find out whether the data that we need is available in the source systems and whether it is accessible. We will research the amount of data, the condition of the data, and the quality of the data and try to identify any potential risks in the project that could prevent us from delivering a data warehouse system that satisfies those functional and nonfunctional requirements.

Identifying Business Areas

In the case study, Amadeus Entertainment is a worldwide online and offline retailer specializing in music, films, and audio books, with outlets in eight countries. Let's name the key people in this case study: the business project manager is Grace, the data warehouse architect is

David, and the project manager is Natalie. They met with various managers and directors from various parts of the business and talked about the business operations and the business issues that the managers were facing. They then visited several physical stores, talked to the store managers and employees, and studied the details of how the business works in the stores.

They also visited the online stores and looked at the product categories and the sales order process. They also created a few orders in WebTower9 (the online store system) and followed up these orders into the back end of the system. Let's say that from these activities they found the following business challenges and issues:

- Because Amadeus Entertainment spans several countries and operates on three different systems, it has difficulty aggregating worldwide sales (including returns) at any time. The company also needs to analyze sales by product and geographic area.

- The company needs to evaluate supplier performance based on delivery lead time and promptness, order volume and quantity, trading and payment history, and store stock fluctuation records, regardless of brand, country, and transaction system. Historically, this activity has also been laborious.

- The company wants to be able to select certain customers based on demographic attributes, order history, and communication permissions and send them newsletters via e-mails containing promotional offers, regardless of which systems they are on, and record the customer responses, such as opening the e-mails and visiting the company web sites.

They then grouped these issues and challenges into three business areas: sales, purchasing, and CRM.

Understanding Business Operations

Grace (the business project manager) and David (the data warehouse architect) then went back to the business users and drilled down into each area to understand the business operations in each area. They tried to understand the processes, the roles, and the issues in each area. In particular, they were looking for business events, status, levels, and roles.

- An *event* is an activity that happens repeatedly every few seconds or minutes. Or it could be every few hours or days. For example, in the purchasing area, we have a document called a *purchase order*. This document contains a request to the supplier (a music record company, for example) to supply the company with some products (CDs or MP3 songs, for example). Every week Amadeus Entertainment creates hundreds of these documents and sends them to various suppliers. This purchase order creation is an event. Another example of an event is when a customer buys a record or downloads a song from the online stores.

- A *status* is a condition of an object at a particular point in time. For example, a song can have a status of active or obsolete. A customer subscription can have a status of subscribed, unsubscribed, or does not exist.

- A *level* is a quantitative measurement of an object at a particular point in time, such as account balance, inventory level, and number of customers. These quantitative measurements change from time to time.

- *Roles* are the who, whom, and what involved in the event. For example, the roles in the purchase order event are supplier, account manager, and product. The account manager raises a purchase order for a supplier for a particular product. The roles in the subscriber event are customer, package, and store; in other words, a customer subscribes to a package in a store.

After talking to business users about these three areas, Grace and David found out that the events, status, and levels in Amadeus Entertainment were as follows: sales event, browsing event, subscribe event, customer class, customer band, purchase order event, campaign sent event, campaign opened event, campaign click-through event, inventory level, package revenues, and package costs. They then worked with the business people to get all the roles and attributes associated with each event and process. In this activity, they tried to understand the business terminology and the business principles in the corporation.

David and Grace spent some time again exploring the WebTower9, Jupiter, and Jade systems. They examined in detail how these processes happen and how these events are captured in these systems. David then sat down with the SQL Server, DB/2, and Informix DBAs for a few hours and conducted a brief walk-through of the database of each system.

Defining Functional Requirements

After understanding the business operations in each area, the business project manager (Grace) discussed with the business users the functional requirements, that is, the features and functions of the data warehouse. In other words, what does the system do? In the end, they agreed that the Amadeus Entertainment data warehouse system has the functional requirements shown in Table 4-1. The users collectively agreed that the business priorities of the requirements are as per the Priority column in Table 4-1.

Table 4-1. *Amadeus Entertainment Data Warehouse System Functional Requirements*

No.	Requirement	Priority
1	The business users need to be able to analyze "product sales" (that's when a customer is buying a product rather than subscribing to a package) over time by geographic area, by customer demographic, by stores and sales territory, and by product hierarchy. The users also need to know the revenues, the costs, and the margin in U.S. dollars. Local currencies will be converted to U.S. dollars.	High
2	The business users need to be able to analyze "subscription sales" (that's when a customer is subscribing to a package rather than purchasing a product) over time by geographic area, by customer demographic, by stores and sales territory, and by product hierarchy. In addition, the users also need to analyze subscription sales by subscription duration and lead source (in other words, where the customers are coming from). The users need to know the revenues, costs, and margins, evaluated every day for a period of one month.	High

Continued

Table 4-1. *Continued*

No.	Requirement	Priority
3	The business users will be able to analyze "subscriber profitability," which is defined as the projected annual revenue of the subscribing customer minus the annualized costs (including proportional indirect costs), expressed as a percentage of the projected annual revenue. This is analyzed over time, by geographic area, by customer demographic attributes, by stores and sales territory, and by product package.	High
4	The business users need to be able to allocate subscribers to specific "classes" based on the customer's projected annual revenue and allocate them to certain "bands" based on the profitability. The classes and bands are used in the loyalty programs. These two attributes are updated daily.	Medium
5	The business users will be able to analyze "supplier performance," which is the weighted average of the totals spent, costs, value of returns, value of rejects, title and format availability, stock outages, lead time, and promptness.	Low
6	The system will enable CRM users to select customers based on communication permissions (subscribed/unsubscribed, e-mail/phone/post, and so on), geographic attributes (address, city, and so on), demographic attributes (age, gender, occupation, income, hobby, and so on), interests (music taste, book topic interests, favorite film types, and so on), purchase history (order values, order dates, number of items, store locations, and so on), subscription details (details of packages, subscription dates, durations, store locations, and so on), and the attributes of the products purchased (for example, music genre, artist, film type, and so on) for the purpose of sending CRM campaigns.	High
7	The system will enable CRM users to analyze campaign results by viewing the following measures for each campaign sent to customers: the number of messages sent by communication channels (mobile phone text message, e-mail, or post), the number of messages delivered successfully, and the number of messages failed to be delivered (including the reason). For e-mail messages, the users need to analyze the following additional information: open rate, click-through rate, complaint rate, spam verdict, and trap hit rate.	Medium
8	For CRM analysis purposes, the data warehouse will store the customers' old occupations, incomes, addresses, e-mail addresses, and telephone numbers, especially the subscribers (as opposed to the purchasers).	Low
9	The data warehouse will store the previous region and division of each store. There is a plan to reorganize the store hierarchy; that is, currently there are only five regions in the United States, but in a few months' time there will be eight regions. Online stores are currently in a separate division, but in the future they will be in the same division as their offline colleagues. Reorganization like this rarely happens. This is the first time it has happened in the six-year history of Amadeus Entertainment. You can expect the new structure to last at least three years.	Low
10	For requirements 1 to 7, when the data warehouse goes live, two years of historical transactional data needs to be loaded into the warehouse, except requirement 5, which should be one year.	Medium
11	The data warehouse will store the data up to five years online and five years offline. The offline data should be able to be accessed online with two days of notice.	Low
12	The system will enable the store managers to view the data of just their own stores. This is because each store manager is responsible for different stores. This is applicable for both offline and online store managers.	High

No.	Requirement	Priority
13	At the store level, the ability to view the daily data in the past few weeks is important. The system should enable the store managers to see the ups and downs of sales, costs, and profitability, and they need to be able to drill down to any particular day to understand the causes of low sales or low profitability, that is, which products, titles, media, or customers caused the issue.	High
14	The data warehouse system will enable the global managers to understand the global trends and break them down by country. They do not need store-level data or daily data. If a certain store or country is having a problem with a particular media, title, or product (for example when they are experiencing negative trends), then the managers needs to be able to communicate this to all stores as early as possible.	Medium
15	The report and OLAP will have an easy-to-use user interface. As long as the user interface enables the company to perform the analysis in this table and it is easy to use, the users do not really care about the details of the user interface. The numbers are much more important to the users than the layout. The data warehouse users understand that their job is to deliver business performance, and these numbers are the enabler.	Low
16	The system will be able to display the figures and charts and will be able to print. The users collectively agree that they will need charts and graphs, but if this feature is not available, they can export to Excel and do the graphs there. They will need an export to Excel (or to CSV) feature.	Low

David, Grace, and Natalie reviewed these functional requirements, documented them, and obtained the necessary sign-off. They reviewed the requirements in terms of completeness, feasibility, and data availability. They documented them in the form of use cases. The business users reviewed the use cases and signed off on them.

Defining Nonfunctional Requirements

Meetings with the IT architecture and operations teams and discussions with the business users revealed the nonfunctional requirements described in Table 4-2. Functional requirements determine what the system does (the features), whereas nonfunctional requirements do not specify the features. Instead, nonfunctional requirements provide guides and constraints to the system architecture. Some of them are from the company IT standards, some are from the IT architecture team, some are from source system restrictions (requests from the source system DBAs and operations manager), and some are from the user needs (requirements from the business users). There are also nonfunctional requirements related to project management or how the project should run, such as requirements related to the time, resources, locations, and budgets.

Table 4-2. *Amadeus Entertainment Data Warehouse System Nonfunctional Requirements*

No.	Requirement
1	All data warehouse users must be able to access the data warehouse front-end applications (reports and OLAP) without logging in again. They just need to log in once to Windows on their PC or laptop.
2	The data warehouse front-end applications must not be accessible from outside the company network.
3	All front-end applications are ideally web-based, accessible from anywhere within the company network.
4	All users access the front-end applications from a central portal. The user interface layout and design need to follow company standards and guidelines.
5	Some users are allowed to access data from their own country only, but some users are allowed to access data from any country.
6	Some "power" users are given access to the dimensional store to perform direct SQL queries.
7	Certain sensitive data is viewable by certain people only.
8	The maximum response time for any report, query, or OLAP view is 30 seconds.
9	The standard minimum specification for the client is Internet Explorer 6 on Windows XP running on a PC or laptop with Intel Pentium D 820 (or mobile/AMD equivalent) with 512MB memory and SVGA resolution (1024×768 pixel).
10	The data warehouse must be available for 24 hours a day, 7 days a week. The downtime is expected to be no more than one hour a month.
11	The downloads from Jupiter can occur only from 4 a.m. to 5 a.m. U.S. Eastern standard time.
12	It is preferred that no application or database changes are made in the WebTower9, Jupiter, and Jade systems, including trigger or schema changes.
13	The data warehouse system must notify the appropriate data owner within 24 hours when a data quality issue arises.
14	The company preference is to use Microsoft SQL Server to build the data warehouse from end to end, including the ETL tool, reporting, and OLAP. Specific front-end BI applications may be used if required. The data warehouse should be upgradable to SQL Server future versions.
15	We need to utilize this project to satisfy data integration needs too. As you know, Amadeus Entertainment has disparate front-end applications. In particular, it would be ideal if this project could create a stepping-stone for master data management.
16	The data warehouse needs to be flexible so we can enhance it easily and adapt to changes that happen in the transaction systems. In particular, it needs to include enhancements such as bringing new pieces of data into the warehouse, adding new reports/cubes/data quality rules, or modifying existing ones.
17	"Who accessed what and when" must be auditable.
18	All servers must be rack mountable, preferably from the Amadeus Entertainment's favored hardware supplier.
19	The data warehouse must be backed up to offline media daily, and the backup must be tested every six months by restoring it from the media. Fairly recent media must be stored off-site.

No.	Requirement
20	If the ETL failed because of power failure in the data center, the data in the data warehouse should not be corrupted or compromised; it must be recoverable, and there should not be any data loss.
21	The number of users is estimated to be between 300 and 500. About 20 percent of these users are estimated to be heavy and frequent users; the rest are occasional.
22	To protect investments, we need to use the same storage area network (SAN) as the file and e-mail servers rather than creating a new, separate SAN.

David, Grace, and Natalie reviewed these requirements, documented them, and obtained the necessary sign-off. They reviewed the requirements in terms of completeness, feasibility, and effect on the system architecture. They documented these requirements in supplementary specification format, with the following sections: usability, reliability, performance, supportability, design constraints, user documentation and help, interfaces, and applicable standards. The business users, IT architecture group, and operations team reviewed the documents and signed off on them.

Conducting a Data Feasibility Study

After defining the functional and nonfunctional requirements, now it is time to understand the data and the source system in detail. A data feasibility study is a process to explore the source system, to understand the data by listing the main data risks and verifying them, and to determine whether it is possible to deliver the project as per the requirements. Exploring the source system means examining the database platform, examining the database structure, and querying the tables. Understanding the data means finding out where the data is located for each functional requirement and understanding the meaning and the quality of the data. The risks are identified by finding out whether there are gaps between the requirements and the data, that is, whether for each requirement the data is available and accessible.

The purpose of doing a data feasibility study is to get an idea about whether there are any data risks that could fail the project. Data risks are project risks associated with data availability and data accessibility. Data availability risks are risks of not being able to satisfy a requirement because the data is not available. For example, a requirement could specify two years of historical data, but you have only six months worth of data. Data accessibility risks are project risks of not being able to satisfy a requirement because the ETL system cannot extract the data and bring it into the warehouse. For example, we may not be able to identify updates in a table because there is no "last updated" timestamp, because we are not allowed to install a trigger in the source table, and because the table is too big to extract the whole table every time.

For the Amadeus Entertainment case study, Table 4-3 lists a few examples of the data risks.

Table 4-3. *Amadeus Entertainment Data Warehouse Risks*

No.	Risk
1	It is impossible to do data extraction in Jupiter in the one-hour limitation, as specified in the nonfunctional requirements.
2	The functional requirements cannot be satisfied because we do not have the data in the source systems. The way to identify this is to go through the functional requirements and query the source system to find out whether we have the data for each requirement.
3	The data is there, but we cannot get to it. Similarly, the way to identify this is to go through the functional requirements, locate the data for that requirement, and check whether we can query the data.
4	We can get to the data, but it is a mess and needs to be restructured and cleansed first. In this case, we need to find out how much effort would be required to cleanse the data.
5	A requirement states that we need to use the same SAN as the file and e-mail servers rather than creating a new, separate SAN. There is a risk here that we are not able to use the same SAN because the amount of data in the data warehouse exceeds the maximum capacity of the existing SAN. Of course, we will buy new disks, but there is a risk that the maximum number of disks that the SAN can handle is less than what we require. For example, the existing SAN may be able to hold only 120 disks and 50 are already used by the file and e-mail servers. If the data warehouse requires more than 70 disks, then we cannot use the existing SAN.
6	The daily incremental load may slow the source system down. We can determine whether the incremental load will slow down the source system by simulating the data extraction runs while the source system is being used. This is preferably done in the test environment.
7	The users may not be able to use the front-end application without logging into the data warehouse. The first nonfunctional requirement states that all data warehouse users must be able to access the data warehouse front-end applications without logging in again. They just need to log in once to Windows on their PC or laptop. We need to investigate whether we would be able to implement Windows integrated security to enable this.
8	The initial data load could take considerably longer than predicted, such as a month, impacting the project timeline. This could happen if we use the operational ETL to do initial data load, particularly when the operational ETL is in a message-based architecture.

It is important to verify these risks and make sure they are mitigated. If we don't do that, we are really risking the data warehouse project to fail. So, let's address these risks one by one.

For risk 1, is it possible to extract data from Jupiter within the one-hour limitation? We cannot answer that until we know what data to extract from Jupiter. And for that we need to model the data first. But we know it's going to be inventory data that we need from Jupiter (sales data is from WebTower9 and Jade). We can quickly build a simple SQL Server Integration Services (SSIS) package to extract one-week data from Jupiter inventory tables. If this package takes five minutes to run, then roughly speaking we are safe from this risk. If this is too simplistic for your project, build a package that extracts one day of equivalent data from several large tables from the source system.

For risk 2, is there any data that is not available or difficult to get? Speak to the business project manager or somebody who knows the front end of the source systems very well. Ask them whether, to their knowledge, there is data required by the business requirements that is unavailable in Jupiter, Jade, or WebTower9. Data such as the company fiscal calendar, performance targets, product costs, holiday data, customer classification, and overhead costs may not be available in the source system. Discuss with the business project manager whether someone can arrange these data items to be supplied to you in text files or spreadsheets.

For risk 3, we need to find out whether we can get to the data. We need to understand what RDBMS the source systems are running on. Most companies uses popular RDBMSs for their OLTP systems, such as Oracle, Informix, DB/2, Ingress, Progress, mysql, Sybase, or SQL Server, and these RDBMSs supports ADO.NET, ODBC, JDBC, or OLEDB, so we can get to the data using SSIS, assuming we have cleared the security permission. But if we hear that one of the source systems is on a proprietary system, not on an RDBMS, then we need to find out whether we can get to the data. If we can't find any ODBC or JDBC drivers for this proprietary system, we need to speak to the DBA about whether it is possible to arrange for the data to be exported periodically to text files.

Connectivity is another obstacle that could prevent us from getting to the data. For example, the production database server may sit behind a firewall. We may need to open a firewall hole, that is, raise a network request allowing database traffic through the firewall to and from a particular database server.

For risk 4, some data in the source system may require cleansing. We can find this out by querying the source system. Some of the data quality issues are incomplete data, incorrect/inaccurate data, duplicate records (because no hard database constraints are applied, such as primary keys or unique constraints), data is in free text format, a column is available but most values are null, orphan records, and so on.

For risk 5, unfortunately, without designing the DDS and NDS, we would not be able to understand the size of the data stores. If we try to estimate the storage at this stage, it could be inaccurate. I don't suggest we shouldn't estimate it, though. We should. The earlier we do the estimate, the better. But we need to be aware of how accurate the estimate is. When we complete data modeling (discussed in the next chapter), then we will be able to estimate the storage much more accurately.

Here is how we can estimate the data storage at this stage, without having the data model in hand:

- For each point in business requirements 1 to 7, assume there will be a fact table and a summary table. At this stage, we do not know the data structure of our dimensional model, so we need to make a lot of assumptions. Estimate the width of the fact table by assuming the number of key columns and fact columns. For a rough estimate, assume 5 key columns for a simple fact table and 15 for a complex one.

- Estimate the width of dimension tables by assuming the number of columns. For a rough estimate, assume 10 columns for a simple dimension and 50 columns for a complex dimension. Most columns are 4 to 8 characters, but some are 100 to 200 characters, so for an estimate assume that on average each column is 50 characters.

- Assume that the size of the summary table is 10 to 20 percent of the fact tables.

- The depth of the fact table depends on volume. For transactional fact tables, look at the source system to figure out how many transactions there are a day. For daily snapshot fact tables, look at the source system to figure out how many records there are per snapshot. Multiply this by the period—how long you plan to use the storage (take two to three years if you have no idea). For example, if on average there are 500,000 purchases a day, the size of the Product Sales fact table would be $500,000 \times 365 \times 2 \times$ the width of fact table as estimated earlier.

- Query the source system to estimate the number of records for each dimension. For example, for the product dimension, we query the inventory master table in Jupiter.

- Estimating the size of the NDS or ODS could vary widely. We cannot estimate it based on the size of the DDS. We can query the source system tables to estimate the size of each of the NDS or ODS tables.

Risk 6, the risk that the daily incremental load may slow the source system down, also depends on the data model and source system mapping, which we will do in the next chapter. But it is possible to mitigate this risk by building some simple SSIS packages that extract the data specified in the business requirements. The SSIS packages simulate the daily incremental load, extracting data from the main tables on the source systems. When this package is running, we use the source systems as normal for OLTP activities and measure whether there is any degradation in performance. For example, entering an order that usually takes a split second when saving to a database now takes three to four seconds. If this is the case, we should schedule the daily incremental load to run after-hours, such as from 2 a.m. to 4 a.m. I will go through how to build an ETL package using SSIS in Chapters 7 and 8.

For risk 7, the single login requirement can be mitigated by building a simple report and a simple OLAP cube and then applying the security. To enable the single login requirement (the customer doesn't need to log in again to the data warehouse system once they log in to Windows), we need to apply Windows integrated security, both on SQL Server Reporting Services (SSRS) and on SQL Server Analysis Services (SSAS). I will go through the steps of building reports in Chapter 11 and building OLAP cubes in Chapter 12.

Risk 8, initial data load, can be estimated by querying the source system according to the criteria specified in functional requirement 10. We can query the main transaction tables in the source system to find out how many records you have to load to the data warehouse to satisfy the historical data requirement. In the case of Amadeus Entertainment, functional requirement 10 specifies that we need to load two years of historical data for sales and CRM and one year for purchasing. We can then go to the source system and query the sales order table with something like select count(*) where sales order date >= [2 years ago] to find out how many historical rows we need on the initial data load for sales data. We then do the same for the CRM subscription data and purchase order data.

Summary

In this chapter, we defined the functional requirements for the case study. We also defined the nonfunctional requirements and verified that the data and the source systems support the requirements, meaning that, up to this point, we don't see anything that poses a serious risk to the project or prevents us from delivering the data warehouse.

In the next chapter, I will show how to design a data model that satisfies these requirements. The discussion about events, levels, status, and roles in this chapter will be useful in the next chapter.

■ ■ ■

CHAPTER 5

Data Modeling

In this chapter, we will design the data stores for the Amadeus Entertainment case study. We will use the NDS + DDS architecture. Apart from the benefits outlined in Chapter 2, the purpose of choosing this architecture for this case study is so that you can have the experience of designing a normalized store and a dimensional store.

We will begin by looking at the business requirements and then design the dimensional data store (DDS) accordingly. We will define the meaning of the facts and dimensional attributes. We will also define the data hierarchy.

Then we will map the data in the DDS with the source systems; that is, we will define the source of the columns in the fact and dimension tables. Sometimes one column in the DDS is populated from several tables in the source system (for example, from column 1 of table A and column 1 of table B) and sometimes from more than one source system. We will define the transformations (formula, calculation logic, or lookups) required to populate the target columns.

Then we will design the normalized data store (NDS) by normalizing the dimensional data store and by examining the data from the source systems we have mapped. The normalization rules and the first, second, and third normal forms are described in the appendix. We will use these rules to design the NDS.

Designing the Dimensional Data Store

So, let's start by designing the DDS. The users will be using the data warehouse to do analysis in six business areas: product sales, subscription sales, subscriber profitability, supplier performance, CRM campaign segmentation, and CRM campaign results. So, we need to analyze each business area one by one to model the business process in order to create the data model. Let's do the first business area: product sales. An order-item data mart in the retail industry is a classic example of data warehousing.

A product sales event happens when a customer is buying a product, rather than subscribing to a package. The roles (the who, where, and what) in this event are the customer, product, and store. The levels (or in dimensional modeling terms, the *measures*) are the quantity, unit price, value, direct unit cost, and indirect unit cost. We get these levels from the business requirements in Chapter 4; in other words, they're what users need to perform their tasks. We put the measures in the fact table and the roles (plus dates) in the dimension tables. The business events become the fact table row. Figure 5-1 describes the result.

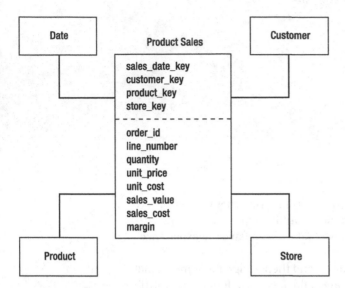

Figure 5-1. *Product Sales fact table and its dimensions*

quantity, unit_price, and unit_cost measures are derived from the source system, but the other three measures (sales_value, sales_cost, and margin) are calculated. They are defined as follows:

- sales_value = unit_price × quantity

- sales_cost = unit_cost × quantity

- margin = sales_value – sales_cost

The four keys in the Product Sales fact table link the fact table with the four dimensions. According to Ralph Kimball, it is important to declare the grain of the fact table. *Grain* is the smallest unit of occurrence of the business event in which the event is measured. In other words, grain is completing this sentence: "One row in the fact table corresponds to. . . ." In this case, the grain is each item sold—one row in the Product Sales fact table corresponds to each item sold.

It is easy to define simple measures for our case study such as sales value, sales cost, and margin, but in practice when doing data modeling we have to deal with complex events, features, exceptions, and logic that are industry specific, such as discounts, taxes, promotional items (for example, "three for the price of two," "buy one get one free," and so on), bundles, and returns.

The general rule for dealing with complex events and exceptions is to always look at the source system. We have to replicate or mimic the source system logic. This is because the output of the data warehouse application must agree with the source system. If the source system includes the discount in the unit price, we should not implement discounts as line items because if we aggregated the discount, it would not match the source system. In any case, always talk to the businesspeople first about the business logic because they know the business rules. Then it is wise to always confirm the data model and business logic with the source system. It is important to get the data model and business logic correct to ensure that the output of the data warehouse reflects the correct business conditions.

Some of the business logic is quite complex, such as cost allocations and customer profitability calculations. Cost allocation is where you need to allocate a total cost to each business event. Usually, it is an overhead or indirect cost occurring periodically, such as the cost of renting a building. Customer profitability is where you calculate the profit you are making for each customer for a certain period. For complex business logic such as this, you could have a disagreement between the businesspeople and the source system code, meaning that the businesspeople want the data warehouse business logic to be different from the one implemented in the source system. In this case, advise the business project manager of the discrepancy you found and ask her to decide which one to implement in the data warehouse. This happens in practice, and I have experienced it myself several times: "I know that the source system calculates the annual revenue with that logic, but in the data warehouse I want to calculate the annual revenue differently." In this case, my belief is that you should implement as per the requirement from the businesspeople; however, it is essential to always let the business project manager facilitate this. It should be documented and should require sign-off. The reason for this is it is perfectly valid for the data warehouse users to have a requirement (about business logic) that is different from the source system. For instance, perhaps there have been some changes in the business situation, or perhaps they want to analyze the data differently.

In retail, alongside sales transactions, you also have sales tax (value-added tax [VAT]) that varies depending on country, state, and product. VAT can be implemented in several ways. In some implementations, VAT is not included in the sales fact table because the business wants to analyze product sales only (to them, taxes obscure the real transaction value). In other implementations, they build a sales tax fact table, with the granularity at one row per order line. In this fact table, they analyze the taxes. In still other implementations, discounts are included in the unit price (rather than as a transaction line). In other words, if the normal price is $5 and there is a 20 percent discount, the unit price is reduced to $4.

Let's now return to the fact table and continue our dimensional design. In Figure 5-1, you can see there are two columns in the fact table: order_id and line_number. They are called *degenerate dimensions*. A degenerate dimension is a dimension with only one attribute, and therefore the attribute is put in the fact table. order_id and line_number are the identifiers of the order line in the source system. We need to always bear in mind that we may be dealing with more than one source system, so it is possible that two source systems have the same order ID. Because of this, we want to include a source system ID column to differentiate them. Also, it is a good idea to always put a timestamp column in the fact table, that is, the time when the record was loaded into the fact table. This column enables us to determine when the fact row (or dimension row) was loaded into the data warehouse data store. In many cases, we need a second timestamp column to store the time the record was last updated. This column enables us to determine when the fact row (or dimension row) was last modified. These two columns are in addition to the transactional date/timestamp column. The transaction timestamp explains when the order (or order line) was created, shipped, canceled, or returned, but it does not explain when the record was loaded into the data warehouse and when it was last modified.

The next step in the fact table design is to determine which column combination uniquely identifies a fact table row. This is important because it is required for both logical and physical database design in order to determine the primary key(s). We ordinarily would be able to uniquely identify a fact table row by using the combination of all dimensional columns in the fact table. However, it is still possible to have duplicate rows. Sometimes we need to use the degenerate dimension to make it unique. In our Amadeus Entertainment case study, the fact table contains one row for each item sold. So, it seems that the combination of the customer, date, product, and store dimensions will be enough to uniquely identify a fact table row. What if customer A bought song B in online store C on date D at 10 a.m. and then she came back at 7 p.m. on the same day to the same store and bought the same song again? Ah, we have two rows with those four dimensional columns having identical values. But the order ID and line number are different. So, to differentiate these two fact rows, we use the order ID and line number. Therefore, we can use order_id and line_number for the primary key candidates. Or we can create a new fact table key column and use it as the primary key candidate.

Note I will discuss the primary keys and cluster indexes in the next chapter because determining primary keys and cluster indexes are part of the physical database design process.

This collection of a fact table and its dimension tables is called a *data mart*. There are more complex forms of data marts, such as when you have more than one fact table, but for now let's consider only one fact table. Bear in mind that this concept of a data mart is applicable only if the data warehouse is in a dimensional model. If the data warehouse is not in a dimensional model—that is, when we are talking about a normalized data store—there is no data mart. A data mart is a group of related fact tables and their corresponding dimension tables containing the measurements of business events, categorized by their dimensions. Data marts exist in dimensional data stores.

With the timestamp columns, the Product Sales fact table (and its dimensions) now looks like Figure 5-2.

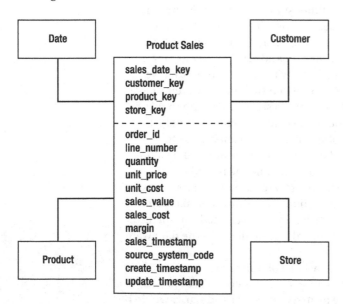

Figure 5-2. *Product Sales table (and its dimensions) with timestamp columns*

We then define the data type for each column. All key columns have integer data types because they are surrogate keys, that is, simple integer values with one increment. The measure columns are usually numeric or currency, so in SQL Server, their data types are decimal or money. The three timestamp columns have datetime data types. The source system code is an integer because it contains only the code, and the description is stored in the source system table in the metadata database.

Then we add the description for each column. We also provide a sample value so we are clear about the data we are going to store in each column. We can get a sample value by querying the source system. Table 5-1 describes the final form of the Product Sales fact table.

Table 5-1. *Product Sales Fact Table*

Column Name	Data Type	Description	Sample Value
sales_date_key	int	The key of the date the customer purchased the product	108
customer_key	int	The key of the customer who purchased the product	345
product_key	int	The key of the product purchased by the customer	67
store_key	int	The key of the store where the customer made the purchase	48
order_id	int	WebTower9 or Jade order ID	7852299
line_number	int	WebTower9 or Jade order line number	2
quantity	decimal(9,2)	How many units of the product the customer purchased	2
unit_price	money	Price of one unit of the product purchased in the original currency	6.10
unit_cost	money	Direct and indirect costs for one unit of the product in the original currency	5.20
sales_value	money	quantity × unit_price	12.20
sales_cost	money	quantity × unit_cost	10.40
margin	money	sales_value − sales_cost	1.80
sales_timestamp	datetime	When the customer purchased the product	02/17/2008 18:08:22.768
source_system_code	int	The key of the source system from which this record was coming from	2
create_timestamp	datetime	When the record was created in DDS	02/17/2008 04:19:16.638
update_timestamp	datetime	When the record was last updated	02/17/2008 04:19:16.638

In multinational companies, you may need to define additional columns to store the measures in the "global enterprise currency," along with the currency rate. When a business has branches in many countries, the business transactions occur in different local currencies. These transactions are stored in the fact table columns listed in Table 5-1. Usually, there are also requirements to analyze transaction data globally. To do this analysis, the transactions need to be converted and stored in a single global currency. The currency rates that were used to convert the transaction values from the local currencies to the global currency are also stored in the fact table. In addition, we need to have a currency key column in the Product Sales fact table, containing the currency in which the transaction occurred. This key column is linked to the currency dimension where the name of the currency is stored. To accommodate these multicurrency requirements in the fact table, we can create the additional columns shown in Table 5-2.

Table 5-2. *Additional Columns on the Product Sales Fact Table*

Column Name	Data Type	Description	Sample Value
currency_key	int	The key of the currency in which the transaction occurred	3
unit_price_usd	money	Price of one unit of the product purchased in U.S. dollars	6.10
unit_cost_usd	money	Direct and indirect costs for one unit of the product in U.S. dollars	5.20
sales_value_usd	money	quantity × unit_price, in U.S. dollars	12.20
sales_cost_usd	money	quantity × unit_cost, in U.S. dollars	10.40
margin_usd	money	sales_value – sales_cost, in U.S. dollars	1.80
currency_rate	money	Conversion rate between the local currency and U.S. dollars	1.97

Dimension Tables

Now that we have discussed the fact table, let's discuss the dimension tables. A *dimension table* is a table that contains various attributes explaining the dimension key in the fact table. As mentioned earlier in this chapter, the fact table stores business events. The attributes explain the conditions of the entity at the time the business event happened. For example, in the fact table in Figure 5-1, we have a dimension key called customer_key. Table 5-1 says that this column contains the key (or the ID) of the customer purchasing the product. In Figure 5-1, you can see that the customer dimension table is "linked" to the fact table using the customer_key column. The customer_key column is a *primary key* in the customer dimension table, and it is a *foreign key* on the fact table. This is known in the database world as *referential integrity*.

Referential integrity is a concept of establishing a parent-child relationship between two tables, with the purpose of ensuring that every row in the child table has a corresponding parent entry in the parent table. The referential integrity can be "hardened" or "enforced" physically as a physical database constraint (data warehouse people call this *hard RI*). A database constraint is a rule governing the permissible values on a certain column. Alternatively, the referential integrity can managed by the ETL and not enforced as a physical data constraint (data warehouse people call this *soft RI*). The ETL checks that the values on the fact table dimensional keys exist in the dimension tables.

The dimension tables contain various attributes explaining the conditions of the entities involved in the business event stored in the fact table. The attributes are stored as columns in the dimension tables. They are known as *dimensional attributes*. The customer dimension contains columns that describe the condition of the customer who made the purchase, including the data about customer name, address, telephone number, date of birth, e-mail address, gender, interest, occupation, and so on. The product dimension contains columns that describe conditions of the product purchased, including the data about product name, product type, product category, media, SKU, minimum order level, product code, unit cost, and unit price.

Now that you understand what a dimension is, let's go through the four dimensions in Figure 5-1—date, customer, product, and store—to complete the design of the product sales data mart. We will define each dimension one by one. We will begin with the date dimension first and then discuss the other three dimensions. We will also talk about the concept of slowly changing dimension (SCD). SCD is a data modeling technique to store historical values of dimensional attributes. It is important to discuss it in the context of dimensions because of its capability to preserve historical attribute values. OK, let's start with the date dimension.

Date Dimension

Almost every single data mart has the date dimension in it. This reflects the nature of a dimensional data mart in that the fact table rows are business events that happened on certain dates. Because the date dimension is used in almost every data mart in the data warehouse, it is important to model the date dimension correctly. It is important for the date dimension to contain the attributes required by *all* fact tables in all data marts.

Why don't we have a time dimension instead of a date dimension? Well, it is not practical. A date dimension with 10 years of data has 3,650 rows. If it were a time dimension with precision to the second, it would have 315 million rows and would impact the data warehouse performance because it's used everywhere. Instead, we use either the timestamp column in the fact table (99 percent of the cases) or a time of day dimension (1 percent of the cases). A timestamp column in the fact table stores the date and time the business event happened and, therefore, eliminates the need to have a time dimension. A time of day dimension contains all the possible minutes (or seconds) in one day. A time of day dimension is used when a different period in a day has a different meaning or label, such as "happy hour," "off-peak period," "night shift," and "migration slot." If labels such as these are not required, the timestamp column is easier (for calculation) and better (for performance).

The columns or attributes in a date dimension can be categorized into four groups:

Date formats: The date format columns contain dates in various formats.

Calendar date attributes: The calendar date attributes contain various elements of a date, such as day, month name, and year.

Fiscal attributes: The fiscal attribute columns contain elements related to the fiscal calendar, such as fiscal week, fiscal period, and fiscal year.

Indicator columns: The indicator columns contain Boolean values used to determine whether a particular date satisfies a certain condition, such as whether it is a national holiday.

Typically used date format columns in the date dimension are as follows (with examples for February 17, 2008):

- date such as "02/17/2008"

- sql_date such as "02/17/2008 00:00:00.000"

- ansi_date such as "2008-02-17"

The sql_date column contains the date in the SQL Server datetime data type, whereas the date and ansi_date columns contain the date in the varchar data type. The date column can be formatted according to the custom in the local geography; for example, mm/dd/yyyy is usually used in the United States. We can also create a column for other places; for example, the dd/mm/yyyy format is usually used in the United Kingdom.

The calendar date attribute columns contain the parts or elements of a date. Table 5-3 shows typically used calendar date attributes in the date dimension, with examples for February 17, 2008. The columns are listed from the smallest unit of measure.

Table 5-3. *Calendar Date Attributes Columns*

Column	Sample Values	Notes
week_day	7	Monday = 1, Tuesday = 2, …, Sunday = 7.
week_day_name	Sunday	
day	17	You can call it day_of_the_month, but most users prefer the short version.
day_of_the_year	48	
week_number	7	The week starts on Monday.
month	2	
short_month_name	Feb	
long_month_name	February	
quarter	Q1	
year	2008	

The columns that end with the word name (such as short_month_name and week_day_name) probably need to be in several languages if you are a multinational organization. If we use several languages, we also need to correctly set the SQL collation of the database according to the character set used by the languages.

It is true that we can derive the attributes in the date dimension (such as month name, week number, day name, and so on) by using Transact SQL functions such as datepart. The reason for providing those attributes in the date dimension is because when we are in the fact table, all we have is the date key, so in the date dimension rather than going to the sql_date column and then deriving the month, we can go directly to the month column.

After the calendar date attribute columns, the next group of columns in the date dimension is the fiscal attribute columns. These columns contain the fiscal property of a date, such as the fiscal year and fiscal week. The values of fiscal attributes are dependent upon when the fiscal year starts and when it ends. Those values are also affected by how many fiscal periods exist in a fiscal year and how many fiscal weeks exist in a fiscal period. Some companies have 13 equal fiscal periods of 4 weeks each. Some companies use a fiscal calendar that has fiscal periods containing an unequal number of fiscal weeks.

Assuming that the fiscal year starts on September 1 and that there are 12 fiscal periods in a year with four or five weeks each, the fiscal calendar attributes commonly used in the date dimension are shown in Table 5-4, with examples for February 17, 2008. The columns are listed from the smallest unit of measure.

Table 5-4. *Fiscal Calendar Attribute Columns*

Column	Sample Values
fiscal_week	27
fiscal_period	9
fiscal_quarter	FQ2
fiscal_year	FY2008

The final columns in the date dimension are the indicator columns. Indicator columns are columns in the date dimension that have only two possible values: 1 or 0 (Boolean). Indicator columns are used to determine whether a particular date satisfies a certain condition such as whether the day is a weekend. Each indicator column serves a different purpose, so you need to choose the ones suitable to your case. The following indicator columns are commonly used: week_day (1 if it's Monday to Friday; 0 otherwise), national_holiday (1 if it is a holiday; several columns if you operate in several countries), last_day_in_month (1 if it is the last day in the month; sometimes this would come in handy), period_end (1 if it is the last day in a fiscal period), and short_day (1 if the offline stores' opening hours are shorter than normal opening hours).

Table 5-5 describes the date dimension of all four groups of columns explained earlier. A surrogate key is an incremental integer. It is unique and not null.

Table 5-5. *Date Dimension*

Column Name	Data Type	Description	Sample Value
date_key	int	The surrogate key of date dimension. This is the primary key of the date dimension. It is unique and not null.	2019
date	char(10)	Full date in mm/dd/yyyy format.	02/17/2008
ansi_date	char(10)	Full date in yyyy-mm-dd format.	2008-02-17
sql_date	datetime	Full date in SQL Server datetime data type.	17/02/2008 00:00:00.000
day	int	The day of the month.	17
day_of_the_week	int	The day of the week; 1 for Monday, 7 for Sunday.	7
day_name	varchar(9)	The name of the day in a week.	Sunday
day_of_the_year	int	The number of elapsed days since January 1, aka *Julian date*.	48

Continued

Table 5-5. *Continued*

Column Name	Data Type	Description	Sample Value
week_number	int	The number of elapsed weeks since January 1; weeks start on Monday.	7
month	int	The number of the month.	2
month_name	varchar(9)	The full name of the month in English.	February
short_month_name	char(3)	The short name of the month in English.	Feb
quarter	char(2)	Three-month period in calendar year, Qn format.	Q1
year	int	The calendar year of the date.	2008
fiscal_week	int	The number of elapsed weeks since September 1.	27
fiscal_period	char(4)	A period consists of four or five weeks depending on the fiscal calendar. Usually, the pattern used in this company is 454, 544, or 445, in FPn format. A fiscal year always consists of 12 periods.	FP9
fiscal_quarter	char(3)	A fiscal quarter is three fiscal periods, from September 1, FQn format.	FQ2
fiscal_year	char(6)	Fiscal year begins on September 1, in FYnnnn format.	FY2008
week_day	tinyint	1 if it is Monday to Friday; 0 otherwise.	0
us_holiday	tinyint	1 if it is a national holiday in the United States; 0 otherwise.	0
uk_holiday	tinyint	1 if it is a statutory holiday in the United Kingdom; 0 otherwise.	0
month_end	tinyint	1 if it is the last day in the month; 0 otherwise.	0
period_end	tinyint	1 if it is the last day in a fiscal period; 0 otherwise.	0
short_day	tinyint	1 if on that day the offline stores' opening hours are shorter than normal opening hours; 0 otherwise. This is applicable only for offline stores.	0

The date_key column is the primary key of the date dimension. In SQL Server implementations, it is also the cluster index.

Slowly Changing Dimension

Now that I have discussed the date dimension, before I discuss the other three dimensions, I'll cover something called SCD, which is a technique used to store the historical value of dimension attributes. The values of dimensional attributes change as time goes by. When these attribute values change, you can overwrite the old values with the new ones, or you can preserve the old value. There are two methods of preserving the old attribute values: you can store the old values as rows, or you can store them as columns. For example, say that store 7 was in region 1, but it is now in region 2. You want to store the historical information—the fact that it was in region 1. You can do this in two ways: by storing it as a row or by storing it as a column. Table 5-6 shows an example of historical information stored as a row.

Table 5-6. *Storing Historical Information As a Row*

key	store	region	status
1	7	1	expired
2	7	2	active

In Table 5-6, you can see that the active row is row 2, but you still have the previous region (region 1) stored in the first row. To understand *when* row 1 became expired and when row 2 became active, you can add two columns in Table 5-6: effective_date and expiry_date.

You can also store the historical information (the old attribute values) as columns instead of rows. Table 5-7 shows how historical information is stored as a column. In Table 5-7, the current region of store 7 is region 2, and previously store 7 was in region 1.

Table 5-7. *Storing Historical Information As a Column*

key	store	current_region	old_region	effective_date
1	7	2	1	11/18/2007

In Table 5-7, you can see that there is a column called old_region that stores the previous value of the region (region 1). To record the date when store 7 moved from region 1 to region 2, you can add a column called effective_date, such as the one shown in Table 5-7.

Of course, the question now is, what if store 7 moves region again, to region 3, for example? Well, because you have only two columns, the oldest value is not stored. You can store only the last two values. If you want to store three values, you need to have three columns: current_region, old_region, and old_region2. What if you want to store ten values? Well, you need to have ten columns. This is the distinct disadvantage of storing the historical value as columns, compared to storing them as rows.

Now that you understand how historical values are stored in the dimension table (that is, as rows or columns), I'll talk about three types of SCD:

- SCD type 1 overwrites the old values of the attributes so the old values are not kept.

- SCD type 2 keeps the old values by creating a new row for each change, just like Table 5-6.

- SCD type 3 keeps the old values by putting them in another column, just like Table 5-7.

Generally, SCD type 2 is more flexible for storing the historical value of dimensional attributes, because you can store as many old versions as you want without altering the table structure. SCD type 3 is using columns to store old values, which is why it is not flexible. It is ideal for situations where you don't have many old versions (five or fewer) and you know there will be only a certain number of versions. Type 3 is also ideal when the changes in this attribute affect a large number of rows. In other words, a lot of dimension rows change the value of this attribute at the same time (simultaneously). For a detailed explanation of SCD, please refer to Ralph Kimball and Margy Ross' book, *The Data Warehouse Toolkit* (Wiley, 2002). You can store the historical values using other ways, such as by putting them in another table, but SCD types 1, 2, and 3 are the most popular, so let's just get on with it.

OK, now you understand that SCD is about storing historical values. The question that some people ask me is, how slow is slow? The perception about how slow is slow (in SCD) is different from industry to industry. As a guide, if on average the dimension attribute changes once a quarter or less, the attribute is slowly changing. If on average the dimension attribute changes once a month or more frequently, the dimension is rapidly changing and is handled differently (as explained in a moment).

This guide of classifying a dimension attribute as slowly or rapidly changing is not a firm rule and has several considerations. The first consideration is the size of the dimension, namely, the number of rows. The larger the dimension, the greater the tendency to classify the attribute as rapidly changing. The second consideration is the relationship between the attribute with the other attributes in the dimension. The looser the coupling between the attribute with the other attributes in the dimension, the more tendency to classify the attribute as rapidly changing. The third consideration is how often the other attributes in the dimension change. The less often the other attributes change, the more we tend to classify the attribute as rapidly changing.

The other questions about SCD that people ask me are, how about the rapidly changing dimension (RCD)? How do we store the historical information? If, on average, the rows in the dimension tables change once a month or more frequently, how do we store the historical value of dimensional attributes? The answer is that we store them in the fact table. Say we have a customer dimension with ten attributes. Attributes 1 to 9 change once a year. Attribute 10 changes every day. We should remove the 10th column from the customer dimension and put it as a degenerate dimension column in the fact table, as shown in Figure 5-3. As mentioned, a degenerate dimension column is a dimension with only one attribute. Because it has only one attribute, rather than putting this attribute in a separate dimension table, you put it in the fact table. A degenerate dimension doesn't have a dimension key.

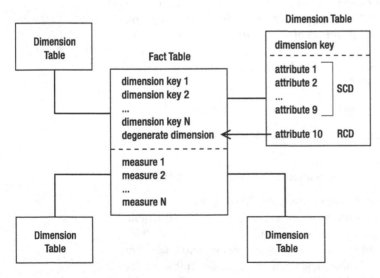

Figure 5-3. *Moving a rapidly changing dimension attribute to the fact table as a degenerate dimension column*

Product, Customer, and Store Dimensions

Now that we have discussed the concept of SCD, let's discuss the other three dimensions: the product dimension, the customer dimension, and the store dimension. Unlike the date dimension that we just discussed, product attributes vary widely from industry to industry. Hence, when you model data in a different industry, keep in mind that the product attributes can be totally different from the ones discussed in this section. This is where industry experience becomes useful. For Amadeus Entertainment, the product attributes are product ID (just a number to identify the product, which is maintained by Jupiter), name, description, title (the title of the song/film/book), artist (the singer, cast, or author), product type (music, film, or book), product group (which is a large grouping; that is, for film, it is thriller, comedy, action, documentary, children, Asian, and so on), product category (a smaller grouping; that is, for an Asian film it is Indian, Chinese, and martial arts), media (WMA, MP3, and so on), unit price, and unit cost.

Business requirements 8 and 9 in Chapter 4 mentioned that we need to store the old attribute values of the customer and store dimensions, but nothing was mentioned about the product dimension. Because we don't have a requirement to store historical values of the product attribute, we will use SCD type 1, meaning we will overwrite the old attribute values.

To create the product dimension, we look at the source system. The case study in Chapter 2 specifies that the inventory and products in Amadeus Entertainment are managed in the Jupiter system, not in the Jade or WebTower9 system. So, we get the product dimension columns from the product tables in the Jupiter system. In the operational source system, the product tables may be normalized, and we need to denormalize them to get a flat structure for the product dimension. We do this by joining the product tables in the source system on their primary and foreign key columns. We then get data types and the length for each column from the source system. We write a description for each column and provide a sample value. Table 5-8 describes the complete structure of the product dimension. As we discussed, a surrogate key is simply an incremental integer. It is unique and not null.

Table 5-8. *Product Dimension*

Column Name	Data Type	Description	Sample Value
product_key	int	The surrogate key of the product dimension. It is unique, is not null, and is the primary key of product dimension.	3746
product_code	varchar(10)	Natural key. Product code is the identifier and primary key of the product table in Jupiter. It is in AAA999999 format.	FGA334288
name	varchar(30)	Product name.	The Panama Story DVD
description	varchar(100)	Product description.	Panama Story movie in DVD format
title	varchar(100)	The song/film/book title.	The Panama Story
artist	varchar(100)	The singer, star, or author.	Mark Danube

Continued

Table 5-8. *Continued*

Column Name	Data Type	Description	Sample Value
product_type	varchar(20)	Level 1 of the product hierarchy, such as music, film, book.	Film
product_category	varchar(30)	Level 2 of the product hierarchy; for film, it could be thriller, western, comedy, action, documentary, children, Asian, and so on.	Action
media	varchar(25)	Format of the media, such as MP3, MPG, CD, or DVD.	DVD
unit_price	money	Price for one item.	4.75
unit_cost	money	Allocated direct and indirect costs.	3.62
status	varchar(15)	Upcoming if we have signed contract with the supplier, Active if it is still being offered to the customer, and Expired if it is no longer being offered.	Active
source_system_code	int	The key of the source system where this record was coming from.	2
create_timestamp	datetime	When the record was created in DDS.	02/05/2008
update_timestamp	datetime	When the record was last updated.	02/05/2008

The product_key column is the primary key of the product dimension, and it is also the cluster index. product_code is the primary key of the product table in the Jupiter system. We call product_code the *natural key*, which is a column in the source system that we can use to identify the record. It must be unique and not null, and it is usually a primary key in the source system table.

Now let's look at the customer dimension with SCD type 2. A customer dimension table looks like the one described in Table 5-9.

Table 5-9. *Customer Dimension*

Column Name	Data Type	Description	Sample Value
customer_key	int	The surrogate key of customer dimension.	84743
customer_id	varchar(10)	Natural key. The primary key of the customer tables in WebTower9 and Jade. WebTower9 customer_id format is AA999999. and Jade is AAA99999.	DH029383
account_number	int	The account number for subscription customers. 0 for nonsubscription customers.	342165
customer_type	char(1)	Subscriber, purchaser, or member.	S
name	varchar(100)	Customer's full name.	Charlotte Thompson
gender	char(1)	M for male; F for female.	F

Column Name	Data Type	Description	Sample Value
email_address	varchar(200)	Customer's e-mail address.	charlotte. thompson@ earthlink.net
date_of_birth	smalldatetime	Customer's date of birth.	04/18/1973
address1	varchar(50)	First line of address.	570 Greenfield Boulevard
address2	varchar(50)	Second line of address.	Suite 2100
address3	varchar(50)	Third line of address.	
address4	varchar(50)	Fourth line of address.	
city	varchar(50)	Village, town, or city of customer's residence.	Jacksonville
state	varchar(40)	For non-U.S. address, it's county or region.	Florida
zipcode	varchar(10)	Postal code.	32228
country	varchar(50)	Country.	USA
phone_number	varchar(20)	Telephone number including area code.	(904) 402-8294
occupation	varchar(50)	Customer's job/profession.	DBA
household_income	varchar(20)	Range of household income in U.S. dollars.	50–60k
date_registered	smalldatetime	The date when the customer first purchased or subscribed.	11/23/2007
status	varchar(10)	Active if the customer is currently a member or made a purchase in the last 12 months.	Active
subscriber_class	varchar(3)	Classification of subscribers based on projected annual revenue.	R1
subscriber_band	varchar(3)	Classification of subscribers based on profitability.	A
effective_timestamp	datetime	For SCD type 2, when the data in the row becomes effective; this defaults to 1/1/1900.	1/1/1900
expiry_timestamp	datetime	For SCD type 2, when the data in the row is no longer valid; this defaults to 12/31/2999.	12/31/2999
is_current	int	For SCD type 2, 1 if this is the current record; 0 otherwise.	1
source_system_code	int	The key of the source system where this record was coming from.	2
create_timestamp	datetime	When the record was created in DDS.	02/05/2008
update_timestamp	datetime	When the record was last updated.	02/05/2008

According to business requirement 8 in Chapter 4, the columns that we need to preserve the history are occupation, household_income, address1, address2, address3, address4, city, state, zipcode, country, phone_number, and email_address. In Chapter 8, we'll discuss how to monitor and maintain the changes in these columns. The is_current column, effective_timestamp column, and expiry_timestamp column are for accommodating SCD type 2. I will discuss how to maintain these columns in Chapter 8.

To accommodate multiple e-mail/postal addresses and landline/cell phone numbers for a customer, we can have multiple sets of addresses, telephones, and e-mail addresses in the customer dimension if we use a star schema. If we use a snowflake schema, we normalize the customer dimension by putting the e-mail/postal address and phone numbers in subtables branching out from the customer dimension.

In Table 5-9, we have the subscriber_class and subscriber_band columns. The purpose of these two columns is to satisfy business requirement 4 from Chapter 4. The requirement was to allocate each subscriber to a specific "class" based on their projected annual revenue. The business requirement also expected us to allocate each customer to a certain "band" based on the profit that the customer generated. The class and band are used in the loyalty program.

Now let's design the final dimension: store. Business requirement 9 in Chapter 4 indicates that there could be a reorganization of the stores. That is, currently there are only five regions in the United States, but in a few months there will be eight regions. Online stores are currently in one division, but in the future they will be in the same division as their offline colleagues. It is said that a reorganization like this rarely happens. This will be the first time in six years, and we can expect the new structure to last at least three years.

This store dimension is an ideal case for SCD type 3 because, as we discussed earlier, type 3 is suitable if we don't have many changes in the attributes (five or fewer) and if we know that there will be only a certain number of old versions. We also discussed that type 3 is suitable when the change involves a large number of rows in the dimension. In other words, a lot of rows are updated simultaneously. We will have a column for the current region, a column for the old region (and the date), and a similar one for the division. Table 5-10 describes the structure.

Table 5-10. *Store Dimension*

Column Name	Data Type	Description	Sample Value
store_key	int	The surrogate key of the store dimension.	12
store_number	int	Natural key. The common store identifier used in Jupiter, WebTower9, and Jade.	56
store_name	varchar(40)	Name of the store, usually based on location.	Los Angeles
store_type	varchar(20)	Store size, in terms of product variety.	Large
store_address1	varchar(50)	First line of store address.	725 South Pacific Avenue

Column Name	Data Type	Description	Sample Value
store_address2	varchar(50)	Second line of store address.	Suite 800
store_address3	varchar(50)	Third line of store address.	
store_address4	varchar(50)	Fourth line of store address.	
city	varchar(50)	Town or city where the store is located.	Los Angeles
state	varchar(40)	For non-U.S. address, it's county or region.	California
zipcode	varchar(10)	Postal code.	90017
country	varchar(50)	Country.	USA
phone_number	varchar(20)	Store's main/public telephone number.	(213) 454-5555
web_site	varchar(100)	Direct URL to store website.	http://www.amadeus.com/LA
region	varchar(30)	Current allocated region.	West
prior_region	varchar(30)		
prior_region_date	datetime		
division	varchar(30)	Current allocated division.	USA
prior_division	varchar(30)		
prior_division_date	datetime		
source_system_code	int	The key of the source system where this record was coming from.	2
create_timestamp	datetime	When the record was created in DDS.	02/05/2007
update_timestamp	datetime	When the record was last updated.	02/05/2007

When the new store organization is announced, the current region will be moved to the prior_region column, and the new region will be placed in the region column. The date the move happens will be recorded in the prior_region_date column. We will also do similar things for division. This way, after the new organizational structure has been implemented, the business users use both the old store organizational structure and the new structure.

To do a sales analysis of different periods by comparing the old organization structure and the new structure, we query the product sales data mart by joining the fact table with the date and store dimensions. We pick region, prior_region, division, and prior_division columns from the store dimension and use this information to organize the data from the fact table in a report or a BI application.

Figure 5-4 shows the final diagram of the data mart. It is a good idea to write the fact table grain just underneath the fact table name to remind us what facts can and cannot go into the fact table.

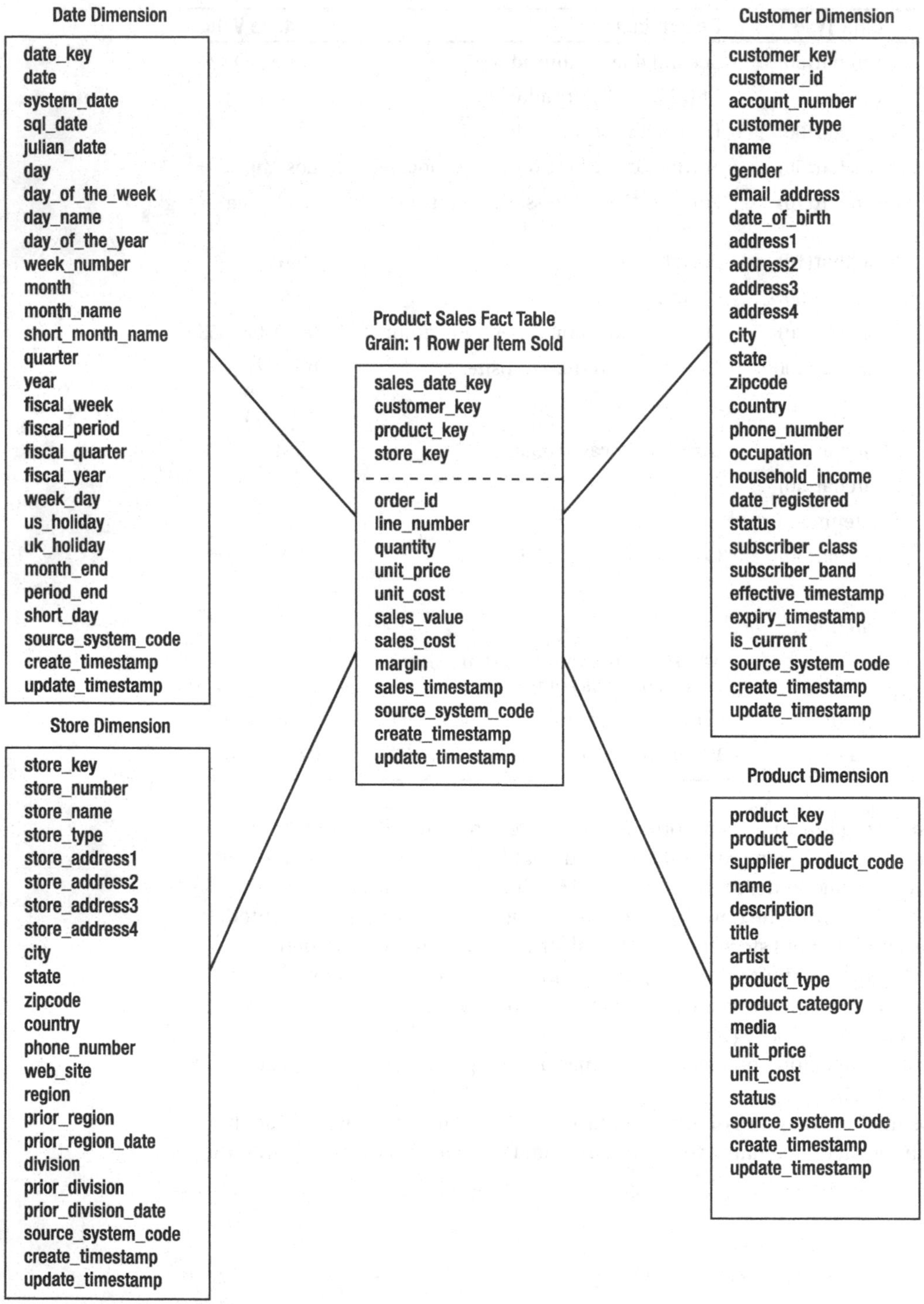

Date Dimension

```
date_key
date
system_date
sql_date
julian_date
day
day_of_the_week
day_name
day_of_the_year
week_number
month
month_name
short_month_name
quarter
year
fiscal_week
fiscal_period
fiscal_quarter
fiscal_year
week_day
us_holiday
uk_holiday
month_end
period_end
short_day
source_system_code
create_timestamp
update_timestamp
```

Customer Dimension

```
customer_key
customer_id
account_number
customer_type
name
gender
email_address
date_of_birth
address1
address2
address3
address4
city
state
zipcode
country
phone_number
occupation
household_income
date_registered
status
subscriber_class
subscriber_band
effective_timestamp
expiry_timestamp
is_current
source_system_code
create_timestamp
update_timestamp
```

Product Sales Fact Table
Grain: 1 Row per Item Sold

```
sales_date_key
customer_key
product_key
store_key
- - - - - - - - - - -
order_id
line_number
quantity
unit_price
unit_cost
sales_value
sales_cost
margin
sales_timestamp
source_system_code
create_timestamp
update_timestamp
```

Store Dimension

```
store_key
store_number
store_name
store_type
store_address1
store_address2
store_address3
store_address4
city
state
zipcode
country
phone_number
web_site
region
prior_region
prior_region_date
division
prior_division
prior_division_date
source_system_code
create_timestamp
update_timestamp
```

Product Dimension

```
product_key
product_code
supplier_product_code
name
description
title
artist
product_type
product_category
media
unit_price
unit_cost
status
source_system_code
create_timestamp
update_timestamp
```

Figure 5-4. *Dimensional star schema for product sales data mart*

Subscription Sales Data Mart

Now that we have done the product sales data mart, we can do the other data marts the same way. In other words, we start with the fact table, determine the dimensional key column in the fact table, set the fact table grain, and then create the dimension tables, taking into account the SCD. If the dimension table in this new data mart already exists in the previous mart, we don't create a new one. Instead, we reuse the existing dimension. If this new mart needs an attribute that does not exist in the dimension yet, we add that attribute to the existing dimension.

The other requirements that we have from the case study are subscription sales, subscriber profitability, supplier performance, CRM campaign segmentation, and CRM campaign results. Generally, the steps to design these marts are the same; they just require different business knowledge to design them. A data mart (the fact table and its dimensions) stores a collection of business events in a certain business area. To design the fact tables and dimensions, we need to have business knowledge in that business area. For example, to determine what columns we need to have in the Campaign Results fact table, we need to have a certain level of business knowledge in CRM.

There are a few things that I want to mention at this point. First, for performance reasons as well as design simplicity and consistency, it is better to stick to a star schema rather than a snowflake, at least as much as we can. As I discussed in Chapter 1, a star schema is simpler and is more consistent than a snowflake schema because it has only one level in all dimensions. Because a star schema is simpler, it is easier for the ETL processes to load the data into it. A snowflake schema is when you normalize a dimension into several smaller tables with a hierarchy structure. It is used when you want to benefit from less data redundancy. The benefit of a snowflake schema is that some analytics applications work better with a snowflake schema than a star schema. The other benefit of a snowflake schema is that less disk space is required. A snowflake schema can decrease query performance, but it can also increase query performance. It decreases the fact table query performance because we have to join more tables to the fact table. It increases the query performance when we want to get the distinct value of a particular dimension attribute. If this attribute is normalized into its own subdimension table, the select distinct query runs more quickly.

Second, if the dimension already exists, we use the existing one instead of creating another version. For example, do not create another customer dimension. If we need more attributes, extend the dimension columns. We need to be careful when doing this so we don't repeat columns with the same meaning. Also, we need be careful not to make the dimension table too wide (more than 40 columns). Also, we should not put nonrelated attributes into the same dimension table; they need to go to their own dimension tables linked separately to the fact table. If we need a higher level of granularity (such as a week dimension), we create a view on top of it. This means we create a view that takes the data solely from the dimension physical table. When creating the view, we filter irrelevant rows on the where clause and select only required columns on the select clause of the view definition.

Third, we have to be consistent with our data definitions. The definition for each measure and each dimension attribute must be accurate and unique. The same term used as a measure or attribute should not be used anywhere else in the data warehouse with a different meaning. For example, if date_registered is defined as "the date when the customer first purchased or subscribed," we should use this term consistently with the same meaning throughout the data warehouse. We should not use this term elsewhere in the data warehouse to mean something else.

Now, let's do the other data marts one by one. Subscription sales analysis (that is when a customer subscribes to a package rather than buying a product) and subscriber profitability analysis can be satisfied with one data mart, as mentioned in business requirements 2 and 3 in Chapter 4. Business requirement 4 is also relevant to this fact table. Let's repeat those three requirements here:

Requirement 2: The system will be able to analyze subscription sales over time by geographic area, by customer demographic, by stores and sales territory, and by product package. In addition, the users need to analyze by subscription duration and lead source (where the customers are coming from). They need to know the revenues, costs, and margins, evaluated every day for a period of one month. So, they have monthly revenue, monthly direct costs, monthly indirect costs, and monthly margin.

Requirement 3: The system will be able to analyze the subscriber profitability, which is defined as the projected annual revenue of the subscribing customer minus the annualized costs (including proportional indirect costs), expressed as a percentage of the projected annual revenue. This is analyzed over time by geographic area, by customer demographic attributes, by stores and sales territory, and by product package.

Requirement 4: The system will be able to allocate subscribers to a specific "class" based on their projected annual revenue and allocated to a certain "band" based on the profitability. The class and band are used in the loyalty program. These two attributes are updated daily.

For this, we will need to create a *periodic snapshot fact table*. A periodic snapshot fact table captures the state or condition of the business at a particular point in time. A periodic snapshot fact table is different from the one we did for the Product Sales fact table, where each row in the fact table corresponds to a certain business event. A fact table that contains a collection of business events is called a *transaction fact table*.

To design a period snapshot fact table that satisfies these three requirements, the first thing we need to do is determine the period, that is, how often we need to capture the business condition or state and put the snapshot in the fact table. Requirement 2 states that "the revenues, costs, and margins need to be evaluated every day," so the period is daily.

The next step is to determine the measures. The measures are determined based on what data the user needs to analyze. Requirement 2 mentioned that the users need to analyze monthly revenue, monthly direct costs, monthly indirect costs, and month margin. These are the measures. These measures are calculated from quantity and unit costs, so we need to include them as measures.

Then we need to determine the dimensions for this fact table. To do this, we need to find out *by what* the users need to analyze the measure. Requirement 2 mentioned that the users need to analyze the data by geographic area, by customer demographic, by stores and sales territory, by product package, by subscription duration, and by lead source. The geographic area and customer demographic are covered by the customer dimension. Stores and sales territory are covered by the store dimension. So, we need to have customer, store, product package, start + end subscription dates, and lead time as the dimensions of this fact table.

Next, we need to determine the fact table grain, that is, what constitutes a row in the fact table. The lowest level that we can capture the monthly revenue, monthly direct costs, monthly indirect costs, and monthly margin is per individual subscription. We can capture it per customer, but subscription is a lower level. So, the grain of this fact table is one row per subscription, and the period is daily.

If Amadeus Entertainment has 500,000 customer subscriptions, every day we will create 500,000 rows in this fact table. Each row will contain the revenues and costs of each subscription. This enables us to analyze the profitability of each customer by the hierarchical attributes, for example, by city, by state, by country, by occupation, by gender, and by household income, on a daily basis and compare them with other days.

The business requirement states that we need to evaluate the subscription sales every day. This is described in functional requirement 2 in Chapter 4 (and earlier in this chapter). The revenues and costs are dynamic, and they change every day. If the customer downloads more songs this week, the cost increases. If the customer downloads fewer films, the cost goes down. If the title unit cost increases, the cost incurred by Amadeus Entertainment for that customer increases. If the customer gets some single titles, the revenue increases.

It is important to be clear about the grain of the fact table. The grain of this fact table is one row for each subscription per day, not one row for each subscriber (customer) per day. It is possible for a customer to have more than one subscription, for example, when a customer subscribes to two different packages.

When drawing the dimensional star schema, I like to write the fact table grain underneath the fact table name to remind me what fact can and cannot go into the fact table. This fact table has six dimensional key columns: three of them already exist (we created them when we did the product sales data mart), and three of them are new dimensions. The three existing dimensions are date, customer, and store. The three new dimensions are package (for example, with a basic package, you can download *x* quantity of film, music, and audio books), format (as in type of media), and lead (the source where the subscription sales were originated from).

Figure 5-5 describes the Subscription Sales fact table and its dimensions. The three existing dimensions were mentioned in Figure 5-4, so the column names are not shown here.

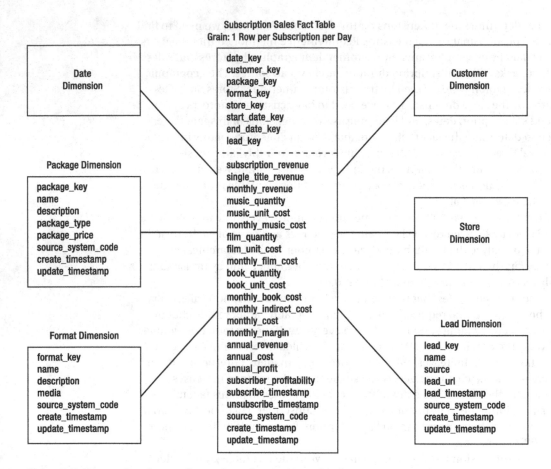

Figure 5-5. *Dimensional star schema for subscription sales data mart*

Let's go through the measures in the fact table one by one. You need to understand the definition of the measures in order to populate them correctly. These descriptions will be used to drive the ETL processes. Table 5-11 describes each measure in the Subscription Sales fact table, along with the data type, description, and sample value.

Table 5-11. *Subscription Sales Fact Table*

Column Name	Data Type	Description	Sample Value
subscription_revenue	money	Last four weeks of income from membership payments.	25.00
single_title_revenue	money	Last four weeks of income from additional single-item downloads (some items are outside the subscription coverage and are billed separately).	7.50
monthly_revenue	money	subscription_revenue + single_title_revenue.	32.50

Column Name	Data Type	Description	Sample Value
music_quantity	int	Number of music products downloaded by the subscriber in the last four weeks.	18
music_unit_cost	money	Weighted average of the unit cost of all music items, regardless of subscriber, in the last four weeks.	0.65
monthly_music_cost	money	music_quantity × music_unit_cost.	11.70
film_quantity	int	Number of films downloaded by the subscriber in the last four weeks.	5
film_unit_cost	money	Weighted average of the unit cost of all films, regardless of subscriber, in the last four weeks.	1.25
monthly_film_cost	money	film_quantity × film_unit_cost.	6.25
book_quantity	int	Number of audio books downloaded by the subscriber in the last four weeks.	2
book_unit_cost	money	Weighted average of the unit cost of all audio books, regardless of subscriber, in the last four weeks.	3.65
monthly_book_cost	money	book_quantity × book_unit_cost.	7.30
monthly_indirect_cost	money	Last four weeks of store, head office, infrastructure, and technology costs, allocated to each subscriber. The allocation is weighted on price and quantity of the items downloaded by the customers.	2.14
monthly_cost	money	monthly_music_cost + monthly_film_cost + monthly_book_cost + monthly_indirect_cost.	27.39
monthly_margin	money	monthly_revenue − monthly_cost.	5.11
annual_revenue	money	One-year projection of monthly_revenue, using the last three months of data. If the subscriber was registered within the last three months, we use all data that we have about that subscriber.	131.47
annual_cost	money	One-year projection of monthly_cost, using the last three months of data.	103.25
annual_profit	money	annual_revenue − annual_cost.	28.21
subscriber_profitability	money	annual_profit calculated as a percentage of annual revenue.	21.46

For the subscription sales data mart shown in Figure 5-5, every day we need to take a snapshot of all subscription data and put it in the fact table. If we have 1 million subscriptions, we will add 1 million new records every day. This way we can analyze the revenue, cost, and profitability of each customer and can roll it up by any of the criteria defined in the requirement, that is, by geographic area, by customer demographic, by stores and sales territory, by product package, by subscription duration, and by lead source. We can analyze the data by all these criteria because they are defined as dimensions.

We created this fact table as a periodic snapshot because we need to capture the revenues, costs, and margins at a regular interval. We cannot create this fact table as a transaction fact table because unlike the Product Sales fact table, the Subscription Sales fact table does not capture business events.

Business requirement 4 mentioned that we need to calculate the subscriber class and band based on annual revenue and annual profitability daily. This means we need to update the value of the `subscriber_class` and `subscriber_band` columns in the customer dimension based on today's set of customer subscription data. For this purpose, it is best to keep today's set of data in a separate table. It is faster to calculate today's value of the subscribers' classes and bands on a table that contains today's data only rather than on a table that contains months or years of subscription data. It is also faster than querying the source system because today's subscription data is stored locally on the DDS and because the annual revenue and annual profitability have been calculated.

Supplier Performance Data Mart

Figure 5-6 shows the dimensional star schema for the supplier performance data mart.

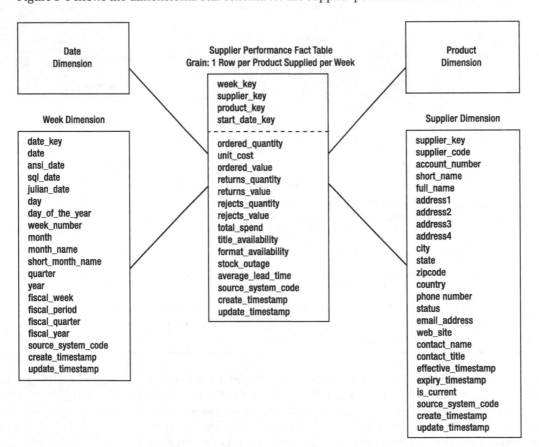

Figure 5-6. *Dimensional star schema for the supplier performance data mart*

The grain of the fact table is one row per product supplied per week. It is not one row per supplier per week. This enables us to drill down to the product level and to roll up to the supplier level. The type of the fact table is a periodic snapshot.

It has a week dimension in addition to the date dimension. The week dimension is referred to by the week_key, which is the week when the supplier performance was evaluated. The date dimension is referred to by the start_date_key, which is the date the supplier started supplying that product to Amadeus Entertainment. The week dimension is a view created on top of the date dimension, filtering columns that are not relevant at week level, by constraining on a particular day. It has the same key as the date dimension.

The supplier performance data mart has four dimensions: date, week, supplier, and product. The supplier dimension supports SCD type 2, indicated by the effective and expiry timestamp and the is_current column. The address columns in the supplier dimension are similar to the columns in the customer dimension, except contact_name and contact_title, which indicate the contact person in the supplier's organization.

The purpose of this data mart is to support the user to analyze "supplier performance," which is the weighted average of the total spent, costs, value of returns, value of rejects, title and format availability, stock outages, lead time, and promptness. To define the measure on the fact table, we need to determine the period on which we want to evaluate the performance. This can be done by discussing the requirement with the business. In this example, we will assume that the cost is calculated based on the last three months.

Table 5-12 contains the column names of the measures on the fact table, as well as the description, data type, and sample values. These definitions will be required to populate the fact table. These descriptions will be used to drive the ETL processes.

Table 5-12. *Supplier Performance Fact Table*

Column Name	Data Type	Description	Sample Value
order_quantity	int	How many units of that product were ordered from that supplier in the last three months.	44
unit_cost	money	The average price that Amadeus Entertainment paid to its supplier for this product in the last three months.	2.15
ordered_value	money	order_quantity × unit_cost.	94.6
returns_quantity	int	How many units of this product Amadeus Entertainment received back from the customer and subsequently returned to the supplier in the last three months.	1
returns_value	money	returns_quantity × unit_cost.	2.15
rejects_quantity	int	How many units were returned to the supplier without it being supplied to a customer first, in the last three months.	1
rejects_value	money	rejects_quantity × unit_cost.	2.15
total_spend	money	ordered_value – returns_value – rejects_value.	90.3

Continued

Table 5-12. *Continued*

Column Name	Data Type	Description	Sample Value
title_availability	decimal (9,2)	The percentage of product titles available in the last three months when Amadeus Entertainment ordered them.	100 percent
format_availability	decimal (9,2)	The percentage of products available in the format that we requested in the last three months when ordering them.	100 percent
stock_outage	decimal (9,2)	The number of days our inventory was out of stock in the last three months for that particular product, divided by total days in the last three months.	0
average_lead_time	smallint	The number of elapsed days between the date the order was placed and the product was delivered, averaged for the last three months.	4

CRM Data Marts

The business requirements for the CRM campaign segmentation are (from Chapter 4): to enable CRM users to select customers based on communication permissions (subscribed/unsubscribed, e-mail/phone/post, and so on), geographic attributes (address, city, and so on), demographic attributes (age, gender, occupation, income, hobby, and so on), interests (music taste, book topic interests, favorite film types, and so on), purchase history (order values, order dates, number of items, store locations, and so on), subscription details (details of packages, subscription dates, durations, store locations, and so on), and attributes of the products purchased (for example, music genre, artist, film type, and so on) for the purpose of sending CRM campaigns.

Communication subscriptions need to be added in a separate fact table (for enabling subscription to multiple communications). Communication permissions and communication preferences (or interests) need to be added to the customer dimension. Purchase history and subscription details are available in the product sales and subscription sales data marts. Attributes of the products purchased are also available in the product sales data mart.

Before we proceed, I'll clarify some CRM terminology first. *Communication subscription* is when a customer subscribes to a communication, such as a weekly newsletter. *Communication permission* is when a customer allows us or third-party partners to contact them (or communicate with them) either via telephone, e-mail, post, and so on. *Communication preferences* has two meanings: communication channel preferences and communication content preferences. The channel is about how they want to be contacted, such as via telephone, post, e-mail, or text messages. The content is about the subject they want to know, such as pop music, comedy films, or certain favorite authors. Communication content preferences are also known as *interests*.

Let's put the communication subscription in a fact table, and let's put the communication permission and communication preferences in the customer dimension. Figure 5-7 shows the communication subscription fact table and its dimensions.

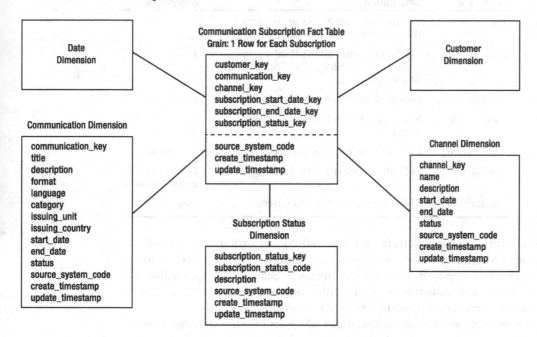

Figure 5-7. *Dimensional star schema for communication subscription data mart*

For simplicity in this case study, a customer has only one e-mail address, one telephone number, and one postal address. But in a real CRM data warehouse, of course this is not the case. A customer can have multiple e-mail/postal addresses and landline/cell phone numbers. If this is the case, in the subscription fact table in Figure 5-7 we need to have contact_ address_key, and we need to have a "contact address" dimension. This dimension stores which e-mail address is subscribed to the newsletter. This dimension also stores which cell phone number is subscribed to the SMS feed and which postal address is subscribed to promotional mailings. This enables the same customer to be subscribed to a newsletter using different e-mail addresses, which is not the case when we have only one e-mail address for a customer. When we design the normalized data store later in this chapter, we will accommodate having multiple postal/e-mail addresses and phone numbers for each customer by normalizing the data.

Now let's add communication permission and preferences in the customer dimension. Table 5-13 shows the additional attributes in the customer dimensions to incorporate permission and preferences. Content preferences or interests are usually obtained via customer surveys, and the questionnaire can be based on the product hierarchy.

Table 5-13. *Additional Customer Dimension Attributes to Incorporate Communication Preferences*

Column Name	Data Type	Description	Sample Value
permission1	int	1 if the customer allows us to contact them; 0 otherwise. The default is 0.	1
permission2	int	1 if the customer allows third-party partners to contact them; 0 otherwise. The default is 0.	1
preferred_channel1	varchar(15)	First preferred communication channel.	E-mail
preferred_channel2	varchar(15)	Second preferred communication channel.	Text
interest1	varchar(30)	First interest/preferred content.	Pop music
interest2	varchar(30)	Second interest/preferred content.	Computer audio books
interest3	varchar(30)	Third interest/preferred content.	New films

With the Communication Subscriptions fact table and additional attributes in the customer dimension, the CRM users can now select the customers based on various criteria for the purpose of sending CRM campaigns. This selection process is called *campaign segmentation*. A campaign is communication sent to customers either regularly or on an ad hoc basis via a delivery mechanism such as e-mail, posts, RSS, or text messages.

So, that's business requirement 6, which is to enable CRM users to select customers. Now we get to business requirement 7, which is to let CRM users analyze campaign results by viewing the several measures for each campaign sent to customers. Those measures are as follows:

- The number of messages sent by communication channel (mobile phone, text message, or e-mail)

- The number of messages delivered successfully

- The number of messages failed to be delivered (including the reason)

The same business requirement also states that for e-mail messages the users will analyze the open rate, click-through rate, complaint rate, spam verdict, and trap hit rate. *Open rate* is the number of mail messages that were opened by the customer, divided by the number of messages sent. *Click-through rate* is the number of hyperlinks embedded in the e-mail messages that were clicked, divided by the number of e-mail messages sent. *Complaint rate* is the number of customers who rated the e-mail as spam, divided by the total number of e-mails sent. *Spam verdict* is the probability that an e-mail would be classified as spam either by the ISP or by the spam filter software. *Trap hit rate* is the number of e-mails delivered to dummy e-mail addresses created by the ISP.

To satisfy this requirement, we need to design a Campaign Results fact table and introduce two new dimensions: campaign and delivery status. Figure 5-8 describes the Campaign Results fact table and its dimensions. Some of the measures in the fact table such as opened, clicked_through, and spam_verdict are not applicable for postal campaigns.

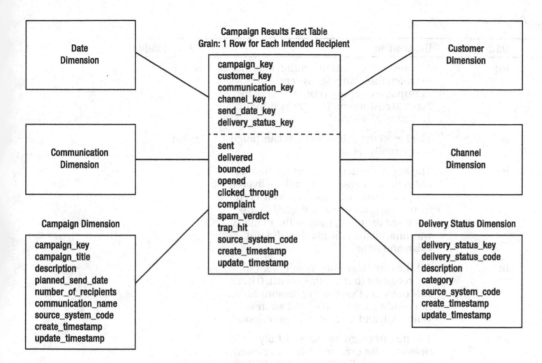

Figure 5-8. *Dimensional star schema for campaign results data mart*

Now let's discuss the data mart shown in Figure 5-8. The grain of the Campaign Results fact table is one row for each intended campaign recipient. If a campaign is planned to be sent to 200,000 recipients, then there will be 200,000 rows in this table for that campaign, even though the campaign was actually sent to 199,970 recipients because (for example) 10 had invalid e-mail addresses and 20 customers explicitly asked not to be contacted for any marketing purposes.

Table 5-14 defines the fact table columns.

Table 5-14. *Campaign Results Fact Table*

Column Name	Data Type	Description	Sample Value
campaign_key	int	The key of the campaign that was sent to customers.	1456
customer_key	int	The key of the customer who was intended to receive this campaign.	25433
communication_key	int	The key of the communication to which the campaign belongs. For example, this campaign is an instance of a communication called "Amadeus music weekly newsletter" dated 02/18/2008.	5

Continued

Table 5-14. *Continued*

Column Name	Data Type	Description	Sample Value
channel_key	int	The key of the communication channel to which this campaign is sent. For example, a campaign could be sent to 200,000 customers, 170,000 by e-mail and 30,000 by RSS.	3
send_date_key	int	The key of the date when this campaign was actually sent.	23101
delivery_status_key	int	The key of the delivery status. 0 means not sent. 1 means successfully delivered. 2 to N contains various reasons why the campaign failed to be delivered to the intended recipient, such as the mailbox was unavailable, the mailbox did not exist, and so on.	1
sent	int	1 if the campaign was actually sent to the recipient (out of our system); 0 if it was not sent. Examples of reasons for not sending are failed e-mail address validation and no customer permission.	1
delivered	int	1 if the campaign was successfully delivered (for example, if it is an e-mail campaign, it is SMTP reply code 250 on the DATA command); 0 if it failed to be delivered. If it failed, the delivery_status_key column will contain the reason.	1
bounced	int	1 if the campaign was hard-bounced (SMTP client received permanent rejection message); 0 otherwise.	0
opened	int	1 if the campaign e-mail was opened or viewed; 0 otherwise.	1
clicked_through	int	1 if the customer clicked any of the links in the campaign e-mails; 0 otherwise.	1
complaint	int	1 if the customer clicked the Spam button (available on some e-mail providers such as Yahoo, AOL, Hotmail, and MSN and we get the information via feedback loop); 0 otherwise.	0
spam_verdict	int	1 if the content of the campaign is identified as spam either by the ISP or by spam filter software such as Spam Assassin; 0 otherwise.	0
source_system_code	int	The key to the source system where this record was coming from.	2
create_timestamp	datetime	When the record was created in DDS.	02/05/2007
update_timestamp	datetime	When the record was last updated.	02/05/2007

The Delivery Status dimension contains the failure reason codes if the delivered fact is 0. If the delivered fact is 1, then `delivery_status_key` is 1, which means OK. `delivery_status_key` being 0 means that the campaign was not sent out to the particular customer. The category column in this dimension contains, for example, a severity level based on SMTP reply codes. If the reply code is 550 (mailbox unavailable), then we can categorize it as severe.

Data Hierarchy

In dimension tables, there is a certain structure called *hierarchy*. Hierarchy is important because it provides you with paths that you can use to roll up and drill down when analyzing the data. In this section, I will discuss data hierarchy in the dimension tables and how it can be used for rolling up the data.

In the dimension tables, sometimes an attribute (column) is a subset of another attribute, meaning that the attribute values can be grouped by the other attribute. The attribute that can be used to group is said to be on a *higher level* than the attribute that is being grouped. That is, if A is a subset of B, then A is on a higher level than B. These levels in the dimensions tables are called *dimensional hierarchy*. For example, a year consists of four quarters, and a quarter consists of three months. In this case, the highest level is year and then quarter, and the bottom level is month. You can roll up a fact from a lower level to a higher level. For example, if you know the sales value of each month in the quarter, you know the sales value of that quarter.

All four dimensions of the Product Sales fact table have hierarchies. The hierarchies of the date, store, customer, and product dimensions are shown in Figure 5-9 and Figure 5-10.

Figure 5-9 shows that fiscal week rolls up to fiscal period, but week does not roll up to month. The `sqldate`, `system_date`, `julian_date`, `day`, `day_of_the_week`, `day_name`, and so on are at the same level as date, so they can also roll up to week, month, and fiscal week.

Figure 5-10 shows that store can roll up to regional structure and geographical structure. Customers roll up to their geographical locations.

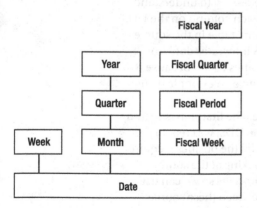

Figure 5-9. *Hierarchy of the date dimension*

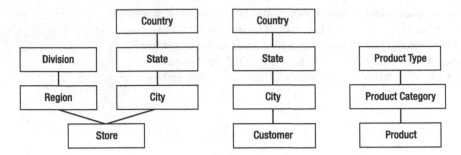

Figure 5-10. *Hierarchies of the store, customer, and product dimensions*

To apply hierarchy in your own situation, first look at the columns (attributes) in the dimension tables to find whether there are any groupings or subsets. Arrange the attributes in the appropriate levels, meaning that you need to put the higher-level attribute on top of the lower-level attribute. Test the data to prove that all the members of the lower-level attribute can be grouped by the higher-level attribute. Identify whether there are multiple paths (branches) in the hierarchy structure; for example, store in Figure 5-10 can be grouped by both city and region. You can do all this by using the data profiling tool. Hierarchy is an integrated part of dimension design.

Source System Mapping

In this section, I will discuss why and how to do source system mapping. Source system mapping is an exercise in mapping the dimensional data store to the source systems.

After we complete the DDS design, the next step is to map every column in the DDS to the source systems so that we know where to get the data from when populating those columns. When doing this, we also need to determine the transformations or calculations required to get the source columns into the target column. This is necessary to understand the functionality that the ETL logic must perform when populating each column on the DDS tables. Bear in mind that a DDS column may come from more than one table in the source system or even from more than one source system, because the ODS integrates data from multiple sources. This is where the source_system_code column becomes useful because it enables us to understand from which system the data is coming. I'll give an example using the Product Sales data mart.

Refer to Table 5-1 again, which shows the Product Sales fact table. The first step is to find out from which tables the columns are coming. When we designed the DDS, we created the DDS columns (fact table measures and dimensional attributes) to fulfill the business requirements. Now we need to find out where we can get the data from by looking at the source system tables. We write the source tables and their abbreviations in brackets so we can use them later in the mapping table. Then we write the join conditions between these source tables so that we know how to write the query later when we develop the ETL.

The following list specifies the target table, the source tables, and the join conditions. It shows where the Product Sales fact table is populated from and how the source tables are joined.

Target table in DDS: Product Sales fact table

Source: WebTower9 `sales_order_header` [woh], WebTower9 `sales_order_detail` [wod], Jade `order_header` [joh], Jade `order_detail` [jod], Jupiter `item_master` [jim], Jupiter `currency_rate` table [jcr]

Join condition: `woh.order_id = wod.order_id`, `joh.order_id = jod.order_id`, `wod.product_code = jim.product_code`, `jod.product_code = jim.product_code`

In this case study, the inventory is managed in Jupiter, and the sales transaction is stored in the two front-office systems, WebTower9 and Jade, which is why we have the link between the Jupiter inventory master table and the order detail tables in WebTower9 and Jade. If you need to recall the Amadeus Entertainment case study, see Chapter 2.

Then we add two columns to Table 5-1: source and transformation. In the source column, we refer to the source table abbreviations that we wrote earlier—woh, wod, joh, jod, and jim. We can determine which table we sourced the column from by understanding the data in the source system. So, Table 5-1 becomes like Table 5-15. I removed the data types and sample values so there's enough space, but I kept the Description column to remind us of what those columns are.

Table 5-15. *Product Sales Fact Table Source System Mapping*

Column Name	Description	Source	Transformation
sales_date_key	The date the customer purchased the product	woh.order_date, joh.order_date	Key lookup on date dimension based on date column.
customer_key	The customer who purchased the product	woh.customer_id, joh.customer_number	Key lookup on customer dimension based on customer_id column.
product_key	The product purchased by the customer	wod.product_code, jod,product_code	Key lookup on product dimension based on product_code column.
store_key	The store where the customer made the purchase	woh.store_number, joh.store_number	Key lookup on store dimension based on store_number column.
order_id	WebTower9 or Jade order ID	woh.order_id, joh.order_id	Trim and convert to uppercase character if required.
line_number	WebTower9 or Jade order line number	wod.line_no, jod.line_no	Remove leading zeros.
quantity	How many units of the product were purchased by the customer	wod.qty, jod.qty	None.
unit_price	Price of one unit of the product purchased in U.S. dollars	wod.price, jod.price	Divided by jcr.rate for that date. Round to four decimal digits.
unit_cost	Direct and indirect costs for one unit of the product in U.S. dollars	jim.unit_cost	Divided by jcr.rate for that date. Round to four decimal digits.

Continued

Table 5-15. *Continued*

Column Name	Description	Source	Transformation
sales_value	quantity × unit_price	This fact table	quantity column × unit_price column. Round to four decimal digits.
sales_cost	quantity × unit_cost	This fact table	quantity column × unit_cost column. Round to four decimal digits.
margin	sales_value – sales_cost	This fact table	sales_value – sales_cost column. Round to four decimal digits.
sales_timestamp	When the customer purchased the product	woh.timestamp, joh.timestamp	Convert to mm/dd/yyyy hh:mm:ss.sss format.
source_system_code	The source system from which this record is coming from	1 for WebTower9, 2 for Jade, 3 for Jupiter	Lookup in source system table in metadata database.
create_timestamp	When the record was created in DDS	Current system time	None.
update_timestamp	When the record was last updated	Current system time	None.

We don't need to map the time dimension because it does not come from any source system. Instead, it is calculated internally in the data warehouse. I recommend spending a few hours writing a SQL script that generates the values for calendar columns, with beginning and end dates as input parameters. You can do this by looping from the start date to the end date and inserting a record at a time containing various date attributes. You can find an example of such a script in the dim_date.sql file in the /Scripts/DDS folder on the book's website. I prefer that approach than calculating them in a spreadsheet because we can rerun the script repeatedly. This comes in handy when developing, testing, and migrating to production.

Fiscal and holiday columns are usually imported from the source system or spreadsheets by loading them into a temporary table using SSIS and then imported into the DDS by the previous script. These sources need to be mapped to a date dimension, as shown in Table 5-16, by comparing the source system columns with the DDS columns. The purpose of doing this mapping is to enable us to write the date dimension population script that I mentioned earlier.

```
Source: Jupiter fiscal_calendar table [jfc], holidays.xls [xh],
Jade store_hours [jsh]
```

Table 5-16. *Date Dimension Source System Mapping*

Column Name	Description	Source	Transformation
fiscal_week	The number of elapsed weeks since September 1.	jfc.week	None
fiscal_period	A period consists of four or five weeks depending on the fiscal calendar. Usually, the pattern used in this company is 454, 544, or 445, in FPn format. A fiscal year always consists of 12 periods.	jfc.period	Remove leading zero, prefix with FP
fiscal_quarter	A fiscal quarter is three fiscal periods, from September 1, in FQn format.	jfc.quarter	Add FQ prefix
fiscal_year	Fiscal year begins on September 1, in FYnnnn format.	jfc.year	Add FY prefix
us_holiday	1 if it is a national holiday in the US; 0 otherwise.	xh.us.date	Lookup to convert to 1 and 0
uk_holiday	1 if it is a statutory holiday in the UK; 0 otherwise.	xh.uk.date	Lookup to convert to 1 and 0
period_end	1 if it is the last day in a fiscal period; 0 otherwise.	Calculated based on fiscal period column	select max (date) group by fiscal period
short_day	1 if the offline stores' opening hours is shorter than normal opening hours; 0 otherwise.	jsh.start, jsh.end	1 if (start-end) < 12, else 0

As usual, we write the source tables with abbreviations in square brackets. We also write the join criteria between the source tables, as follows:

```
Source: Jupiter item_master [jim], Jupiter product_type [jpt],
Jupiter category table [jc], Jupiter media table [jm],
Jupiter currency rate [jcr], Jupiter product_status [jps]
Join criteria: jim.type = jpt.id, jim.category = jc.id,
jim.media = jm.id, jim.status = jps.id
```

Table 5-17 shows the source system mapping for the product dimension.

Table 5-17. *Product Dimension Source System Mapping*

Column Name	Description	Source	Transformation
product_key	The surrogate key of product dimension. It is unique, is not null, and is the primary key of product dimension.	Identity column with seed 1 and increment 1.	None
product_code	Natural key. Product code is the identifier and primary key of the product table in Jupiter. It is in AAA999999 format.	jim.product_code	Convert to uppercase
name	The product name.	jim.product_name	None
description	The product description.	jim.description	None

Continued

Table 5-17. *Continued*

Column Name	Description	Source	Transformation
title	The song/film/book title.	jim.title	None
artist	The singer, star, or author.	jim.artist	None
product_type	Level 1 of product hierarchy, such as music, film, or book.	jpt.description	None
product_category	Level 2 of product hierarchy; for film, it could be thriller, western, comedy, action, documentary, children, Asian, and so on.	jc.name	None
media	Format of the media, such as MP3, MPG, CD, or DVD.	jm.name	None
unit_price	Price for one item.	jim.unit_price	Divide by jcr.rate for that date
unit_cost	Allocated direct and indirect costs.	jim.unit_cost	Divide by jcr.rate for that date
status	Upcoming if we have signed contract with the supplier, Active if it is still being offered to customer, Expired if it is no longer being offered.	jps.description	None

Now we need to complete similar exercises with the customer and store dimensions, that is, write down the source system tables with abbreviations in square brackets, write the join criteria between the source system tables, map the dimension columns to the source system tables and columns, and write the transformations. Then we do the same thing with all the other fact and dimension tables in other data marts.

The end result is that the dimensional data store that we designed in the previous section will be completely mapped to the source systems. Therefore, we know where every single column will be sourced from, including the transformations.

Designing the Normalized Data Store

Now that we have designed the dimensional data store and mapped every column in every table to the source systems, we are ready to design the normalized data store, which is a normalized database that sits between the stage and the DDS. Please refer to the data flow architecture diagram in Figure 2-5 in Chapter 2. The NDS is a master data store containing the complete data sets, including all historical transaction data and all historical versions of master data. The NDS contains master tables and transaction tables. A *transaction table* is a table that contains a business transaction or business event. A *master table* is a table that contains the persons or objects involved in the business event. In this section, you will learn how to design the data model for NDS.

First, we list all the entities based on the source tables and based on the fact and dimension attributes in the DDS. We list all the tables in the source system that we have identified during the source system mapping exercise in the previous section. We then normalize DDS fact and dimension tables into a list of separated normalized tables. We then combine the two lists by eliminating the same tables and separating them into different subject areas. Figure 5-11 shows the results; it contains several groups of tables that have been categorized into business areas. Related tables are put into the same group.

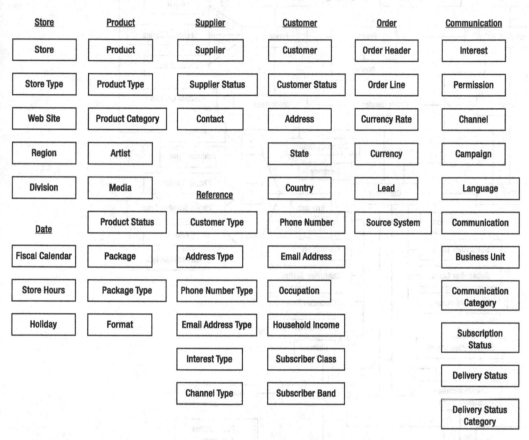

Figure 5-11. *Listing the entities*

We then arrange the entities according to their relationships to enable us to establish the referential integrity between the entities. We do this by connecting the parent table to the child table. A child table has a column containing the primary key of the parent table. Figure 5-12 shows the result; it shows the tables listed in Figure 5-11, but the parent and child tables have been connected. The DDS fact tables become child (transaction) tables in NDS. The DDS dimension tables become parent (master) tables in the NDS.

As an example, let's take the Subscription Sales fact table. This fact table in the DDS has six dimensions: lead, package, format, store, customer, and date. So, the subscription sales transaction table in the NDS in Figure 5-12 is connected to lead, package, format, store, and customer. We don't model the DDS date dimension in the NDS because we put the date in the transaction tables. We normalize the package type column in the package table into a separate table. We normalize the media column in the format table into a separate table.

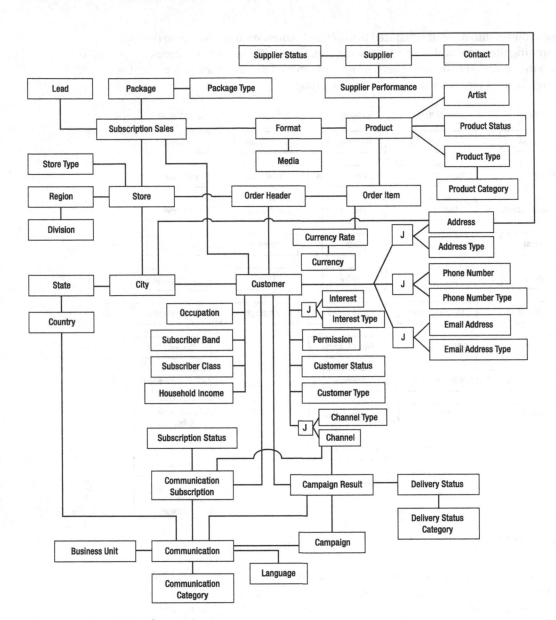

Figure 5-12. *Arranging the entities*

Ideally, the NDS diagram includes the cardinality in "crow's feet" format to reflect the relationship between entities such as one-to-many. The crow's feet format consists of the symbols of circle (zero), line (one), or fork (many) near a table, as shown in Figure 5-13.

Figure 5-13. *Crow's feet symbols*

The J boxes are *junction tables* to enable many-to-many relationships. Some people call them *bridge tables*. For example, the customer_address junction table links between the customer table and the address table. This junction table has three main columns: customer_address_id, customer_id, and address_id. The first column is the primary key of this table. The last two columns are the primary key of the customer table and the address table. Some people prefer to make the customer_id and address_id columns a composite primary key and not use customer_address_id at all. This junction table also has the standard supporting columns such as create_timestamp and update_timestamp.

To support multiple DDSs consistently, all data warehouse keys need to be defined and maintained in the NDS so that all DDSs have consistent keys. In addition to the natural keys from the source system, all the NDS tables in Figure 5-12 need to have a data warehouse key. I will discuss NDS key maintenance in Chapter 8 when I discuss ETL. Some people disagree with this approach and say it is better to generate the DW keys in DDS because surrogate keys are used in the DDS. If you have only one DDS or if you source the secondary DDSs from one main DDS, I agree this is the best approach because you don't have to have a surrogate key in two places (the NDS and the DDS). But if you have more than one DDS and you intend to generate the DDSs from NDS, it is better to maintain the data warehouse keys in the NDS because it will maintain surrogate key's consistency between multiple DDSs.

From a data integration point of view, we need to have a DW key for every table in the NDS. We need it for mapping the reference data from several source systems. To create the mapping, we identify the primary key of the table in the source system and match it with the DW key in the NDS table. When populating the NDS tables, we build ETL according to this mapping. For example, if Jade has 30,000 artists and WebTower9 has 60,000 artists, we need to have an artist_key in the NDS artist table and map Jade artist_id and WebTower9 artist_id to it. Not only does this make the DDS population easier (because it deals only with one system), but also makes the data integration from many source systems easier in the NDS.

The date table is maintained in the NDS too. As we defined in the previous section, the date table is sourced from the fiscal_calendar table, holiday table, and opening_hours tables. But most columns of the date table are generated internally using a population script. This includes the week number, last day flag, system date, Julian date, week day name, month name, and so on.

When designing the NDS, we need to follow the normalization rules. The purpose of normalization is to remove redundant data and make it easier to maintain the data. We need to bear in mind that normalization could impact the performance. There is no definitive rule that we need to design the NDS to the third normal form. In some cases, it makes more sense to design some tables to the second normal form. In other cases, we need to implement other normal forms such as the Boyce-Codd normal form (BCNF) or the fourth normal form.

■**Note** Please refer to the appendix for normalization rules and a quick summary of the first, second, third, Boyce-Codd, fourth, and fifth normal forms.

When doing normalization, we need to be careful when reaching 3NF and BCNF. They are best practice, but there are cases when they are not practical. For example, if we want to bring the customer table to 3NF, we need to break some columns into their own table. Gender and status, which probably have only two or three possible values, according to 3NF rules, need to go into their own tables, linked by a foreign key to the customer table.

The next step is to list the columns. We base this on the DDS columns and on the source system columns. We don't want to bring all source system columns into the NDS. We want to bring only the relevant ones. We get the data types from the source systems. If a particular column is sourced from two different source systems, take the longest one. For example, perhaps email in Jade is varchar(100) and in WebTower9 it is varchar(255). If one is an integer and the other is a varchar (in the case of the order ID, for example), make it a varchar. Be careful when defining decimal and float, because different RDBMSs have different precision. Also, we need to be careful when dealing with date and timestamp data types; again, different RDBMSs have different formats and behaviors.

As in many cases, an example is the best way to understand. Let's do a customer table for an example, as shown in Table 5-18.

Table 5-18. *NDS Customer Table*

Column Name	Data Type	Description	Sample Value
customer_key	int	The surrogate data warehouse key of customer table.	84743
customer_id	varchar(10)	Natural key. The primary key of the customer tables in WebTower9 and Jade. The WebTower9 customer_id format is AA999999, and Jade is AAA99999.	DH029383
account_number	int	For subscription customer; blank otherwise.	342165
customer_type_id	int	Foreign key (FK) to customer_type table where the customer type is stored.	2
name	varchar(100)	Customer's full name.	Charlotte Thompson
gender	char(1)	M for male; F for female.	F
date_of_birth	smalldatetime	Customer's date of birth.	04/18/1973
occupation_id	int	FK to occupation ID where the customer occupation is stored.	439
household_income_id	int	FK to household income table where the customer household income is stored.	732
date_registered	smalldatetime	The date when the customer first purchased or subscribed.	11/23/2007
status	int	FK to customer_status table where the customer status is stored (active if the customer is currently a member or made a purchase in the last 12 months).	Active
subscriber_class_id	int	FK to subscriber_class table where the subscriber class is stored. It is a classification of subscribers based on projected annual revenue.	3

Column Name	Data Type	Description	Sample Value
subscriber_band_id	int	FK to subscriber_band table where the subscriber band is stored. It is a classification of subscribers based on profitability.	5
effective_timestamp	datetime	For SCD type 2, when the data in the row becomes effective; defaults to 1/1/1900.	1/1/1900
expiry_timestamp	datetime	For SCD type 2, when the data in the row is no longer valid; defaults to 12/31/2999.	12/31/2999
is_current	int	For SCD type 2, 1 if this is the current record; 0 otherwise.	1
source_system_code	int	The key to the source system where this record was coming from.	2
create_timestamp	datetime	When the record was created in NDS.	02/05/2008
update_timestamp	datetime	When the record was last updated.	02/05/2008

Then we do the same thing with all the NDS tables; in other words, we list their columns. The next step is to write down the source and transformation. This should not be difficult because we defined them when we did the source system mapping in the DDS.

Now the NDS is complete. It has all the tables necessary to create the DDS. It is highly normalized. We have defined all columns in all tables, along with the source and transformation for each column. We can now return to the DDS and redefine the source for each DDS column in the NDS. This is required for building the ETL between NDS and DDS. We can do this by identifying the source table in the NDS for each DDS table. Then we identify the corresponding NDS column that contains the source data for each DDS column.

Summary

In this chapter, we designed the dimensional data store and the normalized data store of the Amadeus Entertainment case study. We started from the business requirements and modeled the DDS. We defined the fact tables and the dimension tables. We did the source system mapping where we identified the source for each column and the required transformation.

Then we designed the NDS. We listed all the entities and then defined the relationships. Next, we listed the required columns, and we defined their sources and transformations. We went back to the DDS and redefined the source of each column in the NDS.

In the next chapter, you'll see how to physically implement these databases on the SQL Server platform.

■ ■ ■

CHAPTER 6

Physical Database Design

Having designed the logical model of the dimensional data store and normalized data store in the previous chapter, this chapter will cover how we implement those data stores physically as SQL Server databases. For an experienced DBA, this should not be a problem. In the previous chapter, we defined all the columns, all the data types, and the relationships between tables. It should be quite straightforward to now create those tables, right?

Although this is partially true, we need to consider a few details before taking the plunge and creating those tables. For example, we need to deal with issues such as the hardware platform, storage considerations, partitioning, and indexes. I will cover these topics in this chapter.

Hardware Platform

In Chapter 2, we drafted the system architecture for Amadeus Entertainment. Figure 6-1 shows the system architecture diagram for your convenience.

In the system architecture shown in Figure 6-1, we have one ETL server, two database servers (clustered), two report servers (load balanced), and two OLAP servers. We have 12TB raw disk space in the SAN consisting of 85 disks, each with 146GB capacity and 15,000 RPM. All the network connections to the SAN are via a fiber network, and for high availability we have two Fibre Channel switches. We estimated that the number of client PCs that will be using the data warehouse is between 300 and 500.

Note In this chapter, we will be doing the physical database design. To do the physical database design, it is important to understand the physical system architecture on which the database will be operating. Physical database design is a fundamental part of data warehouse design. The performance of a data warehouse is largely affected by the physical design of the underlying databases and the environment where the databases are running.

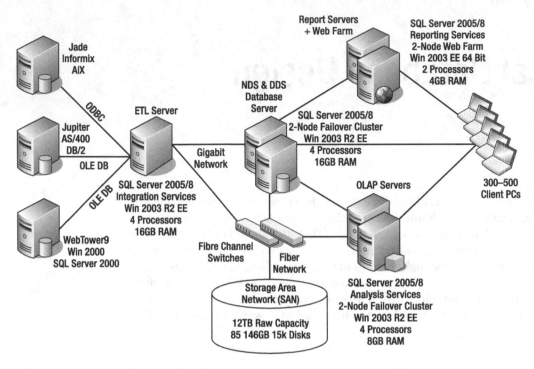

Figure 6-1. *System architecture for the Amadeus Entertainment data warehouse*

Now let's look once again at the nonfunctional requirements from Chapter 4. Nonfunctional requirement 10 mentioned that the data warehouse must be available for 24 hours a day, 7 days a week, and the downtime is expected to be no more than one hour a month. The Amadeus Entertainment data warehouse is used to support CRM activities, both customer analytics and campaign management operations. This means the campaign response data needs to be loaded into the data warehouse many times a day, and the campaign segmentation needs to query the data warehouse many times a day. Users need to run purchase analyses against the order data in the data warehouse several times a day. As such, it is important for the data warehouse to be available 24 hours a day, because it supports the revenue generation from CRM activities.

The previous high-availability requirement means we cannot implement the SQL Server database engine on a single server, because the data warehouse must be available all the time. As we know, it must not be down more than one hour a month. Therefore, we need to implement it in a failover cluster. A *failover cluster* is a configuration of SQL Server installations on several identical servers (nodes). The SQL Server database instances are running on an active node, but when the active node is not available, the database instances automatically switches over to a secondary node.

SQL Server Reporting Services (the web or Windows service part) also needs to be deployed in a network load balanced (NLB) cluster, and the Reporting Services database is installed in the failover cluster described in the previous paragraph. NLB is a configuration of servers where the incoming traffic is distributed to several identical servers. SQL Server Reporting Services (SSRS) has two components: a web service and a database. To make SSRS available all the time, the SSRS web service needs to be installed on NLB servers. The SSRS database needs to be running on a failover cluster so that when one server is not available, the database will still be operational because the system automatically switches to another server.

To support this high availability requirement, Analysis Services also needs to be installed in a failover cluster, either in the same cluster as the database engine or in a separate cluster. In SQL Server 2005 and 2008, unlike SQL Server 2000, Analysis Services is cluster-aware. If your budget permits, I recommend installing Analysis Services in a separate cluster, because you can optimize and tune the memory and CPU usage separately. This means you need to create another failover cluster (separate from the failover cluster that we use for the database engine) specifically for running Analysis Services. This is shown in Figure 6-1, where Analysis Services is installed in a two-node failover cluster.

The allocated disk space on the SAN for Analysis Service should ideally be separated from the database server for the same reason—so that you can optimize and tune the disk usage separately. This is done by configuring the disks on the storage area network (SAN) into two separate sets of logical drives. One is attached to the database engine to store the databases, and the other one is attached to the Analysis Services server to store the multidimensional databases (cubes).

Unfortunately, SQL Server Integration Services is not a cluster-aware application. This means we cannot put SSIS in a failover cluster, which means that if the SSIS server is unavailable, there is no secondary server to take over. This also means that (unlike other ETL software such as Informatica), we cannot distribute the ETL load to several SSIS servers in the NLB configuration. But SSIS does not impact the 24×7 availability requirement to the end users. The data warehouse data stores are still available to the applications and to the end users to query. But if SSIS is down for a period of time, it will impact the *data currency*. The system architecture diagram in Figure 6-1 shows SSIS installed on a single server.

Some considerations in the network that you may want to consider are as follows. Between the SSIS server and the database server, and between the database server and the OLAP server, try to put in a Gigabit network (capable of performing at 1Gbps throughput), rather than the normal 100Mbps Ethernet. This will help Analysis Services performance, especially when you use relational OLAP (ROLAP), where the aggregates are stored on the relational database server. It also improves SSIS performance because it increases the data-loading rate from the SSIS into the data stores on the database server.

In many organizations, the SAN is typically used not only for data warehousing but for other systems too, such as Microsoft Exchange and a file server, so it's probably worth putting in a fiber network (2Gbps or 4Gbps), depending on the network traffic to the SAN. If many other applications are utilizing the SAN, you need to put in a fiber network. To match the high availability of the SAN's RAID disks and the OLAP and database server failover cluster, you need to use two redundant Fibre Channel switches. There is no point in having a high-speed network but a single point of failure.

The next questions that your hardware and network department will be asking you are about the server technical specifications. Typical questions involve how much memory, how many CPUs, how much disk space, which version of Windows Server, and which version of SQL Server to license. I will explain several considerations here, but the answers depend on many factors and vary from project to project. I will also discuss the SSRS server, SSIS/ETL server, SSAS server, and database server.

The Reporting Services web farm (also known as a *scale-out deployment*) does not require a high server specification. For a situation like Amadeus Entertainment, with 300–500 users, two or three nodes with two CPUs and 2GB or 4GB RAM on each node would probably be enough, depending on the report complexity. If you have 1,000 users, consider adding one or two other nodes, depending on light or heavy usage. Sizing a Reporting Services web farm is similar to sizing the web servers for a web site. It all depends on the amount of traffic served by the servers. If the performance statistics show a lot of contention in the WWW service, consider adding another web server.

Several factors determine the specification of the ETL server. The ETL server typically performs intense calculations and therefore will benefit from CPU power. This is determined from the complexity of transformation logic in the ETL processes. The amount of memory required depends on the size of the online lookup in the transformations. For the Amadeus Entertainment case study, based on the data model we did in Chapter 5 and based on the business requirements and data feasibility study we did in Chapter 4, four CPUs with 8GB to 16GB memory will be more than enough for its current condition, and this will also guarantee future growth. In other words, it will be safe for the next two to three years. If the CPUs are hyperthreaded and/or dual-core, we need to adjust the number of CPUs accordingly. A dual-core CPU practically halves the number of CPUs (minus overhead), while a hyperthreaded CPU performs better than single-threaded ones. So, for the Amadeus Entertainment case study, if we use a dual-core hyperthreaded CPU, we use two CPUs instead of four. For an ETL server, you need to take into account the future growth by estimating new data warehouse/ETL projects and enhancement requests that may happen in the future. You may have only ten SSIS packages on the first day to start with, but after a year you may have 100 packages running on it, some of which might not be data warehousing packages but other projects/systems.

Some considerations for OLAP server cluster hardware are the number of large cubes that will be running on Analysis Services, the number of partitions (the more partitions we have, the more memory we need), whether there will be OLAP queries running while the partitions are being processed (if there are, we need more memory), the requirements of a large file system cache (the larger the cache, the more memory we need), the requirements of a large process buffer (the larger this is, the more memory we need), the number of large replicas required (a *replica* is a subset of a dimension to accommodate dynamic security), and the number of heavy relational database queries and OLAP queries running simultaneously (lots of parallel queries require more memory). All of these factors affect the memory requirement. The number of CPUs affects the aggregate calculations and cube-processing times. For current requirements and the amount of data in the Amadeus Entertainment case study, four CPUs with 8GB RAM on each node will be enough, including accommodating the future growth of more cubes and data. The best guide for sizing Analysis Services is the SQL Server 2005 Analysis Services Performance Guide document, available on the Microsoft web site at http://www.microsoft.com/technet/prodtechnol/sql/2005/ssas2005perfguide.mspx.

The database server is probably the most difficult one to size, because it is largely dependent on how heavily and frequently applications access the databases, but we can't really determine how heavy the queries are until the applications are built. We are doing active/passive failover clustering, so it's only the performance of each server that matters. Active/passive failover means that only one node is working at a time. So, even though we have two servers, only the performance of one server matters, because only one server is working. The second server is not working. Some considerations for sizing the database server of a data warehouse are as follows:

The number and complexity of reports, applications, and direct queries hitting the DDS: The main factor that determines the specification of the database server is the workload from application queries. As I discussed in Chapter 2, the DDS is the user-facing database. So, it is the one that the users and BI/CRM applications will be querying. A database server used for data warehousing is predominantly used for queries. It is probably 10 to 20 percent of the time used for loading the data (such as one to three hours a day), and the rest (80 to 90 percent of the time) is used to satisfy user and application queries. The heavier the queries, the more memory and CPU we need in the database server.

Whether we're taking an ELT or ETL approach in populating the NDS/ODS: An ELT approach loads the data into the database server in raw format (in other words, the same as the source system format) and then uses the power of the database server to transform the data into the NDS or ODS format in a set-based operation via stored procedures, whereas the ETL approach transforms the data using the power of the ETL server. If we use the ELT approach in loading the data, we need a more powerful database server than the ETL approach.

Calculation from the stage to the NDS/ODS and the complexity of firewall rules: If these processes run on a separate ETL server, then they don't affect the database server sizing. But if they run on the database server (as stored procedure or triggers), then they impact the performance of the database server. The more complex the calculation and the firewall rules, the more CPU we need.

The number and size of data stores: The more user-facing data stores we have, the more memory and CPUs we need because we would have more connections from the users. The size of the data stores affects the number of records involved in the ETL processes. The larger the size of the data store, the more records inserted/updated/selected/deleted by the ETL processes. To complete a larger ETL process in the same amount of time, we need more powerful hardware for the database server (faster disk, larger memory, and better CPU).

How the data stores are physically designed (indexing, partitions, and so on): Physical database design affects database server configuration because if we utilize certain physical database features, we can improve loading and query performance without significant changes to the server hardware. For example, we can load data into the data warehouse faster if we partition the table physically and if we put the tables in databases on different disks.

The number of other databases hosted in the same server and future growth: For cost reasons, the database server may be utilized to host other databases, not just the data warehouse. This will affect the number of CPUs, the cache size, and the amount of memory we need on the database server. We also need to take into account two to three years of projected growth.

For a system like Amadeus Entertainment, four CPUs with 8GB to 16GB RAM will be suitable for the database server considering the data warehouse workload and its future growth. This is determined based on the business requirements in Chapter 4, the data model in Chapter 5, the architecture in Chapter 2, and all the considerations I described

previously, as well as from Microsoft's RDBMS Performance Tuning Guide for Data Warehousing at http://www.microsoft.com/technet/prodtechnol/sql/2000/maintain/
rdbmspft.mspx. It is on SQL Server 2000, but the principles are highly applicable for SQL
Server 2005. Microsoft's Project REAL (http://www.microsoft.com/sql/solutions/bi/
projectreal.mspx) is also a good reference.

Once we have determined the server configurations for the SSIS, SSAS, SSRS, and database servers, we need to determine which operating system and SQL Server editions we need
and which licensing model best suits the architecture. I'll discuss the operating system first,
then the SQL Server hardware levels (32-bit or 64-bit), then the SQL Server editions (Standard
Edition or Enterprise Edition), and finally the licenses.

Regarding the operating system, Windows 2003 R2 Enterprise Edition (EE) supports up
to eight processors and 64GB RAM, so it is suitable for the Amadeus Entertainment database
server mentioned previously (four CPUs with 8GB to 16GB RAM). The next level up is Windows 2003 R2 Datacenter Edition, which supports up to 64 processors and 128GB RAM, but
in the Amadeus Entertainment case study, there is no need to use this.

We need to determine whether we need the SQL Server 32-bit or 64-bit edition for the
Amadeus Entertainment case study. On the 32-bit platform, even though the SQL Server database engine can use all the RAM available in the server (limited only by the operating system),
Analysis Services can use only 3GB RAM. So if we use the 32-bit edition for the SSAS server, it
won't be able to use the entire 8GB RAM that we have in the server. Because of this, we need
the 64-bit edition.

Regarding the database server, on the 32-bit edition some SQL Server database engine
resources such as sort space, join hash tables, aggregate hash tables, and index creation do not
use RAM more than 3GB. For these reasons, in the Amadeus Entertainment case study, we
need to use the 64-bit version.

SQL Server is available in six editions: Express, Evaluation, Developer, Workgroup, Standard, and Enterprise. The first four are for trial, development, and small applications. For
enterprise-class data warehousing solutions in a production environment like in the Amadeus
Entertainment case study, practically speaking we can use only the last two, the Standard Edition or Enterprise Edition. SQL Server Standard Edition supports four CPUs and unlimited
RAM. These capabilities suit the Amadeus Entertainment case study. But because of the high-
availability and performance requirements, for the Amadeus Entertainment case study we
need SQL Server Enterprise Edition. The primary reason is that the following features are not
available in the Standard Edition:

Table and index partitioning: These features enable us to physically divide a table into
smaller chunks that we can load and query separately. When dealing with a fact table containing billions of rows, this feature is a must-have if we need to have good performance.

Report server scale-out deployment: This means we can run Reporting Services on multiple web servers, all accessing the same reporting services database in the same SQL
Server instance. This enables us to serve hundreds or thousands of users simultaneously
and achieve high availability. Both are requirements in the Amadeus Entertainment case
study: 300–500 client PCs/laptops and 24×7 availability, with only one hour of downtime
per month (99.86 percent uptime).

Analysis Services partitioned cubes: This feature enables us to divide a cube into smaller chunks that we can load and query separately. This is important because it means less cube-processing time and higher query performance.

Semiadditive aggregate functions: These are functions that work with measures that can be summed up in some dimensions but not in other dimensions. This is important because it enables us to deal with semiadditive measures such as account balances.

Parallel index operations: This feature enables us to create or rebuild an index using multiple processors simultaneously. It is useful in data warehousing when we deal with large fact tables.

Online index operation: This enables us to create or rebuild an index when users are querying or updating data on the table being indexed. This is important in data warehousing to maximize data store availability.

Number of nodes for failover clustering: In Standard Edition, the maximum number of nodes is two, which limits future growth because we cannot add more active nodes when we need more capacity or performance. In Enterprise Edition, we don't have a limitation on the number of nodes.

Now that I have discussed the editions, we need to deal with the licenses. Generally speaking, there are two SQL Server licensing models:

Per-processor license: We buy a license for each processor in the server. It does not matter how many users we have. Prices vary between countries, but in the United States the retail price of Enterprise Edition for a per-processor license is about $25,000.[1]

Server + CAL license: We buy a license for the server and a client access license (CAL) for each client accessing the server. A client can be per user or per computer. For Enterprise Edition in the United States, the retail price for one server license is about $14,000 (which includes 25 CALs). Each additional client license is about $162.

The way SQL Server is licensed means that for every single component we need to buy a separate license. Because for the Amadeus Entertainment case study we are installing SSIS, SSRS, SSAS, and the database engine on separate servers, this means we need to buy SQL Server licenses *separately* for each of those servers.

For the Amadeus Entertainment case study, if we license it per processor, we will need 16 per-processor licenses: four for the database cluster (the passive node does not require a license), four for the Analysis Services cluster, four for the report server farm (two servers × two CPUs each, because each node requires a license), and four for the SSIS server. The cost would be 16 × $25,000 = $400,000. If we use Server + CAL licenses, for 500 users we need five server licenses (one for the database cluster, one for the Analysis Services cluster, two for the report server farm, and one for the SSIS server) and 375 additional CALs (from the five server licenses we get 5 × 25 CALs). So, the cost would be (5 × $14,000) + (375 × $162) = $130,750. In this case, the server + CAL licensing model is better.

Storage Considerations

The next thing we need to purchase for the infrastructure is the disk space. In Chapter 4, I said it was not possible to estimate the amount of storage properly at that stage, because we had not completed the DDS and NDS design. Now that we have completed the database design, we can do the estimation.

This is done by calculating the size of the fact and dimension tables to get the size of the DDS. Then we estimate the size of the NDS based on the row size and the number of rows for each table. Then we estimate the size of the stage database based on the source system tables and data extraction method. Let's start with the DDS, then the NDS, then the stage database, then the metadata database, and finally the disk configuration.

Let's examine the Product Sales fact table illustrated in Table 5-1 in Chapter 5. It has eight int columns, one decimal column, ten money columns, and three datetime columns. Integers are 4 bytes, decimals are 5 bytes, and money and datetime are 8 bytes, so the row size is $8 \times 4 + 1 \times 5 + (10 + 3) \times 8 = 141$ bytes. Allow 50 percent to accommodate extra columns in the future, which makes it 212 bytes. The percentage is determined based on how many columns we will add in the future. If the source system shows that on average there are 500,000 sales per day (make it 600,000 to allow for growth—or more, based on projected growth) and we are planning to purchase storage capacity for two years (see Chapter 4), then the size of the fact table is $600,000 \times 365 \times 2 \times 212$ bytes = 86GB. We will add fill factor and overhead later for the whole database, not per table.

The Subscription Sales fact table has 12 int columns, 16 money columns, and 4 datetime columns, so the row size is 208 bytes. Some people call row size *record length*, which is the term inherited from the sequential file era. Allowing 50 percent for extra columns makes it 312 bytes. If the store system shows that Amadeus Entertainment has 800,000 subscribers (make it 1 million to allow for growth) and we store daily data for the last four weeks and weekly data for the last two years (refer to Chapter 5), the size of the fact table is 1 million $\times$ $(4 \times 7 + 2 \times 52) \times 312$ bytes = 38GB.

We do the same exercise for all fact and dimension tables, and we will get the size of all tables in the DDS. It's the same principle in the NDS. We calculate the row size by multiplying the number of columns of each data type with the bytes for that data type. We estimate the number of rows by querying the source system. The number of rows in the NDS table would be roughly the same as the number of rows in the source system. We need to keep in mind that if we have several source systems, the number of rows in the NDS depends on how much overlap we have between the source systems. For example, if the product table in source system A contains 600,000 rows and the product table in source system B contains 400,000 rows, of which 250,000 exist in source system A, then the number of rows in the NDS product table would be $600,000 + 150,000 = 750,000$.

To estimate the size of the stage database, we need to list all the source tables that we did in Chapter 5 when we did the source system mapping. For each table, query the source system to determine the row size and the number of rows. If the extraction method to the stage is incremental, count how many rows are inserted or updated per day in the source system. For example, say there are 300 million rows in the sales order item table but there are only 900,000 rows updated or inserted for each day. If the extraction method to the stage is "truncate and reload," use the number of rows in the whole table. We will go through data extraction from the source system in Chapter 7.

Remember that you may need to get only some columns from the source system table into the data warehouse, not all columns in the table. Let's say the width of the sales order table in WebTower9 is 2,000 bytes but the total bytes of the columns that you download is only half of this. This affects the sizing of the stage database. Another factor that affects the stage database sizing is that you may want to store three or five days' worth (or more, depending on backup strategy) of data in the stage before purging it in case you need to reload it to the NDS for some reason. So in this case, the size of the order item stage table would be 1.1 million × 5 × 1000 bytes = 5GB. We adjust the daily rows from 900,000 to 1.1 million to allow for two years of growth.

The other database that we will create is metadata. It is not big, probably 10–20GB. Allocating 50GB will be sufficient. This is estimated based on the content of the metadata database. The metadata database stores seven kinds of metadata: data definition and mapping metadata, data structure metadata, source system metadata, ETL processes metadata, data quality metadata, audit metadata, and usage metadata.

You may also want to allocate some space for two or three smaller DDSs, such as for data mining purposes or specific analysis projects. The reason for having a separate DDS for these projects and activities is because they may need to update the data to reflect certain business scenarios.

Say, for argument's sake, the result of the previous calculation is as follows: the DDS is 400GB, the NDS is 300GB, the stage is 100GB, the metadata database is 50GB, so the total is 850GB. To get the size of the data files (MDB), we need to allow some space for indexes and for RDBMS overhead such as the table header, row ID, block header and trailer, fill factor, page splits, and other SQL Server internal DBMS mechanisms. Take 30 percent for indexes and 15 percent for internal mechanisms, which makes it 1233GB. Allow 20 percent for estimation tolerance, which makes it 1479GB. The percentages for indexes vary depending on how heavily we index the tables; in other words, it can be 50 percent for some tables, and it can be 10 percent for other tables. My general estimate of 30 percent for index space is just a high-level estimate. If you need a more precise estimation, use the Microsoft guide at http://msdn2.microsoft.com/en-us/library/ms190620.aspx (this page is also available in Books Online). The 20 percent estimation tolerance is to cover unknown factors—those things we are not aware of at the time we do the estimating.

TERMINOLOGY

Let's clear up some terminology commonly used in data storage, especially disk and volume, before we continue. We will use the terminology later in this chapter. A *disk* is a single SCSI drive (we tend not to use IDE drives for database servers because the IDE is perceived more for home use rather than for industrial use because of their reliability and durability). The capacity of a SCSI drive varies from 36GB to 73GB to 146GB to 300GB. The speed varies from 10,000 RPM to 15,000 RPM. Some people use the term *spindle* to refer to a disk. A *volume* is several disks arranged together according to a certain RAID configuration. Redundant Array of Inexpensive Disks (RAID) is a method to configure several disks as one unit to make them more resilient by creating some physical data redundancy.

The popular RAID configurations (some people say *RAID level*) are RAID 0, RAID 1, RAID 5, and RAID 1+0 (some people say RAID 10). If you have four 146GB SCSI disks and arrange them in RAID 0 configuration, the resulting volume is 146 × 4 = 584GB. If you arrange them in RAID 5, the resulting volume is 146 × 3 = 438GB. If you arrange them in RAID 1+0, the resulting volume is 146GB. RAID 1 can be made only with two disks. If you have two 146GB disks, the resulting RAID 1 volume is 146GB. We will use these four RAID levels in this example.

We will place each database in several data files spread over several physical volumes. For this we will create as many RAID 5 volumes as we can (at least four, but ideally eight or more—spreading the database files onto more disk volumes makes the loading and query performance better), but we don't want the size of each volume to be too small. The ideal size is between 300 and 500GB. Less than 250GB is not practical for maintaining large databases. This will give you a lot better performance than a single RAID 1+0 volume, because we're spreading the workload across more physical disks. Let's put the transaction log file (LDF) of each database on different volumes to increase the data-loading performance because the work is distributed across several disks. So, we'll create four RAID 1 volumes for transaction logs: one for the DDS, one for the NDS, one for the stage, and one for the data quality and metadata.

TempDB is one data file per CPU, possibly 10–20GB each, depending on query complexity (SQL Server uses TempDB to store the immediate results of a query). TempDB is ideally located on a separate RAID 1+0 volume and is set to a large initial size with autogrow. RAID 1+0 would help get us optimum performance because this RAID level is both striped (efficient in reading and writing) and resilient (safe in the case of failure). Putting TempDB on a separate dedicated volume will ensure there is no contention with other SQL Server disk read and write activities. The backup volume is expected to be between one and two times the size of the data disk (the log files are usually small), depending on backup strategy, located on RAID 0 or RAID 5 volumes.

A file system volume is used for ETL temporary storage, probably 20 percent to 30 percent of the size of the data volume, in RAID 5. This percentage is determined based on which source system tables would need to be staged in files rather than in a database. In reality, the file system volume is usually used to store other files too, such as project and application files, not just for ETL, so allow for this by reserving some extra space. The OLAP volume is probably the most difficult to estimate; in the Amadeus Entertainment case study, it is probably between two to five times the size of the DDS, depending on aggregate density, ideally spread over several volumes.

We also need to create a quorum volume to support the failover cluster, on RAID level 1. A quorum volume is a drive accessible by any node in the cluster. It is used for arbitration between cluster nodes and to store data that is used for recovery after a communication failure within the cluster.

With an individual disk raw size of 146GB (formatted capacity 133GB), the disk space calculation is described in Table 6-1.

Table 6-1. *Disk Space Calculation*

Volume	Required Size (GB)	RAID Level	No. of Disks	Actual Size (GB)
Data 1-6	1479	6 × RAID 5	6 × 4	6 × 399
Log 1-4	200	4 × RAID 1	4 × 2	4 × 133
TempDB	100	RAID 1+0	4 × 1	133
Quorum	10	RAID 1	2 × 1	133
Backup	2200	RAID 5	1 × 18	2261
File system	600	RAID 5	1 × 6	665
OLAP 1-4	1600	RAID 5	4 × 5	4 × 532
Total			82	8246

Eighty-two disks are required, and the total usable space is 8.2TB. The previous exercise is known as *logical unit number* design. With 85 disks in the cabinet, we have three disks for SAN hot spare. *Hot spare* is a standby disk used automatically to replace a failed disk. It is best to use disks with the same capacity and RPM throughout the SAN. If you use disks with a different capacity or RPM, you must remember that they require different hot spare disks. A RAID volume is built from several disks. If one of these disks fails, the SAN controller automatically assigns the hot spare disk to temporarily replace the failed one. For this to happen, the hot spare disk must have the same capacity as the one being replaced.

If you can afford it, a large quantity of smaller disks (such as 73GB) is better than fewer bigger disks (such as 146GB). This is because the workload is distributed to more disks. A high RPM (such as 15,000) is absolutely essential in any case, because it gives better performance than a lower RPM (such as 10,000). Hewlett-Packard has reported that the I/O throughput performance of a 15,000 RPM disk can be as much as 25 percent higher than the equivalent 10,000 RPM,[2] whereas IBM has reported 50 percent.[3] TempDB is ideally in a RAID 1+0 volume, as explained earlier. It is faster than RAID 5 or RAID 1, both at reading and writing. For data warehousing, a very large TempDB (10–20GB per CPU, depending on the query complexity) on a good-performance RAID 1+0 volume is crucial. The default is 8MB, which is way too small for DW.

I've heard suggestions to partition the RAID 1 quorum volume and allocate a little portion (say 10GB) for the quorum and the remainder (say 123GB) for the log files. I am against this idea because the quorum is the core of a cluster build; I prefer not to risk it. Get a smaller disk if you want for the quorum (36GB, for example), but dedicate it just for the quorum alone. Microsoft recommends assigning a dedicated LUN for quorum resources and not storing user data on any volume on the quorum LUN.[4]

Bear in mind that you need to allocate some amount of disk space for your QA environment. Ideally, the QA environment has the same capacity as production. This enables us to unload production data into the QA environment to test a modification or enhancement to ensure that the modifications will run OK in production. Having a QA environment with the same capacity as the production environment is also useful for performance testing, when we load the QA environment with the same amount of data (if not more) as the production environment. With some calculation, we also can get a reasonable idea about how a production environment will perform based on tests in a smaller QA environment.

Configuring Databases

Now that we have designed the databases, let's create them in SQL Server. Here are some points you may want to consider when creating the databases. Let's take the Amadeus Entertainment case study as an example in these points:

---

2. http://h20223.www2.hp.com/NonStopComputing/cache/117086-0-0-225-121.html

3. http://www-01.ibm.com/common/ssi/cgi-bin/ssialias?subtype=ca&infotype=an&appname=iSource&supplier=897&letternum=ENUS105-324

4. http://technet2.microsoft.com/windowsserver/en/library/dba487bf-61b9-45af-b927-e2333ec810b61033.mspx?mfr=true

- Keep database names short and concise. DDS, NDS, Stage, and Meta will do. We need to keep them short because they will be used as prefixes to ETL process names and stored procedure names.

- Remember to keep the collation of all data warehouse databases the same, preferably as per the company's SQL Server installation standard defined by the SQL Server DBA. Database collation defines how SQL Server handles character and Unicode data, such as case-sensitivity, sort order, and code page. If they are different, there will be conversion problems when populating the NDS from the stage and populating the DDS from the NDS; for example, when trying to do column comparisons for UPSERT, set the server collation as well in case you need to create a new DDS in the future.

- Consider case sensitivity very carefully. Query results will be different depending on the case sensitivity. We need to set case according to the user requirements for sorting order. For the Amadeus Entertainment case study, we will use SQL Server default collation, SQL_Latin1_General_CP1_CI_AS, so it will be case-insensitive.

- For each database we will create six filegroups, located on six different physical disks on RAID 5, with one transaction log file located in the designated log disk of RAID 1. Filegroups are a collection of database files. Set the database default location in the server property to match this. This is necessary so that when we create a new database (for example, a new DDS), SQL Server will put the database data and log files in the correct locations. This is done by right-clicking the SQL Server name in Management Studio and choosing Properties. Click Database Settings, and modify the default database locations.

- Arrange the data files to support the previous filegroup arrangement, meaning that when creating the database, place data files as per the filegroup locations. We have six physical disks for data, so use them well by spreading the filegroups into different physical disks. Put the log files of each database on different log disks, as specified in the previous section. Set the initial size of the data files for six to twelve months of growth by specifying the initial size correctly when creating the database. Maintain the data and log files manually; do not rely on autogrowth. If there is a data load operation that requires more log space than what's available, the operation will take a long time to complete because it has to wait until the grow operation completes. Growing a database by little increments causes a performance problem because of file and disk fragmentation. We still need to turn on autogrow (with a large increment) but use it only for emergency measures.

- Based on the estimated database size in the previous section (400 and 300 over two years), aiming for six months I would set the initial size of the DDS to 100GB with a growth increment of 25GB and the initial size of the NDS to 75GB with a 15GB growth increment. The initial sizes for the DDS and the NDS (100 and 75GB) are calculated by taking the linear proportion of the two-year projection (400GB and 300GB) for six months. If you have initial load, then add this amount to the initial sizes. For example, if the initial load is 30GB, then the initial sizes for the DDS and the NDS become 130GB and 105GB. We need to remember that these initial sizes are collective overall figures, so we need to divide them among the six files. Set the growth increment to 20 to 25 percent of the initial sizes to minimize the SQL Server grow operation. Remember that we need to maintain the size of the data and log files manually (say every six months, with monitoring every month); we should use autogrowth only for emergencies.

- If the expected daily load is 5GB to 10GB and we keep five days of data on the stage, set the stage database's initial size to 50GB with a growth increment of 10GB. For the metadata database, we expect it would be about 10GB in a year and to be 20GB in two years, so let's set the initial size to 10GB with a 5GB increment. The principle to setting the increment is that it is only for emergencies; we should never have to use autogrowth because we increase the file size manually. The increment for the earlier stage database was set to 20 percent to 25 percent as per the DDS and the NDS. This large percentage is selected to minimize fragmentation if the database file did become full. The increment for the metadata database is set to 50 percent (5GB) because the metadata database contains audit and usage metadata that could fluctuate by significant amounts depending on ETL processes.

- The log file size depends on the size of the daily load, recovery model, and the loading method (ETL or ELT, stage or not stage; I'll discuss this in the next chapter) as well as index operations. Let's set it to a 1GB initial size with a 512MB increment for both the DDS and the NDS. For the stage, set a 2GB initial size with a 512MB increment. For metadata, set it to 100MB with a 25MB increment. The transaction log contains database changes. The transaction log space required depends on how much data we load into the database. One way to estimate how much log space is required is to use the ETL processes to load one day's data into the stage and then into the NDS and then into the DDS. If we set the initial size and the increment of these three databases to a small amount (say 1MB to 2MB), during this process the log file will grow so that after the ETL processes are completed, the transaction log sizes of these three databases will indicate the required log sizes.

- For the recovery model, choose simple rather than bulk. All the changes in the data warehouse are from the ETL processes. When recovering from failure, we can roll forward using ETL by reapplying the extracted source system data for the particular day. We don't require the bulk recovery model to roll forward to a certain point in time using differential backup or transaction log backup. We fully control the data upload on the ETL, and the ETL process is the only process that updates the data warehouse. For the stage, the NDS, and the DDS, the full recovery model is not necessary and causes overhead. The full recovery model requires log backup, whereas the simple recovery model doesn't. The simple recovery model reclaims the log space automatically. The full recovery model is suitable for OLTP systems where inserts and updates happen frequently all day from many users and we want to be able to recover the database to a certain point in time. In data warehousing, we can recover the data store by restoring the last full backup followed by applying differential backups and then applying the daily ETL loads.

- If you use the ODS + DDS architecture, you may want to consider the full recovery model in the ODS especially if ETL is not the only process that updates the ODS. Unlike the NDS, the ODS is updatable. End-user applications can retrieve data from the ODS, but they can also update the ODS (please refer to Chapter 2 where ODS + DDS architecture is explained). Because the ODS is continuously updated by the users, it is useful to implement the full recovery model so we can recover the ODS to any point in time.

- For a metadata database, we need to set the recovery mode to full. The data quality and front-end application will also write to metadata, in addition to the daily ETL process, mainly for audit purposes such as report stored procedures, data quality stored procedures, and the administration of ETL processes. Because the metadata database is continuously updated, it is useful to implement the full recovery model so we can recover the metadata database to any point in time.

- Leave the maximum degree of parallelism at 0 to utilize all processors. The degree of parallelism is the number of processors used to execute a single SQL statement in parallel. If we leave it set to 0 (which is the default), SQL Server will utilize all the available processors.

- Disable full-text indexing if you are not using it. Full-text indexing enables us to search for patterns in character columns a lot faster than the LIKE predicate in SELECT statements. The Microsoft Search service uses system memory for the full-text indexing process.

- It is different from DBA to DBA, but you may want to disable autoshrink and enable automatic statistics update, especially in the DDS. A database with autoshrink may lead to fragmentation and cause performance issues. Automatic statistics updating is necessary for the SQL Server query optimizer to know the best path to execute the query. SQL Server collects the statistics of the indexes and column data in the database. The query optimizer uses these database statistics to estimate the selectivity of a column or index and to estimate the costs of different query plans.

For an example, let's create the DDS database. Say we want to make the total size of the data files 100GB. Because we will have six files located on six different physical files, we allocate 100GB / 6 = 17GB for each file. A few months later, these files will not be the same size. A few months later, file 1 could be 18GB, file 2 could be 30GB, and file 3 could be 20GB. To allow for this natural possibility of uneven growth, we will set the initial size for each file to 30GB—the maximum growth. The size of each disk is 399GB, so you can set the max size of each file to 150GB or 170GB if you want, which is 40 percent of the disk size, not 100 percent, because other databases will reside on the same disk too.

The growth increment for the DDS, as mentioned previously, is 25GB. Spread over six disks, that's 4.2GB each, roughly. A growth increment is a figure that tells SQL Server how much we want to expand the file when it's full. It doesn't have the uneven growth problem mentioned previously, so we will allocate 5GB in each file. As I said previously, we should not rely on autogrowth, because the DWA should have a script monitoring this allocated data space. This script shows the percentage of data files used for each data warehouse data store.

The database creation script for the DDS is as follows. It shows that the initial size is 30GB, as mentioned previously, and the file growth is 5GB. It uses six data files. The log file is 1GB with a 512MB increment, as discussed previously. This script is included in the /script folder

at the book's web site (http://www.apress.com/). To execute this script on a stand-alone laptop or desktop, you just need to replace the drive letter (h) with a local drive such as c or d.

```
use master
go

if db_id ('DDS') is not null
   drop database DDS;
go

create database DDS
on primary (name = 'dds_fg1'
, filename = 'h:\disk\data1\dds_fg1.mdf'
, size = 30 GB, filegrowth = 5 GB)
, filegroup dds_fg2 (name = 'dds_fg2'
, filename = 'h:\disk\data2\dds_fg2.ndf'
, size = 30 GB, filegrowth = 5 GB)
, filegroup dds_fg3 (name = 'dds_fg3'
, filename = 'h:\disk\data3\dds_fg3.ndf'
, size = 30 GB, filegrowth = 5 GB)
, filegroup dds_fg4 (name = 'dds_fg4'
, filename = 'h:\disk\data4\dds_fg4.ndf'
, size = 30 GB, filegrowth = 5 GB)
, filegroup dds_fg5 (name = 'dds_fg5'
, filename = 'h:\disk\data5\dds_fg5.ndf'
, size = 30 GB, filegrowth = 5 GB)
, filegroup dds_fg6 (name = 'dds_fg6'
, filename = 'h:\disk\data6\dds_fg6.ndf'
, size = 30 GB, filegrowth = 5 GB)
log on (name = 'dds_log'
, filename = 'h:\disk\log1\dds_log.ldf'
, size = 1 GB, filegrowth = 512 MB)
collate SQL_Latin1_General_CP1_CI_AS
go

alter database DDS set recovery simple
go
alter database DDS set auto_shrink off
go
alter database DDS set auto_create_statistics on
go
alter database DDS set auto_update_statistics on
go
```

   h:\disk\data1 to h:\disk\data6 and h:\disk\log1 to h:\disk\log4 are the mount points
of the six data volumes and four log volumes that we built in the SAN (please refer to the previous section). A mount point is the drive letter assigned to a volume created from several
physical disks in a RAID configuration. This drive letter is used by the operating system to

access the data in that volume. For other databases, the scripts are similar, apart from the file locations and sizes. Put the NDS log file on h:\disk\log2, the stage on h:\disk\log3, and the metadata on h:\disk\log4.

For the stage database, we don't need automatic statistic updating because we don't usually index tables. We still want the simple recovery model, and we still don't need autoshrink for the stage database. Remember to put the stage log file on a different disk from the NDS and DDS logs; this is important for ETL performance because it minimizes the contention of log traffic between data stores. Because of the size and the nature of loading, we don't need to split the stage database over six disks. Three of four would be more than enough because we can allocate different stage tables in three to four different disks that can be loaded simultaneously. We can use data disks 1–4 for the stage.

Remember to set the recovery mode to full for the metadata database. Because the size of the metadata database is small and because the way we use the metadata database is more like an OLTP type query than a data warehouse query (in other words, it is frequently updated), we don't need to spread it across six disks. Two disks are good enough because the size is only 10–20GB, as discussed previously. We can use data disks 5 and 6 for metadata. We still need to put the metadata log file on a separate disk, though, not for the benefit of the metadata database itself but so that we don't affect the performance the NDS, the DDS, and the stage log files.

■**Note** Because you will be creating the databases in your development environment, which in the case of a stand-alone desktop or laptop probably doesn't have multiple disks or drivers and a large amount of disk space, you can reduce the figures from gigabytes to megabytes so the databases will be enough for your disk space. Just create a folder called disk and create ten folders called data1 to data6 and log1 to log4 under this disk folder. This simulates the six data disks and four log disks discussed earlier. You can put the database data files and log files in these ten folders.

Now that we have created all four databases, we are ready to create the database structure—the tables.

Creating DDS Database Structure

After we created the databases, we can now create the tables based on the logical design that we created in the previous chapter. Let's start with the DDS. It has five fact tables and fourteen dimensions. Let's do the Product Sales fact table first. We'll do the four dimensions that it uses first and then the fact table. We defined these four dimension tables in the previous chapter. So, open SQL Server 2005 Management Studio, connect to your development SQL Server instance, and start creating the tables. You can use Management Studio's point-and-click functionality if you want, or you can script it.

Either way, create the date dimension table as follows:

```
use DDS
go

if exists
  (select * from sys.tables
   where name = 'dim_date')
drop table dim_date
go

create table dim_date
( date_key            int        not null
, date                char(10)   not null
, system_date         char(10)   not null
, sql_date            datetime   not null
, julian_date         int        not null
, day                 tinyint    not null
, day_of_the_week     tinyint    not null
, day_name            varchar(9) not null
, day_of_the_year     smallint   not null
, week_number         tinyint    not null
, month               tinyint    not null
, month_name          varchar(9) not null
, short_month_name    char(3)    not null
, quarter             char(2)    not null
, year                smallint   not null
, fiscal_week         tinyint
, fiscal_period       char(4)
, fiscal_quarter      char(3)
, fiscal_year         char(6)
, week_day            tinyint    not null
, us_holiday          tinyint
, uk_holiday          tinyint
, month_end           tinyint    not null
, period_end          tinyint
, short_day           tinyint
, source_system_code  tinyint    not null
, create_timestamp    datetime   not null
, update_timestamp    datetime   not null
, constraint pk_dim_date
  primary key clustered (date_key)
  on dds_fg6
) on dds_fg6
go
```

```
if exists
  (select * from sys.indexes
   where name = 'sql_date'
   and object_id = object_id('dim_date'))
drop index dim_date.sql_date
go

create unique index sql_date
  on dim_date(sql_date)
  on dds_fg6
go
```

In SQL Server 2005 and 2008, the sys.tables catalog view replaces sysobjects used in SQL Server 2000. You can use sys.objects if you want (notice the dot there), but you need to specify where type = 'U'. The sys.objects catalog view contains all the database objects such as tables, views, triggers, primary keys, and stored procedures. By specifying type = 'U', we filter the rows for user-defined tables only. Catalog views contain information used by the SQL Server database engine, such as tables, columns, and primary keys.

The dimension key needs to be assigned as the primary key of the table and as the clustered index. This means that the table will be physically ordered on the date_key column. This will be useful for query performance. We don't need to make the dimensional key column an identity column because all keying will be done in the NDS. Columns that should not contain NULL such as weekdays and month ends should have the NOT NULL constraint.

I don't advise putting a check constraint in the DDS dimensions because it will negatively affect the loading performance. Instead, it would be better to put it in the data quality (DQ) routine inside the ETL because the check will be processed in a set-based statement rather than row by row, so it's faster. I'll talk about DQ in Chapter 9. Don't put default gettime() in the create_timestamp or update_timestamp column, because we want all rows inserted or updated during the same batch to have the same timestamp, so we will set this timestamp in the ETL.

You may want to put in a bit of code that checks and drops the foreign key constraints before dropping and creating the table, like in the following code. This prevents orphan or invalid foreign keys on the related tables.

```
if exists
  (select * from sys.foreign_keys
   where name = 'fk_fact_campaign_result_dim_date'
   and parent_object_id = object_id('fact_campaign_result'))
alter table fact_campaign_result
  drop constraint fk_fact_campaign_result_dim_date
go
```

And after creating the table, re-create the foreign key that you dropped, like this:

```
if exists
  (select * from sys.tables
   where name = 'fact_campaign_result')
alter table fact_campaign_result
  add constraint fk_fact_campaign_result_dim_date
  foreign key (send_date_key)
  references dim_date(date_key)
go
```

This way, the individual script can be executed independently of the other scripts. Don't forget to use Unicode (nchar and nvarchar) if you operate in countries with non-Latin characters. If the width is fixed, such as date, use char rather than varchar; char is slightly faster because it has a fixed position and is slightly smaller because it doesn't have the 2 bytes offset. If you have three varchar(10) columns, the storage is 2 + (3 × 2) + (3 × 10 bytes) = 38 bytes. If you use three char(10) columns, the storage is 30 bytes. To get the row size, you need to add 4 bytes for the row header and 3 bytes for the null bitmap (this is the total for the row, not for each column). The null bitmap is an indicator whether a column may contain null. So, if we use varchar, the row size is 45 bytes, and if we use char, the row size is 37 bytes. If, however, you know that on average the varchar column will be only 60 percent full, use varchar, because the storage is 2 + (3 × 2) + (3 × 10 bytes × 60 percent) = 26 bytes.

Every time you use int, ask yourself whether the value of that column will ever reach 2 billion. In many cases, you can use tinyint (up to 255) and smallint (up to 32k). If you use decimal or number, always specify the precision, 9 or lower if possible. Precision 9 uses 5 bytes, whereas precisions 10 to 19 use 9 bytes. The default precision is 18. For dimension tables, you can just set all columns to Unicode and int because they are small (probably a few thousand rows except for the customer dimension, which could be millions). But for a fact table with billions of rows, you may want to consider the right data type to save the disk space and maximize data loading and query performance.

Every time you use money (8 bytes), ask yourself whether the value will ever reach 214,000. If not, use smallmoney, which is only 4 bytes. Also, ask yourself whether you need more than four digits after the decimal point, for example, for the currency rate. If you do, use decimal rather than money. Some people use smalldatetime rather than datetime when they need only the date and don't need the time element. You probably want to reconsider this because smalldatetime is only up to year 2079, and it starts from 1900.

Perhaps you also noticed there are two dds_fg6 on the create table statement previously mentioned. They are the filegroups. *Filegroups* are collections of database files. You need to specify the filegroup; otherwise, it will be stored in the primary filegroup, which is on disk 1. The first one is where the primary key's clustered index is physically stored. The second one is where the table is physically stored. To keep track of what table goes to which filegroup, it is useful if you make a filegroup allocation table, as shown in Table 6-2. As we discussed earlier, it is important to spread the tables in the data store on different disks, using filegroups, to maximize query performance and data-loading performance.

Table 6-2. *Filegroup Allocation Table for the DDS*

Table Name	Table Type	Filegroup
dim_week	Dimension	6
dim_store	Dimension	6
dim_campaign	Dimension	6
dim_channel	Dimension	6
dim_communication	Dimension	6
dim_customer	Dimension	6
dim_date	Dimension	6
dim_delivery_status	Dimension	6
dim_format	Dimension	6
dim_lead	Dimension	6
dim_package	Dimension	6
dim_product	Dimension	6
dim_subscription_status	Dimension	6
dim_supplier	Dimension	6
fact_product_sales	Fact	2
fact_subscription_sales	Fact	3
fact_supplier_performance	Fact	3
fact_communication_subscription	Fact	5
fact_campaign_result	Fact	5
Fact tables' PKs and indexes		4
Dimension tables' PKs and indexes		6

To maximize query performance and data-loading performance on the DDS database, in Table 6-2 we allocate all dimension tables to filegroup 6, the Product Sales fact table to filegroup 2, the Subscription Sales and Supplier Performance fact tables to filegroup 3, the two CRM fact tables to filegroup 5, and the fact table indexes to filegroup 4. We won't use the primary filegroup yet. We will use this for the summary fact table later.

If we put a fact table and dimension table on different disks, we reduce the disk contention and therefore increase the query performance. The performance increase depends on how large the dimension tables being joined to the fact table in the query are. We reduce the contention further by putting the fact indexes on a separate disk from the fact tables. Ideally, the dimension table and index should also be separated, but because they are a lot smaller than fact tables, I prefer to put the dimension indexes in filegroup 6 together with dimension tables rather than, for example, putting them in filegroup 2 with the large Product Sales fact table.

OK, let's continue creating the product dimension as follows:

```
use DDS
go

if exists
  (select * from sys.objects
   where name = 'dim_product')
drop table dim_product
go

create table dim_product
( product_key          int not null
, product_code         varchar(10)
, name                 varchar(30)
, description          varchar(100)
, title                varchar(100)
, artist               varchar(100)
, product_type         varchar(20)
, product_category     varchar(30)
, media                varchar(25)
, unit_price           money
, unit_cost            money
, status               varchar(15)
, source_system_code   tinyint
, create_timestamp     datetime
, update_timestamp     datetime
, constraint pk_dim_product
  primary key clustered (product_key)
  on dds_fg6
) on dds_fg6
go
```

And then let's create the customer dimension:

```
use DDS
go

if exists
  (select * from sys.tables
   where name = 'dim_customer')
drop table dim_customer
go
```

```
create table dim_customer
( customer_key          int not null
, customer_id           varchar(10)
, account_number        int
, customer_type         char(1)
, name                  varchar(100)
, gender                char(1)
, email_address         varchar(200)
, date_of_birth         datetime
, address1              varchar(50)
, address2              varchar(50)
, address3              varchar(50)
, address4              varchar(50)
, city                  varchar(50)
, state                 varchar(40)
, zipcode               varchar(10)
, country               varchar(50)
, phone_number          varchar(20)
, occupation            varchar(50)
, household_income      varchar(20)
, date_registered       datetime
, status                varchar(10)
, subscriber_class      varchar(3)
, subscriber_band       varchar(3)
, permission            tinyint
, preferred_channel1    varchar(15)
, preferred_channel2    varchar(15)
, interest1             varchar(30)
, interest2             varchar(30)
, interest3             varchar(30)
, effective_timestamp   datetime
, expiry_timestamp      datetime
, is_current            tinyint
, source_system_code    tinyint
, create_timestamp      datetime
, update_timestamp      datetime
, constraint pk_dim_customer
  primary key clustered (customer_key)
  on dds_fg6
) on dds_fg6
go
```

And then let's create the store dimension:

```
use DDS
go

if exists
  (select * from sys.tables
   where name = 'dim_store')
drop table dim_store
go

create table dim_store
( store_key            int not null
, store_number         smallint
, store_name           varchar(40)
, store_type           varchar(20)
, store_address1       varchar(50)
, store_address2       varchar(50)
, store_address3       varchar(50)
, store_address4       varchar(50)
, city                 varchar(50)
, state                varchar(40)
, zipcode              varchar(10)
, country              varchar(50)
, phone_number         varchar(20)
, web_site             varchar(100)
, region               varchar(30)
, prior_region         varchar(30)
, prior_region_date    datetime
, division             varchar(30)
, prior_division       varchar(30)
, prior_division_date  datetime
, source_system_code   tinyint
, create_timestamp     datetime
, update_timestamp     datetime
, constraint pk_dim_store
  primary key clustered (store_key)
  on dds_fg6
) on dds_fg6
go
```

And finally, we'll create the Product Sales fact table:

```
use DDS
go

if exists
  (select * from sys.objects
   where name = 'fact_product_sales' and type = 'U')
drop table fact_product_sales
go

create table fact_product_sales
( sales_date_key      int        not null
, customer_key        int        not null
, product_key         int        not null
, store_key           int        not null
, order_id            int        not null
, line_number         int        not null
, quantity            int
, unit_price          smallmoney
, unit_cost           smallmoney
, sales_value         money
, sales_cost          money
, margin              money
, sales_timestamp     datetime
, source_system_code  tinyint    not null
, create_timestamp    datetime   not null
, update_timestamp    datetime   not null
, constraint pk_fact_product_sales
  primary key clustered (order_id, line_number)
  on dds_fg4
, constraint fk_fact_product_sales_dim_date
  foreign key (sales_date_key)
  references dim_date(date_key)
, constraint fk_fact_product_sales_dim_customer
  foreign key (customer_key)
  references dim_customer(customer_key)
, constraint fk_fact_product_sales_dim_product
  foreign key (product_key)
  references dim_product(product_key)
, constraint fk_fact_product_sales_dim_store
  foreign key (store_key)
  references dim_store(store_key)
) on dds_fg2
go
```

```
create index fact_product_sales_sales_date_key
  on fact_product_sales(sales_date_key)
  on dds_fg4
go

create index fact_product_sales_customer_key
  on fact_product_sales(customer_key)
  on dds_fg4
go

create index fact_product_sales_product_key
  on fact_product_sales(product_key)
  on dds_fg4
go

create index fact_product_sales_store_key
  on fact_product_sales(store_key)
  on dds_fg4
go
```

I'll discuss the indexes and how to choose primary keys in more detail when I talk about indexing later in this chapter because it is closely related with how to choose a cluster index. For now let's suffice it to say that for the primary key we need to choose a column or columns that make the row unique. There could be several candidates for the primary key.

Some people prefer not to put referential integrity (foreign keys) in a data warehouse. They say that data integrity is controlled in the ETL so we don't need a foreign key. The second argument is that a foreign key slows down the loading. But on the other hand, the query optimizer uses constraint definitions such as the primary key and the foreign key to build a high-performance query execution plan. If you have a primary key - foreign key relationship between two tables, it indicates to SQL Server that the two tables have been optimized to be combined in a query that uses the key as its criteria. This is particularly useful on optimizing queries that join several tables, the choice is yours. I prefer putting the foreign key on first and seeing how the loading performs. If loading is slow at a particular table, consider taking that particular foreign key off (not all of them) before the loading begins and put it back afterward.

About the column names, some people prefer to abbreviate the column name such as sh_mon_nm. I think it is better to use the full words because they are easier to understand.

Note Regarding table naming, some people prefix table names with dim_ and fact_, some prefix them with d and f, some put the word dim or fact at the end as in order_fact, and some people don't use underscores as in PurchaseOrderFact (this is what Microsoft recommends in MSDN, but many SQL Server 2005 system views use underscores, as in sys.foreign_key). Again, the choice is yours, but please be consistent.

We do the same thing with all other tables in DDS. For the complete DDS table creation scripts, please refer to the web site accompanying this book at http://www.apress.com/; the scripts are in the /script folder.

When you have completed all five fact tables and fourteen dimension tables, create a batch file using sqlcmd, as shown next, and call those scripts one by one. sqlcmd is a SQL Server utility that enables you to enter Transact SQL statements and script files at the command prompt. Start with the database creation, then the dimensions, and finally the facts. They need to be in this order because of the foreign key in the fact tables.

```
h:
cd "h:\dw\scripts\dds"
sqlcmd -i db_dds.sql                            >> ddsout.txt
sqlcmd -i dim_campaign.sql                      >> ddsout.txt
sqlcmd -i dim_channel.sql                       >> ddsout.txt
sqlcmd -i dim_communication.sql                 >> ddsout.txt
sqlcmd -i dim_customer.sql                      >> ddsout.txt
sqlcmd -i dim_date.sql                          >> ddsout.txt
sqlcmd -i dim_delivery_status.sql               >> ddsout.txt
sqlcmd -i dim_format.sql                        >> ddsout.txt
sqlcmd -i dim_lead.sql                          >> ddsout.txt
sqlcmd -i dim_package.sql                       >> ddsout.txt
sqlcmd -i dim_product.sql                       >> ddsout.txt
sqlcmd -i dim_store.sql                         >> ddsout.txt
sqlcmd -i dim_subscription_status.sql           >> ddsout.txt
sqlcmd -i dim_supplier.sql                      >> ddsout.txt
sqlcmd -i dim_week.sql                          >> ddsout.txt
sqlcmd -i fact_product_sales.sql                >> ddsout.txt
sqlcmd -i fact_subscription_sales.sql           >> ddsout.txt
sqlcmd -i fact_supplier_performance.sql         >> ddsout.txt
sqlcmd -i fact_communication_subscription.sql   >> ddsout.txt
sqlcmd -i fact_campaign_result.sql              >> ddsout.txt
```

The parameter -i [filename] means "input file." Instead of >> [filename], you use -o [filename] or > [filename] to create the output file, but it will replace the content of the output file. If your development SQL Server environment is not local, you need to specify -S followed by the server name: sqlcmd -S server1. You may also need to specify the username and password using the -U and -P parameters: sqlcmd -S server1 -U user1 -P password1. You can specify the password just once in the environment variable using set sqlcmdpassword=. If you don't specify -U and -P, the default is -E, which means use a trusted connection. You can also string all the script file names together in one line: sqlcmd -i file1, file2, file3, ...

Here are two examples:

```
sqlcmd -i file1.sql -S server1 -U user1 -P password1
sqlcmd -i file1.sql file2.sql -S server1 -E
```

The first example connects to server1 using user1 and password1 credentials and then executes the statements in file1.sql.

The second example connects to server1 using a trusted connection (Windows integrated security) and executes the statements in file1.sql and file2.sql.

Creating the Normalized Data Store

The NDS is a little bit different from the DDS. The main difference is the normalization. In the next few pages, I will discuss the tables in Figure 6-2 and how to create them physically. I will also discuss how to arrange the tables in different filegroups located on different disks.

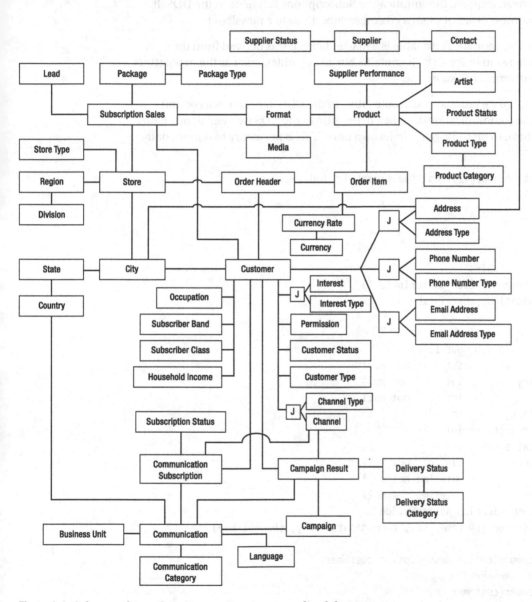

Figure 6-2. *Schema of Amadeus Entertainment normalized data store*

The tables in the NDS can be categorized into three groups: transaction tables, master tables, and attribute tables. Transaction tables contain business events and are derived from the DDS fact tables. Master tables contain business entities and are derived from the DDS dimension tables. Attribute tables contain the attributes of business entities and are derived from dimension attribute columns. For example, let's discuss the three tables at the bottom of the diagram:

communication_subscription: The communication_subscription table is a transaction table. It was derived from the Communication Subscriptions fact table in the DDS. It contains the business event of when a customer subscribes to a newsletter.

communication: The communication table is a master table. It was derived from the communication dimension in the DDS. It contains business entities, such as the newsletters to which the customers can subscribe.

language: The language table is an attribute table. In the DDS, language is a column (attribute) in the communication dimension. Because in the NDS we need to normalize the tables, we have to place language in its own table. This is necessary to remove data redundancy.

The communication_subscription table is created as follows:

```
use NDS
go

if exists
  (select * from sys.tables
   where name = 'communication_subscription')
drop table communication_subscription
go

create table communication_subscription
( customer_key            int      not null
, communication_key       int      not null
, channel_key             int      not null
, subscription_start_date int
, subscription_end_date   int
, subscription_status_key int
, source_system_code      tinyint  not null
, create_timestamp        datetime not null
, update_timestamp        datetime not null
, constraint pk_communication_subscription
  primary key clustered (customer_key, communication_key, channel_key)
  on nds_fg6
, constraint fk_communication_subscription_customer
  foreign key (customer_key)
  references customer(customer_key)
, constraint fk_communication_subscription_communication
  foreign key (communication_key)
  references communication(communication_key)
, constraint fk_communication_subscription_channel
  foreign key (channel_key)
```

```
    references channel(channel_key)
, constraint fk_communication_subscription_subscription_status
    foreign key (subscription_status_key)
    references subscription_status(subscription_status_key)
) on nds_fg4
go
```

The primary key of the `communication_subscription` table has the same granularity as the fact table—one row per subscription. If the customer unsubscribes, we will just mark it in the same row, `subscription_end_date`. If the customer resubscribes to the same newsletter, we will mark the `subscription_start_date` column and clear the unsubscribe date. We don't create a new row. We need to include a channel in the primary key because it is possible that a customer subscribes to (for example) the Amadeus Entertainment Music weekly newsletter via two channels: e-mail and RSS feed.

Just as we did in the DDS, we need to place the tables in different filegroups located on a different physical disk. The main principle here is to avoid putting large transaction tables on the same disk. For the NDS, I usually split them according to the subject areas, as follows (please refer to Figure 6-2):

- Subject area 1 is sales, physically located on the primary filegroup.

- Subject area 2 is customer, physically located on filegroup 2.

- Subject area 3 is geographic, physically located on filegroup 3.

- Subject area 4 is CRM, physically located on filegroup 4.

- Subject area 5 is supplier, physically located on filegroup 5.

Table 6-3 lists all the NDS tables, along with the table type (master, transaction, or attribute), the subject area (one of the five mentioned previously), and the filegroup where they are located.

Table 6-3. *Filegroup Allocation Table for NDS*

Table Name	Table Type	Subject Area	Filegroup
supplier	Master	Supplier	5
contact	Attribute	Supplier	5
supplier_performance	Transaction	Supplier	5
product	Master	Product	5
format	Master	Product	5
media	Attribute	Product	5
product_status	Attribute	Product	5
product_type	Attribute	Product	5
product_category	Attribute	Product	5
package	Master	Sales	Primary
package_type	Attribute	Sales	Primary

Continued

Table 6-3. *Continued*

Table Name	Table Type	Subject Area	Filegroup
lead	Master	Sales	Primary
subscription_sales	Transaction	Sales	3
order_header	Transaction	Sales	Primary
order_item	Transaction	Sales	Primary
currency	Master	Sales	Primary
currency_rate	Attribute	Sales	Primary
store_type	Attribute	Geographic	3
store	Master	Geographic	3
region	Attribute	Geographic	3
division	Attribute	Geographic	3
city	Attribute	Geographic	3
state	Attribute	Geographic	3
country	Attribute	Geographic	3
customer	Master	Customer	2
occupation	Attribute	Customer	2
interest	Attribute	Customer	2
interest_junction	Junction	Customer	2
permission	Attribute	Customer	2
subscriber_band	Attribute	Customer	2
subscriber_class	Attribute	Customer	2
customer_status	Attribute	Customer	2
customer_type	Attribute	Customer	2
address	Attribute	Geographic	3
address_type	Attribute	Geographic	3
address_junction	Junction	Geographic	3
phone_number	Attribute	Customer	2
phone_number_type	Attribute	Customer	2
phone_number_junction	Junction	Customer	2
email_address	Attribute	Customer	2
email_address_type	Attribute	Customer	2
email_address_junction	Junction	Customer	2
communication_subscription	Transaction	CRM	4
subscription_status	Master	CRM	4
campaign	Master	CRM	4
channel	Master	CRM	4
channel_junction	Junction	CRM	2

Table Name	Table Type	Subject Area	Filegroup
communication	Master	CRM	4
campaign_result	Transaction	CRM	4
business_unit	Attribute	CRM	4
communication_category	Attribute	CRM	4
language	Attribute	CRM	4
delivery_status	Master	CRM	4
delivery_status_category	Attribute	CRM	4

We then put indexes in filegroup 6 to separate them from the tables. For performance reasons, we generally want to have indexes and tables on separate disks. The Primary filegroup has three transaction tables, so to balance everything, we can put the Subscription Sales table in filegroup 3. Filegroup 2 doesn't have a transaction table, but the customer master and attribute tables are generally larger than other subject areas.

The communication table contains (amongst other things) the newsletter that we send to customers. It is created as follows:

```
use NDS
go

-- Remove FK if exists (otherwise you can't drop the table):
if exists
  (select * from sys.foreign_keys
   where name = 'fk_communication_subscription_communication'
   and parent_object_id = object_id('communication_subscription'))
alter table communication_subscription
  drop constraint fk_communication_subscription_communication
go

if exists
  (select * from sys.foreign_keys
   where name = 'fk_campaign_result_communication'
   and parent_object_id = object_id('campaign_result'))
alter table campaign_result
  drop constraint fk_campaign_result_communication
go

-- Drop the table if exists:
if exists
  (select * from sys.tables
   where name = 'communication')
drop table communication
go
```

```sql
-- Create the table:
create table communication
( communication_key    int not null identity(1,1)
, title                varchar(50) not null
, description          varchar(200)
, format               varchar(20)
, language_key         int
, category_key         int
, issuing_unit_key     int
, start_date           smalldatetime
, end_date             smalldatetime
, status               varchar(10)
, source_system_code   tinyint not null
, create_timestamp     datetime not null
, update_timestamp     datetime not null
, constraint pk_communication
  primary key clustered (communication_key)
  on nds_fg6
, constraint fk_communication_language
  foreign key (language_key)
  references language(language_key)
, constraint fk_communication_communication_category
  foreign key (category_key)
  references communication_category(communication_category_key)
, constraint fk_communication_business_unit
  foreign key (issuing_unit_key)
  references business_unit(business_unit_key)
) on nds_fg4
go

-- Create FK:
alter table communication_subscription
  add constraint fk_communication_subscription_communication
  foreign key (communication_key)
  references communication(communication_key)
go

alter table campaign_result
  add constraint fk_campaign_result_communication
  foreign key (communication_key)
  references communication(communication_key)
```

```
-- Build indexes:
if exists
  (select * from sys.indexes
   where name = 'communication_title'
   and object_id = object_id('communication'))
drop index communication.communication_title
go

create unique index communication_title
  on communication(title)
  on nds_fg6
go
```

The language table is an attribute table of the previous communication table. The communication table has a foreign key pointing to the language table. The language table is created as follows:

```
use NDS
go

-- Remove FK if exists:
if exists
  (select * from sys.foreign_keys
   where name = 'fk_communication_language'
   and parent_object_id = object_id('communication'))
alter table communication
  drop constraint fk_communication_language
go

-- Drop the table if exists and create the table:
if exists
  (select * from sys.tables
   where name = 'language')
drop table language
go

create table language
( language_key          int not null identity(1,1)
, language_code         char(3) not null
, language_name         varchar(20) not null
, source_system_code    tinyint not null
, create_timestamp      datetime not null
, update_timestamp      datetime not null
, constraint pk_language
  primary key clustered (language_key)
  on nds_fg6
) on nds_fg4
go
```

```
-- Create FK:
alter table communication
  add constraint fk_communication_language
  foreign key (language_key)
  references language(language_key)
go

-- Build indexes:
if exists
  (select * from sys.indexes
   where name = 'language_code'
   and object_id = object_id('language'))
drop index language.language_code
go

create unique index language_code
  on language(language_code)
  on nds_fg6
go
```

When using the sys.foreign_keys catalog view to find out whether a foreign key already exists, you need to specify the table name to which the foreign key belongs. For example:

```
select * from sys.foreign_keys where name = 'name1'
and parent_object_id = object_id('table1')
```

This is important to ensure that the foreign key belongs to the correct table. It is possible that two foreign keys belonging to two different tables have the same name.

Likewise, when checking indexes on sys.indexes, always specify object_id. For example:

```
select * from sys.indexes where name = 'name1'
and object_id = object_id('table1')
```

When naming the primary key and the foreign key, use a consistent convention. I usually name the primary key as pk_tablename and the foreign key as fk_childtable_parenttableN where N is a number from 1,2,3…. N is used only if we have more than one foreign key between the same two tables. Microsoft recommends mixed case without any underscores.

The relationship between the communication_subscription table, the communication table, and the language table is simple. This is essentially a fact table connected to a master table, of which an attribute table describes a particular attribute in the master table.

The relationships between the transaction table, master table, and attribute table are not always that simple. One fact table in the DDS may need to be normalized into two transaction tables in the NDS. For example, the Product Sales fact table in the DDS is normalized into an order_header table and an order_item table in the NDS.

A dimension table may not link directly to the attribute table. If the relationship is many-to-many, we need to use a junction table (aka *bridge table*). The junction table contains the primary key of both the dimension table and the attribute table, which is the customer dimension. In the NDS, the customer dimension is normalized into 18 tables. There are 17 attribute tables. Attribute tables that are one-to-many, such as the occupation table, are connected directly to the customer table. Attribute tables that are many-to-many, such as the email_address table, are connected to the customer table using a junction table.

The customer table is the most complex table in the NDS. It has 17 attribute tables. It references six other tables and is being referenced by eight other tables. This table is the core table in this system. We will create it in filegroup 2, with the index in filegroup 6. The customer table is created as follows:

```
use NDS
go

-- Remove FK if exists:
if exists
  (select * from sys.foreign_keys
   where name = 'fk_address_junction_customer'
   and parent_object_id = object_id('address_junction'))
alter table address_junction
  drop constraint fk_address_junction_customer
go

if exists
  (select * from sys.foreign_keys
   where name = 'fk_phone_number_junction_customer'
   and parent_object_id = object_id('phone_number_junction'))
alter table phone_number_junction
  drop constraint fk_phone_number_junction_customer
go

if exists
  (select * from sys.foreign_keys
   where name = 'fk_email_address_junction_customer'
   and parent_object_id = object_id('email_address_junction'))
alter table email_address_junction
  drop constraint fk_email_address_junction_customer
go

if exists
  (select * from sys.foreign_keys
   where name = 'fk_interest_junction_customer'
   and parent_object_id = object_id('interest_junction'))
alter table interest_junction
  drop constraint fk_interest_junction_customer
go
```

```sql
if exists
  (select * from sys.foreign_keys
   where name = 'fk_subscription_sales_customer'
   and parent_object_id = object_id('subscription_sales'))
alter table subscription_sales
  drop constraint fk_subscription_sales_customer
go

if exists
  (select * from sys.foreign_keys
   where name = 'fk_communication_subscription_customer'
   and parent_object_id = object_id('communication_subscription'))
alter table communication_subscription
  drop constraint fk_communication_subscription_customer
go

if exists
  (select * from sys.foreign_keys
   where name = 'fk_campaign_result_customer'
   and parent_object_id = object_id('campaign_result'))
alter table campaign_result
  drop constraint fk_campaign_result_customer
go

if exists
  (select * from sys.foreign_keys
   where name = 'fk_channel_junction_customer'
   and parent_object_id = object_id('channel_junction'))
alter table channel_junction
  drop constraint fk_channel_junction_customer
go

-- Create customer table (drop it first if exists):
if exists
  (select * from sys.tables
   where name = 'customer')
drop table customer
go

create table customer
( customer_key          int not null identity(1,1)
, customer_id           varchar(10) not null
, account_number        int
, customer_type_key     int
, name                  varchar(100) not null
, gender                char(1)
```

```
, date_of_birth           datetime
, occupation_key          int
, household_income_key     int
, date_registered          datetime
, customer_status_key      int
, subscriber_class_key     int
, subscriber_band_key      int
, permission_key           int
, effective_timestamp      datetime not null
, expiry_timestamp         datetime not null
, is_current               tinyint not null
, source_system_code       tinyint not null
, create_timestamp         datetime not null
, update_timestamp         datetime not null
, constraint pk_customer
  primary key clustered (customer_key)
  on nds_fg6
, constraint fk_customer_occupation
  foreign key (occupation_key)
  references occupation(occupation_key)
, constraint fk_customer_household_income
  foreign key (household_income_key)
  references household_income(household_income_key)
, constraint fk_customer_customer_status
  foreign key (customer_status_key)
  references customer_status(customer_status_key)
, constraint fk_customer_subscriber_class
  foreign key (subscriber_class_key)
  references subscriber_class(subscriber_class_key)
, constraint fk_customer_subscriber_band
  foreign key (subscriber_band_key)
  references subscriber_band(subscriber_band_key)
, constraint fk_customer_permission
  foreign key (permission_key)
  references permission(permission_key)
) on nds_fg2
go

-- Create FK from other tables to this table:
alter table address_junction
  add constraint fk_address_junction_customer
  foreign key (customer_key)
  references customer(customer_key)
go
```

```
alter table phone_number_junction
  add constraint fk_phone_number_junction_customer
  foreign key (customer_key)
  references customer(customer_key)
go

alter table email_address_junction
  add constraint fk_email_address_junction_customer
  foreign key (customer_key)
  references customer(customer_key)
go

alter table interest_junction
  add constraint fk_interest_junction_customer
  foreign key (customer_key)
  references customer(customer_key)
go

alter table subscription_sales
  add constraint fk_subscription_sales_customer
  foreign key (customer_key)
  references customer(customer_key)
go

alter table communication_subscription
  add constraint fk_communication_subscription_customer
  foreign key (customer_key)
  references customer(customer_key)
go

alter table campaign_result
  add constraint fk_campaign_result_customer
  foreign key (customer_key)
  references customer(customer_key)
go

alter table channel_junction
  add constraint fk_channel_junction_customer
  foreign key (customer_key)
  references customer(customer_key)
go
```

```
-- Build indexes:
if exists
  (select * from sys.indexes
   where name = 'customer_id'
   and object_id = object_id('customer'))
drop index customer.customer_id
go

create unique index customer_id
  on customer(customer_id)
  on nds_fg6
go
```

As you can see, it has its own data warehouse key called customer_key. The DDS will be using this key too. We do key management in the NDS. The NDS is where the key is assigned and maintained. If you notice, there is no address_key, email_address_key, or phone_number_key in the Customer table. This is because we are using junction tables to implement a many-to-many relationship for these three entities. The customer table has occupation_key, household_income_key, customer_status_key, subscriber_class_key, subscriber_band_key, and permission_key, because they have a many-to-one relationship.

For key columns, to avoid confusion and maintain consistency, I prefer to use int rather than tiny or small int, even though it takes up more space. This is because if you have a foreign key on a key column, the data type must match exactly. If one table uses tinyint and the other table uses smallint, SQL Server won't create the foreign key. With so many tables to link, 14 in this customer table, remembering which one is smallint, which one is tinyint, and which one is int causes a headache.

The additional space is not that much anyway; in other words, using 2 or 3 bytes extra and the dimensions that can use tinyint as their dimension keys means that they have less than 255 rows anyway. Remember that key columns are identity (1,1), meaning that even though the number of rows is currently 200, it is possible that the max(key) is 300, because the other 100 rows have been deleted over time. If we set the key column as tinyint, we would have a problem.

Here is the order_header table:

```
use NDS
go

-- Remove FK if exists:
if exists
  (select * from sys.foreign_keys
   where name = 'fk_order_detail_order_header'
   and parent_object_id = object_id('order_detail'))
alter table order_detail
  drop constraint fk_order_detail_order_header
go
```

```
-- Create the table (drop it first if exists):
if exists
  (select * from sys.tables
   where name = 'order_header')
drop table order_header
go

create table order_header
( order_id              int not null
, sales_date            datetime
, customer_key          int
, store_key             int
, source_system_code    tinyint not null
, create_timestamp      datetime not null
, update_timestamp      datetime not null
, constraint pk_order_header
  primary key clustered (order_id)
  on nds_fg6
) on [primary]
go

-- Create FK:
alter table order_detail
  add constraint fk_order_detail_order_header
  foreign key (order_id)
  references order_header(order_id)
go

-- Build indexes:
if exists
  (select * from sys.indexes
   where name = 'order_header_order_id'
   and object_id = object_id('order_header'))
drop index order_header.order_header_order_id
go

create unique index order_header_order_id
  on order_header(order_id)
  on nds_fg6
go

if exists
  (select * from sys.indexes
   where name = 'order_header_sales_date'
   and object_id = object_id('order_header'))
drop index order_header.order_header_sales_date
go
```

```
create unique index order_header_sales_date
  on order_header(sales_date)
  on nds_fg6
go

if exists
  (select * from sys.indexes
   where name = 'order_header_customer_key'
   and object_id = object_id('order_header'))
drop index order_header.order_header_customer_key
go

create unique index order_header_customer_key
  on order_header(customer_key)
  on nds_fg6
go

if exists
  (select * from sys.indexes
   where name = 'order_header_store_key'
   and object_id = object_id('order_header'))
drop index order_header.order_header_store_key
go

create unique index order_header_store_key
  on order_header(store_key)
  on nds_fg6
go
```

Notice that we created four indexes for the order_header table, because the query traffic could come from those four possible directions. The order_header table references customer and store tables and is being referenced by the order_detail table.

Here is the email_address_table, with the email_address_junction and email_address_ type tables:

```
use NDS
go

if exists
  (select * from sys.foreign_keys
   where name = 'fk_email_address_junction_email_address'
   and parent_object_id = object_id('email_address_junction'))
alter table email_address_junction
  drop constraint fk_email_address_junction_email_address
go
```

```sql
if exists
  (select * from sys.foreign_keys
   where name = 'fk_supplier_email_address'
   and parent_object_id = object_id('supplier'))
alter table supplier
  drop constraint fk_supplier_email_address
go

if exists
  (select * from sys.tables
   where name = 'email_address')
drop table email_address
go

create table email_address
( email_address_key    int not null identity(1,1)
, email_address        varchar(200)
, source_system_code   tinyint not null
, create_timestamp     datetime not null
, update_timestamp     datetime not null
, constraint pk_email_address
  primary key clustered (email_address_key)
  on nds_fg6
) on nds_fg2
go

alter table email_address_junction
  add constraint fk_email_address_junction_email_address
  foreign key (email_address_key)
  references email_address(email_address_key)
go

alter table supplier
  add constraint fk_supplier_email_address
  foreign key (email_address_key)
  references email_address(email_address_key)
go

if exists
  (select * from sys.indexes
   where name = 'email_address_email_address'
   and object_id = object_id('email_address'))
drop index email_address.email_address_email_address
go
```

```
create unique index email_address_email_address
  on email_address(email_address)
  on nds_fg6
go
```

Here is the email_address_junction table:

```
use NDS
go

if exists
  (select * from sys.tables
   where name = 'email_address_junction')
drop table email_address_junction
go

create table email_address_junction
( email_address_junction_key  int not null
, customer_key                int not null
, email_address_key           int not null
, email_address_type_key      int
, source_system_code          tinyint not null
, create_timestamp            datetime not null
, update_timestamp            datetime not null
, constraint pk_email_address_junction
  primary key clustered (email_address_junction_key)
  on nds_fg6
, constraint fk_email_address_junction_customer
  foreign key (customer_key)
  references customer(customer_key)
, constraint fk_email_address_junction_email_address
  foreign key (email_address_key)
  references email_address(email_address_key)
, constraint fk_email_address_junction_email_address_type
  foreign key (email_address_type_key)
  references email_address_type(email_address_type_key)
) on nds_fg2
go

if exists
  (select * from sys.indexes
   where name = 'email_address_junction_customer_key_email_address_key'
   and object_id = object_id('email_address_junction'))
drop index
  email_address_junction.email_address_junction_customer_key_email_address_key
go
```

```
create unique index email_address_junction_customer_key_email_address_key
  on email_address_junction(customer_key, email_address_key)
  on nds_fg6
go
```

Here's the email_address_type table:

```
use NDS
go

-- Remove FK if exists:
if exists
  (select * from sys.foreign_keys
   where name = 'fk_email_address_junction_email_address_type'
   and parent_object_id = object_id('email_address_junction'))
alter table email_address_junction
  drop constraint fk_email_address_junction_email_address_type
go

-- Create the table (drop it first if exists):
if exists
  (select * from sys.tables
   where name = 'email_address_type')
drop table email_address_type
go

create table email_address_type
( email_address_type_key    int not null identity(1,1)
, email_address_type_code   char(2)
, email_address_type        varchar(10)
, description               varchar(30)
, source_system_code        tinyint not null
, create_timestamp          datetime not null
, update_timestamp          datetime not null
, constraint pk_email_address_type
  primary key clustered (email_address_type_key)
  on nds_fg6
) on nds_fg2
go

-- Create FK:
alter table email_address_junction
  add constraint fk_email_address_junction_email_address_type
  foreign key (email_address_type_key)
  references email_address_type(email_address_type_key)
go
```

The `email_address_type` table is used to determine, for example, which e-mail address is the home e-mail address and which e-mail address is an office e-mail address. Similarly, `address_type` and `phone_number_type` are used for the same purpose. If you use a junction table, you don't have key columns on both child and parent tables. Both child and parent key columns are in the junction table. Remember to set all primary key columns in all tables to identity (1,1).

■**Tip** It is useful to name the foreign key as `fk_childtable_parenttable`. If, for example, you make a small change in the `email_address` table and want to run the script and it says "Cannot drop the email address table because it is being used in FK relationship with other table," then you need to find out which table referenced to it. But with this naming, you can query with `select * from sys.foreign_keys where name like '%email_address'`.

With that, we have finished creating the NDS. Just like we did in the DDS, you just need to create a batch file that contains `sqlcmd` to call all these scripts. Be careful with the sequence of how you build the tables. Because of the referential integrity (foreign keys), you need to build them in a particular order. And the script may need several passes to build successfully because the foreign key creation is put on the table creation script (if we create all tables first and then create all the foreign keys afterward, we need only one pass). For a complete list of scripts for all the tables in the NDS, please refer to http://www.apress.com/. The NDS table creation scripts are located in the /script folder.

Using Views

A *view* is a database object with columns and rows like a table but not persisted on disks. A view is created using a SELECT statement that filters columns and rows from a table or a combination of several tables using a JOIN clause. In a data warehouse, views are used for three purposes:

To create conform dimensions in dimensional data stores: Conformed dimensions mean they are either the same dimension table or one is the subset of the other. As I discussed in Chapter 1, dimension A is said to be a subset of dimension B when all columns of dimension A exist in dimension B and all rows of dimension A exist in dimension B.

To shield users from physical tables, making it simpler for the users as well as to restrict access: A view creates a virtual layer on the top of physical tables. Users do not access the physical tables anymore. Instead, they are accessing the views. This additional layer enables us to create a virtual table that gets data from several tables. The additional layer also enables us to restrict users from accessing certain columns or certain rows.

To increase the availability, particularly to make the data warehouse up and running when we are populating it: This is used in user-facing data stores such as the DDS. For every dimension table and every fact table, we create two physical tables and one view that selects from one of these two tables. When table 1 is being populated, the view selects from table 2. Conversely, when table 2 is being populated, the view selects from table 1.

Let's discuss these three uses of views one by one.

The first one is to create a conform dimension. Sometimes when creating a data mart, the dimension that we need in that mart already exists. But we can use the existing dimension because the granularity is different. We need a dimension with higher granularity, and therefore only certain columns are applicable. In this case, we create a view from that existing dimension to select only certain rows and certain columns. We make this view a new dimension with a higher grain for that data mart.

The new dimension conforms to the existing dimension. When we have conformed dimensions between two data marts, we can drill across from one mart to another mart. The benefit of using views to create conform dimensions is that we don't have to populate the higher-grain dimension. When the data in the underlying dimension changes, the data in the higher-grain dimension automatically changes.

For example, in the supplier performance data mart, there is a dimension called week. The week dimension contains one row for each week in the year. This dimension is not a physical table but a view created from the date dimension. It is created by filtering only certain days (this can be any day of the week) and selecting only relevant columns, as follows:

```
use DDS
go

if exists
  (select * from sys.objects
    where name = 'dim_week' and type = 'V')
drop view dim_week
go

create view dim_week as select
date_key, date, system_date, sql_date, julian_date, day,
day_of_the_year, week_number, month, month_name, short_month_name,
quarter, year, fiscal_week, fiscal_period, fiscal_quarter, fiscal_year,
source_system_code, create_timestamp, update_timestamp
from dim_date where day_of_the_week = 1
go
```

The week dimension and date dimension are conformed. This is an example of conformed dimensions that consist of two entities. Two dimensions are said to be conformed if they are identical or one is a subset of the other.

The second usage is to create a virtual layer on top of the physical tables to make it simpler for the users. Three typical uses are the data mart view, last month view, and specific store view. Two other uses are for SCD type 2 and SCD type 3 current view. A slowly changing dimension contains both the current values and the historical values. We use a current view to select only the current values.

A data mart view is where we create a view on top of a fact table and its dimension tables, giving the end users who have direct DDS access a single virtual table sourced from many physical tables. For example, in the Amadeus Entertainment case study to analyze product sales by date, customer, product, and store, the SQL query is as follows:

```
select f.quantity, f.price, f.value, f.cost, f.margin
d.date, d.day_name, d.fiscal_week, d.fiscal_period,
c. name, c.email_address, c.city, c.country, c.subscriber_class,
p.name, p.title, p.artist, p.product_type, p.product_category,
s.city, s.country, s.store_type, s.region, s.division
from fact_product_sales
left join dim_date t on f.date_key = d.date_key
left join dim_customer c on f.customer_key = c.customer_key
left join dim_product p on f.product_key = p.product_key
left join dim_store s on f.store_key = s.store_key
```

These key columns from the main dimension tables are accessed over and over again, and every time users have to type those long left-joins. In certain cases, the column names on the tables are not short and nice like previously shown but rather long and confusing, such as wk_rev_sub_sgl_ttl, fs_prd_nm, and tot_rgn_div. To avoid this problem in the first place, we should use descriptive names for all database objects including columns, tables, views, indexes, primary keys, and foreign keys. For these users, a view like the following would make it a single table with the necessary columns:

```
create view sales as
select f.quantity, f.price, f.value, f.cost, f.margin
d.date, d.day_name, d.fiscal_week, d.fiscal_period,
c. name, c.email_address, c.city, c.country, c.subscriber_class,
p.name, p.title, p.artist, p.product_type, p.product_category,
s.city, s.country, s.store_type, s.region, s.division
from fact_product_sales
join dim_date t on f.date_key = d.date_key
join dim_customer c on f.customer_key = c.customer_key
join dim_product p on f.product_key = p.product_key
join dim_store s on f.store_key = s.store_key
```

I have experienced this myself: some users are so used to writing these queries that they know the date_key value for yesterday and the store_key value for their stores, as in select * from fact_sales where date_key = 12201 and store_key = 324. In the first few weeks, they write this:

```
select * from sales_fact f
join dim_date d on f.date_key = d.date_key
join dim_store s on f.store_key = s.store_key
where d.sql_date = 'mm/dd/yyyy' and s.name = 'Paris'
```

but because they get so used to it (also to make it shorter), in the end they type date_key and store_key directly. My point is, if they use the views, it would be much easier for them.

Another example where a view is used to create a virtual layer to make it simpler for the users is the last month view. The last month view is a view with the where clause where d.month = datepart(m,getdate())-1. This is frequently used because last month was a complete month, and it was recent. This month is not complete yet, so you can't really compare it.

A specific store (or country, or branch, or locale, or region) is another view that is frequently used, as shown previously but with a `where` clause to limit to a certain store, branch, or region. This is because the users are responsible only for that store or region.

When you have a slowly changing dimension, most of the time the users just want the current view. So, a view with a `where` clause such as `where is_current = 1` is greatly welcomed by the users. That's for SCD type 2. For type 3, the view is something like `create view as select store_id, address, city, region2 as region, division2 as division`, ignoring the prior region and prior division. This is especially useful when your current region is called region2, but last year it was region1.

The last usage of view is to increase availability. When you populate a fact table, chances are, you will be locking this table from access. There are two purposes of locking the table when loading data: to speed up loading and to avoid data volatility, such as in ever-changing values, which could cause user confusion. So, your infrastructure is excellent, is clustered, and has a web farm with dual fiber switches, but still the data warehouse will be inaccessible for three hours every day. If the data warehouse is used worldwide, there is no "nighttime." Nighttime in the United States is daytime in Asia. You can't schedule the batch-loading process for 3 a.m. EST because Singapore and London are using the data warehouse.

A common technique is to use a view. We have two physical tables and one view that point to one of these two tables. For example, say we have two physical tables: `fact_product_sales_1` and `fact_product_sales_2`. We create a view called `fact_product_sales` as `create view fact_product_sales as select * from fact_product_sales_N`, with N = 1 or 2, depending on which day. Monday it is 1, Tuesday it is 2, Wednesday it is 1, Thursday it is 2, and so on. Assume that today is Monday. Your active fact table is `fact_product_sales_2`. On the stage, you have a table containing today's data. So, you load this data (Monday data) into `fact_product_sales_1`. After you load it, you drop the `fact_product_sales` view and do this: `create view fact_product_sales as select from fact_product_sales_1`. Notice that now `fact_product_sales_2` is out-of-date because it contains Sunday data.

Tomorrow, your stage table contains Monday data and Tuesday data. You load the Monday and Tuesday data from the stage into `fact_product_sales_2`. Then you drop the `fact_product_sales` view and do this: `create view fact_product_sales as select from fact_product_sales_2`. Notice that now `fact_product_sales_1` is out-of-date because it contains Monday data. The BI or CRM applications are shielded from what's happening. From an application point of view, they only access a fact table called `fact_product_sales`, which is always available, and the data is always up-to-date. In reality, the fact table is actually a view sourced alternately from two different physical tables.

This technique is not only for loading fact tables but also for loading dimension tables. Rather than a multiday implementation as described previously, you can also use this technique for an intraday implementation, as follows:

1. Set the view to point to table 2.

2. Load today's data into table 1.

3. Set the view to point to table 1.

4. Load today's data into table 2.

By using this technique, your data warehouse will be up all the time. Dropping and re-creating a view takes only a few seconds. This technique is commonly used to increase the data warehouse availability, both in packaged applications running on a normalized data warehouse as well in custom-developed data warehouses.

Summary Tables

Out of the many things that can improve data warehouse performance, the summary table is at the top of the list. (The second one is table partitioning, and the third one is indexing.) This is because the data that the users need is already precalculated. We will discuss these three things one by one in the next three main sections.

Say you have a report that displays a graph of the summary of weekly sales data for the last 12 weeks by product group or by stores. Let's say that within a week you have 1 million rows. So the stored procedure behind that report must process 1 million rows and display the data on the screen as a graph, while the user waits. Let's say that this takes 45 seconds.

If you produce a table called weekly_sales_summary, which runs the same query, and put the result in this summary table, when the user accesses the report, the stored procedure or the SQL statement behind the report needs to access only this summary table. The response time of the report is greatly improved; it's probably only one or two seconds now.

The summary table needs to be at least 10 times smaller (in terms of the number of rows), ideally 100 times smaller or more. Otherwise, there is no point creating a summary table. If you wonder where 10 and 100 come from, the guideline to determine whether it is worth creating the summary table is to compare the performance improvement with the time required to build it. What I meant by "performance improvement" is how much faster querying the summary table compared to querying the underlying table directly is. If the performance improvement is insignificant (say less than 10 percent), if it takes a long time to build the table (say one hour), and if the query is not used frequently, then it's not worth building a summary table. Remember that a summary table needs to be updated every time the underlying fact table is updated. If the number of rows in the summary table is much less than the underlying table, such as 10 or 100 times smaller, usually the performance improvement is significant. The ideal time to refresh the summary tables is immediately after the population of the underlying fact table.

As we discussed in Chapter 5, we have three types of fact table: the transactional fact table, the periodic snapshot fact table, and the accumulative snapshot fact table. A summary fact table is suitable for a transaction fact table. For a periodic snapshot fact table, we have the "latest summary table." A latest summary table contains only today's version of the snapshot. For example, the Subscription Sales fact table contains a daily snapshot of all the membership subscriptions. If we have 1 million customer subscriptions, the table would contain 1 million records every day. Over two years, there would be 730 million rows in the fact table. In this case, we can create a table called fact_subscription_sales_latest that contains only today's rows so it contains only 1 million rows and is therefore faster. This latest summary table is useful if you need information that depends on the today value only.

Partitioning

Out of many things that can improve the performance of a data warehouse, I would say partitioning is the second most important. In SQL Server 2005 and 2008, we have a new feature for partitioning for a physical table. Previously, in SQL Server 2000, we could partition only a view; we could not partition a table.

There are two types of partitioning: vertical partitioning and horizontal partitioning. *Vertical partitioning* is splitting a table vertically into several smaller tables, with each table containing some columns of the original table. *Horizontal partitioning* is splitting a table horizontally into several smaller tables, with each table containing some rows of the original table. In this section, I'm talking about horizontal partitioning, not vertical partitioning.

Imagine if the Subscription Sales fact table were horizontally partitioned like the one in Figure 6-3.

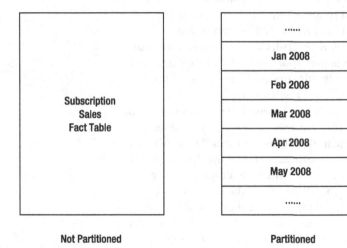

Figure 6-3. *Partitioned and nonpartitioned Subscription Sales fact table*

The nature of the fact tables in dimensional data warehouses is that their content is chronological according to time. If it is a transactional fact table, such as Product Sales, the rows coming into the fact table are the sales records from the previous day. If it is a periodic snapshot fact table, such as Subscription Sales, the rows coming into the fact table are the snapshot of all subscriber records as they were on that day.

Because of this natural characteristic, it is best to physically organize the table by date. It makes the loading a lot quicker. It makes the query faster if the information you need is from the same month or the same year. The left part of Figure 6-4 shows the loading and query of a nonpartitioned Subscription Sales fact table, physically clustered on store_key. The records are loaded to various parts of the table. The queries fetch the data also from various different places within the table.

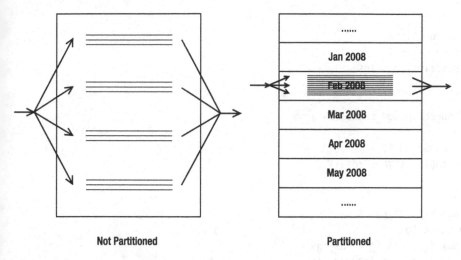

| Not Partitioned | Partitioned |

Figure 6-4. *Loading and query of partitioned and nonpartitioned table*

The right part of Figure 6-4 shows a partitioned Subscription Sales fact table. The loading of today's data hits only a particular partition, which is faster because the data is loaded into one place (physically clustered sectors on disk), rather than scattered over different sectors and disks. Queries are faster too. The response time of a query with `where column1 = value1` is better if run on a partitioned table with `column1` as the partitioning key, compared to running it on a nonpartitioned table because it encourages SQL Server to execute the query in parallel. A test on SQL Server 2005 running on Unisys ES7000 with EMC Clarion SAN managed to load 2.5 billion rows into a partitioned fact table in about one hour.[5]

Let's partition our Subscription Sales table. In this example, we have a fact table storing customer subscriptions. We will partition the table into monthly partitions; in other words, each month will go into its own partition. In this example, we will use January until December 2008. Here is the table creation script:

```
use dds
go

if exists
  (select * from sys.tables
   where name = 'fact_subscription_sales')
drop table fact_subscription_sales
go

if exists
  (select * from sys.partition_schemes
   where name = 'ps_subscription_sales')
drop partition scheme ps_subscription_sales
go
```

---

5. http://www.microsoft.com/technet/prodtechnol/sql/2005/spdw.mspx#ESGAC

```
if exists
  (select * from sys.partition_functions
   where name = 'pf_subscription_sales')
drop partition function pf_subscription_sales
go

create partition function pf_subscription_sales (int)
as range left for values
(10365, 10396, 10425, 10456, 10486, 10517
, 10547, 10578, 10609, 10639, 10670, 10700, 10731)
go

create partition scheme ps_subscription_sales
as partition pf_subscription_sales to
(dds_fg2, dds_fg3, dds_fg5, dds_fg2, dds_fg3, dds_fg5
, dds_fg2, dds_fg3, dds_fg5, dds_fg2, dds_fg3, dds_fg5
, dds_fg2, dds_fg3)
go

create table fact_subscription_sales
( date_key                int       not null
, customer_key            int       not null
, package_key             int       not null
, format_key              int       not null
, store_key               int       not null
, start_date_key          int       not null
, end_date_key            int       not null
, lead_key                int       not null
, subscription_id         int       not null
, subscription_revenue    money
, single_titles_revenue   money
, monthly_revenue         money
, music_quantity          int
, music_unit_cost         money
, monthly_music_cost      money
, film_quantity           int
, film_unit_cost          money
, monthly_film_cost       money
, book_quantity           int
, book_unit_cost          money
, monthly_book_cost       money
, monthly_indirect_cost   money
, monthly_cost            money
, monthly_margin          money
, annual_revenue          money
, annual_cost             money
, annual_profit           money
```

```
, subscriber_profitability   decimal(9,2)
, subscribe_timestamp        datetime
, unsubscribe_timestamp      datetime
, source_system_code         tinyint
, create_timestamp           datetime
, update_timestamp           datetime
, constraint pk_fact_subscription_sales
  primary key clustered
  ( date_key, customer_key, subscription_id )
  on ps_subscription_sales(date_key)
, constraint fk_fact_subscription_sales_dim_date1
  foreign key (date_key)
  references dim_date(date_key)
, constraint fk_fact_subscription_sales_dim_customer
  foreign key (customer_key)
  references dim_customer(customer_key)
, constraint fk_fact_subscription_sales_dim_package
  foreign key (package_key)
  references dim_package(package_key)
, constraint fk_fact_subscription_sales_dim_store
  foreign key (store_key)
  references dim_store(store_key)
, constraint fk_fact_subscription_sales_dim_date2
  foreign key (start_date_key)
  references dim_date(date_key)
, constraint fk_fact_subscription_sales_dim_date3
  foreign key (end_date_key)
  references dim_date(date_key)
, constraint fk_fact_subscription_sales_dim_lead
  foreign key (lead_key)
  references dim_lead(lead_key)
) on ps_subscription_sales(date_key)
go
```

First we drop the table, the partition function, and the partition scheme, if they exist. Then we create a partition function called pf_subscription_sales. We specify the boundary values. Because we will partition the table based on the date_key column, we need to specify the boundary values of each partition. Partition 1 is for records before 1/1/2008, partition 2 is for January 2008, partition 3 is for February 2008, partition 4 is for March 2008, partition 5 is for April 2008, ..., partition 13 is for December 2008, and partition 14 is for records on or after 1/1/2009.

In the data warehouse, we'll set date_key for 1/1/2007 as 10,000. This enables us to go back 10,000 days if necessary; in other words, if we need to create 2006 records (which we do need at some point before we go live to load the history), it would be assigned date_key 9635 to 9999. You don't have to set it to 10,000. You can customize it to your needs. Setting the date_key of the first operational day of the data warehouse to 10,000 enables us to go back 27 years. If you need only three years, then you can start the date key with 1100 (3 × 365).

The date keys for 2008 records are 10365 to 10730. So in the partition function, we specify that the boundary values are 1/1/2008 (date_key 10365), 2/1/2008 (date_key 10396), and so on. We then create the partition scheme by assigning the partitions to filegroups.

After creating the partition scheme, we then create the table by specifying the partition scheme with the partitioned column in brackets at the end of the DDL. This is to inform SQL Server that we want to partition the table using that partition scheme. A common mistake is to specify a filegroup for the clustered primary key as follows: constraint pk_tablename primary key clustered(PK columns) on dds_fg4. This will produce the following message:

```
The filegroup 'dds_fg4' specified for the clustered index
 'pk_fact_subscription_sales' was used for table
'fact_subscription_sales' even though partition scheme
'ps_subscription_sales' is specified for it.
```

What happened was that SQL Server put the table and the clustered index on dds_fg4, rather than on dds_fg2, dds_fg3, and dds_fg5 as we specified in the partition scheme. This is because the leaf nodes of the clustered index are the physical table pages. When creating a partition table, if the constraint filegroup is different from the table filegroup, SQL Server will do whatever is specified in the constraint filegroup and ignore the table filegroup.

The partition index is best placed in the same filegroup as the partition table because it enables SQL Server to switch the partitions efficiently. In this case, we say that the index is *aligned* with the table. Aligning the partition index with the partition table helps when we implement a sliding window for archiving partitions and when we add new partitions to the table. To enable us to switch or move partitions, the index must be aligned with the table. When we move or transfer a partition, we don't actually move the data. Instead, we change the metadata only around where the data is.

Partition maintenance is the activity of administering a partitioned table so that it is ready for data loading and query. If we implement partitioning using monthly sliding windows, we can do partition maintenance monthly or annually. Every month we can drop the oldest partition (and archive it) and add this month's partition. Or we can do this every December: drop 12 partitions for the oldest year and add 12 new partitions for the coming year.

Indexes

Indexing can significantly improve the query and loading performance of data warehousing. In this section, I will discuss how to implement indexing in a data warehouse. I will discuss choosing the primary key and clustered index and indexing small tables, including indexes and partitioned indexes.

In the DDS, we have fact tables and we have dimension tables. They require different indexing and primary keys. I will discuss dimension tables first and then the fact tables. Each dimension table has a surrogate key column. This is an identity (1,1) column, and the values are unique. We make this surrogate key column the primary key of the dimension table. We also make this surrogate key column the clustered index of the dimension table. The reason for doing this is because in the DDS, the dimension tables are joined to the fact table on the surrogate key column. By making the surrogate key a clustered primary key, we will get good query performance because in SQL Server a clustered index determines the order of how the rows are physically stored on disk. Because of this, we can have only one clustered index on each table.

Dimension tables contain attribute columns, typically having a character data type. Attribute columns that are often used in the where clause of the queries need to be set as a nonclustered index—but only if the selectivity is high. If the attribute column has many duplicate values, it may not be worth indexing.

For the fact table in SQL Server data warehousing, we have two approaches in terms of determining the primary key and the clustered index. Note that this is specifically for SQL Server; it does not apply to other database engines such as Oracle or Teradata.

- The first approach is to create a fact table surrogate key column. This is an identity (1,1) column that functions as a single-column unique identifier of the fact table row. We set this column as the primary key and the clustered index of the fact table.

- The second approach is not to have a fact table surrogate key column. Instead, we select the minimum combination of columns that make a row unique as the primary key. In some cases, the combination of all dimensional surrogate key columns makes a row unique. In other cases, they don't, and we have to identify other columns that make a row unique, such as the degenerate dimension columns.

If you want to implement the first approach, create a new column for every single fact table. Call this column fact_key. It is an identity (1,1) column. The data type is bigint. It is not worth taking the risk of using the int data type to save 4 bytes, unless you are certain you are not going to hit 9 billion. Remember that the max(key) can be higher than the number of rows, as I explained earlier. The bigint data type is 9 quintillion (18 zeros), so it should be enough. Create a clustered primary key in this column. The advantages of this approach are that the loading can be twice as fast (because the clustered index key is an identity column, so there is no need to reorganize the fact table rows when loading new data), and the nonclustered indexes can be four to five times smaller than the second approach (because the clustered index key is 8 bytes).

If you want to implement the second approach, find out what makes the fact table row unique. For example, in our Subscription Sales fact table, the grain is one row for each customer subscription per day. So, date_key and customer_key must be part of the primary key. What if the customer subscribes to two packages? We need to include the subscription_id in the primary key to make it unique, so the primary key is date_key, customer_key, and subscription_id. We cluster the table in these primary key columns, so the table will physically be organized/sorted according to date, customer, and then subscription ID.

This will make the query fast if the where clause contains the date and customer, because the table is physically sorted by the date and then the customer. This could be 10 times faster than if the date and customer are not indexed. That's the advantage of the second approach. The loading speed of the second approach could be twice as slow as the first approach (as discussed previously), but we have fewer indexes to maintain. Overall, on the SQL Server platform, the fact table surrogate key approach is preferred because there is no need to reorganize the clustered index when loading, which results in better loading performance, while the query performance can be supported by a nonclustered index. The second reason is functionality: we can uniquely identify a fact table row using a single column, which is useful when we need to refer to a fact table row either from another fact table (drilling across) or from the same fact table itself (self-join).

For the Communication Subscriptions fact table, the grain is one row for each subscription, so the columns that make a row unique are `customer_key`, `communication_key`, and `start_date_key`. So, we make these three columns the clustered primary key. For the Supplier Performance fact table, the grain is one row per week for each product supplied. The columns that make a row unique are `week_key`, `supplier_key`, and `product_key`, so we make these three columns the clustered primary key. For the Campaign Results fact table, the grain is one row for each intended recipient. The columns that make a row unique are `campaign_key`, `customer_key`, and `send_date_key`, so we make them the clustered primary key.

For the Product Sales fact table, the grain is one row for each item sold. The columns that make a row unique are `order_id` and `line_number`, so we make them the clustered primary key. The disadvantage of the second approach is that, potentially, the nonclustered indexes are three to four times larger, because the clustered index may consist of three or four columns. The disadvantage of the first approach (the fact table surrogate key) is that there are more indexes to maintain, which could impact query performance. How much it impacts the query performance depends on whether the index covers the column on the `where` clause of the query.

The Subscription Sales fact table has eight dimensional key columns and one degenerate dimension column (`subscription_id`). If you create the fact table clustered primary key based on the combination of eight dimension keys plus `subscription_id`, all nonclustered indexes would become very large, in other words, nine columns (which is as big as the table itself). This is not a good idea because in SQL Server the clustered index key is used by all nonclustered indexes. The loading performance could be two times slower (or worse) as SQL Server and must physically reorganize the fact table based on these nine columns as the data is loaded into the fact table.

It is not worth indexing the small tables, such as some dimension tables and some attribute tables on the NDS. The overhead (index maintenance at loading) outweighs the benefit (query performance). The guideline I usually use is 1,000 rows (this is determined by querying two tables with and without an index). If it is less than 1,000 rows, I generally don't index. Dimension tables between 1,000 and 10,000 rows I rarely index; I think twice or even three times before indexing them, probably examining the execution plan first. For example, in the Amadeus Entertainment `store` table, the query `where city = value1` takes 0 milliseconds, whether we have a nonclustered index on `city` or not. The loading is impacted, though. An `insert select` into the table (empty) takes 0 milliseconds without an index, 93 milliseconds with an index only on the `city` column, and 2560 milliseconds with indexes on 17 columns.

Indexing is a two-step process. The first step is to determine what column to index based on application and business knowledge. If the column will be used when analyzing the data, we consider that column for indexing. This is done when doing data modeling and physical database design. For example, on the customer dimension, we think we need to put a nonclustered index on the occupation column because the business user needs to analyze the product and subscription sales by income. We also need to index on the permission column, because the CRM segmentation process will need to get a list of customers who have given their permissions.

The second step is to fine-tune the indexes based on the query workload using the Query Execution Plan and the Database Engine Tuning Advisor. This is done after we load the data into the NDS and DDS, still in the development environment. We can identify slow-running queries by measuring how many milliseconds each query runs. This is done using SQL Server

Profiler to capture the SQL statement execution duration into a table that we can analyze. After we identify the slow-running queries, we examine the execution plan of those queries. For example, we may find some SQL queries use columns that we have not indexed in their where clause. We can improve these queries by creating a nonclustered index on those columns.

OK, let's move on with our indexing. In the dimension table, let's create the indexes in columns that are used in the queries. For example, the day of the week column is used on dim_week, so we index on that column, like this:

```
if exists
  (select * from sys.indexes
   where name = 'dim_date_day_of_the_week'
   and object_id = object_id('dim_date'))
drop index dim_date.dim_date_day_of_the_week
go

create index dim_date_day_of_the_week
  on dim_date(day_of_the_week)
  on dds_fg6
go
```

Which dimension column do we index? In the first step of indexing, during data modeling and physical database design, we create the indexes based on our application and business knowledge. In the second step, we fine-tune the indexes based on the result of query execution results that we capture using SQL Server Profiler.

For a fact table, it generally helps the performance of queries that join the fact table and the dimension tables if we create one column nonunique nonclustered index for each dimensional surrogate key column in the fact table. The SQL Server query optimizer can then use the combination of these one-column indexes when executing the query with where dim_key1 = ... and dim_key2 = ... and dim_key3 = ... Some people call this type of indexing *index intersection*, and some people call it *index bitmapping*. Here is an example of index intersection that creates an index for each dimensional surrogate key column in the fact table:

```
create index fact_product_sales_sales_date_key
  on fact_product_sales(sales_date_key)
  on dds_fg4
go

create index fact_product_sales_customer_key
  on fact_product_sales(customer_key)
  on dds_fg4
go

create index fact_product_sales_product_key
  on fact_product_sales(product_key)
  on dds_fg4
go
```

```
create index fact_product_sales_store_key
  on fact_product_sales(store_key)
  on dds_fg4
go
```

To help index intersection and speed up certain queries, sometimes it is better to create a covering index. A *covering* index is an index that contains all the columns referenced in the query. The benefit of using a covering index is that the SQL Server query engine doesn't have to go to the table itself to get any data. It can find all the data it needs on the index. For example, if the where clause in the SQL statement is where column1 = value1, column2 = value2, then the covering index needs to contain column1 and column2.

The order of columns in the where clause does not matter, but the order of columns in the covering index does matter. So, be careful when specifying the order of columns in the covering index. For the first column, we need to choose the most used dimension key. For the second column, choose the second most-used dimension key. For the Product Sales fact table, I'll set the three covering indexes as follows:

- Date, customer, store, product

- Date, store, product, customer

- Date, product, store, customer

We may have to swap the third and fourth columns depending on the queries. Note that even if you have all columns covered, the SQL Server query optimizer may not use the index if the selectivity is low. *Selectivity* is the ratio between the number of rows that satisfy the criteria and the total rows. If this ratio is high, the selectivity is low, and the index is not useful and may not be useful. A unique index has the highest selectivity because it returns only one row.

To create indexes in a partitioned table, we just have to mention the partition schema instead of the normal filegroup. Here are some of examples for the Subscription Sales fact table we partitioned earlier:

```
create index date_key
on fact_subscription_sales(date_key)
on ps_subscription_sales(date_key)
go

create index package_key
on fact_subscription_sales(package_key)
on ps_subscription_sales(package_key)
go

create index customer_key
on fact_subscription_sales(customer_key)
on ps_subscription_sales(customer_key)
go
```

The indexed column must be of the same data type as the partitioning function. This is another reason why we need to keep all the dimension key column data types as int (not smallint or tinyint), in addition to the foreign key reason we discussed earlier.

Summary

Well, this was quite a long chapter. Database design is the cornerstone of data warehousing. We will build the ETL and applications on this foundation, so we must get it right. In this chapter, we discussed the details of the hardware platform and system architecture, the disk space calculation, database creation, and table and view creation.

We also covered the top three factors that can improve data warehouse performance: summary table, partitioning, and indexing. We need to make sure they are set correctly from the beginning—in other words, when we create the databases, not later when we have performance problems.

Now that we have built the databases, in the next two chapters you will learn how to extract the data from the source systems and populate our NDS and DDS databases, widely known as ETL, which stands for Extract, Transform, and Load.

CHAPTER 7

■ ■ ■

Data Extraction

Now that we have created the tables in the NDS and the DDS, it is time to populate them. Before we can populate them, though, we need to retrieve the data from the source system. This is what data extraction is all about.

First I'll discuss the general principles of data extraction, different kinds of source systems, and several data extraction techniques. Then I'll introduce the tool that we will be using, SQL Server Integration Services. After introducing the tool, I'll then show how to use it to extract the data from the source systems in our case study: Jade, WebTower, and Jupiter.

Introduction to ETL

ETL stands for Extract, Transform, and Load. It is the process of retrieving and transforming data from the source system and putting it into the data warehouse. It has been around for decades, and it has developed and improved a lot since its inception.

There are several basic principles to understand when extracting data from a source system for the purpose of populating a data warehouse. First, the volume of data being retrieved is large, probably hundreds of megabytes or tens of gigabytes. An OLTP system is designed so that the data is retrieved in little pieces, not in large amounts like this, so you have to be careful not to slow the source system down too much. We want the extraction to be as fast as possible, such as five minutes if we can, not three hours (this depends on the extraction method, which I'll cover later in this chapter). We also want it to be as small as possible, such as 10MB per day if we can, not 1GB per day. In addition, we want it to be as infrequent as possible, such as once a day if we can, not every five minutes. We want the change in the source systems to be as minimal as possible, such as no change at all if we can, not creating triggers for capturing data changes in every single table.

The previous paragraph talks about a fundamental principle in data extraction. If there is only thing that you will take away from this chapter, I hope it is this: when extracting data from a source system, you have to be careful not to disturb the source system too much.

After we extract the data, we want to put it into the data warehouse as soon as possible, ideally straightaway, without touching the disk at all (meaning without storing it temporarily in a database or in files). We need to apply some transformations to the data from the source system so that it suits the format and structure of the data in the NDS and the DDS. Sometimes the data transformation is just formatting and standardization, converting to a certain number or date format, trimming trailing spaces or leading zeros, and conforming into standards. Other times the modification is a lookup, such as translating customer status 2 to Active or translating the product category "Pop music" to 54. Another transformation that is frequently used in data warehousing is aggregation, which means summarizing data at higher levels.

We also want the data we put into the warehouse to be clean and of good quality. For example, we don't want invalid telephone numbers, an e-mail address without the character @ in it, a product code that does not exist, a DVD with a capacity of 54GB, an address with a city of Amsterdam but a state of California, or a unit price of $0 for a particular audio book. For this purpose, we need to do various checks before putting the data into the warehouse.

Two other important principles are *leakage* and *recoverability*. Leakage happens when the ETL process thinks it has downloaded all the data completely from the source system but in reality has missed some records. A good ETL process should not have any leakage. Recoverability means that the ETL process should be robust so that in the event of a failure, it can recover without data loss or damage. I will discuss all this in this chapter.

ETL Approaches and Architecture

There are several approaches of implementing ETL. A traditional approach is to pull the data from the source systems, put it in a staging area, and then transform it and load it into the warehouse, as per the top diagram of Figure 7-1. Alternatively, instead of putting the data in a staging area, sometimes the ETL server does the transformation in memory and then updates the data warehouse directly (no staging), as shown in the bottom diagram of Figure 7-1. The staging area is a physical database or files. Putting the data into the staging area means inserting it into the database or writing it in files.

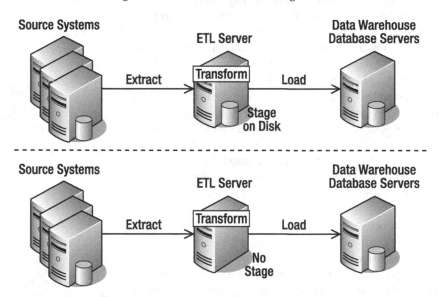

Figure 7-1. *To stage on disks or do transformation in memory*

Transforming the data in memory is faster than putting it on disk first. If the data is small enough, you can transform in memory, but if the data is big, you need to put it on disk first. Whether you can put the data into memory depends on how much memory the ETL server has.

The alternative to the two ETL approaches shown in Figure 7-1 is called Extract, Load, and Transform (ELT), as shown in the bottom half of Figure 7-2. In the ELT approach, we pull the data from the source systems, load it into the data warehouse, and then apply the transformation by updating the data in the warehouse. In the ELT approach, essentially we copy the source system (OLTP) data into the data warehouse and transform it there. People usually take the ETL approach if they have a strong ETL server and strong software that is rich with all kinds of transformation and data quality processes.

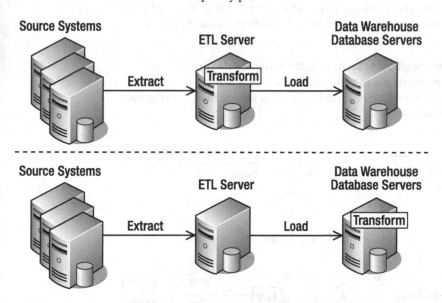

Figure 7-2. *ETL and ELT: choices of where to perform the transformations*

People usually take the ELT approach if they have a strong data warehouse database system, usually MPP database systems. Massively parallel processing (MPP) is a group of servers (called *nodes*), and each node has its own memory, processor, and disk. Examples of MPP database systems are Teradata, Netezza, and Neoview. When you cluster two or more SQL Servers, you get high availability and each node has its own memory and processor, but you still share the disks. In MPP database systems, each node has its own memory, processor, and disk. It is known as a *share nothing* architecture. An MPP database system is more powerful than systems with shared disks because data loading is happening in parallel across multiple nodes that have their own disks.

The main advantage of MPP database systems is that the performance increase is linear. If you put ten SQL Servers in an active-active cluster, the performance increases, but not 10✕ a single SQL Server. In MPP database systems, if you put in ten nodes, the performance is almost ten times the performance of a single node.

In terms of *who* moves the data out of the source system, we can categorize ETL methods into four approaches (see Figure 7-3):

- An ETL process pulls the data out by querying the source system database regularly. This is the most common approach. The ETL connects to the source system database, queries the data, and brings the data out.

- Triggers in the source system database push the data changes out. A database trigger is a collection of SQL statements that executes every time there is an insert, update, or delete on a table. By using triggers, we can store the changed rows in another table.

- A scheduled process within the source system exports the data regularly. This is similar to the first approach, but the program that queries the database is not an external ETL program. Instead, it is an *internal* exporter program that runs in the source system server.

- A log reader reads the database log files to identify data changes. A database log file contains a record of the transactions made to that database. A log reader is a program that understands the format of the data in the log file. It reads the log files, gets the data out, and stores the data somewhere else.

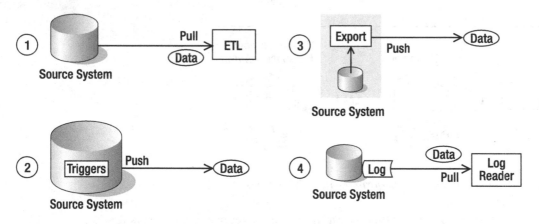

Figure 7-3. *Four ETL approaches based on who moves the data out of the source system*

In terms of *where* the processes that move the data out are executed, we can categorize ETL into three approaches (see Figure 7-4):

- Execute the ETL processes in a separate ETL server that sits between the source system and the data warehouse server. This approach provides the highest performance. The ETL runs on its own server, so it does not use the resources of the data warehouse server or the source system server at all. It is more expensive than the next two options because you have to purchase additional server and software licenses.

- Execute the ETL processes in the data warehouse server. This approach can be used if we have spare capacity in the data warehouse server or if we have a time slot when the data warehouse is not used (at night for example). It is cheaper than the first approach because we don't need to provide additional servers.

- Execute the ETL processes in the server that hosts the source system. This approach is implemented when we need real-time data warehousing. In other words, the moment the data in the source system changes, the change is propagated to the data warehouse. This is can be achieved using database triggers in the source system. In practice, this approach is implemented in conjunction with either of the previous approaches. That is, this approach is used only for a few tables, and the remaining tables are populated using the first two approaches.

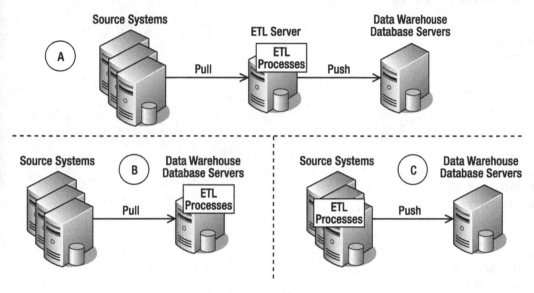

Figure 7-4. *Choices of where to put ETL processes*

General Considerations

The system we are extracting from may not be a database. It could be a file system, a queue, a service, or e-mails. If the data is in a database, usually we retrieve the data using ADO.NET, ODBC, OLEDB, JDBC, or proprietary database connectivity. These days, most databases are relational, but occasionally we come across hierarchical databases, such as Adabas and ISM, or sequential file storage, such as ISAM. To extract the data from them, we need to have the right database driver or write a data export script using the database-specific language.

If the data is in a file or files, it could be structured, semistructured, or unstructured. A structured file is like this:

```
ID      Date     Store   Product   Quantity
2893    2/1/08   32      A160      150
2897    2/4/08   29      B120      240
```

which is a fixed position file, meaning that the fields are in certain column positions. Or it could be like this:

```
ID|Date|Store|Product|Quantity
2893|2/1/08|32|A160|150
2897|2/4/08|29|B120|240
```

which is a delimited file. In this case, it is pipe delimited.

A structure file contains tabular (table) data, meaning that the data is essentially in columns and rows format. A semistructured file contains tabular data and nontabular data. A semistructured file looks like this XML file:

```
<order ID="2893">
    <date>2/1/08</date>
    <store>32</stores>
    <product>A160</product>
    <quantity>150</quantity>
</order>

<order ID="2897">
    <date>2/4/08</date>
    <store>29</stores>
    <product>B120</product>
    <quantity>240</quantity>
</order>

<customer ID="83">
    <name>John Smith</name>
    <email>jsmith@aol.com</email>
</order>
```

The first two sections (order data) are tabular, but the third one (customer data) is not tabular.

Unstructured data is like this: "On 2/1/2008 we received order ID 2893 from store 32, requiring 150 units of product A160. Three days later store 29 asked for 240 pieces of B120." It is the typical content of e-mails. We extract the information in unstructured data using text mining.

Sometimes, the data extraction can be done only during certain times, such as after a batch, or it cannot be done at certain times, such as at backup times or during month-end processing. Sometimes, if we are lucky, we can access the source data at any time, such as when there is a secondary read-only server specifically provided for ad hoc queries and ETL. Table 7-1 lists the potential problems in data extraction, the scenarios, and the common techniques in those scenarios.

Table 7-1. *Potential Problems in Data Extraction*

Potential Problem	Scenario	Common Technique to Overcome
Data is available only at certain times.	A long batch schedule runs overnight followed by a big database backup. Extracting data during the day would slow the OLTP.	Negotiate a time slot with the OLTP DBA. Break the extraction into smaller chunks.
The OLTP database is not available on certain days.	On the first day of every month, OLTP runs a month-end batch for the whole day.	Skip extraction on that day. Tell users the reasons for this limitation.
The OLTP DBA is concerned that our ETL could "mess up" their system.	The project team consists of external consultants who are just learning the OLTP internals.	Ask the DBA to give "read-only" access. Ask the OLTP DBA to export data for you.
There is a concern that ETL will strain/overload the OLTP database.	There are no "quiet times" because the OLTP is a global database.	Read from the secondary OLTP database. Use a less frequent extract for large tables, such as only Sundays.
The OLTP DBA is concerned that they can't stop ETL processes in an emergency.	There is an emergency situation in OLTP that requires server restart.	Tell the DBA they may terminate you at any time (tell them how) but rerun afterward (manual invoke).
They can't start ETL processes.	There is an OLTP backup overrun.	Program the ETL to rerun automatically later.

One of the most important things at this stage of the project (the beginning of ETL) is to get to the data, that is, to be able to connect to the source data. Sometimes it takes time to be in a position where we can query the source system (if it is a database) or read the files (if it a file system). Sometimes the source database server is physically located on another continent and there is no connectivity to that server. I've worked on several projects where we had to arrange for the network connectivity to be opened, that is, to allow certain TCP traffic to flow through the firewall so that we could get to the data. Table 7-2 lists the common reasons for not being able to get to the source data, as well as their common solutions.

Table 7-2. *Reasons for Not Being Able to Get the Source Data*

Reason	Common Solution
There is no connectivity to the target database, probably because of no routing or the traffic is blocked on the firewall.	Ask the network engineer to open the firewall. Provide the source IP address, the destination IP address, and the port number to open. Use the NATed IP address if required.
The target database requires a specific driver. We cannot use ODBC, ADO.NET, or OLEDB.	Obtain or purchase the driver and install it on the ETL server.
The target server name is not recognized.	Try it with IP first. If this works, ask the network team to add the name on the DNS. Some database systems such as Teradata add a suffix to the name.

Continued

Table 7-2. *Continued*

Reason	Common Solution
We can reach the database but cannot query because we have no access to the tables or views.	Ask the OLTP DBA to create two accounts: a personal account for development and a functional account for production. Always ask for read-only access.
The database version of the OLTP is newer than the driver on the ETL server.	Upgrade the driver.
The RDBMS requires a specific language or tool, such as Progress 4GL.	Either obtain the ODBC version of the driver (which accepts normal SQL queries) or ask the DBA to write a script to export the data.

In the next three sections, I'll discuss extracting data from databases, file systems, and other source types.

Extracting Relational Databases

After we connect to the source data, we can then extract the data. When extracting data from a relational database that consists of tables, we can use one of four main methods:

- Whole table every time
- Incremental extract
- Fixed range
- Push approach

Whole Table Every Time

We use the whole table every time when the table is small, such as with a table with three integer or varchar(10) columns consisting of a few rows. A more common reason is because there is no timestamp or identity column that we can use for knowing which rows were updated since the last extract. For example, a general decode table like Table 7-3 could be extracted using the "whole table every time" method.

Table 7-3. *A General Decode Table*

Table	Code	Description
PMT	1	Direct debit
PMT	2	Monthly invoice
PMT	3	Annual in advance
STS	AC	Active
STS	SU	Suspended
STS	BO	Balance outstanding
SUB	S	Subscribed
SUB	U	Unsubscribed
...		

This code-decode table is used throughout the system. Rather than creating a separate table for the payment code, customer status, subscription status, and so on, some business systems use a common table, that is, a single decode table serving the whole system. Of course, this is less flexible, but I've seen this implemented in a source system. Because there was no timestamp, no transaction date (it's not a transaction table), and no identity column either, there was no way we could possibly download the data incrementally, because we couldn't identify which rows were new, updated, or deleted. Luckily, the table was only about 15,000 rows and took about a minute to extract to the stage.

In my experience, a table that contains 1,000 to 5,000 rows (say 10 to 30 columns, or up to 500 bytes in width) on a 100Mbps LAN normally takes one to five seconds to download from DB/2 on an AS/400 using an iSeries OLE DB driver, or from Informix on Unix using an Informix native OLE DB driver into a staging table with no index in SQL Server 2005 or 2000 on a Windows 2000 or 2003 server, configured with RAID 5 for MDF and RAID 1 for LDF using 15,000 RPM disks, running on Dell 2850 with 8MB memory, performed using SSIS or DTS, with no transformation or scripting (just plain column-to-column mapping with data conversion). I cannot give you the formula of how to calculate the time it would take in your environment because different hardware and software configurations have different results, but I can give you a guide: you can estimate the time it would take in your production environment by measuring how long it takes to run the ETL routine on your development or test environment against the test OLTP system.

If the table is small enough, say up to 10,000 rows (this number is based on my experience; it may be different in your environment), it is usually quicker to download the whole table than to constrain the query with a certain where clause in the query. If we specify, for example, `select * from stores where (createtimestamp > 'yyyy-mm-dd hh:mm:ss' and createtimestamp <= 'yyyy-mm-dd hh:mm:ss') or (updatetimestamp > 'yyyy-mm-dd hh:mm:ss' and updatetimestamp <= 'yyyy-mm-dd hh:mm:ss')`, it will take the source database engine a few seconds to do the previous four comparisons with every row to identify the rows that we are looking for. This is especially true if the table is not indexed in any of those four columns (and most tables are not indexed in timestamp columns). It would be faster to put just `select * from stores` so that the source database engine can start returning the rows straightaway, without doing any preprocess calculation first.

For tables with fewer than 10,000 rows, I recommend you measure the time it takes to download the whole table and compare it with the time to download it incrementally with some constraints on. We can measure the time it takes to download by using SQL Profiler, by storing "before" and "after" timestamps into a table/file, or by looking at the SSIS log.

Incremental Extract

The transaction tables in major organizations are large tables, containing hundreds of thousands of rows or even hundreds of millions of rows (or more). It could take days to extract the whole table, which is a very disk-intensive operation, decreasing the transactional performance on the front-end application because of a database bottleneck. It is not a viable option (because of the time required to extract), so we need to find a way to extract the data incrementally.

Incremental extraction is a technique to download only the changed rows from the source system, not the whole table. We can use several things to extract incrementally. We can use timestamp columns, identity columns, transaction dates, triggers, or a combination of them. Let's explore and study these methods one by one.

Imagine that the order header table in Jade is like the one in Table 7-4.

Table 7-4. *Jade Order Header Table*

Order ID	Order Date	Some Columns	Order Status	Created	Last Updated
45433	10/10/2007	Some Data	Dispatched	10/11/2007 10:05:44	10/12/2007 11:23:41
45434	10/15/2007	Some Data	Open	10/16/2007 14:10:00	10/17/2007 15:29:02
45435	10/16/2007	Some Data	Canceled	10/16/2007 11:23:55	10/17/2007 16:19:03
...					

This table is ideal for incremental extract. It has a "created" timestamp column and a "last updated" timestamp column. It has an incremental order ID column. It has an order date that shows when the order was received.

First we need to check whether the timestamp columns are reliable. A reliable timestamp means that every time the row in the table changes, the timestamp is updated. This can be done by examining the value in both timestamp columns and comparing them with the order date. If they contain dummy values such as 1900-01-01, blank, or null, or if they differ from the order date significantly (say by five months), or if the "last updated" date is less than the "created" date, it's an indication that we may not be able to rely on them.

We can also do further checks by comparing the timestamp columns to the order ID column; that is, the created date of an order between order ID 1 and order ID 2 should be between their created dates. Note that this does not apply in situations where IDs are assigned in blocks to multiple DB servers. If the timestamp columns are in a good order, we can then use them for incremental extraction in SSIS as follows (see Figure 7-5).

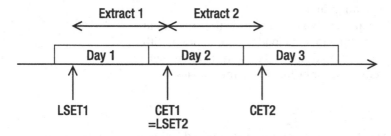

Figure 7-5. *Incremental extraction logic using LSET and CET*

Here's how to extract incrementally using the current extraction time (CET) and the last successful extraction time (LSET):

1. Retrieve the LSET from the metadata database. LSET acts like a watermark. It memorizes the time when data was last extracted.

2. Get the CET, which is passed in by the top-level ETL package. CET is the time the ETL package started, not when the current task started. The purpose of using the start time of the ETL package rather than the task start time is so that all ETL tasks in the package have the same CET so it's easier to restart if the package failed.

3. Extract the data using `select * from order_header where (created >= LSET and created < CET) or (last_updated >= LSET and last_update < CET)`.

4. If the extract is successful, update the metadata database by writing CET as the new LSET value.

This logic is fault tolerant, meaning that if it doesn't run or it failed to run, we could just rerun it with no risk of missing the data or loading data that we loaded earlier. For example, if the ETL has not been running for two days because of a connection problem to the source system (or the extraction failed for other reasons), it will pick up two days of data because the LSET would still be two days ago.

The purpose of restricting the upper limit with the CET is to exclude orders that were created after the ETL process started. This way, the next time the ETL process runs, it will pick up the orders created after the ETL process started. If we don't put CET as the upper limit, the orders created after the extract begins will be extracted twice.

If the timestamp is not in good order, we can use the order date column. It is a transaction date that reflects when the event happened. But we need to be careful when using the order date column. Although the two timestamp columns are system generated, the order date column is input. Therefore, it is possible that the operative set it to last week's data instead of today, because the order happened last week but just entered into the system today (past-dated orders).

If we apply the previous logic to the `order_date` column, we will miss past-dated orders. To pick up the past-dated orders, we need to add a grace period, as follows: `select * from order_header where order_date >= (LSET - 28 days) and created < CET`. The grace period is obtained from the business rule implemented in the source system application as a restriction or validation; for example, if you try to put the order date as 29 days ago, Jade wouldn't allow it and would generate an error message. This is not ideal, compared to a reliable last-updated date column, so use it as the last resort and test for data leakage (which I'll discuss in a moment).

If there is no source application restriction on the order date, another way of doing incremental extract is to use the order ID as follows (see Figure 7-5, where the logic is the same):

1. Retrieve the Last Successfully Extracted ID (LSEI) from the metadata database.

2. Select `max(order_id)` from `order_header`, and put this in CEI variable as the current extraction ID.

3. Extract the rows between the LSEI and CEI as follows: `select * from order_header where order_id >= LSEI and order_id < CEI`.

4. If the extract is successful, store the CEI in the metadata database as the LSEI.

The previous discussion of fault-tolerant and missed orders still applies; that is, the LSEI provides a fault-tolerant mechanism, and the CEI prevents the orders created after the extract begins from being missed. The past-dated orders and the grace period are also applicable.

How about deletion? How do we know which orders have been deleted? The source systems don't delete the order header records from the previous table. Instead, the orders that have been canceled are marked as canceled in the order status column. This is the ideal condition for ETL, which is known as a *soft delete*, meaning that they don't physically delete the record in the table but mark them only in certain columns.

If for some reason the rows are physically deleted, then there are two ways we can detect the deletion:

By comparing the primary key between the source table and the warehouse table: If we find a primary key that exists in the warehouse table but not in the source table, it means that the row was deleted from the source system. We can then mark the data warehouse row as deleted.

Using deletion trigger; that is, when a record is deleted, the trigger inserts a row into an audit or event table containing the primary key of the deleted row: The ETL then reads the audit table incrementally to find out which rows were deleted from the source system, and we mark the data warehouse rows as deleted.

In addition to detecting deletion, we can use triggers to detect updates and inserts too, which benefits us because it provides a means of capturing the data changes in the source system so we can extract incrementally. We can create separate triggers for delete, update, and insert. A trigger is the most reliable approach in ETL. It is the best way to detect the changes happening in the source systems. The drawback of installing triggers in the source system is an overhead of about 20 to 100 ms per trigger depending on the complexity (these are typical values; I've seen 16 and 400 ms too). This may or may not be a problem depending on your OLTP application, that is, whether it can wait that long or not for a database transaction to complete.

There is one thing we need to be careful of when installing triggers that insert the primary key of the deleted row into an event table: multiple updates. If we write the primary key only of the updated row, we may not be able to get the changed value if there is another update before we read the row. Here is the scenario: in the customer table, row 37 contains the name John. That row was updated at 10:47, changing the name to Alex. The update trigger fired and inserted the primary key of row 37 into the event table. At 10:48, row 37 was updated again, changing the name to David. The trigger fired again and inserted the primary key of row 37 into the event table again. When we read the event table, there were two rows there, both pointing at row 37. When we read the customer table, the name is now David. There is no way we can get the intermediate value (Alex) because it has been overwritten.

In some situations, it is acceptable not to get the intermediate value, but in certain cases it is not acceptable. If it is not acceptable, we can create an audit table that contains all the columns of the source table. When the update trigger fires, it inserts a row into the audit table containing the values of all columns of the updated row, as well as inserting a row into the event table containing just the primary key and a timestamp. Compared with implementing an event table, it takes more overhead to implement an audit table, but we can see the full history of data changes.

Fixed Range

If it is not possible to extract the whole table because the table is too large—and it is not possible to do incremental extraction, for example, because there are no timestamp columns or the timestamp columns are not reliable, because there is no reliable incremental identity column, and because it is not possible to install triggers in the source system—there is one more approach we can do. We can use the "fixed range" method.

Basically, we extract a certain number of records or a certain period of time. For example, say we extract the last six months of data, based on the transaction date. As before, we get the duration of the period from the source application if there is a restriction on the front-end application. For example, once the month-end processing is done, the rows can't be changed. In this case, we can download the last five weeks of data every time the ETL process runs or where the transaction date is after the month-end date.

If there is no transaction date column in the table and we cannot extract the whole table because it is a huge table, we can use the system-assigned row ID to extract a fixed range, such as the last 100,000 rows. What I meant by row ID is a hidden column in every table containing system-assigned sequential values. Not all database systems have row IDs; for example, Oracle and Informix have row IDs, but SQL Server and DB/2 don't. (In DB/2, the row ID is a data type, not a hidden column.) When using the row ID, we have no restrictions on the front-end application, so we need to monitor the source system and find out how many we need to extract every time. Download the primary key column(s) every day, and compare between each daily download to detect the changes. Identifying new rows and deleted rows by comparing primary keys is quite straightforward. Let's have a look at Table 7-5.

Table 7-5. *Comparing Daily Download to Detect New and Deleted Rows*

10/1	10/2	10/3	10/4	10/5
5467	5467	5467	5467	5467
8765	8765	3422	3422	3422
	3422	6771	6771	6771
			1129	1129

In this table, 8765 was deleted on 10/3, 6771 was created on 10/3, and 1129 was created on 10/4. But identifying updates is more difficult. For example, it seems that there are no new or deleted rows on 10/5, but in fact there is an update on row 3422. Updates can be detected using checksum, but we need to download the columns that we want to compare to the stage first, and this will be time-consuming if the table is large. Assuming table1 contains yesterday's data and table2 contains today's data, we can do the checksum comparison as illustrated here:

```
create table table1 (col1 int, col2 int, col3 int)
insert into table1 values(3434, 4565, 2342)
insert into table1 values(2345, 3465, 6321)
insert into table1 values(9845, 9583, 8543)
go
```

```
create table table2 (col1 int, col2 int, col3 int)
insert into table2 values(3434, 4565, 2342)
insert into table2 values(2345, 8888, 8888)
insert into table2 values(9845, 9583, 8543)
go

alter table table1 add col4 as checksum(col1, col2, col3)
alter table table2 add col4 as checksum(col1, col2, col3)
go

select * from table1
select * from table2
select * from table1 t1
where not exists
( select * from table2 t2
  where t1.col4 = t2.col4 )
go
```

After we are able to identify the changed rows, we can now define how far back we need to download the data every time the ETL process runs, that is, the last 10,000 rows, the last 100,000 rows, the last three weeks, the last two months, and so on.

Related Tables

If a row in the source table is updated, we need to extract the corresponding row in the related table too. For example, if order ID 34552 in the order header table is updated and extracted to the data warehouse, the rows for order ID 34552 in the order detail table need to be extracted to the data warehouse too, and vice versa. For example, if a row in the order detail is updated and that row is extracted into the data warehouse, the corresponding row in the order header needs to be extracted too.

This is also the case for inserts and deletes. If a new row (a new order) is inserted into the order header in the source system, the corresponding order detail rows need to be inserted into the data warehouse order detail table too. If a row is marked as canceled (soft delete) in the order header in the source system, the corresponding order detail rows need to be canceled too. We can do this in the data warehouse application too, but ideally it is done in the data warehouse database. If a row is physically deleted in the order header, it needs to be marked as deleted in the data warehouse order detail.

To do this, we identify the changed rows in the first table, and then using the primary key and foreign key relationship, we identify the rows in the second table, and vice versa. For example, in the case of the order header and order detail tables, we find the changed rows on the order header first, then we identify the changed rows in the order detail, and finally we extract *both sets of rows* from *both tables* into the data warehouse.

Testing Data Leaks

If we do either incremental extraction or period range extraction, it is essential that we test for data leaks. Say we think we have extracted all changes in the source system into our data warehouse. Now let's test it. We need to build the incremental or fixed-range ETL and run it every day (or four times a day or any other frequency). After a few weeks, we compare the number of rows between the source system and the data warehouse. Then we identify whether there are any missing rows or missing updates by comparing the checksum. That is, table1 contains the data from the ETL that has been running for two weeks, and table2 contains the data from the source system as it is today, so we compare the checksum columns from both tables:

```
select * from table2 where not exists
( select * from table1
  where table1.checksum_column = table2.checksum_column )
```

The reverse is also true. For rows that exist in table1 but do not exist in table2, use this:

```
select * from table1 where not exists
( select * from table2
  where table1.checksum_column = table2.checksum_column )
```

If we don't have any missing rows or any missing updates, then our incremental ETL process is reliable. Let it run for a few more weeks while you develop other parts of the DW system, and then do the previous test again. If you find missing rows, check your ETL logic, the LSET, the CET, and so on. If the ETL logic is correct, then consider another approach; for example, use a trigger to capture data changes or use a fixed-period extract if there is no reliable timestamp column.

If we extract from a relational database, it is very important to always test for data leaks. If we missed some rows or some updates, it means that the data in our data warehouse is not reliable. Remember that no matter how good the data warehouse functionality is, if the data in our warehouse is wrong, then it is unusable.

Extracting File Systems

The most common type of *files* acting as sources in the ETL process are flat files. Two examples of flat files, fixed-position files and pipe-delimited files, were shown earlier in the chapter. Flat files are common because they provide the best performance. Importing or exporting from a flat file is probably the fastest, compared to importing from other types of files (XML, for example). SQL Server's bulk insert and bulk copy utility (bcp) work with flat files.

bulk insert is a SQL command to load data from a file into a SQL Server table. bulk insert is executed from within the SQL Server query editor like a regular Transact SQL command. A typical usage of bulk insert is to load a pipe-delimited file into a table:

```
bulk insert table1 from 'file1' with (fieldterminator = '|')
```

The bulk copy utility is executed from a command prompt. To use the bulk copy utility to load data from a pipe-delimited file into a table, a typical usage is as follows:

```
bcp db1.schema1.table1 in file1 -c -t "|" -S server1 -U user1 -P password1
```

It is quite a common practice in data warehousing for the source system to export the data into flat files, and then an ETL process picks them up and imports them into the data warehouse. Here are some of the things you need to consider when importing from flat files:

- Agree with the source system administrator about the structure of the file system. This includes the file naming convention (fixed file name such as `order_header.dat` or dynamic file names such as `order_header_20071003.dat`), the directory structure (one directory per day), and so on. *Guidelines*: In my experience, it is more useful to use dynamic file names so we can leave the last *n* days of extract files on disk before deleting them.

- Make sure you have access to the agreed-upon location. It could be a shared network folder. It could be an FTP server. Whatever and wherever the location is, you need to have access to it. You may need permissions to delete files as well as read the files. Find out what user ID you must use to connect to the file server or FTP server. Do not underestimate this, because it can take a long time. *Guidelines*: Start raising the change requests for having read-write access to the file location as soon as possible. Do this for the development, QA, and production environments.

- Agree on the process; for example, after processing each file, do you need to delete the files or move them to an archive directory? If you move them to an archive directory, who will be deleting them from there later? How long will the files be stored in the archive directory? Will it be a year, six months, and so on? *Guidelines*: Determine the archive period based on backup procedure. That is, don't delete from disk before it's backed up to tape. Modify the extraction routine to include the movement of extracted files to the archive directory and to delete archived files older than the archive period.

- Agree on failure handling. For example, if for some reason the source systems are unable to produce the files yesterday, when their export process works again today, will the files be placed in the yesterday directory or the today directory? If both the yesterday and today data goes into the today directory, will it be two files or one file? *Guidelines*: I'd put them in the today directory. The main principle of failure handling is that the ETL process must be able to be rerun (or miss a run) without causing any problems.

- Agree on the frequency that the source systems run their export. Is it once a day, four times a day, and so on? *Guidelines*: This loading frequency depends on how often they export and on how often the business needs to see the data. The ideal loading frequency is the same as the export frequency (loading: put the data into the DW; exporting: retrieve the data from the source system).

- Agree on the file format. Will it contain a column heading, is it going to be a delimited file or a fixed-position file (delimiter is better, because the file sizes are smaller), what is the delimiter (don't use commas because the data can contain a comma; a pipe is a good choice), are you enabling Unicode (the 2-byte characters), what's the maximum line length, and what's the maximum file size? *Guidelines*: In my experience, it is not good to use tabs, commas, colons, backslashes, or semicolons. I usually test the OLTP data for pipes (|). If the data does not contain a pipe, then I use a pipe as the delimiter. Otherwise, I use a tilde (~) or this character: ¬. Both are rarely used/found in the data. Also test for newline characters, and if you find any, replace them when exporting.

- Agree on which columns are going to be exported by the source system and in what order. This is so that you can prepare column-to-column mapping for your import routine, whether you are using SSIS or bcp. *Guidelines*: For simplicity, consider leaving the order as is but choose and export only required columns. Refrain from exporting all columns. This is useful to minimize incremental extract size, especially if the table is very large (more than 1 million rows) and the data changes frequently.

If you are importing spreadsheet files such as Excel files, the guidelines are more or less the same as the previous ones. The main difference is that you don't need to worry about the delimiter. You can't use bcp or bulk insert for importing Excel files. In SQL Server we use SSIS for importing Excel files. Spreadsheets are quite commonly used for source files because they are widely used by the business users. For example, annual budgets or targets may be stored in Excel files.

Web logs are the log files of a web site, located within the web servers. Each web log is a text file containing the HTTP requests from the web browsers to the servers. It contains the client IP address, the date and time of the request, which page was requested, the HTTP code reflecting the status of the request, the number of bytes served, the user agent (such as the type of web browser or search engine crawlers), and the HTTP referrer (the page this request came from, that is, the previous page from which the link was followed).

People are interested in web logs because they can give useful browsing and shopping information in an e-commerce web site, that is, who browsed for what and when. The purpose of extracting from web logs into a data warehouse (instead of using web analysis software) is to integrate the web traffic data with the data already in the warehouse, such as to monitor the results of a CRM campaign, because the page requests in the campaign have additional query strings identifying the particular e-mail campaign from which they originated.

Web logs come in different formats. Apache HTTP Server 1.3 uses Common Log Format and Combined Log Format. IIS 6.0 uses W3C Extended Log Format. Once we know the format, we can parse each line of the log files into a separate entry/field, including the client IP address, username, date, time, service, server name, and so on. We can then map each field into a column in the data warehouse target table and load the data.

Although they're not as common as flat files and spreadsheets, database transaction log files and binary files can also be used as a source of ETL processes. Database transaction log files (in Oracle this is known as *redo logs*) are utilized by applying the transactions in the log files into a secondary copy of the database by using log shipping or by reading the files and processing them using specialized software (a different tool is used for each RDBMS). Transaction logs are very useful because we do not touch the primary database at all. They come at no cost to us. The transaction logs are produced and backed up for the purpose of recovering the database in the event of a failure. They are there doing nothing if you like. By reading them and extracting the transactions into our data warehouse, we avoid touching the source database. And the logs are quite timely too; for example, they contain a constant stream of data from the database. This is probably the only extraction method that does not touch the source relational database.

To do this, you need a specific tool or software that can read the transaction log files of your source system database. Different database systems have different log file formats and transaction log architecture. An example of such a tool or software is DataMirror. If the source system is a SQL Server, we can apply the transaction log files into a secondary server using log shipping. Then we read the data from the secondary server.

Binary files containing images, music samples, film trailers, and documents can also be imported into a data warehouse by using tools such as ADO.NET (or other data access technologies) and storing them as binary or varbinary data types in SQL Server tables.

These days, XML files are becoming more and more commonly used as source data in the ETL. We can use SSIS to read, merge, validate, transform, and extract XML documents into SQL Server databases. To do this, we use the XML task in the SSIS control flow and specify the operation type. Validation can be done using the XML schema definition (XSD) or document type definition (DTD). To do this, we specify the operation type as Validate in the SSIS XML task. Note that the DTD is now superseded by XSD. We can also use XML bulk load COM objects or OpenXML Transact SQL statements to read and extract XML documents. To use OpenXML, we call `sp_xml_preparedocument` first to get the document handle. We can then do `select * from openxml (doc handle, row pattern, mapping flag) with (schema declaration)` to read the content of the XML document.

Extracting Other Source Types

Relational database and flat files are the most common types of source data for the ETL processes of a data warehouse system. I have also briefly mentioned spreadsheet files, web logs, hierarchical databases, binary files, database transaction logs, and XML files. Other types of source data are web services, message queues, and e-mails. I'll discuss these types in this section so you can understand what they are, how they are normally used, and how to extract them in our ETL processes into a data warehouse.

A *web service* is a collection of functions that perform certain tasks or retrieve certain data, exposed by a web interface to receive requests from web clients. Well, we don't really extract a web service, but we *use* a web service to get the data. In a service-oriented architecture (SOA) environment, we don't access the database directly. Instead, the data is "published" using a collection of web services. We can, for example, request a list of products (with their attributes) that were updated in the last 24 hours.

The benefit of using a web service to get the data is that the source system can have a single, uniform mechanism to publish its data. All the consumers of this data are sure that the data they receive is consistent. I have been on a data warehouse project where the source system had already published its data using a web service so the data consumers (the data warehouse is one of them) can just tap into this service. Although this is fine for operational purposes where the data is a trickle feed (in other words, a small amount), the web service approach cannot be used for initial bulk loading where we need to load large volumes of data. The performance would be poor. For example, if each transaction takes tens or hundreds of milliseconds, it would take weeks or months to load millions of rows of initial data. We need to use another mechanism for initial data loading.

A message queue is a system that provides an asynchronous communication protocol, meaning that the sender does not have to wait until the receiver gets the message. System A sends messages to the queue, and system B reads the messages from the queue. A queue manager starts and stops the queue, cleans up unprocessed messages, sets threshold limits (maximum number of messages in the queue), logs the events, performs security functions such as authentications, deals with errors and warnings such as when the queue is full, governs the order of the queue, manages multicasting, and so on. To put a message queue into ETL context and to understand the implementation of message queues for ETL systems, let's go through an example from a project.

A source system captures the changes using insert, update, and delete triggers. The system has several event log tables to record the changes that happened in the system. At certain periods (typically between one and four hours, which is determined based on the business requirement, that is, how recent we need the DW data to be), the ETL routines read the event logs incrementally and retrieve the changed data from the source database using web services that return the data in XML format. The ETL routines then wrap the XML in outer envelopes (also in XML format) and send them as XML messages to message queues over a VPN. These message queues are located in the global data warehouse, so other subsidiary companies also use the same message queues for sending their data. The global data warehouse then reads the messages in the message queues in a multicast mode; that is, there were two redundant ETL routines reading each message from the same queue into two redundant relational stores within the data warehouse. In this case, the global data warehouse reads the MQ as an ETL source.

E-mails are stored in e-mail servers such as Microsoft Exchange and Java Email Server (JES). E-mails are accessed using application programming interfaces (APIs), Collaboration Data Objects (CDO), ADO.NET, or an OLEDB provider. For example, OLE DB for Exchange Server enables us to set up an Exchange Server as a linked server in SQL Server so that the e-mails stored in Exchange Server are exposed in a tabular form and so we can use a normal SQL select statement within SSIS to retrieve the data.

Extracting Data Using SSIS

Now let's try to extract data from Jade into the stage database using SSIS. Before we start, let's go through an overview of what we are going to do. To extract data from Jade into the stage database, in the next few pages we will be doing the following steps:

1. Create the source system database and a user login.
2. Create a new SSIS project.
3. Create data sources for Jade and the stage.
4. Create a Data Flow task.

5. Probe the source system data.

6. Create a data flow source.

7. Create a data flow destination.

8. Map the source columns to the destination.

9. Execute the SSIS package.

Before we open Business Intelligence Development Studio and start creating SSIS packages to extract data from Jade, we need to create a Jade database first. To simulate a Jade database, which in the Amadeus Entertainment case study is an Informix database, we will create a database called Jade in SQL Server. To create this database, we will restore it from a backup available on the Apress web site using the following steps:

1. Download the file called Jade.zip (about 6MB) from this book's page on the Apress web site at http://www.apress.com/.

2. Uncompress it to get Jade.bak from that file.

3. Put Jade.bak in your development SQL Server, say on c:\. This file is a backup of a SQL Server database named Jade, which we will use to simulate Jade as the source system.

4. Open SQL Server Management Studio, and restore the Jade database from Jade.bak, either by using SQL Server Management Studio or by typing the following in a query window, replacing [sqldir] with the SQL Server data directory:

```
restore database Jade from disk = 'c:\Jade.bak'
with move 'Jade_fg1' to '[sqldir]\Jade_fg1.mdf',
move 'Jade_log' to '[sqldir]\Jade_log.ldf'
```

We need a stage database for the target, and we created a stage database in Chapter 6. We also need to create a login to access Jade and the stage databases. To create a login called ETL with db_owner permission in both the stage and Jade databases, and with the default database set to the stage, do the following:

```
create login ETL with password = '[pwd]', default_database = stage
go
use Jade
go
create user ETL for login ETL
go
sp_addrolemember 'db_owner', 'ETL'
go
use Stage
go
create user ETL for login ETL
go
sp_addrolemember 'db_owner', 'ETL'
```

```
go
use Meta
go
create user ETL for login ETL
go
sp_addrolemember 'db_owner', 'ETL'
go
```

Replace [pwd] with a complex password that meets SQL Server security standards, or use Windows integrated security (Windows authentication mode). In the previous script, we also create a user for that login in the metadata database. This is to enable the ETL login to retrieve and store the extraction timestamp in the metadata database, which we will do in the next section.

Open Business Intelligence Development Studio. Click File ➤ New ➤ Project, select Integrated Services Project, and name the project **Amadeus ETL**. Click OK to create the project. The screen will look like Figure 7-6.

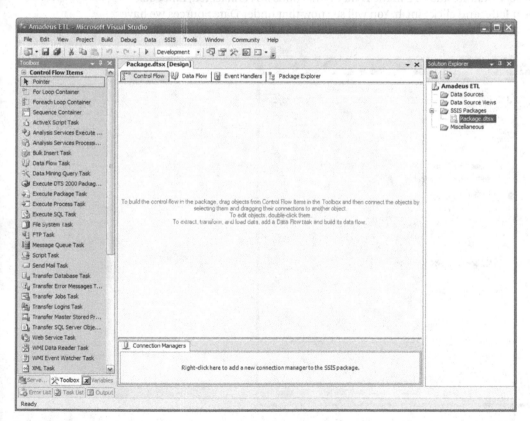

Figure 7-6. *Business Intelligence Development Studio initial project screen*

Now let's set up a data source for Jade:

1. In the top-right corner, right click Data Sources, and choose New Data Source. In the Data Source Wizard, click New.

2. In the Provider drop-down list, you would select IBM OLE DB Provider for Informix, but for this case study we will choose Microsoft OLE DB Provider for SQL Server in order to simulate the connection to Informix (in practice, if your source system is SQL Server, choose SQL Native Client).

3. Enter your development server name, select Use SQL Server Authentication, type **ETL** as the username along with the password, check "Save my password," and select Jade for the database name. If you use Windows integrated security, choose Use Windows Authentication.

4. The screen should look like Figure 7-7. Click Test Connection, and click OK.

5. Ensure that servername.Jade.ETL in the Data Connections box is selected, and click Next. Name it **Jade**, and click Finish. You will see now that under Data Sources we have Jade.ds.

Figure 7-7. *Using the Connection Manager dialog box to set up a connection to Jade*

Repeat the same process to set up another data source for the stage, as follows:

1. Choose SQL Native Client as the provider.

2. Type the server name, username, and password the same as before.

3. Enter the database name as **Stage**.

4. Click Test Connection, and click OK if succeeds.

5. Make sure servername.Stage.ETL in the Data Connections box is selected, and click Next.

6. Name it **Stage**, and click Finish. Notice that you now have two data sources in the top-right corner.

Double-click the Data Flow task in the Toolbox on the left side. A Data Flow task will appear in the top-left corner of the design surface. Double-click that Data Flow task in the design surface, and the design surface will change from Control Flow to Data Flow. Double-click OLE DB Source under Data Flow Sources in the Toolbox on the left side. The OLE DB Source box will appear in the design surface, as shown in Figure 7-8.

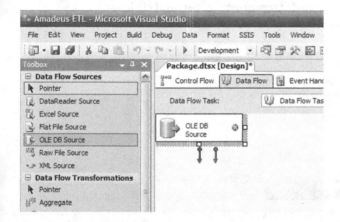

Figure 7-8. *Creating the OLE DB source in the Data Flow task*

When we are facing an unknown source system, we need to be careful. It could be a huge table containing 500 million rows. It could contain strange characters in Extended Binary Coded Decimal Interchange Code (EBCDIC). Perhaps we are not even familiar with the table names and column names. Perhaps we are even not familiar with the syntax of the SQL language in that platform. The last thing we want is to cripple that source system with our queries. Here I will illustrate how we can "probe" an unknown source system carefully.

First we need to know how many rows are in the source table. In practice, the source system may not be an SQL Server, so we can't query it directly. Therefore, we use SSIS to count the rows as follows:

1. Click the OLE DB Source box on the design surface.

2. Hit F2, and rename it to **Jade order_header**.

3. Double-click the "Jade order_header" box.

4. In the OLE DB Connection Manager, click New.

5. Select servername.Jade.ETL, and click OK.

6. In the Data Access Mode drop-down list, choose SQL Command.

7. Click Build Query, and Query Builder window opens.

8. Click the rightmost icon, Add Table. This is so that we know what the tables are in the source system.

9. Click Close.

10. In the SELECT FROM section of the window, type **select count(*) from order_header**, and click OK.

11. Click Preview. If it takes a long time and it shows a big number (such as a few million or more), we need to be careful not to extract the whole table.

12. Click Close to close the table list.

Modify the SQL Command Text box to say `select top 10 * from order_header`, and click Preview. Every RDBMS has a different syntax, as follows:

```
Informix: select first 10 * from order_header
Oracle: select * from order_header where rownum() <= 10
DB/2: select * from order_header fetch first 10 rows only
Mysql and Postgres: select * from order_header limit 10
Sybase: set rowcount 10; select * from order_header;
Teradata: select * from order_header sample 10
```

Figure 7-9 shows the result.

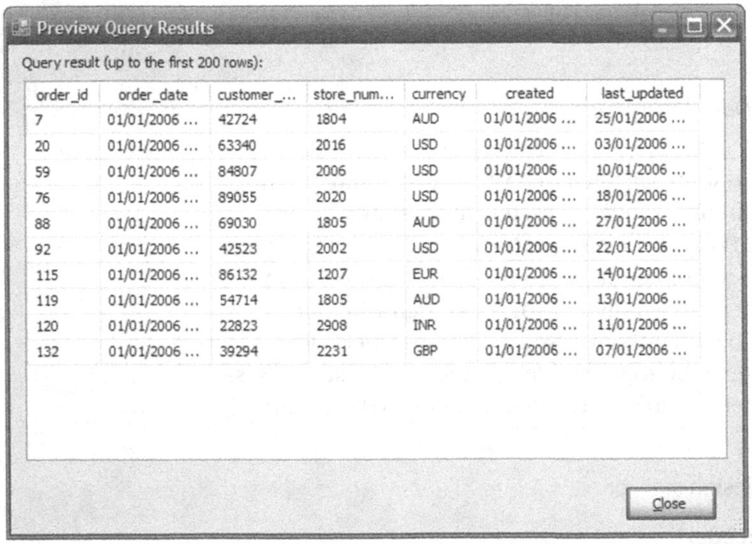

Figure 7-9. *Previewing the first ten rows*

This selection of the first ten rows has three purposes:

- To know the column names. We need these names for further queries. If the source system DBA provides us with the data dictionary, that's great. If not, here the names are. If you are familiar with the system tables of your source system and your user account has administrative privileges, you can query the source system metadata to get the column names. For example, in SQL Server it's catalog views, in Teradata it's DBC, and in Oracle it's system tables.

- To understand the content of the data for each column, scroll the window to the right. In particular, look for columns containing nonstandard characters (usually shown as little blank rectangles) and the date format.

- If count(*) is large, this "ten rows" query enables us to understand whether the source system has good response time or is very slow. If the table is huge but it is partitioned and indexed well, we should expect the first "ten rows" query to return in less than two seconds. Bear in mind that the response time is also affected by other factors such as system load, hardware and software configuration, throttling, and so on.

Then select the changed data by typing this in the SQL Command Text window:

```
select * from order_header
where (created > '2007-12-01 03:00:00'
and created <= '2007-12-02 03:00:00')
or (last_updated > '2007-12-01 03:00:00'
and last_updated <= '2007-12-02 03:00:00')
```

Change the dates to yesterday's date and today's date, and click Preview. Don't worry about the dates being hard-coded; later in this chapter you'll learn how to make this dynamic by retrieving and storing into the metadata database. Don't worry about the risk that it will return 400 million rows in 4 hours; SSIS will return only the first 200 rows because SSIS limits the output when previewing data. Scroll down and scroll to the right to examine the data. If everything looks all right, change the data access mode to Table or View, choose order_header as the name of table, click Preview, click Close, and then click OK.

Scroll down in the Toolbox. Under Data Flow Destination, double-click SQL Server Destination. The SQL Server Destination box will appear in the design surface. Click that box, press F2, and rename it to **Stage order header**. Resize the box if necessary. Click the "Jade order header" box, and pull the green arrow to the "Stage order header" box. Double-click the "Stage order header" box. In the "OLE DB connection manager" drop-down list, click New. In the Data Connection box, select servername.Stage.ETL, and click OK.

You can create the destination table in the stage manually, based on the source system column data types. You can also create it on the fly using the New button to the right of the table or the View drop-down list. I prefer to create it manually so I can be sure of the data types, table name, column name, constraints, and physical location/filegroup, as follows (of course you can use SQL Server Management Studio rather than typing the SQL statement):

```
create table order_header
( order_id            int
, order_date          datetime
, customer_number     int
, store_number        int
, created             datetime
, last_updated        datetime
) on stage_fg2
go
```

Click OK in Create Table window to create the order_header table in the stage database. In the table or view, choose order_header that we just created. Click Preview, and it shows an empty table. Click Close, and then click Mapping on the left side. Figure 7-10 shows the outcome.

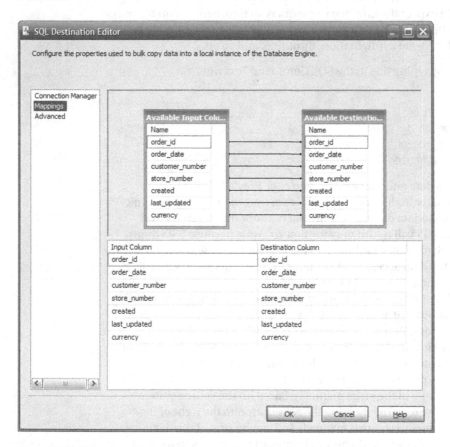

Figure 7-10. *Mapping source columns to the stage table columns*

If the column names are different, you need to map them manually. If the column names are the same, they are mapped automatically. Click OK to close this window. Press F5 or the green triangle icon in the toolbar to run the package. It will fail with a "Stage order_header" box marked in red, as shown in Figure 7-11.

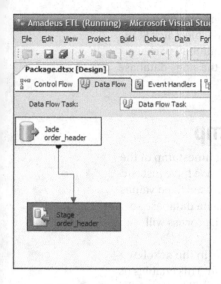

Figure 7-11. *Running the SSIS package*

Click the Progress tab. You will see that it says "You do not have permission to use the bulk load statement." Press Shift+F5 or the blue rectangle to stop running the package. SSIS shows the Execution Results tab, displaying the same error message. This is a common error. The cause was that the user ETL does not have the bulk insert.

Click the Data Flow tab, and then click the "Stage order_header" box. Scroll down the properties on the right side, as shown in Figure 7-12.

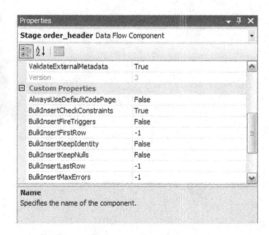

Figure 7-12. *Bulk insert properties*

The SQL Server destination uses the bulk insert to load data into SQL tables. Therefore, the login that we use needs to have a bulkadmin server role. You can use SQL Server Management Studio or SQL statement to assign this role. The SQL statement is sp_addsrvrolemember 'ETL', 'bulkadmin'.

Rerun the package. Now both boxes in the Data Flow tab should be green, meaning that SSIS has successfully imported those rows from the source table to the stage table. Click Stop, or press Shift+F5. Click the blue disk button (or select File ➤ Save) to save your SSIS package. Go to SQL Server Management Studio, and query the order_header table in the stage database to verify that you have the rows in the stage.

Memorizing the Last Extraction Timestamp

Memorizing the last extraction timestamp means that we memorize the last timestamp of the data we extracted so that on the next extraction we can start from that point. We have just successfully extracted the order header records from Jade into the stage. But we used fixed values for the date range. Now let's store the last extraction timestamp in the metadata database so that every time the ETL process runs it will extract different records. The ETL process will extract only those records that were added after the last extract.

Before we begin, let's go through an overview of what we are going to do. In the next few pages, we will use the last extraction timestamp to control the next extraction. This enables us to extract the source table incrementally. To do that, in the next few pages we will be doing the following steps:

1. Create a table in the metadata database to store the timestamps.

2. Create a data source for the metadata database.

3. Modify the data flow as follows:

    a. Store the current time.

    b. Get the last extraction timestamp from the table.

    c. Add timestamps to the extraction query as parameters.

    d. Update the timestamps in the table.

4. Clear the target table in the stage database.

5. Set the initial timestamps in the metadata table.

6. Execute the package to populate the target table.

So first, let's create the data_flow table as follows:

```
use meta
go

if exists
  ( select * from sys.tables
    where name = 'data_flow' )
drop table data_flow
go
```

```
create table data_flow
( id        int         not null identity(1,1)
, name      varchar(20) not null
, LSET      datetime
, CET       datetime
, constraint pk_data_flow
  primary key clustered (id)
)
go

create index data_flow_name
on data_flow(name)
go

declare @LSET datetime, @CET datetime
set @LSET = '2007-12-01 03:00:00'
set @CET = '2007-12-02 03:00:00'
insert into data_flow (name, status, LSET, CET)
  values ('order_header', 0, @LSET, @CET)
insert into data_flow (name, status, LSET, CET)
  values ('order_detail', 0, @LSET, @CET)
insert into data_flow (name, status, LSET, CET)
  values ('customer', 0, @LSET, @CET)
insert into data_flow (name, status, LSET, CET)
  values ('product', 0, @LSET, @CET)
go
```

Note LSET stands for Last Successful Extraction Timestamp, and CET means Current Extraction Timestamp.

Verify that we have that order_header row in the data_flow table: select * from data_flow. You should see four rows, as shown in Table 7-6.

Table 7-6. data_flow *Table*

id	name	LSET	CET
1	order_header	2007-12-01 03:00:00.000	2007-12-02 03:00:00.000
2	order_detail	2007-12-01 03:00:00.000	2007-12-02 03:00:00.000
3	customer	2007-12-01 03:00:00.000	2007-12-02 03:00:00.000
4	product	2007-12-01 03:00:00.000	2007-12-02 03:00:00.000

OK, now let's modify our order_header Data Flow task in our Amadeus ETL package so that it first sets the CET to the current time and then reads the LSET. If the data flow is successfully executed, we update the LSET and status for that data flow. If it fails, we set the status to fail, and we don't update the LSET. This way, the next time the data flow is run, it will pick up the records from the same LSET.

So, let's create a new data source called Meta that connects to the metadata database using the ETL user. The procedure is the same as the last time. This is why in the previous section, when we created the Jade database, we also assigned the user ETL as db_owner in the metadata database. Now we will set the CET to the current time for all rows.

1. In the Toolbox on the left side, double-click the Execute SQL task. There will be a new box on the design surface labeled Execute SQL Task. Right-click, and rename this box as **Set CET**.

2. Double-click this box. In the SQL Statement section, click the Connection drop-down list, and select <New connection...>, as shown in Figure 7-13.

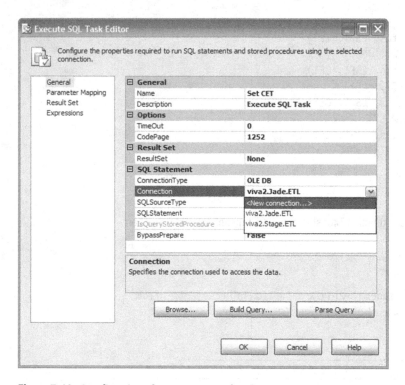

Figure 7-13. *Configuring the connection for the Execute SQL Task*

3. Choose the servername.Meta.ETL data connection, and click OK.

4. In the SQL Statement field, type update data_flow set CET = getdate() where name = 'order_header'. Click OK to close the Execute SQL Task Editor dialog box.

In steps 5 to 7 we are going to retrieve the last successful extraction time and the current extraction time from the data flow metadata table.

5. In the Toolbox, double-click the Execute SQL task again to create a new task in the design surface. Rename this box to **Get LSET**.

6. Double-click the box to edit it. Set the connection to servername.Meta.ETL. Set Result-Set to Single Row.

7. In the SQL Statement field, type **select LSET, CET from data_flow where name = 'order_header'**. Click Parse Query to verify.

   In steps 8 to 12, we are going to store the query result in variables. They will be used later to limit the order header query.

8. In the left column, click Result Set. Click Add. Change NewResultName to **LSET**.

9. Click the Variable Name cell, expand the drop-down list, and choose <New variable...>. Leave the container set to Package, which means that the scope of the variable is the SSIS package, not just the Get LSET task, which means we can use the variable in other tasks.

10. Change the name to **dtLSET**. Leave Namespace set to User.

11. Change Value Type to **DateTime**. Set the value as **2007-10-01 00:00:00** (or any date you like), and click OK.

12. Click Add again to add another variable. Set Result Name as **CET** and Variable Name as a new variable called **dtCET** of type DateTime. The result will look like Figure 7-14.

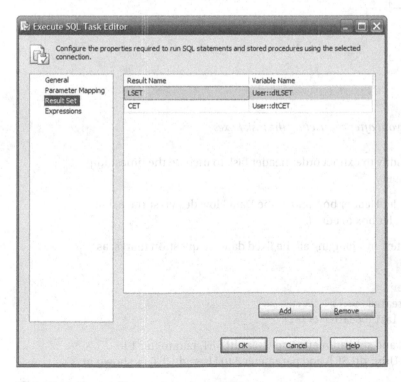

Figure 7-14. *Storing the result set in variables*

13. Click OK to close the Execute SQL Task Editor dialog box.

In steps 14 to 16 we will connect the tasks on the design surface and tidy up the layout.

14. Connect the green success arrow from the Set CET box to the Get LSET box. Rename the Data Flow task to **Extract Order Header**, and connect the green arrow from the Get LSET box to this box.

15. In the Toolbox, double-click the Execute SQL task to create a new box, and rename it to **Set LSET**. Connect the green arrow from Extract Order Header box to this Set LSET box.

16. Let's tidy up the layout a little bit. In the menu bar, select Format ➤ Auto Layout ➤ Diagram. The result looks like Figure 7-15.

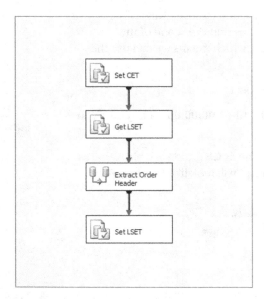

Figure 7-15. *Arranging the layout after connecting the task boxes*

In steps 17 to 20, we will modify to extract order header task to include the timestamp as parameters to limit the query.

17. Double-click the Extract Order Header box, and in the Data Flow design surface double-click the Jade Order Header box to edit it.

18. Update the SQL command text by changing all the fixed dates to question marks, as follows:

```
select * from order_header
where (created > ? and created <= ?)
or (last_updated > ? and last_updated <= ?)
```

19. Click the Parameter button, and set parameter 0 to User::dtLSET, parameter 1 to User:dtCET, parameter 2 to User::dtLSET, and parameter 3 to User::dtCET, as shown in Figure 7-16.

Figure 7-16. *Making the date range in the Data Flow task dynamic*

20. Click OK, and click OK again to close the windows and return to the data flow design surface.

In steps 21 to 22 we will modify the Set LSET task to update the timestamps stored in the `data_flow` table.

21. On top of the design surface, click the Control Flow tab. Double-click the Set LSET box, and set the connection to servername.Meta.ETL.

22. Set the SQL statement to `update data_flow set LSET = CET where name = 'order_header'`, and click OK. Save the package by pressing Ctrl+S.

In steps 23 to 25, we will prepare for the package execution by emptying the target table and setting the timestamp value.

23. Before we run the package, delete all rows from the `order_header` table in the stage, as follows: `truncate table stage.dbo.order_header`.

24. Set the CET column for `order_header` on the `data_flow` table in the metadata database to yesterday's date and the LSET column to the day before yesterday, as follows: `update meta.dbo.data_flow set LSET = getdate()-2, CET = getdate()-1 where name = 'order_header'`.

25. Verify the rows in Jade's `order_header` table that we are going to extract by using the following query:

```
select * from jade.dbo.order_header
where (created between getdate()-1 and getdate())
or (last_updated between getdate()-1 and getdate())
```

Note how many rows this query returns.

In steps 26 to 29, we will execute the package and check the execution results.

26. Go back to Business Intelligence Development Studio, and press F5 (or click the green triangle button in the toolbar) to run the package. All four boxes become yellow and then green one by one, as shown in Figure 7-17.

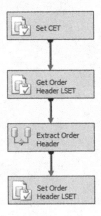

Figure 7-17. *Running SSIS package that memorizes the last extraction time*

27. If one of them becomes red, don't panic. Click the last tab (Progress) and see the error message. You can debug by right-clicking the boxes on the control flow and choosing Edit Breakpoints. The Set Breakpoints dialog box will pop up, as shown in Figure 7-18, and you can choose when you want the breakpoint to occur. You can also specify whether the breakpoint always happens or only at a certain count, that is, how many times the breakpoint is ignored before the execution is stopped.

You can also see the value of the variable by clicking the Watch 1 or Locals tabs in the bottom-left corner of the screen. Figure 7-19 shows that we can observe the value of the local variables when the execution is suspended at a breakpoint. For example, the value of user variable dtCET_OH is 06/10/2007 21:47:22 and the data type is DateTime.

28. Press Shift+F5 to stop the package running. Click the Execution Results tab, and verify that all tasks were executed successfully.

29. Open SQL Server Management Studio, and check that the LSET and CET columns for order_header in the data_flow table in the metadata database are updated correctly to current time. Also check that order_header in the stage database contains the correct number of rows from the Jade order_header table, as noted earlier.

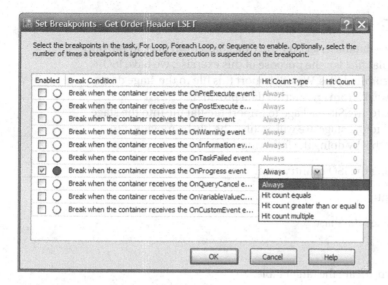

Figure 7-18. *Setting up a breakpoint*

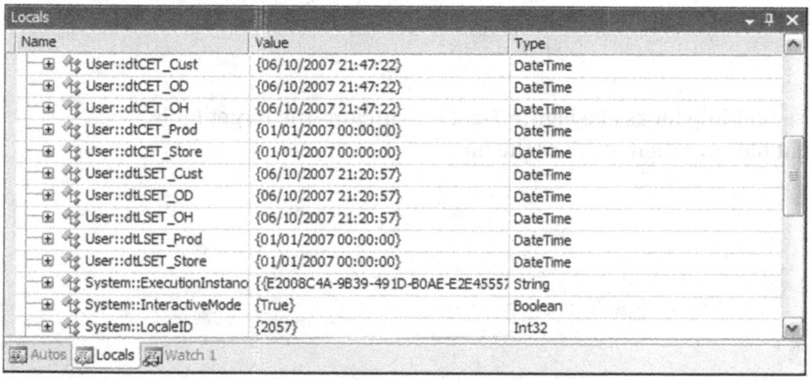

Figure 7-19. *The Locals window showing the variable value and data type*

30. At the moment, the name of the SSIS package in Solution Explorer is Package.dtsx. Rename it to order_header.dtsx by right-clicking it. When asked "Do you want to rename the package object as well," click Yes. By default SSIS renames only the package file, but internally the object name is not changed (you can see the object name by clicking the View menu and choosing Properties Window). By answering yes, we rename the package object as well as the package file.

31. Click the File menu, and choose Save All to save the entire solution. Click the File menu, and choose Close Project to close the package.

With that, we're finished going through the basics of extracting data incrementally from a relational database. Before we close this chapter, let's do a data extract from a file because in real data warehouse projects this happens a lot.

Extracting from Files

Now that we have extracted data from a database, let's try to extract data from files. In the next few pages, we will extract data from a flat file. For the purpose of this exercise, we have ISO country data supplied to us in pipe-delimited files. We will import this file to the stage database. The file will be supplied once a week, from an external data provider.

In the following pages we will create an SSIS package to import the flat file into the stage database. After importing successfully to the stage, we will archive the file by moving it to another directory. We will accomplish this by doing the following steps:

1. Download the flat file containing the ISO country data.

2. Open the flat file to see the content.

3. Create the target table in the stage database.

4. Create a new SSIS package.

5. Create an Execute SQL task to truncate the target table.

6. Create a Data Flow task to load the flat file to the stage database.

7. Create a File System task to archive the file.

8. Execute the package.

The SSIS package that we are building looks like Figure 7-20. It truncates the target table, extracts data from the country flat file, and then archives the file.

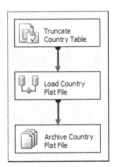

Figure 7-20. *SSIS package to extract data from file*

OK, so let's get started. First download the flat file from the book's web site at http://www.apress.com/. It is located in the folder /data/external. The file name is country.dat (8KB). Put this file in your local drive, for example: c:\.

Let's open the country.dat file using Notepad to see the content. It looks like this:

```
Code|Country
ad|Andorra
ae|United Arab Emirates
af|Afghanistan
ag|Antigua and Barbuda
ai|Anguilla
al|Albania
```

This consists of two columns, and it is pipe delimited. The first column is a two-character ISO country code, and the second column is the country name. The first line contains the column header: Code for the first column and Country for the second column.

Now that we know the content and format of the file, let's create the SSIS package to load this file into the stage. But before that, we need to create the stage table first. If we look at the data file, the longest country name is 34 characters (Saint Tome (Sao Tome) and Principe), so for this exercise we will set the width of the country name column to 50 characters. Let's open Management Studio and create the target table called country on the stage database as follows:

```
create table country
( country_code      char(2)
, country_name      varchar(50)
)
```

Now we can create the SSIS package:

1. Open Business Intelligence Development Studio, and open the Amadeus ETL project (select File ➤ Open ➤ Project, navigate to Amadeus ETL.sln, and double-click it).

2. In Solution Explorer, right-click SSIS Packages, and choose New SSIS Package. A blank design surface opens.

3. To be able to run the package many times, we need to truncate the target table before we load the data. Click the Control Flow tab, and double-click the Execute SQL task in the Toolbox.

4. Rename the box **Truncate Country Table**, and double-click the box to edit it. Set the connection to servername.Stage.ETL.

5. Set the SQL statement to truncate table country, and click OK. Click OK again to close the Execute SQL Task Editor dialog box.

6. Now let's create a Data Flow task to load the flat file to the stage database. Double-click Data Flow Task in the Toolbox, and rename the new box **Load Country Flat File**. Connect the green arrow from Truncate Country Table to Load Country Flat File.

7. Double-click Load Country Flat File to edit it. Let's add the country flat file as a source. Double-click Flat File Source in the Toolbox, and rename the new box **Country Flat File**.

8. Double-click the Country Flat File box, and click the New button.

9. The Flat File Connection Manager Editor dialog box opens, as shown in Figure 7-21. Set the name and description as Country Flat File, click Browse, and choose the country.dat file you downloaded earlier. Set the other properties as shown on Figure 7-21.

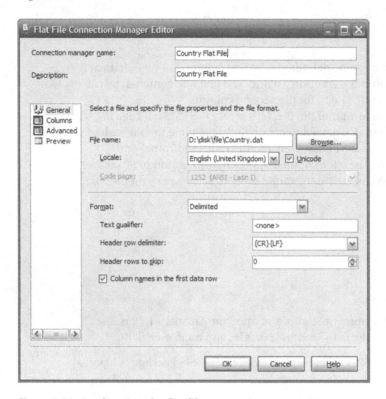

Figure 7-21. *Configuring the flat file connection properties*

10. In the pane on the left, click Columns, and specify the column delimiter as Vertical Bar {|}. Leave the row delimiter as {CR}{LF}.

11. Because the country code is two characters wide, we need to set the output column width accordingly. In the page on the left, click Advanced, and change the Output-ColumnWidth for the Code column from 50 to 2, as shown in Figure 7-22. Leave the Country column width as 50 because this column is 50 characters, as we discussed earlier.

12. Click OK to close the Flat File Connection Manager Editor and return to the Flat File Source Editor window. Click Preview to see the sample data, and then click Close. Click OK return to the design surface.

13. Now let's create a Data Conversion transformation to convert the flat file output, which is in Unicode, to suit the column on target table, which is an ANSI character string. Double-click the Data Conversion transformation in the Toolbox, and connect the green arrow from Country Flat File to Data Conversion.

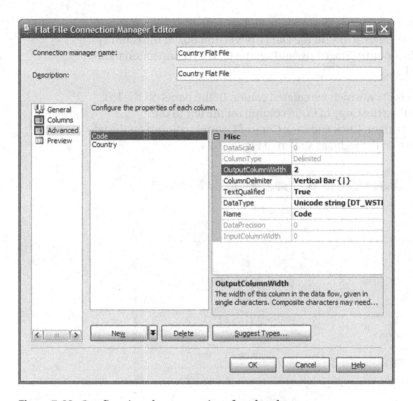

Figure 7-22. *Configuring the properties of each column*

14. Double-click Data Conversion to edit it, and check both the Code and Country columns under Available Input Columns. In the Data Type column, choose string [DT_STR] for both the Code and Country columns, as shown in Figure 7-23.

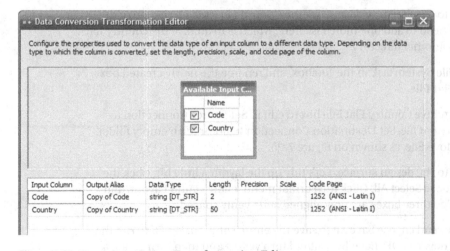

Figure 7-23. *Data Conversion Transformation Editor*

15. In the Toolbox, double-click SQL Server Destination, and rename the new box to **Country Stage**. Connect the green arrow on the Data Conversion box to the Country Stage box. Double-click the Country Stage box, and set the OLE DB connection manager to servername.Stage.ETL.

16. Set "Use table or view" to country, which we created earlier. In the panel on the left, click Mappings. Click and drag the Copy of Code column on the left to the country_code column on the right. Click and drag Copy of Country column on the left to the country_name column on the right, as shown in Figure 7-24.

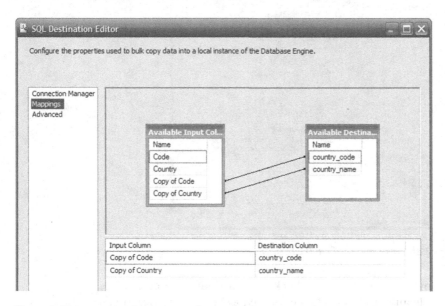

Figure 7-24. *Mapping the source columns to the target columns*

17. Click OK to return to the design surface. Click the Control Flow tab on the top of the design surface. We need to add one more task here, which is to archive the country flat file by moving it to another directory.

18. Double-click the File System task in the Toolbox, and rename the newly created box **Archive Country Flat File**.

19. Double-click the Archive Country Flat File box to edit it. Set Source Connection to point to the country flat file. Set Destination Connection to point to an empty folder. Set Operation to Move File, as shown on Figure 7-25.

20. Click OK to return to the design surface. Let's tidy up the layout a little bit. Click the Edit menu, and choose Select All. Click the Format menu, choose Auto Layout, and choose Diagram. The three boxes are now aligned and evenly spaced.

21. Click the File menu, and choose Save All to save the entire solution. Hit F5 to run the package. It should now run OK. Each box should turn yellow and then turn green, as shown in Figure 7-26.

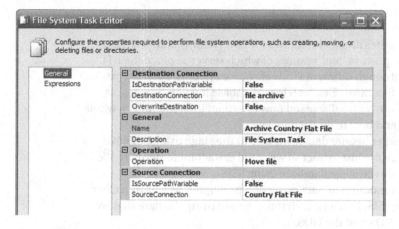

Figure 7-25. *Configuring the File System task to archive the file*

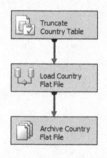

Figure 7-26. *Importing country data from flat files into the stage*

Even though we are not extracting incrementally here, we still have to add the metadata bit as we did previously when extracting the order header. This means we need to store the last successful run timestamp in the data_flow table. Recording the result of every single ETL data flow is important so that when the ETL fails and we want to restart from failure, we know where to restart from because we know which tasks were successful and which tasks failed to run. We do this by storing the execution result in the same data_flow metadata table as shown in Figure 7-27. (I will be discussing metadata in Chapter 10.)

key	name	status	LSET	CET
1	stg_order_header	2	2007-10-06 21:20:57.730	2007-10-06 21:47:22.750
2	stg_order_detail	2	2007-10-06 21:20:57.730	2007-10-06 21:47:22.750
3	stg_customer	2	2007-10-06 21:20:57.730	2007-10-06 21:47:22.750
4	stg_product	2	2007-10-06 21:20:57.730	2007-10-06 21:47:22.750
5	stg_product_status	1	2007-04-22 13:13:58.560	2007-04-22 13:13:58.560
6	stg_product_category	1	2007-04-22 13:13:58.560	2007-04-22 13:13:58.560
7	stg_product_type	1	2007-04-22 13:13:58.560	2007-04-22 13:13:58.560
27	stg_country	1	2007-10-07 16:43:19.733	2007-10-07 16:43:19.733

Figure 7-27. *The* data_flow *metadata table stores execution status, the LSET, and the CET*

Summary

This chapter started with the approaches and architectures for ETL systems, that is, ETL, ELT, using a dedicated ETL server or not, push vs. pull, choices of which server to place the ETL processes, and so on. Then it went through different kinds of source systems, such as relational databases, spreadsheets, flat files, XML files, web logs, database log files, images, web services, message queues, and e-mails. It also discussed how to extract incrementally a whole table every time using fixed ranges and how to detect data leaks.

Then I showed how to extract order header data from Jade to the stage using SSIS. We put some processes in place to memorize the last extract so we could extract incrementally. We also extracted the country flat file into the stage database using SSIS.

This chapter gave you a good foundation of data extraction principles, as well as a clear understanding of how to do it using SSIS. In the next chapter, we will bring the data that we have imported to the stage into the NDS and the DDS.

■ ■ ■

CHAPTER 8

Populating the Data Warehouse

Now that we have extracted the data from the source system, we'll populate the normalized data store and dimensional data store with the data we have extracted. In this chapter, I will discuss five main subjects regarding data warehouse population in the sequence they occur in a data warehouse system:

1. *Loading the stage*: We load the source system data into the stage. Usually, the focus is to extract the data as soon as possible without doing too much transformation. In other words, the structure of the stage tables is similar to the source system tables. In the previous chapter, we discussed the extraction, and in this chapter, we will focus on the loading.

2. *Creating the data firewall*: We check the data quality when the data is loaded from the stage into the NDS or ODS. The check is done using predefined rules that define what action to take: reject the data, allow the data, or fix the data.

3. *Populating a normalized data store*: This is when we load the data from the stage into the NDS or ODS, after the data passes through the data firewall. Both are normalized data stores consisting of entities with minimal data redundancy. Here we deal with data normalization and key management.

4. *Populating dimension tables*: This is when we load the NDS or ODS data into the DDS dimension tables. This is done after we populate the normalized data store. DDS is a dimensional store where the data is denormalized, so when populating dimension tables, we deal with issues such as denormalization and slowly changing dimension.

5. *Populating fact tables*: This is the last step in populating the data warehouse. It is done after we populate the dimension tables in the DDS. The data from the NDS or ODS (or from the stage, depending on the architecture; see Chapter 2) is loaded into DDS fact tables. In this process, we deal with surrogate key lookup and late-arriving fact rows.

In this chapter, I will also discuss and compare batches, mini-batches, and the near real-time approach, because the latter two approaches are becoming more and more popular these days. I will close the chapter by discussing real-time ETL, which means that the data is pushed into the warehouse rather than being pulled.

I will also cover how to use SSIS for populating the NDS and managing data warehouse keys and how to use SSIS to populate the dimension tables and fact tables in the DDS. I will also show how to use related SSIS tasks and transformations (such as the Slowly Changing Dimension transformation, the Lookup transformation, and the Execute SQL task) to populate NDS and DDS.

Stage Loading

In the previous chapter, we extracted the data from the source system into a stage. The stage can be a file system or a database.

When using files as a data warehouse stage, it is necessary to plan the file naming and directory structure carefully, in particular when incorporating the dates into the file names or directory names. We need to have access rights and permission to the stage folders. We need to define the deletion and archiving process, the failure handling, and the loading frequency. Most important, we need to define the details of the file format. Capacity on the allocated disk is also important at the planning stage. This is a simple point but has caused problems, so ensure that you won't run out of disk space, and ensure that your ETL process will be able to handle this situation gracefully rather than abruptly. The disk space for the stage area is planned based on the maximum daily data extraction volume from the source system and how long we will be archiving the data for.

If your stage is a database, which is common, it is better *not* to put any indexes or constraints (such as not null, primary keys, or check constraints) in the stage database. The main reason for this is not because of performance but because we want to capture and report the "bad data" in the data quality process. We want to allow bad data such as null and duplicate primary keys into the stage table so we can report it. If we restrict our stage table to reject null and duplicate primary keys, then the data quality process that sits between the stage and the NDS would not be able capture these DQ issues and report them for correction in the source system. For example, if we restrict the stage table with a unique constraint on the primary key column, when we have two duplicate rows, the second row will not be inserted into the stage. It is better to allow them into the stage. This way, when we populate the NDS, we can implement a set of comprehensive and stringent rules that filter out bad data into the data quality quarantine area for reporting and further processing such as cleansing, fixing, reimporting, or archiving.

Indexing stage tables is generally not necessary. This is because of the way the stage tables are structured and selected. The best way to do this is to load the data into empty stage tables without any indexes and then select all records from those tables for loading into the NDS. If you plan to keep, say, five days of stage data, in case you need them in the event of failures, it is better not to keep the previous day's data in the same table. The first reason why we can't go back to the source system and restage is because the source system data may have changed. The second reason is performance. In other words, it is quicker to reload the NDS from the stage than to retrieve data from the source system again.

Figure 8-1 shows three different approaches of how stage tables are structured:

Approach 1 keeps the previous day's data in the same table: This approach is simple to implement because you have only one table. You store the time each record was loaded into the stage table by having a column called `loaded_timestamp` in the stage table. The `loaded_timestamp` column is a datetime column that indicates when the record was loaded into the stage.

Approach 2 keeps each day in a separate table: Even though it is more complex than approach 1, approach 2 gives better performance because you load into an empty table and select all records when retrieving the data. When implementing approach 2, you create the Today table before the loading begins and drop the Day 1 table after the loading has completed successfully.

Approach 3 is to have just one table and truncate the table every time before loading: This approach is even simpler than approach 1. We don't keep the previous day's data in the stage database. If we need to restore the stage data retrieved a few days ago, we have to restore from database backup. Well, the number of days of the stage database backup to keep is different for each company. It is determined based on the extraction frequency (from the source system into the stage) and the loading frequency (from the stage to the NDS, ODS, or DDS).

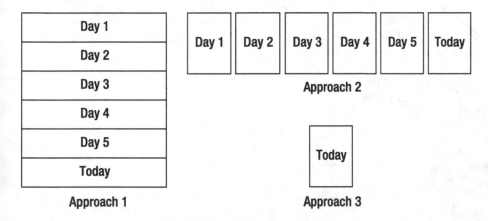

Figure 8-1. *Different approaches for stage loading*

I said earlier that indexing the stage table is *generally* not necessary. So, when is it necessary to index the stage table? It may be necessary to index a stage table when you implement approach 1 (keeping the previous day's data in the same table) and the stage table is used by multiple applications, not just the data warehouse. It depends on the data volume. In other words, indexing is useful only if the volume is large enough. In this case, indexing the stage table on the `loaded_timestamp` column will assist the application's ETL in selecting the rows relevant to a particular day when loading from the stage into the application's data store.

Data Firewall

The data firewall is important in data warehousing because the data firewall blocks bad data from going into the data warehouse. In this section, I will discuss what a data firewall is and how it is used to filter out bad data.

The term *data firewall* was probably inspired by the functionality of a firewall in networking. In networking, when you have a firewall between network segments, by default everything is blocked. So, to have connectivity between segment A and segment B, you need to allow certain network traffic through the firewall. It is like making a hole in the firewall. The "hole" is different for each type of network traffic, meaning that when you allow certain network traffic through the firewall, you have to specify the type of traffic. You do this by specifying the port number. For example, the hole for web HTTP traffic is different from the hole for ODBC traffic.

To help visualize this, please refer to Figure 8-2. The figure shows three holes. Each hole is applicable only for a certain type of network traffic. For argument's sake, let's say that the circle hole allows HTTP traffic, the rectangle hole allows ODBC traffic, and the triangle hole allows FTP traffic. Each hole on the firewall has a specific purpose.

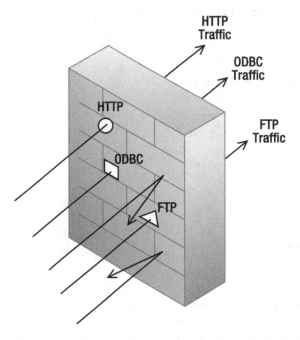

Figure 8-2. *Different holes in the firewall are for different types of traffic.*

The concept of a data firewall is similar to the firewall concept in networking. The data firewall is a program that checks the incoming data. Physically, it is an SSIS package or a stored procedure. We place a data firewall between the stage and the NDS, which will allow or reject data depending on the data quality rules that we set. Like network firewalls, data firewalls also have mechanisms to report what data has been rejected, by what rule, and when.

This is because every time the data firewall captures or finds bad data (as defined by the data quality rule), the bad data is stored in the data quality database, along with which rule was used to capture the bad data, what action was taken, and when it happened. We can then report from this data quality database. We can also set the data quality system to notify the appropriate people when certain data quality rules are violated.

Unlike a network firewall, a data firewall can also fix or correct bad data. When the data firewall detects bad data, we can set it to do one of these three actions: reject the data (not load it into the data warehouse), allow the data (load it into the data warehouse), or fix the data (correct the data before loading it into the data warehouse).

A data firewall is an important part of data warehouse loading because it ensures data quality. Before we load the data into the normalized data store (or into a DDS if we use DDS-only architecture), we check the data by passing the data through firewall rules.

Populating NDS

In the NDS + DDS architecture, we need to populate the tables in the NDS before we populate the dimension and fact tables in the DDS. This is because we populate the DDS based on the NDS data. Populating a normalized data store is quite different from populating the stage. This is because when populating the NDS, we need to normalize the data, while when populating the stage, we don't need to normalize the data. We extract some data from the stage table or straight from the source system and then load it into the NDS database. If the record does not exist in the NDS, we insert it. If the record already exists, we update it.

When populating the NDS, we need to consider several issues:

Normalization: In the NDS, the tables are normalized, so when loading the data from the stage, we need to normalize it to fit the NDS structure. This means we need to populate certain tables first before we can populate the main table.

External data: It is possible that the data from external sources does not match the data from the source system. This means that when we load data into the NDS, we may need to do some data conversion.

Key management: In the NDS, we need to create and maintain internal data warehouse keys, which will also be used in the DDS. When loading data into the NDS, we need to manage these keys.

Junction tables: The junction tables enable us to implement many-to-many relationships. When populating junction tables, we need to follow a certain sequence.

We will discuss each of these four topics one by one in the following pages. Let's begin with the first one, normalization. The NDS is a normalized store. But the source systems may not be normalized, so we have to normalize the data to fit the NDS normalized structure. For example, consider the store table in the source system, shown in Table 8-1.

Table 8-1. *Non-normalized* store *Table in the Source System*

store_number	store_name	store_type
1805	Perth	Online
3409	Frankfurt	Full Outlet
1014	Strasbourg	Mini Outlet
2236	Leeds	Full Outlet
1808	Los Angeles	Full Outlet
2903	Delhi	Online

We need transform it into the table shown in Table 8-2.

Table 8-2. *A Normalized* store *Table in the NDS*

store_number	store_name	store_type_key
1805	Perth	1
3409	Frankfurt	2
1014	Strasbourg	3
2236	Leeds	2
1808	Los Angeles	2
2903	Delhi	1

The store_type column in the source system in Table 8-1 is normalized into its own table, as shown in Table 8-3.

Table 8-3. store_type *Table in the NDS*

store_type_key	store_type
1	Online
2	Full Outlet
3	Mini Outlet

Figure 8-3 shows the entity relationship diagram of the store and store_type tables in the source system and in the NDS. The diagram on the right shows that the store table is normalized in the NDS. Each store has one store type. Each store type relates to zero or many stores.

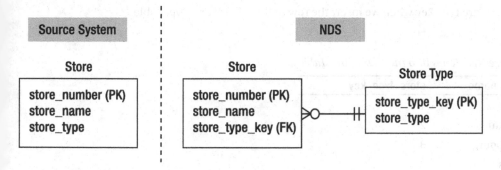

Figure 8-3. *Entity relationship diagram of the* store *table in the source system and the NDS*

If in the source system we have the store_type table, we just need to bring it to the NDS. But if we don't have a store_type table in the source system, we need to populate the NDS store_type table using the data in the store table. If the store table contains a new store type, we need to insert it into the store_type table. In practice, whether you use an ODS or NDS in your data warehouse architecture, many of the reference entities are available in the source system.

But there are always a few entities that are not available in the source system, so you need to create them based on the data in the main entities. You can do this by inserting new data from the main entity into the subentity. In the store example, the source system doesn't have a store_type table. So in the NDS, you need to create and populate the store_type table based on the data available in the store table. Suppose we get the three rows from the source system, as shown in Table 8-4.

Table 8-4. *Incoming Data from the Source System*

store_number	store_name	store_type
2009	Dallas	Online
2237	London	Full Outlet
2014	San Francisco	Distribution Center

The first and second rows (Dallas and London) are fine because their store types already exist in the NDS store_type table (shown earlier in Table 8-3). But the third row (San Francisco) has a store type of Distribution Center. We don't have this store type in the NDS store_type table. So, we insert this new Distribution Center store type into the NDS store_type table, as shown in Table 8-5.

Table 8-5. *Adding a New Store Type*

store_type_key	store_type
1	Online
2	Full Outlet
3	Mini Outlet
4	Distribution Center

Then we use the new store type key when we insert the row in the NDS store_type table, as shown in Table 8-6.

Table 8-6. *Adding the Three New Rows into the NDS* store *Table*

store_number	store_name	store_type_key
1805	Perth	1
3409	Frankfurt	2
1014	Strasbourg	3
2236	Leeds	2
1808	Los Angeles	2
2903	Delhi	1
2009	Dallas	1
2237	London	2
2014	San Francisco	4

The second thing we want to consider when populating the NDS (or the ODS) is that we may bring data from external sources, such as the ISO country table that we loaded in the previous chapter. So, the country table in the NDS has several more columns than the stage or the source, as illustrated in Table 8-7.

Table 8-7. *The* country *Table in NDS with Additional Columns*

country_key	country_code	country_name	source_system_code	active	created	last_updated
1	cg	Congo	4	1	09/15/2007	10/02/2007
2	ch	Switzerland	4	1	10/21/2007	11/14/2007

The issue with using external data is not how to look up the country key for a particular country name or how to find out whether a country is still active. The issue here is whether a country exists in the table but under a different name. For example, in the source system, the customer record in Kinshasa has the country name "Congo (Zaire)," whereas the external data is "Congo." Therefore, when we do a lookup for the country name, we won't find it. In this case, if we create "Congo (Zaire)" as a new row, we will end up having two entries in the country table for "Congo." This is similar for "Bosnia-Herzegovina" and "Yugoslavia." In this case, we may want to consider applying a rule in the data quality routine to replace "Congo (Zaire)" with "Congo" as we bring the data into the NDS. This problem occurs because we are using external data for reference data that does not match the master data in the source system.

In Figure 8-4, the source system supplies "Congo (Zaire)" in the customer table, and the external data supplies "Congo" for the country table. The country table in the NDS is populated with "Congo" from the external data. The data firewall replaces "Congo (Zaire)" from the customer table in the source system with "Congo" so that when the NDS ETL looks up "Congo" in the NDS country table, it finds it. This is necessary to prevent the ETL from creating duplicate entries in the NDS country table. This example illustrates the data matching that needs to be done when we have more than one data source. When populating the NDS, matching is the base activity for integrating the data.

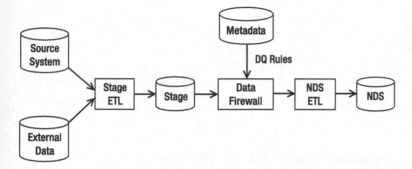

Figure 8-4. *Using the DQ rule to correct incoming data to prevent duplicate data in the NDS*

The third consideration is key management. We want to implement key management when doing NDS population. Consider a simple table in Jade like the one shown in Table 8-8.

Table 8-8. product_status *Table in Jade*

status_code	description
AC	Active
QC	Quality Control
IN	Inactive
WD	Withdrawn

The product_status table in the NDS has a surrogate key column and an unknown row, as shown in Table 8-9.

Table 8-9. product_status *Table in NDS*

product_status_key	product_status_code	product_status	other columns
0	UN	Unknown	
1	AC	Active	
2	QC	Quality Control	
3	IN	Inactive	
4	WD	Withdrawn	

The purpose of having our own keying system in the data warehouse is twofold. First, it enables integration with the second source system, and second, we want to be able to adapt the key changes in the source system(s). Data warehouse keying is in the form of simple incremental integers (1, 2, 3, 4, and so on). The data warehouse key is known as a *surrogate key* (SK). The source system key is known as a *natural key* (NK). The SK enables the integration of several source systems because we can map or associate the NK with the SK. For example, say Jupiter has the product status shown in Table 8-10.

Table 8-10. product_status *Table in Jupiter*

status_code	description
N	Normal
OH	On Hold
SR	Supplier Reject
C	Closed

The SK in the data warehouse enables us to arrange in the ETL to have Normal in Jupiter associated with Active in Jade. In addition, both should be mapped to SK 1, both Inactive and Closed should be mapped to SK 3, and the remaining two codes from both systems are maintained so that the resulting product_status table looks like Table 8-11. Figure 8-5 shows the mapping.

Table 8-11. product_status *Table in NDS Combining Jade and Jupiter*

product_status_key	product_status_code	product_status	control columns
0	UN	Unknown	...
1	AC	Active	...
2	QC	Quality Control	...
3	IN	Inactive	...
4	WD	Withdrawn	...
5	OH	On Hold	...
6	SR	Supplier Reject	...

What I meant by "control columns" in Table 8-11 are active flag, source system code, created, and last updated. In the NDS, we have a source_system table that contains a list of source systems feeding the NDS. In this source system table, we define 1 for Jade, 2 for WebTower, 3 for Jupiter, and 0 for unknown or not applicable, as shown in Figure 8-5. We set the source system code for On Hold and Supplier Reject to 3, Unknown to 0, and the remaining four rows to 1. Figure 8-5 shows the mapping between the source system tables and the NDS. It also shows the source_system table.

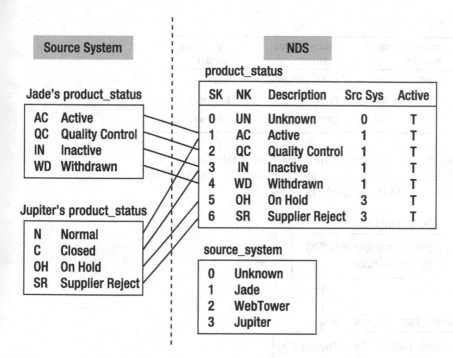

Figure 8-5. *The mapping for the* product_status *table between the source systems and the NDS*

If Quality Control was deleted later from Jade, we would change the active flag for Quality Control from T to F (please see the active column on the NDS product_status table in Figure 8-5). It is better to apply soft deletion in the NDS, rather than hard deletion. Some regulations in certain countries may require hard deletion on certain data; for example, French and UK customers may request that their e-mail addresses be physically deleted from a marketing-related database.

Junction tables are the fourth and last consideration. In Chapter 5 when we did the data modeling, we created five junction tables in the NDS: address_junction, phone_number_junction, email_address_junction, channel_junction, and interest_junction. The purpose of these tables is to implement many-to-many relationships between the customer table and address, phone_number, email_address, channel, and interest tables. Now we need to populate these junction tables. Let's take one junction table for this example: the phone_number_junction. Table 8-12 shows the customer table in the source system. It has three customers with their phone numbers. Some are home phone numbers, some are office phone numbers, and some are cell phone numbers.

Table 8-12. customer *Table in Source System*

customer_id	customer_name	home_phone_number	office_phone_number	cell_phone_number
56	Brian Cable	(904) 402-8294	(682) 605-8463	N/A
57	Valerie Arindra	(572) 312-2048	N/A	(843) 874-1029
58	Albert Amadeus	N/A	(948) 493-7472	(690) 557-3382

The target tables in the NDS are the customer table, the phone_number table, the phone_number_junction table, and the phone_number_type table. Figure 8-6 shows the entity relationship diagram, and Tables 8-13 to 8-16 shows the NDS tables.

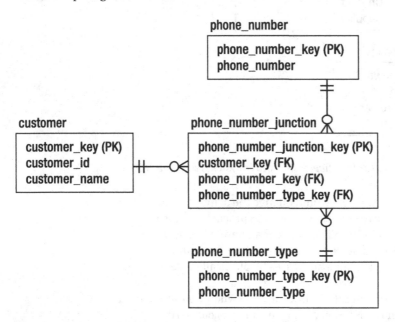

Figure 8-6. *Entity relationship diagram for NDS phone number tables*

Table 8-13. *NDS* customer *Table*

customer_key	customer_id	customer_name
801	56	Brian Cable
802	57	Valerie Arindra
803	58	Albert Amadeus

Table 8-14. *NDS* phone_number_junction *Table*

phone_number_junction_key	customer_key	phone_number_key	phone_number_type_key
101	801	501	1
102	801	502	2
103	802	503	1
104	802	504	3
105	803	505	2
106	803	506	3

Table 8-15. *NDS* phone_number *Table*

phone_number_key	phone_number
0	unknown
501	(904) 402-8294
502	(682) 605-8463
503	(572) 312-2048
504	(843) 874-1029
505	(948) 493-7472
506	(690) 557-3382

Table 8-16. *NDS* phone_number_type *Table*

phone_number_type_key	phone_number_type
0	Unknown
1	Home phone
2	Office phone
3	Cell phone

In the previous case, we remove all three phone columns in the customer table and put them in the junction table, with the customer_key, phone_key, and phone_type_key columns each referring to their own table. Alternatively, rather than linking the phone_number_type table to the phone_number_junction table, we can link the phone_number_type table to the phone number table, as shown in Figure 8-7.

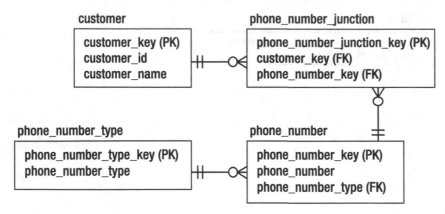

Figure 8-7. *Alternate ERD for NDS phone number tables*

The NDS tables are normalized, which is good in terms of no data redundancy. This means there is only one place to update if you have a data change. It's just that this transformation is a little bit tricky to do in the ETL. In the ETL, we need to populate the customer table and phone_number table first, and then we populate the junction table by looking up the customer key and phone number key. The phone_number_type table is static; we populate it when we initiate the data warehouse.

Using SSIS to Populate NDS

In this section, you will learn how to populate a table in the NDS using the Slowly Changing Dimension Wizard in SSIS. The best way to learn about data warehouse population is by doing it. It is good to know the theory, but if you haven't actually done it, then you won't encounter any problems (or their solutions). So, let's populate the NDS using SSIS. Open BIDS, and open the Amadeus ETL SSIS package that we created in the previous chapter.

In the previous chapter, we created SSIS packages that populate the stage tables from the source systems. In this chapter, we will create packages for populating the NDS and DDS tables. All the packages that populate the stage tables are available on this book's web page at http://www.apress.com/. In the /ETL folder, there is an SSIS solution file called Amadeus ETL.sln. The stage packages are named according to the frequency they are run and the extraction method, as follows:

```
[destination data store] [frequency] [extraction method]
```

The first element is the target data store, such as the stage, the NDS, or the DDS. The second element is the frequency that the ETL package is executed, such as daily, weekly, monthly, or ad hoc. The third element is the extraction method, such as incremental, full reload, or external data. There are five stage packages in the Amadeus ETL SSIS solution:

- Stage daily incremental.dtsx contains the order header, order detail, customer, product, and store.

- Stage monthly incremental.dtsx contains the currency rate.

- Stage daily full reload.dtsx contains the product status, customer status, product type, household income, product category, interest, currency, package, and package type.

- Stage weekly external data.dtsx contains the country and language.

- Stage adhoc full reload.dtsx contains the region, division, and state.

In the previous chapter, we loaded country data from an external source into the stage. Now let's create a package to load the country data from the stage to the NDS. We will do this using the Slowly Changing Dimension Wizard. If the country already exists in the NDS country table, the Slowly Changing Dimension Wizard will update the target row. But if the country code doesn't exist in the NDS country table, the Slowly Changing Dimension Wizard will insert it as a new row. The stage country table contains only the country_code and country_name columns, but the NDS country table contains three additional columns: source_system_code, create_timestamp, and update_timestamp. In this exercise, we will also populate these three additional columns.

1. Create a new package in SSIS. In Solution Explorer, right-click SSIS Packages, and choose New SSIS Package to create a new SSIS package.

2. We want to load the data from the stage to the NDS. The task suitable for this job is the Data Flow task, so let's create a Data Flow task on the design surface and rename it to **Country**.

3. Double-click it to edit the data flow and create an OLE DB source. Call this OLE DB source **Stage Country**, and point the connection to the servername.Stage.ETL OLE DB connection. Set the data access mode to Table or View and the table name to country.

4. Click Preview to see the data, and click Close. Click OK to close the OLE DB source editor window.

5. In the Toolbox, find a transformation called Derived Column, and drag it onto the design surface. Connect the green arrow from the stage's Country column to the Derived Column. Double-click Derived Column to edit it.

6. Click the cell under Derived Column Name, and type **source_system_code**. Then set Expression to 2 and Data Type to a single-byte unsigned integer, as shown in Figure 8-8. The source_system_code data type is defined as a single-byte unsigned integer because the destination data type in the NDS is tinyint. The source_system_code value is defined as 2 because the data originated from Jupiter (Jade = 1, Jupiter = 2, WebTower = 3).

7. Create two more columns called create_timestamp and update_timstamp, set Expression to getdate() for both columns, and set Data Type to database time-stamp, as shown in Figure 8-8. Click OK to close the Derived Column Transformation Editor dialog box.

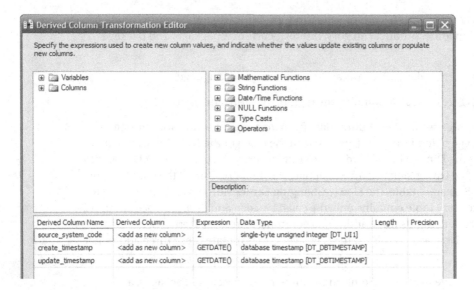

Figure 8-8. *Setting the constants in the Derived Column transformation*

8. In the Toolbox, scroll down and find Slowly Changing Dimension. Drag it onto the design surface, and put it under the Derived Column box. Connect the green arrow from the Derived Column box to this new Slowly Changing Dimension box.

9. Double-click the Slowly Changing Dimension box, and the Slowly Changing Dimension Wizard will open. Click Next. Set the connection manager to servername.NDS.ETL by clicking the New button. Set the "Table or view" drop-down list to country. Click "Not a key column" for country_code, and change it to "Business key." Figure 8-9 displays the result.

10. Click Next. On the next page, click the blank cell under Dimension Columns, and select country_name. Set Change Type to "Changing attribute." Do the same for source_system_code and update_timestamp. We don't want to update the create_timestamp column for existing records because it is set once at record creation only. Figure 8-10 shows the result. We set the three columns shown in Figure 8-10 to "Changing attribute" because we want them to be updated when the stage data changes. But we want the create_timestamp column to be static because it shows when the row was created.

11. The "Changing attribute" option is for SCD type 1 (overwriting existing values), and "Historical attribute" is for SCD type 2 (preserving history by writing the new values into new records). Click Next. Leave the Changing Attribute check box unchecked because we don't have outdated records in the country dimension.

12. Click Next. Uncheck "Enable inferred member support." Inferred dimension member happens when a fact table references a dimension row that has not been loaded yet. We will map the unknown dimensional value in the fact table to the unknown dimension record later in this chapter.

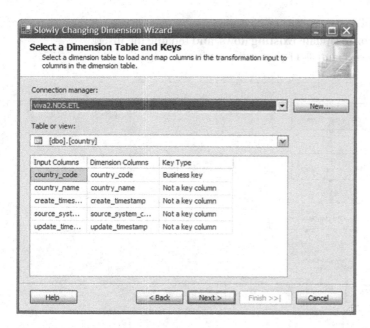

Figure 8-9. *Selecting dimension table and keys in the Slowly Changing Dimension Wizard*

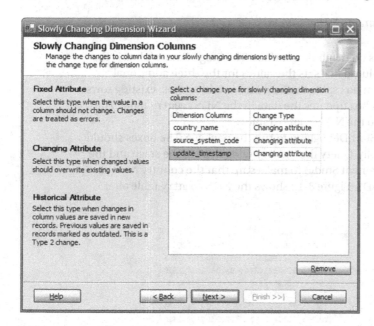

Figure 8-10. *Setting the change type for dimension columns*

13. Click Next, and then click Finish to complete the Slowly Changing Dimension Wizard. Rename the OLE DB Command box to **Update Existing Rows**, and rename the Insert Destination box to **Insert New Rows**. Figure 8-11 shows the result.

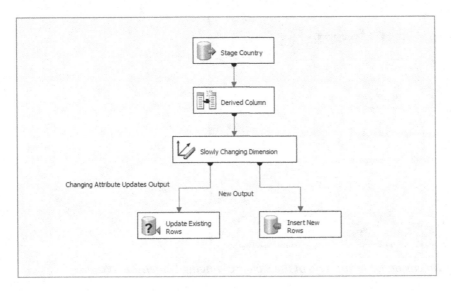

Figure 8-11. *Completed Slowly Changing Dimension task*

Figure 8-11 shows we have five boxes on the design surface. The Stage Country box is the source table in the stage. The Derived Column box sets the values for the three additional columns. The Slowly Changing Dimension box splits the data into two branches: existing rows and new rows. The Update Existing Rows box updates the data in the NDS country table. The Insert New Row box inserts new rows into the NDS country table.

Click the Debug menu, and choose Start Debugging to run the package. The boxes should all be green if the package runs successfully. Query the country table in both the stage and the NDS databases using SQL Server Management Studio to make sure that the country records have been loaded successfully into the NDS. Figure 8-12 shows the NDS country table after loading.

	country_key	country_code	country_name	source_system_code	create_timestamp	update_timestamp
1	0	UN	Unknown	0	1900-01-01 00:00:00.000	1900-01-01 00:00:00.000
2	1	ad	Andorra	2	2007-10-10 21:38:42.873	2007-10-10 21:38:42.873
3	2	ae	United Arab Emirates	2	2007-10-10 21:38:42.873	2007-10-10 21:38:42.873
4	3	af	Afghanistan	2	2007-10-10 21:38:42.890	2007-10-10 21:38:42.890
5	4	ag	Antigua and Barbuda	2	2007-10-10 21:38:42.890	2007-10-10 21:38:42.890
6	5	ai	Anguilla	2	2007-10-10 21:38:42.890	2007-10-10 21:38:42.890
7	6	al	Albania	2	2007-10-10 21:38:42.890	2007-10-10 21:38:42.890
8	7	am	Armenia	2	2007-10-10 21:38:42.890	2007-10-10 21:38:42.890
9	8	an	Netherlands Antilles	2	2007-10-10 21:38:42.890	2007-10-10 21:38:42.890
10	9	ao	Angola	2	2007-10-10 21:38:42.890	2007-10-10 21:38:42.890
11	10	aq	Antarctica	2	2007-10-10 21:38:42.890	2007-10-10 21:38:42.890
12	11	ar	Argentina	2	2007-10-10 21:38:42.890	2007-10-10 21:38:42.890

Figure 8-12. *NDS* country *table after loading*

Figure 8-12 showed that there is a row with country_key set to 0. This row is called the *unknown record*. On every master table in the NDS, we need to add the unknown record with the data warehouse key equal to 0. An unknown record is a row with all the columns set to dummy values, used when we have an unknown value in the main table. We can create the unknown record using the following Transact SQL:

```
set identity_insert country on
insert into country
( country_key, country_code, country_name, source_system_code,
  create_timestamp, update_timestamp )
values
( 0, 'UN', 'Unknown', 0,
  '1900-01-01', '1900-01-01' )
set identity_insert country off
```

We need to set identity_insert to ON because the country_key column is an identity column and we are inserting a specific value in this column. Some people prefer to set the key value to 0 for the unknown records, and others prefer to set it to –1. I have seen some implementations with the key value equal to 1 for unknown records; 0 or –1 is better than 1 because you can have your surrogate key as a positive integer. Whatever the value is, you need to be consistent; for example, once you have defined it as 0, use 0 throughout (in the DDS too).

Generally, the value of an unknown record is 0 for numeric columns; Unknown or a blank string for char or varchar columns; and a low-value date for the date columns, such as 1900-01-01 for smalldatetime, 1753-01-01 for datetime, and 0001-01-01 for the new SQL 2008 datetime2 data type. We should not use NULL in the unknown record to differentiate from a row that doesn't actually have a value. The purpose of having an unknown record is so that the referential integrity in the NDS is maintained, even if the code value in the transaction table is not known.

Now that we have populated the country table, let's do the state table using the same process. The SQL command for the OLE DB source is as follows:

```
select state_code, state_name, formal_name,
  admission_to_statehood, population,
  capital, largest_city,
  cast(2 as tinyint) as source_system_code,
  getdate() as create_timestamp,
  getdate() as update_timestamp
from state
```

The unknown record initialization is comprised of the following SQL statements:

```
set identity_insert state on
insert into state
( state_key, state_code, state_name, formal_name,
  admission_to_statehood, population,
  capital, largest_city, source_system_code,
  create_timestamp, update_timestamp )
```

```
values
( 0, 'UN', 'Unknown', 'Unknown',
  '1900-01-01', 0,
  'Unknown', 'Unknown', 0,
  '1900-01-01', '1900-01-01' )
set identity_insert state off
```

When you execute the package for the first time, it should insert records into the destination, but when you run it for the second time, it should update the records in the destination, as shown in Figure 8-13.

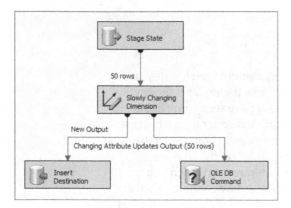

Figure 8-13. *Using SCD transformation for loading the* state *table*

Figure 8-14 shows the NDS state table. It consists of all the columns in the stage state table from state_code to largest_city, plus three control columns (source_system_code, create_timestamp, and update_timestamp). It has an unknown record with state_key equal to 0.

	state_key	state_code	state_name	formal_name	admission_to_statehood	population	capital	largest_city	sour...	create_timestamp	update_timestamp
1	0	UN	Unknown	Unknown	1900-01-01 00:00:00.000	0	Unknown	Unknown	0	1900-01-01 00:00:00.000	1900-01-01 00:00:00.000
2	2	AK	Alaska	State of Alaska	1959-01-03 00:00:00.000	670053	Juneau	Anchorage	2	2007-10-13 12:20:49.297	2007-10-13 12:20:49.297
3	3	AL	Alabama	State of Alabama	1819-12-14 00:00:00.000	4599030	Montgomery	Birmingham	2	2007-10-13 12:20:49.297	2007-10-13 12:20:49.297
4	4	AR	Arkansas	State of Arkansas	1836-06-15 00:00:00.000	2810872	Little Rock	Little Rock	2	2007-10-13 12:20:49.297	2007-10-13 12:20:49.297
5	5	AZ	Arizona	State of Arizona	1912-02-14 00:00:00.000	6166318	Phoenix	Phoenix	2	2007-10-13 12:20:49.297	2007-10-13 12:20:49.297
6	6	CA	California	State of California	1850-09-09 00:00:00.000	36457549	Sacramento	Los Angeles	2	2007-10-13 12:20:49.297	2007-10-13 12:20:49.297
7	7	CO	Colorado	State of Colorado	1876-08-01 00:00:00.000	4753377	Denver	Denver	2	2007-10-13 12:20:49.297	2007-10-13 12:20:49.297
8	8	CT	Connecticut	State of Connecticut	1788-01-09 00:00:00.000	3504809	Hartford	Bridgeport	2	2007-10-13 12:20:49.297	2007-10-13 12:20:49.297
9	9	DE	Delaware	State of Delaware	1787-12-07 00:00:00.000	853476	Dover	Wilmington	2	2007-10-13 12:20:49.297	2007-10-13 12:20:49.297
10	10	FL	Florida	State of Florida	1845-03-03 00:00:00.000	18089888	Tallahassee	Jacksonville	2	2007-10-13 12:20:49.297	2007-10-13 12:20:49.297
11	11	GA	Georgia	State of Georgia	1788-01-02 00:00:00.000	9363941	Atlanta	Atlanta	2	2007-10-13 12:20:49.297	2007-10-13 12:20:49.297
12	12	HI	Hawaii	State of Hawai'i	1959-08-21 00:00:00.000	1285498	Honolulu	Honolulu	2	2007-10-13 12:20:49.297	2007-10-13 12:20:49.297
13	13	IA	Iowa	State of Iowa	1846-12-28 00:00:00.000	2982085	Des Moines	Des Moines	2	2007-10-13 12:20:49.297	2007-10-13 12:20:49.297
14	14	ID	Idaho	State of Idaho	1890-07-03 00:00:00.000	1466465	Boise	Boise	2	2007-10-13 12:20:49.297	2007-10-13 12:20:49.297
15	15	IL	Illinois	State of Illinois	1818-12-03 00:00:00.000	12831970	Springfield	Chicago	2	2007-10-13 12:20:49.297	2007-10-13 12:20:49.297
16	16	IN	Indiana	State of Indiana	1816-12-11 00:00:00.000	6313520	Indianapolis	Indianapolis	2	2007-10-13 12:20:49.297	2007-10-13 12:20:49.297
17	17	KS	Kansas	State of Kansas	1861-01-29 00:00:00.000	2764077	Topeka	Wichita	2	2007-10-13 12:20:49.297	2007-10-13 12:20:49.297
18	18	KY	Kentucky	Commonwealth of ...	1792-06-01 00:00:00.000	4206074	Frankfort	Louisville	2	2007-10-13 12:20:49.297	2007-10-13 12:20:49.297
19	19	LA	Louisiana	State of Louisiana	1812-04-30 00:00:00.000	4287768	Baton Ro...	New Orlea...	2	2007-10-13 12:20:49.297	2007-10-13 12:20:49.297
20	20	MA	Massachu...	Commonwealth of ...	1788-02-06 00:00:00.000	6437193	Boston	Boston	2	2007-10-13 12:20:49.297	2007-10-13 12:20:49.297
21	21	MD	Maryland	State of Maryland	1788-04-28 00:00:00.000	5615727	Annapolis	Baltimore	2	2007-10-13 12:20:49.297	2007-10-13 12:20:49.297
22	22	ME	Maine	State of Maine	1820-03-15 00:00:00.000	1321574	Augusta	Portland	2	2007-10-13 12:20:49.297	2007-10-13 12:20:49.297
23	23	MI	Michigan	State of Michigan	1837-01-26 00:00:00.000	10095643	Lansing	Detroit	2	2007-10-13 12:20:49.297	2007-10-13 12:20:49.297
24	24	MN	Minnesota	State of Minnesota	1858-05-11 00:00:00.000	5167101	Saint Paul	Minneapolis	2	2007-10-13 12:20:49.297	2007-10-13 12:20:49.297

Figure 8-14. *NDS* state *table after loading*

As before, we query both the stage and the NDS state table to make sure that all data has been correctly loaded into the NDS. We can do this using the following query, which tests the existence of each stage row in the NDS. If no row is returned, it means all the rows in the stage have been loaded into the NDS.

```
select * from stage.dbo.state a
where not exists
( select * from nds.dbo.state b
  where a.state_code = b.state_code )
```

Now that the "initial loading" is done, let's test whether a change in the stage data will be correctly loaded into the NDS by the previous SCD transformation. For that purpose, let's update the population of Arizona in the stage database. Issue the following SQL statements one by one against the stage database in SQL Server Management Studio:

```
use stage
select population from state where state_code = 'AZ' --6166318
update state set population = 6167318 where state_code = 'AZ'
```

Notice that the population was 6,166,318 and we updated it to 6,167,318. Before we run the SSIS package, run this query to check the value of the Arizona population in the NDS:

```
select population from nds.dbo.state where state_code = 'AZ'
```

Notice that in the NDS the population is 6,166,318. Now let's run the SSIS package and then run the previous NDS query. The population in the NDS should now be 6,167,318 as expected. Set the stage back to 6,166,318, and rerun the SSIS package to put it back as it was.

Upsert Using SQL and Lookup

What the previous SCD transformation does is commonly known as *upsert*—in other words, update if exist, insert if not exist. It is a basic operation in data warehousing, and you will come across this operation many times when building a data warehouse ETL system. There are two other methods that are commonly used in practice to do upsert using SSIS. The first one is using a SQL statement. The second one is using the Lookup transformation.

The following Transact SQL shows how to do an UPSERT operation using a SQL statement. I'll use the same example as mentioned previously: country, which is simpler than the state example. The first statement (update ...) updates the rows in the NDS table that have country names different from the ones on the stage table. The second statement (insert ...) loads the rows on the stage table that do not exist in the NDS.

```
update nds.dbo.country
set country_name = s.country_name,
  source_system_code = 2,
  update_timestamp = getdate()
from the stage.dbo.country s
inner join nds.dbo.country n
  on n.country_code = s.country_code
where n.country_name <> s.country_name
and n.country_key <> 0
```

```
insert into nds.dbo.country
( country_code, country_name, source_system_code,
  create_timestamp, update_timestamp )
select s.country_code, s.country_name,
  2 as source_system_code,
  getdate() as create_timestamp,
  getdate() as update_timestamp
from the stage.dbo.country s
left join nds.dbo.country n
  on s.country_code = n.country_code
where n.country_key is null
```

To implement the previous SQL statement approach in SSIS, create a new SSIS package, and rename it to **NDS country using SQL**. In the Toolbox, drag the Execute SQL task onto the design surface, and rename it to **Update NDS Country**. Drag another Execute SQL task onto the design surface, and rename it to **Insert NDS Country**. Set the connection to servername. NDS.ETL for both of them. Set the SQL statement to the previous statements, and leave SQL-SourceType as direct input. Connect the green arrow from the Update NDS Country box to the Insert NDS Country box. Figure 8-15 describes the package execution result. The resulting data is the same as in Figure 8-12.

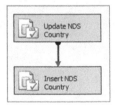

Figure 8-15. *Using Execute SQL tasks to do an upsert operation*

The second method is to use a Lookup transformation. Let's use the same example as mentioned previously (country) so it is easy to understand the differences between the two:

1. In Solution Explorer, right-click SSIS Packages, and choose New SSIS Package to create a new SSIS package.

2. Drag a Data Flow task from the Toolbox onto the design surface, and double-click the box to edit it.

3. To set the country table in the stage as a source, drag an OLE DB source from the Toolbox onto the design surface, and rename it to **Stage Country**. Configure the connection to point to the stage. To retrieve both columns from the source table and add the three additional columns, set the data access mode to SQL Command, and set the SQL command to the following:

```
select country_code, country_name,
  cast(2 as tinyint) as source_system_code,
  getdate() as create_timestamp,
  getdate() as update_timestamp
from country
```

4. Click Preview to make sure the SQL statement is correct and the data is there, and then click OK.

5. Let's create a Lookup transformation to check whether the row already exists in the NDS. In the Toolbox, under the Data Flow Transformation section, find an icon called Lookup, and drag it onto the design surface. Name this box **Lookup Country Code**. Connect the green arrow from Stage Country to the Lookup Country Code box. Double-click the box to edit it.

6. Now we need to configure the Lookup transformation to check whether the country code exists in the NDS country table. To do that, set the connection to NDS. Select "Use the results of an SQL query," and set the query as select country_code from country. This is so that only one column is retrieved from disk into memory. If you select "Use table or view," all columns will be retrieved into memory. Click Preview to make sure the data is there. Figure 8-16 shows the settings.

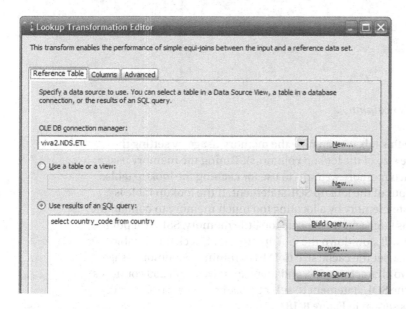

Figure 8-16. *Configuring the data source and SQL query for the Lookup transformation*

7. Click the Columns tab. There should be a line connecting `country_code` from Available Input Columns on the left to the `country_code` from Available Lookup Columns on the right, as shown in Figure 8-17. If there isn't, drag `country_code` from the left to the right to map it. You don't need to check the box on `country_code`; in fact, leave it unchecked. We are not using any output column from this Lookup transformation. We use the Lookup transformation only for checking whether all the country codes on the stage table exist on the NDS table.

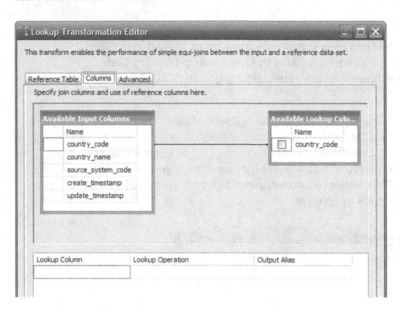

Figure 8-17. *Specifying the join column*

8. Click the Advanced tab. On this tab, we can tune the memory usage by setting the cache size closer to the byte size of the lookup column(s). Tuning the memory usage means we allocate how much memory we want to use for caching the lookup table. The lookup table is the output of the lookup SQL statement. If the lookup table is small, we don't want to waste memory by allocating too much memory to contain the output. If the lookup table is large and we allocate too little memory, SSIS will put the lookup table on disk, and it will slow down the lookup process. Check the "Enable memory restriction" box, and set the cache size to 1MB to minimize memory usage. The country code is only two characters wide, and there are fewer than 250 countries in the stage table. Change the SQL statement to `select country_code from country where country_code = ?`, as shown in Figure 8-18.

9. Click OK to close the Lookup Transformation Editor dialog box.

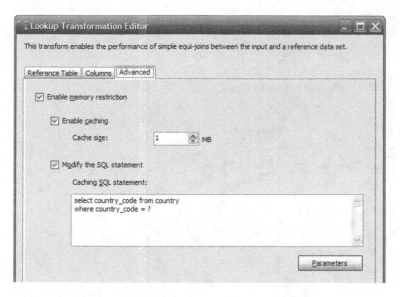

Figure 8-18. *Configuring the cache memory size and SQL statement*

10. Next, we need to update the countries that already exist in the NDS, setting the country names to be the same as the ones in the stage table. In the Toolbox, find the OLE DB command, and drag it onto the design surface. Name it **Update Existing Row**. Connect the green arrow from Lookup Country Code to the Update Existing Row box. Double-click the box to edit it.

11. To set the country name of the row in the NDS table to be the same as the country name in the stage table, under the Connection Manager column set the Connection drop-down list to servername.NDS.ETL. Click the Component Properties tab, and set SqlCommand to this:

```
update country
set country_name = ?,
  source_system_code = 2,
  create_timestamp = getdate(),
  update_timestamp = getdate()
where country_code = ?
```

12. In the previous Transact SQL, we have two question marks. They are parameters. The first question mark is Param_0, and the second question mark is Param_1. To feed the input columns coming from the Lookup Country Code box to these parameters, click the Column Mappings tab, and connect country_code to Param_1 and country_name to Param_0, as shown in Figure 8-19. Click OK to close this editor.

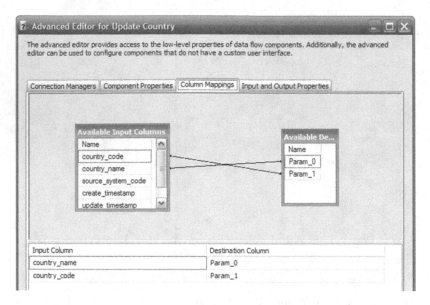

Figure 8-19. *Configuring column mappings in the OLE DB command*

13. Next, we need to insert rows in the stage table that do not exist in the NDS table. In the Toolbox, find SQL Server Destination, and drag it onto the design surface. Name it **Insert New Rows**. Connect the red arrow from the Lookup Country Code box to this box. Click OK in the dialog box.

14. Double-click the Insert New Rows box to edit it. Set the connection to NDS. Set Table to country, and click Preview to verify that it is country table that we selected.

15. Click Mappings, and configure the mappings between the input columns and destination columns, as shown in Figure 8-20.

16. Click OK to close the SQL Server Destination Editor dialog box.

17. To test the package, we can prepare the data by issuing the following SQL statements against the NDS database. The first statement updates Andorra's country name in the NDS to Andorra1 and is, therefore, not the same as the country name in the stage. The second statement deletes Turks and Caicos Island from the NDS.

```
update nds.dbo.country set country_name = 'Andorra1'
where country_code = 'ad'

delete from nds.dbo.country where country_code = 'tc'
```

18. Query the NDS country table to check that the data changes were successfully made. To execute the package, click the Debug menu, and choose Start Debugging (F5). Figure 8-21 shows how the final package looks.

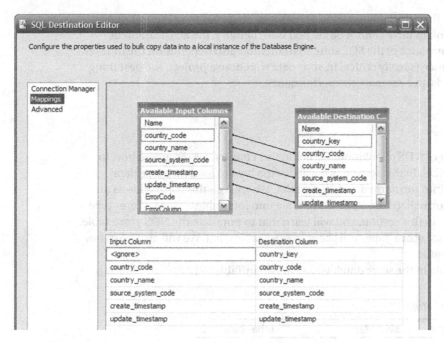

Figure 8-20. *Mapping the columns on the SQL Server destination*

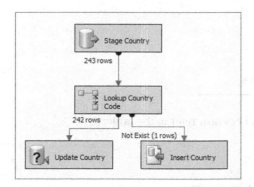

Figure 8-21. *Upsert using the Lookup transformation*

19. Check the NDS country table to see whether Andorra was corrected and whether Turks and Caicos Island was reinserted into the table. Also, check that both the create_timestamp and update_timestamp columns for these two records are set to today.

The question that many people ask is, which one is the best method, or which one gives the best performance? The SQL method is simpler and easier to use. Which method gives the best performance depends on the size of data, the complexity of the lookup, and the specification of the ETL server, in particular the memory. If the lookup table can be cached into the memory of the ETL server, then the lookup and SCD methods are faster than the SQL statement method. But if the lookup table cannot be cached into memory, the SQL statement method is faster. The performance of the SQL statement method also depends on the indexes and partitions. If performance is really critical in your data warehouse project, the best thing to do is to test both methods and compare the performance.

Normalization

Normalization is a key part of NDS population. Earlier in this chapter, we discussed how to normalize stage tables in NDS. In this section, we will discuss how to load the stage data (which is not normalized) into the normalized NDS tables. We will use the store table as an example. In the NDS, we normalized the stage store table into four tables: store, store_type, address, and phone_number. In this section, you will learn that to populate the NDS store table, you need to load the address, store_type, and phone_number tables first. We will also learn how use SSIS to load the store table.

Consider the store table in the stage database, as shown in Table 8-17.

Table 8-17. store *Table in the Stage Database*

store_number	store_name	store_type	other columns
1010	Paris	Mini Outlet	...
1011	Lyon	Full Outlet	...
1012	Toulouse	Full Outlet	...
1013	Nice	Full Outlet	...
1014	Strasbourg	Distribution Center	...
1015	Nantes	Mini Outlet	...

We can see that the store_type column is not normalized. Let's now refer to the target table in the NDS, as shown in Table 8-18.

Table 8-18. store *Table in the NDS*

store_key	store_number	store_name	store_type_key	other columns
0	0	Unknown	0	...
562	1010	Paris	19	...
607	1011	Lyon	18	...
576	1012	Toulouse	18	...
531	1013	Nice	18	...
585	1014	Strasbourg	17	...
547	1015	Nantes	19	...
515	2703	Osaka	18	...

In the previous table, we can see that to load the NDS store table we need store_type_ key. We get this store_type_key from the store_type table. This is also the case with the address and phone_number columns. To insert a record into the store table, we need store_ type_key, address_key, and phone_number_key, so we need to do a lookup on those three tables. But before we can do a lookup, if there is any new store type, address, or phone number, we need to load them first. So, diagrammatically, the process is like the one described in Figure 8-22.

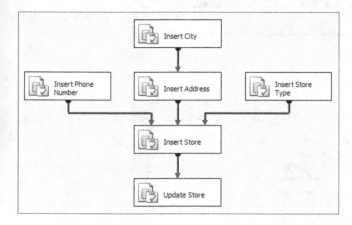

Figure 8-22. *Loading the NDS* store *table*

When populating the address table, we need to check whether there are any new cities because we need the city key to populate the address table. If there are new cities, we need to insert them into the city table. The state and country tables have their own data feed from the source system, so we do not need to normalize them. We only need to do a lookup to get their key values.

So, let's create the SSIS package for loading the store table:

1. Open BIDS, create a new package, and call it **NDS store**. Drag the Execute SQL task from the Toolbox onto the design surface, and call it **Insert New Store Types**.

2. Double-click it to edit it, and set the connection to NDS. Set the SQL statement as follows:

```
insert into nds.dbo.store_type
( store_type, source_system_code,
  create_timestamp, update_timestamp )
select
  distinct store_type as store_type,
  1 as source_system_code,
  getdate() as create_timestamp,
  getdate() as update_timestamp
from stage.dbo.store s
where not exists
( select * from nds.dbo.store_type t
  where t.store_type = s.store_type )
```

The earlier SQL statement looks for new store types—those that exist in the stage `store` table but do not exist in the NDS `store_type` table. It then inserts the new store types into the NDS `store_type` table.

You can also build the SQL statement by clicking the Query Builder button in the SSMS. This will open the Query Builder, which is shown in Figure 8-23.

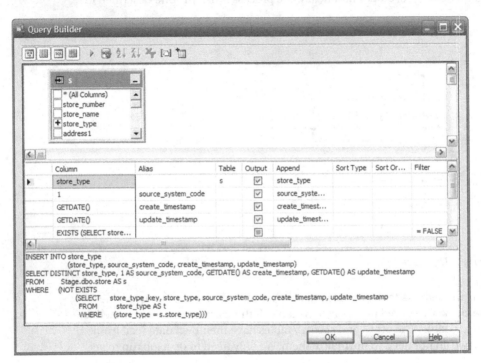

Figure 8-23. *Using Query Builder to build the SQL statement*

3. Similarly, create an Execute SQL task, call it **Insert New Phone Number** pointing to the NDS database, and set the SQL statements as follows. The following SQL statement looks for new phone numbers that exist in the stage but not in the NDS and then inserts these new phone numbers into the NDS phone_number table.

```
insert into nds.dbo.phone_number
( phone_number, source_system_code,
  create_timestamp, update_timestamp )
select
  distinct s.phone_number as phone_number,
  1 as source_system_code,
  getdate() as create_timestamp,
  getdate() as update_timestamp
from stage.dbo.store s
where not exists
( select * from nds.dbo.phone_number p
  where p.phone_number = s.phone_number )
```

4. We then insert new cities and addresses, using the Execute SQL task, with the SQL statements as follows. The first statement inserts the new cities into the NDS city table, and the second statement inserts the new addresses into the NDS address table.

```
insert into city
( city_name, source_system_code,
  create_timestamp, update_timestamp )
select
  distinct s.city as city_name,
  1 as source_system_code,
  getdate() as create_timestamp,
  getdate() as update_timestamp
from stage.dbo.store s
where not exists
( select * from nds.dbo.city c
  where c.city_name = s.city )

insert into nds.dbo.address
( address1, address2, address3, address4,
  city_key, post_code, state_key, country_key,
  source_system_code, create_timestamp, update_timestamp)
select
  distinct s.address1, s.address2, s.address3, s.address4,
  c.city_key, s.zipcode, st.state_key, co.country_key,
  1 as source_system_code,
  getdate() as create_timestamp,
  getdate() as update_timestamp
from stage.dbo.store s
left join nds.dbo.city c
  on s.city = c.city_name
left join nds.dbo.state st
  on case when s.state = 'N/A' then 'Unknown'
     else s.state end = st.state_name
left join nds.dbo.country co
  on s.country = co.country_code
where not exists
( select * from nds.dbo.address a
  where coalesce(a.address1,'') = coalesce(s.address1,'')
  and   coalesce(a.address2,'') = coalesce(s.address2,'')
  and   coalesce(a.address3,'') = coalesce(s.address3,'')
  and   coalesce(a.address4,'') = coalesce(s.address4,'')
  and   coalesce(a.city_key,0) = coalesce(c.city_key,0)
  and   coalesce(a.post_code,'') = coalesce(s.zipcode,'')
  and   coalesce(a.state_key,0) = coalesce(st.state_key,0)
  and   coalesce(a.country_key,0) = coalesce(co.country_key,0) )
```

In the previous SQL statement, we have a case statement in the join with the state table. The purpose of this case statement is to map N/A in the source data to the unknown record. This is because for online stores, the address columns are populated with N/A, which essentially means unknown. If we don't do this mapping, we will end up with two unknown records in the address table: one for N/A and 1 for unknown. In a more sophisticated data warehouse system, this comparison is ideally performed in metadata so that it is easier to maintain.

As you saw earlier, unlike the store type, phone number, and city, the identification of a unique record in the address table depends not only on one column, but on eight columns. This is why, in the earlier where clause, we see eight conditions. The purpose of those eight conditions is to identify whether a record in the address already exists in the NDS.

Tip When comparing a nullable column to another nullable column, use coalesce to replace NULL with either '' (blank string) or 0. This is because NULL cannot be compared to NULL. For example, if you write a.post_code = s.zipcode, the value of both sides of the equation can be NULL, and the comparison will fail. To avoid that, you need to add coalesce to convert NULL to a blank string as follows: coalesce(a.post_code,'') = coalesce(s.zipcode,'').

---

5. Now we are ready to create the Execute SQL task for the store table using the following SQL statement. This statement finds the new stores that do not exist in NDS; converts their store type, address, phone number, and region into their keys; and then inserts the new stores into the NDS.

```
insert into nds.dbo.store
( store_number, store_name, store_type_key,
  address_key, phone_number_key, web_site, region_key,
  source_system_code, create_timestamp, update_timestamp )
select
  s.store_number as store_number,
  s.store_name as store_name,
  t.store_type_key as store_type_key,
  z.address_key as address_key,
  p.phone_number_key as phone_number_key,
  s.web_site as web_site,
  r.region_key as region_key,
  1 as source_system_code,
  getdate() as created_timestamp,
  getdate() as update_timestamp
from stage.dbo.store s
inner join nds.dbo.store_type t
  on s.store_type = t.store_type
```

```
inner join
  ( select a.address_key, a.address1, a.address2, a.address3,
      a.address4, a.post_code as zipcode, c.city_name as city,
     st.state_name as state, upper(co.country_code) as country
    from address a
    inner join city c on a.city_key = c.city_key
    inner join state st on a.state_key = st.state_key
    inner join country co on a.country_key = co.country_key
  ) z
  on coalesce(s.address1,'') = coalesce(z.address1,'')
 and coalesce(s.address2,'') = coalesce(z.address2,'')
 and coalesce(s.address3,'') = coalesce(z.address3,'')
 and coalesce(s.address4,'') = coalesce(z.address4,'')
 and coalesce(s.zipcode,'') = coalesce(z.zipcode,'')
 and coalesce(s.city,'') = coalesce(z.city,'')
 and coalesce(case when s.state = 'N/A' then 'Unknown'
     else s.state end,'') = coalesce(z.state,'')
 and coalesce(s.country,'') = coalesce(z.country,'')
inner join nds.dbo.phone_number p
  on s.phone_number = p.phone_number
inner join nds.dbo.region r
  on s.region = r.region_name
where not exists
( select * from nds.dbo.store n
  where n.store_number = s.store_number )
```

In the previous SQL statement, we join the address table with the store_type, address, phone_number, and region tables to get the surrogate key. We use inner joins rather than left joins because we previously made sure that all store types, addresses, phone numbers, and regions exist; if they don't, we insert them.

The previous SQL statements filter out the stores that already exist in the NDS store table. They use coalesce to avoid comparing NULL to NULL. They also use the case statement to map N/A to Unknown.

6. Next, we update the NDS store table for records that already exist and for which the value has changed. For that, create another Execute SQL task, label it as **Update Store**, set the connection to NDS, and set the SQL statements as follows:

```
update nds.dbo.store
set store_name = s.store_name,
  store_type_key = st.store_type_key,
  address_key = a.address_key,
  phone_number_key = pn.phone_number_key,
  region_key = r.region_key,
  web_site = s.web_site,
  update_timestamp = getdate()
```

```
from stage.dbo.store s
inner join nds.dbo.store n
  on s.store_number = n.store_number
inner join nds.dbo.store_type st
  on n.store_type_key = st.store_type_key
inner join nds.dbo.address a
  on n.address_key = a.address_key
inner join nds.dbo.phone_number pn
  on n.phone_number_key = pn.phone_number_key
inner join nds.dbo.region r
  on n.region_key = r.region_key
inner join nds.dbo.city c
  on a.city_key = c.city_key
inner join nds.dbo.state sta
  on a.state_key = sta.state_key
inner join nds.dbo.country co
  on a.country_key = co.country_key
where coalesce(s.store_name,'') <> coalesce(n.store_name,'')
or coalesce(s.store_type,'') <> coalesce(st.store_type,'')
or coalesce(s.address1,'') <> coalesce(a.address1,'')
or coalesce(s.address2,'') <> coalesce(a.address2,'')
or coalesce(s.address3,'') <> coalesce(a.address3,'')
or coalesce(s.address4,'') <> coalesce(a.address4,'')
or coalesce(a.city_key,0) <> coalesce(c.city_key,0)
or coalesce(a.post_code,'') <> coalesce(s.zipcode,'')
or coalesce(a.state_key,0) <> coalesce(sta.state_key,0)
or coalesce(a.country_key,0) <> coalesce(co.country_key,0)
or coalesce(s.phone_number,'') <> coalesce(pn.phone_number,'')
or coalesce(s.web_site,'') <> coalesce(n.web_site,'')
```

This SQL statement updates the NDS stores that have a different store name, store type, address, phone number, or web site from the ones in the stage. Just like the insert statement, in the previous SQL statement we join the address table with the city, state, and country tables to compare the address. We also use coalesce to avoid the NULL-against-NULL comparison.

7. The control flow of the package now looks like Figure 8-22, which we discussed earlier. Save and run the package.

8. Query the five NDS tables (city, address, phone number, store type, and store) to ensure that they are populated properly by comparing them to the source system. Figure 8-24 shows the result (the NDS store table).

	store_key	store_number	store_name	store_type_key	address_key	phone_number_key	web_site	region_key	sour...	create_timestamp	update_timestamp
1	0	0	Unknown	0	0	0	Unknown	0	0	1900-01-01 00:00:00.000	1900-01-01 00:00:00.000
2	715	1805	Perth	17	199262	200	http://www.amadeus...	1	1	2007-03-22 22:49:44.407	2007-03-22 22:49:44.407
3	716	3409	Frankfrut	17	199190	182	http://www.amadeus...	3	1	2007-03-22 22:49:44.407	2007-03-22 22:49:44.407
4	717	1209	Zaragoza	17	199247	194	http://www.amadeus...	4	1	2007-03-22 22:49:44.407	2007-03-22 22:49:44.407
5	718	1014	Strasbourg	17	199241	177	http://www.amadeus...	6	1	2007-03-22 22:49:44.407	2007-03-22 22:49:44.407
6	719	2903	Delhi	17	199266	111	http://www.amadeus...	7	1	2007-03-22 22:49:44.407	2007-03-22 22:49:44.407
7	720	2705	Sapporo	17	199233	193	http://www.amadeus...	8	1	2007-03-22 22:49:44.407	2007-03-22 22:49:44.407
8	721	2236	Leeds	17	199264	167	http://www.amadeus...	9	1	2007-03-22 22:49:44.407	2007-03-22 22:49:44.407
9	722	1808	Canberra	18	199181	176	http://www.amadeus...	1	1	2007-03-22 22:49:44.407	2007-03-22 22:49:44.407
10	723	1803	Sydney	18	199212	141	http://www.amadeus...	1	1	2007-03-22 22:49:44.407	2007-03-22 22:49:44.407
11	724	1804	Darwin	18	199245	135	http://www.amadeus...	1	1	2007-03-22 22:49:44.407	2007-03-22 22:49:44.407
12	725	1806	Brisbane	18	199261	144	http://www.amadeus...	1	1	2007-03-22 22:49:44.407	2007-03-22 22:49:44.407
13	726	2022	El Paso	18	199183	153	http://www.amadeus...	2	1	2007-03-22 22:49:44.407	2007-03-22 22:49:44.407
14	727	2009	Dallas	18	199197	192	http://www.amadeus...	2	1	2007-03-22 22:49:44.407	2007-03-22 22:49:44.407
15	728	2237	London	18	199229	186	http://www.amadeus...	9	1	2007-03-22 22:49:44.407	2007-03-22 22:49:44.407
16	729	2027	Portland	18	199174	138	http://www.amadeus...	10	1	2007-03-22 22:49:44.407	2007-03-22 22:49:44.407
17	730	2011	San Jose	18	199186	155	http://www.amadeus...	10	1	2007-03-22 22:49:44.407	2007-03-22 22:49:44.407
18	731	2024	Seattle	18	199213	174	http://www.amadeus...	10	1	2007-03-22 22:49:44.407	2007-03-22 22:49:44.407
19	732	2014	San Francisco	18	199226	181	http://www.amadeus...	10	1	2007-03-22 22:49:44.407	2007-03-22 22:49:44.407
20	733	2007	San Diego	18	199257	106	http://www.amadeus...	10	1	2007-03-22 22:49:44.407	2007-03-22 22:49:44.407
21	734	2244	Liverpool	18	199191	129	http://www.amadeus...	9	1	2007-03-22 22:49:44.407	2007-03-22 22:49:44.407
22	735	2231	Glasgow	18	199220	171	http://www.amadeus...	9	1	2007-03-22 22:49:44.407	2007-03-22 22:49:44.407

Figure 8-24. *The NDS* store *table after loading*

Practical Tips on SSIS

So, we have covered how we populate the NDS. Before I discuss how to populate the DDS, I'll share some practical tips on SSIS. I hope you will find them useful in doing your work later.

- To format your data flow quickly, press Alt+O, and then press Enter twice. This will invoke Auto Layout, which will arrange the boxes on your data flow design surface (sources, transformation, and targets) in a nice top-to-bottom order. If you want to do the same on the control flow design surface, press Alt+O, then press L, and finally hit Enter.

- On a data conversion task, to quickly select all columns, press Alt+A, and tick one check box. This is useful when the table has many columns.

- To quickly build a data flow similar to an existing one, select the objects, and then copy and paste. First you need to create an empty data flow. Then you open an existing data flow, select the object you want to copy, and press Ctrl+C to copy the object into memory. Open the new empty data flow, and press Ctrl+V to paste the objects from memory. This is useful when you have a lot of similar data flows to create in a package.

- To see the variable in a package, right-click the design surface, and choose Variable. This will open the Variables window. This is useful when you have several data flows all using LSET and CET datetime variables. You can select which columns to display by clicking the Properties button. The value column is very useful because it enables you to know the values of all variables in one go.

- It is better to define the variables when creating the Execute T-SQL Statement task (on the Result Set pane) rather than in the Variables window mentioned earlier. This is because in the Result Set pane you can define the scope of the variable, such as which container you want to create the variable in.

- If your SSIS package is big and doesn't fit into one screen, click the four arrow icons at the bottom-right corner of the design surface to navigate around the design surface. It's much better and quicker to move around the workflow to control flow objects than using scroll bars.

- In the Lookup transformation, on the Columns tab, to delete all lines between the left table and the right table, click the background, press Ctrl+A, and then press Delete.

- On the Data Conversion transformation, set the output data type according to the target column (see Table 8-19); otherwise, SSIS will produce a data conversion error when you run the package. In Table 8-19, I list some of the most popular used data types (in the target column) and what the data conversion output should be.

Table 8-19. *Data Conversion Output for Popular Data Types*

Target Column	Conversion Output	Notes
int	4-byte signed integer [DT_I4]	
tinyint	Single-byte unsigned integer [DT_UI1]	
datetime	Database timestamp [DT_DBTIMESTAMP]	
decimal	Numeric [DT_NUMERIC]	Don't choose decimal because you can specify only the scale and cannot specify the precision.
money	Currency [DT_CURRENCY]	There is only one data type for currency.
char, varchar	String [DT_STR]	Don't forget to specify the correct length; otherwise, a data conversion warning or error occurs.

Populating DDS Dimension Tables

Now that I have discussed how to populate the NDS, I'll discuss how to populate the DDS. The DDS is a dimensional store. The tables in the DDS are denormalized. Just like when loading data into the NDS, when loading data into the DDS, we also do an UPSERT operation to update or insert the source row depending on whether it exists in the target.

We have two main types of DDS tables: fact tables and dimension tables. In this section, I will discuss how to load data into dimension tables. In the next section, I will discuss how to load data into the fact tables. I will show how to use SSIS to load the data. I will show how to use the Slowly Changing Dimension Wizard to load the data into dimension tables. When loading data into dimensional tables in the DDS, you need to consider several issues: incremental loading, key management, denormalization, and slowly changing dimension. I'll discuss these four topics first, and then we will create an SSIS package to load the data into customer dimension.

Incremental loading: When populating the dimension tables in the DDS, we have the luxury of incremental loading. We don't have to worry about how to extract the data incrementally from the NDS because in the NDS everything is timestamped. When loading the stage data into the NDS, we always put the current time on the last-updated timestamp column. So, we know when each record was last updated. This enables us to load the NDS data into the DDS incrementally. In other words, we load only the NDS rows that changed since the last ETL run.

Key management: In the DDS, we don't have to maintain the surrogate keys. Surrogate keys are managed in the NDS. This makes the UPSERT operation simpler, because every row in the dimension table has a surrogate key. The surrogate keys that we use in the DDS are the same as the surrogate key that we use in the NDS. Bear in mind that in the NDS + DDS architecture we can have multiple DDS data stores. Because we define and manage the data warehouse surrogate key in the NDS, we can guarantee that *all* DDSs use the same surrogate key.

ODS, on the contrary, does not have surrogate keys, and we need to create and manage the surrogate keys in the DDS. In the ODS + DDS architecture, we can have only one DDS, so we don't have an issue of synchronizing the surrogate keys between DDSs. Earlier in this chapter when I discussed populating the NDS, I talked about surrogate key management. If you use the ODS + DDS architecture, you need to apply this method to manage the surrogate key in the DDS.

Denormalization: The dimension tables in the DDS are denormalized, whereas in the NDS they are normalized. Therefore, to load a single dimension table in the DDS, we need to get data from several tables in the NDS by joining them. For example, to load the store dimension in the DDS, in the NDS we need to join the store table with the store_type table. This is because the NDS store table has only the store type *keys*. Please refer to Figure 8-3 and Tables 8-1 to 8-3. To get the store type, we need to join the store table with the store_type table.

Slowly changing dimension (SCD): The dimension tables in DDS have either SCD type 1 (overwrite), SCD type 2 (rows), or SCD type 3 (column). Please refer to Chapter 5 for more information about SCD. In the Amadeus Entertainment case study, the product dimension is SCD type 1, the customer dimension is SCD type 2, and the store dimension is SCD type 3. If the dimension is SCD type 1, we just overwrite the old attribute values with the new values. If the dimension is SCD type 2, we need to create a new row containing the new attribute values and expire the old row. If the dimension is SCD type 3, we need to put the old values into another column and put the new values in the main attribute column.

A good way to learn more about these four topics in SQL Server data warehousing is by implementing them using SSIS. So, let's populate our customer dimension using SSIS, and I'll explain these topics as we go along:

1. Open BIDS. Create a new SSIS package, and name it **DDS Customer.**

2. Drop an Execute SQL task onto the design surface, name it **Set Customer CET**, set the connection to the metadata database, and set the SQL statement as follows:

```
update data_flow
set status = 3, CET = getdate()
where name = 'dds_customer'
```

This statement sets the status of the dds_customer data flow in the ETL metadata to in progress and sets the current extraction time to now.

3. To extract incrementally from the NDS, we need to retrieve the last successful extraction time (LSET) into a variable so that we can use it in the Execute SQL task to limit the extraction query. To do this, create a row for the dds_customer task in the data_flow table in the metadata database by issuing the following SQL statement using SQL Server Management Studio (set the LSET to last week and CET to today). You can use Query Builder to compose the SQL statement by clicking the Query menu and choosing Design Query in Editor.

```
insert into data_flow (name, status, LSET, CET)
values ('dds_customer', 0, 'yyyy-mm-dd', 'yyyy-mm-dd')
```

4. Now let's read the LSET from the data_flow table in the metadata database into a variable. Drop an Execute SQL task onto the design surface, name it **Get Customer LSET**, set ResultSet to "Single row," set the connection to NDS, and set the SQL statement to select LSET, CET from dataflow where name = 'dds_customer', as shown in Figure 8-25.

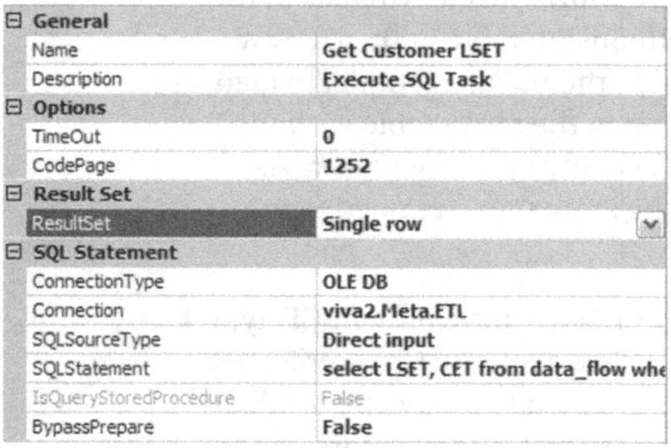

General	
Name	**Get Customer LSET**
Description	**Execute SQL Task**
Options	
TimeOut	**0**
CodePage	**1252**
Result Set	
ResultSet	**Single row**
SQL Statement	
ConnectionType	**OLE DB**
Connection	**viva2.Meta.ETL**
SQLSourceType	**Direct input**
SQLStatement	**select LSET, CET from data_flow whe**
IsQueryStoredProcedure	False
BypassPrepare	**False**

Figure 8-25. *Retrieving the last successful extraction time into a variable to extract incrementally*

5. To map the output of the query to variables, click Result Set on the left side, click Add, and set the result name to CET. In the Variable Name column, create a new variable called dtCET_Customer, set the namespace to User, set the value type to DateTime, type **2007-01-01** in the Value field, and leave the "Read only" box unchecked. Do the same for LSET; map it to a new variable called dtLSET_Customer with the Namespace, Value type, Value, and "Read only" boxes set the same as you did for CET, as shown in Figure 8-26.

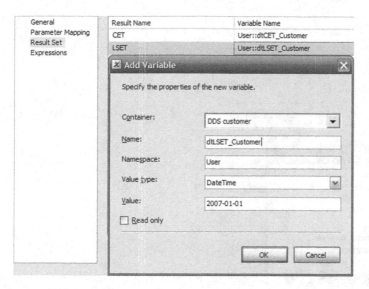

Figure 8-26. *Mapping the result set to variables*

6. Now we can create a task to retrieve the data from NDS incrementally using the CET and LSET that we have put into variables. To do this, drop a Data Flow task (some people call it DFT) onto the design surface, and name it **Populate Customer Dimension**. Double-click it to edit it. Add an OLE DB source, name it **Customer NDS**, set the connection to NDS, set the data access mode to SQL Command, and set the command text as follows:

```
select * from customer
where (create_timestamp >= ? and create_timestamp < ?)
or (update_timestamp >= ? and update_timestamp < ?)
```

The previous SQL statement gets customer records from the NDS that were created or updated within a certain date range.

7. The previous SQL statement has four parameters (indicated by four question marks). We need to map these parameters to the CET and LSET variables so that the where clause in the previous SQL statement is limited by the variables. Click the Parameters button, and specify the variables for each parameter, as shown in Figure 8-27. Then click OK.

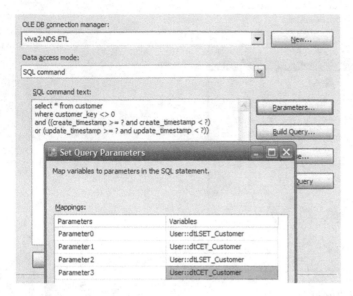

Figure 8-27. *Mapping the parameters to variables to extract incrementally*

8. We need to denormalize the customer dimension by looking up the values of `customer_type_key`, `customer_status_key`, `occupation_key`, `household_income_key`, and `permission_key` to get the customer type, customer status, occupation, household income, and permission, and then we need to insert the whole record into the customer dimension. We will use the Lookup transformation to look up the surrogate keys. Drop a Lookup transformation onto the design surface, name it **Customer Type**, connect the green arrow from the `customer` NDS into it, set the connection to NDS, select "Use results of an SQL query," and set the query as follows:

```
select customer_type_key, customer_type_code
from customer_type
```

9. Next, we need to specify the lookup column and the output column. On the Columns tab, map the `customer_type_key` column, and select the `customer_type_code` check box, as shown in Figure 8-28.

10. Now that we have completed the lookup of `customer_type`, let's do the same with `customer_status`, `occupation`, `household_income`, and `permission`. Figure 8-29 shows the data flow with the NDS `customer` table as the source and the five Lookup transformations that search surrogate keys to obtain the customer type, customer status, occupation, household income, and permission.

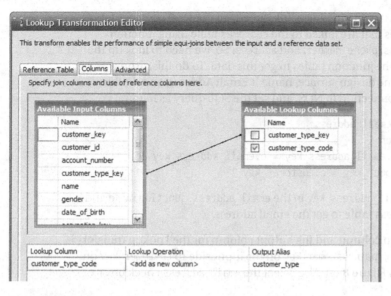

Figure 8-28. *Mapping the customer type columns on the Lookup transformation*

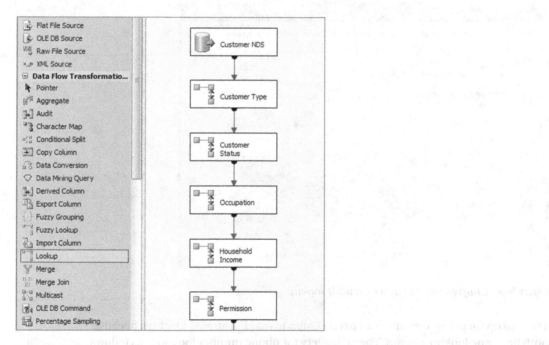

Figure 8-29. *Lookup transformations for populating the customer dimension*

11. The five attributes we did in the previous step link directly to the NDS customer table. But there are some attributes that are linked to the customer table using junction tables, such as email_address, phone_number, and address. So, we need to look up the customer surrogate keys in the junction tables to get this data. To do this, drop a Lookup transformation on the design surface, name it **Email Address**, and double-click it to edit it. Point the connection to NDS, and set the SQL query as follows:

```
select j.customer_key, e.email_address
from email_address_junction j
join email_address e on j.email_address_key = e.email_address_key
join customer c on j.customer_key = c.customer_key
```

This SQL statement gets email_address_key in the email_address_junction table and then goes to the email_address table to get the email address.

12. We need to define the lookup column and the output column for the Lookup transformation. On the Columns tab, map customer_key on the input side to customer_key on the lookup side, as shown in Figure 8-30. Also select the email_address check box to output that column.

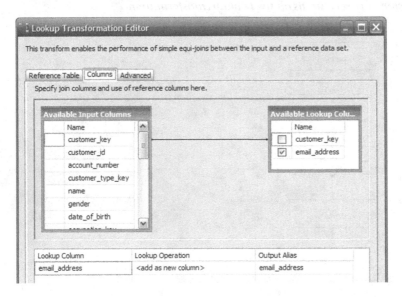

Figure 8-30. *Configuring the junction table lookup*

13. The lookup for phone_number_junction is similar to email_address_junction because both have one lookup column. The SQL query for phone number lookup is as follows. This SQL statement finds phone_number_key for the customer and then gets the phone number:

```
select j.customer_key, p.phone_number
from phone_number_junction j
join phone_number p on j.phone_number_key = p.phone_number_key
join customer c on j.customer_key = c.customer_key
```

14. The lookup for the address junction is a little bit different because we need to join with three other tables and because it has multiple output columns. The SQL query for the address lookup is as follows. This SQL statement gets the address key from the junction table and then gets the customer address, including the city name, state name, and country name.

```
select j.customer_key, a.address1, a.address2,
  a.address3, a.address4, ci.city_name as city,
  a.post_code, st.state_name as state,
  co.country_name as country
from address_junction j
join address a on j.address_key = a.address_key
join customer c on j.customer_key = c.customer_key
join city ci on a.city_key = ci.city_key
join state st on a.state_key = st.state_key
join country co on a.country_key = co.country_key
```

The purpose of naming the previous output columns (city, state, and country) is to match the column names in the dimension table so that the SCD transformation can automatically map the columns. Figure 8-31 shows the key mapping and output columns.

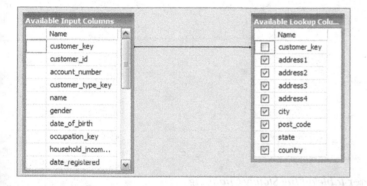

Figure 8-31. *Key mapping and output columns for address lookup*

In this data flow, so far we have looked up all the customer attributes from the corresponding tables: customer_type, customer_status, occupation, household_income, permission, email_address, phone_number, and address. We now have a full customer record from the NDS, ready to be loaded into the customer dimension in the DDS. Remember that the customer dimension has SCD type 2 (see Chapter 5 for more information). We are going to load the customer data into the DDS using the Slowly Changing Dimension Wizard. The Slowly Changing Dimension Wizard will produce a data flow that will do the UPSERT operation into the DDS customer dimension table. This means loading new customers and updating existing customers.

1. Open the Slowly Changing Dimension Wizard. Drop the Slowly Changing Dimension from the toolbar onto the design surface. Double-click it to edit.

2. Define a new connection to the DDS database. Choose `dim_customer` as the target table. Immediately after choosing the table name, you should see that most columns are automatically mapped because they have the same names and the same data types, as shown in Figure 8-32.

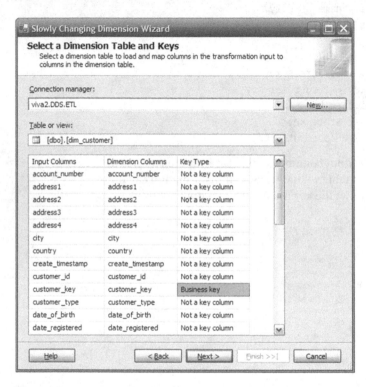

Figure 8-32. *Mapping the columns of* `customer` *table on the Slowly Changing Dimension Wizard*

3. Select `customer_key` as the business key, as shown in Figure 8-32. Some columns are not mapped automatically because they have different names. For these columns, choose the right input columns. In the case study, we need to map the `post_code` column to `zipcode`. Leave `effective_date`, `expiry_date`, and `is_current` unmapped. We will be using them for SCD later. After you have mapped all the columns, click Next to move to the next step.

4. The next screen is Slowly Changing Dimension Columns, shown in Figure 8-33. On this screen, we define the change type for each column such as "Fixed attributes," "Changing attributes," or "Historical attributes." Let's go through what these three change types mean.

Fixed attributes means that the value should not change; changes are treated as errors (by processing the error output). For example, you may want to consider create_timestamp, date_of_birth, date_registered, and gender columns to be fixed attributes.

Changing attributes means that the new values will overwrite existing values. Select this type when you don't need to store the history, such as when you need only the latest version. For example, you may want to consider source_system_code, update_timestamp, subscriber_band, subscriber_class, interest, and preferred_ channels columns as changing attributes because you don't need to store their previous values.

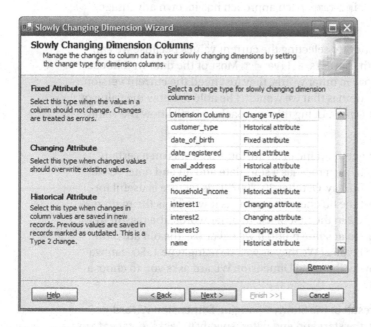

Figure 8-33. *Assigning the change type for each dimension attribute*

Historical attributes means SCD type 2; in other words, SSIS will create a new row containing the new attribute values. The existing row will be marked as outdated. The new row will be marked as current, meaning that it is the active row containing the valid attribute values. Most columns in the customer dimension would be in this category. For example, you may want to make the address columns (including city, state, country, and post_code), phone_number, email_address, customer_type, customer_id, status, name, occupation, and household_income historical attributes, if you need to store the previous values either for analysis purposes or for data traceability. When you have assigned the correct change type to every column, click Next to go to the next screen.

5. For the fixed attributes, we have the option to fail the SCD transformation when changes are detected, meaning that the package execution will stop. If you prefer this option (for example, because you can't load the target table), select the check box. For changing attributes, we have the option to change all matching records when changes are detected. This includes outdated records. If you prefer this option, select the check box. For this case study, leave both check boxes unselected.

6. Click Next to go to Historical Attribute Options, as shown in Figure 8-34. On this screen, we have two options to implement SCD 2: we can use a single column, or we can use start and end dates. In the customer dimension, I have prepared for both options so you can learn both of them. We have an is_current column, and we have effective_timestamp and expiry_timestamp. Each approach has its own advantage and disadvantage.

   Using the is_active column is better for selecting the current values because we can constrain the dimension table with where is_active = 1. Most of the data warehouse queries are asking for the active row. In other words, they just need the current version. The drawback of using a single column is that we wouldn't be able to know the value of an attribute *at a certain point in the past*. Using this approach, we will know the value of an attribute only as it is now.

   Using date columns enables us to get the value of an attribute as it was on a certain date in the past. With this approach, each row has a start date and an end date, so we can find out which row was active on, say, October 30, 2007. This feature is useful for business analysis, such as to report the business situation "as it was." It is the main reason why we implemented SCD type 2 in the first place. In other words, the reason to preserve the old values is to use them at some point. If we never use the old attribute values, why do we need to use SCD type 2? We may as well be using type 1. So, can we have both? Unfortunately, the Slowly Changing Dimension Wizard asks you to choose only one, as shown in Figure 8-34.

7. Fortunately, you can modify the result of the Slowly Changing Dimension Wizard to add the other one. So, let's choose the start and end dates, specify effective_timestamp as the start date column, and specify expiry_timestamp as the end date column. Set "Variable to set date values" to dtCET_Customer, which we created earlier, and click Next.

8. The next screen is Inferred Dimension Members, as shown in Figure 8-35.

   In a dimensional data store, a fact row may arrive before the corresponding dimension row. There are three common solutions to this: not loading the fact row, loading the fact row and pointing it to the dimension's unknown record, or creating a dummy row in the dimension table. The screen shown in Figure 8-35 enables us to create a dummy dimension row. In this case, the fact table will reference a customer dimension row, which has not been loaded. This is done by creating a dummy row in the dimension table that contains just the customer key. When the dimension row is finally loaded, SSIS will update that dummy row. This dummy row is called an *inferred dimension member*. This situation is commonly referred to as *late-arriving dimension rows*. There is another situation called *late-arriving fact* (see the next section).

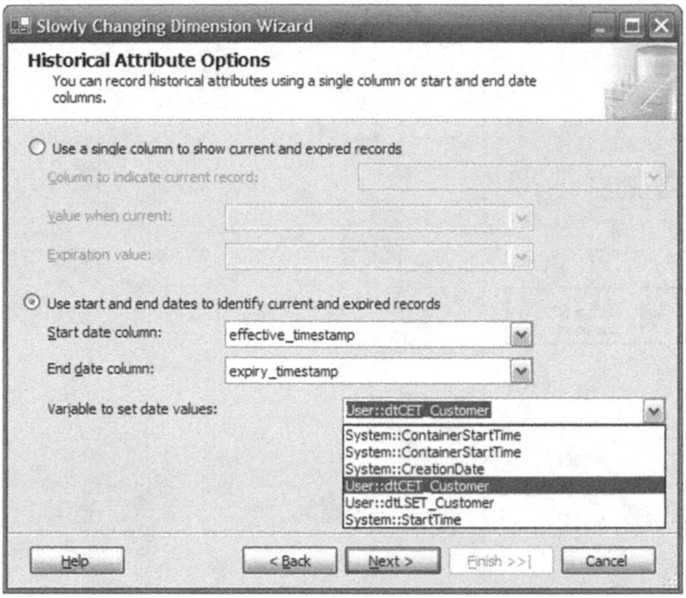

Figure 8-34. *Historical attribute options in the Slowly Changing Dimension Wizard*

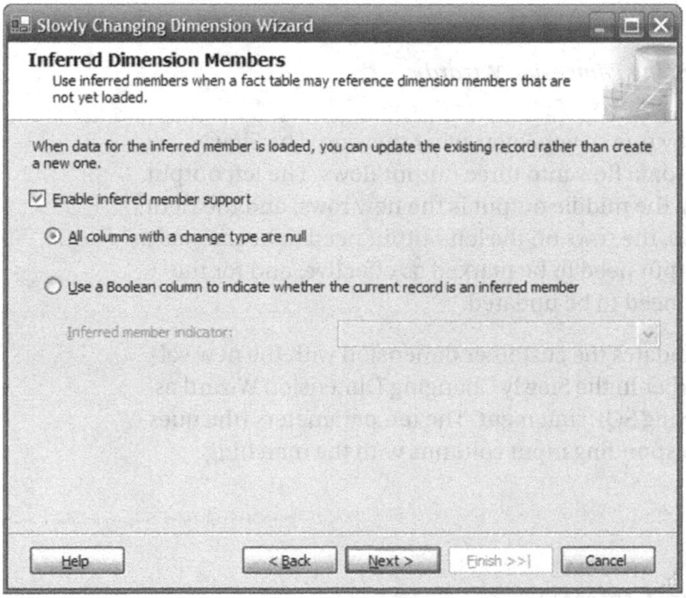

Figure 8-35. *Inferred Dimension Members screen*

There are two ways to tell SSIS that a row is an inferred member: when an indicator column is true or when all columns are null (except the key column). Let's enable the inferred member support and leave the option as "all columns with a change type are null."

9. Click Next, and then click Finish. Rename the boxes as shown in Figure 8-36.

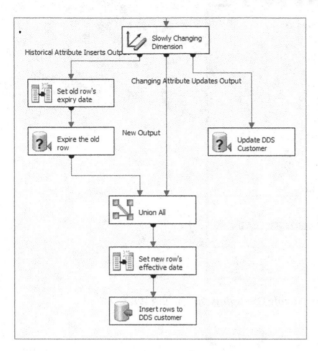

Figure 8-36. *Result of the Slowly Changing Dimension Wizard*

I'll discuss the resulting boxes one by one so you know what they are. The Slowly Changing Dimension box splits the data flow into three output flows. The left output is the historical attributes/old rows, the middle output is the new rows, and the right output is the changing attributes. So, the rows on the left output need to be marked as expired, the rows on the middle output need to be marked as effective, and for the rows on the right output the values need to be updated.

10. The "Update DDS Customer" box updates the customer dimension with the new values for columns that we marked earlier in the Slowly Changing Dimension Wizard as changing attributes using the following SQL statement. The ten parameters (the question marks) are mapped to the corresponding input columns with the matching names.

```
UPDATE dim_customer
SET interest1 = ?, interest2 = ?, interest3 = ?,
  preferred_channel1 = ?, preferred_channel2 = ?,
  source_system_code = ?, subscriber_band = ?,
  subscriber_class = ?, update_timestamp = ?
WHERE customer_key = ? AND expiry_timestamp IS NULL
```

11. The "Set old row's expiry date" box assigns the dtCET_Customer variable to the expiry_timestamp column so that the expiry date of the old row is updated with the current extraction time. The "Expire the old row" box updates the expiry_timestamp column of the old row, using the following SQL statement, to the dtCET_Customer variable set previously. The purpose of doing this is to expire the old row because we are going to insert a new row containing the current attribute values.

```
UPDATE dim_customer SET expiry_timestamp = ?
WHERE customer_key = ? AND expiry_timestamp IS NULL
```

12. The Union All box (shown in Figure 8-37) combines the output of the previous "Expire the old row" box with the middle output of the SCD box (the new rows to be inserted). This prepares the new customer rows containing the current, valid attribute values. Double-click the Union All box to see the properties in Figure 8-37.

Figure 8-37. *Union All transformation to combine two outputs*

13. The "Set new row's effective date" box assigns the `dtCET_Customer` variable to the `effective_timestamp` column so that the new rows that will be inserted have the correct start dates.

14. The last box, which is marked as "Insert rows to DDS customer," inserts the new rows into the customer dimension in the DDS. You can double-click this box to see the column mapping, which is shown in Figure 8-38.

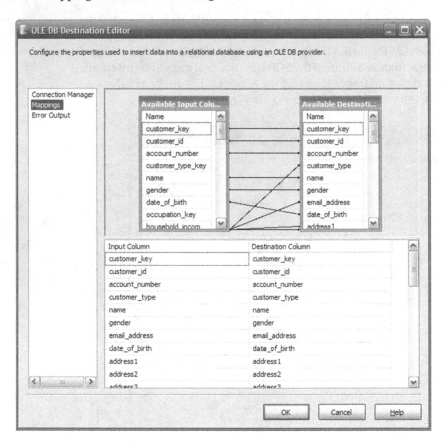

Figure 8-38. *Final mapping of the columns before inserting into dimension table*

Sometimes you get a warning saying truncation may happen on column X, such as if the subscriber class lookup is varchar(30) but on the customer dimension it is varchar(20). To solve this error, you can adjust the column width on the customer dimension table.

If there is no warning or error, save the package and run it. Check that the customer dimension is populated properly by comparing it to the NDS tables. Change some values in various columns in the `customer` table in the source system (the Jade database), and run the stage and NDS package to bring the data to the NDS. Do this by opening the SSIS package and then clicking the Debug menu and choosing Start Debugging (or pressing F5 for short). Then run the package we just created by pressing F5 to bring the data to the customer dimension and check whether the changes have been propagated properly. This is done by checking that the changes we made in the Jade database are propagated to the customer dimension in the DDS.

So, I have now covered the four points mentioned at the beginning of this section: incremental loading, key management, denormalization, and slowly changing dimension. Two more topics are worth mentioning here: *deletion* and *SCD type 3*. If you detect deletion in the source system (using delete triggers or primary key comparison; please refer to Chapter 7) and if the dimension is SCD type 2, then the deleted row is simply marked as expired. If you use the is_current flag, set the flag to 0.

If your dimension is SCD type 3 (preserve previous attributes in columns), such as the store dimension in the case study, unfortunately you cannot use the Slowly Changing Dimension Wizard because there is no facility for it in SSIS. I'll explain the mechanism for loading SCD type 3 dimension tables using a simplified store dimension in Figure 8-39. I have removed the nonrelevant columns from the diagram (address, phone_number, web_site) so we can concentrate on the region and division columns.

	store_key	store_number	store_name	store_type	region	prior_region	prior_region_date	division	prior_division	prior_division_date
1	0	0	Unknown	Unknown	Unknown	Unknown	1900-01-01 00:00:00.000	Unknown	Unknown	1900-01-01 00:00:00.000
2	715	1805	Perth	Distribution Centre	Australia		1905-03-12 00:00:00.000	America, Asia and Australia		1905-03-12 00:00:00.000
3	717	1209	Zaragoza	Distribution Centre	Spain		1905-03-12 00:00:00.000	Europe, Middle East & Africa		1905-03-12 00:00:00.000
4	762	1011	Lyon	Full Outlet	France		1905-03-12 00:00:00.000	Europe, Middle East & Africa		1905-03-12 00:00:00.000
5	810	1705	US Site	Online	Online		1905-03-12 00:00:00.000	Online Business		1905-03-12 00:00:00.000
6	815	1706	DE Site	Online	Online		1905-03-12 00:00:00.000	Online Business		1905-03-12 00:00:00.000

Figure 8-39. *A simplified store dimension with SCD type 3*

Both region and division are SCD type 3. They both have a prior value column, and they both have a prior date column. Although the previous example has only one prior value column, in practice we can have many prior value columns. In this scenario, we have 11 regions and three divisions, as shown in Figure 8-40.

	region_code	region_name	division_code
1	AU	Australia	AAA
2	CUS	Central US	AAA
3	DE	Germany	EMEA
4	ES	Spain	EMEA
5	EUS	Eastern US	AAA
6	FR	France	EMEA
7	IN	India	AAA
8	JP	Japan	AAA
9	UK	UK	EMEA
10	WUS	Western US	AAA
11	ON	Online	O

	division_code	division_name
1	AAA	America, Asia and Australia
2	EMEA	Europe, Middle East & Africa
3	O	Online Business

Figure 8-40. *Regions and divisions of Amadeus Entertainment before reorganization*

Let's suppose that Amadeus Entertainment does reorganize and there are only two divisions: High Street Business and Online Business. Under the High Street Business division there are three regions (North and South America, Europe and Africa, and Asia and Australia), and under the Online Business there are also three regions (North and South, Europe and Africa, and Asia and Australia).

We need to create a temporary table (we can use a table variable if the rows are not that numerous) containing the map between the old regions and divisions to the new ones. We then put the current values in the prior value column, and we put today's date in the prior date column. Then, using the map table, we update the current columns to the new values, as shown in Figure 8-41.

	store_key	store_number	store_name	store_type	region	prior_region	prior_region_date	division	prior_division	prior_division_date
1	0	0	Unknown	Unknown	Unknown	Unknown	1900-01-01 00:00:00.000	Unknown	Unknown	1900-01-01 00:00:00.000
2	715	1805	Perth	Distribution Centre	A&A	Australia	1905-03-12 00:00:00.000	High Street	America, Asia and Australia	1905-03-12 00:00:00.000
3	717	1209	Zaragoza	Distribution Centre	E&A	Spain	1905-03-12 00:00:00.000	High Street	EMEA	1905-03-12 00:00:00.000
4	762	1011	Lyon	Full Outlet	E&A	France	1905-03-12 00:00:00.000	High Street	EMEA	1905-03-12 00:00:00.000
5	810	1705	US Site	Online	N&SA	Online	1905-03-12 00:00:00.000	Online Business	Online Business	1905-03-12 00:00:00.000
6	815	1706	DE Site	Online	E&A	Online	1905-03-12 00:00:00.000	Online Business	Online Business	1905-03-12 00:00:00.000

Figure 8-41. *The simplified store dimension after the changes are loaded*

In this section, I discussed how to load dimension tables in the DDS. I discussed incremental loading, key management, denormalization, and SCD. In the next section, I will discuss how to populate the fact tables in the DDS.

Populating DDS Fact Tables

In this section, I will discuss the mechanism for loading the data from the NDS into the fact tables in DDS. I will also discuss updating and deleting fact table rows, populating a periodic snapshot fact table, and loading a fact table row where the corresponding dimension row has changed.

The basic mechanism in populating the fact table is reading the source rows from the NDS, looking up the dimensional keys, and inserting the keys into the fact table, as shown in Figure 8-42. Therefore, fact table population needs to be done after the dimension tables are populated.

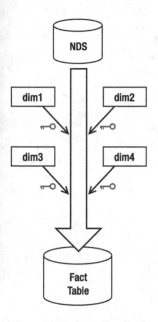

Figure 8-42. *Data flow in fact table population*

The data flow in SSIS is similar to the one shown in Figure 8-29. In other words, one OLE DB source is followed by a series of Lookup transformations. We can also use the Execute SQL approach, similar to the one I discussed earlier in this chapter when populating the NDS. For example, the SQL statement for inserting into the Product Sales fact table is as follows:

```
insert into fact_product_sales
( sales_date_key, customer_key, product_key,
  store_key, order_id, line_number, quantity,
  unit_price, unit_cost, sales_value,
  sales_cost, margin, sales_timestamp,
  source_system_code,
  create_timestamp, update_timestamp )
select oh.order_date, oh.customer_number, od.product_code,
  oh.store_number, oh.order_id, od.line_no, od.qty,
  od.price, od.unit_cost, od.qty * od.price as sales_value,
  od.qty * od.unit_cost as sales_cost,
  od.qty * (od.price - od.unit_cost) as margin,
  oh.order_date as sales_timestamp,
  1 as source_system_code,
  getdate() as create_timestamp,
  getdate() as update_timestamp
from nds.dbo.order_header oh
left join nds.dbo.order_detail od
on oh.order_id = od.order_id
```

The previous SQL statement selects the rows from the order_header and order_detail tables in the NDS and inserts them into the Product Sales fact table in the DDS. In the fact table, we don't store the natural keys such as customer number, product code, and store number; instead, we store the surrogate keys. So, we need to get the surrogate key from the dimension tables. The SQL statement to do that is as follows:

```
select coalesce(dd.date_key, 0) as date_key,
  coalesce(dc.customer_key, 0) as customer_key,
  coalesce(dp.product_key, 0) as product_key,
  coalesce(ds.store_key, 0) as store_key,
  oh.order_id, od.line_no, od.qty,
  od.price, od.unit_cost, od.qty * od.price as sales_value,
  od.qty * od.unit_cost as sales_cost,
  od.qty * (od.price - od.unit_cost) as margin,
  oh.order_date as sales_timestamp,
  1 as source_system_code,
  getdate() as create_timestamp,
  getdate() as update_timestamp
from nds.dbo.order_header oh
left join nds.dbo.order_detail od
on oh.order_id = od.order_id
left join dim_date dd
on dd.sql_date = oh.order_date
left join dim_customer dc
on dc.customer_number = oh.customer_number
left join dim_product dp
on dp.product_code = od.product_code
left join dim_store ds
on ds.store_number = oh.store_number
```

The previous SQL statement selects rows from the NDS order_header and order_detail tables and then gets the surrogate keys from the relevant DDS dimension tables. It then inserts the fact rows into the Product Sales fact table in the DDS.

In some data warehouses, we only do INSERTs on the fact tables. In other systems, we do both INSERTs and UPDATEs. If we need to update the fact table as well, we use the UPSERT technique. We can use either the SQL statement method or the Lookup transformation method. Fact tables are normally large tables (in terms of the number of rows). Table partitioning can speed up the update operation significantly when correctly applied to a fact table.

Whether it is better to drop the indexes before updating the fact table depends on what portion of the fact table we are updating and whether the fact table is partitioned. If we are updating a large number of rows, then it is probably worth it to drop the indexes. I'm talking about the index *on the measure columns*, not the dimensional key indexes. The dimensional key index is required to find the row that we want to update, so we should not drop them.

To determine whether it is beneficial to drop the measure column indexes, compare the time required to update the rows (without dropping the index) with the time required to drop the index first, update the rows, and then re-create the index. In most cases, I have found that dropping fact table indexes is not necessary. If the table is partitioned, there is no need to drop the indexes and re-create them afterward. Indexes do not slow down insert operations too much (depending on how many indexes exist on the table); it is the update operation that is more affected by indexes.

We don't usually delete from the fact table (except when purging). Cancellations or returns are implemented as inserts with negative quantities or with different transaction types. For example, in our case study, if a customer returns a product, we can insert a row in the Product Sales fact table with the quantity set to −1.

A periodic snapshot fact table requires a different loading method because it does not contain incremental transactional data. A periodic snapshot fact table is a fact table that captures the state or condition of the business at a particular point in time at a certain interval. An example of a periodic snapshot fact table is the Subscription Sales fact table in our Amadeus Entertainment case study (see Figure 5-5).

The source of this fact table is not from the order header and order detail in the NDS but from the customer dimension where customer type = subscriber. We read all active customers from the customer dimension; then join (or look up) with the store, lead, date, package, and format dimensions to get the dimensional keys; and then we load the rows into the fact table.

One interesting phenomenon in fact table population is a *late-arriving fact*. This is different from a late-arriving dimension row, which I discussed earlier. A late-arriving fact happens when we receive fact table rows with transaction dates in the past (say, a few weeks ago or a few months ago). As usual, we do a lookup in the dimension tables to get the dimensional keys and then load the row into the fact table.

But, when the transaction is a few months old, the dimension row may have changed. If the dimension table is using SCD type 2, we will have several rows in the dimension table. We need to find which row corresponds to the transaction that we load into the fact table. To do this, we use the effective date and expiry date columns in the dimension table. The correct dimension row for this transaction is the one where the fact table transaction date is between the effective date and expiry date.

For example, the customer dimension we populated in the previous section uses SCD type 2. The customer dimension row for this late-arriving fact row may have changed; for example, there may be four rows for this customer. Three of them are marked as inactive, and one of them is marked as active. Because we have the effective date and the expiry date, we can find which one of those three inactive rows is the correct one to apply for this late-arriving fact table transaction.

Batches, Mini-batches, and Near Real-Time ETL

Most of the data warehouse ETL processes run daily, weekly, or monthly. Many people refer to these ETL processes as *batches*. When people say *daily batch*, for example, they are referring to the ETL processes that run daily.

In recent years (the past two to three years), I have heard the term *mini-batch* more and more often. When people talk about a mini-batch, what they mean is a group of ETL processes (that brings data into the data warehouse) that runs hourly, typically between one to six hours. Only some of the ETL processes are included in the mini-batch. The rest still run in batches, such as daily, weekly, monthly, and so on.

In the Amadeus Entertainment case study, there is no business benefit in populating the Subscription Sales fact table hourly. The business requirement indicates that the revenues, costs, and margin associated with the subscription sales, subscription duration, and lead sources need to be evaluated every day (please refer to Chapter 4). There is also no business benefit for the Supplier Performance fact table to be loaded hourly. But it could be beneficial to run the Product Sales mart hourly in order to manage the inventory better, for example. The Campaign Results fact table could benefit from a mini-batch too. For example, it would enable the marketing department to know within an hour which customers clicked which links in the campaign e-mails so marketing can respond accordingly.

Because of this latest development (in other words, the mini-batch), data warehouses now have a new function. Ten years ago, data warehouses were intended for analysis purposes and not as operational systems. Now they can have an operational role.

Near real-time ETL is the term people use when the time lag between the data in the data warehouse and the data in the source systems is less than one hour, typically between 10 and 30 minutes. Again, in near real-time ETL, only some tables are set in that fashion. In the Amadeus Entertainment case study, not only could the Campaign Results fact table benefit from mini-batch, but also it would benefit from near real-time ETL. For example, to enable the marketing department to know within ten minutes which customers are interested in which products, they can react accordingly by using automated response rules.

Just like batch processes, both the mini-batch and near real-time ETL are based on pull approaches. The ETL processes *pull* the data from the source system into the data warehouse. The main difference between the three of them is the frequency they run. The batch ETL runs daily, weekly, or monthly; the mini-batch runs hourly; and the near real-time ETL typically runs every 10 to 30 minutes. The near real-time ETL is also known as a *micro-batch*.

To apply a micro-batch or near real-time ETL, you need to analyze the DDS fact tables and determine which one would benefit if they were loaded every few hours (or less). Ideally, you need to pick only one or two fact tables to minimize the negative impact on performance. The next step is to determine which dimensions associated with these fact tables need to be loaded at the same frequency. Then you can change the execution interval of the ETL processes.

Pushing the Data In

Data warehouse population has traditionally been done using ETL. The ETL processes *pull* the data from the source system and then load it into the data warehouse. In recent years, because of their operational functions, some data warehouses need to be updated as soon as the source system changes. In this case, the source systems push the data into the warehouse. In this approach, the source systems have triggers. They typically contain insert and update triggers but sometimes delete triggers too. Please refer to Figure 8-43.

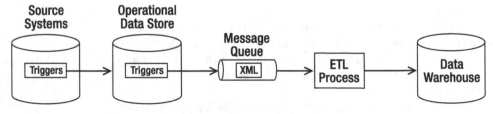

Figure 8-43. *Push approach for loading data*

As the application inserts or updates or deletes data from the source system database, these triggers are invoked, and they insert the changed data into the ODS. The tables in the ODS also have triggers that send the data changes to a message queuing (MQ) system in the form of XML messages. On the other end of the MQ, an ETL application constantly polls and processes the XML messages from the MQ, unwraps them, shreds them, assigns or looks up the data warehouse keys, and inserts them into appropriate dimensions and fact tables in the data warehouse. Or, leaving the MQ out, in the case of a DDS-only architecture (please refer to Chapter 2), the triggers in the source system update the DDS directly. A DDS-only architecture is more suitable for the push approach because there is no intermediary data store such as an NDS or an ODS. The typical lead time is between 5 and 30 seconds, happening in real time.

Three years ago, we heard this approach implemented only for enterprise application integration (EAI). Today, it is implemented for data warehouse population. Some people refer to this push approach as *real-time data integration*.

Let's understand how we can benefit from this technology. If we can push the data changes into the warehouse within 30 seconds, then in the case of Amadeus Entertainment, the marketing department can respond to customer *shopping* behavior. When an online customer is currently browsing the site looking for products or subscriptions but then abandons the shopping process and leaves the site, marketing can respond accordingly using the CRM system in almost real time.

One important consideration when loading large fact tables in real time is that we need to arrange the ETL so that we can insert into the fact table only. We can't possibly do an update or a delete, because this will take a few seconds and we don't have a few seconds. We have only a few milliseconds. When the daily batch runs, along with flipping the fact table views (see Chapter 6), we can process today's inserted data and do the updates in batches.

Summary

This chapter started with a brief discussion on stage loading, including the three approaches of stage tables. Then I talked a little bit about the data firewall, followed by several points that you need to consider when loading the NDS: normalization, external data, key management, and the many-to-many relationship. Then I showed how to load the data into the NDS using SSIS.

I showed how to use three different methods in SSIS to load the data: SQL statements, Slowly Changing Dimension transformations, and Lookup transformations. Then we populated the dimension tables and fact tables in the DDS, including SCD. And finally I discussed the batch, mini-batch, and near real-time (or micro-batch) ETL approaches, followed by the push approach.

CHAPTER 9

■ ■ ■

Assuring Data Quality

In this chapter, we'll explore why data quality is important, and I'll explain why there is no point having a data warehouse if we cannot trust the data in the warehouse. Then I will discuss the data quality process and explore the architecture elements that are involved in the process.

In addition, I will discuss data cleansing and explore the three types of matching logic: exact, fuzzy (approximate), and rule based. I'll show how to do a Fuzzy Lookup transformation in SSIS to identify duplication in artist names based on the similarity scores. I will also discuss cross-checking with external sources. Then I'll talk about the three categories of data quality rules: incoming data, cross-references, and internal rules.

I'll discuss the three choices of what to do with the data when a data quality rule is violated: we can reject it, allow it into the warehouse, or fix/correct it. I'll also talk about logging, which is basically storing the failed rows in the data quality (DQ) database, along with additional audit information, such as the time it happened, which rule was violated, and the correction status; this is for the purpose of auditing and reporting later. We will then end the chapter with reporting and notification so that someone can correct the data.

So, why is data quality important? It is easy to answer this simple question. Say you can't trust the data in your data warehouse, perhaps because some data is incorrect (accuracy), because some data is missing (completeness), because some data is not in sync with other data (consistency), because some data is only a rough estimate (precision), or because some data is out-of-date (timeliness). In these cases, would it still be possible for you to use the data warehouse? If you use the data for making important decisions and the data is incorrect, how much will the mistake cost the company? And how bad will it be for your career?

Further, if you cannot trust the data in your data warehouse, what is the point of having a data warehouse? To prevent this disaster, when building a data warehouse, it is important to think about data quality as early as possible, preferably at the beginning of the project. The essence of maintaining data quality is to prevent bad data from getting into the data warehouse and to fix the bad data as early as possible in the process chain (ideally at the source system). To implement this, we need to set up rules that define what "bad data" is and put additional components in the architecture to filter the bad data out and to enable reporting, monitoring, and cleaning mechanisms.

Data Quality Process

The data quality process includes the activities to make sure the data in the data warehouse is correct and complete. This is usually done by checking the data on its way into the data warehouse. The data quality process also includes the mechanism to report the bad data and to correct it. So, there are three aspects of the data quality process: checking, reporting, and correcting.

For example, in the Amadeus Entertainment case study, customers can purchase a product, or they can subscribe to a package. The date a customer subscribes to a package for the first time is called the *first subscription date*, and the most recent date they canceled their subscriptions is called the *last cancellation date*. Suppose one day the ETL process extracted a customer record with the last cancellation date earlier than the first subscription date. This is not a valid condition. Either the last cancellation date is wrong or the first subscription date is wrong, or both. The data quality process detects this condition and reports it to the people responsible for the subscription data. They then correct the data in the source system, and the data is loaded into the data warehouse.

To understand the mechanism of how the data quality process works, look at Figure 9-1. It shows the ODS + DDS architecture discussed in Chapter 2, with the data quality components added.

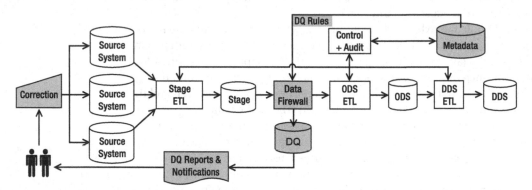

Figure 9-1. *Data quality components in the data warehouse architecture*

The DQ components in Figure 9-1 are shaded and are as follows:

- The data firewall is a program that checks the incoming data. Physically it is an SSIS package or a stored procedure.

- Metadata is a database that stores the data quality rules, such as "The last cancellation date must be greater than the first subscription date."

- The DQ database stores the bad data detected by the data firewall.

- DQ reports and notifications read the DQ database and inform the people responsible for data quality.

- Correction is a process to correct the data in the source system.

In Figure 9-1, the stage ETL extracts the data from the source system and loads it into the stage database. The data firewall then checks the data according to the data quality rules from the metadata database, such as "The first subscription date is greater than or equal to the last cancellation date." If the data satisfies the DQ rule, the data is passed to the ODS ETL, which will then put the data into the ODS. If the data fails the DQ rule, it is put in the DQ database.

When the data is placed in the DQ database, certain auditing information is recorded too, such as which source system the data is coming from, which table in the source system it is from, what time (and date) this happened, which rule(s) failed the data, and what table/mart/area this data is for.

DQ reports and notifications read the DQ database at regular intervals, such as daily. In the DQ database, we have many records from different DQ rules. For example, we could have 2,000 records from 100 different DQ rules, or an average of 20 for each rule. The DQ database also contains information about who is responsible for each rule; for example, the customer service department is responsible for rules 1 to 10, which are about customer data, and the finance department is responsible for rules 11 to 20, which are about financial data.

DQ reports and notifications read the records in the DQ database rule by rule and report them to the appropriate people at a regular interval. The people fix the data in the source system so that the next time that data is extracted by the stage ETL, it is already correct. The purpose of these reports and notifications is to notify the users to get the data corrected. They contain the previous day's (or previous week's) errors.

There is another group of data quality reports whose purpose is to analyze the data quality in the data warehouse. One indicator of the quality of the data in the data warehouse is the number of times each rule was violated. The reports contain the number of DQ rule violations for a certain period.

This analysis can also be done using data quality dashboards. *Dashboards* are business intelligence applications that give a quick summary of the data quality in graphical gadgets, typically gauges, charts, and indicators. By clicking these gadgets, we can drill down to lower-level details. We will discuss more about data quality dashboards later in this chapter.

Tip If you implement a data warehouse for the purpose of business intelligence, you may think it is a good idea to use the same notification mechanism for alerting certain managers about time-dependant business warnings such as a period of low sales. This idea is usually inspired by the fact that this is the earliest point in the system where the data is coming into the warehouse. The earlier the managers know about this alert, the better, right? Well, no. The data coming into the data firewall is not a complete set where you can examine it in a true business sense. For business alerts like this, your notification service needs to operate off the ODS (or the DDS) after it is fully loaded, not in the middle of the loading process; for example, we can put it at the end of the ETL batch.

In the box marked as Correction in Figure 9-1, the people responsible for the appropriate areas (product sales, subscriptions, customers, products, currency, and so on) then fix the data in the source system so that when the data is loaded again the next day (or whenever), the data is already correct. We can fix the data automatically on its way into the data warehouse, but generally this is not a good practice because it is still wrong in the source system. Other applications that may be using the same data (or the source system itself) will publish incorrect data.

Can the correction in the source system be automated? The simple answer is yes. But we need to be careful when doing this. First, the rule for automatic correction must be checked and double-checked to make sure it is 100 percent correct. Second, it is generally better to understand how the bad data is created in the source system and why this happens. If it is within our control, let's fix it so it doesn't happen again. That is better than automatically correcting it every day.

In reality, the boundary between good data and bad data is not always clear. For example, if the data value is 5,000 or more, it is good. If the value is 3,000 or less, it is bad. But if the value is between 3,000 and 5,000, it is not good but not too bad. So, in practice, we need to set how we want to react accordingly. For example, we may have a different treatment for each range. Or, a certain range qualifies as a "warning," and a certain range qualifies as an "error," and so on. In this example, if the data value is between 3,000 and 5,000, we want to classify it as a warning, but if the value is lower than 3,000, it is an error.

In Figure 9-1, instead of putting the data firewall before the ODS ETL, we can put it before the stage ETL. The data quality checks the data as the data is being loaded into the stage tables. If the data satisfies the DQ rule, it is loaded into the stage tables. If it fails the DQ rules, the data is placed in the DQ database for reporting and correction. The extraction process is slower, but this means the bad data does not touch any area of the data warehouse at all, not even the stage.

We can also check the data on the source system and not extract bad data; in other words, the where clause is dynamically set. For example, we can use select product_code, product_name, description, status, … etc… where product_code <> 19331. The data from the source is clean, but the extraction is slower. The other disadvantage is that we can't report the bad data comprehensively because that data is not extracted.

The problem in data quality is usually not about a particular record but about a collection of records. For example, usually in a medium-sized branch there are about 20,000 to 60,000 transactions a day, with total sales of $0.6 million to $6 million (for small or large branches, the metrics are different). If the number of transactions is less than 10,000 or the total sales is $0.5 million, it is probably an indication of extraction or loading failure, so we want this condition to be reported.

One way to do this is to have what we call an *ODS firewall*, in Figure 9-2. The ODS firewall is a program that runs after the data has been loaded into the ODS but before it is loaded into the DDS. The ODS firewall reads the ODS database and checks the data according to the DQ rules from the metadata database.

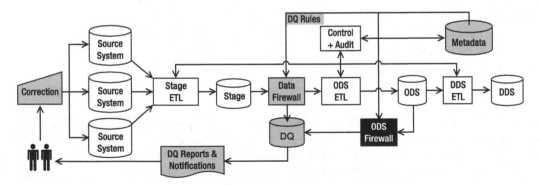

Figure 9-2. *The ODS firewall (bottom right) checks the data against the DQ rules.*

If the collection of data fails the DQ rules, we put the data on the DQ database, along with the auditing information such as which table in the source system it is from, what time (and date) this happened, which rule(s) failed the data, and what table/mart/area this data is for. We could let the data remain in the ODS (and be subsequently loaded into the DDS), or we can remove the data from the ODS (and not be loaded into the DDS) until the problem is fixed. The approach we need to take depends on the nature of the data. If it is more important for the data to be present in the data warehouse even though it is not complete, then we load the data into the DDS. But if the incompleteness causes problems in the business analysis or decision making, then we remove the data from the ODS.

If we allow the data to stay in the ODS (and load it into the DDS), we need to mark the data quality. We do this by adding up to five data quality keys on each row of data: accuracy, precision, timeliness, completeness, and consistency. These keys refer to the five data quality dimensions. We don't have to use all five keys. We can just use two of them (such as accuracy and precision), depending on which ones we need.

Alternatively, we can just have a single DQ key on each row. This single DQ key is called *reliability*, which is calculated based on the scores of the five DQ base dimensions. For example, the calculation can simply be a weighted average such as reliability = A * accuracy + B * precision + C * timeliness + D *completeness + E * consistency, where A, B, C, D, and E are percentages that add up to 100 percent. This reliability "stamp" on each row enables the users to know how much they can trust the data. The disadvantage of this approach is that the calculation could become a little bit tricky. For example, if an aggregate is calculated by averaging fifty rows all with an accuracy of 5 but there are two rows with an accuracy of 1, how would you score the accuracy of the aggregate?

Now that you understand the mechanism of data quality in the data warehouse, how data quality is implemented in the architecture, which components are affected, and the alternative approaches, I'll discuss the details of each component, such as the rules, the actions, the logging and auditing, and the reporting. But before I do that, I'll talk about two other areas in data quality, namely, data cleansing and external data.

Data Cleansing and Matching

What is data cleansing? Why is it important in data quality? Put simply, data cleansing, or *data scrubbing*, is the process of identifying and correcting dirty data. *Dirty data* means incomplete, wrong, duplicate, or out-of-date data. I'm not sure why, but people in the data warehousing community prefer to use the words *cleanse* and *scrub* rather than *clean*, which is simpler and more descriptive. An example of data cleansing is checking stores' tables to make sure the store names, store numbers, store types, and store addresses are all correct. Other examples are making sure that there are no duplicate customer records, that the price lists are correct, that obsolete products are flagged accordingly, that all subscriptions refer to existing packages, and that the song and film titles are correctly spelled.

In data cleansing, it is important to be able to determine that one data item is the same as another data item. This is called *data matching*. Data matching is used to identify duplicate records when doing a lookup on reference data. Matching is particularly relevant for character-based data types, including large value data types, such as varchar(max), because for numerical or datetime data types, we can simply use the equal sign. For character-based data types, it may not be that clear. For example, when loading the address table in the NDS, we may find that the city name is "Los Angles," which does not exist in the city table. In this case, we need to match "Los Angles" to "Los Angeles." Another example is the customer name "Robert Peterson." We need to match/recognize that "Robert Peterson" is the same as "Bob Peterson."

Numeric data is not as tricky as character data. We can just use the equal sign; 5 is 5 whatever way we look at it, and 5 is different from 6. So, we can just use = for matching numeric data. For example, "if A = B, then…." The only possible problem is rounding; for example, is 5.029 the same as 5.03? If the precision is two decimal digits, they are the same, but if the precision is three decimal digits, then they are different.

For date and time data, if the data is stored as a datetime data type, it's not a problem. We can just use the equal sign like the numeric data. But if it is stored as a character data type, it could be a little bit tricky because of the date format and time zone. For example, is 03/01/2008 the same as 01/03/2008? Is it the same as 2007-03-01T00:00:00Z+06? We need a little bit of logic here to match them, such as by comparing the components or by comparing the date, month, and year.

In SQL Server we have three types of matching logic: exact, fuzzy (approximate), and rule based. Exact matching is where all characters are the same, for example "Los Angeles" and "Los Angeles." In SSIS this is done using a Lookup transformation. Fuzzy logic matching finds how similar a set of data is to another set of data. For example, using the Fuzzy Lookup transformation in SSIS, "You can't hurry love" and "You cannot hurry love" have a similarity score of 0.81666672 and a confidence level of 0.59414238. You can then decide for example that if the similarity score is greater than 0.75 and the confidence level is greater than 0.5, then it's a match.

To determine the threshold for the similarity score and confidence level (0.75 and 0.5 in the previous case), we need to run the data through a Fuzzy Lookup transformation with the similarity threshold set to zero. This will output the similarity scores for all the rows in the source data. We then manually examine the score to find the appropriate threshold. We will do this (finding the threshold) later in this section.

Rule-based logic is where we use certain rules and data to identify a match. For example, we can define (in a table) that for name data the string "Bill" is the same as "William" or in product names "movie" is the same as "film." In SSIS this is implemented with database lookup. We can also define a rule, such as "For product code, omit the spaces when comparing" so that "KL 7923 M" is the same as "KL7923M." Here's another example: "Omit prefix 9000 in the supplier number" so that "900089123" and "89123" are the same. SSIS logic like the previous can be implemented with Script Component.

Let's open Business Intelligence Development Studio (BIDS) and construct a fuzzy logic and a rule-based logic solution. As they say, the devil is in the details. And without trying it, we wouldn't know the details. In this scenario, we have a table in Jade called artist2. The table contains 20 artists that we are going to load into NDS. The artist2 table also contains city and country, as shown in Table 9-1.

Table 9-1. `artist2` *Table in the Jade Source System*

artist_code	artist_name	genre	country	city
CAT011	Catherine Jarrette	CJ	Poland	Warsaw
NIC003	Nicoleta Jadyn	BF	Andorra	Andorra la Vella
ADE006	Adellais Clarinda	BX	Zambia	Lusaka
CHE019	Cheyanne Chantelle	BA	Australia	Canberra
HUG005	Hughie Violet	BE	Norway	Oslo
PAL002	Palmira Charlie	BE	Israel	Jerusalem
LUC003	Luciana Chrysanta	CC	Nigeria	Abuja
CEL008	Celeste Vitolia	AH	Nicaragua	Managua
EVE002	Evete Mona	CH	Mauritius	Port Louis
ALI004	Alienor Hambert	CG	Kazakhstan	Astana
CHL003	Chloe Ignatius	AJ	United States	Washington DC
HUG005	Hugh Clarity	AW	Taiwan	Taipei
SUS002	Susan Johansen	BN	Belgium	Brussels
TAN001	Tania Balumbi	AW	Pakistan	Islamabad
VIC001	Victor Robinson	CE	Luxembourg	Luxembourg
THO001	Thomas Clark	AJ	Japan	Tokyo
TIM001	Tim Lewis	AJ	Germany	Berlin
LAU002	Laura Scott	AN	Congo	Kinshasa
PET001	Peter Hernandez	AP	Spain	Madrid
ADA001	Adam Baxter	BQ	Egypt	Cairo

Out of these twenty artists, nine are new artists. Eleven of those twenty, however, actually already exist in the NDS, but their names are slightly different. For example, one that already exists in the NDS is "Catherine Jarrett," but the incoming data is "Catherine Jarrette."

We are going to use a Fuzzy Lookup transformation with certain similarity levels to determine whether the artists already exist in the NDS. If they exist, we update the NDS. If they don't exist, we will insert them into the NDS. In this case, we will find first what the confidence level should be by pointing the output of the Fuzzy Lookup transformation to a file and setting up a data viewer. The city and country need be translated into keys using normal lookup (exact match). As with every NDS table, we also need to populate the source_system_code, create_timestamp, and update_timestamp columns. We'll use a Derived Column transformation to populate these three columns. Using a Derived Column transformation, we can create new columns containing constant values or calculations based on the input columns.

In Chapters 7 and 8 I discussed how to extract and load data using SSIS and gave quite a lot of detailed exercises, so you should be quite familiar with it by now. Let's get started:

1. Define a new SSIS package, and call it **NDS Artist**.

2. Create a Data Flow task on the design surface, and call it **Load Artist**.

3. Double-click it to edit it.

4. Create an OLE DB connection (please refer to Chapter 7), call it **Jade Artist**, and point this connection to the Jade database.

5. Set Data Access Mode to table or view and the name of the table to **Artist2**. Click Preview to check; there should be 20 rows. In the column pane, ensure that all columns are selected.

6. Create a Lookup transformation, name it **Lookup City**, and connect the green arrow from Jade Artist to it. Point the connection to the NDS, set the SQL as select city_key, city_name from city, and map the incoming city column to the city_name column on the lookup table. Define one output column, and call it **city_key**, as shown in Figure 9-3. Click OK to close Lookup City.

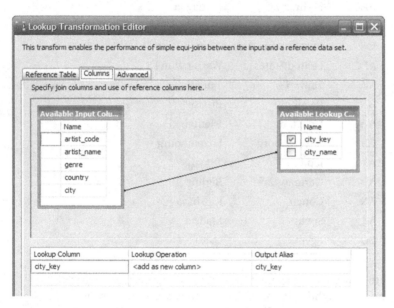

Figure 9-3. *Looking up the city key using a normal lookup*

7. Repeat step 6 for country. When doing a lookup like this, you can (you should, really) redirect the error output to a file for further processing (for example, to prevent the next step from loading the data into the DDS or for analyzing the failed data) as well as for auditing purposes.

8. After you are done with country, create a Derived Column transformation. This is to add the source_system_code, create_timestamp, and update_timestamp columns. Name the transformation **Source Code & Timestamps**, and configure it as per Figure 9-4.

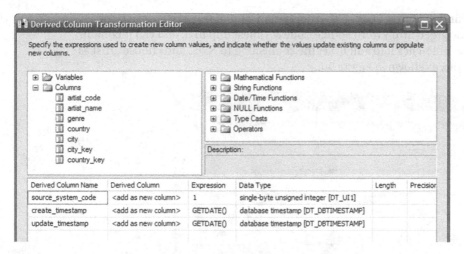

Figure 9-4. *Using derived column to define source system code and timestamps*

9. The resulting data flow will be similar to the one in Figure 9-5. The last two boxes in Figure 9-5 (Lookup Artist Names and Flat File Destination) are not done yet. We'll do them next.

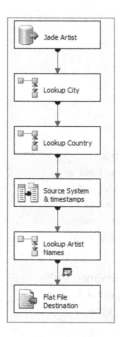

Figure 9-5. *Data flow for loading the* artist2 *table using fuzzy lookup*

10. In the Toolbox, find the Fuzzy Lookup transformation, and drag it to the design surface. Connect the green arrow from Source Code & Timestamp to it, and call it **Lookup Artist Names**. Double-click it to edit it, set the connection to NDS, and choose artist as the reference table, as shown in Figure 9-6.

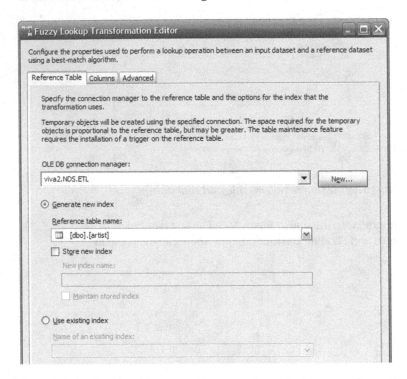

Figure 9-6. *Setting the reference table on the Fuzzy Lookup transformation*

11. Now we want to look up the artist record in the NDS (target) based on the artist name on the stage (source). For that, click the Columns tab. Ensure that all the Pass Through check boxes are checked so that the input columns are included in the output. Delete the artist_code and genre mappings, leaving only artist_name. This is because we want to do the lookup based only on the artist name. Check artist_name in the Available Lookup Columns list, and set Output Alias to artist_name1, as shown in Figure 9-7.

12. Click the Advanced tab. Leave the maximum number of matches at 1. Leave the similarity threshold at 0, and leave the token delimiters as they are, as shown in Figure 9-8. The purpose of doing this is so that we get the similarity score for all the rows in the table. Click OK to close the Fuzzy Lookup Transformation Editor dialog box.

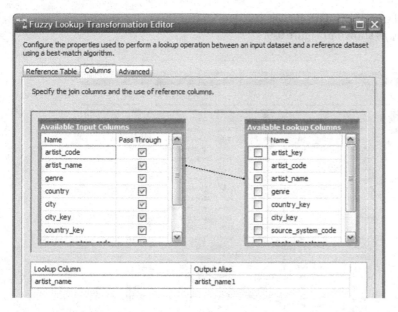

Figure 9-7. *Configuring the lookup columns on the Fuzzy Lookup transformation*

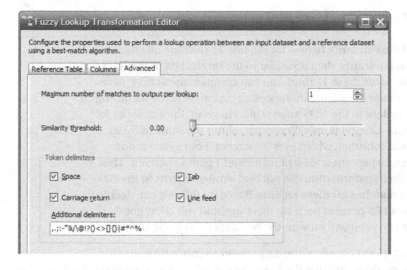

Figure 9-8. *Advanced tab of the Fuzzy Lookup transformation*

13. Now let's add a file destination and a data viewer so we can see and examine the data, along with the similarity score and confidence level. Create a flat-file destination. Point it to a new folder called Output in your ETL directory. Set the format to Delimited. In the column pane, set the column delimiter to a vertical bar (|). Leave everything else as is, and click OK. Right-click the green connector between the Fuzzy Lookup and the Flat File destination, and select Data Viewers. Click Add, and choose Grid. Click the Grid tab, and select all columns. Click OK twice to return to the Data Flow transformation.

14. Run the package, and it will stop at the data viewer. The data viewer shows the similarity and confidence columns, as shown in Figure 9-9.

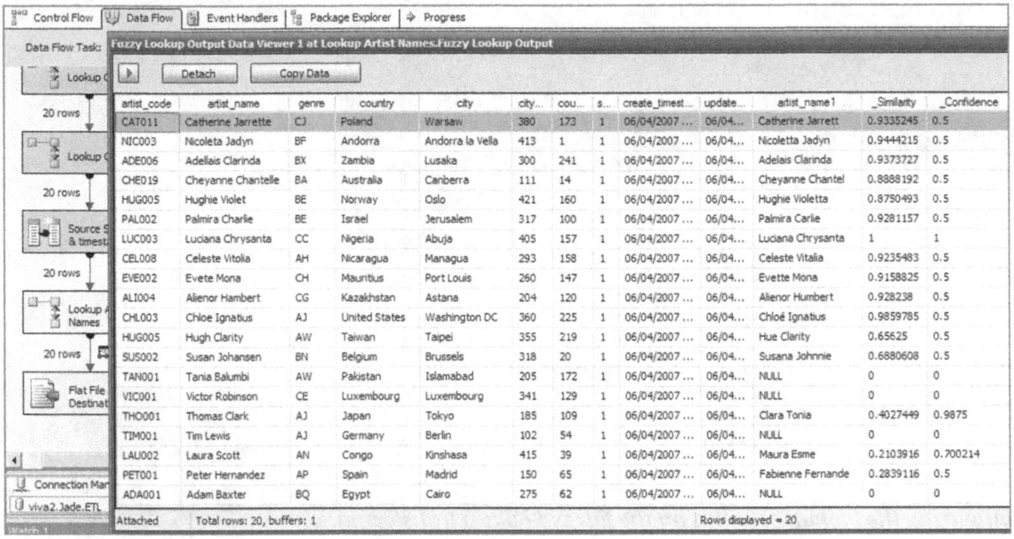

artist_code	artist_name	genre	country	city	city...	cou...	s...	create_timest...	update...	artist_name1	_Similarity	_Confidence
CAT011	Catherine Jarrette	CJ	Poland	Warsaw	380	173	1	06/04/2007 ...	06/04...	Catherine Jarrett	0.9335245	0.5
NIC003	Nicoleta Jadyn	BF	Andorra	Andorra la Vella	413	1	1	06/04/2007 ...	06/04...	Nicoletta Jadyn	0.9444215	0.5
ADE006	Adelais Clarinda	BX	Zambia	Lusaka	300	241	1	06/04/2007 ...	06/04...	Adelais Clarinda	0.9373727	0.5
CHE019	Cheyanne Chantelle	BA	Australia	Canberra	111	14	1	06/04/2007 ...	06/04...	Cheyanne Chantel	0.8888192	0.5
HUG005	Hughie Violet	BE	Norway	Oslo	421	160	1	06/04/2007 ...	06/04...	Hughie Violetta	0.8750493	0.5
PAL002	Palmira Charlie	BE	Israel	Jerusalem	317	100	1	06/04/2007 ...	06/04...	Palmira Carlie	0.9281157	0.5
LUC003	Luciana Chrysanta	CC	Nigeria	Abuja	405	157	1	06/04/2007 ...	06/04...	Luciana Chrysanta	1	1
CEL008	Celeste Vitolia	AH	Nicaragua	Managua	293	158	1	06/04/2007 ...	06/04...	Celeste Vitalia	0.9235483	0.5
EVE002	Evete Mona	CH	Mauritius	Port Louis	260	147	1	06/04/2007 ...	06/04...	Evette Mona	0.9158825	0.5
ALI004	Alienor Hambert	CG	Kazakhstan	Astana	204	120	1	06/04/2007 ...	06/04...	Alienor Humbert	0.928238	0.5
CHL003	Chloe Ignatius	AJ	United States	Washington DC	360	225	1	06/04/2007 ...	06/04...	Chloé Ignatius	0.9859785	0.5
HUG005	Hugh Clarity	AW	Taiwan	Taipei	355	219	1	06/04/2007 ...	06/04...	Hue Clarity	0.65625	0.5
SUS002	Susan Johansen	BN	Belgium	Brussels	318	20	1	06/04/2007 ...	06/04...	Susana Johnnie	0.6880608	0.5
TAN001	Tania Balumbi	AW	Pakistan	Islamabad	205	172	1	06/04/2007 ...	06/04...	NULL	0	0
VIC001	Victor Robinson	CE	Luxembourg	Luxembourg	341	129	1	06/04/2007 ...	06/04...	NULL	0	0
THO001	Thomas Clark	AJ	Japan	Tokyo	185	109	1	06/04/2007 ...	06/04...	Clara Tonia	0.4027449	0.9875
TIM001	Tim Lewis	AJ	Germany	Berlin	102	54	1	06/04/2007 ...	06/04...	NULL	0	0
LAU002	Laura Scott	AN	Congo	Kinshasa	415	39	1	06/04/2007 ...	06/04...	Maura Esme	0.2103916	0.700214
PET001	Peter Hernandez	AP	Spain	Madrid	150	65	1	06/04/2007 ...	06/04...	Fabienne Fernande	0.2839116	0.5
ADA001	Adam Baxter	BQ	Egypt	Cairo	275	62	1	06/04/2007 ...	06/04...	NULL	0	0

Figure 9-9. *Data viewer showing the similarity and confidence columns*

15. The data viewer shows that the similarity figures for the first 11 rows are all greater than 87 percent. This means the source data is similar to the target data in the NDS. In other words, we found a match for these 11 rows. You can compare the `artist_name` and `artist_name1` columns to see the slight differences. `artist_name` is the incoming data, and `artist_name1` is the data in the NDS artist table. However, the similarity for Hugh Clarity (NDS record Hue Clarity) is only 65 percent, about the same as Susan Johansen (NDS record Susana Johnnie), which gets 69 percent. Four gets 0 (none matching), two gets between 20 percent and 30 percent, and 1 gets 40 percent. This means that the Fuzzy Lookup transformation did not find similar records in the NDS. In other words, there are no matches for these records. Based on this, we can decide to set the similarity level to about 85 percent because this threshold will allow good records to be loaded onto NDS, yet it will prevent the bad data from going through.

16. Click the green arrow in the top-left corner of the data viewer to continue executing the package. The package completes, and the flat file is populated. The first ten lines of the flat file are shown here:

```
artist_code|artist_name|genre|country|city|city_key|country_key|
source_system_code|create_timestamp|update_timestamp|
artist_name1|_Similarity|_Confidence
```

```
CATO11     |Catherine Jarrette|CJ|Poland|Warsaw|380|173|
1|2007-04-06 22:30:42.546000000|2007-04-06 22:30:42.546000000|
Catherine Jarrett|0.93352449|0.5|0.93352449
NICO03     |Nicoleta Jadyn|BF|Andorra|Andorra la Vella|413|1|
1|2007-04-06 22:30:42.546000000|2007-04-06 22:30:42.546000000|
Nicoletta Jadyn|0.94442153|0.5|0.94442153
ADE006     |Adellais Clarinda|BX|Zambia|Lusaka|300|241|
1|2007-04-06 22:30:42.546000000|2007-04-06 22:30:42.546000000|
Adelais Clarinda|0.93737274|0.5|0.93737274
CHE019     |Cheyanne Chantelle|BA|Australia|Canberra|111|14|1|
2007-04-06 22:30:42.546000000|2007-04-06 22:30:42.546000000|
Cheyanne Chantel|0.88881922|0.5|0.88881922
HUG005     |Hughie Violet|BE|Norway|Oslo|421|160|
1|2007-04-06 22:30:42.546000000|2007-04-06 22:30:42.546000000|
Hughie Violetta|0.87504929|0.5|0.87504929
PAL002     |Palmira Charlie|BE|Israel|Jerusalem|317|100|
1|2007-04-06 22:30:42.546000000|2007-04-06 22:30:42.546000000|
Palmira Carlie|0.92811567|0.5|0.92811567
LUC003     |Luciana Chrysanta|CC|Nigeria|Abuja|405|157|
1|2007-04-06 22:30:42.546000000|2007-04-06 22:30:42.546000000|
Luciana Chrysanta|1|1|1
CEL008     |Celeste Vitolia|AH|Nicaragua|Managua|293|158|
1|2007-04-06 22:30:42.546000000|2007-04-06 22:30:42.546000000|
Celeste Vitalia|0.92354828|0.5|0.92354828
EVE002     |Evete Mona|CH|Mauritius|Port Louis|260|147|
1|2007-04-06 22:30:42.546000000|2007-04-06 22:30:42.546000000|
Evette Mona|0.91588253|0.5|0.91588253
ALI004     |Alienor Hambert|CG|Kazakhstan|Astana|204|120|
1|2007-04-06 22:30:42.546000000|2007-04-06 22:30:42.546000000|
Alienor Humbert|0.92823803|0.5|0.92823803
```

17. Press Shift+F5 to stop the package and return to the designer. Now let's delete the Flat File destination because we want to direct the output of the Fuzzy Lookup transformation to the NDS. To load the output into the NDS, we need to split the output into two depending on whether the artist record already exists in the NDS. If the record already exists, we update it. If it does not exist, we insert it. For that let's add a Conditional Split transformation and connect the green arrow from Fuzzy Lookup to it. Name the box **Split Based on Similarity**, and double-click it to edit it. Under Output Name, type **Similar**, and under Condition, type **[_Similarity]>=0.85**, as shown in Figure 9-10.

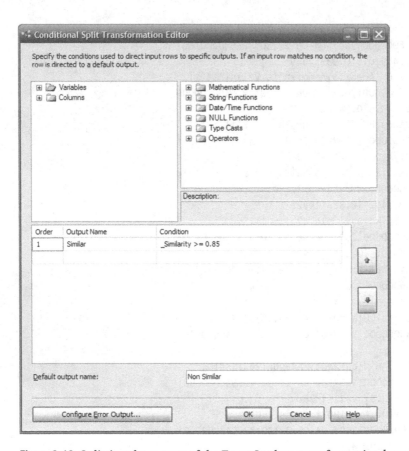

Figure 9-10. *Splitting the output of the Fuzzy Lookup transformation based on similarity*

18. Now that we have split the output into two branches, we need to feed both branches into two separate destinations. The first destination is for insert, and the second one is for update. If the artist name is the same or similar to the ones in the target (the NDS), we want to update the target. On the other hand, if the artist name does not exist (Not Similar), we want to insert (create) that artist into the NDS. For that, let's set Default Output Name to Not Similar and click OK. Now we need to configure the insert and update. Let's do the insert first. Drag an SQL Server destination onto the design surface, and name it **Insert to NDS Artist**. Connect the green arrow from the Split Based on Similarity box, and the Input Output Selection will pop up. In the Output drop-down list, select Not Similar, and click OK. Double-click the SQL Server destination, and set the connection to NDS. Point it to the artist table, and configure the column mappings as per Figure 9-11.

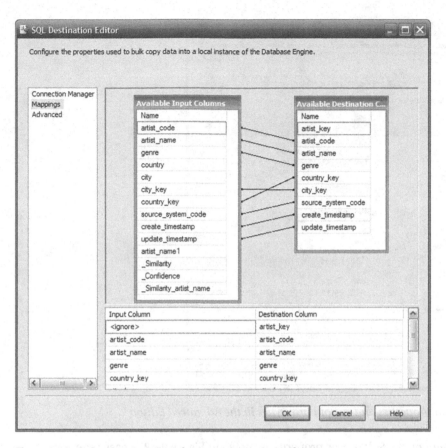

Figure 9-11. *Column mappings for inserting nonsimilar rows*

19. From the Toolbox, drag an OLE DB Command transformation onto the design surface, and call it **Update NDS Artist**. Connect the green arrow from the Split box onto it; this time the Input Output Select doesn't pop up. It will just choose Similar because Similar is the only output left from the Split box without connection. Double-click the Update NDS Artist box to edit it. Set Connection Manager to NDS.

20. Click the Component Properties tab to display the common and custom properties, as shown in Figure 9-12. On this tab we need to set the SQL statement that updates the artist record in the NDS.

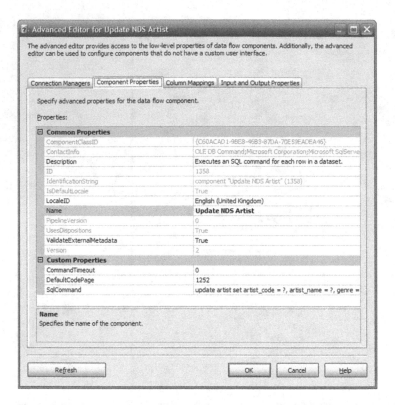

Figure 9-12. *Common properties and custom properties in the Advanced Editor*

21. Set the SQL statement on the `SqlCommand` property, as shown in Figure 9-12. Please note that `SqlCommand` here is a property of the OLE DB `Command` SSIS transformation, not the .NET Framework class on the `System.Data.SqlClient` namespace. We need to set the `SqlCommand` property as follows:

```
update artist set artist_code = ?,
artist_name = ?, genre = ?,
city_key = ?, country_key = ?, source_system_code = ?,
update_timestamp = ?
where artist_name = ?
```

Notice that we don't update `create_timestamp` in the previous SQL because we are updating the row, not creating the row. On the Column Mappings tab, configure the mappings as shown in Figure 9-13, and click OK to close the Update NDS Artist OLE DB command.

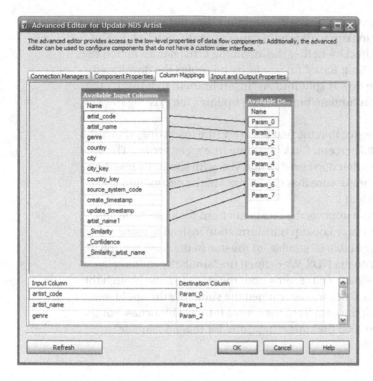

Figure 9-13. *Column mappings for the OLE DB command for updating similar rows*

Add two data viewers, one for the update branch and one for the insert branch, as shown in the bottom two boxes in Figure 9-14.

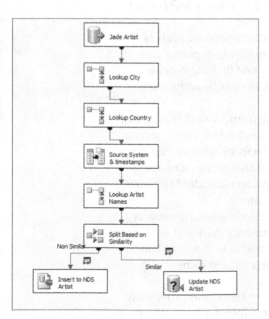

Figure 9-14. *The data flow after adding split, insert, and update components*

The bottom part of Figure 9-14 is basically an UPSERT operation (insert if it does not exist and update if it exists), but it uses fuzzy lookup to determine approximate matches. In Figure 9-14, the Lookup Artist Names box checks whether the incoming artist names match the NDS artist table using fuzzy lookup. The Split Based on Similarity box splits the flow based on the fuzzy lookup similarity score. The flow is split into an "insert branch" that inserts the incoming data into the artist table and an "update branch" that updates the existing rows in the artist table.

Save and execute the package, and notice that the first data row (the insert one) shows the eleven rows with similarity greater than 85 percent. Click Continue (the green arrow). The second data viewer then shows the nine rows that don't exist in the NDS with similarity less than 70 percent. Check the NDS artist table to make sure that eleven rows in the destination artist NDS table are updated and nine are inserted.

So, we have created a SSIS package that imports the artist data from the stage table and loads it into the NDS database, using the Fuzzy Lookup transformation instead of using an exact match. If the artist name on the stage table is "similar" to the one in the NDS, we update the NDS record. Otherwise, we insert it into the NDS. We defined the "similarity" criteria by determining the similarity threshold by allowing all records from the stage to flow through the Fuzzy Logic transformation to score them. Once we determined the similarity threshold, we set the Fuzzy Logic transformation to split the data from the source into two branches. For the "similar" branch, we update the NDS based on the source data, and for the "nonsimilar" branch we insert the source data into NDS.

Cross-checking with External Sources

Some data-cleansing activities are done internally, such as checking 100 stores including their store types, locations, phone numbers, web sites, store numbers, regions, and divisions. In this case, we manually verify that the store details in the system are accurate and correct them if they are wrong.

Some data cleansing is done by cross-referencing with external data sources, such as checking and fixing names and addresses in the customer table, identifying duplicate customer records (individual level, household level, or company level), and flagging deceased customers. We can also use external sources for enriching our data, such as by adding telephone numbers to the customer data.

Cross-referencing with external data can be done by using data from post office organizations such as Address Information Systems (AIS) and NCOA Link from the U.S. Postal Service. Or, in the United Kingdom, this can be done using the Royal Mail Postcode Address File (PAF). In some countries, other possible data sources are voter registration and the electoral roll. Another example of external data is reference data from the International Standard Organization, such as country names and languages, as we discussed in Chapter 7.

External data sources are delivered in various formats and in various ways. This affects the way we integrate the external data with our data warehouse. Some are delivered as files on CD-ROMs, some are delivered as a system (you need to install the system to use it, with automatic weekly updates via the Internet, for example), some are using EDI, and some are delivered online using web services.

We need to work with the providers to be able to use their data or services appropriately in our data warehouse. Looking at how the external data is integrated into the data warehouse, we can classify these different delivery mechanisms into two big approaches. With the first approach, we bring the external data into the data warehouse. The provider gives us the data, and we store it in the data warehouse. With the second approach, we don't bring the external data into our data warehouse. Instead, we leave the data with the provider, and we "tap" the data as and when we need it. This "tapping" is done, for example, using web services.

Data Quality Rules

Data quality rules are essentially filters to prevent dirty data from getting into the warehouse. Based on the data location, there are three kinds of data quality rules:

- Incoming data validation

- Cross-reference validation

- Data warehouse internal validation

Incoming data validation is where we check the incoming data only on its own, without referring to the data already in the warehouse (the ODS, NDS, or DDS). Incoming data validation is performed on the fly when the data is being loaded into the warehouse. These rules verify that the data from the source systems is valid, in other words, within the expected range and in the right format. Examples are that the product code is in AAA999AA format, the prices for a certain product range are greater than $1, the song duration is between one and ten minutes, and the subscription duration is greater than or equal to one month. Here are three real examples from my projects:

- $\sum$ (col1, col2, col3) > 0 where col4 > 0 and col5 > 0

- Value of data limited to list: value1, value2, value3, value4

- Fiscal period <= 13

Cross-reference validation is where we check the incoming data against the data in the warehouse. The objective is to make sure that the value of the incoming data is within a certain range that is calculated based on the data already in the warehouse: the incoming data is expected to be within a 25 percent range of the average of col1, the number of downloaded songs per week is less than 50 times the registered devices (the number of registered devices is data already in the warehouse, while the number of downloaded songs is incoming data from the source systems), and the incoming unit cost is within 15 percent of the average of the last three months of supplier costs. Like incoming data validation, cross-reference validation is performed on the fly when the data is being loaded into the warehouse.

Data warehouse internal validation is where we check the data already in the warehouse. We don't check the incoming data. The purpose of doing this is to verify the quality of the data in the warehouse at the aggregate level. In other words, the details data (record level) might be correct, but the totals might be incorrect. This can be done by comparing the totals over a period of time against a known standard value. Examples of data warehouse internal validation are that the number of new subscriptions last week is less than or equal to 5,000; the average number of copies for each title in the last three weeks is between 10 and 20; and the average unit cost of last week's title is within 10 percent of the average of the last three months.

Unlike the previous two, data warehouse internal validation is performed after the incoming data is fully loaded into the warehouse.

The DQ rules for internal data warehouse validation have different running frequencies. That is, some are run every few hours, some are daily, and some are weekly or monthly. The frequency depends on how critical the data is and how quickly the business needs to be informed if some inaccuracies happen. If the data is critical (such as data that has direct impact on the revenue or has potential risks of breaking government regulations), the business may need to know quickly, so we need to set up the DQ rules at short frequencies such as every four hours or twice a day. The frequency also depends on the volume and seasonality of data. For example, if the number of subscriptions varies widely every day, we may want to compare it weekly rather than daily.

We need to be careful with the last two categories (cross-reference validation and data warehouse internal validation), because it can potentially impact the ETL performance. Here's why. When the DQ rules involve a statistical calculation, such as "within 15 percent of the average of the last three months of supplier costs," it could take a long time to calculate the statistics. So if we tried to calculate the statistics on the fly, we would face a bottleneck, and the ETL process would be very slow. One common technique is to calculate the statistical figures beforehand, such as the day before. This way, when the DQ rule runs, the statistics are already calculated and stored in the warehouse as constant numbers. So, the validation will be fast because we are comparing against constant numbers rather than a formula.

Not all DQ rules are errors. Some DQ rules are only warnings. For warnings, we still want the occurrence to be reported, but we are not rejecting the data. We allow the data to be loaded into the warehouse. For example, if the data is more than 35, it is good, and if it is less than 30, it is an error. But if it is between 30 and 35, it is a warning. Even though we load the data into the warehouse, the data still needs to be reported to the business users and subsequently corrected in the source systems so that the next time that data is loaded into the warehouse, it is already correct.

Some DQ rules are neither an error nor a warning but are informational only. In other words, there is no issue whatsoever with the data. An example of this kind of DQ rule is if the national sales amount on a weekday is more than $3 million, we need to inform the national sales manager. This is neither an error nor a warning, but is informational only. On the contrary, the reverse (too little rather than too much) might be an error or a warning; for example, if the national sales amount on a weekday is less than $300,000, then there may be a problem with the ETL, perhaps because not all source sales data is loaded properly into the data warehouse for that day.

I have found that it is good practice in a data warehouse project for the business user to write a document called *Data Quality Business Rules*. It essentially describes all the business rules, what type they are, which data warehouse attributes they are applicable to, what is the appropriate course of action (for example, reject, allow, or fix; see the next section), and who should be notified when a violation to a rule occurs. The document is written in pure English with no SQL code or pseudocode. For example, rather than `where (prd_type = 'FL' and unit_cost < 2.25) or (prd_type = 'AB' and unit_cost < 1.43)`, we should describe it as "The incoming unit cost should be less than 2.25 for films and less than 1.43 for audio books." The developer can then translate this to SQL when implementing the rules in SSIS. I have found that throughout the development process we kept referring to this handy document.

Tip When defining DQ rules, define them based on the risk, in other words, the impact or damage. It is useful to know that if rule #34 is violated, all the marts will be totally inaccurate and useless, whereas if rule #17 is violated, the impact is almost negligible, and we have nothing to worry about. It is very useful to have this attribute in the previously mentioned document and on the DQ reports (see the DQ report section later in this chapter). We can then define the urgency and service-level agreement (SLA) based on the risk level. For example, risk level 5 rules need to be solved next day, whereas risk level 1 has a four-week period.

The DQ rules are described in a table called dq_rules. The purpose of this table is to describe the details of each data quality rule including the following:

- The objective of the rule (including the calculation if any, in English)

- Whether it is an error, is a warning, or is informational

- What type of validation it is (whether it is an incoming data validation, cross-reference validation, or internal validation)

- How critical the rule is (measured by the risk), from level 1 (low risk) to level 5 (high risk)

- What actions to take, such as reject the data, allow the data into the warehouse, or fix it

- The status of the rule (whether it is active or disabled)

- Who to notify when there is a violation to this rule

This table is used by the data firewall to check the incoming data before loading it into the NDS or ODS. In some implementations, the DQ rule table is placed in the metadata database; in other implementations, the DQ rule table is placed in the DQ database. For performance reasons, in my opinion, it is better to put it in the DQ database because it is referenced by the DQ tables, even though technically it is a metadata table (I'll discuss metadata in the next chapter). Essentially the DQ rule table contains the same columns as the *Data Quality Business Rules* document, in other words, rule_id, rule_name, rule_description, rule_type (error or warning), category (incoming data, cross-reference, or internal), risk_level (1 to 5), status, action, notification, create_timestamp, and update_timestamp. This table will be cross-referenced by the DQ audit tables. DQ audit tables store the records that fail the DQ rule validation. We'll discuss DQ rules table in more detail in the next chapter.

Action: Reject, Allow, Fix

When a data quality rule is violated, we have three choices of what to do with the data: we can reject the data, allow the data into the warehouse, or fix/correct the data. These are known as *actions*. Which action is appropriate for a particular piece of data depends on the situation, the risk level, the rule type (error or warning), and so on.

The reject action means that we do not allow the data into the warehouse. We put it in an audit table in the DQ database. The data will then be reported to the business users and corrected before it is loaded into the data warehouse. Typically, the structure of the audit table is the same as the structure of the source system table, but with five additional columns: dq_id, rule_id, dq_timestamp, dq_action, and dq_status. If on the source system we have 60 tables, then there will be 60 audit tables in the DQ database. If these are your 60 tables in your source system:

```
artist
channel
customer
customer_status
customer_type
format
...
product_type
store
```

then these are the audit tables in the DQ database:

```
artist
channel
customer
customer_status
customer_type
format
...
product_type
store
```

Yes, the table names are the same, and they have all the columns in the original table, plus five additional columns: dq_key, rule_key, dq_timestamp, dq_action, and dq_status. dq_key contains a sequential identity(1,1) column. rule_key is the identifier of the DQ rule that causes this row to be rejected by the data firewall and put in the quarantine table (see the previous section for the dq_rule table). dq_timestamp is the time when this row was rejected by the data firewall. dq_action is the action taken to the incoming data (reject, allow, or fix). dq_status is the correction status (fixed or not fixed).

So, if we reject a row of address data, instead of going into the address table in the NDS (or the ODS or the DDS, depending on your DW architecture), the row goes to the address audit table in the DQ database. The row will be reported (see the section "Data Quality Reports and Notifications" later in this chapter) to the relevant people, fixed in the source system, and reloaded into the NDS (or the ODS or the DDS). If the address table is extracted using "the whole table every time" approach, it's not a problem. In other words, the row will be loaded automatically in the data warehouse on the next ETL batch that occurs after the row is corrected. If the address table is extracted incrementally, we need to "memorize" the failed row, and we need to keep extracting the row on the ETL batch until it is corrected. One way to do this is by modifying the extraction SQL, adding something like this: ... union select [columns] from source.dbo.address src join dq.dbo.address d on src.address_id = dq.address_id and `dq_status <> 'C'`. And when the row has been loaded successfully, we mark the row on the audit table as *C* (or closed). In SSIS, as an alternative to the Execute SQL task, we can also use a merged join or a Lookup transformation for this purpose.

Instead of fixing it in the source system, we can also take the approach of correcting the failed row stored in the DQ database and reloading it to the data warehouse. Although this is less favorable because we leave the source system incorrect, at times it is more practical, because it has a quicker turnaround time, resulting in the row being loaded into the warehouse sooner. The drawback of choosing this approach is that the source system is still incorrect so that the next time the data is retrieved from the source system, we will still face the same problem. That's why it is usually used for data that does not change frequently, such as reference data. This approach is usually used as a temporary measure, while waiting for the data change request to be implemented in production (which could take, say, two to three weeks).

Instead of rejecting the dirty data, we can allow it into our warehouse. Wait a minute, why do we want to do this? Well, there are several reasons. One reason is because perhaps it is only a warning, not an error; for example, the rule may say that single-title revenue should be between $1 and $4. If it is between 0 and 1 or between 4 and 10, allow it in. But if it is less than 0 or greater than 10, reject it. This is because (for example) the majority of the products (say, 99 percent) are priced between $1 and $4. Sometimes (the 1 percent) products are priced very low for sale or promotional reasons (between 0 and $1) and very high for seasonal reasons (between $4 and $10). That is why these two ranges are only a warning, not an error. But a negative price or prices more than $10 never happens in the business for that product type, so that is why in this example the "< 0" and "> 10" are classified as errors.

The second reason for allowing the data into the warehouse is that other data in the same row is required for data integrity. Each fact table row is essentially a business transaction. If we don't load some rows, the total of that day would not be correct because there is some missing data. For example, a Subscription Sales fact table contains eight dimension keys and nineteen facts. Say one column does not satisfy a DQ rule; for example, the `subscribe_timestamp` column contains an invalid date. All the other facts are OK; `subscription_revenue`, `single_title_revenue`, `monthly_revenue`, `music_quantity`, `music_unit_cost`, `monthly_music_cost`, `film_quantity`, `film_unit_cost`, `monthly_film_cost`, `book_quantity`, `book_unit_cost`, `monthly_book_cost`, `monthly_indirect_cost`, `monthly_cost`, `monthly_margin`, `annual_revenue`, `annual_cost`, `annual_profit`, and `subscriber_profitability` are all correct. We have two choices: if we reject the fact row, the total of all these facts will be incorrect. If we allow the row in, the total of all these facts will be correct, and the `subscribe_timestamp` will be set to unknown. The invalid date will still be logged, reported, fixed, and reloaded next time.

The third possible action is to automatically fix the data based on certain rules. In this case, when the data firewall detects a certain value, it automatically replaces it with another value, based on certain criteria. For example, say in the source system we have "NA," " N/A," "N.A.," and "Not Applicable." We create a DQ rule to replace "NA," "N/A," and "N.A." with "Not Applicable." This way, the data in the data warehouse is clean, even though the data in the source system is not. Here's another example: in the source system store 17 is in region 1. This is incorrect. Store 17 should be in region 2. We create a DQ rule to update the region automatically. Here's another example: when the total customer purchase is between $500 and $1,000 in the source system, it is classified as band C. In the data warehouse, this range is classified as band D. We create a DQ rule to update the customer band from C to D. Note that in a way, this is like an ETL transformation, because we update the data as we load it into the data warehouse. We need to be careful when implementing autofix actions like this, because the data in the source system is still wrong. It is (always) better to fix the data in the source system than to fix it in the data warehouse. But if we cannot change it in the source system, this could be an alternative solution. Or perhaps it's possible to fix the data in the source system, but it will take a long time. In that case, we could implement this temporarily.

One example of a good use of a DQ rule with autofix action is formatting, for example, to convert to mixed case or to remove spaces. For example, in the format column of the product table in the source system, we have the following entries: "DVD 5," "DVD-5," and "DVD5," and in the ODS or NDS the entry is "DVD-5." When loading the product table from the source system, we can create a DQ rule with an action to convert them to "DVD-5." Some people argue that this should be implemented as a normal "transformation" in the ETL logic, so why would we want to put it as a DQ rule? Well, the main difference between an ETL transformation and a DQ rule is the reporting aspect. We know that this inconsistency between "DVD 5," "DVD-5," and "DVD5" is an issue in the source system. In other words, there is no referential integrity from the product table to the format table. We have reported this to the source system owner and the data will be fixed in the next few weeks, but in the meantime we need to keep the data warehouse up and running, so we put this rule in. Because it is a DQ rule with an autofix action, it is reported to the appropriate people regularly, so we know when it is fixed. If it is implemented as an ETL transformation, it won't be reported and monitored. Well, actually you can report and monitor ETL transformation, but it will slow the ETL processes down if you need to report and monitor all the transformations. Also, an ETL transformation is not as rich as a DQ rule; for example, it doesn't have the following:

- The objective of the rule (including the calculation if any)

- Whether it is an error, is a warning, or is informational

- What type of validation it is (whether it is an incoming data validation, cross-reference validation, or internal validation)

- How critical the rule is (measured by the risk), for example from level 1 (low risk) to level 5 (high risk)

- What actions to take, such as reject the data, allow the data into the warehouse, or fix it

- The status of the rule (whether it is active or disabled)

- Who to notify when there is a violation to this rule

Logging and Auditing

When a DQ rule is violated, we store that event in the data quality database. We store the time that violation happened, which rule was violated, what action was taken, and the correction status. We store all of this information in a table called the *data quality log*, or *DQ log* for short. We also need to store the rows that failed the DQ rule. This process of recording the DQ rule violation events, along with the rows that failed the DQ rules, is called *data quality logging*.

The failed rows are also stored in the DQ database, but not in the DQ log table. They are stored in a number of tables called *data quality audit tables*. The structures of the audit tables are the same as the target data warehouse tables. So if the target table has ten columns, the audit table also has ten columns, with each column having the same name and the same data types as the target tables. This process of analyzing the data quality rules violation by querying the DQ log table and DQ audit tables is called *data quality audit*.

We store the failed rows in the corresponding audit table; for example, if the failed rows were for the customer table, we store them in the customer audit table. If the failed rows were for the subscription table, we store them in the subscription audit table. Whether the action of the DQ rule is to reject, allow, or fix, we still need to put the failed rows in the audit tables.

One additional column in the audit tables makes them different from the target data warehouse table: the primary key. The primary key of an audit table is a surrogate integer column. This primary key is stored in the DQ log table as a foreign key. This is how the audit tables are linked to the DQ log table, as shown in Figure 9-15.

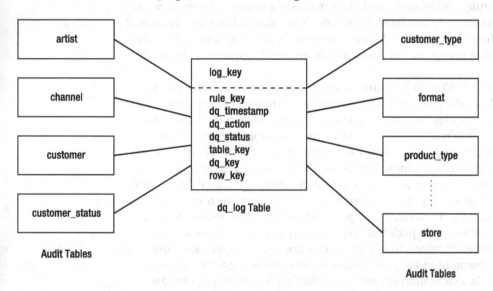

Figure 9-15. *The DQ log table and the DQ audit tables*

As we can see in Figure 9-15, the DQ log table stores four pieces of information related to the violation event: which rule was violated (rule_key), when it happened (dq_timestamp), what action was taken (dq_action), and the correction status (dq_status). In Figure 9-15, log_key is the primary key of the dq_log table.

Figure 9-15 shows that the DQ log tables contain three other key columns: table_key, dq_key, and row_key. These three key columns point to the failed rows stored in the DQ audit tables.

- The first column, table_key, determines on which audit table the failed row is stored. table_key contains the SQL Server object_id of the audit table. We can get the table name by querying the data structure metadata tables.

- The second column, dq_key, is the primary key of the audit tables. Together with table_key, dq_key can pinpoint the exact location of the failed row.

- The third column, row_key, contains the row identifier. It is the natural primary key. It is the primary key of the row in the source table. For example, for the address table, row_key is address_id. We can also use the combination of table_key and row_key to point to the failed row.

This way, if the same source row failed two rules, there would be only one copy of that row stored in the audit table, but we'll have two rows in the DQ log table.

A data quality audit means querying the DQ audit tables and DQ log table for the purpose of finding out when a DQ rule was violated, which/how many data rows are impacted, which/how many source/target tables were impacted, what action was taken, what is the status, and what were the values of the source data. All of these questions should be able to be answered just by querying the log table, except the last one, which is answered by querying the associated audit table.

The ultimate purpose of a DQ audit is to find out the quality of the data in the data warehouse. This can be done by evaluating how many DQ rules were violated in the recent months (say, the last three months or the last six weeks), how many cases of each rule, and whether the rule is critical to the continuity of the business. Of course, one other important factor is how long the DQ problem occurred before being fixed. If a business critical accuracy issue is left opened for two weeks, the impact is more serious than if it were open for only two days.

The audit tables and log table need to be purged regularly. *Purging* means deleting (permanent removal) or archiving (moving the data somewhere else) to keep the number of rows in the main table to a minimum. Of course, we purge or archive only those records that have been resolved. Purging is necessary for performance, especially when doing dynamic SQL for joining the log table and the audit tables. To give you a picture of the frequency and duration, a typical purging scenario for audit and log tables (they are always done together) is done once a month, keeping the last six months of rows in the main table and the prior twelve months of rows in the archive table. It is rarely necessary to purge on a weekly basis.

Data Quality Reports and Notifications

The main purpose of DQ reports and notifications is to get somebody correcting the data. In any DQ system, it is important to have a "closed loop," in other words, the corrections. The correction forms a closed loop in the data quality process because, if you refer to Figure 9-1 at the beginning of this chapter, the correction connects the reporting and notifications back to the source systems.

The secondary purpose of DQ reports and notifications is to make the users aware that a particular area of the warehouse has a data quality issue, such as when the subscription sales for the introductory package were late by one week. Say that usually we receive the sales figures within a day after the sale transactions happened. But because of log file problem, in that particular month we received the subscription sales data one week late. This made the introductory package have zero sales for a week. This would subsequently be flagged by the data quality reports and notifications, showing that there is a problem with the subscription sales for the introductory package.

When a DQ system is first put into operation, sometimes the number of DQ issues reported is high. Afterward, when the system is running, corrections are done, so the DQ issues should be decreasing steadily. For example, Figure 9-16 shows the exponential decrease for a six-month implementation. The decrease will be faster if a person is dedicated for this responsibility. Have you heard the old saying "You get what you measure"?

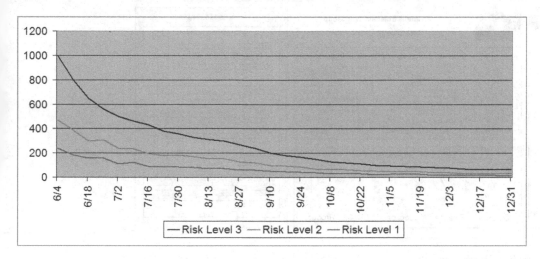

Figure 9-16. *Decreasing number of DQ issues reported*

Note that the tail in the chart in Figure 9-16 is not zero. It will never be. There will always be DQ issues happening, and that is normal. Also, we need to be aware that a valid possible course of action is to change the DQ rule itself rather than doing data correction, perhaps because some rules are capturing unnecessary events or because those events do not need to be captured.

We can e-mail different DQ reports to different users, according to their groups. For example, in the case of Amadeus Entertainment, we can classify users into four business areas: product sales, subscription sales, supplier performance, and customer relationship management. So, we can create four groups, one for each of these business areas, and put the business users into these groups. When we have any DQ issues related to product sales, we send the DQ reports to the product sales group. When we have a DQ issue related to CRM, we send the DQ report to the CRM group. This can be done using SQL Server Reporting Services (SSRS), which enables data warehouse users to subscribe to the different data areas for which they are responsible. Reporting Services enables the reports to be web-based so that on the DQ e-mail we can just put the links (URLs) to the reports, rather than the reports themselves. There are two benefits of this:

- Lighter e-mail content

- More flexible because the users can set different report parameters themselves

The DQ rule violations can also be sent to the users using notifications. For this we can use SQL Server Notification Services. For example, we can set the Notification Services to read the DQ log table and DQ audit tables and deliver the newest records to the users.

We can also create a dashboard application to display the overall data quality status for the whole warehouse, along with the key data quality indicator of each business area. The dashboard can also contain some data quality reports and selected data quality charts, such as the one shown in Figure 9-17.

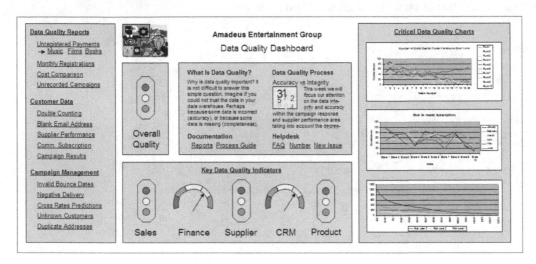

Figure 9-17. *Data quality dashboard*

Summary

In this chapter, I discussed what data quality is and why it is so important. I discussed the data quality process and the components involved in the process. I talked about data cleansing and data matching, and I showed how to do a Fuzzy Lookup transformation in SSIS.

I discussed the categories of data quality rules in terms of validation and the choices of what to do with the data when a data quality rule is violated: reject, allow, or fix. I talked about logging and auditing, and I finished the chapter by talking about reporting and notification in order to get somebody correcting the data.

Of all the various aspects of data warehousing, data quality is probably the most important one. Simply speaking, this is because if the data is wrong, we cannot use the data warehouse.

CHAPTER 10

■ ■ ■

Metadata

In general, *metadata* means data that describes data. For example, in photography, we store our photographs as RAW or JPG files. That is the data. But we also store the following information: which camera we used to take the photographs, the aperture and ISO settings of the camera, the resolution of each photograph, where it was taken, when it was taken, and a few words describing the content of the photo. That is all metadata.

Metadata in data warehousing is different from photography, though. In this chapter, I will discuss what metadata is in a data warehousing context, why metadata is important in data warehousing, what it is used for, how to store it, and how to maintain it.

Metadata in Data Warehousing

In data warehousing, metadata contains the definitions of data (the meaning and source of each column), the definition of the data warehouse itself (in other words, the data store structure, the ETL processes, and the data quality), the definition of the related systems (for example, the source systems), the audit information (what processes ran and when they ran), and the usage (which reports and cubes are used by whom and when). So, we have seven kinds of metadata:

- Data definition and mapping metadata contains the meaning of each fact and dimension column and where the data is coming from.

- Data structure metadata describes the structure of the tables in each data store.

- Source system metadata describes the data structure of source system databases.

- ETL process metadata describes each data flow in the ETL processes.

- Data quality metadata describes data quality rules, their risk levels, and their actions.

- Audit metadata contains a record of processes and activities in the data warehouse.

- Usage metadata contains an event log of application usage.

I'll discuss these briefly here, and in the subsequent sections I will discuss them in more depth.

The data definition metadata contains the meaning of each fact, dimension key, and dimension attribute within the data warehouse. "Meaning" is the business description of the data in the context of the organization where the data warehouse is implemented or used.

This is necessary so that all users have a common understanding about what the facts and attributes mean. For example, in Chapter 5, we defined *title availability* as the percentage of the product titles being available in the last three months when Amadeus Entertainment ordered them. Having a definitive meaning of title availability stored in a metadata database and viewable by the users is useful to avoid confusion and misperception. The users can view the data definitions either via reports created using SSRS or via direct query using Enterprise Manager. Data definition metadata also contains the business description of each column in the NDS or ODS.

Data mapping metadata (sometimes called *data lineage metadata*) is about where each piece of data is coming from. For example, the music_unit_cost fact in the Subscription Sales fact table in the DDS is from the unit_cost column in the product table in the NDS. The unit_cost column in the product table in the NDS is from the unit_cost column in the product table in the stage database. And the unit_cost column in the product table in the stage database is from the unit_cost column in the product table in the Jade source system. The data lineage metadata makes it easier to perform the impact analysis. Impact analysis is an activity to understand the effect of a particular change to different elements of the data warehouse. For example, when the source system DBA says that the unit_cost column in the Jupiter product table will not contain intercompany trading figures, we can understand what columns on the ODS, NDS, and DDS will be impacted.

Data structure metadata describes the structure of the DDS, NDS, ODS, and stage databases. It contains an entry for every table in the data warehouse. It contains the data types for each column in every table, including the collation, whether the column is a primary or a foreign key, and whether the column is an identity column or can contain null. For the DDS, it also contains the dimensional hierarchy and SCD details and the index, view, and partition information. Why don't we just use SQL Server object catalog views directly instead of building data structure metadata? The reason is that we need to reference the database objects in the ETL metadata, DQ metadata, and data description metadata in order to understand their structure.

Source system metadata describes the data structure of all the source systems feeding into the data warehouse. It contains the data type, collation, primary key, foreign key, view, index, and partition. It also contains volumetric data and data profiling information. Source system metadata is used to help users understand the source of the data.

Audit metadata contains the results of all processes and activities in the data warehouse, such as ETL processes, data modification, DQ rule validation, security log, system patches, purging, indexing, and partitioning activities. Audit metadata is used for administering the data warehouse such as to verify whether the ETL processes ran successfully.

Usage metadata contains a log that records which reports and cubes are used by whom and when. Usage metadata is used to understand the access and usage pattern of the data warehouse applications. For example, how many times is a particular report accessed and by which users or departments?

ETL metadata contains the description of each data flow, where they extract from, what the destination is, what transformation is applied, the parent process, and the schedule when it is supposed to run. Along with the data mapping metadata, ETL metadata is useful to understand the data flow and transformation. ETL metadata is also used to determine the sequence each task is run in an ETL batch.

Data quality metadata describes each data quality rule, along with the rule types, which table and column they are applicable for, their risk level, and their actions. Data quality metadata is used to determine what action to take when "bad data" is detected.

Why do we need metadata? The primary reason is to describe and explain the data and the data warehouse (the structure and processes) to the users. This explanation enables the users to use the data warehouse better. This explanation also makes it easier to enhance and maintain the data warehouse. For example, data definition metadata helps new users understand the meaning of each fact and dimension attribute, along with its sample values. Data definition metadata also helps avoid misunderstanding among existing users about the meaning of certain columns. Data mapping metadata helps us understand the impact if a column in the source system is deprecated or if we want to add a new column in the data warehouse. This is possible because data mapping metadata explains the source of each piece of data.

The secondary reason is for audit purposes to understand what happened, where it happened, and when it happened. For example, when an ETL process stopped unexpectedly, the audit metadata helps us understand which steps have been executed, what the results of those steps are, and which steps have not been executed so we can pinpoint the exact point in the ETL process where it failed. This is because audit metadata contains the results of all processes and activities in the data warehouse, including ETL processes, data modification, and DQ rule validation. That will make it easier to find out the cause of failure, and it enables the ETL processes to recover from the point of failure the next time it runs.

Metadata is also used by the system to run operational tasks, such as determining the required action when "bad data" is detected by a data quality rule and the order the ETL tasks need to be executed.

For maintainability, we use normalized forms in the metadata database; in other words, the table names and column names are stored in data structure metadata. Data definition, data mapping, ETL metadata, and audit metadata refer to the data structure metadata by storing the table keys and column keys. By using normalized forms, we need to modify only one place when we want to change something in the metadata database.

Data Definition and Mapping Metadata

Data definition metadata is a list of all columns from every table in the DDS, ODS, and NDS (depending on which architecture we chose; see Chapter 2), along with their meanings and sample values. Instead of mentioning the data store names, table names, and column names, data definition metadata uses the table key and column key defined in the data structure metadata.

Mapping metadata describes where each piece of data comes from in the source system. Mapping metadata is also known as *data lineage metadata*. If the mapping metadata contains only the source system column name, it can be put on the same table as the data definition metadata. But if the mapping metadata contains the complete data lineage between the DDS, the NDS/ODS, the stage, and the source systems, then it is usually placed in a separate table. The benefit of putting the mapping metadata in the same table as the data definition metadata is that the structure is simpler. The benefit of putting mapping metadata in separate tables is that the structure is more flexible and has less data redundancy.

Table 10-1 contains an example of data definition and mapping metadata. Table 56 is the product table, and table 68 is the campaign result fact table. The source column is located on the database one step earlier in the process; in other words, if it is a DDS column, we put the NDS column as the source. If it is an NDS column, we put the stage column as the source. If it is stage column, we put the source system column as the source.

Table 10-1. *Data Definition Metadata*

table_key	column_key	description	sample_value	source_column_key
56	112	The surrogate key of the product dimension. It is unique, is not null, and is the primary key of the product dimension.	3746	88
56	113	Natural key. Product code is the identifier and primary key of the product table in Jupiter. It is in AAA999999 format.	FGA334288	89
56	114	The product name.	The Panama Story DVD	90
56	115	The product description.	The Panama Story movie on DVD format	91
56	116	The song/film/book title.	The Panama Story	92
56	117	The singer, star, or author.	Mark Danube	93
56	118	Level 1 of product hierarchy; in other words, music, film, or book.	Film	94
56	119	Level 2 of product hierarchy; in other words, for film, it could be thriller, western, comedy, action, documentary, children, Asian, and so on.	Action	95
56	120	Format of the media; in other words, MP3, MPG, CD, or DVD.	DVD	96
56	121	Price for one item.	4.75	97
56	122	Allocated direct and indirect costs.	3.62	98
56	123	Upcoming if we have signed contract with the supplier, active if it is still being offered to the customer, expired if it is no longer being offered.	Active	99
68	251	The key of the campaign that was sent to customers.	1456	124
68	252	The key of the customer who was intended to receive this campaign.	25433	145
68	253	The key of the communication to which the campaign belongs. For example, this campaign is an instance of a communication called "Amadeus music weekly newsletter" dated 02/18/2008.	5	165
68	254	The key of the communication channel to which this campaign is sent. For example, a campaign could be sent to 200,000 customers, 170,000 by e-mail and 30,000 by RSS.	3	178
68	255	The key of the date when this campaign was actually sent.	23101	189

table_key	column_key	description	sample_value	source_column_key
68	256	The key of the delivery status. 0 means not sent. 1 means successfully delivered. 1 to N contains various different reasons why the campaign failed to be delivered to the intended recipient, such as the mailbox was unavailable, the mailbox does not exist, and so on.	1	193
68	257	1 if the campaign was actually sent to the recipient (out our door); 0 if it was not sent. Examples of reasons for not sending are failed e-mail address validation and no customer permission.	1	204

The Data Definition Language (DDL) of the data definition table in Table 10-1 is as follows so you can create the table for the case study:

```
use meta
go

create table data_definition
( column_key          int  not null
, table_key           int  not null
, column_type_key     int  not null
, description          varchar(200)
, sample_values        varchar(50)
, source_column_key    int  not null
, create_timestamp     datetime not null
, update_timestamp     datetime not null
, constraint pk_data_definition
  primary key clustered (column_key)
)
go

create index data_definition_description
on data_definition(description)
go
```

The table_key column is optional, because the column key links to the data structure metadata column table that also has a table key. The index on the description column helps querying a column with a particular meaning. To enable sophisticated word searches, you may want to build a full-text index on the description column instead, as follows:

```
create fulltext catalog data_definition_fulltext_catalog
in path 'd:\disk\data6'
as default
go
```

```
create fulltext index
on data_definition (description)
key index pk_data_definition
go
```

Columns in data warehouse tables serve different purposes. A column type indicates these purposes. A column type helps differentiate, for example, dimensional attributes from the fact column. Table 10-2 lists various column types and their descriptions. Column types can be put on data structure metadata or on data definition metadata.

Table 10-2. *Column Types*

Column Type	Location	Description
Surrogate key	DDS dimension tables	A single not null column that uniquely identifies a row in a dimension table.
Natural key	DDS dimension tables	Uniquely identifies a dimension row in the source system.
Dimensional attribute	DDS dimension tables	Describes a particular property of a dimension.
Degenerate dimension	DDS fact tables	Identifies a transaction in the source system. A natural key of a dimension without any attributes.
SCD support	DDS dimension tables	Columns that support slowly changing dimension such as is_active, effective_date, and expiry_date.
Measure	DDS fact tables	Columns in the fact table that contain business measurements or transaction values.
Fact key	DDS fact tables	A single not null column that uniquely identifies a row on a fact table.
System	All data stores	Auxiliary columns created by the system for system usage such as create_timestamp and update_timestamp.
Transaction	ODS and NDS tables	Column in normalized tables containing business transaction values, such as order tables.
Master	ODS and NDS tables	Columns in normalized tables that contain master data such as stores, products, and campaigns.
Stage	Stage tables	Columns in stage tables containing business data.

In addition to table columns, we can also include report columns in data definition metadata. We do this by adding the report columns in the metadata_definition table. This way, the meaning of every column in every report is explained properly. This helps avoid confusion among the users about the meaning of particular columns in a report. For example, a column called *profitability* can have many different meanings.

As I described earlier, if we want to describe full data lineage, we need to put data mapping metadata in a separate table. If we put the source column in the data definition table shown in Table 10-1, we can refer to only one level of data source, in other words, only the source system. But if we put the source column on data mapping metadata, we can refer to multiple levels of data stores, not only the source system but also the DDS, NDS, and stage.

It also enables us to refer to more than one source, which is useful if a column is sourced from two or three different sources. There are two benefits of sourcing a column from multiple sources: the ability to perform calculations based on several source columns and getting more complete data as the source columns complement each other.

The Data Definition Language (DDL) of the data mapping table is as follows:

```
use meta
go

if exists
  ( select * from sys.tables
    where name = 'data_mapping')
drop table data_mapping
go

create table data_mapping
( data_mapping_key    int not null identity(1,1)
, column_key          int not null
, source_column_key   int
, create_timestamp    datetime not null
, update_timestamp    datetime not null
, constraint pk_data_mapping
  primary key clustered (data_mapping_key)
)
go
```

Figure 10-1 shows the data flow diagram between data stores in a data warehouse. It shows the three DW data stores: the stage, the ODS, and the DDS, along with the source systems and the application layer. The solid stripes are columns on the tables within the data store. For example, column 249 is on a table in the ODS. Figure 10-1 shows the data lineage (or data mapping) for two columns in the DDS: column 378, which is populated from column 249 in the ODS, and column 442, which is populated from columns 251 and 289 in the ODS. Table 10-3 shows the corresponding sample data on the data mapping table for the data flow in Figure 10-1.

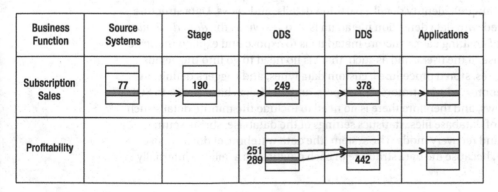

Business Function	Source Systems	Stage	ODS	DDS	Applications
Subscription Sales	77	190	249	378	
Profitability			251 289	442	

Figure 10-1. *Data flow diagram showing data lineage between data stores*

Table 10-3. *Data Mapping Table for the Data Flow in Figure 10-1*

data_mapping_key	column_key	source_column_key	create_timestamp	update_timestamp
1	378	249	2007-10-24 09:23:48	2007-11-18 14:10:08
2	249	190	2007-10-24 09:28:36	2007-11-19 11:05:16
3	190	77	2007-10-24 09:31:13	2007-10-24 09:31:13
4	442	251	2007-11-04 17:01:55	2007-12-18 15:09:42
5	442	289	2007-11-04 17:03:29	2007-11-04 17:03:29

DDS tables are populated from the ODS. The ODS tables are populated from the stage tables. The stage tables are populated from the source systems' tables. Because of that, the data mapping table is a linked list. Both column_key and source_column_key refer to the column table in the data structure metadata (see the next section). To query the data mapping table, we need to use a recursive query. A recursive query is a SQL query from a table that joins to the same table (self-join). We need to be careful when doing a recursive query because we could potentially be caught in an endless loop. To prevent it, we need to limit the number of loops/self-joins.

It is better if the source system metadata is put in the same place with the data warehouse data structure metadata. This way, source_column_key in the data mapping table needs to refer to only one table. Source system metadata contains a list of tables and columns in all source systems, along with their data types. Data structure metadata contains a list of tables and columns in the data warehouse (for example, stage, ODS, DDS), along with their data types. If we put both of them in the same table, the data mapping table needs to refer to this one table. But if we put them in two different tables, the data mapping needs to go to two different tables to get the data structure. If it is a source system data store, it goes to table 1, and if it is a data warehouse data store, it goes to table 2.

Data Structure Metadata

Data structure metadata contains the tables and columns in all data stores in the data warehouse (for example, DDS, NDS/ODS, and stage) along with their data types. Data structure metadata also contains table definitions, indexes, referential integrity (primary keys, foreign keys), constraints (null, unique), identity details, partition details, and views. Data structure metadata when combined with data definition metadata is also known as the *data dictionary*.

The main purpose of creating data structure metadata is to expose and explain the structure of the data warehouse to the users, and as such, there is no need to go into the details such as the full-text indexes, stored procedures, custom data types, and trigger's definition. Database and data warehouse administrators, developers, and architects have access to SQL Server object catalog views, and therefore there is no need to include the minute details such as the physical location of database files, statistics settings of the database, shrink settings, database access mode, and recovery mode. The system (the data warehouse) does not use data structure metadata, because the data structure of each database is available internally to the system.

We do need to describe, however, at the very least, the data store, tables, and columns. In other words, we need to describe—with good business descriptions—how many data stores there are in the data warehouse; how many tables are in the DDS, NDS, and stage; and how many columns there are in each table. It is absolutely useless for the business users if we describe dim_communication as *communication dimension* and dim_channel as *channel dimension*. What the business users need, especially those who are new to CRM, is an explanation of what communication and channel are. So, descriptions such as these are much more useful: "A communication is printed or electronic media issued at a regular or irregular interval that customers can subscribe to, such as a newsletter or an RSS feed" and "A channel is a medium to deliver communications to customers, such as an e-mail, an RSS feed, a cell/mobile phone text message, and a telephone call."

The second purpose of creating data structure metadata is for a reference to other metadata. Data structure metadata contains the name, data type, and description of all the tables and columns in all data stores. Other metadata needs to refer to data structure metadata to get this information. As listed earlier, these are seven types of metadata. Many of them refer to data structure metadata. For example, as you learned in the previous section, data definition and mapping metadata refer quite frequently to the data structure metadata. Rather than rewriting the column names and data types, they simply refer to the column table in the data structure metadata.

Data structure metadata consists of five tables: ds_data_store, ds_table, ds_table_type, ds_column, and ds_column_type. (DS stands for data structure.) Table 10-4 lists the tables for data structure metadata.

Table 10-4. *Data Structure Metadata Tables*

Table Name	Description
ds_data_store	Lists all data stores in the data warehouse
ds_table	Lists tables in each data store
ds_table_type	Lists table types such as dimension table, fact table, and so on
ds_column	Lists all columns in each table
ds_column_type	Lists column types such as the surrogate key column, measure, and so on

Tables 10-5 to 10-8 describe an example of the data structure metadata tables.

Table 10-5. *Data Structure Metadata:* ds_data_store *Table*

key	data_store	description	collation	current_ size	growth
1	Stage	Staging area	SQL_Latin1_General_CP1_CI_AS	70	10
2	NDS	Normalized data store	SQL_Latin1_General_CP1_CI_AS	125	25
3	DDS	Dimensional data store	SQL_Latin1_General_CP1_CI_AS	150	25
4	Meta	Metadata	SQL_Latin1_General_CP1_CI_AS	10	5

Table 10-6. *Data Structure Metadata:* ds_table *Table*

key	name	entity_type	data_store	description
1	dim_campaign	1	3	DDS campaign dimension. A campaign is an instance of a communication, such as "Amadeus weekly music newsletter dated 19 December 2007."
2	dim_channel	1	3	DDS channel dimension. A channel is a medium to deliver a communication to customers, such as e-mail, RSS feed, mobile phone text, and telephone calls.
3	dim_communication	1	3	DDS communication dimension. A communication is printed or electronic media that issues at a regular or irregular interval that customers can subscribe to, such as a newsletter or an RSS feed.
4	dim_customer	1	3	DDS customer dimension. A customer is an individual or organization that purchased a product, subscribed to a communication, subscribed to a package, or registered on a web site.
11	fact_product_sales	2	3	DDS Product Sales fact table. Contains purchases made by customers.
12	fact_subscription_sales	2	3	DDS Subscription Sales fact table. Contains subscriptions made by customers to packages.
13	fact_campaign_result	2	3	DDS Campaign Result fact table. Contains the send and delivery status of the campaign to each intended recipient.
28	product	3	2	NDS product master table. Contains active products offered to customers for purchase including artist, format, and unit cost, as well as inactive products.
29	order_detail	4	2	NDS order detail transaction table. Contains order line records for each purchase including product code, quantity, and price.
...				

Table 10-7. *Data Structure Metadata:* ds_table_type *Table*

key	table_type	description
1	dimension	Dimension table
2	fact	Fact table
3	master	Master table
4	transaction	Transaction table
5	stage	Stage table
6	metadata	Metadata table

Table 10-8. *Data Structure Metadata:* ds_column *Table*

column_key	table_key	column_name	data_type	is_PK	is_FK	is_null	is_identity
...							
126	21	customer_key	int	Y	Y	N	N
127	21	communication_key	int	Y	Y	N	N
128	21	channel_key	int	N	Y	N	N
129	21	subscription_start_date_key	int	Y	Y	N	N
130	21	subscription_end_date_key	int	N	Y	N	N
131	21	subscription_status_key	int	N	Y	N	N
132	21	source_system_code	tinyint	N	N	N	N
133	21	create_datetime	datetime	N	N	N	N
134	21	update_datetime	datetime	N	N	N	N
...							

Some data structure metadata can be populated from SQL Server object catalog views, as follows (other tables are populated manually):

```
use dds
go

select coalesce(t2.table_key, 0) as table_key
, c.name as column_name
, case when ty.name in ('char', 'varchar')
  then ty.name + '(' + convert(varchar, c.max_length) + ')'
  else
    case when ty.name in ('decimal', 'float')
    then ty.name + '(' + convert(varchar, c.precision)
      + ',' + convert(varchar,c.scale) + ')'
    else ty.name
    end
```

```
    end as data_type
, case coalesce(a.index_column_id, 0) when 0 then 'N' else 'Y' end as is_PK
, case coalesce(fkc.parent_column_id, 0) when 0 then 'N' else 'Y' end as is_FK
, case c.is_nullable when 0 then 'N' else 'Y' end as is_null
, case c.is_identity when 0 then 'N' else 'Y' end as is_identity
from sys.tables t
inner join sys.columns c
  on t.object_id = c.object_id
inner join sys.types ty
  on c.system_type_id = ty.system_type_id
left join
( select i.object_id, ic.index_column_id
from sys.indexes i
inner join sys.index_columns ic
  on i.object_id = ic.object_id
 and i.index_id = ic.index_id
 and i.is_primary_key = 1
) a
 on t.object_id = a.object_id
and c.column_id = a.index_column_id
left join sys.foreign_key_columns fkc
 on t.object_id = fkc.parent_object_id
and c.column_id = fkc.parent_column_id
left join meta.dbo.ds_table t2
  on t.name = t2.table_name
order by table_key, c.column_id
go
```

Table 10-9 shows the output of the previous script.

Table 10-9. *Output of the Script to Populate Data Structure Metadata*

table_key	column_name	data_type	is_PK	is_FK	is_null	is_identity
...						
11	customer_key	int	Y	Y	N	N
11	communication_key	int	Y	Y	N	N
11	channel_key	int	Y	Y	N	N
11	subscription_start_date_key	int	N	Y	N	N
11	subscription_end_date_key	int	N	Y	N	N
11	subscription_status_key	int	N	Y	N	N
11	source_system_code	tinyint	N	N	N	N
11	create_timestamp	datetime	N	N	N	N
11	update_timestamp	datetime	N	N	N	N
...						

The core of the previous query is interrogating the sys.tables and sys.columns object catalog views to list all the columns in the data store, including getting the null and identity attributes of the column. The query then goes to sys.index_columns and sys.foreign_key_columns to identify whether the column is a primary key or a foreign key. The output columns are converted into Y and N using a case statement. The data_type column is then formatted using a case statement as follows:

- If the column is char or varchar, it includes the maximum length.

- If the column is a decimal or float, it includes the precision and scale.

Finally, the table names are converted into table keys.

It is, of course, possible to populate the data structure metadata manually, but it is handy to be able to populate it automatically using scripts like the previous one for consistency and accuracy. The output of the previous script needs to be "upserted" into the column table, in other words, updated when it exists and inserted when it does not exist. But, regardless of the script, the table description columns still need to be filled in manually with meaningful and useful business descriptions. There are tools that can produce data structure information of a database, such as table and column names, data types, and data length, but we still have to type the business description of each column and table manually.

Source System Metadata

Source system metadata is similar to data structure metadata. In other words, it contains the data structure of the source system. Like data structure metadata, at the least it needs to contain the database level, table level, and column level. This information is required because data mapping metadata stores only the column key. When the application needs to display the column names and data types, it gets this information from the source system metadata. Additionally, source system metadata can also contain other information such as the refresh frequency for particular tables. The refresh frequency is useful when we try to optimize the ETL process. Other information that is useful on source system metadata is a data profile, such as minimum and maximum values, row count, and the number of NULLs.

The main purpose of creating the source system metadata is to expose and explain the structure of the source systems to the data warehouse users. This, in a way, acts as an extension to the data warehouse structure exposed by the data structure metadata. As such, there is no need to go down to the technical details of the source systems, such as the indexes, backup interval, triggers, and detailed database properties.

The second purpose of creating source system metadata is to serve as a reference for the other metadata. For example, the source column on the data mapping metadata refers to the columns on the source systems, which exist in the source system metadata. ETL processes metadata and data quality metadata also contain the source system columns, and therefore they need to refer to the source system metadata. This other metadata stores only the column key. When the application needs to display the column name and data types, it gets this information from the source system metadata.

As I explained earlier, it is best to place the source system metadata in the same place as the data structure metadata, rather than creating it on its own set of tables. They have the same structure, so they can be put in the same set of tables. This way, it is easier to query because we don't have to conditionally join two different set of tables, which will make the query slower. For example, on the full data lineage/mapping table, if we place the source system metadata columns in the data structure metadata column table, we have only the table to link to, regardless of whether it is a stage, NDS, or source system column.

Tables 10-10, 10-11, 10-12, and 10-13 show the data structure metadata tables. Data structure metadata consists of three core tables: ds_data_store contains a list of data stores, ds_table contains a list of tables, and ds_column contains a list of columns. In these tables we put the data stores, tables, and columns of both the data warehouse and the source systems. Table 10-10 shows the ds_data_store table, which contains both the data warehouse data stores and the source system data stores. Table 10-11 shows the ds_tables table, which contains both the data warehouse tables and the source system tables. Table 10-12 shows the ds_table_type table, which describes the types of tables, such as dimension table or fact table. Table 10-13 shows the ds_column table, which contains both the data warehouse columns and the source system columns.

Table 10-10. *Data Structure + Source System Metadata:* ds_data_store *Table*

data_store_key	data_store_name	description	DBMS	collation	current_size	growth
1	Stage	Staging area.	SQL Server 2005	SQL_Latin1_General_CP1_CI_AS	70	10
2	ODS	Operational data store.	SQL Server 2005	SQL_Latin1_General_CP1_CI_AS	225	25
3	DDS	Dimensional data store.	SQL Server 2005	SQL_Latin1_General_CP1_CI_AS	350	25
4	Meta	Metadata database.	SQL Server 2005	SQL_Latin1_General_CP1_CI_AS	10	5
5	Jade	A custom Java-based system running on Informix. This includes sales, customer service, subscriptions, and front-office functions.	Informix Dynamic Server 10	Unicode	430	30
6	WebTower	A custom-developed .NET-based system for dynamic web sites, multimedia trading, broadcasting, sales order processing, and subscription management, running on Oracle Database.	Oracle 10g R2	ANSI	845	65
7	Jupiter	The back-end enterprise resource planning (ERP) system. An off-the-shelf AS/400-based business system running on DB2.	DB2 Enterprise 9	EBCDIC	800	50

Table 10-11. *Data Structure + Source System Metadata:* ds_table *Table*

table_key	table_name	table_type	data_store	description
1	dim_campaign	1	3	DDS campaign dimension. A campaign is an instance of a communication, such as "Amadeus weekly music newsletter dated 19 December 2007."
2	dim_channel	1	3	DDS channel dimension. A channel is a means to deliver a communication to customers, such as e-mail, an RSS feed, a mobile phone text, and a telephone call.
3	dim_communication	1	3	DDS communication dimension. A communication is printed or electronic media that issues at a regular or irregular interval to which customers can subscribe, such as a newsletter or an RSS feed.
4	dim_customer	1	3	DDS customer dimension. A customer is an individual or organization that purchased a product, subscribed to a communication, subscribed to a package, or registered on a web site.
11	fact_product_sales	2	3	DDS Product Sales fact table. Contains purchases made by customers.
12	fact_subscription_sales	2	3	DDS Subscription Sales fact table. Contains subscriptions made by customers to packages.
13	fact_campaign_result	2	3	DDS Campaign Result fact table. Contains the send and delivery status of the campaign to each intended recipient.
28	product	3	2	NDS product master table. Contains active products offered to customers for purchase including artist, format, and unit cost, as well as inactive products.
29	order_detail	4	2	NDS order detail transaction table. Contains order line records for each purchase including product code, quantity, and price.

Continued

Table 10-11. *Continued*

table_key	table_name	table_type	data_store	description
71	artist	7	5	Jade artist table. Contains artist reference data including artist name, genre, and country, mainly used by the Jade product table.
79	supplier_performance	8	5	Jade Supplier Performance table. Contains supplier and purchase order transaction data such as ordered, rejected and returned quantities (and their associated values), title and format availability, stock outage, and lead time.

...

Table 10-12. *Data Structure + Source System Metadata:* ds_table_type *Table*

key	table_type	description
1	dimension	Dimension table
2	fact	Fact table
3	master	Master table
4	transaction	Transaction table
5	stage	Stage table
6	metadata	Metadata table
7	source reference	Source system reference table
8	source transaction	Source system transaction table

Table 10-13. *Data Structure + Source System Metadata:* ds_column *Table*

column_ key	table_ key	column_ name	data_ type	PK	FK	null	identity
...							
126	21	customer_key	int	Y	Y	N	N
127	21	communication_key	int	Y	Y	N	N
128	21	channel_key	int	N	Y	N	N
129	21	subscription_start_date_key	int	Y	Y	N	N
130	21	subscription_end_date_key	int	N	Y	N	N
131	21	subscription_status_key	int	N	Y	N	N
132	21	source_system_code	tinyint	N	N	N	N
133	21	create_datetime	datetime	N	N	N	N
134	21	update_datetime	datetime	N	N	N	N
192	79	supplier_id	integer	Y	Y	N	N

column_ key	table_ key	column_ name	data_ type	PK	FK	null	identity
193	79	product_id	integer	Y	Y	N	N
194	79	start_date	date	N	N	Y	N
195	79	ordered_quantity	integer	N	N	Y	N
...							

How do we populate source system metadata? Unlike data structure metadata, which can be obtained automatically (well, semiautomatically to be precise, because we still have to put in the description), in most cases we are not able to populate the source system metadata automatically, because it is not under our control. We need administrative rights to the source system databases, and this kind of access is usually possessed only by the DBA. So, we need to populate the source system metadata manually. We usually get the information that we need to populate the source system metadata when we do source system analysis (also known as the *data feasibility study*; please refer to Chapter 4). For some of us who are lucky enough (or unlucky, depending on how you look at it) to be the DBA of the source systems, we will be able to automate the population by accessing the system information schema or table definitions and be able to create a script in the source system to export its structure into a text file, which we can then import into metadata tables.

There is one thing that source system metadata has but that does not exist in data structure metadata: a source data profile. A source data profile contains statistics and volumetric information describing the source data such as minimum value, maximum value, average value, and number of distinct values for each column. It also contains the number of rows, row size, and number of columns for each table. A source data profile is useful when creating ETL processes to extract the data out of the source system. It is also useful when we need to modify the ETL processes after the data warehouse has been deployed in production.

We get the information required for populating the source data profile usually when doing source system analysis. Tables 10-14 and 10-15 show an example of a source data profile. To put it into context, in the following example, table 71 is the artist table, 72 is the customer table, and 79 is a supplier performance table, all from the Jade source system.

Table 10-14. *Source System Metadata: Source Table Data Profile*

table_key	rows	row size	columns	has_timestamp
...				
71	5768	240	5	N
72	2415832	877	28	Y
79	4103841	85	15	N
...				

Table 10-15. *Source System Metadata: Source Column Data Profile*

column_key	table_key	unique_values	minimum	maximum	average	max length	null
..							
192	79	12894	110921	219032	159281		0
193	79	45120	3	50394	27291		0
194	79	1609	03/19/1998	12/19/2007	05/07/2002		120
195	79	78	0	134	2		0
..							

In Table 10-14, we can see the number of rows, row size, and number of columns for each table. Table 10-15 lists the number of unique/distinct values, the minimum value, the maximum value, and the average value for each column. Table 10-15 also shows the number of rows with nulls in that column. For char or varchar columns, we can have minimum length, maximum length, and average length. We can also have other useful statistics such as the count of the most and least frequent values for each column.

ETL Process Metadata

ETL process metadata consists of a data flow table, a package table, and a status table. The data flow table describes the name and description of each SSIS data flow, what table they extract from, the destination table, what transformations are applied (only a descriptive text, not the exact formula), the parent package, their current status, the last successful extraction time (LSET), and the current extraction time (CET). This information is used by the ETL processes to determine which records to extract from the source system. Sometimes on the data flow table, we have a column called order. This column contains the sequential order when the data flow needs to run, in relative position to other data flow. When using SSIS, we don't actually need this column, because we have precedence constraints defining the workflow between data flows. We need it when we use stored procedures for ETL.

The package table contains the name and description of each SSIS package, their schedule (only descriptive text; the actual schedule is set when creating the SQL Server Agent Job to execute the SSIS package), their status, and the last time they ran. The status table contains the status code and description. To be able to restart an ETL batch from the point of failure (not from the beginning), we need to know exactly where it failed, what was executed, and what was not executed. The status column on both the data flow table and the package table enables this. In its simplest form, the status values are success, failed, and in progress. In a more sophisticated implementation, other status values are "about to run" and "canceled." These two additional statuses enable us to understand the more precise state of each ETL process, which helps us troubleshoot when there is a problem with the ETL.

Tables 10-16 to 10-18 show the tables that form the ETL processes metadata. There are three tables: data_flow, package, and status. The data_flow table contains a list of ETL processes. An ETL process contains several ETL tasks, such as transformations. The package table contains a collection of ETL processes. The status table contains the state of each data flow.

Table 10-16. *ETL Processes Metadata:* data_flow *Table*

key	name	description	source	target	transformation	package	status	LSET	CET
...									
8	stage_product	Extracts Jade and Jupiter product tables incrementally based on the last-updated date and puts them in the product stage table.	Jade.product, Jade.product_detail, Jupiter.prod_hd, Jupiter.prod_dt	stage.product	Adds 9000 on Jupiter product code; dedupe two source systems based on product group and product code.	4	1	11/27/2007 04:06:09	11/27/2007 04:06:09
9	nds_product	Loads product data from the stage to the NDS.	state.product	stage.product	Upsert and keying; DQ unit_cost with rule 29	11	1	11/27/2007 04:07:11	11/27/2007 04:07:11
...									

Table 10-17. *ETL Processes Metadata:* package *Table*

key	name	description	schedule
...			
4	Stage daily incremental	This SSIS package extracts the following data from the source system incrementally and loads it onto the stage: customer, permission, product, store, product purchases, package subscription, and communication subscription.	Runs every day including weekends at 3 a.m.
5	Stage daily full reload	This SSIS package extracts the following data from the source system by downloading the whole table: customer type, customer status, interest, household income, occupation, currency, artist, product status, product type, product category, package, and package type.	Runs every day at 3 a.m.
11	NDS product	This loads product-related tables from the stage to the NDS, in other words, the ones with product, product status, product type, product category, package, and package type data.	Runs daily at 3 a.m.
12	NDS customer	This loads customer-related tables from the stage to the NDS, in other words, the ones with customer, customer status, customer type, address, address type, e-mail address, e-mail address type, permission, phone number, phone number type, household income, occupation, and interest data.	Runs daily at 3 a.m.
...			

Table 10-18. *ETL Processes Metadata:* status *Table*

key	status
...	
0	Unknown
1	Success
2	Failed
3	In progress
...	

Table 10-17 shows that the stage ETL packages are grouped into packages according to the frequency they run (daily, weekly, monthly, ad hoc, and so on) and the extraction method (full reload, incremental, or fixed period). Table 10-17 also shows that the NDS ETL packages are grouped into packages according to the subject area, such as product, customer, product purchase, package subscription, CRM subscription, and so on.

The main purpose of having ETL metadata is to control the ETL packages in SSIS. For example, as we did in Chapter 7, the LSET and CET columns enable us to extract incrementally by memorizing the last time a successful extract was run. The status columns enable the SSIS packages or the whole ETL batch to restart from the point of failure. When we restart an ETL package, we can use the status column to determine which ETL processes have not been executed, and we can restart from that process onward, rather than from the beginning. To be able to restart from failure, the ETL processes need to be re-runnable. In other words, we need to be able to run the same process over and over without causing any problem.

The second purpose of having ETL metadata is to describe the ETL processes. It describes what the ETL process or package does, such as "Stage daily incremental: this SSIS package extracts the following data from the source system incrementally and loads it into the stage: customer, permission, product, store, product purchases, package subscription, and communication subscription. Runs every day including weekend at 3 a.m." Being able to query such descriptive text for every package and data flow is very useful to most data warehouse administrators, provided that the descriptions are kept up-to-date. We can automate it a little bit, such as by querying sysjobs, sysjobsteps, sysjobschedules, and sysschedules tables in the msdb database to determine the SQL Server Agent job steps and schedule. We can also query sysjobhistory to determine what jobs have been executed.

Data Quality Metadata

Data quality metadata contains the data quality rules that we discussed in the previous chapter, including the rule name and description, rule type (for example, error or warning), rule category (for example, incoming data validation, cross reference validation, or internal data warehouse validation; see Chapter 9), risk level (for example, business or financial risk if this rule is violated, on the scale of 1 to 5), status (active or not), action (reject, allow, or fix; see Chapter 9), notification, create timestamp, and update timestamp. The notification column contains a link to the DQ notification table that contains who to notify and how to notify them (for example, an e-mail or a cell/mobile phone text message). We can have other features such as how many times to notify, at what interval, acknowledgment status, escalation timeframe, escalation person/second level, and so on. We also need to have a third table containing the user details, in other words, name, department/business area, role/position, e-mail address, cell phone number, group number, and so on. And potentially we need a fourth table for describing the user groups when we have a lot of users and we want to assign the data quality tasks to a group of users rather than to individual users. It is usually better to start with something simple, such as without escalation/second level. If it is proven to be successful, we can enhance it further.

Tables 10-19 to 10-21 contain data quality metadata. There are three main tables: DQ rules, DQ notification, and DW user. The DQ rules table contains the data quality rules. The DQ notification table specifies which DW users to notify for each rule. The DW user table describes the data warehouse users including their e-mail addresses.

Table 10-19. *Data Quality Metadata: DQ Rules Table*

rule_ key	rule_ name	description	rule_ type	rule_ category	risk_ level	status	action	create_ timestamp	update_ timestamp
...									
7	The product code format	Product code needs to be in AAA999AA format. Reject if it is not in this format, and notify product manager by e-mail.	E	I	3	A	R	10/21/2007 11:41:33	11/27/2007 14:07:11
8	The unit price	Within 25% of last three months' average.	W	C	1	A	A	09/18/2007 12:04:33	10/12/2007 09:27:55
...									

Table 10-20. *Data Quality Metadata: DQ Notification Table*

key	rule_key	recipient_type	recipient	method
...				
11	7	I	3	E
12	8	G	9	E
...				

Table 10-21. *Data Quality Metadata: Data Warehouse User Table*

key	name	department	role	email_address	phone_number	group
...						
3	Brian Hill	Merchandising	Product Manager	brian.hill@ amadeus.com	0983475052	9
4	Sarah Fairbank	Finance	Costing Assistant	sarah.fairbank@ amadeus.com		9
...						

In Table 10-19, the `rule_type` column is linked to the `rule_type` table, which has two entries: E for errors and W for warnings. This enables us to determine whether it is an error or warning. The `rule_category` column is linked to the `rule_category` table, which has three entries: I for incoming data validation rules, C for cross-reference validation rules, and D for internal data warehouse validation rules (see Chapter 9). This enables us to determine the type of data quality issue we are facing.

The `risk_level` column is linked to the `rule_risk_level` table, which has five entries: level 1 for no business impact to level 5 for severe damage to business financial positions. This enables us to determine how big the impact of the data quality issue is. The `status` column is linked to the `rule_status` table, which has two entries: A for active and D for decommissioned. This enables us to add new rules and deactivate obsolete rules. The `action` column is linked to the `rule_action` table, which contains R for reject, A for allow, and F for fix. This enables us to determine what kind of action was taken against each data quality issue.

Tip *rule* is a SQL Server keyword, which specifies the acceptable values that can be inserted into a column. In SQL Server 2008, it is replaced by check constraints. So, be careful when you want to use *rule* as a table name, because you need to use brackets (`[rule]`) every time you use the table name. A practical approach is to change the table name to `dq_rule`, which is more descriptive. For consistency, you need to name the rule type, rule category, and rule status tables as `dq_rule_type`, `dq_rule_category`, and `dq_rule_status`. Underscores are used for naming SQL Server system views, such as `sys.foreign_keys`, `sys.default_constraint`, `sys.service_queues`, `sys.sql_modules`, and `sys.backup_devices`. I prefer to use underscores because it gives better readability compared to joined words with no underscore.

In Table 10-20, the recipient type column is linked to the `recipient_type` table, which has two entries: I for individual and G for group. This enables us to send the notification to a group of users, rather than to an individual user. The `recipient` column contains the key of the individual or the group on the user table, depending on the value of the `recipient_type` column. Table 10-21 contains the user details, with the last column (group) being the group key of each user to enable sending a DQ notification for a particular rule to several people simultaneously.

This is only one design. Of course, you could and should alter or enhance it according the needs of your projects and situations. The purpose of giving the previous example is just for illustration to help you understand the practical implementation. For instance, in some projects, it is required to extend the DQ rule table by creating a parameter column. This column contains a value that is used in the rule. For example, if the rule is "the unit cost of product family AG9 needs to be greater than 1.25," then the number 1.25 is actually stored as a value in the parameter column, not hard-coded in SSIS data flow logic. This makes it easier to update the value later. To accommodate more than one parameter, the parameters are placed in a separate parameter table and linked to the DQ rule table on the rule key column. You can add "data type" column in the parameter table to handle the issue of parameters being of different data types.

Audit Metadata

Audit metadata contains the results of every process and activity in the data warehouse, including data loading process (ETL), creation of specific purpose DDS (mart), manual data modification (for example, updating DQ user table), DQ rule validation, security log/breach (for example, web portal login), system enhancements and modifications (for example, patches, schema changes and upgrades), data purging and archiving, database tuning, and maintenance (indexing and partitioning activities).

Audit metadata is used for administering the data warehouse, including monitoring ETL processes, monitoring data quality, enhancements requests, installation patches, and monitoring security access. For example, the purpose of one of the daily operation reports (or manual query using SQL script) is to verify whether the ETL processes ran successfully. This report or script accesses the audit metadata to get the number of rows loaded for each table. It is used to see when the last purging, indexing, or partitioning was done on a particular table. Another example of administrative usage is to support enhancement requests. By examining or querying the audit metadata, we know what patch was applied and when. We will go though these administrative tasks in Chapter 17 when we discuss data warehouse administration.

The secondary usage of audit metadata is for troubleshooting. When there is a problem or issue, you can query audit metadata to know what happened in the last few hours. Say you got a call from a user saying that a package subscription report or cube is missing some data. You know that this cube is fed from the Subscription Sales fact table in the DDS, and it turns out that today this fact table was not loaded. In this case, you can query how many records were loaded into the stage, how many into NDS, and how many into DDS. It helps you to pinpoint where the cause of the problem lies.

In its simplest form, audit metadata is an event log table containing every single event that happened in the data warehouse populated by every single process and activity in the data warehouse. The processes use insert SQL statements to add rows into the event log table. It contains the event type, event category, which data warehouse object is involved in the event (linked to data structure metadata), the data flow initiating the event (linked to the data flow table), the number of rows involved, the timestamp when the event occurred, and a note. Table 10-22 gives an example of this event log table.

In the event_type table described in Table 10-22, the key column is an identity (1,1) containing a sequential number for identifying the log entry. The type column contains the event type, linked to the event_type table shown in Table 10-23. The category column contains the event category, linked to the event_category table shown in Table 10-24. The object column contains the table key, linked to the ds_table table in the data structure metadata. For ETL processes, the data_flow column contains the SSIS data flow, linked to the data_flow table in the ETL processes metadata. For ETL processes, the rows column contains the number of rows affected. The event_log table is purged regularly, such as every month, leaving only the last 12 months of data. This enables us to maintain query and reporting performance. The purge frequency and number of months to keep depends on the administrative requirements, performance requirements, regulatory issues, and company standards.

Table 10-22. *Audit Metadata:* event_log *Table*

key	event_type	event_category	timestamp	object	data_flow	rows	note
...							
12418	26	5	2007-11-24 03:04:09	56	12	23102	
12419	27	6	2007-11-24 03:05:19	87	23	23102	
12420	28	7	2007-11-24 03:06:11	112	38	23102	
12581	39	18	2007-11-25 14:36:06	29			Login successful
15013	59	21	2007-11-26 00:09:15	35			Applying patch 19
...							

Table 10-23. *Audit Metadata:* event_type *Table*

key	event_type
...	
26	Load Stage customer
27	Run DQ rule17
28	Load NDS customer
39	Login
59	Bug fix
...	

Table 10-24. *Audit Metadata:* event_category *Table*

key	event_category
...	
5	Stage ETL
6	Data Quality
7	NDS ETL
18	Security
21	System modification
...	

Usage Metadata

Usage metadata is similar to the audit metadata in that it contains an event log. But this time, the events are the usage of the Reporting Services reports, Analysis Services cubes, and data mining model. In one implementation, the reports, cubes, and mining model could be accessed via a web portal. Before the link on the portal redirects to the report (or cubes or mining model), it inserts a record into this usage metadata first. So, we know which reports or cubes were accessed and when they were accessed. The access patterns are useful for doing performance tuning and capacity planning. For example, they enable us to avoid the busy times when processing the cubes.

Another implementation is to populate the usage metadata from the SQL Server stored procedures, which are invoked by the Reporting Services reports. For this, the reports must not contain direct SQL statements; instead, they must call the stored procedures.

Usage metadata is used to understand (for example) how many times a particular report is accessed and by which users or departments. We can use an IIS log to record the number of hits on the links on the data warehouse portal page, but usage metadata is more flexible. It could be reported using SSRS, so it would have a more consistent look with other data warehouse reports. An IIS log, on the other hand, requires some kind of web log analysis software in order for us to understand how many times a report is accessed and by which users. Each entry on the IIS log contains the date and time the activity occurred, the client IP address, the username of the authenticated user who accessed the server, the target page or report, the Universal Resource Identifier (URI) query, the bytes sent, and the length of time that the action took (in milliseconds). Each hit on the report produced an IIS log entry with all the previous information. This way, a full collection of IIS log entries enables us to determine the usage or access pattern of the report.

One simple implementation of usage metadata is a usage_log table. The log table contains the user, the object, and the timestamp, and if applicable, it also contains the parameters. Table 10-25 shows an example of this usage_log table.

Table 10-25. *Usage Metadata:* usage_log *Table*

key	user	object	timestamp	parameters	note
...					
7834	12	56	2007/11/03 16:09:33	FG45	
7892	20	114	2007/12/05 11:39:05		
...					

The user column on Table 10-25 is linked to the data warehouse user table shown in Table 10-21. The object column is linked to the ds_table table in the data structure metadata shown in Table 10-6. The timestamp column shows when the object is accessed.

When the authentication method in SSRS is Windows integrated security, the user ID can be obtained using system_user. system_user is a SQL Server internal system variable that contains the login name (if using SQL authentication) or the Windows login identification name (if using Windows authentication).

Maintaining Metadata

It is important to keep the metadata up-to-date. An out-of-date data structure or outdated data mapping metadata, for example, may lead the users to the wrong understanding of the data warehouse. Also, the system may take an incorrect action if the metadata is incorrect.

Conducting a change request impact analysis based on out-of-date data mapping metadata could lead to ETL problems, such as because we misinterpreted where a piece of data is coming from or because the data type was not correct.

Data definition and mapping metadata is usually defined and created at an early phase of a data warehousing project. Once created, they are then maintained through change request procedures. Rather than changing it directly on the metadata tables, the change needs to be implemented using a data change script. The data change script is a Transact SQL script containing the rollback section, the change request details (which go to the event log table), and the roll forward.

The DW administrator needs to prepare a script to change the metadata and submit this script to be executed under a change request process. The script contains three sections: log, rollback, and implementation.

- The log section records the change request details into the event log table. The reason for doing this is for traceability and troubleshooting if something goes wrong.

- The rollback section tries to "undo" the change. This is necessary to prove that we can revert the changes.

- The implementation section applies the change to the metadata database.

The following is an example of a metadata change request. This example updates the risk level of rule 8 in Table 10-19 from level 1 to level 2.

```
/* Change request number: CR023
Date created: 12/14/2007
Created by: Vincent Rainardi
Description of change: Change the risk level for rule 8 from 1 to 2
Schedule for production implementation: 12/18/2007
*/

use meta -- switch to metadata database

-- Event Log section
insert into event_log (event_type, event_category,
event_timestamp, object, dataflow, rows, note)
values (7, 3, getdate(), 371, 0, 8,
'update risk level from 1 to 2')

-- Rollback section
update dq_rules set risk_level = 1 where rule_key = 8

-- Implementation section
update dq_rules set risk_level = 2 where rule_key = 8
```

Some data structure metadata can be maintained automatically using SQL Server object catalog views. A query gets the data from the object catalog views and inserts or updates the appropriate metadata tables. For example, we can use the query shown earlier in this chapter. Some data structure metadata still needs to be maintained manually, such as object business descriptions, dimensional hierarchy, and SCD details. Source system metadata is usually created and populated during the source system analysis phase and then maintained during the development phase by using a data change script to update the metadata tables (illustrated earlier), according to the change request process. After the data warehouse is released, the source system metadata is maintained using data change scripts, governed by a change request procedure.

ETL process metadata is created and populated during the development of the SSIS packages. We need to update the ETL process metadata every time we modify the SSIS packages. Similarly, data quality metadata (DQ rule table, and so on) needs to be updated every time we modify the SSIS packages. Ideally, we need to use a standardized data change script to update the metadata tables, rather than using direct SQL statements to update the tables. All updates to metadata need to be recorded on the audit metadata event log table. So, this needs to be included in the data change scripts.

Audit metadata and usage metadata are maintained as the data warehouse is used. Audit metadata is populated by the ETL processes, patch release processes, and security processes. Usage metadata is populated by the stored procedure or the web portal.

Summary

This chapter defined what metadata in a data warehouse is and what it contains. It listed seven kinds of metadata: data definition and mapping metadata, data structure metadata, source system metadata, ETL processes metadata, data quality metadata, audit metadata, and usage metadata. I discussed them one by one so you can understand what they are used for, how to create them, and how to populate/maintain them.

Metadata helps us understand the structure and definition/meaning of the data in the data warehouse. It also helps us understand the structure and definition of the data warehouse itself. Metadata is also used for auditing and troubleshooting purposes, in other words, to understand what happened (and what is happening) in the data warehouse, where it happened, and when it happened.

In the next few chapters, I will discuss how to get the data out of the data warehouse. I will discuss how to use SQL Server Reporting Services and SQL Server Analysis Services to create reports and cubes to bring the data from the data warehouse to the users.

■ ■ ■

CHAPTER 11

Building Reports

Earlier in this book, you learned how to build a data warehouse, including defining the architecture, selecting the methodology, gathering the requirements, designing the data models, and creating the databases. In the past few chapters, I discussed how to populate the data warehouse, including extracting from the source system, loading the data stores, maintaining the data quality, and utilizing the metadata.

Now that we have loaded the data into the warehouse, in this chapter and the next few chapters, I will discuss how to get the data out to the users and how to use the data in the warehouse. Two of the most popular ways to present the data to the users are using reports and using multidimensional databases. So in this chapter, I will discuss reports, and in the next chapter, I will talk about multidimensional databases.

Two of the most popular uses of data warehouses are for business intelligence (BI) and customer relationship management (CRM). In Chapters 13 and 14, I will discuss these two uses, and in Chapter 15, I will discuss other uses such as customer data integration and unstructured data. Reporting and multidimensional databases are used quite intensively in BI.

In this chapter, you will learn how to use SQL Server 2005 Reporting Services to create reports to bring the data from the data warehouse to the users. I'll first explain what data warehouse reports are, and then I will show how to use Reporting Services to actually build a report. When building the report, you will learn some key features in reporting such as querying the data, arranging the report layout, using parameters, sorting the data, and filtering the data. I will also discuss how to create a pivot table report, how to follow the principle of simplicity, and how to report from a multidimensional database. I will close this chapter by discussing how to deploy and administer the reports.

This chapter will give you enough knowledge to start building the reports for your data warehouse. There is no doubt that you will need to refer to Books Online along the way for more detailed instructions, but this chapter will provide you with a good starting point.

Data Warehouse Reports

In the data warehousing context, a report is a program that retrieves data from the data warehouse and presents it to the users on the screen or on paper. Users also can subscribe to these reports so that they can receive them automatically by e-mail at certain times (daily or weekly, for example) or in response to events.

Which data stores do data warehouse reports usually retrieve data from? Data warehouse reports usually retrieve data from a dimensional data store (DDS), an operational data store

(ODS), a data quality database, or a metadata database. They can also retrieve data from a multidimensional database (MDB). (Please refer to Chapter 1 for an explanation of what a multidimensional database is.)

In the next few pages, I will show you two examples of BI reports. The first one is a simple store listing. The second one is Amadeus Entertainment's Weekly Product Sales report, which contains the total sales amount for each product type for every single week in a particular quarter in a particular division. Keep in mind that there are data warehouse (DW) reports that are not for BI. (For a definition of what BI is and what DW is, please refer to Chapter 1.) A data quality report, a campaign effectiveness report, and an audit report are three examples of DW reports that are not BI reports.

A simple report retrieves a few columns from a database table and presents them in tabular format on the screen. Figure 11-1 shows an example of such a report.

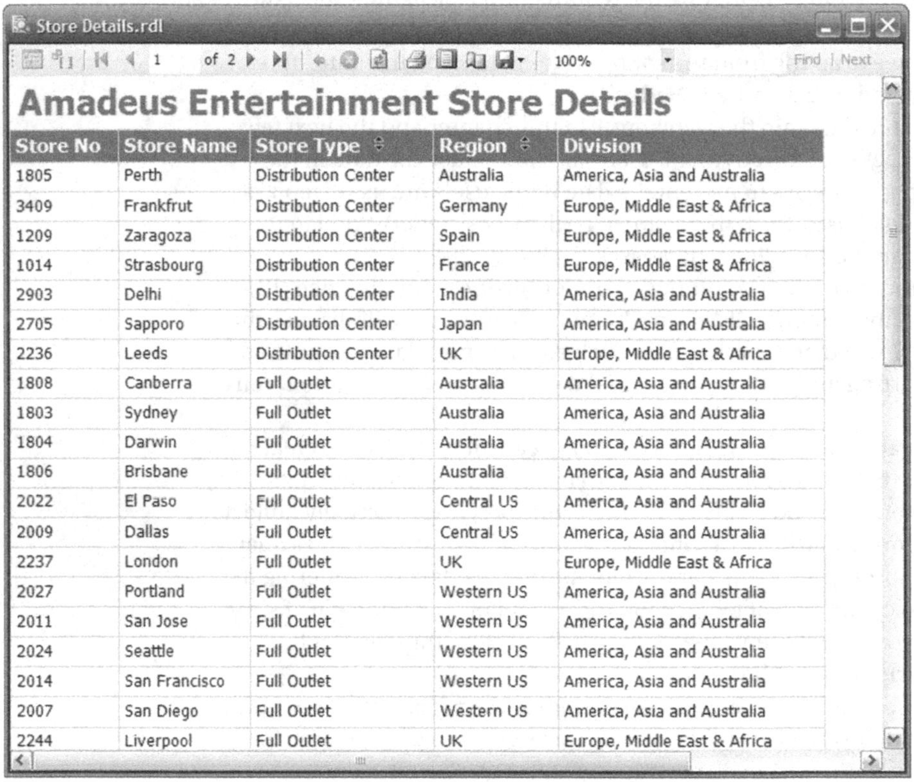

Store No	Store Name	Store Type	Region	Division
1805	Perth	Distribution Center	Australia	America, Asia and Australia
3409	Frankfrut	Distribution Center	Germany	Europe, Middle East & Africa
1209	Zaragoza	Distribution Center	Spain	Europe, Middle East & Africa
1014	Strasbourg	Distribution Center	France	Europe, Middle East & Africa
2903	Delhi	Distribution Center	India	America, Asia and Australia
2705	Sapporo	Distribution Center	Japan	America, Asia and Australia
2236	Leeds	Distribution Center	UK	Europe, Middle East & Africa
1808	Canberra	Full Outlet	Australia	America, Asia and Australia
1803	Sydney	Full Outlet	Australia	America, Asia and Australia
1804	Darwin	Full Outlet	Australia	America, Asia and Australia
1806	Brisbane	Full Outlet	Australia	America, Asia and Australia
2022	El Paso	Full Outlet	Central US	America, Asia and Australia
2009	Dallas	Full Outlet	Central US	America, Asia and Australia
2237	London	Full Outlet	UK	Europe, Middle East & Africa
2027	Portland	Full Outlet	Western US	America, Asia and Australia
2011	San Jose	Full Outlet	Western US	America, Asia and Australia
2024	Seattle	Full Outlet	Western US	America, Asia and Australia
2014	San Francisco	Full Outlet	Western US	America, Asia and Australia
2007	San Diego	Full Outlet	Western US	America, Asia and Australia
2244	Liverpool	Full Outlet	UK	Europe, Middle East & Africa

Figure 11-1. *An example of a simple tabular report*

Figure 11-1 shows the store number, store name, store type, region, and division of all Amadeus Entertainment stores from our case study. The report simply lists the data in a tabular format. The report was created using SQL Server Reporting Services (SSRS). On the top of the report there are buttons to navigate to the next page, zoom in/zoom out, set up the page layout, and print the report. The disk icon exports the report to Excel, a text file, a PDF, or XML.

The report queries the store dimension in the DDS using the SQL query shown in Listing 11-1.

Listing 11-1. *SQL Query for the Store Details Report*

```
select store_number, store_name,
store_type, region, division
from dim_store
where store_key <> 0
```

As you can see, the Transact SQL query in Listing 11-1 retrieves data only from the store dimension table where the store key is not 0 (the store key 0 is the unknown record). You can replace the <> in the SQL statement with > because store_key is an identity (1,1) column. In other words, it's a positive integer, with the exception of 0 for the unknown record, as I discussed in Chapters 5 and 6.

A more typical data warehouse report retrieves data from fact and dimension tables in a dimensional data store. Figure 11-2 shows an example of such a report.

Amadeus Entertainment Product Sales.rdl

| Year | 2007 | | Quarter | Q1 | | | | | | | | | View Report |

| Division | Online Business | | | | | | | | | | | | View Report |

| ◀ 1 of 2 ▶ ▶| | 100% | | Find | Next |

Amadeus Entertainment Product Sales

Product by Week	1	2	3	4	5	6	7	8	9	10	11	12	13
A cappella Msc	8.88	1.98	0.89		3.68		1.99	5.18	12.99			13.88	4.99
Action Books	1.99	0.89			3.08	4.99							
Action Films				2.59			24.55		0.89	2.18	2.67		17.99
Adventure Books	1.09		1.09				1.99	1.99	12.99			27.65	
Blues Music	2.67		1.38	51.96	17.99	4.99	0.69			3.76	3.08	2.68	1.09
Cartoon Films	2.67	13.88			17.99			38.97		1.09	1.98		
Childrens Books	1.99		0.69	6.27	12.99			0.69		0.89	2.59		15.58
Childrens Films		2.59	3.56	27.97	6.27		12.99	4.99	1.09	1.78			
Childrens Music		1.09	1.99	0.89	17.99	1.99	56.44		5.97				2.59
Classical Music							1.09			1.09			
Comedy Books	2.59	4.99		9.05					1.99		2.59		
Comedy Films					2.59		0.89	14.98	1.99				
Cooking Books	7.99	4.36	2.18		1.78				1.99	2.59	0.89	1.99	
Culture Books		7.99		7.99		7.58		5.18		2.59	1.99		0.69
Dance Music	7.99			1.99		14.98							
DIY Books	0.89	13.96	6.57	20.58	2.68	2.59	10.53	12.99	0.89	5.97	4.05	0.69	31.03
Documentary	14.77	1.09				4.58				7.99			
Drama Films	2.88				1.99			8.66				5.97	7.04
Engineering Bk		1.99	1.38	30.32	12.99	1.99				5.07	9.98		
Family Films	1.99				5.97	1.09			2.59	1.99			1.09
Fiction Books	0.89			2.67	12.99		51.96				2.67		

Figure 11-2. *A typical report presenting data from a dimensional data warehouse*

The report in Figure 11-2 shows the weekly product sales of Amadeus Entertainment in a particular quarter for a particular division. On the top of the report there are three drop-down lists that enable the users to select the year, quarter, and division. The report was created using SSRS by querying data from the Product Sales fact table and joining with the date, product, and store dimensions, as shown in Listing 11-2.

Listing 11-2. *SQL Query for Weekly Product Sales Report*

```
select d.week_number, p.product_type
, sum(f.sales_value) as [Sales Value]
from fact_product_sales f
inner join dim_date d
  on f.sales_date_key = d.date_key
inner join dim_product p
  on f.product_key = p.product_key
inner join dim_store s
  on f.store_key = s.store_key
where d.quarter = @pQuarter
  and d.year = @pYear
  and (s.division = @pDivision
  or @pDivision = ' All')
group by d.week_number, p.product_type
```

The output columns of this query (week number, product type, and sales value) are then arranged into a cross-tab table. The columns of the cross-tab table are the week numbers, the rows are the product types, and the cells are the sales values.

When to Use Reports and When Not to Use Them

Data warehouse reports are used to present the business data to users, but they are also used for data warehouse administration purposes. Reports such as the one shown in Figure 11-2 are called *dimensional reports*. Their main purpose is to present DDS data to the users in a cross-tab format. Other data warehouse reports have different purposes or different ways of operating:

Data quality reports: These report the statistics of data quality rule violation events. They primarily query a metadata database. I discussed them in Chapter 9.

Audit reports: These reports read the event log table in a metadata database to get the results and status of data warehouse processes and activities, such as ETL processes, mart creation, security logs, system enhancements, data purging, database maintenance, and so on.

Usage reports: These reports read the usage log table to retrieve which reports, cubes, and mining models were used/ran, when, and by whom.

ODS reports: In the ODS + DDS architecture, the ODS acts as an integration point from multiple source systems, as well as acts as the data store for an operation application such as a customer service center application. ODS reports read the ODS to check that the data from various source systems is integrated correctly, as well as check that the dimension hierarchies are correct, including the customer and product hierarchies.

DDS single dimension reports: Some DDS reports do not join a fact table to several dimensions but report only from a single dimension for a specific business purpose, such as to check the store/region/division structure.

DDS drill-across dimensional reports: Some DDS reports drill across from a fact table to another fact table, such as combining the Subscription Sales fact table, the Communication Subscriptions fact table, and the Campaign Results fact table to understand the effectiveness of particular campaigns and their impact on revenue streams.

The previous are examples of where and when data warehouse reports are used. But not all cases are suitable for reports. Sometimes it is not appropriate to use data warehouse reports:

- Some operational reporting such as "when was order X dispatched?" and "what is the address of customer X?" are best performed using the reports in the source system, such as OLTP, rather than using data warehouse reports. Source system reports contain more up-to-date data than data warehousing reports. The data in the source system reports is up-to-the-minute, whereas the data in the data warehouse reports could be one day old or one week old depending on how frequently the ETL updates the data warehouse.

- In some cases, it is more suitable to use OLAP tools to explore the data in the warehouse (particularly the DDS) than using reports. Reports are more rigid. For example, it is difficult for the users to change the dimensions and the attributes they want to view. We can use drop-down lists to make them a little bit more flexible, but that's about it. OLAP tools such as Analysis Services enable the users to choose the dimensions and attributes they require. Well, we also have some degree of flexibility in SSRS. For example, we have other methods of entering parameters and the ability to toggle views including charts, and so on, but it's less flexible than OLAP tools.

On the other hand, you need to be aware of the following in regard to the previous two cases:

- Regarding the first point, sometimes we need to report not just from one source system but from several source systems. In this case, it may be more appropriate to report from the data warehouse because it integrates several operational source systems.

- Regarding the second point, in certain cases reports are preferred over OLAP tools:

  - To use OLAP tools, the users need to understand how the data is structured and organized, while to use reports we don't, so it is easier for the users.

  - If we use OLAP tools, we need to populate and process the OLAP cubes every day to refresh the data in the cubes, but when using reports, we don't need to populate and process. So, reports are simpler to maintain.

  - OLAP tools are suitable to report from the DDS because the DDS is in dimensional format. It is easy and natural to create OLAP cubes from the DDS. Creating OLAP cubes from the ODS is not that easy, because the ODS is in normalized format, not in dimensional format. So if you need to report from the ODS, it is easier to use reporting tools than to use OLAP tools.

Now that you understand what data warehouse reports are and when to use them, let's create a report. I've found that "learning by doing" is the fastest way to learn data warehousing reports, so like Chapter 7 when you learned ETL and SSIS, you'll complete a hands-on exercise in this chapter. We'll create the report shown in Figure 11-2. We'll build it gradually. In the next section, we'll build the query. In the section after that, we will define the report layout, and then we will add the parameters, and so on. At the end of each section, I will add some other points that are useful to know but are not covered by the exercise. By the end of the whole exercise, you should have practical knowledge to build a data warehouse report that you can then expand upon.

If you are new to data warehousing and also new to SSRS, following the exercise in the next few sections is probably the fastest way to get you into the heart of the matter. This exercise will take a only few hours to do, yet you will get first-hand experience in dimensional reporting, which is used quite a lot for BI, as well as basic and advanced topics in Reporting Services such as data sets, queries, matrixes, layout, parameters, grouping, subtotals, filtering, and sorting.

In choosing and explaining the exercise, I will focus on the core functionalities that are relevant for data warehousing reports. Out of hundreds of features that SSRS has, I will probably cover only 30 percent of them. But those 30 percent are the ones you need to build the simple report and dimensional report illustrated in the previous section. After finishing this chapter, you will have enough knowledge to build simple data warehouse reports and complex dimensional reports, using SSRS, for your own data warehouse project. If you want to master the remaining 70 percent functionality, you need to complete your knowledge by reading a book that specifically explains every aspect of SSRS from cover to cover. The most complete source of documentation for SSRS is, of course, Books Online.

OK, enough about the approach. Let's start building the dimensional report shown in Figure 11-2 by using SSRS. The first step is to use the Report Wizard to create the report including defining the SQL query.

Report Wizard

Follow these steps to start creating the report:

1. Let's begin by restoring the DDS database on your development SQL Server. The backup file of the DDS database that you need to restore is dds.bak, located in the /data folder on the book's page on the Apress web site at http://www.apress.com/. Ensure that you have a login called ETL, and create a user with db_owner permission on the DDS database. (Please refer to Chapter 7 for information on how to restore a database and create the user.)

2. After restoring the DDS database, open Business Intelligence Development Studio, and start a new project (File ➤ New ➤ Project). Choose the Business Intelligence Projects project type, choose the Report Server Project Wizard template, enter **Amadeus Reports** as the project name, set the location to a working directory on your computer, keep the solution name as Amadeus Reports, and ensure that "Create directory for solution" is ticked. Verify that it looks similar to Figure 11-3, and click OK.

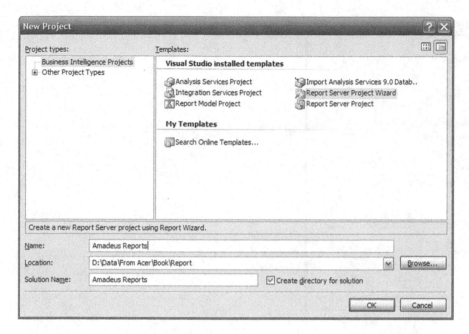

Figure 11-3. *Creating a new report server project*

3. Click Next on the welcome page. On the Select the Data Source page, set the name to DDS, keep the type as Microsoft SQL Server, and click Edit. The Connection Properties dialog box will open. Set the server name as your development SQL server. Choose Use Windows Authentication, or use the username ETL and the password (we created this login in Chapter 7). Under "Select or enter a database name," choose DDS from the drop-down list. The dialog box should look like Figure 11-4.

4. Click Test Connection. Microsoft Visual Studio should respond with "Test connection succeeded." Click OK to close the response window. Click OK to close the Connection Properties dialog box. If you want to reuse this data source for other reports, check the "Make this a shared data source" box. The Select the Data Source page should look like Figure 11-5.

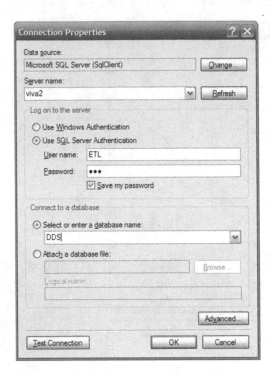

Figure 11-4. *Setting the database connection in the Report Wizard*

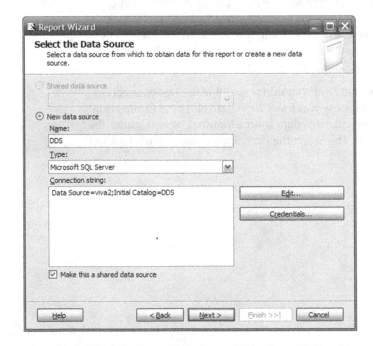

Figure 11-5. *Select the Data Source page in the Report Wizard*

5. Click Next on the Select the Data Source page. You should now see the Design the Query page. Click the Query Builder button. Click the Generic Query Designer button (the leftmost button). The Query Builder page pops up. Maximize the Query Builder dialog box so you can see it better. On the toolbar on the top of the page, click Add Table (the rightmost icon with a yellow + on it). Using the Control button, select these three tables: dim_date, dim_product, and fact_product_sales. Then click Add to add these tables to Query Builder. Click Close. Query Builder now looks like Figure 11-6. Please notice that Query Builder automatically adds the relationship between the three tables because we have defined the relationship on the database using foreign keys.

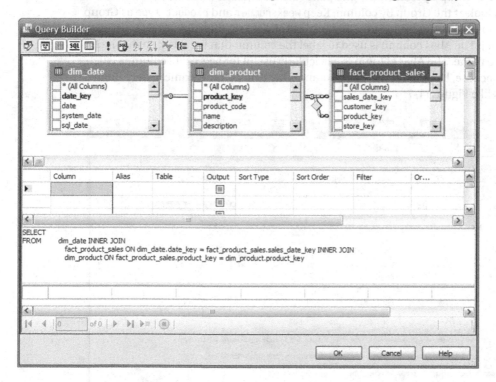

Figure 11-6. *Building the query*

In Query Builder, the top pane is called the *diagram pane*. The middle pane is called the *grid pane*. The bottom pane is called the *SQL pane*. In the diagram pane, we define which tables we want to query from, the relationship between tables, and which columns we want to use.

We use the grid pane to define which column we want to display on the report, the filter criteria (the where clause), the summary values (the group by clause), and the sort order (the order by clause). The SQL pane displays the SQL statement of the query, which we can edit if we need to do so.

6. Scroll down on the date dimension (the dim_date table in the diagram pane), and find the week_number column. Select this column by ticking its check box. Selecting a column in the diagram pane brings the column to the grid pane so we can use it later either for displaying the column on the report or for applying a filter, grouping, or sorting order.

   Select the product_type column from the product dimension and the sales_value column from the Product Sales fact table.

7. Click the Use Group By icon on the grid pane (the second one from the right). In the grid pane, look at the Group By column. Keep week_number and product_type as Group By, but change sales_value to Sum. In the Alias column, set the alias of sales_value to [Sales Value]. The Alias column is used to label the column that we select so that it can have a nice name. The Alias column is particularly useful for aggregate columns (such as SUM) because, by default, aggregate columns have no column name. Query Builder now looks like Figure 11-7.

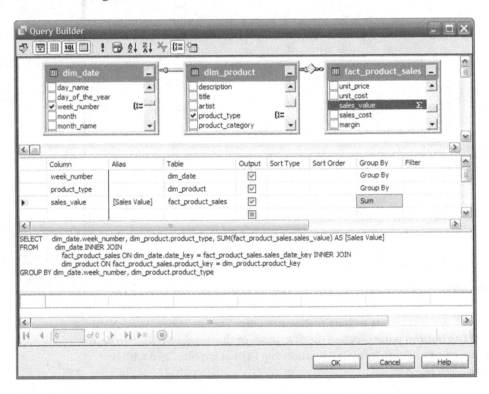

Figure 11-7. *Selecting the columns and creating a grouping*

8. Click OK to close Query Builder, and click Next on the Design the Query page. On the Select the Report Type page, choose Matrix, and click Next. On the Design the Table page, put week_number as Columns, product_type as Rows, and sales_value as Details, as shown in Figure 11-8.

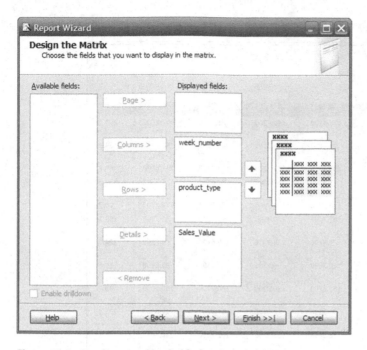

Figure 11-8. *Configuring the fields for the matrix*

9. Click Next. Choose the report style, and click Next. Type **Amadeus Entertainment Product Sales** as the report name, and click Finish. The Business Intelligence Development Studio Report Wizard will open a new project, create the report, and display the layout of the report on the screen, as shown in Figure 11-9.

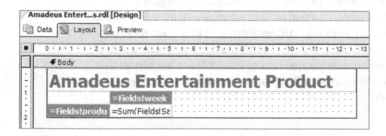

Figure 11-9. *The output of the Report Wizard*

10. Notice that there are three tabs: Data, Layout, and Preview. We are now on the Layout tab. The Layout tab displays the design of the report. The Data tab displays the SQL query. The Preview tab shows how the report looks when it's running. The data on the Preview tab is retrieved from the database based on the SQL query on the Data tab. Click the Data tab to see the design of the SQL query. It looks exactly like Query Builder with its three panes: the diagram pane, grid pane, and SQL pane. Click the Preview tab to see how the report looks, which is shown in Figure 11-10.

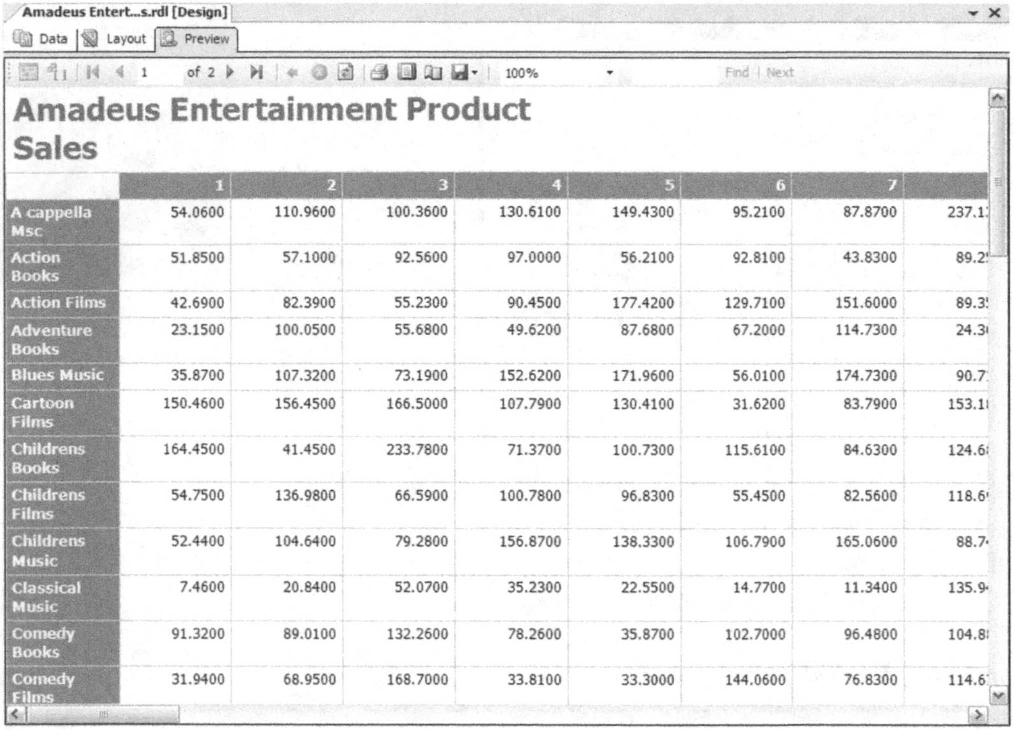

Amadeus Entertainment Product Sales

	1	2	3	4	5	6	7	
A cappella Msc	54.0600	110.9600	100.3600	130.6100	149.4300	95.2100	87.8700	237.1
Action Books	51.8500	57.1000	92.5600	97.0000	56.2100	92.8100	43.8300	89.2
Action Films	42.6900	82.3900	55.2300	90.4500	177.4200	129.7100	151.6000	89.3
Adventure Books	23.1500	100.0500	55.6800	49.6200	87.6800	67.2000	114.7300	24.3
Blues Music	35.8700	107.3200	73.1900	152.6200	171.9600	56.0100	174.7300	90.7
Cartoon Films	150.4600	156.4500	166.5000	107.7900	130.4100	31.6200	83.7900	153.1
Childrens Books	164.4500	41.4500	233.7800	71.3700	100.7300	115.6100	84.6300	124.6
Childrens Films	54.7500	136.9800	66.5900	100.7800	96.8300	55.4500	82.5600	118.6
Childrens Music	52.4400	104.6400	79.2800	156.8700	138.3300	106.7900	165.0600	88.7
Classical Music	7.4600	20.8400	52.0700	35.2300	22.5500	14.7700	11.3400	135.9
Comedy Books	91.3200	89.0100	132.2600	78.2600	35.8700	102.7000	96.4800	104.8
Comedy Films	31.9400	68.9500	168.7000	33.8100	33.3000	144.0600	76.8300	114.6

Figure 11-10. *Preview of the report after finishing the Report Wizard*

The query we just built is quite simple, but it reflects the most popular type of query used in dimensional reporting. We joined a fact table with two dimension tables. We group on two columns and sum a column from the fact table. In a real project when querying a dimensional data store, it is likely that you will be dealing with more dimensions and more numbers of facts or measures. But the principles are the same. Now let's continue with perfecting the report layout. By that I mean enhancing the report appearance such as fixing the report title, formatting the numbers, adding column headings, and adjusting the column size. We will then add some parameters to the report.

Report Layout

In Figure 11-10, the word *Sales* in the title falls on the second row. The figures on the cells contain four decimal points, but the third and fourth ones are all zero. They need to be changed to two decimal points. The first column has no title, and the product types are wrapped onto two lines. So, let's tidy up the layout.

1. First, let's fix the word *Sales* in the report title. Click the Layout tab. Click the title. Notice that now there are eight little white boxes around the title. Click the right-center box, and drag it to the right until the word *Sales* appears on the title line. Click the Preview tab to verify that the title is now on one line.

2. Now let's change the figures on the report cells to two decimal points. Click the Layout tab. Right-click the report cell, the one that contains =Sum(Fields!Sa..., and select Properties. The Textbox Properties dialog box appears. Click the Format tab. Click the ... button next to the "Format code" text box. Underneath Standard, select Number, and click 1,234.00, as illustrated in Figure 11-11. Click OK to close the Choose Format dialog box. Then click OK again to close the Textbox Properties dialog box.

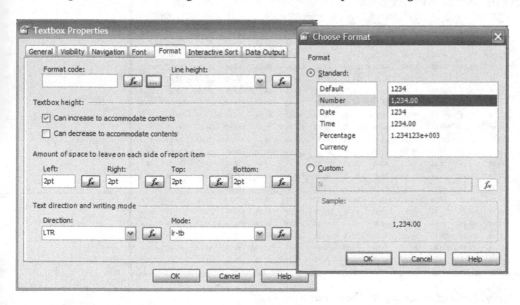

Figure 11-11. *Setting the format of the report cells*

3. Click the Preview tab to check that the figures on the report cells have been formatted correctly to two decimal points.

4. Now let's fix the width of the first column. Click the Layout tab. Click the first column. Notice on the ruler that the width of the first column is 2.5 centimeters. Click the vertical line between the first and second columns, and drag it to the right to make the column width 4 centimeters. Click the Preview tab to verify that the product types are not wrapped onto two lines.

5. Now let's give the first column a heading. Click the Layout tab. Double-click the first cell of the first column. Type **Product by Week**, and click the Preview tab to verify that the first column now has a heading.

6. Last, let's resize the columns containing the weekly sales figure. Click the Layout column. Click the second column. Click the line on the right of the second column, and drag the line to the left to make the column width 1.5 centimeters; for example, on the ruler it should be from 4.0 to 5.5 centimeters. Click Preview to verify.

Now that we have completed fixing the layout, let's run the report by pressing F5. Business Intelligence Development Studio should say, "The project cannot be debugged because no starting report is specified." This is because we have not specified the starting point of the project, so we need to specify which report to execute when we run the project. So, click the Project menu, and select Amadeus Reports Properties. On the StartItem, select Amadeus Entertainment Product Sales. Click OK. Press F5 again to run the report. Figure 11-12 shows how the report looks.

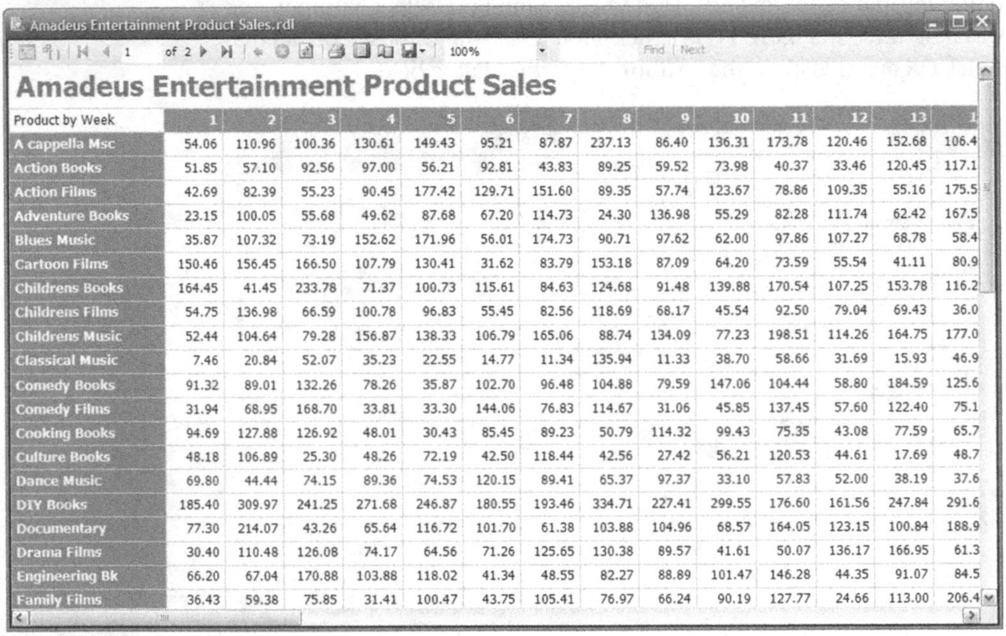

Product by Week	1	2	3	4	5	6	7	8	9	10	11	12	13	1
A cappella Msc	54.06	110.96	100.36	130.61	149.43	95.21	87.87	237.13	86.40	136.31	173.78	120.46	152.68	106.4
Action Books	51.85	57.10	92.56	97.00	56.21	92.81	43.83	89.25	59.52	73.98	40.37	33.46	120.45	117.1
Action Films	42.69	82.39	55.23	90.45	177.42	129.71	151.60	89.35	57.74	123.67	78.86	109.35	55.16	175.5
Adventure Books	23.15	100.05	55.68	49.62	87.68	67.20	114.73	24.30	136.98	55.29	82.28	111.74	62.42	167.5
Blues Music	35.87	107.32	73.19	152.62	171.96	56.01	174.73	90.71	97.62	62.00	97.86	107.27	68.78	58.4
Cartoon Films	150.46	156.45	166.50	107.79	130.41	31.62	83.79	153.18	87.09	64.20	73.59	55.54	41.11	80.9
Childrens Books	164.45	41.45	233.78	71.37	100.73	115.61	84.63	124.68	91.48	139.88	170.54	107.25	153.78	116.2
Childrens Films	54.75	136.98	66.59	100.78	96.83	55.45	82.56	118.69	68.17	45.54	92.50	79.04	69.43	36.0
Childrens Music	52.44	104.64	79.28	156.87	138.33	106.79	165.06	88.74	134.09	77.23	198.51	114.26	164.75	177.0
Classical Music	7.46	20.84	52.07	35.23	22.55	14.77	11.34	135.94	11.33	38.70	58.66	31.69	15.93	46.9
Comedy Books	91.32	89.01	132.26	78.26	35.87	102.70	96.48	104.88	79.59	147.06	104.44	58.80	184.59	125.6
Comedy Films	31.94	68.95	168.70	33.81	33.30	144.06	76.83	114.67	31.06	45.85	137.45	57.60	122.40	75.1
Cooking Books	94.69	127.88	126.92	48.01	30.43	85.45	89.23	50.79	114.32	99.43	75.35	43.08	77.59	65.7
Culture Books	48.18	106.89	25.30	48.26	72.19	42.50	118.44	42.56	27.42	56.21	120.53	44.61	17.69	48.7
Dance Music	69.80	44.44	74.15	89.36	74.53	120.15	89.41	65.37	97.37	33.10	57.83	52.00	38.19	37.6
DIY Books	185.40	309.97	241.25	271.68	246.87	180.55	193.46	334.71	227.41	299.55	176.60	161.56	247.84	291.6
Documentary	77.30	214.07	43.26	65.64	116.72	101.70	61.38	103.88	104.96	68.57	164.05	123.15	100.84	188.9
Drama Films	30.40	110.48	126.08	74.17	64.56	71.26	125.65	130.38	89.57	41.61	50.07	136.17	166.95	61.3
Engineering Bk	66.20	67.04	170.88	103.88	118.02	41.34	48.55	82.27	88.89	101.47	146.28	44.35	91.07	84.5
Family Films	36.43	59.38	75.85	31.41	100.47	43.75	105.41	76.97	66.24	90.19	127.77	24.66	113.00	206.4

Figure 11-12. *How the report looks after tidying up the layout*

We can tweak the layout in many other ways, including adding columns, adding a page header and footer, changing the font, setting the alignment, and setting the spacing as well as specifying all the text box properties shown in Figure 11-11. You can also create a report in tabular form instead of matrix form. I encourage you to explore those Reporting Services layout features and use them in your reports.

Report Parameters

Report parameters are an important feature in a data warehouse dimensional report. In a dimensional model, the core data is stored in a fact table, which has links to dimension tables so that we can filter and group by the dimensional attributes. Refer to the SQL query in Listing 11-2. In this query, we can choose any fact columns from the Product Sales fact table—grouped by any columns from the date, product, customer, or store dimension table, as well as filtered by any conditions in any dimension columns. That is a very powerful query!

In the report we just created in the previous two sections, we have not put any conditions on the query. There is no where clause in the query (refer to Figure 11-6). We have select, from, and group by clauses, but we don't have a where clause. In this section, you will learn how to add some conditions to the query, such as the where clause, using parameters.

We'll add three parameters to the report (Year, Quarter, and Division) as three drop-down lists. The values of these parameters will then be passed to the SQL query. These parameters will be passed to the where clause of the SQL query, as shown in Listing 11-3.

Listing 11-3. *The* where *Clause of Weekly Product Sales Query*

```
where d.quarter = @pQuarter
  and d.year = @pYear
  and (s.division = @pDivision
  or @pDivision = ' All')
```

A parameter name always begins with @. I usually name the parameter the same as the column but add a p prefix. For example, for the quarter column, I name the parameter @pQuarter. This is so that I can find out quickly which parameter is for which column. But you can name your parameters differently; there are no restrictions for this. OK, let's start.

1. Let's return to our report in Business Intelligence Development Studio. If the report is still running, close it. Click the Layout tab. Click the Report menu, and choose Report Parameters. Click Add. Set the name to **pYear**, the data type to **String**, and the prompt to **Year**. Leave everything else as is, and click OK.

   The reason why I add the p prefix in the parameter name is because in the Report Parameters dialog box (see the later Figure 11-14), we don't have the @ sign on the parameter names. So if we name the table column Year, the parameter Year, and the data set Year, it's difficult for us to know which one is which. If we name the column Year, the parameter pYear, and the data set dsYear, it is easier to differentiate them. I'll explain about data sets in the next paragraph. This is not really a Hungarian naming convention because the prefix does not indicate the data type. In Hungarian naming conventions (such as sSupplierName, nQuantity, and dOrderDate), the prefix indicates the data type (s = string, n = numeric, and d = date).

2. When the user clicks the Year drop-down list, we want the list to display all the years that exist in the orders in the Product Sales fact table. For that, we need to create a data source for the drop-down list. So, click the Data tab. Click the DDS data set drop-down list, and choose <New Dataset...>. Set the name to dsYear, the data source to DDS, and the command type to Text, as shown in Figure 11-13.

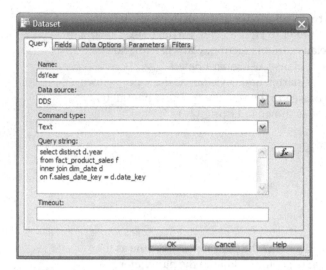

Figure 11-13. *Setting up the data source for the Year parameter*

3. Set the query string as shown in Listing 11-4, and click OK to close the Dataset dialog box.

Listing 11-4. *SQL Query for dsYear Data Set*

```
select distinct d.year
from fact_product_sales f
inner join dim_date d
on f.sales_date_key = d.date_key
```

I need to mention here that populating the Year drop-down list by selecting from a fact table like this is quite an expensive query to run, especially on large databases. If the performance is not satisfactory, consider creating a little parameter table containing the distinct year values of the sales date column on the fact table. You can then use this little parameter table to populate the Year drop-down list. The year values on this little table need to be maintained by the ETL process to keep them up-to-date.

4. Click the exclamation mark (!) to run the query. It displays 2006 and 2007 on the output grid.

5. Click the Report menu, and choose Report Parameters. Click the pYear parameter to select it. Under Available Values, click From Query. Set the data set to dsYear, the Value field to Year, and the Label field to Year, as shown in Figure 11-14.

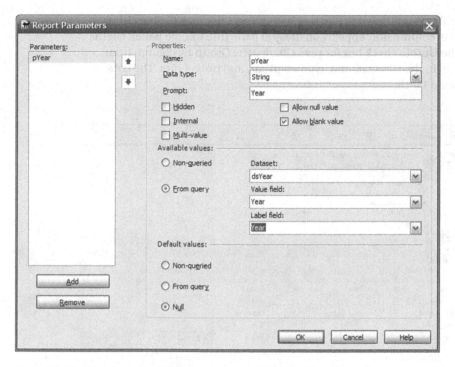

Figure 11-14. *Setting up the Year parameter*

6. We have just created a parameter. So, let's see how the report looks now. Click the Preview tab. There is a drop-down list called Year there, as shown in Figure 11-15. Click this drop-down list to see its list of values. It contains 2006 and 2007 as per our query.

Figure 11-15. *Year parameter as it looks on the report*

7. Now let's link this parameter to the SQL query so that when the user selects 2007 and clicks View Report, the report will contain only 2007 data. For that, click the Data tab, and make sure that the DDS data set is selected; if not, select the DDS data set. Click the ... button next to the DDS data set drop-down list. Click the Parameters tab. In the Name column, type **@pYear**, and under the Value column, select =Parameters!pYear.Value from the drop-down list. Click OK to close the Dataset dialog box.

8. For the dim_date table, scroll down to find the year column, and tick the check box. Notice that the year column now appears on the grid pane (the middle pane). On the grid pane, clear the Output check box for year. Change the Group By column from Group By to Where. In the Filter column, type **=@pYear**, and press Enter. The data set now looks like Figure 11-16.

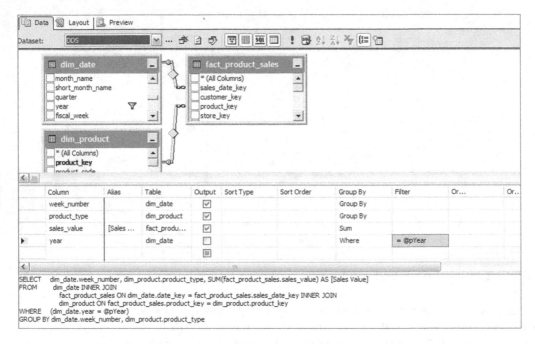

Figure 11-16. *Adding the Year parameter to the* where *clause of the data set query*

9. Notice that there is a where clause in the query now. Also notice there is a funnel icon on the dim_date's year column.

10. Now that we have added the Year parameter to the data set query (on the where clause), let's test the report. Click Preview. In the Year drop-down list, select 2006, and click View Report. Memorize the value of the data in a few cells. Now select 2007, and click View Report again. Notice that the values on those cells are different.

11. Now let's add the second parameter: Quarter. This second parameter (Quarter) is dependent on the first parameter (Year). For 2006, we have four quarters of data in the Product Sales fact table. But for 2007, we have only Q1 and Q2 data. So, when we choose 2006 on the Year parameter, the Quarter parameter should show four quarters. But when we choose 2007 on the Year parameter, the Quarter parameter should show only Q1 and Q2. The same technique can be implemented on the Division and Region parameters on the store dimension hierarchy.

12. Let's now create the Quarter parameter. Click the Report menu. You'll find that Report Parameters is grayed out. This is because we are currently on the Preview tab. Report Parameters is not available on the Preview tab; it is available only on the Data and Layout tabs. Click the Layout tab. Now click the Report menu again. Now Report Parameters is active. Click Report Parameters. Click Add. Set the name to pQuarter, the type to String, and the prompt to Quarter, and then click OK. Click the Data tab, create a new data set, and then set the name to dsQuarter and the query string to Listing 11-5.

Listing 11-5. *SQL Query for dsQuarter Data Set*

```
select distinct d.quarter
from fact_product_sales f
inner join dim_date d
on f.sales_date_key = d.date_key
where d.year = @pYear
```

I shall repeat my previous warning that this is quite an expensive query to run, especially on large fact tables. To enhance the performance, we can enhance the little parameter table I mentioned previously. We can enhance the little table so that it contains a distinct year-quarter combination from the sales_date column. We can then source the dsQuarter data set from this little table.

13. Click OK to close the Dataset dialog box. Click the exclamation mark (!) to run the query. In the Define Query Parameters dialog box, enter **2007** in the Parameter Value column, as shown in Figure 11-17, and click OK.

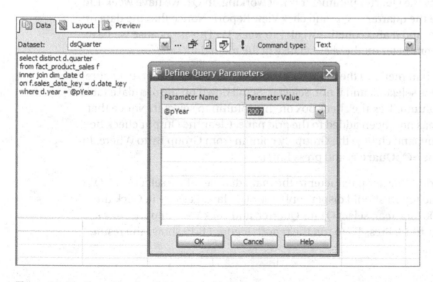

Figure 11-17. *Creating the* dsQuarter *data set*

14. You should see Q1 and Q2 in the result set window. Now run the data set query again, but this time enter **2006** as the parameter value for pYear. You should see Q1, Q2, Q3, and Q4 in the result set window.

15. Now that the data set for Quarter is created, let's use it on the parameter. Click the Report menu, and select Report Parameters. Click pQuarter. Under Available Values, click From Query. Set the data set to dsQuarter, and select quarter for both Value Field and Label Field. Click OK to close the Report Parameters dialog box.

Please notice that you don't have to click the Parameters tab of the data set to define the pQuarter parameter. This is an optional step. Reporting Services will automatically create it for you if you don't define it.

16. Click the Preview tab to see the report. Notice that the Quarter parameter is there but is grayed out. This is because it is dependent on the value of the Year parameter. Select 2006 for Year. Notice that now the Quarter parameter is active, and it contains Q1, Q2, Q3, and Q4. Select 2007 for Year, and notice that the Quarter parameter contains Q1 and Q2 only, as shown in Figure 11-18.

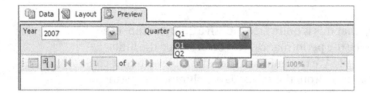

Figure 11-18. *A parameter that is dependent on the value of another parameter*

17. Select Q1, and click View Report. Notice that it still contains data from week 1 until week 17, which means the Quarter parameter is not working. In Q1, we have week 1 to week 13 only. Change the quarter to Q2, and click View Report. Notice that the data on the report is the same, and it also contains week 1 to week 17. This is because we have not put the Quarter parameter on the where clause of the main data set.

18. Let's add the Quarter parameter to the main data set query. Click the Data tab. Ensure that the DDS data set is selected, and if not, select it. Scroll down on the dim_date table to find the quarter column. Tick the check box on this column to select it. Notice that the quarter column has now been added to the grid pane. Clear the Output check box for the quarter column, and change the Group By column from Group By to Where. In the Filter column, type **=@pQuarter**, and press Enter.

19. Now that we have added Quarter parameter to the main data set, if we select 2007 Q1 on the parameters, the report should display only 2007 Q1 data. Let's try it. Click the Preview tab. Select 2007 for Year, select Q1 for Quarter, and click View Report. Now it contains only weeks 1 to 13. Press F5 to run the report. Figure 11-19 shows the result.

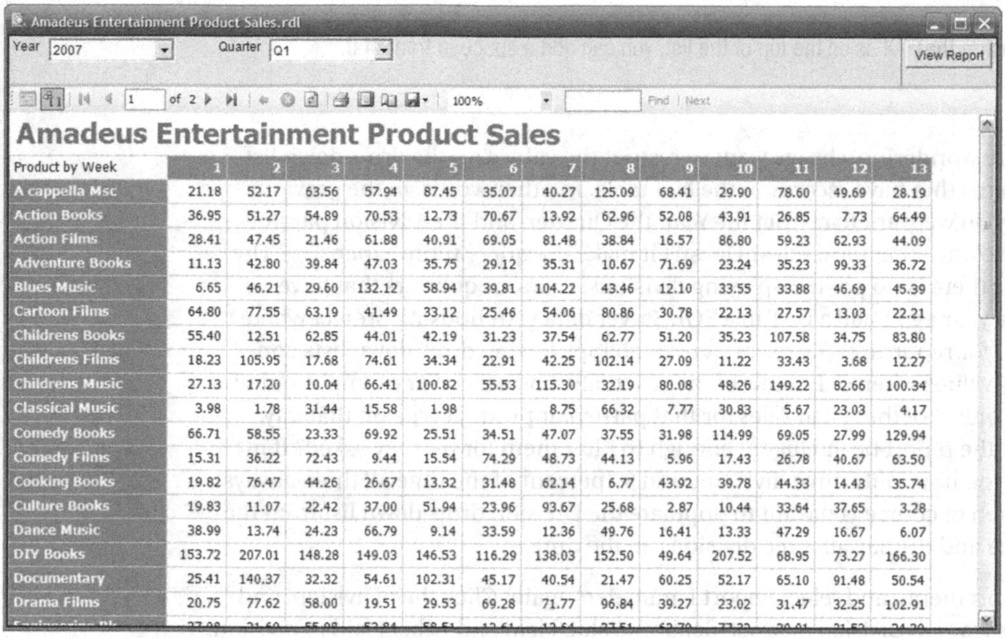

Product by Week	1	2	3	4	5	6	7	8	9	10	11	12	13
A cappella Msc	21.18	52.17	63.56	57.94	87.45	35.07	40.27	125.09	68.41	29.90	78.60	49.69	28.19
Action Books	36.95	51.27	54.89	70.53	12.73	70.67	13.92	62.96	52.08	43.91	26.85	7.73	64.49
Action Films	28.41	47.45	21.46	61.88	40.91	69.05	81.48	38.84	16.57	86.80	59.23	62.93	44.09
Adventure Books	11.13	42.80	39.84	47.03	35.75	29.12	35.31	10.67	71.69	23.24	35.23	99.33	36.72
Blues Music	6.65	46.21	29.60	132.12	58.94	39.81	104.22	43.46	12.10	33.55	33.88	46.69	45.39
Cartoon Films	64.80	77.55	63.19	41.49	33.12	25.46	54.06	80.86	30.78	22.13	27.57	13.03	22.21
Childrens Books	55.40	12.51	62.85	44.01	42.19	31.23	37.54	62.77	51.20	35.23	107.58	34.75	83.80
Childrens Films	18.23	105.95	17.68	74.61	34.34	22.91	42.25	102.14	27.09	11.22	33.43	3.68	12.27
Childrens Music	27.13	17.20	10.04	66.41	100.82	55.53	115.30	32.19	80.08	48.26	149.22	82.66	100.34
Classical Music	3.98	1.78	31.44	15.58	1.98		8.75	66.32	7.77	30.83	5.67	23.03	4.17
Comedy Books	66.71	58.55	23.33	69.92	25.51	34.51	47.07	37.55	31.98	114.99	69.05	27.99	129.94
Comedy Films	15.31	36.22	72.43	9.44	15.54	74.29	48.73	44.13	5.96	17.43	26.78	40.67	63.50
Cooking Books	19.82	76.47	44.26	26.67	13.32	31.48	62.14	6.77	43.92	39.78	44.33	14.43	35.74
Culture Books	19.83	11.07	22.42	37.00	51.94	23.96	93.67	25.68	2.87	10.44	33.64	37.65	3.28
Dance Music	38.99	13.74	24.23	66.79	9.14	33.59	12.36	49.76	16.41	13.33	47.29	16.67	6.07
DIY Books	153.72	207.01	148.28	149.03	146.53	116.29	138.03	152.50	49.64	207.52	68.95	73.27	166.30
Documentary	25.41	140.37	32.32	54.61	102.31	45.17	40.54	21.47	60.25	52.17	65.10	91.48	50.54
Drama Films	20.75	77.62	58.00	19.51	29.53	69.28	71.77	96.84	39.27	23.02	31.47	32.25	102.91

Figure 11-19. *Product Sales report with the Year and Quarter parameters*

20. Now that we have added two parameters to the report, let's add the third one. This time it is not from the date dimension but from the store dimension. This third parameter is Division. This time it has one additional value in the drop-down list, which is All. So, the users will be able to select a division, but they can also select all divisions.

21. Because we have already done it twice, this time I'll skip the details. Add a parameter called pDivision with a label called Division. Define a data set called dsDivision, with the query string as shown in Listing 11-6.

    Listing 11-6. *SQL Query for* `dsDivision` *Data Set*

    ```
    select distinct s.division
    from fact_product_sales f
    inner join dim_store s
    on f.store_key = s.store_key
    union
    select 'All' as division
    ```

    The query retrieves the distinct values on the `division` column from the Product Sales fact table. It adds one more value, which is 'All,' using the `union` operation.

■ **Tip** If you want to ensure that 'All' is on the top of the list, you can add a space in front of it.

Perhaps you're wondering why we want to restrict the values on the drop-down list only to the items that have records in the fact table. In other words, in the previous example, why do we want to restrict the Year, the Quarter, and the Division parameters to only the ones that have sales? Doesn't it make the query more expensive? The answer is that there is no point displaying divisions, years, or quarters that have no sales. About a year ago I had a UAT in a SQL Server data warehousing project where we used SSRS for reporting. The users were not happy having drop-down lists containing many values when only a few of them actually had sales. For example, out of 50 branches, only 5 of them had sales for that particular product type on that day. Why couldn't the report be intelligent enough to filter them for us, they asked? If in your project you have only three divisions and 99 percent of the time all three always have sales, then of course you want to populate the Division drop-down list from the division table and display all three divisions all the time.

22. Click the Report menu, and select Report Parameters again. Click the pDivision, and get the values from dsDivision data set. Set both Value Field and Label Field to division.

23. On the DDS data set, click the Add Table icon (the rightmost icon), and add the dim_store table. Click Close. Scroll down in the dim_store table until you find the Division column, and select it. On the grid pane, clear the Output check box, and change the Group By column to Where. In the Filter column, enter **=@pDivision**.

24. Click the Preview tab, and you should see three parameters now: Year, Quarter, and Division. Select 2007 for Year, Q1 for Quarter, and Online Business for Division, and then click View Report. Notice that the report is now sparser than before; that is, there are some blank cells. This is because it displays only the Online Business division. Change the Division parameter to All, and click View Report. The report is blank. Why is the report blank? Well, there is no division called All. So, the query returns no results.

25. To fix this, click the Data tab. Click the Generic Query Designer icon (the one with a yellow pencil). Update the where clause from WHERE (dim_date.year = @pYear) AND (dim_date.quarter = @pQuarter) AND (dim_store.division = @pDivision) to what's shown in Listing 11-7.

Listing 11-7. *Updating Main Data Set's* where *Clause to Include All*

```
WHERE dim_date.year = @pYear
  AND dim_date.quarter = @pQuarter
  AND (dim_store.division = @pDivision or @pDivision = 'All')
```

So now if you select All on the Division parameter, the @pDivision = 'All' will evaluate to true so the expression in parentheses will also evaluate to true.

26. Let's test it now. Click the Preview tab. Select 2007 for Year, Q1 for Quarter, and All for Division, and click View Report. It displays all data for 2007 Q1. Change the division to Europe, Middle East & Africa (EMEA), and click View Report. The report displays only EMEA sales data, as shown in Figure 11-20.

Product by Week	1	2	3	4	5	6	7	8	9	10	11	12	13
A cappella Msc	7.44	15.73	8.27	8.07	6.12	23.16	19.78	14.77	15.21	21.65	16.94	14.33	2.68
Action Books	10.20	3.68	11.75	15.98	1.99	59.71	11.04	5.18	2.87	9.71	0.89	3.08	13.25
Action Films	23.54	23.45	17.98	29.46	16.64	55.32	5.06	30.98	6.24	9.76	34.95	44.15	7.17
Adventure Books	6.36	1.98	20.76	44.15	3.98	1.58	7.77	7.99	6.74	1.78	3.68	21.14	17.98
Blues Music		1.99	6.27	6.55	18.72	5.18	6.15	29.46	5.75		7.77	10.17	41.34
Cartoon Films	61.04	21.86	5.47	22.64		6.75	11.72	10.65	1.38	15.86	12.61	8.66	8.33
Childrens Books	9.08	6.56	1.78	5.54	15.58	28.64	13.88	21.13	33.44	16.83	43.80	5.43	11.54
Childrens Films	4.37	45.93	2.18	3.76	20.03	4.16	18.32	63.03	19.04	5.96	16.96	3.68	5.95
Childrens Music	21.06	14.13	0.89	24.74	67.39	14.72	43.51	1.38	7.44	0.89	116.48	31.44	20.16
Classical Music			12.99	12.99			1.09	2.18	2.59	13.68	1.99		3.28

Figure 11-20. *Weekly Product Sales report after adding the Division parameter*

If you want, you can also set the value of the parameters as a list of static/constant values. To do this, in the Report Parameters window, choose Non-Queried. On the report that we have just built, when the report starts, the parameters are blank. You can define a value that will automatically be selected when the report starts. For example, you may want the division to be set to Online Business when the report starts. To set this in the Report Parameters window, change the default value from null to either From Query or Non-Queried. You can also set the starting value to a function. For example, you may want the year to be set to this year when the report starts. To do this, enter **=year(now)** in the Non-Queried box, or click the fx button to get a list of functions and their descriptions.

Grouping, Sorting, and Filtering

So far, you have learned how to use the Report Wizard to produce a matrix report, how to specify SQL queries, how to touch up the layout, and how to use parameters to dynamically change the query. Now you'll learn about grouping, sorting, and filtering. *Grouping* means classifying multiple rows (or columns) into one collection. You can group data by fields or expression. Grouping is usually used to provide logical selection of data within a table or matrix or to calculate subtotals, counts, or any other expression in the group header or footer. *Sorting* is used to order a particular column as either ascending or descending.

Filtering means limiting the rows according to a certain criteria. Using parameters, you can filter the data at run time. For example, when the users select Online Business for the Division parameter, Reporting Services adds `where division = 'Online Business'` to the SQL query. This will then filter the data that is displayed on the report. There is another way to filter the data that we display on the report—by adding a where clause to the main data set query at design time. This type of filtering cannot be changed by the users at run time. The purpose of doing this is to limit the rows returned by the query according to certain criteria. For example, you may want to have a report that specifically deals with business customers. In this case, we filter the query with where customer_type = 'Business' or something similar. In this section, we will be doing the type of filtering that uses the where clause at design time.

First, we'll include the product category column on the SQL query, and then we'll add it as a group to the Weekly Product Sales report that we built. Then, we will change the order of the column, add a sorting order, and, finally, apply a filter.

1. To start, click the Data tab. Add dim_product.product_category on both the select clause and group by clause, and reformat the query a little bit, as shown in Listing 11-8.

Listing 11-8. *Adding the Product Category on the SQL Query*

```
select dim_date.week_number, dim_product.product_type,
  sum(fact_product_sales.sales_value) AS [Sales Value],
  dim_product.product_category
from dim_date
inner join fact_product_sales
  on dim_date.date_key = fact_product_sales.sales_date_key
inner join dim_product
  on fact_product_sales.product_key = dim_product.product_key
inner join dim_store
  on fact_product_sales.store_key = dim_store.store_key
where dim_date.year = @pYear
  and dim_date.quarter = @pQuarter
  and (dim_store.division = @pDivision or @pDivision = 'All')
group by dim_product.product_type, dim_date.week_number,
  dim_product.product_category
```

In SSRS, we have two tools to build queries. One is called Query Builder, and the other is Generic Query Designer. Query Builder is the graphical tool that we used with the Report Wizard. Generic Query Designer is the plain-text editor that we used to add @pDivision or @pDivision = 'All' to the report query.

A lot of SQL developers find that SQL query formatting is sometimes annoying if it is not up to their standards or their style. For example, where to break to a new line, the abbreviation of table names, the number of spaces for indentation, the choice of uppercase or lowercase, whether to put the comma at the beginning or at the end of the line, and where to put brackets…all these are little things that sometimes make us uncomfortable if the formatting is different from our own style.

Other than the ability to control the details such as the join syntax, style is another reason (but not the primary one) why some SQL developers choose to not use Query Builder and instead use the plain-text Generic Query Designer.

2. We want to add the product category to the report to understand how the sales figure splits between music, film, and audio books. For that, let's now add the product category as a new group to the report. Click the Layout tab. Click the heading of column 1 (Product by Week). Right-click the cell above Product by Week, and choose Add Row Group. The Grouping and Sorting Properties dialog box will pop up. Set the name to ProductCategory, and set Expression to '=Fields!product_category.Value, as shown in Figure 11-21. Next, click OK.

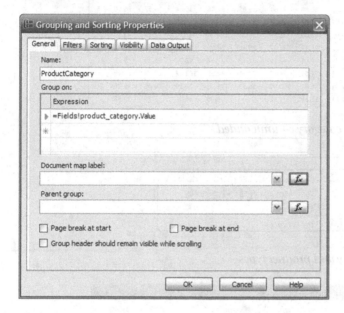

Figure 11-21. *Setting the properties of the product category group*

3. Click the Preview tab, fill in the parameters (such as 2007, Q1, and All Divisions), and click View Report. The product category is positioned as the second column in the report, as shown in Figure 11-22.

4. There are only three product categories (music, films, and audio books), but there are many product types. The product category is on a higher level than the product type. One product category contains many product types. So in Figure 11-22, the product category should be located to the left of the product type. Let's now swap the product category column and the product type column. Click the Layout tab. Click the product category cell. Click the line surrounding the product category cell, and drag it to the left of the product type column, as shown in Figure 11-23.

5. Click the Preview tab, and view the report again. It now looks like Figure 11-24.

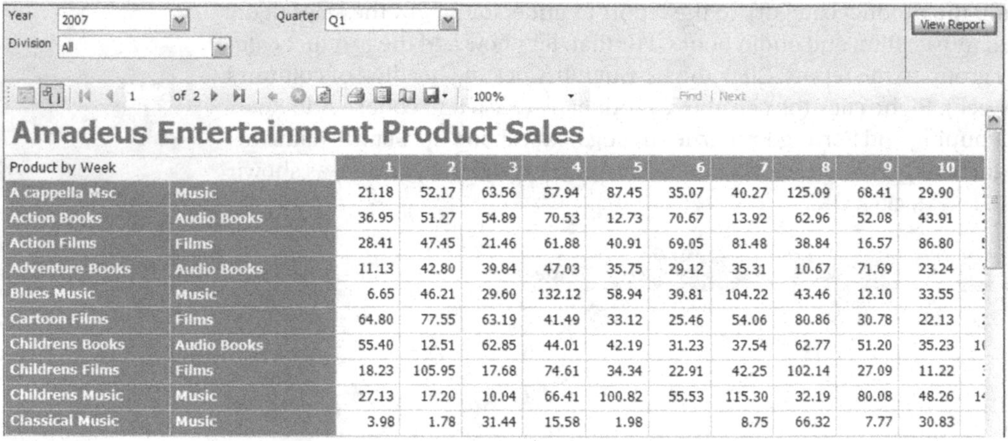

Figure 11-22. *Product Sales report with product category column added*

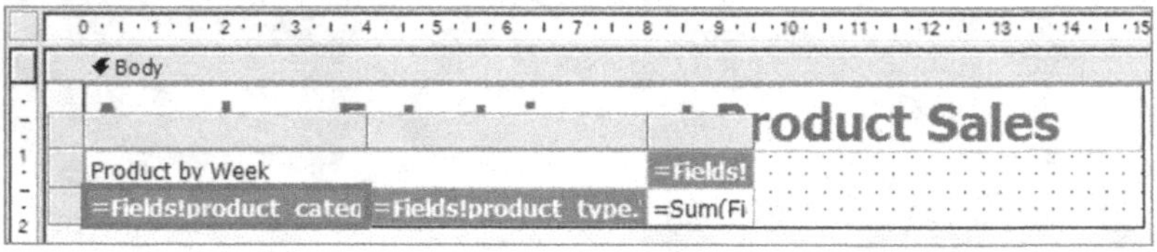

Figure 11-23. *Swapping product category and product types*

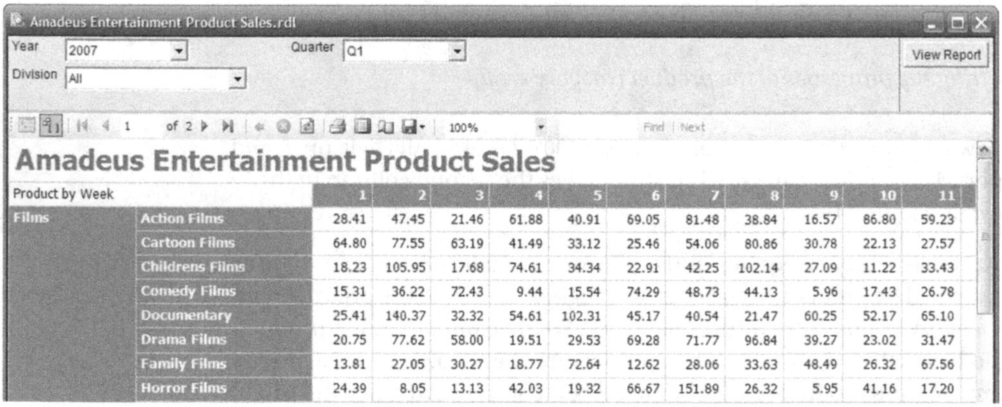

Figure 11-24. *Product Sales report after swapping the product category and product type columns*

I'll now discuss the sorting order for groups. Let's put the sorting order on the product category column so that Music is at the top, Films is second, and Audio Books is at the bottom. Click the Layout tab. Right-click the product category cell, and choose Edit Group. The Grouping and Sorting Properties dialog box appears. Click the Sorting tab, set Expression to =Fields!product_category.Value, and set Direction to **Descending**. Click OK. Click the Preview tab to view the report.

The sorting order on the product category column is now what we wanted; that is, Music is at the top, Films is in the middle, and Audio Book is at the bottom. But at the very top, before Music, we have Unknown. This is because we have an unknown record on both the product category dimension and the product type dimension in the DDS. So, let's filter out the unknown record.

1. Click the Layout tab. Right-click the Product Category cell, and choose Edit Group.

2. Click the Filter tab, set Expression to =Fields!product_category.Value, Operator to !=, and Value to **Unknown**. Click OK.

3. Click the Preview tab to view the report again. The unknown record is no longer there, and the report now looks like Figure 11-25.

Amadeus Entertainment Product Sales

Product by Week		1	2	3	4	5	6	7	8	9	10
Music	A cappella Msc	21.18	52.17	63.56	57.94	87.45	35.07	40.27	125.09	68.41	29.90
	Blues Music	6.65	46.21	29.60	132.12	58.94	39.81	104.22	43.46	12.10	33.55
	Childrens Music	27.13	17.20	10.04	66.41	100.82	55.53	115.30	32.19	80.08	48.26
	Classical Music	3.98	1.78	31.44	15.58	1.98		8.75	66.32	7.77	30.83
	Dance Music	38.99	13.74	24.23	66.79	9.14	33.59	12.36	49.76	16.41	13.33
	Heavy metal	35.20	54.16	97.40	101.82	19.52	102.54	58.31	95.52	31.47	65.28
	Hip hop Music	4.65	24.04	43.48	31.31	74.21	24.60	37.92	65.91	28.30	59.24
	Indie Music	76.40	50.07	45.45	52.57	73.04	80.34	67.70	37.28	1.58	75.18
	Instrumental Ms	31.05	102.21	64.51	41.27	30.05	31.50	71.80	28.58	45.60	37.20

Figure 11-25. *Sorting on the product category and filtering the unknown record*

Grouping is usually used to provide a logical grouping of data within a table or matrix or for calculating subtotals, counts, or any other expression on the group header or footer. As the last task in this section, let's now add a subtotal in the product category column and a grand total.

1. Click the Layout tab. To add the subtotal to the product category column, right-click the Product Type cell, and choose Subtotal. You will see a new row with Total in the second column with a little green triangle in the corner of the cell.

2. To add the grand total, right-click the product category cell, and choose Subtotal.

3. Click the Preview tab to view the report. Scroll down to see the subtotal for the Music category and the Films category.

4. On the toolbar, click the Next Page icon (the blue triangle) to go to page 2. Verify that you can see the subtotal for the Audio Books category as well as the grand total on the last row, as shown in Figure 11-26.

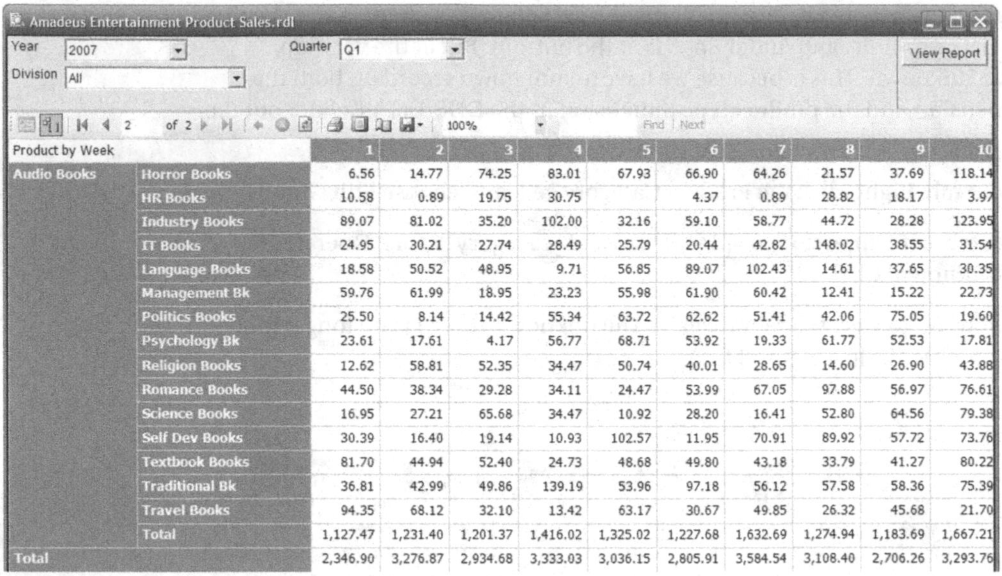

Product by Week		1	2	3	4	5	6	7	8	9	10
Audio Books	Horror Books	6.56	14.77	74.25	83.01	67.93	66.90	64.26	21.57	37.69	118.14
	HR Books	10.58	0.89	19.75	30.75		4.37	0.89	28.82	18.17	3.97
	Industry Books	89.07	81.02	35.20	102.00	32.16	59.10	58.77	44.72	28.28	123.95
	IT Books	24.95	30.21	27.74	28.49	25.79	20.44	42.82	148.02	38.55	31.54
	Language Books	18.58	50.52	48.95	9.71	56.85	89.07	102.43	14.61	37.65	30.35
	Management Bk	59.76	61.99	18.95	23.23	55.98	61.90	60.42	12.41	15.22	22.73
	Politics Books	25.50	8.14	14.42	55.34	63.72	62.62	51.41	42.06	75.05	19.60
	Psychology Bk	23.61	17.61	4.17	56.77	68.71	53.92	19.33	61.77	52.53	17.81
	Religion Books	12.62	58.81	52.35	34.47	50.74	40.01	28.65	14.60	26.90	43.88
	Romance Books	44.50	38.34	29.28	34.11	24.47	53.99	67.05	97.88	56.97	76.61
	Science Books	16.95	27.21	65.68	34.47	10.92	28.20	16.41	52.80	64.56	79.38
	Self Dev Books	30.39	16.40	19.14	10.93	102.57	11.95	70.91	89.92	57.72	73.76
	Textbook Books	81.70	44.94	52.40	24.73	48.68	49.80	43.18	33.79	41.27	80.22
	Traditional Bk	36.81	42.99	49.86	139.19	53.96	97.18	56.12	57.58	58.36	75.39
	Travel Books	94.35	68.12	32.10	13.42	63.17	30.67	49.85	26.32	45.68	21.70
	Total	1,127.47	1,231.40	1,201.37	1,416.02	1,325.02	1,227.68	1,632.69	1,274.94	1,183.69	1,667.21
Total		2,346.90	3,276.87	2,934.68	3,333.03	3,036.15	2,805.91	3,584.54	3,108.40	2,706.26	3,293.76

Figure 11-26. *Product Sales report with subtotal and grand total*

Simplicity

Sometimes users ask for very complex reports. A request to be able to group four facts from the fact table by twelve different attributes from four different dimensions is an example of such complex reports. A request to have five different subreports within a single report is another example of a complex report.

Sometimes users ask for many similar reports querying the same information but presenting it in many different ways. As a result, we have many reports doing similar or the same things.

When you have many complex reports or many similar reports doing the same things, it pays to investigate whether the user requests would be better satisfied using OLAP tools. From the very start of the project, we need to keep in mind the advantages as well as the limitations of reports. Reports are, almost by definition, simple and rigid. In my opinion, products such as Microsoft SQL Server Reporting Services and Business Objects Crystal Report XI have been very successful in taking reporting to its vertical limit. But a report is still a report; it runs according to the design, and there is very little flexibility at run time.

OLAP tools such as Microsoft SQL Server Analysis Services 2005, ProClarity, and Cognos Powerplay, on the other hand, are designed to be extremely flexible at run time. Users can view the totals of any facts against any dimension attributes. They can swap one attribute with another attribute just by dragging and dropping. They can drill down along the dimension hierarchy just by clicking the dimension. OLAP tools are designed to explore the data. Reports are not. So if you get very complex reporting requests, it's worth finding out whether the users need to explore the data. If so, OLAP tools would satisfy their needs better than reports.

Another means of exploring the data is using SQL queries. I have found that if the business user understands a little bit about SELECT statements, it takes only a day or two to explain the structure of the dimensional data store and how to use a join to query the structure. If they don't understand how to use SELECT statements, many tools help build SQL queries through a GUI. Reporting Services has Query Builder, which does this. Excel has Query Wizard, which is a query design tool with a GUI interface. A lot of other BI applications also have reporting tools with GUI interfaces for designing queries.

The business users understand the data and the meaning of each fact and attribute, and that's why it's quicker for them to query the fact and dimension tables. This is especially true if you consistently use a star schema, because once you spend a day explaining how to query one data mart, the other marts have the same structure. Querying can be done from Management Studio or from Excel via an ODBC or OLEDB connection (or SQL Server native if you install the driver on the client's PC).

Different users have different needs. Some users need to use a static report only to view the facts related to their area of responsibility. Some users need to explore and analyze the data to find out the root cause of a particular problem such as a period of low sales. Some users need to run "what if?" scenarios. Some users need to investigate whether the data has certain consistent patterns.

SSRS is a sophisticated reporting tool with a lot of capabilities and features. But we need to keep in mind that there are better ways and tools to satisfy exploration needs. Reports are designed for something simple and fixed. So, we need to keep reporting simple. That's the principle of simplicity in reporting.

Spreadsheets

It is also possible to present or report the data in the data warehouse to the users using spreadsheets such as Excel. Many data warehouse business users are familiar with spreadsheets, and spreadsheets are the perfect compromise between SSRS reports, which are static, and OLAP tools, which are very flexible. Using spreadsheets, users can query the data in the data warehouse and present it either in a simple tabular format or in a pivot table.

I'll show some examples of how it looks if we use spreadsheets to present the data. In these examples, I will use Excel as the spreadsheet. Figure 11-27 shows the Amadeus Entertainment Store Details report, which is in tabular format. It is essentially the same as Figure 11-1, but this one was created in Excel. I'll explain how to create and populate this Excel spreadsheet after the next paragraph.

Figure 11-28 shows the Amadeus Entertainment Weekly Product Sales report that we created earlier in this chapter. It also has the year, quarter, and division parameters like the ones shown earlier in Figure 11-2. Of course, we can also enhance the layout, such as adding a report title, tidying up the column headers, and fixing the column width.

	A	B	C	D	E
1	store_number	store_name	store_type	region	division
2	1805	Perth	Distribution Centre	Australia	America, Asia and Australia
3	3409	Frankfrut	Distribution Centre	Germany	Europe, Middle East & Africa
4	1209	Zaragoza	Distribution Centre	Spain	Europe, Middle East & Africa
5	1014	Strasbourg	Distribution Centre	France	Europe, Middle East & Africa
6	2903	Delhi	Distribution Centre	India	America, Asia and Australia
7	2705	Sapporo	Distribution Centre	Japan	America, Asia and Australia
8	2236	Leeds	Distribution Centre	UK	Europe, Middle East & Africa
9	1808	Canberra	Full Outlet	Australia	America, Asia and Australia
10	1803	Sydney	Full Outlet	Australia	America, Asia and Australia
11	1804	Darwin	Full Outlet	Australia	America, Asia and Australia
12	1806	Brisbane	Full Outlet	Australia	America, Asia and Australia
13	2022	El Paso	Full Outlet	Central US	America, Asia and Australia
14	2009	Dallas	Full Outlet	Central US	America, Asia and Australia
15	2237	London	Full Outlet	UK	Europe, Middle East & Africa
16	2027	Portland	Full Outlet	Western US	America, Asia and Australia
17	2011	San Jose	Full Outlet	Western US	America, Asia and Australia
18	2024	Seattle	Full Outlet	Western US	America, Asia and Australia
19	2014	San Francisco	Full Outlet	Western US	America, Asia and Australia

Figure 11-27. *The Store Details report created using Excel*

	A	B	C	D	E	F	G	H	I	J	K	L	M	N	O
1	year	2007													
2	quarter	Q1													
3	division	(All)													
4															
5	Sum of sales_value	week													
6	product_type	1	2	3	4	5	6	7	8	9	10	11	12	13	Grand Total
7	A cappella Msc	21.18	52.17	63.56	57.94	87.45	35.07	40.27	125.09	68.41	29.9	78.6	49.69	28.19	737.52
8	Action Books	36.95	51.27	54.89	70.53	12.73	70.67	13.92	62.96	52.08	43.91	26.85	7.73	64.49	568.98
9	Action Films	28.41	47.45	21.46	61.88	40.91	69.05	81.48	38.84	16.57	86.8	59.23	62.93	44.09	659.1
10	Adventure Books	11.13	42.8	39.84	47.03	35.75	29.12	35.31	10.67	71.69	23.24	35.23	99.33	36.72	517.86
11	Blues Music	6.65	46.21	29.6	132.12	58.94	39.81	104.22	43.46	12.1	33.55	33.88	46.69	45.39	632.62
12	Cartoon Films	64.8	77.55	63.19	41.49	33.12	25.46	54.06	80.86	30.78	22.13	27.57	13.03	22.21	556.25
13	Childrens Books	55.4	12.51	62.85	44.01	42.19	31.23	37.54	62.77	51.2	35.23	107.58	34.75	83.8	661.06
14	Childrens Films	18.23	105.95	17.68	74.61	34.34	22.91	42.25	102.14	27.09	11.22	33.43	3.68	12.27	505.8
15	Childrens Music	27.13	17.2	10.04	66.41	100.82	55.53	115.3	32.19	80.08	48.26	149.22	82.66	100.34	885.18
16	Classical Music	3.98	1.78	31.44	15.58	1.98		8.75	66.32	7.77	30.83	5.67	23.03	4.17	201.3
17	Comedy Books	66.71	58.55	23.33	69.92	25.51	34.51	47.07	37.55	31.98	114.99	69.05	27.99	129.94	737.1
18	Comedy Films	15.31	36.22	72.43	9.44	15.54	74.29	48.73	44.13	5.96	17.43	26.78	40.67	63.5	470.43
19	Cooking Books	19.82	76.47	44.26	26.67	13.32	31.48	62.14	6.77	43.92	39.78	44.33	14.43	35.74	459.13
20	Culture Books	19.83	11.07	22.42	37	51.94	23.96	93.67	25.68	2.87	10.44	33.64	37.65	3.28	373.45
21	Dance Music	38.99	13.74	24.23	66.79	9.14	33.59	12.36	49.76	16.41	13.33	47.29	16.67	6.07	348.37
22	DIY Books	153.72	207.01	148.28	149.03	146.53	116.29	138.03	152.5	49.64	207.52	68.95	73.27	166.3	1777.07
23	Documentary	25.41	140.37	32.32	54.61	102.31	45.17	40.54	21.47	60.25	52.17	65.1	91.48	50.54	781.74
24	Drama Films	20.75	77.62	58	19.51	29.53	69.28	71.77	96.84	39.27	23.02	31.47	32.25	102.91	672.22
25	Engineering Bk	37.08	31.69	55.98	53.84	58.51	12.61	12.64	37.51	62.79	77.32	30.01	31.52	24.3	525.8
26	Family Films	13.81	27.05	30.27	18.77	72.64	12.62	28.06	33.63	48.49	26.32	67.56	11.53	55.28	446.03
27	Fiction Books	45.36	19.28	14.6	71.68	57.86	22.84	136.63	48.51	31.12	52.73	48.36	43.02	38.16	630.15
28	Finance Books	56.34	61.25	52.92	98.73	41.49	46.97	99.71	22.69	85.49	38.83	9.8	125.9	52.55	792.67
29	Gardening Books	40.34	59.34	23.69	33.76	52.82	35.06	160.84	31.8	25.53	45.18	28.21	26.92	75.75	639.24

Figure 11-28. *The Weekly Product Sales report created using Excel*

Creating these reports is easy. Let's start.

1. Open Excel, and click Data ➤ Import External Data ➤ New Database Query. Define a new data source, and connect to the data source as follows: select <New Data Source> on the Databases tab, as shown in Figure 11-29, and click OK.

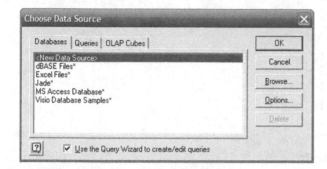

Figure 11-29. *Creating a new data source*

2. In the Create New Data Source dialog box (see Figure 11-30), name the data source DDS. Select SQL Server as the driver, and click Connect.

Figure 11-30. *Filling in the details in the Create New Data Source dialog box*

3. The SQL Server Login dialog box will open, as shown in Figure 11-31. Select your SQL Server, uncheck Use Trusted Connection, and supply the login details (we discussed this in Chapter 7). Click the Options button, and select the DDS database. Click OK to go back to the Create New Data Source dialog box in Figure 11-30. Optionally, you can select dim_store as the default table. Click OK.

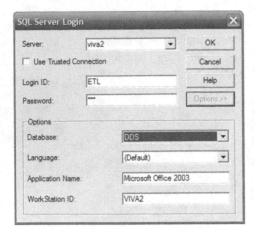

Figure 11-31. *Supplying SQL Server login details*

4. You are now in Excel's Query Wizard. Choose the columns you need from the tables (in this case, it is from the `dim_store` table), as shown in Figure 11-32.

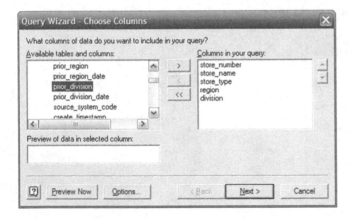

Figure 11-32. *Choosing the columns in Excel's Query Wizard*

5. Click Next. On the Filter Data page, specify `store_number not equal 0` as the criteria, and then click Next. On the Sort Order page, just click Next. On the final page, click Finish.

To create the Weekly Product Sales pivot table report, do the following steps:

1. Click the Data menu, and select Pivot Table. Choose External Data Source, and click Next.

2. Click Get Data, and select DDS as the data source. Choose the columns (week_number, quarter, and year from dim_date; product_code from dim_product; division from dim_store; and sales_value from fact_product_sales). Excel's Query Wizard will say that you can't continue because of the join criteria. This is because it cannot find the date_key column in the fact_product_sales table to join it with the dim_date table. Just click Yes in the dialog box and join date_key on dim_date to sales_date_key on fact_product_sales manually, as shown in Figure 11-33.

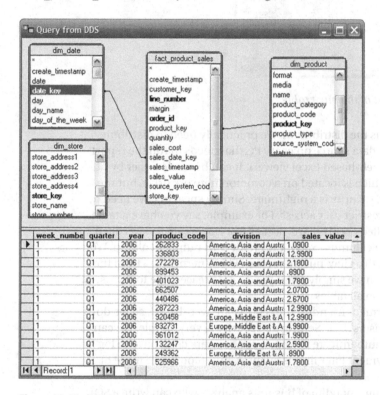

Figure 11-33. *Joining the tables*

3. Click the Return Data icon, and click Next in the dialog box.

4. Click Layout, and specify the layout, including the week number in the column, the product code in the row, the sales value in the cells and year, and the quarter and division on the page, as shown in Figure 11-34.

5. Click OK, and then click Finish. You will get the pivot table shown in Figure 11-28. You can then tidy up the layout by adding a report title, setting the column width, and so on.

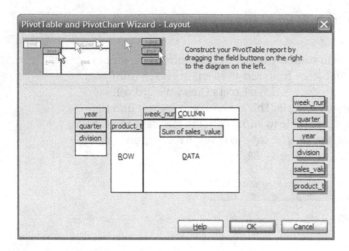

Figure 11-34. *Setting up the layout of the pivot table*

The problem with Excel reporting is the distribution. We practically need to distribute the Excel file to all users and set up the data source on every PC that needs to run the report (unless you put it on a server with the web-based Excel viewer). It can be made easier by utilizing a file data source name (DSN), which is located on a common network drive, but the deployment overhead is still there. And security is a nightmare. Simply speaking, we need to create views in the data warehouse to restrict user access. For example, say you have a table called payment containing a column called credit_card_number. We can create a view called payment_v containing all payment table columns except the credit card number column. We grant SELECT permission to the user on this view, but we revoke SELECT permission from the user on the base table (payment table). If we simply grant the db_datareader role to the users, they will be able to access all columns on all tables.

SSRS, on the other hand, is deployment friendly. The reports are web-based, so we don't have to install anything on any of the users' PCs. Setting up security is very simple. We can even utilize the Windows accounts to authenticate the users so the users don't have to log in again. We'll discuss more about deployment later in this chapter. But, reports are more or less static.

Access to DDS using Excel would suit a handful of business analysts who can write a SQL query, can understand the DDS structure, are very familiar with Excel, are happy to set up DSN themselves, and are able to create the Excel reports. They can manipulate the data in any way they like in their Excel files. They can turn the pivot tables in any way they like. They can format the reports in any way they like, and they can also create some charts.

Multidimensional Database Reports

So far in this chapter, you have learned that from SSRS you can access relational data stores within the data warehouse, such as the DDS database. But a data warehouse may also contain multidimensional databases or cubes. (Please refer to Chapter 1 for an explanation of what a multidimensional database or cube is.) From SSRS, we can also access multidimensional databases.

By their very nature, cubes are meant to be accessed using OLAP tools or cube browsers or by using an application framework such as ADOMD.NET. In most cases, cube data is accessed independently of relational data, but occasionally we need to combine the data from a relational store and from a cube in one report or in one set of reports.

Let's learn how to create a report that retrieves data from a cube. The fastest and best way to learn this is by doing it. So, let's get started. This time we will not use the Report Wizard. Instead, we will create it manually, including the query and the layout. In the next chapter, we will learn how to create a cube, but for now we will use an existing cube. For that, please restore the Amadeus Entertainment.abf cube backup from the /data folder on this book's web site (http://www.apress.com). You can use SQL Server Management Studio to restore the cube backup. You just need to connect to your Analysis Services server, right-click Databases in Object Explorer, and choose Restore.

1. In Solution Explorer of BIDS, define a new data source. To do this, right-click Shared Data Sources, and choose Add New Data Source. Set the name to Cubes, and set the type to Microsoft SQL Server Analysis Services, as shown in Figure 11-35.

2. Click the Edit button. Set the server name to your development SQL Server, and in the database name drop-down list choose the Analysis Services database where the cube is located. Click OK. Leave the Credential tab as Use Windows Authentication (Integrated Security), and click OK.

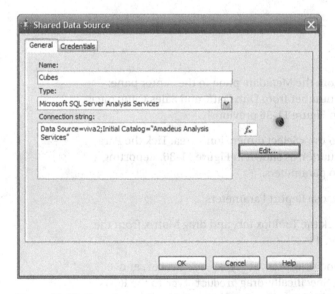

Figure 11-35. *Creating a shared data source for accessing Analysis Services cubes*

3. In the Solution Explorer pane, right-click the Reports, and choose Add ➤ New Item. Choose Report (not Report Wizard). Give it a name, such as Cube Report.rdl, and click Add.

4. In the Dataset drop-down list, choose <New Dataset…>. Give it a name (such as dsCube), choose the Data Source to Cubes (shared), leave the command type set to text, and leave the query string empty. Click OK. MDX Query Designer, similar to the one shown in Figure 11-36, will be displayed.

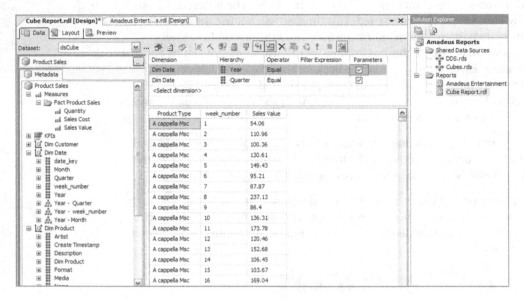

Figure 11-36. *MDX Query Designer*

5. Drag the following fact and attributes from the Metadata pane to the center pane: Product Type from Dim Product, week_number from Dim Date, and Sales Value measure from Fact Product Sales, as shown in Figure 11-36 previously.

6. Drag Year and Quarter from Dim Date to the <Select dimension> area. Tick the Parameters check boxes for both Year and Quarter, as shown in Figure 11-36. Reporting Services automatically creates those two parameters.

7. To verify, click the Report menu, and choose Report Parameters.

8. Click the Layout tab. In the left pane, click the Toolbox tab, and drag Matrix from the Toolbox to the canvas, as shown in Figure 11-37.

9. Click the Datasets tab in the left pane, and drag product_type, week_number, and sales_value from dsCube to the matrix. Specifically, drag product_type to the Rows cell, week_number to the Columns cell, and sales_value to the Data cell.

10. Save the report, and click the Preview tab. Select Year to 2007, Quarter to Q1, and click View Report. The report looks similar to Figure 11-38.

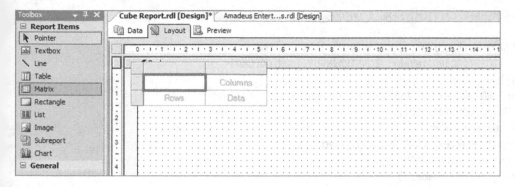

Figure 11-37. *Creating the report layout*

	1	2	3	4	5	6	7	8	9	10	11	12	13
A cappella Msc	21.18	52.17	63.56	57.94	87.45	35.07	40.27	125.09	68.41	29.9	78.6	49.69	28.19
Action Books	36.95	51.27	54.89	70.53	12.73	70.67	13.92	62.96	52.08	43.91	26.85	7.73	64.49
Action Films	28.41	47.45	21.46	61.88	40.91	69.05	81.48	38.84	16.57	86.8	59.23	62.93	44.09
Adventure Books	11.13	42.8	39.84	47.03	35.75	29.12	35.31	10.67	71.69	23.24	35.23	99.33	36.72
Blues Music	6.65	46.21	29.6	132.12	58.94	39.81	104.22	43.46	12.1	33.55	33.88	46.69	45.39
Cartoon Films	64.8	77.55	63.19	41.49	33.12	25.46	54.06	80.86	30.78	22.13	27.57	13.03	22.21
Childrens Books	55.4	12.51	62.85	44.01	42.19	31.23	37.54	62.77	51.2	35.23	107.58	34.75	83.8
Childrens Films	18.23	105.95	17.68	74.61	34.34	22.91	42.25	102.14	27.09	11.22	33.43	3.68	12.27
Childrens Music	27.13	17.2	10.04	66.41	100.82	55.53	115.3	32.19	80.08	48.26	149.22	82.66	100.34
Classical Music	3.98	1.78	31.44	15.58	1.98		8.75	66.32	7.77	30.83	5.67	23.03	4.17
Comedy Books	66.71	58.55	23.33	69.92	25.51	34.51	47.07	37.55	31.98	114.99	69.05	27.99	129.94

Figure 11-38. *Report that retrieves data from a cube*

11. If the product type column is not wide enough, you can adjust it on the Layout tab, as well as the 13 columns containing the sales values. You can also add a report title.

And with that, we have finished created our report that retrieves data from a cube!

If you notice, we did not write any Multidimensional Expressions (MDX) at all. This is because we were using the MDX Query Designer. If you want to see what the MDX looks like, click the Data tab, and click the … button next to the dsCube Dataset drop-down list. You will see that the MDX query is like the one in Listing 11-9.

Listing 11-9. *The MDX Query for the Cube Report*

```
SELECT NON EMPTY { [Measures].[Sales Value] }
ON COLUMNS, NON EMPTY
{ ([Dim Product].[Product Type].[Product Type].ALLMEMBERS
   * [Dim Date].[week_number].[week_number].ALLMEMBERS ) }
```

```
DIMENSION PROPERTIES MEMBER_CAPTION, MEMBER_UNIQUE_NAME ON ROWS
FROM
( SELECT ( STRTOSET(@DimDateQuarter, CONSTRAINED) ) ON COLUMNS
  FROM ( SELECT ( STRTOSET(@DimDateYear, CONSTRAINED) ) ON COLUMNS
        FROM [DDS]))
WHERE ( IIF( STRTOSET(@DimDateYear, CONSTRAINED).Count = 1,
  STRTOSET(@DimDateYear, CONSTRAINED),
  [Dim Date].[Year].currentmember ),
  IIF( STRTOSET(@DimDateQuarter, CONSTRAINED).Count = 1,
  STRTOSET(@DimDateQuarter, CONSTRAINED),
  [Dim Date].[Quarter].currentmember ) )
CELL PROPERTIES VALUE, BACK_COLOR, FORE_COLOR,
  FORMATTED_VALUE, FORMAT_STRING,
  FONT_NAME, FONT_SIZE, FONT_FLAGS
```

It is handy that Reporting Services uses MDX Query Designer to help us create the MDX query. It makes reporting from cubes so much easier.

Deploying Reports

After we have built the reports, we want to publish them in a web server so the business users can access them through their web browsers. This action is commonly known as *deploying reports*. Reports are deployed to a place called Report Manager on the web server. Let's take a step back for a moment and try to understand what a Report Manager is.

When we install Reporting Services on a web server, it creates a web site called Report Manager. Report Manager is usually located at `http://servername/reports` (that's the default location). We use Report Manager to upload reports, view reports, create data sources, organize reports in folders, subscribe users to a report, configure site properties, and manage report security (which users can access which reports). Figure 11-39 shows how Report Manager looks on the web browser.

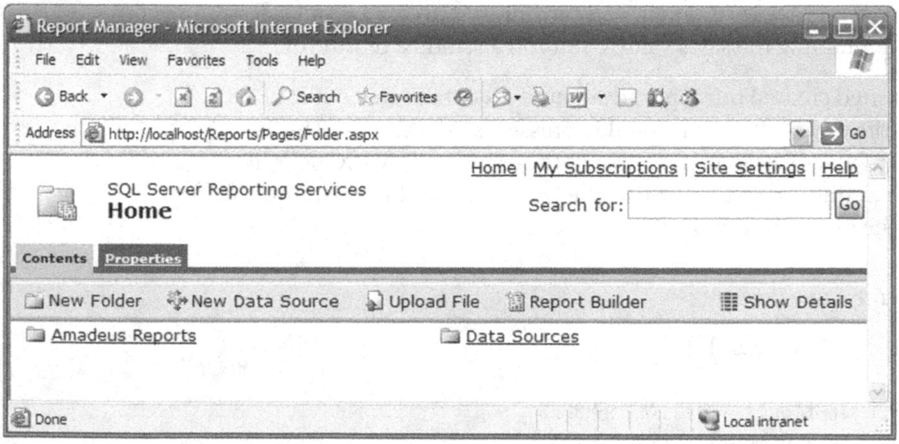

Figure 11-39. *Report Manager*

Now that you understand what deploying a report means and what Report Manager is, I'll explain how to deploy a report. First, we need to make sure that Reporting Services is up and running. Check the SQL Server Configuration Manager, and start it if it's not running. Figure 11-40 shows how to start Reporting Services in Configuration Manager.

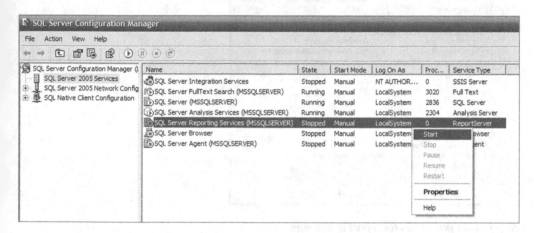

Figure 11-40. *Starting Reporting Services in Configuration Manager*

After starting Reporting Services, we need to configure our report project in BIDS to point to the target server. Click the Project menu, choose Properties, and set the Target Data Source Folder, Target Report Folder, and Target Server URL options, as shown in Figure 11-41. Keep Overwrite Data Source as false, because we don't want to overwrite data source information on the production server. Usually, the data source details on the production server are different from the development server. Target Data Source Folder is the folder name on the Report Manager where we want the data sources to be deployed. Target Report Folder is the folder name on the Report Manager where we want the reports to be deployed. Target Server URL is the web server where Reporting Services is installed.

Now after Reporting Services is started and the report project is configured, we can deploy the reports. To deploy all the reports in our project, as well as the data sources, in Solution Explorer right-click the root folder of the report project, as shown in Figure 11-42, and choose Deploy.

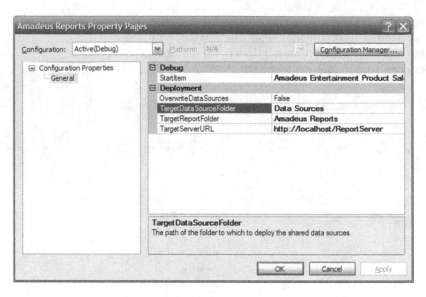

Figure 11-41. *Configuring project properties for report deployment*

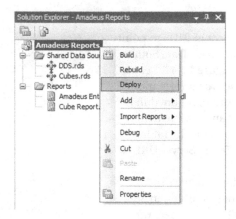

Figure 11-42. *Deploying reports*

Listing 11-10 shows the output log of this deployment.

Listing 11-10. *Deployment Output*

```
------ Build started: Project: Amadeus Reports, Configuration: Debug ------
Build complete -- 0 errors, 0 warnings
------ Deploy started: Project: Amadeus Reports, Configuration: Debug ------
Deploying to http://localhost/ReportServer
Deploying data source '/Data Sources/Cubes'.
Deploying data source '/Data Sources/DDS'.
```

```
Deploying report '/Amadeus Reports/Amadeus Entertainment Product Sales'.
Deploying report '/Amadeus Reports/Cube Report'.
Deploying report '/Amadeus Reports/Store Details'.
Deploy complete -- 0 errors, 0 warnings
========== Build: 1 succeeded or up-to-date, 0 failed, 0 skipped ==========
========== Deploy: 1 succeeded, 0 failed, 0 skipped ==========
```

Instead of deploying all reports and data sources as discussed earlier, you can also deploy only a particular report or a particular data source. To do so, in Solution Explorer, right-click the report or data source you want to deploy, and choose Deploy.

Now that the reports are deployed, you can view them in Report Manager. To do that, open your web browser (Internet Explorer, Firefox, Opera, Safari, or whatever), and go to the Report Manager URL at `http://servername/reports`, where `servername` is the name of the web server (IIS) where Reporting Services is installed. Report Manager will display two folders: Amadeus Reports and Data Sources, as shown previously in Figure 11-39.

Let's view the Product Sales report we created earlier in this chapter. Click the Amadeus Report link. It shows the three reports we have in BIDS: Amadeus Entertainment Product Sales, Store Details, and Cube Report. Click Amadeus Entertainment Product Sales to view it. Figure 11-43 shows the result.

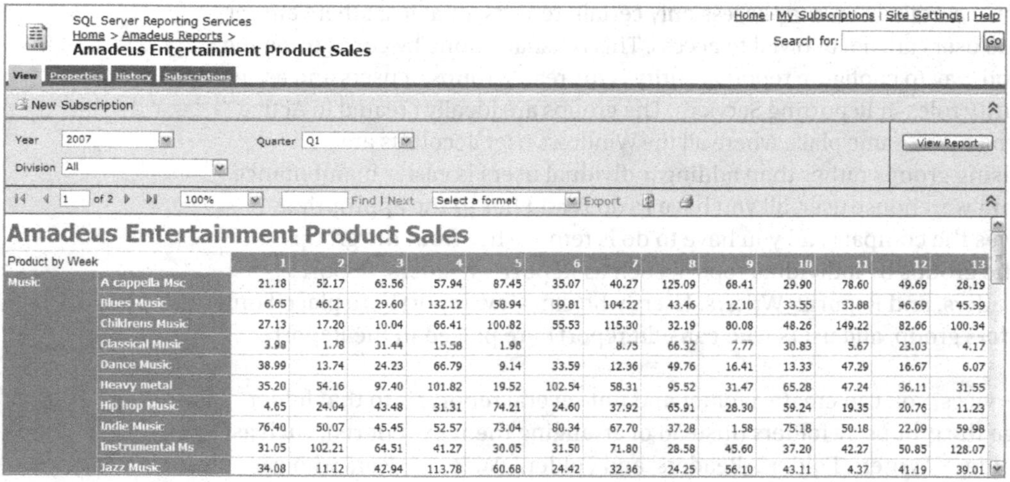

Product by Week		1	2	3	4	5	6	7	8	9	10	11	12	13
Music	A cappella Msc	21.18	52.17	63.56	57.94	87.45	35.07	40.27	125.09	68.41	29.90	78.60	49.69	28.19
	Blues Music	6.65	46.21	29.60	132.12	58.94	39.81	104.22	43.46	12.10	33.55	33.88	46.69	45.39
	Childrens Music	27.13	17.20	10.04	66.41	100.82	55.53	115.30	32.19	80.08	48.26	149.22	82.66	100.34
	Classical Music	3.98	1.78	31.44	15.58	1.98		8.75	66.32	7.77	30.83	5.67	23.03	4.17
	Dance Music	38.99	13.74	24.23	66.79	9.14	33.59	12.36	49.76	16.41	13.33	47.29	16.67	6.07
	Heavy metal	35.20	54.16	97.40	101.82	19.52	102.54	58.31	95.52	31.47	65.28	47.24	36.11	31.55
	Hip hop Music	4.65	24.04	43.48	31.31	74.21	24.60	37.92	65.91	28.30	59.24	19.35	20.76	11.23
	Indie Music	76.40	50.07	45.45	52.57	73.04	80.34	67.70	37.28	1.58	75.18	50.18	22.09	59.98
	Instrumental Ms	31.05	102.21	64.51	41.27	30.05	31.50	71.80	28.58	45.60	37.20	42.27	50.85	128.07
	Jazz Music	34.08	11.12	42.94	113.78	60.68	24.42	32.36	24.25	56.10	43.11	4.37	41.19	39.01

Figure 11-43. *How the Product Sales report looks when deployed*

To increase the scalability, we can also deploy the report on a web farm. Reporting Services also supports the report server database to be installed on a SQL Server cluster. Clustering increases the availability of the reports.

Now that we have deployed the reports, the next thing to do is manage them, which we will discuss next.

Managing Reports

After we deploy the reports to the Reporting Services server, we need to manage them. In particular, we need to manage three areas: security, subscriptions, and execution:

- *Security* is about authentication and authorization. Authentication is verifying the user's identity, for example, by checking the user ID and password. Authorization is about allowing certain users to access certain objects (such as reports) and keeping everybody else out.

- A *subscription* is a request to deliver a particular report to a particular user using a particular method (such as e-mail or a file share) at a particular time in a particular format.

- *Execution* is about the process of running the reports. We can execute a report in three ways: on demand, on demand from the cache, or from a snapshot. A snapshot is a static copy of the report output, produced at a specific time. We can schedule certain reports to run at certain frequencies or for the snapshots to be created at a certain interval.

Managing Report Security

In some data warehouse implementations, all users can access all reports. But that is rare. In most implementations, certain users may access only certain reports, or at least there are certain reports that some users are not allowed to access. This is usually done by configuring the report security. A good way to configure report security is to create groups of users and assign those groups to security roles in Reporting Services. The groups are ideally created in Active Directory on the domain, the same place where all the Windows user accounts are.

The benefit of using groups rather than adding individual users is easier maintenance. If you have a new data warehouse user, all you have to do is add her to the appropriate groups. If a user leaves the company, all you have to do is remove her from the groups. You could arrange the groups by individual report, such as Report1_Readers, Report1_Writers, Report2_Readers, and Report2_Writers. Users who can view report1 are placed only in the Report1_Readers group, and users who can edit report1 are placed in the Report1_Writers group.

In Reporting Services, you can create a folder and put several reports into that folder. You can then arrange the groups by folders (instead of arranging them by reports), such as Folder1_Readers, Folder1_Writers, Folder2_Readers, and Folder2_Writers. Users who can view only those reports in folder1 will be in Folder1_Readers, and users who can create and edit all reports in folder1 will be in Folder1_Writers. You can always go down to the report level if needed. For example, if a particular user needs to view all ten reports in folder1, except report5 that she needs to edit, you still add her to the Folder1_Readers group but on top of that you will add her as an individual user in report5 with write access.

Now that I have discussed the approach, let's configure the security for the reports in our case study. We'll give a group called Group1 read access to all reports in the Amadeus Report folder. In the Report Manager, to assign a user or a group to a folder, we click the Property tab and click the Security link in the menu on the left. OK, open Report Manager by going to http://servername/reports in your web browser. Navigate to the Amadeus Report folder, and then click the Properties tab, as shown in Figure 11-44.

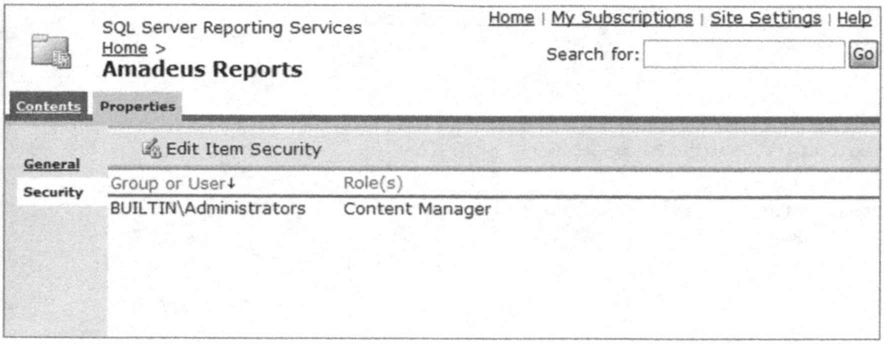

Figure 11-44. *Configuring report security*

Click Edit Item Security. Reporting Services will display a warning that the security is currently inherited from the parent folder. This is because, by default, a folder inherits its parent's security settings. Click OK on this warning. Click New Role Assignment. To give read access on all reports under this folder to Group1, type **Group1** in the "Group or user name" box, and tick the Browser role check box, as shown in Figure 11-45.

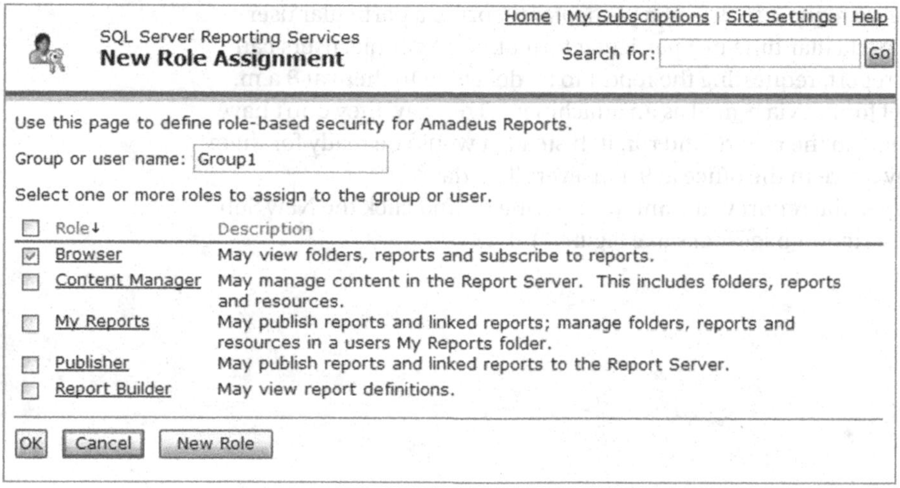

Figure 11-45. *Assigning a Browser role to a security group*

As displayed in Figure 11-45, a user (or a group of users) can have one of five security roles: Browser, Content Manager, My Reports, Publisher, and Report Builder, with the descriptions shown in Figure 11-45. You can also define a new role by clicking the New Role button. Click OK, and Group1 will be added to the list of groups for this folder (and all the reports and folders in it), as shown in Figure 11-46.

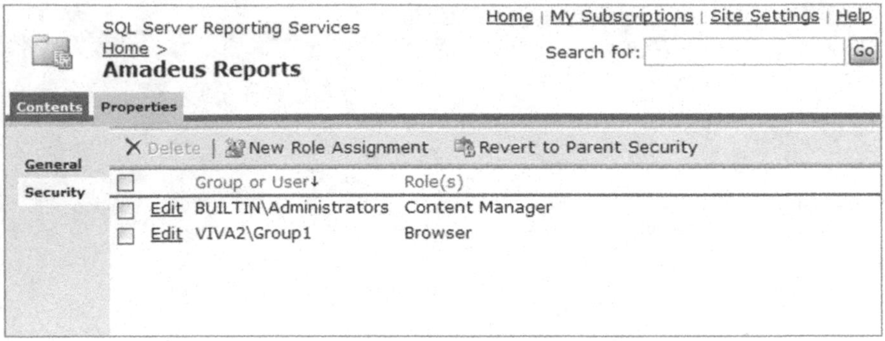

Figure 11-46. *Adding a group with browser role to report security*

Now, if a user who does not belong to Group1 tries to access the Amadeus Report, he will not see any report in the folder. Instead, the folder will be empty, so he cannot access the reports.

Managing Report Subscriptions

As I said earlier, a subscription is a request to deliver a particular report to a particular user using a particular method at a particular time in a particular format. For example, users can subscribe to the Product Sales report, requesting the report to be delivered to them at 8 a.m. every Tuesday morning in Excel format via e-mail as an attachment. This way, they don't have to open Report Manager, navigate to the report, and run it. Instead, it would be ready for them in their e-mail inbox when they arrive in the office at 9 a.m. every Tuesday.

To subscribe to a report, open the report you want to subscribe to, and click the New Subscription button. The New Subscription page looks like Figure 11-47.

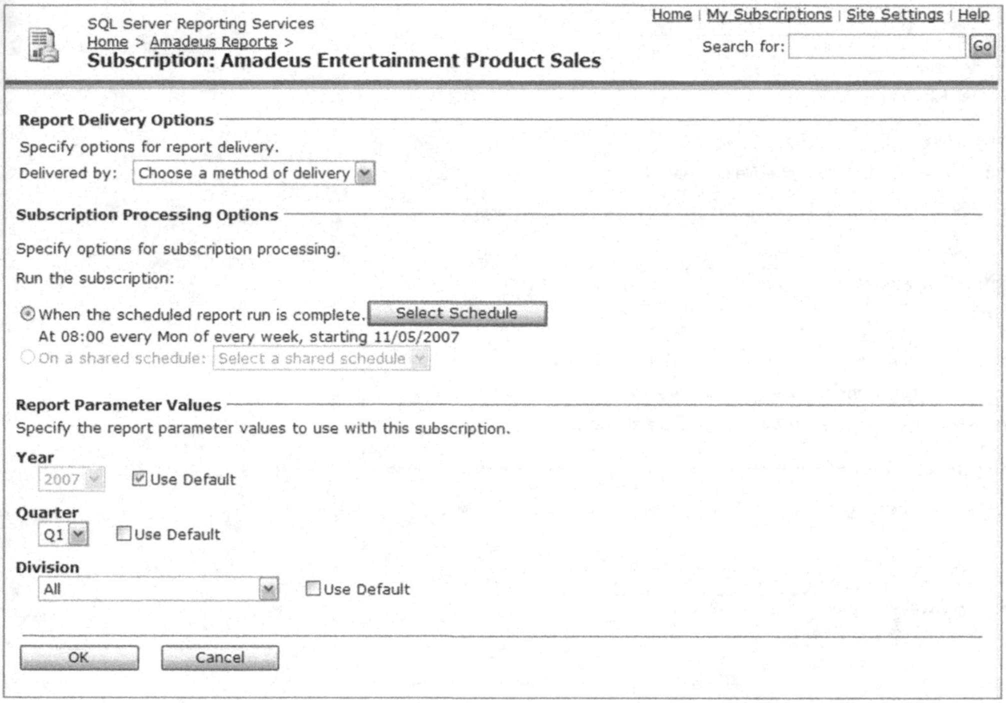
SQL Server Reporting Services
Home > Amadeus Reports >
Subscription: Amadeus Entertainment Product Sales
Home | My Subscriptions | Site Settings | Help
Search for:
Go
Report Delivery Options
Specify options for report delivery.
Delivered by:
Choose a method of delivery
Subscription Processing Options
Specify options for subscription processing.
Run the subscription:
When the scheduled report run is complete.
Select Schedule
At 08:00 every Mon of every week, starting 11/05/2007
On a shared schedule:
Select a shared schedule
Report Parameter Values
Specify the report parameter values to use with this subscription.
Year
2007
Use Default
Quarter
Q1
Use Default
Division
All
Use Default
OK
Cancel

Figure 11-47. *Creating a new subscription*

Then choose the report delivery option, such as e-mail or file share. If you choose e-mail, fill in the To text box with the recipient's e-mail address, and choose the delivery option, either Include Report or Include Link. Include Report means the e-mail will contain the report, whereas Include Link means the e-mail will contain only the URL of the report. For Include Report, if you choose Web Archive as the render format, the report will be embedded in the body of the e-mail. If you choose any other render format (CSV, Excel, PDF, HTM, XML, or TIFF), the report will be sent as an attachment to the e-mail.

If you choose the report delivery option of File Share, specify the file name and folder where you want the file to be created, the format (CSV, Excel, PDF, HTM, XML, or TIFF), the credential to access the file, and whether you want to overwrite the existing file.

Next, you can set the schedule when you want the report to run, such as every Tuesday at 8 a.m. Finally, you can set the parameters. Figure 11-48 shows the result.

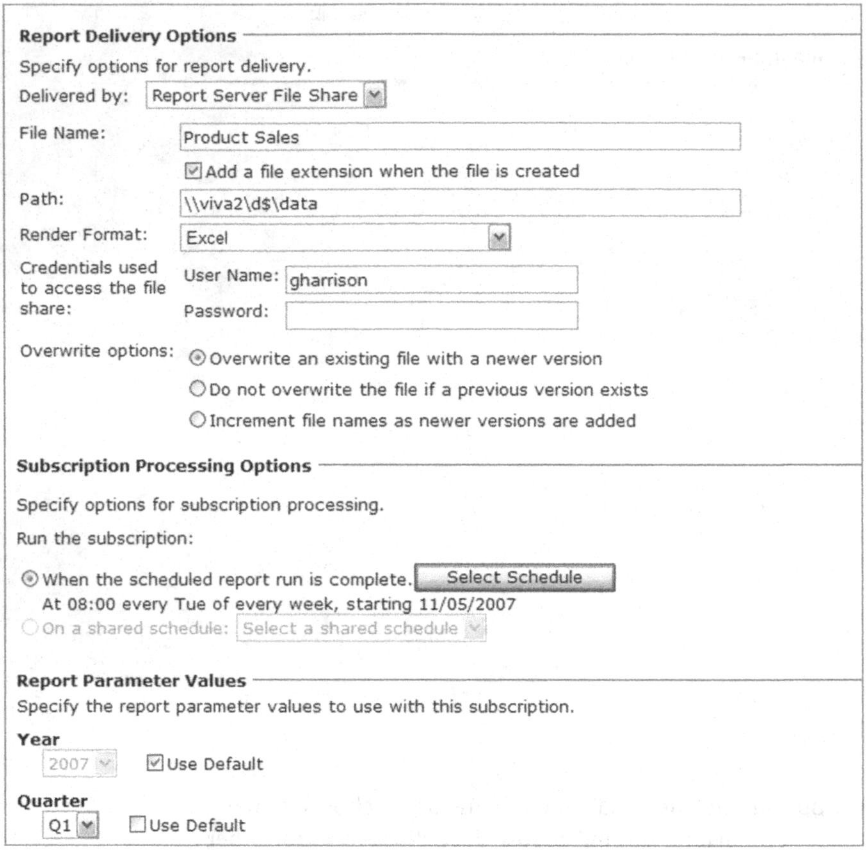

Figure 11-48. *Configuring report subscription*

The users can then monitor the status of their subscriptions using the My Subscription page, which is located in the upper-right corner of the Report Manager. On this page, they can see when the subscription was last run as well as the status of the subscription, such as if the report failed to be sent or if it was successfully written to a file.

Managing Report Execution

We can execute a report in three ways: on demand, on demand from the cache, or from a snapshot. On demand means that when we run the report, Reporting Services will always retrieve the data from the database. On demand from the cache means that when we run the report, Reporting Services will take the data from the cache, not fresh from the database. Reporting Services will still run the report, but not take data from the database. From a snapshot means that every certain period Reporting Services will run the report and store the report output, including the layout and the data. This report output is called a *snapshot*. Snapshots are stored in the report server database. In this case, Reporting Services does not execute the report when the users access the report. It simply displays the snapshot to the screen (or in an e-mail).

To configure the execution method, navigate to the report you want to configure, and then click the Properties tab. Then click the Execution link in the left pane. Figure 11-49 shows the Execution page.

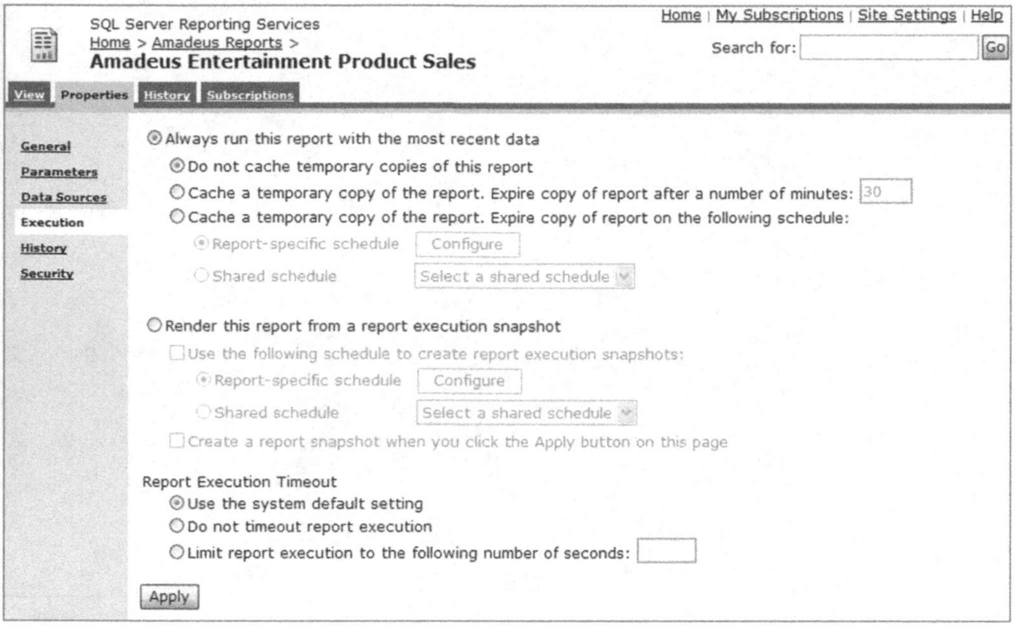

Figure 11-49. *Configuring report execution*

To set the report to be run on demand, choose "Always run this report with the most recent data" and "Do not cache temporary copies of this report." To set the report to be run on demand from the cache, choose "Always run this report with the most recent data" and one of the "Cache a temporary copy of the report. Expire copy of report…" options. To set the report to be run from a snapshot, choose "Render this report from a report execution snapshot."

With that, we've finished going through the three things about reports that we need to manage after we have developed them: security, subscription, and execution. Data warehouse users usually access the reports via a web portal rather than using the Report Manager.

Summary

Reports are one of the two primary means of getting the data out of the data warehouse (the other one is using an OLAP/BI tool). Because of this key role, reports are important in data warehousing. Reports can retrieve data from a relational database as well as from a multidimensional database.

Reports are used by both the business users as well as data warehouse administrators in the form of data quality reports, audit reports, and usage reports. For business purposes, reports are mostly used for business intelligence.

In the next chapter, I will discuss the other way of presenting the data from the data warehouse to the business users: using OLAP tools.

■■■

CHAPTER 12

Multidimensional Database

In the previous chapter, I discussed reporting, which is one of the most popular ways of getting the data out of the data warehouse and presenting it to the users. In this chapter, I will discuss another popular way of getting the data out—using multidimensional databases (MDBs). Multidimensional databases are mainly used for analytics and data mining applications. While you are learning in this chapter what multidimensional databases are, what they are for, how to design them, how to populate them, and how to query them, you need to remember that the final purpose of data warehousing is to get the data to the users, not to get the data into the warehouse.

There is no point in collecting data from various source systems throughout the enterprise into one central place if you are not going to retrieve the data and present it to the users. If you remember only one thing from this book, I hope it is this one: we can spend a million dollars and two years setting up the servers, architecting the data warehouse, designing the databases, building the ETL systems, and populating the data stores, but if the data is not retrieved and presented to the users, then the data warehouse is useless. It is very important to get the data out and presented in such a way that gives good business value to the users. In fact, the entire data warehouse should be designed to support this.

In this chapter, I'll cover, step by step, what MDBs are, what they are for, how to design them, how to populate them, how to query them, and how to administer them.

What a Multidimensional Database Is

In this section, I'll discuss what multidimensional databases are, what they look like, what they are used for, their advantages and disadvantages, how they are different from OLAP, and the system to manage them.

A *multidimensional database* is a form of database where the data is stored in cells and the position of each cell is defined by a number of hierarchical called *dimensions*. Each cell represents a business event, and the value of the dimensions shows when and where this event happened.

The structure stores the aggregate values as well as the base values, typically in compressed multidimensional array format, rather than in RDBMS tables. Aggregate values are precomputed summaries of the base values.

Examples of multidimensional databases are Microsoft Analysis Services, Hyperion Essbase, and Cognos PowerCube. The other terms that people use for a multidimensional database are *hypercube*, *cube*, *OLAP cube*, *multidimensional database* (abbreviated as MDB, MDD, or MDDB), and *multidimensional data store* (MDDS).

Physically, an MDB is a file. To help you understand how an MDB file is internally structured, you can visualize it as a matrix or a cube, as shown in Figure 12-1 and Figure 12-2. Figure 12-1 shows an MDB with two dimensions; it looks like a matrix. The two dimensions are customer and product. The combination of these two dimensions points to a cell in the matrix. The cell contains one or more measurement values (or none/empty). A cell represents a business event. The value of the dimensions shows when and where this event happened. Event A is created by customer C1 and product P1.

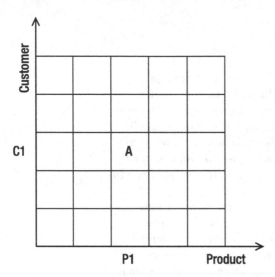

Figure 12-1. *Visualization of a multidimensional database with two dimensions*

Figure 12-2 shows an MDB with three dimensions; it looks like a cube. An MDB with four or more dimensions is called a *hypercube*. Although logically an MDB looks like a cube (for three dimensions) or a hypercube (for four or more dimensions), physically it is stored as compressed multidimensional arrays with offset positioning. The cube in Figure 12-2 has three dimensions: customer, product, and time. The combination of these three dimensions points to a cell in the cube. Each cell represents a business event. The value of the dimensions shows when and where this event happened. In Figure 12-2, the business event is "A customer buys a product." Business event A is a transaction where customer C1 buys product P1 at time T1. In Figure 12-2, the cell contains three measure values: the revenue, the cost, and the profit.

Multidimensional databases are typically used for business intelligence (BI), especially for online analytical processing (OLAP) and data mining (DM). The advantages of using multidimensional databases for OLAP and DM rather than a relational database such as a dimensional data store (DSS) are that they use less disk space and have better performance. A multidimensional database occupies less disk space compared to a relational *dimensional* database (like DDS) because it is compressed and because it does not use indexing like a DDS. Instead, it uses multidimensional offsetting to locate the data. A multidimensional database performs better on OLAP operations because the aggregates are precalculated and because the way the data is physically stored (compressed multidimensional array format with offset positioning) minimizes the number of IO operations (disk reads), compared to storing tables in an RDBMS.

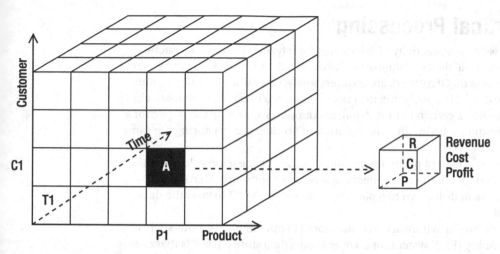

Figure 12-2. *Visualization of a multidimensional database with three dimensions*

On the other hand, the drawback of using a multidimensional database compared to using a relational database is the processing time required for loading the database and calculating the aggregate values. Whenever the relational source is updated, the MDB needs to be updated or reprocessed; in other words, the aggregate cells need to be recalculated (it doesn't have to be done in real time). The second drawback is the scalability: an MDB may not scale well for a very large database (multiple terabytes) or a large number of dimensions.

Note The term *multidimensional database* is often confused with the term *online analytical processing*, but these terms have different meanings. An MDB is the database, and OLAP is the activity used to analyze the database. The confusion is caused by the word *OLAP cube*. An OLAP cube has the same meaning as an MDB; it means a multidimensional database. We'll talk about OLAP in the next section.

Most people in the database world know that an RDBMS is the system that manages a relational database. What do we use to manage multidimensional databases? The system that manages and operates multidimensional databases is called a *multidimensional database system* (MDBMS). Multidimensional database systems are also known as *OLAP servers* or *cube engines*. Examples of an MDBMS are Microsoft SQL Server Analysis Services, Hyperion Essbase, and Cognos PowerCube. Business Objects and MicroStrategy don't have an MDBMS; they use ROLAP (I'll talk about ROLAP in the next section).

The standard interface to connect to an MDBMS is XML for Analysis (http://www.xmlforanalysis.com/), which is known as XMLA. For example, using SQL Server Reporting Services, we can connect not only to Analysis Services cubes but also to Hyperion Essbase cubes using XMLA. Microsoft, Hyperion (now owned by Oracle), SAP, and SAS support XMLA. ADOMD.NET is a .NET data provider that uses XMLA to communicate the analytical data sources.

Online Analytical Processing

Online analytical processing is the activity of interactively analyzing business transaction data stored in the dimensional data warehouse to make tactical and strategic business decisions. Typically, people who do OLAP work are business analysts, business managers, and executives. An example of OLAP is analyzing the effectiveness of a marketing campaign by measuring sales growth over a certain period. Another example is analyzing the impact of a price increase on the product sales in different regions and product groups during the same period of time.

OLAP helps solve these types of problems by summing up the measure values within the MDB according to certain criteria that reflect the business conditions. OLAP also enables the business users to drill down to a particular area of the MDB to view the data at a more detailed level.

How about analyzing business transactions data stored in operational systems such as enterprise resource planning (ERP) systems or an operational data store (ODS)? Is that classified as OLAP? No, it is not OLAP. It is business analysis, but it is not OLAP. For the analysis to be OLAP, it needs to be performed against a dimensional data warehouse, either stored in relational format or stored in multidimensional format.

What if it is not interactive, but only a one-way interaction such as reading and analyzing reports? Is that OLAP? No, that is reporting, not OLAP. OLAP is interactive; in other words, the business analyst queries, and the system responds, repeatedly, as illustrated in Figure 12-3. The response time is typically within seconds, not hours (although certain OLAP scenarios take hours).

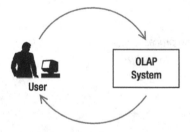

Figure 12-3. *OLAP is interactive.*

OLAP activities are part of BI. There are three widely used BI activities: reporting, OLAP, and data mining. OLAP tools are the interactive tools that business analysts use to query a data warehouse to perform business analysis. Examples of OLAP tools are SSAS, Cognos BI 8 Analysis, Business Objects XI Release 2 Voyager, and ProClarity Analytics 6.

OLAP functionalities can be delivered using a relational database or using a multidimensional database. OLAP that uses a relational database is known as *relational online analytical processing* (ROLAP). ROLAP leaves the data in tables and relies on SQL select statements with sum and group clauses to summarize the detail-level data. The precalculated summary data (called *aggregates*) is stored in summary tables. When receiving queries, ROLAP chooses the best summary tables to be used to satisfy the query and then supplements the results with select statements to the base tables.

OLAP that uses a multidimensional database is known as *multidimensional online analytical processing* (MOLAP). MOLAP precalculates the summary of measure values in the MDB and stores the aggregates within the MDB structure. An example of ROLAP is MicroStrategy OLAP Services. Examples of MOLAP are Cognos BI 8 Analysis and ProClarity Analytics 6. Microsoft SQL Server Analysis Services (SSAS) supports both ROLAP and MOLAP, plus it supports Hybrid Online Analytical Processing (HOLAP). HOLAP uses both relational and multidimensional databases. SSAS databases can store the data in a relational database, a multidimensional database, or both. When we set SSAS to store the data in HOLAP mode, the base data (leaf level) is stored in SQL Server relational database tables, and the aggregate data is stored in an MDB.

Creating a Multidimensional Database

Let's create a multidimensional database from the DDS database in the Amadeus Entertainment case study. In this exercise, we will create the Product Sales multidimensional database that was used for reporting in the previous chapter. For that, open BIDS, and follow these steps:

1. Click the File menu, and select New ➤ Project.

2. Choose Business Intelligence Projects for the project type, choose Analysis Services Project as the template, and name it **Amadeus Analysis Services**, as shown in Figure 12-4. Then click OK.

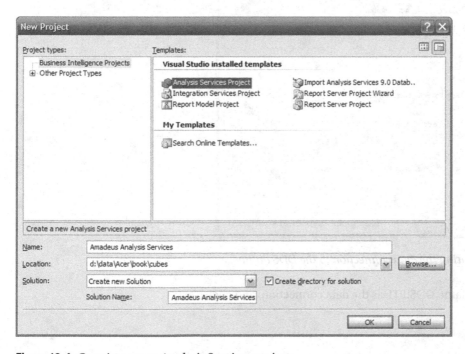

Figure 12-4. *Creating a new Analysis Services project*

3. We need to connect to the DDS database. The scripts mentioned in Chapter 6 created the DDS database and the tables within it. The steps in Chapters 7 and 8 populated the DDS tables. You can also download the completed DDS at the Apress website (http://www.apress.com/). It is in the /data folder, and the file name is dds.zip (7MB). Uncompress this file, and restore the database on your development SQL Server.

4. Let's create a data source pointing to the DDS database so we can use the DDS as a data source for our MDB. In Solution Explorer, right-click Data Sources, and choose New Data Source. Click Next on the welcome page.

5. On the Data Source wizard page, click New to create a new connection. Because the DDS is a SQL Server database, choose SQL Native Client as the provider.

6. Select your development SQL Server in the Server Name drop-down box, and select Use Windows Authentication (or supply the credential if you use SQL Server authentication). Choose DDS for the database to connect to, as shown in Figure 12-5.

Figure 12-5. *Creating the data connection to the DDS database*

7. Choose servername.DDS.ETL as the data connection, and click Next.

8. On the Impersonation Information page, choose "Use the service account" (or supply the credential if you use SQL Server authentication), and then click Next.

9. Name the data source **DDS**, and click Finish. Now in Solution Explorer, there is a new data source called DDS.

Now let's create a data source view, which is the relational model for this data source. In this data source view, we will put in only the dimension and fact table that we need to create the product sales cube, which are: date dimension, product dimension, store dimension, and Product Sales fact table. For that, follow these steps:

1. Right-click Data Source Views in Solution Explorer, and choose New Data Source View.

2. Click Next on the welcome page.

3. Select DDS for Relational Data Sources, and click Next.

4. Double-click the date, product, and store dimensions, as well as the Product Sales fact table, and bring them to the Included Objects box on the right side, as shown in Figure 12-6. Then click Next.

5. Click Finish to complete the wizard.

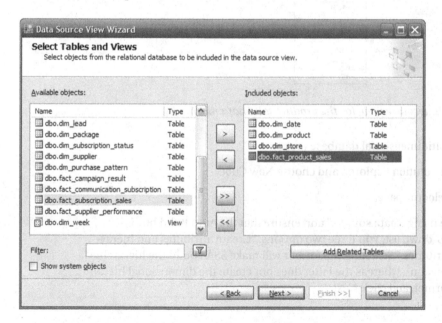

Figure 12-6. *Selecting tables for the data source view*

The result is a new data source view with one fact table and three dimensions, as shown in Figure 12-7.

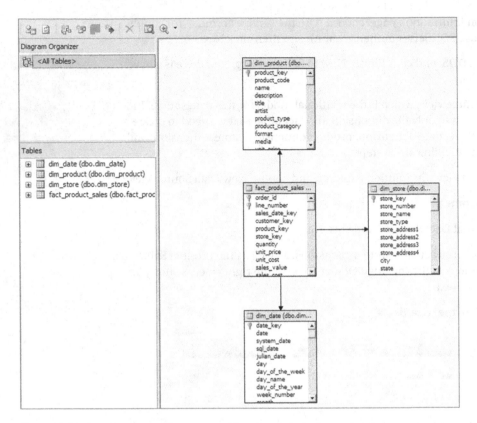

Figure 12-7. *Creating a new data source view for the product sales data mart*

Now let's create the multidimensional database (cube):

1. Right-click Cubes in Solution Explorer, and choose New Cube.

2. Click Next on the welcome page.

3. Choose "Build Cube using a data source," and ensure that the Auto Build box is checked. In the drop-down list, you'll see two options: "Create attributes and hierarchies" or "Create attributes." Selecting the former will make SSAS build the hierarchies (levels) for the dimensions, whereas the latter does not create the dimensional hierarchies. Choose the former, and click Next.

4. Auto Build makes recommendations based on the data source view structure. When building a cube in SSAS, we have two choices: we can either build it manually or select Auto Build. When building the cube manually, we specify the measures in the fact tables, the data types, the dimensions, and the hierarchies. With Auto Build, the Cube Wizard will detect the cube structure based on the tables in the data source view. Select DDS for the data source view, and click Next.

5. The wizard analyzes the relationship between tables in the data source view, as shown in Figure 12-8. The wizard identifies which tables are the fact tables and which tables are the dimension tables. Click Next.

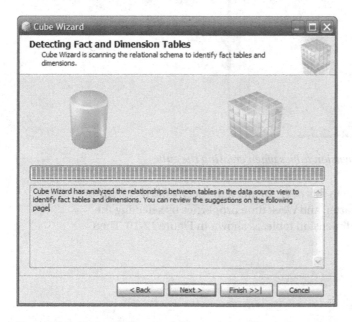

Figure 12-8. *Detecting fact and dimension tables*

6. The wizard correctly identifies dim_product and dim_store as dimension tables, but it incorrectly identifies dim_date as both a fact and dimension table. To correct this, uncheck the fact check box for dim_date so that date, product, and store are set as dimensions and Product Sales is set as a fact table. The wizard does not identify the time dimension, so in the "Time dimension table" drop-down list, choose dim_date, as shown in Figure 12-9.

Figure 12-9. *Selecting the fact and dimension tables when creating the cube*

7. The next page is Select Time Periods. On this page, we need to specify the hierarchy of the time dimension. Set the Year, Quarter, and Week time properties by selecting the appropriate columns from the date dimension table, as shown in Figure 12-10. Then click Next.

Figure 12-10. *Selecting time periods*

8. The next page is Select Measures. On this page, we need to select the measure we want to include in the cube. By default the wizard selects all available measures, but in this case we want to select only some of them. Select Quantity, Sales Cost, and Sales Value, as shown in Figure 12-11. Then click Next.

9. The Cube Wizard will scan the dimensions to detect the hierarchies. For each dimension, the wizard tries to identify whether a column is a parent or a child of another column based on the data values in that column. In the Amadeus Entertainment case study, we have Product Category and Product Type as the hierarchies in the product dimension; Year, Quarter, and Week in the date dimension; and Division and Region in the store dimension. Click Next.

10. The next page is Review New Dimension. Expand each dimension, and check that the wizard has successfully identified the hierarchies. Click Next on this page.

11. Name the Cube **Product Sales**, and click Finish.

Figure 12-11. *Selecting measures*

Figure 12-12 shows the resulting cube. It has three dimensions: store, product, and time. We have created a data source for the DDS database. We then created a data source view for three dimensions and one fact table. And finally, we created a cube based on that data source view.

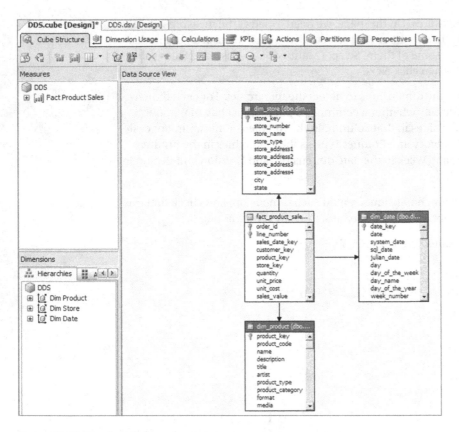

Figure 12-12. *Product Sales cube structure*

Processing a Multidimensional Database

As you have just seen, if you have a dimensional relational data warehouse (also known as a *dimensional data store*), you can easily create the multidimensional database or cube. Before you can browse this cube or query this cube for reporting, though, you need to process the cube first. Processing a cube means calculating the aggregates from the cube cells.

And before you can process the cube, you need to build it and deploy it first:

- Building a cube means checking the internal structure of the cube including the facts, dimensions, hierarchy, and connections to the data source to make sure the structure we created is valid.

- Deploying a cube means creating the cube structure that we have designed in a multi-dimensional database engine (aka OLAP server or cube engine), which, in this case, is an Analysis Services server.

Let's build and deploy the cube we just created:

1. Click the Build menu, and choose Build Amadeus Analysis Services. In the bottom-left corner you'll see "Build started," followed by "Build succeeded."

2. Ensure that the Analysis Services server is up and running. Click Start ➤ All Programs ➤ Microsoft SQL Server 2005 or 2008 ➤ Configuration Tools ➤ SQL Server Configuration Manager. Right-click the SQL Server Analysis Services, and choose Start, as shown in Figure 12-13.

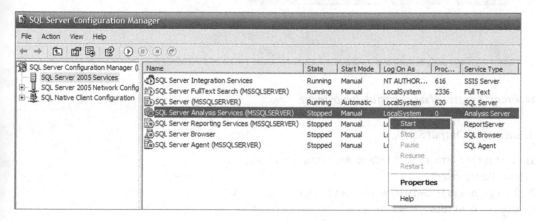

Figure 12-13. *Starting Analysis Services*

3. Now let's deploy the cube. In the Solution Configuration drop-down list on the toolbar (the one next to the green Play button), choose Development. Click the Build menu, and choose Deploy Amadeus Analysis Services.

4. When the project has been successfully deployed to the Analysis Services instance, the deployment progress will be like the one in Figure 12-14, and the output script will be like Listing 12-1. Figure 12-14 tells us that SSAS has successfully created the cube structure in the MDB and populated it with the data from the DDS tables. When it says "Processing Measure Group Fact Product Sales completed successfully," it means that SSAS has loaded all the values on the measure columns in the fact_product_sales table in the DDS into the cube structure. When it says "Processing Dimension dim_store completed successfully," it means that SSAS has loaded the distinct values for each column in the store dimension in the DDS into the cube structure, including the hierarchy structure.

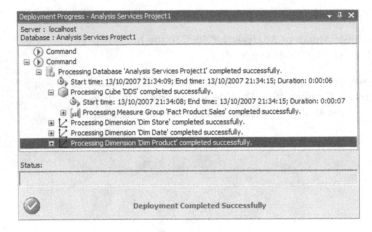

Figure 12-14. *Progress script of a successful deployment*

Listing 12-1. *Successful Output Script*

```
------ Build started: Project: Amadeus Analysis Services,
Configuration: Development ------
Started Building Analysis Services project: Incremental ....
Build complete -- 0 errors, 0 warnings
------ Deploy started: Project: Amadeus Analysis Services,
Configuration: Development ------
Performing an incremental deployment of the 'Amadeus Analysis Services'
database to the 'localhost' server.
Generating deployment script...
    Add RelationalDataSource DDS
    Process Database Amadeus Analysis Services
Done
Sending deployment script to the server...
Done
Deploy complete -- 0 errors, 0 warnings
========== Build: 1 succeeded or up-to-date, 0 failed, 0 skipped ==========
========== Deploy: 1 succeeded, 0 failed, 0 skipped ==========
```

5. What we just did was deploy the cube design into a physical structure. In other words, we were creating the cube in SSAS based on what we designed in BIDS. So, let's see the cube we just created. Open SQL Server Management Studio, and connect to the Analysis Services instance. The Object Explorer shows the measure groups of the cube along with the three dimensions, as shown in Figure 12-15.

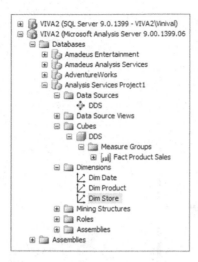

Figure 12-15. *Object Explorer of the deployed Analysis Services project*

6. Now that we have built and deployed the project, we are ready to process the cube. In BIDS, click the Database menu, and choose Process. The Process Database page opens, as shown in Figure 12-16. The Impact Analysis button lists which other SSAS objects are affected by the processing task. There are three main types of SSAS objects: server objects (such as data sources and data source views), dimension objects (such as attributes and hierarchies), and cube objects (such as measures and partitions).

The Change Settings button enables us to change the processing order (whether the objects are processed sequentially, which means one object at a time, or in parallel, which means all objects simultaneously) and the transaction mode if we process sequentially (process in one transaction or in separate transactions); it also enables us to handle dimensional errors (whether to convert to an unknown record or discard the record, how to handle invalid keys, null keys and duplicate keys, and so on) and (whether or not to) process affected objects.

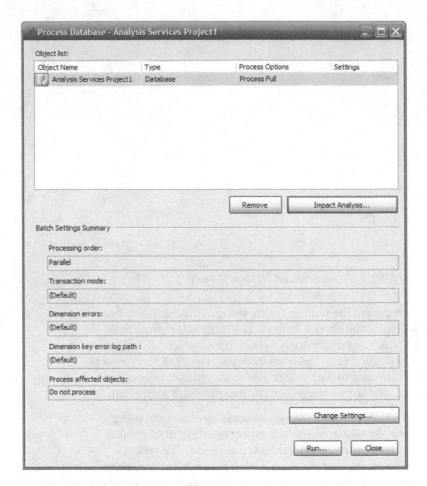

Figure 12-16. *Process Database dialog box*

7. In our case, we are quite happy to go with the default settings, so just click Run. Analysis Services will process the cube and display the progress as it goes along, as shown in Figure 12-17. It will end with a message "Process succeeded." Click Close to close the Process Progress dialog box. Click Close again to close the Process Database dialog box.

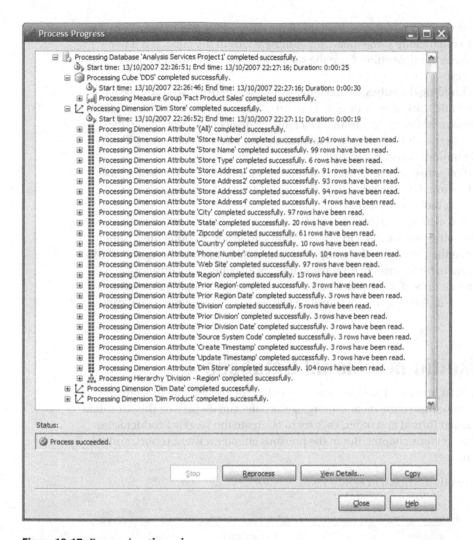

Figure 12-17. *Processing the cube*

So, we have built, deployed, and processed a cube: product sales with its dimensions. The cube is populated from the Product Sales fact table. We have not included all the dimensions and measures from this fact table. We included only three dimensions (date, product, and store) and three measures (quantity, sales value, and sales cost). A typical scenario in a simple data warehouse project is to include most of the dimensions and measures. I prefer to build the cube bit by bit. For example, if the mart has six dimensions and ten measures, I would probably start the cube with three dimensions and three to five measures; add member formulas, additional aggregations, and dimension intelligence; build and deploy the cube; make sure it's working fine before adding the remaining dimensions and measures; and then build and deploy it again. This makes it easier to troubleshoot if we have problems.

When building a cube, we do not have to include all the dimensions and measures in the fact table. It is normal to not include some measures or dimensions in the cube. It is a perfectly valid scenario to have multiple cubes from the same fact table with different sets of dimensions and measures.

Then we move on, building the cubes for the other fact tables. In the case study, we have four other fact tables to build the cubes from: Subscription Sales, Supplier Performance, Communication Subscriptions, and Campaign Results fact tables. Not all fact tables need cubes. Some fact tables are accessed only in their relational format. We build the cubes only if we need to browse them in multidimensional format.

Some BI tools don't require cubes to be built because they are ROLAP or reporting tools. These tools read from relational databases such as the ODS or the DDS. Some tools such as ProClarity and data mining tools work better with cubes.

We don't have to build a cube from just one fact table. We can build a cube from two (or more) fact tables. When doing this, we need to bear in mind dimensional conformity. Conformed dimensions mean they are either the same dimension table or one is the subset of the other. Dimension A is said to be a subset of dimension B when all columns of dimension A exist in dimension B and all rows of dimension A exist in dimension B. In doing this, we are *drilling across*, in other words, joining two (or more) fact tables that have conformed dimensions between them.

Querying a Multidimensional Database

Now that the cube has been processed, we can query the cube. The easiest way to query a cube is by browsing it. Browsing a cube means querying the cube and displaying the cube data on the screen in a particular format and order. Let's try to re-create the Weekly Product Sales report that we did in the previous chapter. But in the previous chapter it was a report, and this time it will be a cube browser.

1. Click the Browser tab, as shown in Figure 12-18.

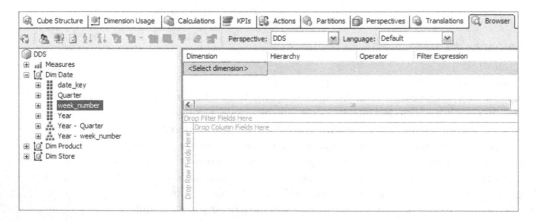

Figure 12-18. *Selecting the row and column to browse a cube*

2. Expand the date dimension by clicking the + sign next to it. Click week_number, and drop it onto the Drop Column Fields Here area, also shown in Figure 12-18.

3. Expand the product dimension by clicking the + sign next to it. Click the Product Type, and drop it onto the Drop Row Fields Here area.

4. Expand Measures, and expand Fact Product Sales by clicking their + signs. Click Sales Value, and drop it onto the Drop Totals or Detail Fields Here area. Figure 12-19 displays the outcome.

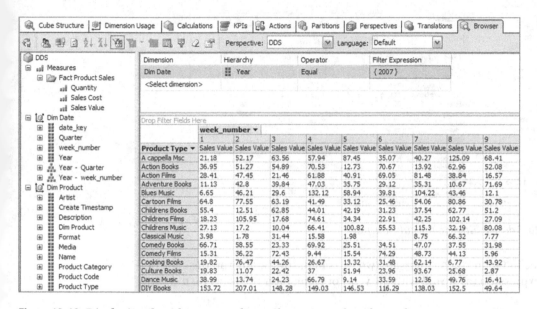

Figure 12-19. *Displaying the sales amount by product type and week number*

5. Remember that in the previous chapter we constrained the output by year and quarter? Let's do the same here. On the tree pane on the left, click Year under Dim Date. Drag and drop it onto the <Select dimension> area.

6. Expand the Filter Expression drop-down list, and select 2007. Notice that the figures in the main table are updated automatically to reflect only 2007.

7. There is another way to filter the result; you can use the Drop Filter Fields Here area. Let's use it to filter the output to a particular quarter. Drag Quarter from the date dimension, and drop it onto the Drop Filter Fields Here area.

8. Click the little blue triangle next to Quarter, and choose Q2. Notice that the output changes automatically. Figure 12-20 shows the result.

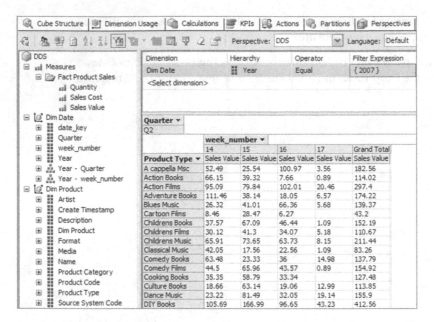

Figure 12-20. *Adding filters to the cube output*

As you can see in Figure 12-20, there are two ways of putting a filter on the cube output: using filter expression (as we did with the year) or using filter fields (as we did with the quarter).

You have just seen that you can query the cube using the Analysis Services cube browser. There are other ways to query an Analysis Services cube to get the data out and present it to the users:

- You can query the Analysis Services cube from Reporting Services using MDX queries, as we did in the previous chapter when I discussed reporting.

- You can browse Analysis Services cubes using a third-party BI tool such as ProClarity.

- You can use data mining to analyze an Analysis Services cube.

- You can use ADOMD or XMLA to query the cube.

Administering a Multidimensional Database

Once we have built, deployed, processed, and queried the cubes, we need to administer them. There are three common administrative tasks with regard to Analysis Services cubes. The first one is to secure the cube; for example, only people who are authorized to access the cubes should be able to access them. The second one is to keep the data within the cubes up-to-date. For this we need to process the cube regularly, such as once a day or a few times a day, depending on the following:

- How frequently the source DDS is updated

- How up-to-date the users need the data to be

The third one is to make sure we can restore the cubes if they are out of order, for example, taking backups regularly.

■Note Before we go through these three items, I'd like to clarify two Analysis Services terms that are often misunderstood and used incorrectly. In the multidimensional world, the term *cube* has the same meaning as the term *multidimensional database*. In Analysis Services, they are different. In Analysis Services, a cube is a single *n* dimensional structure consisting of *n* dimensions and *m* measures, whereas a multidimensional database (or a database for short) is a collection of cubes.

Multidimensional Database Security

To secure the cubes, we need to understand Analysis Services security architecture. Unlike a SQL Server database engine, Analysis Services doesn't have SQL Authentication mode. It has Windows Authentication mode only. So, a user needs to be created in Windows before we can give the user access to Analysis Services cubes. Analysis Services has two different roles: the server role and the database role. Users with server roles have access to everything. They can access all multidimensional databases and the cubes within them, create and delete multidimensional databases, create and delete database users, and perform administrative tasks. Users with database roles can access only a specific multidimensional database and the cubes within them.

To grant a server role to a user, in Management Studio right-click the Analysis Services server instance, and choose Properties. Click Security, and then click Add. Type the username, and click Check Names, as shown in Figure 12-21. Click OK. Alternatively, you can also click the Advanced button and then click Find Now to get a list of users.

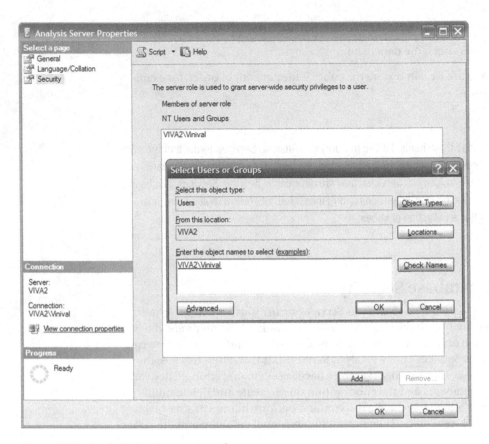

Figure 12-21. *Analysis Services server role*

To give a user access to a particular multidimensional database, in Management Studio go to the multidimensional database that you want to give access to, right-click Roles, and choose New Role. The Create Role dialog box will be displayed, as shown in Figure 12-22.

You'll see the following tabs:

- On the General tab (shown in Figure 12-22), we can give the role a name and a description. We can also choose the database permissions: Full Control has access to everything in the database, Process Database can process a cube or a dimension, and Read Definition can access the definition of the database.

- On the Membership tab, we can add the users to the role.

- On the Data Sources tab, we can give access to the data source (this is mainly used for data mining).

- On the Cubes tab, we can give the user read or write access to the individual cubes within the database and specify whether the user can drill through, create local cubes, or process the cube, as shown in Figure 12-23.

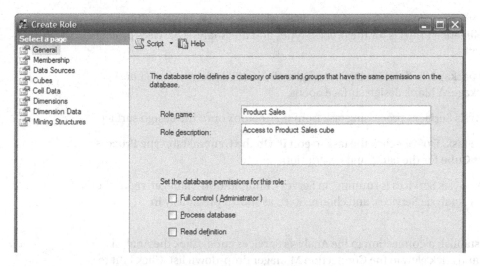

Figure 12-22. *Analysis Services database role*

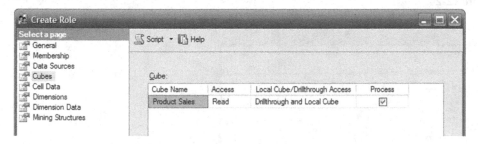

Figure 12-23. *Setting up cube permissions*

- On the Cell Data tab, we can give the user read or write access to the cell data. Note that the cell data is limited by the cube permission. For example, if a role has write access on a cell but the role has only read access on the cube, then the role can only read on that cell.

- On the Dimensions tab, we can give the user read or write access to the individual dimension, read the dimension definition, and process the dimension.

- On the Dimension Data tab, we can specify the access to an individual member and hierarchy within each dimension.

Processing Cubes

Earlier in this chapter, you learned how to process a cube manually using BIDS. In practice, once we have built and deployed the cube in the production server, we need to schedule it to be processed regularly to keep the data up-to-date with the DDS. For this we use SSIS. Open BIDS, and go through the process:

1. Create a new Integrated Services project by clicking File ➤ New ➤ Project. Choose Business Intelligence Projects for the process types and the Analysis Services project for the templates.

2. Create a new package: in Solution Explorer, right-click SSIS Packages, and choose New SSIS Package. A blank design surface opens.

3. Drag the Analysis Services processing task from the Toolbox onto the design surface.

4. Let's name the task. Double-click the task to edit it. On the General tab, type **Process Product Sales Cube** for the name and description.

5. Ensure that Analysis Services is running. In Server Configuration Manager, right-click the SQL Server Analysis Services, and choose Start, as shown previously in Figure 12-13.

6. We need to establish a connection to the Analysis Services cube. Click the Analysis Services tab, and click New in the Connection Manager drop-down list. Click Edit to define a new connection, and enter the details of your Analysis Services server, as shown in Figure 12-24.

Figure 12-24. *Setting the connection to the Analysis Services database*

7. Click Add in the object list, and select the database, cubes, measure groups, partitions, and dimensions to process, as shown in Figure 12-25. In this case, we need to select only the Product Sales cube; there's no need to select any of the dimensions. SSAS will automatically process the measure groups and dimensions for that cube.

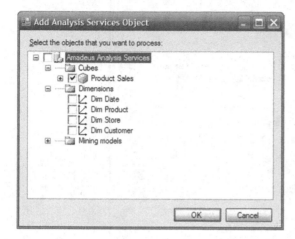

Figure 12-25. *Selecting the Analysis Services object to process*

8. You can also specify the processing order, transaction mode, dimension errors, dimension key error log path, and whether to process affected objects by clicking the Change Settings button, as shown in Figure 12-26.

   The parallel processing order makes the tasks run simultaneously in a single transaction. To do this, click Change Settings, and select Parallel. Sequential processing order means Analysis Services will execute the processes one by one, either in a single transaction or in a separate transaction. If it is a single transaction, when a single process fails, the whole job is rolled back, and the entire job fails. If it is a separate transaction, when a single process fails, only the failed process is rolled back, and the other processes in the job continue.

   Processing affected objects means processing all objects that have a dependency on the object that we selected. It is normally used when processing dimensions; for example, when we process a dimension, we may want to process all the cubes that use that dimension.

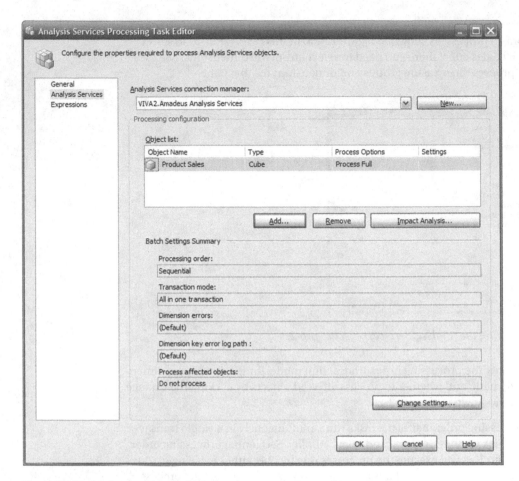

Figure 12-26. *Setting up the Analysis Services processing task*

9. Now that we have set up the task to process the cube, let's execute it. Click OK to close the Analysis Services Processing Task Editor dialog box. Right-click the Process Product Sales Cube task, and execute the task. Figure 12-27 shows the result.

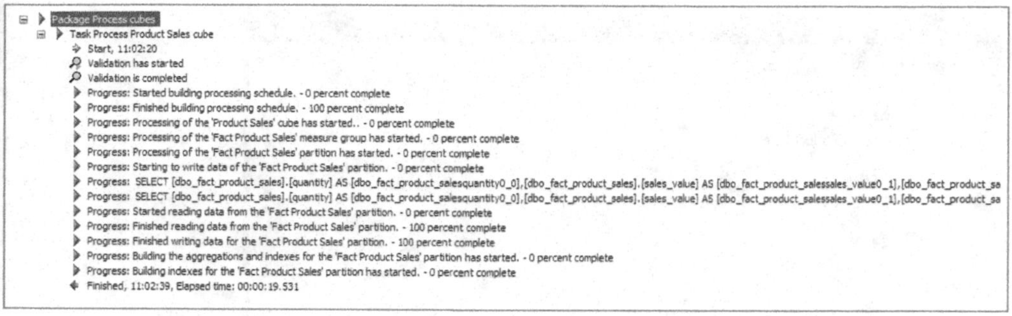

```
☐ ▶ Package Process cubes
  ☐ ▶ Task Process Product Sales cube
      ⇨ Start, 11:02:20
      ♫ Validation has started
      ♫ Validation is completed
      ▶ Progress: Started building processing schedule. - 0 percent complete
      ▶ Progress: Finished building processing schedule. - 100 percent complete
      ▶ Progress: Processing of the 'Product Sales' cube has started.. - 0 percent complete
      ▶ Progress: Processing of the 'Fact Product Sales' measure group has started. - 0 percent complete
      ▶ Progress: Processing of the 'Fact Product Sales' partition has started. - 0 percent complete
      ▶ Progress: Starting to write data of the 'Fact Product Sales' partition. - 0 percent complete
      ▶ Progress: SELECT [dbo_fact_product_sales].[quantity] AS [dbo_fact_product_salesquantity0_0],[dbo_fact_product_sales].[sales_value] AS [dbo_fact_product_salessales_value0_1],[dbo_fact_product_sa
      ▶ Progress: SELECT [dbo_fact_product_sales].[quantity] AS [dbo_fact_product_salesquantity0_0],[dbo_fact_product_sales].[sales_value] AS [dbo_fact_product_salessales_value0_1],[dbo_fact_product_sa
      ▶ Progress: Started reading data from the 'Fact Product Sales' partition. - 0 percent complete
      ▶ Progress: Finished reading data from the 'Fact Product Sales' partition. - 100 percent complete
      ▶ Progress: Finished writing data for the 'Fact Product Sales' partition. - 100 percent complete
      ▶ Progress: Building the aggregations and indexes for the 'Fact Product Sales' partition has started. - 0 percent complete
      ▶ Progress: Building indexes for the 'Fact Product Sales' partition has started. - 0 percent complete
      ✦ Finished, 11:02:39, Elapsed time: 00:00:19.531
```

Figure 12-27. *The execution result of processing the Analysis Services cube*

Now that we have successfully executed the task, we need to schedule the SSIS package like a normal SSIS job. Let's go through how to schedule the job:

1. In Management Studio, connect to the database engine.

2. In Object Explorer, double-click SQL Server Agent. You need to start SQL Server Agent if it doesn't start automatically.

3. Right-click Jobs, and choose New Job. Type **Process Analysis Services cubes** for the name on the General tab.

4. Click the Steps tab. Click New to define a new step, name it **Process Product Sales cube**, and choose the SQL Server Integration Services package for the type.

5. On the General tab, in the Package Source drop-down list, choose File System and select the DTSX file containing the "Process Analysis Services cube" SSIS package we created earlier, as shown in Figure 12-28. Click OK to finish the step creation process.

Note It is also possible to store the SSIS package in the SSIS server. If this is the case, in the "Package source" drop-down list, choose SSIS Package Store instead of "File system."

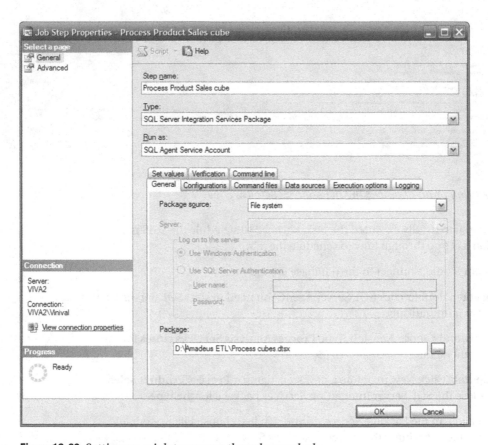

Figure 12-28. *Setting up a job to process the cube regularly*

6. Click the Schedule tab, and click New to create a new schedule to set the regular time when you want the cube to be processed, as shown in Figure 12-29, just like when creating a regular SQL job. Click OK twice to create the scheduled job.

7. In Management Studio Object Explorer, right-click the job you just created, and choose Start Job to execute the job to make sure it runs OK.

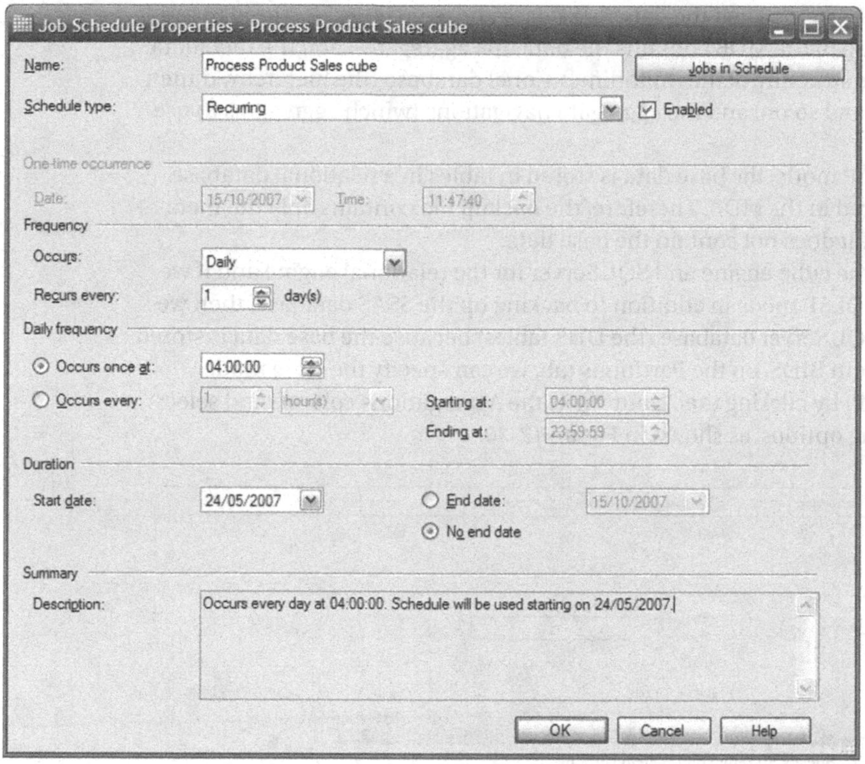

Figure 12-29. *Setting up the schedule to process the cube*

Backup and Restore

Now that we have created the multidimensional database, set up the security access, and arranged for it to be processed regularly, we need to back up the multidimensional database regularly. The backup frequency is determined based on how often the cube is processed. One important thing that some people forget is that when we have backed up the multidimensional database, we need to restore the backup. If we don't prove that the backup can be restored successfully, we still have a great risk. It is necessary to schedule the backup regularly (say, every day), but it is also necessary to schedule the restore regularly (say, every quarter). This is not a real restore, but only a test restore. So, let's go through the process of backing up and restoring an Analysis Services multidimensional database.

Before we get down to the details, let's understand an important concept first when backing up a multidimensional database (MDB). If the MDB storage is in ROLAP mode, the data is not stored in the MDB. The data (both the base data and the aggregates) is stored in the tables in a normal relational database. Therefore, the backup of the MDB contains only the metadata. The backup does not contain the data.

If the MDB is in MOLAP mode, then the data (base data and aggregates) is stored in the MDB. Therefore, the backup of the MDB contains the data, the aggregates, and the metadata. The metadata contains the structure of the multidimensional database (the hierarchy, dimension, measures, partition, and so on) and the aggregate navigations (which aggregates to use for certain conditions).

If the MDB is in HOLAP mode, the base data is stored in tables in a relational database, but the aggregates are stored in the MDB. Therefore, the backup file contains only the metadata and the aggregations. It does not contain the base data.

So if we use SSAS for the cube engine and SQL Server for the relational engine and if we set the SSAS database in ROLAP mode in addition to backing up the SSAS database, then we also need to back up the SQL Server database (the DDS tables) because the base data is stored there. In the cube designer in BIDS, on the Partitions tab, we can specify the store mode (MOLAP, ROLAP, or HOLAP) by clicking the ... button in the Aggregations column and selecting the storage and caching options, as shown in Figure 12-30.

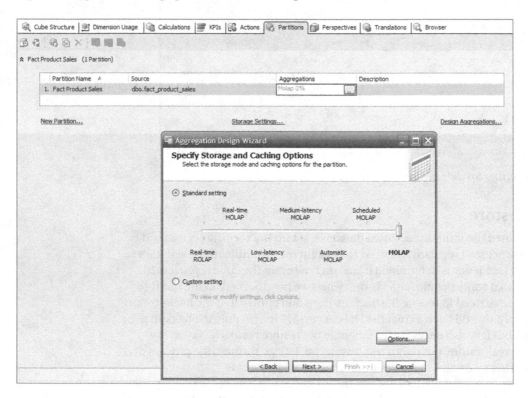

Figure 12-30. *Specifying the storage mode for the partition*

Now that you understand what will be stored and what will not be stored in the backup file, let's go through the backup and restore process. The easiest way to regularly back up the Analysis Services database is to create an XMLA script using Management Studio and execute that script using SSIS. XMLA is the de facto standard for accessing multidimensional databases (MDBs). We then use SQL Server Agent to execute the script.

Let's create the XMLA script for backing up the MDB:

1. In Management Studio's Object Browser, connect to the Analysis Services instance. Right-click the database you want to back up, and select Backup.

2. Set the path and name of the backup file, and set the options to allow overwriting an existing backup file and to compress or encrypt the backup file, as shown in Figure 12-31.

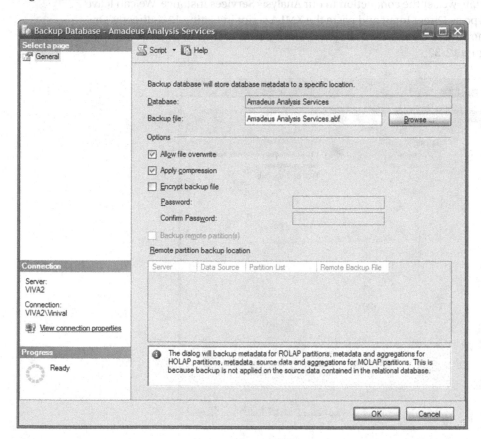

Figure 12-31. *Creating XMLA script for backing up the database*

3. To create the XMLA script, click Script at the top. The result is similar to Listing 12-2.

Listing 12-2. *XMLA for Backing Up a Multidimensional Database*

```
<Backup xmlns="http://schemas.microsoft.com/analysisservices/2003/engine">
  <Object>
    <DatabaseID>Amadeus Analysis Services</DatabaseID>
  </Object>
  <File>h:\data\backup\MDB\Amadeus.abf</File>
  <AllowOverwrite>true</AllowOverwrite>
</Backup>
```

4. Now we need to run this script in SSIS. So, open BIDS, create a new SSIS project, and create a new package.

5. Drag the Analysis Services Execute DDL task from the palette onto the design surface. Double-click it to edit it.

6. On the General tab, we can give the task a name and description.

7. On the DDL tab, we set the connection to our Analysis Services instance. We can leave the SourceType as Direct Input and paste the XMLA script in Listing 12-2 directly. Or, we can set the SourceType as File and specify the file path to the XMLA script, as shown in Figure 12-32.

Figure 12-32. *Configuring an SSIS task to execute the XMLA script*

8. Click OK to close the task editor and execute the task.

9. Check that the backup file is produced at the specified location.

10. Using SQL Server Agent, we can then schedule the SSIS package to run at a specified time, such as after the cube is processed successfully.

To test restoring the backup regularly, we create an XMLA file using the same process as earlier. To restore into a new database with a different name, just modify the <DatabaseName> element in the XMLA file. Then execute it using the SSIS task as done earlier. Alternatively, if it is one time only, we can just use Management Studio to restore the backup.

Summary

In this chapter, you learned about MDBs, OLAP, and the difference between them. I also discussed the differences between ROLAP, MOLAP, and HOLAP. We created a multidimensional database for our Product Sales fact table, and you learned how to process, query, secure, and back up the multidimensional database.

As I emphasized in the beginning of this chapter, the main purpose of having a data warehouse is to get the data out and present it to the user community. In the previous two chapters, I discussed how to get the data out of the data warehouse using reports and analytical tools. In the next three chapters, I'll discuss how to use data warehouses for BI and CRM, as well as for other purposes.

CHAPTER 13

■■■

Using Data Warehouse for Business Intelligence

In this chapter and the next two chapters, I will discuss the applications of data warehouses. In this chapter, I will discuss business intelligence (BI), which is by far the most widely used data warehouse application. The next chapter describes customer relationship management (CRM), and in Chapter 15, I will discuss customer data integration (CDI), unstructured data, and search.

BI is a collection of activities to get an understanding and insights about a business by performing various types of analysis on the company data as well as on external data from third parties to help make strategic, tactical, and operational business decisions and take the necessary actions to improve business performance. The key words here are "improve business performance." The purpose of any BI activity is to improve business performance. Some of the most popular examples of BI implementations are analyzing customer profitability, studying product profitability, evaluating sales figures across different products and regions, exploring accounts profitability, examining supplier performance, and discovering customer risk patterns.

It is important to bear in mind that business intelligence activities are not limited to the data in the data warehouse. Business intelligence applications can query the ODS or ERP or any other systems in the enterprise to perform the necessary analysis for improving business performance. But in this chapter, I'll discuss only BI applications that query the data warehouse.

You can classify the various BI applications into six categories: reporting applications, analytic applications, data mining applications, dashboards, alerts, and portal. Reporting applications query the data warehouse and present the data in static tabular or pivot format. Analytic applications query the data warehouse repeatedly and interactively and present the data in flexible formats that users can slice and dice. Data mining applications explore the data warehouse to find patterns and relationships that describe the data. Reporting applications are usually used to perform lightweight analysis. Analytic applications are used to perform deeper analysis. Data mining applications are used for pattern finding.

Dashboards are a category of business intelligence applications that give a quick high-level summary of business performance in graphical gadgets, typically gauges, charts, indicators, and color-coded maps. By clicking these gadgets, we can drill down to lower-level details. Alerts are notifications to the users when certain events or conditions happen. A BI portal is an application that functions as a gateway to access and manage business intelligence reports, analytics, data mining, and dashboard applications as well as alert subscriptions.

In the rest of the chapter, I will discuss these six categories of BI applications. I'll discuss what they are, why we use them (why are they important), and their advantages and disadvantages, and I will provide some examples of each.

Business Intelligence Reports

As discussed in Chapter 11, reports query the data warehouse and present the data in tabular format or pivot format. We can also produce various types of charts. We can add parameters on the reports to make them dynamic. In a data warehousing context, a report retrieves data from the data warehouse and presents it to the users on the screen or on paper. Users also can subscribe to these reports so that the reports can be sent to the users automatically by email at certain times (daily or weekly, for example). In Chapter 11, we discussed reports in great detail, including when to use reports (and when not to), how to create them, how to deploy them, and how to administer them. So in this section, I'll be brief so as not to repeat the topics I already discussed in Chapter 11.

The main advantage of using reports in BI is their simplicity. Reports are simple to create, simple to manage, and simple to use. We usually use reports (instead of analytics or data mining applications) in BI when the presentation format requirements are fairly simple and static. The disadvantages of using reports are that they are not flexible or interactive. If users want to swap a piece of data with another piece or want to view the data at a higher or lower level, we need to redesign the report. By comparison, the other types of business intelligence applications such as analytic applications are more flexible. We don't have to redesign the application if the user wants to present another piece of information. We just "plug" the analytic application on top of some cubes, and the user can explore all the data in those cubes.

With SSRS we can do charting (line chart, bar chart, pie chart, and so on) or present the data in simple tables or pivot table format. We can group, sort, and filter the data. We can drive the content of the report using parameters and make the report a little bit dynamic. Users can also change the sort order of the report at run time. Users can subscribe to a report to receive it via e-mail automatically at certain intervals. The report can be attached to the e-mail, or the e-mail can just contain the link to the report. We can also create a subreport within a report. We can store or cache the report output for quick retrieval later. We can add a link to another report by passing certain parameters to tailor the content.

BI reports are not limited to just the data warehouse. BI reports can query other data sources within the enterprise. Most relational databases (SQL Server, Oracle, Teradata, DB/2, mySQL, Informix, Sybase, and many others) can be accessed using ADO.NET, OLE DB, Open Database Connectivity (ODBC), and Java Database Connectivity (JDBC). Instead of using ODBC to access SQL Server, we can also use the SQL Native Client driver. Most multidimensional databases can be accessed using XML for Analysis (XMLA) and ADOMD.NET. We can access, for example, data stored in the ERP systems (production, HR, sales, and purchasing information), the call center application (customer applications, complaints, and new contacts), the ODS (integrated master data, reference codes, account and policy information, up-to-date prices, and currency conversion rates), or even Windows Active Directory (security information and usernames). Using reports we can combine the stored results of a saved query and the fresh output of an online query. We can combine the data from ERP systems, the ODS, and the data warehouse in a single report or in a set of reports.

BI reports are usually managed and published in one central place, such as an intranet. Using SSRS we can secure the reports, allowing only the people who should be able to access the reports and keeping everybody else out. We can set the security access so that different people or departments can administer the content of different reports. We can also integrate the report security with Windows Active Directory so the users don't have to login again to access the reports.

Business Intelligence Analytics

Henry Morris coined the term *analytic applications* in 1997. He defined analytic applications as applications that "provide guidance in the decision-making process by accessing time-based data from multiple sources."[1] Users use analytic applications to access a dimensional data warehouse interactively. Analytic applications, or *analytics* for short, are also known as *OLAP applications*. Users can slice and dice the data, drilling up and drilling down.

I'd like to clarify the terminology that people use in analytics (such as slicing, dicing, drilling up, and drilling down) to make sure we have a common understanding. *Slicing* is the process of retrieving a block of data from a cube by filtering on one dimension, as shown in Figure 13-1. *Dicing* is the process of retrieving a block of data from a cube by filtering on all dimensions, as shown in Figure 13-2.

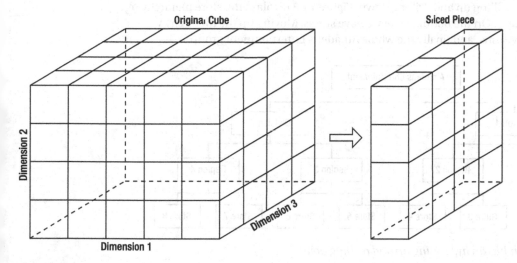

Figure 13-1. *Slicing*

1. Power, D., "Henry Morris Interview: Decision support and analytic applications," DSSResources.com. December 3, 2006.

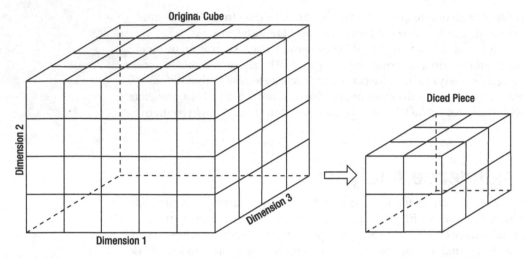

Figure 13-2. *Dicing*

In Figure 13-1, we are filtering only on dimension 1; in other words, dimension 1 = [values]. We do not constrain or filter dimensions 2 and 3. In Figure 13-2, we filter on all three dimensions; in other words, dimension 1 = [values], dimension 2 = [values], and dimension 3 = [values].

Now let's discuss drilling up and drilling down. Figure 13-3 displays the store hierarchy of Amadeus Entertainment. On the bottom level we have stores. Moving up the hierarchy we have regions, then divisions, and finally the whole Amadeus Entertainment group.

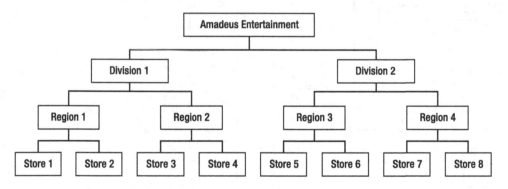

Figure 13-3. *Dimension hierarchy, drilling up and drilling down*

Drilling up means presenting the data at a higher level on the dimension hierarchy (from detail level to summary level), such as going from the store level to the region level. Drilling down means presenting the data at a lower level on the dimension hierarchy (from summary level to detail level), such as going from the region level to the store level.

To illustrate the process of drilling up, please look at the subscription revenue of Amadeus Entertainment stores for a particular week in Table 13-1.

Table 13-1. *Subscription Revenue for a Particular Week at Store Level*

Store	Subscription Revenue
Store 1	72,663
Store 2	61,899
Store 3	36,409
Store 4	61,994
Store 5	75,786
Store 6	34,049
Store 7	34,937
Store 8	41,012

When we drill up from store level to region level, we will get the subscription revenue for each region, as displayed in Table 13-2.

Table 13-2. *Subscription Revenue for a Particular Week at Region Level*

Region	Subscription Revenue
Region 1	134,562
Region 2	98,403
Region 3	109,835
Region 4	75,949

We can then drill up further to division level and to group level. Drilling down is the reverse, going from a higher level to a lower level. When drilling down, we get more detail information.

Analytics are what most people mean when they say *BI applications*. Depending on which industry you are in, you can use analytic applications to evaluate business perform- ance, analyze product and customer profitability, and study how to lower inventory costs. Some analytic applications have their own multidimensional database management system (MDBMS) such as SQL Server Analysis Services, Cognos 8 BI Analysis, Hyperion System 9 BI Essbase Analytics, and SAP Business Warehouse. Some analytic applications can use other vendors' MDBMSs; for example, Business Objects OLAP Intelligence can read Microsoft Analysis Services, Hyperion Essbase, SAP BW, and DB2 OLAP cubes,[2] while ProClarity reads Microsoft Analysis Services cubes.

All these applications are called *MOLAP applications*; they're analytic applications that read from multidimensional databases. Some analytic applications do not read from multidi- mensional databases. They read from relational databases instead, such as MicroStrategy OLAP. These are called *ROLAP applications*. To be able to respond quickly to a query such as "What is the total revenue for fiscal week 4 in 2008 from all stores in region 4?", ROLAP appli- cations store the totals (known as *aggregates*) in summary tables. These aggregates are calculated and stored in summary tables when the ROLAP structure is processed. This way,

---

2. http://www.businessobjects.com/global/pdf/products/queryanalysis/olap_intelligence.pdf

when end users submit their queries, the ROLAP application doesn't need to access a lot of records on the fact table. The ROLAP application can just access the summary table to get the precomputed total.

Some applications can read from both relational and multidimensional sources and combine the data internally before presenting the data to the end users. Whether the applications read from a relational or multidimensional data source, the data source ideally needs to be in dimensional data warehouse (Kimball) form, consisting of fact and dimension tables that make conformed data marts. Some analytic applications can supplement this dimensional data with data from a normalized database; for example, to get more accurate descriptions (product descriptions, account descriptions, and so on).

Using analytic applications, we can get an overview of the current business performance, such as sales, production, purchasing, or profitability (probably by region) and compare it with the budget or targets. We can then drill down into specific areas that have problems and try to find out the cause of the problems. That is a typical scenario of BI analysis. But there are also other scenarios; for example, in the telecommunications industry we can analyze the line usage patterns (by weekly time slots) against the bandwidth cost. Or in the waste management industry we can weigh the revenue stream (which is by volume) vs. the disposal cost (which is by weight). Using analytic applications in monetary and technical organizations, such as combustion engine laboratories, nationwide economic management, and weather measurement stations, are totally different from the "normal" business organizations (companies) mentioned earlier.

We can also do charting, "what if?" analysis, planning exercises, and key performance indicator monitoring from analytic applications. We can swap any dimension with another dimension to get a different business perspective, going up and down the dimensional hierarchy to get different levels of summary, and we can pick certain dimension members and focus our attention on them. Using analytic applications, we can perform ad hoc queries, drill across to another cube, analyze data from several cubes, find and locate certain data, and perform various kinds of formatting and manipulation with regard to the results, such as adding or removing columns and performing calculations.

The main advantage of using analytic applications is the flexibility. If the users don't know what they are trying to find in advance, then this is the right tool for them. Using analytic applications, we have the whole data warehouse at our fingertips. This is especially useful for companies and organizations that make business decisions based on data rather than instincts, such as performing quantitative analysis to justify the decisions. The main disadvantage of analytic applications is the complexity. It takes some time for the users to get familiar with the tools. Also, the multidimensional databases' data sources need to be maintained properly. But once everything is set and ready, then it's easy to keep the operation going.

In analytic applications, a multidimensional database (cube) is fundamental, because that's where the data is stored. In the previous chapter, I discussed how to create, process, and browse cubes using SSAS. I also discussed how to query the cubes and how to administer them. Hence, I'm not going to repeat those topics here, so let's continue with data mining.

Business Intelligence Data Mining

Data mining is the process of exploring data to find the patterns and relationships that describe the data and to predict the unknown or future values of the data. The key value of data mining is the ability to understand why some things happened in the past and the ability to predict what will happen in the future. To refer to predicting the future with regard to data mining, some people use the term *forecasting*, and some call it *predictive analytics*. On the other hand, when data mining is used to explain the current or past situation, it is called *descriptive modeling*, *descriptive analytics*, or *knowledge discovery*.

Implementing data mining in the business is growing by the day, both through descriptive and predictive analytics. Using data mining, we can find the correlation between purchase patterns and customer demographics. For example, in our Amadeus Entertainment case study, we can find whether there is a relation between the sales of a music product type and the customer interest or occupation. In the financial services industry, data mining is traditionally used for credit scoring, for example, to predict the ability and willingness to pay the loan based on (each country has different factors) payment behavior, past delinquency, current debt, credit history, number of inquiries, address, bankruptcies filed, and customer demography.

There are many examples of data mining implementation for CRM, which we will discuss in the next chapter. In business intelligence, popular applications of data mining are for fraud detection (credit card industry), forecasting and budgeting (finance), cellular/mobile package development by analyzing call patterns (telecommunication industry), market basket analysis (retail industry), customer risk profiling (insurance industry), usage monitoring (energy and utilities), and machine service times (manufacturing industry).

We need to do four steps to implement data mining in SQL Server 2005 Analysis Services:

1. *Define what we want to achieve*: In this step, we formulate the question that we will try to answer. For example, in our Amadeus Entertainment case study, the question is this: "Is there a correlation between the sales of music, film, and audio book product types and the customer interest or occupation?"

2. *Prepare the data*: In this step, we make sure we have the relevant data and check the data quality. In our case study, the data is already cleansed and ready in the data warehouse, but to answer the previous question, we need to prepare the data in a separate table that records whether the customers have purchased music, film, or audio book products.

3. *Build the mining models*: We then create a mining structure that consists of one or more data mining models. The mining models can use different mining algorithms. Mining models can be built from relational sources or from OLAP cubes. We then process the models and test how they perform.

4. *Deploy and maintain the models in production*: We can then use the models to create predictions, either using the SQL Server data mining language (DMX) or using Prediction Query Builder. A *prediction* is a forecast or a guess about the future value of a certain variable. For example, in the Amadeus Entertainment case study, we can use the model to forecast the sales of music products in the next quarter. We can also create reports that query the mining models by creating an Analysis Services data set. We may need to process the models regularly to keep them up-to-date, either using XML for Analysis (XMLA) or using Analysis Management Objects (AMO).

Let's go through the process of creating and processing the mining models in SQL Server for the Amadeus Entertainment case study. Open Management Studio, and create the following table in the DDS database. We will use this table to build mining models to find the correlation between the music purchases and demographic attributes. We will also group the rows on this table into ten clusters with similar characteristics to enable us to analyze and predict the behavior of each cluster.

```
create table dm_purchase_pattern
( customer_key  int
, gender        char(1)
, interest      varchar(30)
, occupation    varchar(50)
, music         char(1)
, film          char(1)
, audio_books   char(1)
, constraint pk_dm_purchase_pattern
  primary key clustered (customer_key)
)
go
```

Now let's store music, film, and audio book purchases in this table, along with the customer demographic attributes such as interest, gender, and occupation.

Listing 13-1 inserts customer demographic information into the dm_purchase_pattern table, along with indicators whether they have purchased music, film, or audio book products.

Listing 13-1. *Creating and Populating Purchase Pattern Table for Data Mining*

```
insert into dm_purchase_pattern
(customer_key, gender, interest, occupation, music, film, audio_books)
select c.customer_key, c.gender, c.interest1, c.occupation
, case sum(case p.product_category when 'Music' then 1 else 0 end)
  when 0 then 'N' else 'Y' end as music
, case sum(case p.product_category when 'Films' then 1 else 0 end)
  when 0 then 'N' else 'Y' end as films
, case sum(case p.product_category when 'Audio Books' then 1 else 0 end)
  when 0 then 'N' else 'Y' end as audio_books
from fact_product_sales f
join dim_product p on f.product_key = p.product_key
join dim_customer c on f.customer_key = c.customer_key
group by c.customer_key, c.gender, c.interest1, c.occupation
go
```

Now open BIDS, and open the Analysis Services project we created in Chapter 12. (You can also create a new project if you want.) Edit the DDS data source view by double-clicking it in Solution Explorer. Right-click the canvas, and choose Add/Remove Tables. Add the dm_purchase_pattern table we just created to the data source view.

Right-click Mining Structures in Solution Explorer, and choose New Mining Structure. Click Next on the welcome page, and choose "From existing relational database or data warehouse" on the next page. Choose "Microsoft Decision Trees" for Data Mining Technique, and then choose DDS for the data source view. On the Specify Table Types page, choose dm_purchase_pattern as the *case table*. The case table is a table that contains the training data that we want to use to train the mining model.

On the next page (Specify the Training Data), we have three usage types for each column. We can use a column as a key, as an input, or as a *predictable*. The key column uniquely identifies a row in a table. The input column provides the information used by the mining model to make the predictions. The predictable column is the value we are trying to predict.

Choose `customer_key` for the key column; `gender`, `interest`, and `occupation` for the input columns; and `music` for the predictable column, as shown in Figure 13-4.

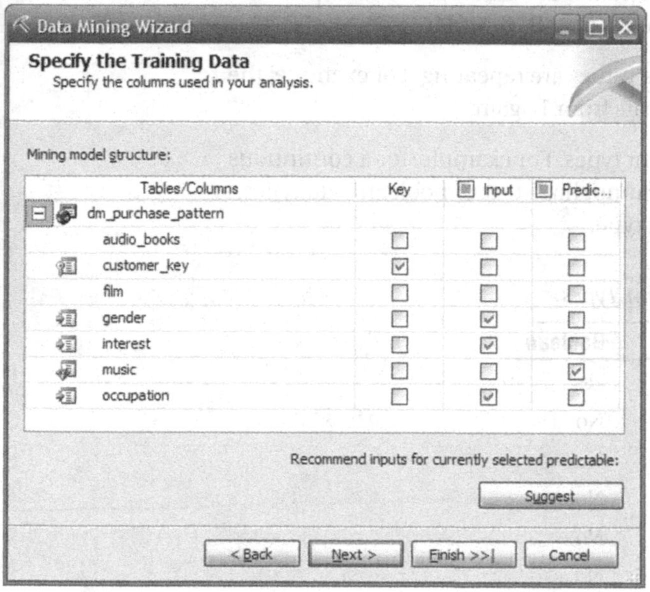

Figure 13-4. *Specifying the training data*

Before we move to the next page, let's go through one concept first: content type. In the database world we have data types, such as integer, varchar, decimal, datetime, and so on. As the name implies, data types define the type of data we can have for a particular column. For example, an integer column can have only "whole" numeric values, such as 1, 2, 3, and so on, whereas a varchar column can contain "string" values. In a mining model, we have five data types for a column: date, double, long, text, and boolean. These data types describe the *type* of data but not the *behavior* of data, such as whether the values are ordered. Because of that, in data mining we have the concept of *content type*, which describes the behavior of the data.

There are eight content types: discrete, continuous, discretized, key, key sequence, key time, ordered, and cyclical:

- A discrete column contains a set of values. There are only certain possible values for that column such as city name and gender.

- A continuous column contains any values of certain types; for example, the revenue column can contain any numerical values.

- A discretized column contains continuous values that have been converted into several buckets of discreet values.

- A key column acts as a unique identifier of the row.

- A key sequence column is a key column, but the values represent a sequence of events. The values are ordered, as in 1, 2, 3, 4, 5, …. They don't have to have the same distance between them. For example, 1, 3, 4, 6, … are valid key sequence values.

- A key time column is a key column, but the values are datetime values. The values are ordered, as in 2007-10-22 00:00:00, 2007-10-23 00:00:00, 2007-10-24 00:00:00, and so on.

- An ordered column is a discreet column, but the values are ordered. For example, the customer class column may contain discreet values of A, B, C, and D.

- A cyclical column is an ordered column, but the values are repeating. For example, the month number goes from 1 to 12 and then repeats from 1 again.

Only certain data types are valid for certain content types. For example, for a continuous column we can have only date, double, and long; we cannot have text or boolean data types. Table 13-3 shows the valid data types for each content type.

Table 13-3. *Valid Data Types for Mining Structure Content Types*

Content Types	Date	Double	Long	Text	Boolean
Discrete	Yes	Yes	Yes	Yes	Yes
Continuous	Yes	Yes	Yes	No	No
Discretized	Yes	Yes	Yes	No	No
Key	Yes	Yes	Yes	Yes	No
Key Sequence	Yes	Yes	Yes	Yes	No
Key Time	Yes	Yes	Yes	No	No
Ordered	Yes	Yes	Yes	Yes	Yes
Cyclical	Yes	Yes	Yes	Yes	Yes

Now that you understand the concepts of content types and data types, let's continue with the Data Mining Wizard. The next page is Specify Columns' Content and Data Type, where we specify the content type and the data type for each column, as shown in Figure 13-5. On this page, we can ask Analysis Services to detect the content types and data types, or we can specify them manually. In this case, click Next because they are already correct.

On the next page, specify the mining structure name as **Purchase Pattern** and the mining model name as **Decision Trees**, and check the "Allow drill through" box. This option allows us to explore the source data. The Mining Structure designer opens, showing the dm_purchase_pattern table, as shown in Figure 13-6.

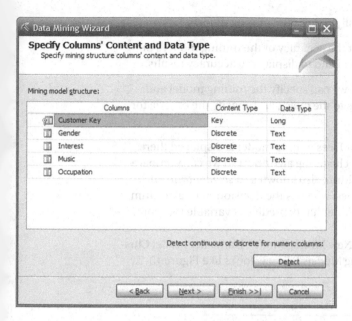

Figure 13-5. *Specifying content types and data types*

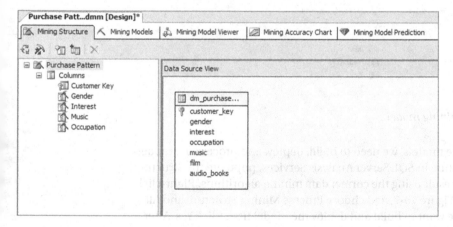

Figure 13-6. *Mining Structure designer*

Before we move on, let's go through the five tabs on the Mining Structure designer:

- The Mining Structure tab (displayed in Figure 13-6) contains the columns in the mining structure and the table that the data source view contains. We can use this tab to modify the mining structure and explore the underlying source data.

- The Mining Models tab contains the mining models we created using the Data Mining Wizard, based on the mining structure displayed on the Mining Structure tab. We use this tab to manage existing models and to create new models.

- The Mining Model Viewer tab is used to visually explore the mining models.

- The Mining Accuracy Chart tab is used to test the accuracy of the mining model's prediction. This tab contains tools to filter the data and to display the accuracy results.

- On the last tab, Mining Model Prediction tab, we can specify the mining model and input tables, map the columns, add functions to the query, and specify the criteria for each column.

Next, click the Mining Models tab. The Decision Trees mining model is displayed there. We'll create another mining model using a different clustering algorithm so we can compare different data mining algorithms. A clustering algorithm, also known as a *segmentation algorithm*, divides data into groups with similar properties, whereas the decision trees algorithm (also known as the *classification* algorithm), on the other hand, predicts a variable (or more) based on the other variables in the data set.

Right-click anywhere on the table, and choose New Mining Model. Name the model **Clustering**, and choose Microsoft Clustering. The Mining Models tab now looks like Figure 13-7.

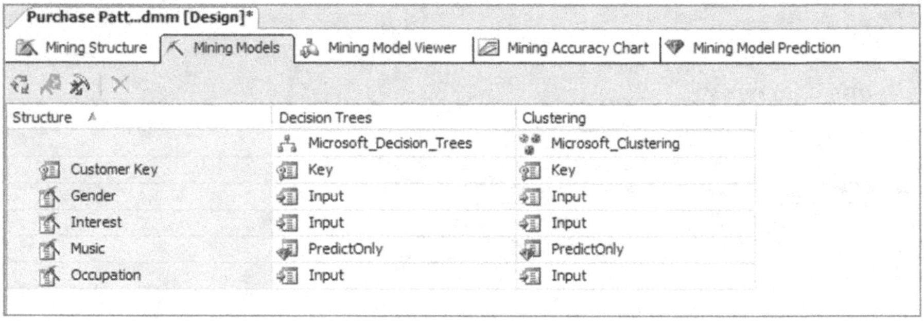

Purchase Patt...dmm [Design]*		
🔲 Mining Structure ⃠ Mining Models 🔲 Mining Model Viewer 🔲 Mining Accuracy Chart 🔲 Mining Model Prediction		
Structure ∧	Decision Trees	Clustering
	🔲 Microsoft_Decision_Trees	🔲 Microsoft_Clustering
🔲 Customer Key	🔲 Key	🔲 Key
🔲 Gender	🔲 Input	🔲 Input
🔲 Interest	🔲 Input	🔲 Input
🔲 Music	🔲 PredictOnly	🔲 PredictOnly
🔲 Occupation	🔲 Input	🔲 Input

Figure 13-7. *Creating the second mining model*

Now that we have created the models, we need to build, deploy, and process the models. This is to create the mining structure in SQL Server Analysis Services, populate the structure with raw data, and calculate the result using the correct data mining algorithms. Right-click anywhere on the table shown in Figure 13-7, and choose Process Mining Structure and All Models. BIDS will ask whether we want to build and deploy the model first. Click Yes. After building and deploying the model, BIDS displays the Process Mining Structure dialog box, as shown in Figure 13-8.

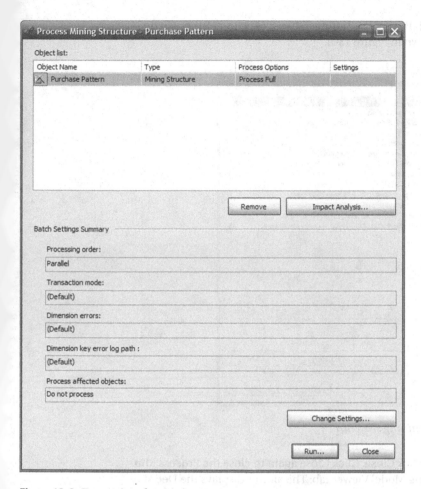

Figure 13-8. *Processing the mining structure*

In this window we specify the settings we want to use when processing the mining structure. When processing a mining structure, we have four process options:

- Process Full drops and repopulates data in all mining models in the mining structure.

- Process Structure populates the mining structure with source data.

- Process Clear Structure removes all training data from the mining structure.

- Unprocess drops the data in all mining models in the mining structure.

The Impact Analysis button lists which other SSAS objects are affected by the processing task. The Change Settings button enables us to change the processing order (whether the mining models are processed sequentially, one model at a time, or parallel, which is all models simultaneously), the transaction mode if we process sequentially (process in one transaction or in separate transactions), how to handle dimensional errors (whether to convert to an unknown record or discard the record, how to handle invalid keys, null keys and duplicate keys, and so on), and whether the processes affected objects.

In this case, we are happy to go with the default settings, so just click Run. BIDS will display the progress as we go along, as shown in Figure 13-9.

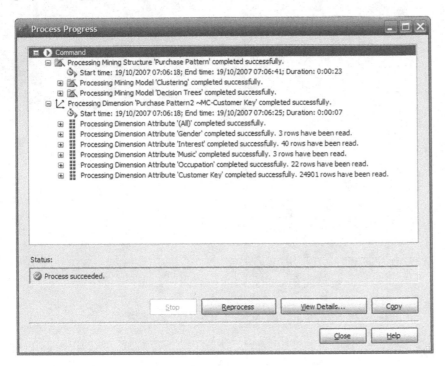

Figure 13-9. *The progress of processing a mining structure*

After the processing is completed, click Close. Click Close again to close the Process Mining Structure dialog box. Click the Mining Model Viewer tab. The viewer displays the Decision Trees model using Microsoft Tree Viewer. As shown in Figure 13-10, there are 298 customers with interest = 'Pop Music', and 264 of them (88 percent) purchased music products from Amadeus Entertainment. The Y and N equates to purchasing music because when populating the case table (dm_purchase_pattern), we store music purchases in the music column (see Figure 13-4), and when creating the mining model, we set music as the predictable column (as shown earlier in Listing 13-1).

In the figure, the shaded part shows how many customers in that segment purchased music products, and the unshaded part shows how many didn't. The group of customers who are interested in romance, management, and business are all unshaded, meaning that none of them purchased the music products. Classic and Asian Music, on the other hand, have long

shaded lines, meaning that the majority of them purchased music products. You can display
the numeric details of each box by placing the cursor on those boxes. We can show more levels
by moving the slider. We can move and navigate around the canvas easier by clicking the +
sign on the bottom-right corner of the canvas.

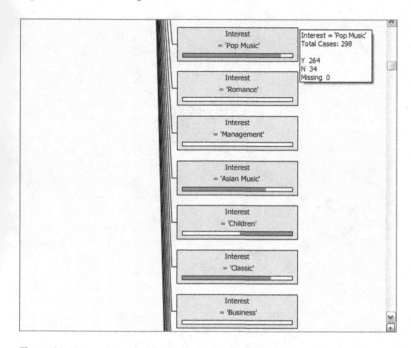

Figure 13-10. *Examining the correlation between interest and music purchase*

Click the Dependency Network tab to see the relationship between the demographic factors (gender, interest, and occupation) and music purchases, as shown in Figure 13-11. You
can understand the strength of the relationship using the slider on the left. When we move the
slider down, the arrow with the weak relationship will disappear.

A *dependency network* diagram shows the relationship or dependency between the
input columns and the predictable columns (please refer to Figure 13-4 when we specified
the columns in our mining model). These columns are called *nodes* (represented as ellipses
in Figure 13-11). When we select a node (by clicking it), the nodes are color-coded; the
selected node is in light blue, the input columns are in red, the predictable columns are in

dark blue, and if a column is used for both input and predictable, it is in purple. For example, although the colors aren't shown in Figure 13-11, Music is the selected node, and Interest and Occupation are the input columns.

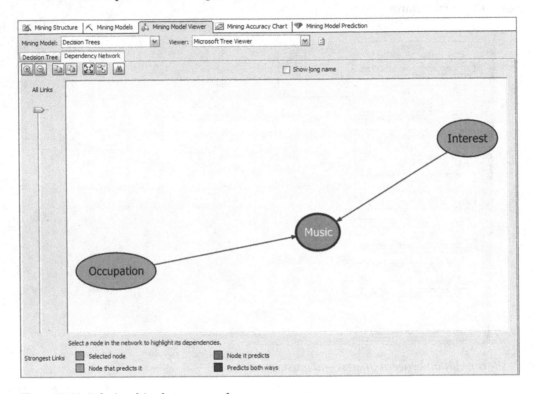

Figure 13-11. *Relationships between nodes*

In the dependency network diagram, only input columns that affect the predictable column are shown. Figure 13-11 shows that only interest and occupation affects music purchase; gender doesn't.

We can move the slider downward to find out which demographic factor has stronger influence on the music purchase: occupation or interest. Figure 13-12 shows what happens when we move the slider downward to the bottom. It shows that occupation has stronger influence because it is the only node with an arrow pointing to music. The arrow on the interest node has disappeared.

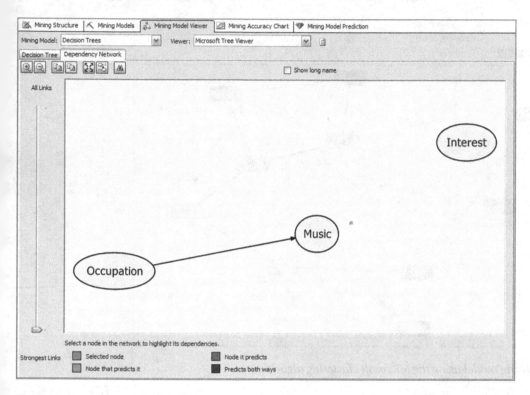

Figure 13-12. *Moving the slider downward shows the strongest link.*

We can also view the other model that we built using the clustering algorithm by choosing the model in the drop-down list. BIDS will ask whether we want to build and deploy the model first. Say Yes to this offer. Figure 13-13 shows the result.

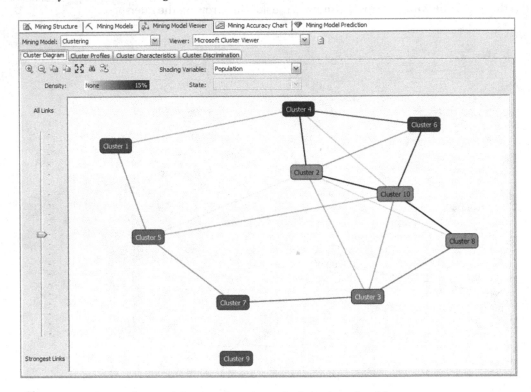

Figure 13-13. *The mining model using the Microsoft clustering algorithm*

The Microsoft clustering algorithm uses iterative techniques to group the rows in our dm_purchase_pattern table into ten clusters that contain similar characteristics. Figure 13-13 shows how the ten clusters are similar to each other; in other words, the darker the line between two clusters, the more similar those clusters are. By default, the graph displays the population size; in other words, the bluer the cluster box, the more customers in that cluster.

In Figure 13-13, we can change what data the shading color is showing. For example, we can show interest in gardening by changing the Shading Variable drop-down list to Interest and the State drop-down list to Gardening, as shown in Figure 13-14.

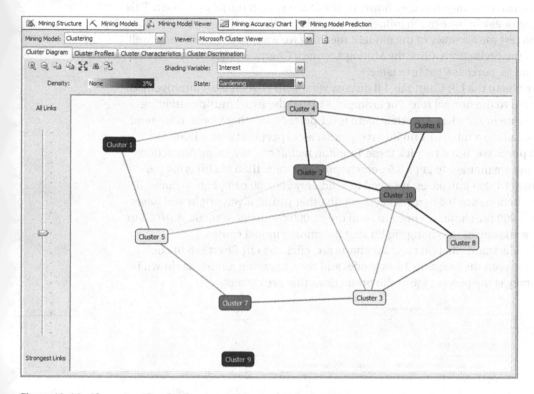

Figure 13-14. *Changing the shading variable on the cluster diagram*

We can see the profile of each cluster by clicking the Cluster Profile tab, as shown in Figure 13-15.

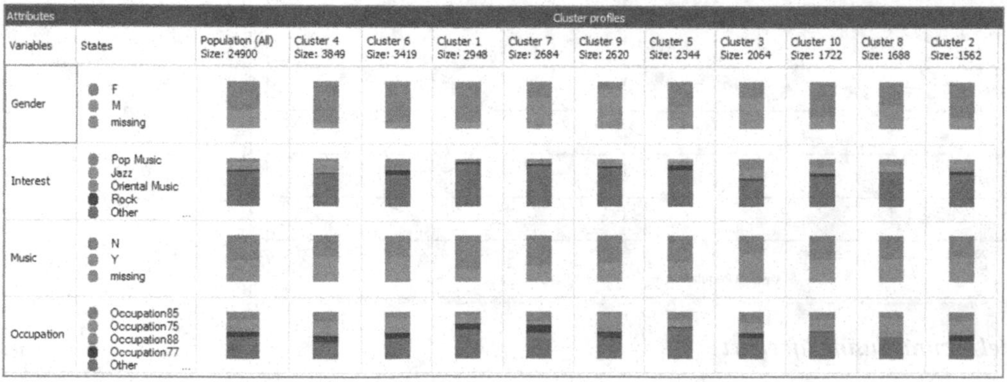

Figure 13-15. *The profile of each cluster*

We can use the cluster profiles to find out whether a particular demographic attribute affects the music purchase. For example, let's compare clusters 2 and 9 in Figure 13-15. Clusters 2 and 9 have similar interests, similar occupations, and very different genders (cluster 2 is mostly female, and cluster 9 is mostly male); however, they have similar music purchases. This indicates that gender does not have much influence on music purchases.

We now need to test the accuracy of the models, meaning we want to determine how well the models perform the predictions. Click the Mining Accuracy Chart tab, click Select Case Table, and choose the dm_purchase_pattern table.

Before we continue to the Lift Chart tab, I'll discuss what a *lift* is. A lift is an improvement in response compared to the normal rate. For example, say that the usual music marketing campaign purchase rate in Amadeus Entertainment is 0.1 percent; in other words, if we send music campaign e-mails to a random 1 million recipients, we expect that about 1,000 customers will make a purchase. But if we pick these 1 million recipients, say, using predictions from data mining and we manage to get a 0.5 percent purchase rate, then the lift is 0.4 percent. In this case, to get 1,000 purchases, we need to send only 200,000 campaign e-mails. If the data mining predictions are 100 percent accurate (in other words, always right and never wrong), then to get 1,000 purchases we need to send only 1,000 campaign e-mails. A *lift chart* is a graphical representation of the change in lift that the mining model causes.

Now that you understand what lifts and lift charts are, click the Lift Chart tab to compare the accuracy between the Decision Trees model and the Clustering model, as shown in Figure 13-16. Accuracy is the percentage of the predictions that are correct.

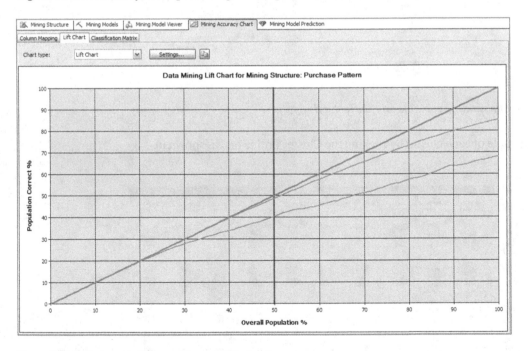

Figure 13-16. *Test model accuracy using lift chart*

In Figure 13-16, the straight line shows the ideal scenario where the prediction is always correct. In this case, the prediction is whether a customer will purchase music products. The line closest to ideal shows the Decision Trees model, and the line below that shows the Clustering model. We can see that when the x-axis is at 100 percent population, the Decision Trees model is 85 percent correct, whereas the Clustering model is 69 percent correct. This means that when using all the data in the dm_purchase_pattern table to guess which customers made music purchases and which ones did not, the Decision Tree model was 85 percent correct, while the Clustering model was only 69 percent correct. This shows that the Decision Trees model is more accurate than the Clustering model for predicting music purchases based on demographic attributes.

You may ask, why is the Decision Tree model more accurate than the Clustering model? Is this always the case? You may also ask, when do I use the Decision Trees model and when do I use Clustering model? Even though in this particular case the Decision Tree model is more accurate than the Clustering model, in other cases it might not always be true. Both the Decision Tree model and the Clustering model are good for predicting a discreet column, such as a music purchase (which is a Yes or No value). But for predicting a continuous column, the Decision Tree model is better. Please refer to the discussion about content types earlier in this section about the differences between discreet and continuous columns. The Clustering model is better for finding groups of similar items, such as segmenting customers into groups based on demographic data for targeted mailings.

The next step is to deploy this mining structure into production and use it to predict whether a potential customer would be interested in purchasing music products. For the purpose of this exercise, we will use data from the same table. For that, let's click the Mining Model Prediction tab, click Select Case Table, and choose dm_purchase_pattern. Set the source, field, show, and criteria/argument columns, as shown in Figure 13-17, to select what columns we want to display in the output.

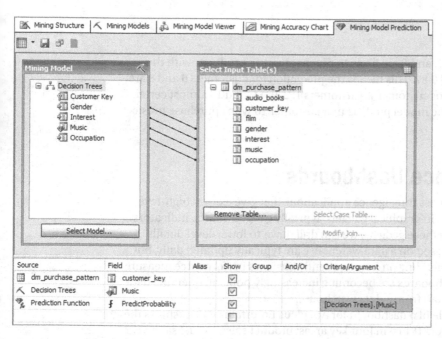

Figure 13-17. *Using the model to predict future values*

The rows on the table at the bottom of Figure 13-17 correspond to the columns we want to display in the prediction output in Figure 13-18. In this case, we want to display three columns in the prediction output: customer key, music, and prediction probability. The first row means we want to display the `customer_key` column from the `dm_purchase_pattern` table in the output. The second row means we want to display music purchases from the Decision Trees model. The third row means we want to display the probability of the music purchase prediction using the PredictProbability function, in other words, how certain we are about the result. The probability level is expressed as a decimal number between 0 and 1; 0 means not sure at all, and 1 means 100 percent certain. PredictProbability is a Data Mining Extensions (DMX) function that users cannot configure. It returns the probability of a given value in a discreet column.

To view the prediction results, click the first icon in the toolbar. Figure 13-18 shows the result.

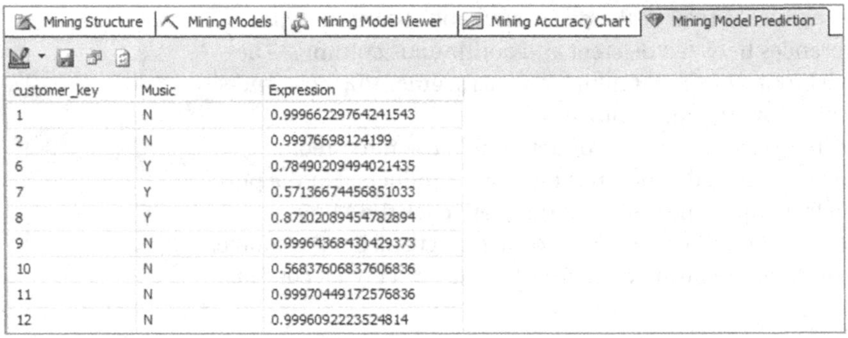

customer_key	Music	Expression
1	N	0.99966229764241543
2	N	0.99976698124199
6	Y	0.78490209494021435
7	Y	0.57136674456851033
8	Y	0.87202089454782894
9	N	0.99964368430429373
10	N	0.56837606837606836
11	N	0.99970449172576836
12	N	0.9996092223524814

Figure 13-18. *The prediction output*

In Figure 13-18, customers 6, 7, and 8 are likely to purchase music products, with the probability levels of 0.78, 0.57, and 0.87. This means the prediction for customers 6 and 8 are more certain than the prediction for customer 7. Customers 1, 2, 9, 11, and 12 almost certainly won't purchase music products. The model predicts that customer 10 won't purchase music either, but it's not so certain.

Business Intelligence Dashboards

Dashboards are a category of business intelligence applications that give a quick high-level summary of business performance in graphical gadgets, typically gauges, charts, indicators, and color-coded maps. By clicking these gadgets, we can drill down to lower-level details. Dashboard applications that are based on a data warehouse are typically updated daily, but sometimes weekly or monthly, depending on how frequently business performance measurements are required. Real-time dashboards are becoming increasingly popular, querying data from operational systems rather than from a data warehouse.

Figure 13-19 shows an example of a dashboard for Amadeus Entertainment. It shows the top-level key performance indicators (KPIs) in four key areas: product sales (actual sales year-to-date vs. target), subscription sales (the number of subscriptions compared to the target), supplier performance (one for each product category plus streaming media), and customer relationship management (bounce rate, open rate, click-through rate, and CRM revenue).

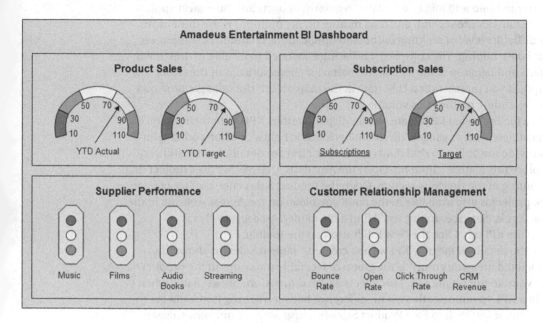

Figure 13-19. *Amadeus Entertainment BI dashboard*

Dashboard applications were initially used by upper-level management (senior managers and C-level executives) to analyze business performance. Today all levels of management use dashboards as the applications become increasingly closer to operational level rather than for analysis. Dashboard applications have become important and useful tools for managing business operations and driving business performance. If there are problems in achieving business targets and budgets, operation managers and directors need to know as early as possible so they have the time to take action to rectify the problems; in other words, if the target is monthly, they want the data daily. The critical factor for the successful implementation of dashboard applications is to determine the correct KPIs and regularly update these indicators with the correct data. The old saying is true: we get what we measure.

Key performance indicators are metrics that reflect business objectives. Different business areas have different KPIs. For sales departments, weekly or monthly sales revenue and profit margin, by region or store, are important KPIs, especially if they are compared against the target figures. For finance, debtor days, operating profit, and return on equity are some KPIs. KPIs are different from organization to organization. Other examples of popular KPIs are customer churns, market share, employee turnover, customer satisfaction rating, and product profitability.

Dashboard applications incorporate these KPIs into visual gadgets that are very clear and easy to understand and keep up-to-date. It can also show the trend or progress (in other words, down or up) of the KPI by comparing the current value to a previous period. The main advantages of dashboard applications are the ability to understand the overall status of the entire business in a quick glance (because of the visual gadgets and because of the correct KPIs) and the ability to drill down to a more detailed level if necessary. The disadvantages are that they are not easy to build and must be updated regularly. Reports are the easiest application to build, OLAP analytics are second, and data mining (in my opinion) is the third most complicated. The difficulty level of building dashboard applications is somewhere between OLAP analytics and data mining. The complexity is because we need to be able to drill down to lower-level details and because of the interactive behavior characteristics of the visual objects. For example, if you mouse over a U.S. state in the map object, the sales gauge shows red/green/yellow depending on the sales volume.

SSAS provides a facility called KPI where we can display various KPIs with their trends in the form of visual gadgets such as gauges, thermometers, traffic lights, or color-coded cylinders. It does not provide the ability to drill down to the lower level of details, but it's still very useful. So, let's explore this feature a little bit. Open the Amadeus Analysis Services project that we used for data mining in the previous section. Open the Product Sales cube that we created in Chapter 12. The project is also available in the book download on the Apress website; in the Cubes\ Amadeus Analysis Services folder you'll find a file named Amadeus Analysis Services.sln. Click the KPI tab. Click the New KPI button on the toolbar.

Let's complete the details of the new KPI we just created. Name it **Sales**, as shown in Figure 13-20. "Associated measure group" is the group of fact table measures in the product sales cube that we want to put on the KPI. This affects which dimensions are available when the users browse this KPI. In our case, there is no difference between setting it to <All> (as shown in Figure 13-20) or setting it to Fact Product Sales because we have only one measure group in the cube.

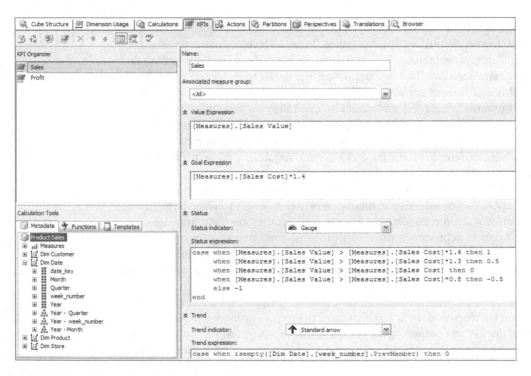

Figure 13-20. *Setting up KPIs*

"Value expression" in Figure 13-20 contains the value of the KPI. To put the sales value as a KPI, let's set this to [Measures].[Sales Value]. "Goal expression" contains the goal value of the KPI. For this exercise, let's set it to [Measures].[Sales Cost]*1.4, which means the target for the KPI is for the sales value to be greater than or equal to 1.4 * Sales Cost.

"Status indicator" determines the type of visual gadget for this KPI. Set it to Gauge. "Status expression" controls the status of the gauge, in other words, when it is green, yellow, or red. The gauge will be green if the status expression is 1, yellow if 0, and red if -1. It will be between green and yellow if the status expression is 0.5 and between yellow and red if the status expression is -0.5. Set the status expression as follows:

```
case when [Measures].[Sales Value] > [Measures].[Sales Cost]*1.6 then 1
  when [Measures].[Sales Value] > [Measures].[Sales Cost]*1.3 then 0.5
  when [Measures].[Sales Value] > [Measures].[Sales Cost] then 0
  when [Measures].[Sales Value] > [Measures].[Sales Cost]*0.8 then -0.5
  else -1
end
```

This language is Multidimensional Expressions (MDX), which is a scripting language that is used to specify a subset of cube data or to specify an expression when dealing with multi-dimensional databases (MDBs). Using MDX, you can do the following:

- Create, drop, and work with MDB objects.

- Retrieve and manipulate data from/in MDB.

- Create MDX scripts to manage the scope, context, and program flow.

- Use MDX operators and functions for manipulating data retrieved from MDB.

We can use MDX in SSIS, SSRS, and SSAS, as well as for performing ad hoc queries in BIDS. Basically, MDX is the scripting language for dealing with cubes.

In Figure 13-20, "Trend indicator" is the graphic that represents the trend value, such as up, down, or flat. There are four choices: standard arrow (black arrow), status arrow (green arrow), reverse status arrow (green arrow but with reverse direction), and faces (yellow smiley). Let's set the trend indicator to a standard arrow (or any other one if you like).

"Trend expression" is an MDX expression that returns the trend value; 1 means up, -1 means down, and 0 means flat. Let's set the trend expression as follows:

```
case when isempty([Dim Date].[week_number].PrevMember) then 0
  when [Measures].[Sales Value] > ([Dim Date].[week_number].PrevMember,
      [Measures].[Sales Value] * 1.2) then 1
  when [Measures].[Sales Value] > ([Dim Date].[week_number].PrevMember,
      [Measures].[Sales Value]) then 0
  else -1
end
```

The previous code sets the trend to up when this week's sales value is higher than 1.2 times last week's sales, flat when it's between 1 and 1.2, and down when this week's sales value is lower than last week.

Let's create another KPI called Profit. This time select the status indicator as a traffic light so we can compare it to the previous KPI, which is a gauge. The settings are similar to the first

KPI that we just set. Set "Associated measure group" to <All>, because we have only one measure group in the cube. Set the value expression to [Measures].[Sales Value]-[Measures].[Sales Cost] to describe that Profit = Sales – Cost. Set the goal expression to [Measures].[Sales Value]*0.5, meaning that the goal is to have a profit equal to half of the sales value. Set the status indicator to a traffic light; in other words, the status is green, yellow, or red. Set the status expression as follows:

```
case when ([Measures].[Sales Value]-[Measures].[Sales Cost]) >
     [Measures].[Sales Value]*0.5 then 1
     when ([Measures].[Sales Value]-[Measures].[Sales Cost]) > 0 then 0
     else -1
end
```

The previous code sets the Profit KPI to green when the profit is greater than 0.5 * sales, yellow when the profit is greater than 0 but less than 0.5 * sales, and red when the profit is negative. Set the trend indicator as a standard arrow and the trend expression as follows:

```
case when isempty([Dim Date].[week_number].PrevMember) then 1
when ([Measures].[Sales Value]-[Measures].[Sales Cost]) >
   1.2 * ([Dim Date].[week_number].PrevMember,
   ([Measures].[Sales Value]-[Measures].[Sales Cost])) then 1
when ([Measures].[Sales Value]-[Measures].[Sales Cost]) >
   1.1 * ([Dim Date].[week_number].PrevMember,
   ([Measures].[Sales Value]-[Measures].[Sales Cost])) then 0.5
when ([Measures].[Sales Value]-[Measures].[Sales Cost]) >
   ([Dim Date].[week_number].PrevMember,
   ([Measures].[Sales Value]-[Measures].[Sales Cost])) then 0
when ([Measures].[Sales Value]-[Measures].[Sales Cost]) >
   ([Dim Date].[week_number].PrevMember,
   0.9 * ([Measures].[Sales Value]-[Measures].[Sales Cost])) then -0.5
else -1
end
```

The previous code sets the profit trend to up when the profit is greater than 1.2 of last week's profit, half up (pointing to 2 o'clock direction) when the profit is between 1.1 and 1.2 of last week's profit, flat (pointing to the right) when the profit is between 1 and 1.1, half down (pointing to 4 o'clock direction) when the profit is between 0.9 and 1, and down when the profit is less than 0.9.

After everything is set up, click the ABC button to check that the syntax is correct. Click the Build menu, and choose Deploy. After deployment is completed successfully, click the Reconnect icon (it's the third icon from the left). This is necessary to reconnect to the Analysis Services cube after the KPIs have been added to the cube to pick up the changes we just made. To see the KPIs, with their values, goals, status, and trends, click the Browser View button (it's the second icon from the right). Let's pick up a certain product category and certain week to check whether the values, goals, status, and trends are correct for that week. Set the product category to Music and the date dimension to week 10 (you can pick other product categories and other weeks if you want), as shown in Figure 13-21.

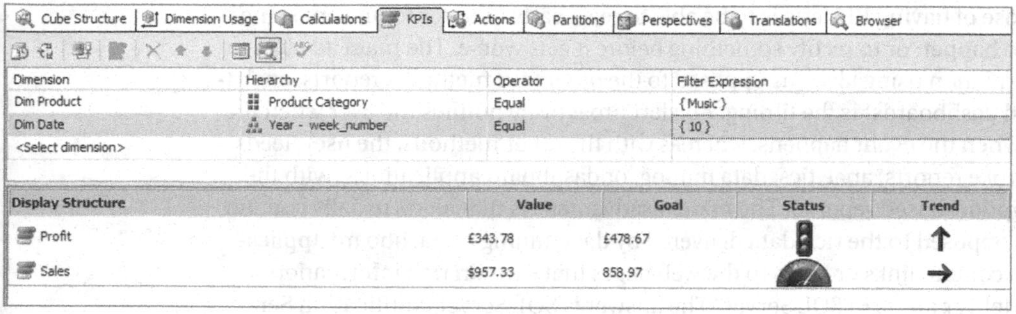

Dimension	Hierarchy	Operator	Filter Expression
Dim Product	Product Category	Equal	{ Music }
Dim Date	Year - week_number	Equal	{ 10 }
<Select dimension>			

Display Structure	Value	Goal	Status	Trend
Profit	£343.78	£478.67		↑
Sales	$957.33	858.97		→

Figure 13-21. *Viewing the KPIs*

The condition of the visual gadgets depends on the criteria that we specify in the MDX. Figure 13-21 shows that the status of Profit is yellow, meaning it is between 0 and 0.5 of the sales value. The trend for Profit is up, meaning it is more than 1.2 times the value in the previous period. The sales status is between yellow and green, which means it is between 1.3 and 1.6 times the sales cost. The sales trend is flat, meaning it's between 1 and 1.2 times the previous period.

In SQL Server, we can deliver a dashboard using SSAS and KPIs, as discussed. We can then put the KPIs that we built in SSAS as web parts and host them in SharePoint to create dashboard applications. ProClarity (now part of Microsoft), Microsoft Office Performance Point, and Business Scorecards Manager also have the ability to deliver dashboard applications.

Business Intelligence Alerts

Alerts are notifications to the users that a certain event or condition has happened. Examples of such events or conditions are the following:

- When a daily sales figure in any particular store falls under a certain percentage of the target

- When the number of account closures across the whole country is beyond a certain figure

- When the profit margins for certain product types across the whole region are lower than a preset limit

Again, remember that BI covers a wider area than just the data warehouse. A BI tool such as alert system can access the ODS and operational systems as well as the data warehouse. Therefore, we can distinctly differentiate BI alerts into two categories according to which system they get the data from: data warehouse alerts and operational system alerts. The main difference between these two is that the scope of operational system alerts is per transaction, whereas data warehouse alerts are at an aggregate level; for example, they can be weekly across product types or daily across regions. Examples of operational system alerts are an e-mail, pager, or SMS notification in the event that the stock level falls below a certain mark or when a booking order value is more than the customer credit limit.

The main purpose of having BI alerts is to be able to react early in order to prevent something that is about to happen or to rectify something before it gets worse. The main advantage of delivering BI information using alerts as opposed to the other four methods (reports, analytics, data mining, and dashboards) is the timing. An alert proactively notifies the user when the situation occurs or when the event happens, whereas with the other methods, the user needs to actively run or invoke reports, analytics, data mining, or dashboard applications (with the exception of subscription-based reports). The main disadvantage is that alerts usually contain only simple data, as opposed to the rich data delivered by data mining or dashboard applications. But, alerts can contain links or URLs to the web pages that contain rich information.

So, how do we deliver alerts in SQL Server? The answer is SQL Server Notification Services. Notification Services is a platform for developing and deploying applications that generate and send notifications to subscribers. Notification Services has four components: Subscription Management, Event Collection, Subscription Processing, and Notification Delivery. The Subscription Management component stores the subscribers, the information to be delivered, and the preferred delivery channels. The Event Collection component gathers the events from databases, file systems, or applications and sends these events to a notification application. Standard event providers are SQL Server (T-SQL queries), Analysis Services (MDX queries), and file system watcher (XML files). The Subscription Processing component evaluates the subscriptions to find a match against the collected events and then generates the notifications. The Notification Distribution component transforms the notification data into a readable message (web, file, or e-mail), formats the message, and sends it to the subscribers via the correct delivery channels.

Business Intelligence Portal

A BI portal is an application that functions as a gateway to access and manage business intelligence reports, analytics, data mining, and dashboard applications as well as alert subscriptions. It can be developed as a custom-built application (using Visual Studio .NET, for example) or using an off-the-shelf solution. Some BI vendors have products to construct a BI portal that put various reports, OLAP, scorecards, and dashboards (usually their own BI applications) into one place for easier and simpler access, including MicroStrategy 8 Dynamic Enterprise Dashboards, Hyperion 9 Interactive Reporting Dashboard Studio, and Cognos Portlets for IBM WebSphere Portal. Microsoft Office Business Scorecard Manager 2005 and Microsoft Office SharePoint Server 2007 also have a BI portal as a built-in sample application.

The main benefit of using a BI portal is that all BI applications are available in one central place. The second benefit is centralized security management. In other words, users need to log in only once to the portal, and they don't need to log in again to access each application. So, it is simpler for the administrator to manage the security. These days most BI portals are web-based so that users across different geographical regions can access them via the company intranet, extranet, or other platform. It is also common to place the BI documentation and user guides, as well as the support phone numbers and the link to the help desk application, on the BI portal for easy access by the users. You can also put BI and data warehouse news and announcements such as when you have new dashboards or when a particular sales report shows good results. Figure 13-22 shows an example of a BI portal.

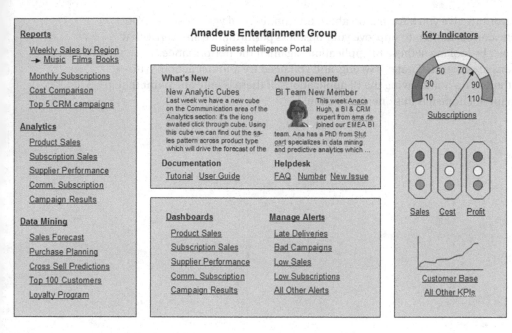

Figure 13-22. *Example of a BI portal*

So, how do we build a BI portal? Well, in its simplest form, it is a web page containing many links to various reports and BI applications. So, we can use ASP.NET to build it. With some documentation, a user guide, and other useful information added, it would become a good starting point for the BI users. For the implementation of business intelligence on the SQL Server platform, some people build the BI portal using SharePoint to take advantage of integrating Reporting Services web parts with SharePoint. (Reporting Services provides SharePoint components that we can include in the SharePoint portal. These components are called *web parts*.) Examples of Reporting Services SharePoint web parts are RsReportInfo, RsReportView, RsReportParameters, and RsReportExport. You can use RsReportInfo to get the report details. RsReportView is used for viewing the reports, so it's probably the most useful web part. RsReportParameters is for setting up reporting parameters. RsReportExport is for exporting reports to PDF, XML, Excel, or text files. On the SharePoint portal, you can also provide the link to the Reporting Services main page, where all the reports are kept in folders.

Summary

There are several types of BI applications such as reporting, analytics, data mining, dashboards, and alerts. In this chapter, I discussed each of these types one by one. I went through the detailed steps of creating key performance indicators in SQL Server Analysis Services 2005. I also discussed BI portals, which unify all the previous applications in one central place and simplify the security administration.

All these BI applications give you information about the condition of your business. You need to implement the correct actions to improve your business performance and verify that these actions are correct by looking at these BI applications again. If the performance is improving, your actions are correct. If not, it's wrong, and you need try another action. Without doing anything, there is no point having the BI applications. If there is only one point that you take from this chapter, I hope it is this one: take action!

CHAPTER 14

■ ■ ■

Using Data Warehouse for Customer Relationship Management

Customer Relationship Management (CRM) is the activity of establishing contact and managing communications with customers, analyzing information about customers, campaigning to attract new customers, performing business transactions with customers, servicing customers, and providing support to customers. Customers are the people (or parties) who a company or an organization serves; they're the ones who consume its products or services. If the organization is not a company or business (for example, a school or university, government agency, nonprofit organization, social club, political party, and so on), you can replace the word *customers* in the earlier definition with *students*, *constituents*, *citizens*, *taxpayers*, *users*, *applications*, *stakeholders*, and so on, whichever is most appropriate.

A CRM application is a system that a company or organization uses to create and send campaigns, analyze customers' personal and demographic information, analyze and predict customer behavior including purchases, perform customer scoring, manage customer permissions, manage customer support/service, integrate customer data, manage customer loyalty programs, and manage customer contacts (including complaints and resolutions). Some CRM applications cover only some of the functionalities listed here. CRM applications can be hosted internally in-house or hosted externally with an application support provider (ASP), meaning the application and data is hosted outside the company and the users access it remotely, usually via the Internet. An example of a hosted CRM solution is Salesforce.com, which offers customer data management, customer analysis, customer response management, and customer relationship history hosted on its servers over the Internet. CRM applications can be sold as part of an Enterprise Resource Planning (ERP) product suite, such as in the case of Siebel, SAP, and PeopleSoft, or it can be a stand-alone product such as Infor (Epiphany), Microsoft Dynamics CRM, and Teradata CRM.

Customer data can be stored centrally in a data warehouse or in an operational data store, where the customer data is integrated to produce a single-customer view (SCV). An SCV is an integrated collection of customer data from various data sources in one central place so you can have a holistic view of your customers. An SCV is important because it gives you a better understanding of your customers. I will discuss SCVs in more detail in the next section. The other major benefit of storing integrated customer data in the data warehouse is to perform customer analytics and data mining—both descriptive analytics (discovering the patterns in customer data) and predictive analytics (forecasting customer behaviors). Also, a dimensional data warehouse is an ideal platform to perform customer scoring (calculating the value of a customer using a particular formula, for example, based on their purchases), especially when the algorithm for scoring involves demographics and purchase analysis.

In this chapter, I will discuss how to use a data warehouse to perform CRM activities, including creating a single customer view, performing campaign segmentation, managing permissions, monitoring deliverability, performing customer analysis, managing customer support, managing personalization, and administering loyalty schemes.

Single Customer View

Organizations make contacts with their customers at various points. This results in various views or definitions of customers. If we asked our order-processing department about who our customers are, they would probably say, "Individuals who have purchased a product or service from us." If we asked our CRM department, they would probably have a different view. Their concept of a customer might be "Individuals who have purchased something from us, plus anybody who is currently subscribed to our newsletters." Another department, such as customer service, could have a different view of a customer. Their concept of a customer may be "Individuals who have put something in a shopping basket, even though they don't continue to the checkout." Finance may have a different view of a customer: "A customer is anybody who has paid us or owes us money."

The previous paragraph illustrates a common situation where different parts of the enterprise have their own view, or definition, of customers. Because of these different views, "the number of customers" is different from department to department. If we ask the order-processing department, they may say that the number of customers is 25 million, whereas the marketing department may say that the number of customers is 60 million.

This situation may be even worse if different departments are using different systems or applications. Marketing may be using Omniture, finance may be using SAP, and CRM may be using Siebel. In this situation, the customer data is scattered across several different systems, and each system has a different list of customers. Therefore, it is very difficult to compose a single definitive list of customers.

The concept of an SCV is to have a single definition about who a customer is. Only when we have a single common definition across all departments can we have a definitive list of customers. An SCV is an integrated collection of customer data from various data sources in one central place so we can have a holistic view of our customers.

Let's illustrate this with our case study, Amadeus Entertainment. A customer in Amadeus Entertainment can be a purchaser, subscriber, registered user, or various other definitions, depending on the department. Say that we have the following definitions of customers. These quantities are just some examples to show the effect of overlaps on the total (they don't come from our DDS sample database).

- Twenty-five million individuals have purchased Amadeus Entertainment's products.

- Thirty-five million individuals subscribe to its communications.

- Twenty million individuals have registered on the web sites.

- Forty-four million individuals have asked for quotes.

- Fifty-five million individuals have browsed its web sites.

- Thirty-one million individuals have downloaded something from the web sites.

- Twelve million individuals have participated in one of its online competitions.

- Seven million individuals have sent the company e-mails or called.

- Twenty-four million individuals have made payments to Amadeus Entertainment.

- Seventeen million individuals have accounts with Amadeus Entertainment.

This situation can be drawn in the Venn diagram shown in Figure 14-1. The circles on the diagram show the different customer definitions. The sizes of the circles reflect the quantities. Each circle intersects with other circles, meaning that the same customers can be included in several definitions. If the common definition of a customer of Amadeus Entertainment includes all of the previous (purchaser, subscriber, registered user, and so on), then the total number of customers that the company has is identified by the total area of the Venn diagram.

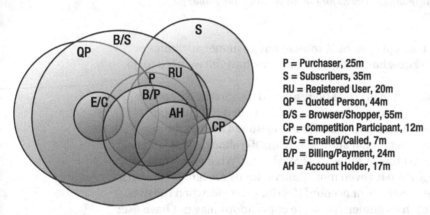

P = Purchaser, 25m
S = Subscribers, 35m
RU = Registered User, 20m
QP = Quoted Person, 44m
B/S = Browser/Shopper, 55m
CP = Competition Participant, 12m
E/C = Emailed/Called, 7m
B/P = Billing/Payment, 24m
AH = Account Holder, 17m

Figure 14-1. *Intersections between different customer definitions*

Because of the overlap, the total number of customers that Amadeus Entertainment has is not 25 million + 35 million + 20 million + 44 million + 55 million + 31 million + 12 million + 7 million + 24 million + 17 million = 270 million, but probably much less than that. In Figure 14-1, the total area is probably 1.5 of the largest circle (B/S, 55 million), giving us only 82.5 million. This situation is illustrated in the customer table shown in Table 14-1.

Table 14-1. *Customer Table Containing Different Customer Definitions*

Name	Email Address	P	S	RU	QP	B/S	CP	E/C	B/P	AH
Chloe Nicoletta	chloe@han.com	Y		Y		Y			Y	Y
Nicolina Luigia	nicolina@earth.org				Y	Y				
Deni Hudd	deni@bc.org					Y			Y	
Bernardine Avril	bavril@msn.com		Y				Y			
	a_ilaria@gmail.com							Y		
Jojo Emilie	jojo@aol.com				Y	Y			Y	
Serafina Hodge	serafin@giant.es	Y		Y		Y				Y
	tina@hans.com		Y							
a_harvey@can.it		Y								
Orsola Velia	man33@yahoo.com		Y				Y			

P stands for Purchaser, S stands for Subscriber, RU stands for Registered User, QP stands for Quoted Person, B/S stands for Browser/Shopper, CP stands for Competitor Participant, E/C stands for E-mailed/Called, B/P stands for Billing/Payment, and AH stands for Account Holder.

Table 14-1 shows the simplified concept of an SCV, without any customer attributes or links to other areas. When we want to know how many customers we have, all we need to do is use select count (*).

Table 14-1 probably looks simple, but in practice there are two things that we need to consider when creating an SCV. First, how do we identify, match, and deduplicate a customer? This is fundamental to SCV. If we have a new customer registered on the web site today, say her name is Orsola Velia and her e-mail address is man33@yahoo.com, is she the same person as the customer on the last row in Table 14-1? Maybe not. What if we know only her e-mail address but not her name? Then it's even more difficult for us to identify or match the customer. Some applications have user IDs or account IDs (for example, when the user is registered) that uniquely identify each customer. But some applications may not have user IDs or account IDs (for example, when a user subscribes to a newsletter). So, we need to agree on the business rules for identifying, matching, and deduplicating customers; for example, we could agree that a customer can be identified by an account ID if available and, if not, by an e-mail address and the source system. Matching (to determine whether two customers are the same customer) is quite a risky business, so we want to get it right the first time. If we are not careful, orders from customer A could be under customer B's name. Surely we don't want that to happen.

The second issue to consider when creating an SCV is the customer attributes. Because the definition of a customer is different across different departments in an organization (as described earlier), the customer attributes have different levels of richness (the number of attributes). For example, if it is a subscriber, we know only the name and e-mail address. If it is a purchaser, we know their name, e-mail address, address, and phone number. If it is a competition participant (they filled in a customer survey), we know their name, e-mail address, address, phone number, date of birth, occupation, and interests. So when using the SCV data, we need to be aware that we don't have all the attributes for all the customers. For example, perhaps we have addresses only for 60 percent of our customers, we have names for 80 percent of our customers, and for email address we have 95 percent coverage.

In many organizations, customer data is scattered across different systems. The systems may have different applications (ERP systems) between the stores and the e-commerce web sites or between marketing contacts and promotions. They may use different agencies for e-mail promotions (which means that the data is even more scattered). For example, an international business group consists of different individual legal entities (companies or agencies), which are composed of many brands that may be located in many countries. Some occurred by acquisitions; in other words, the group purchased a subsidiary company. Some happened via merger; in other words, two big business groups joined together. We could be talking about 30 to 100 individual legal entities (worldwide). There is no way that all these companies are using the same application to manage their business. But if you are talking about a small business with three offices all under one legal entity, it is possible that they have a single application to manage their business, at least with regard to where the customer data is stored. But for an international business that exists in 50 countries, it is unlikely. This means the customer data is likely to be scattered all over the place.

So, is it possible to have a centralized customer database containing personal information, their orders, their preferences, their quotes, their e-mail promotions, their downloads, their contact details, their interests, their subscriptions, their complaints, their queries, their credit score, their loyalty score, their browsing/shopping history, their account details, their competition participations, their payments, their registration details, and their security details all in one central place? Luckily, the answer is yes. It's hard work, but it is possible. Many CRM initiatives started by integrating customer data. Projects such as Customer Data Integration (CDI) hubs and Operational Data Stores (ODS) centralize customer data into one place; they probably also publish this data for other applications to consume via a software as a service (SaaS) scheme in a Service Oriented Architecture (SOA). Sometimes, in less than ideal situations, they don't have CDI hubs or an ODS, and the only place where customer data is integrated is in the data warehouse, in other words, in the customer dimension.

An SCV is important because it gives us a better understanding of our customers; basically, it gives us a more complete view. We get different attributes from different sources. For example, from the registration database, we get their user IDs, names, and addresses. From the order-processing system, we get contact telephone numbers, e-mail addresses, billing addresses (which may be different from the registered address), and perhaps the credit card details. From the promotion and competition system, we could get their occupation, marriage status, number of children, salary range, interests/communication preferences, and permissions (for us to send them marketing-related material), and perhaps they can even subscribe to one or two newsletters. From customer service systems, perhaps we can get information about which products they don't like or which service they like best. Perhaps from customer loyalty programs, we can get their input about what products and services need to be improved, which benefits are valuable or not valuable to them, and what we can do to help them more. When we combine the data from various systems, we get a more complete view about the customers. The more we know about our customers, the more we can tailor our products and services to meet their interests and needs, and the business becomes more successful. So, an SCV is about an integrated view of our customers from various sources.

What are the advantages of having an SCV in the data warehouse, compared to having it in the ODS or CDI, for example? The first advantage is a slowly changing dimension (SCD), particularly type 2. SCD is a technique used in dimensional modeling for preserving historical information about dimensional data. In SCD type 2, we keep the historical information in rows, while in SCD type 3, we keep the historical information in columns. In SCD type 1, we don't keep the historical information. (Please refer to Chapter 5 for more information about SCD.) The advantage of having historical information is the data richness. With an SCD, we have richer customer data in the data warehouse, because of historical information. For example, in the case of the customer dimension, we can use SCD type 2 to store the previous address, the previous occupation, or, more important, the previous loyalty scores and subscriber bands. The last two are calculated based on their purchases and subscriptions and based on the revenue and/or profit the customer produced. So for customers who were previously on higher bands, we may want to tailor our offerings a little bit by presenting them with more suitable products or services, thus potentially resulting in more revenue from customers.

The second advantage of using a data warehouse for an SCV is the analytical nature of a dimensional data warehouse, enabling us to perform better customer analysis, which results in a better understanding of the customers. This can potentially drive the business to be more successful. A dimensional data warehouse is an ideal place for performing analysis, such as analyzing customer purchase behavior or subscription dynamics to get the customer score and subscription band, which can then be persisted as a customer attribute. I'm not saying that we can't do this in the ODS, CDI, or ERP; I'm saying that data warehouse is a better place to perform that analysis. In terms of performance, this analysis is better performed on a dimensional database than on a normalized database, particularly on a star schema. This is because in a normalized database we need to do a lot of joins between tables. Analyzing five years of order data against 20 million customers (with SCD type 2) using data mining algorithms will probably affect the operational performance of our normalized ERP, CDI, or ODS. Say it is 30 million order lines per year. Say that SCD type 2 on average creates one historical row for each customer, so we are talking 40 million rows on customer data. Say we use three algorithms: Decision Trees, Clustering, and Naive Bayes. So, we are talking about running analysis on the ODS or ERP for 150 million order data items against 40 million customer data items and say 10,000 product data items using three algorithms. How long would it take to run? It could take from a few hours to a few days. I'm sure the internal front-end users won't be happy that the system performance is so slow during the hours the analysis runs. Can you imagine the impact on revenue if customers can't add an item to a shopping basket or if the checkout system is affected in any way? No, I don't think anybody would run this kind of analysis on anything that affects the front-end systems. By having SCV customer data on the data warehouse, the customer purchase and subscription analysis results will be better in terms of performance.

The third advantage of using a data warehouse for an SCV is the computational power of a data warehouse system. A data warehouse system is designed and built to be able to handle large data-processing requirements. A data warehouse system is designed to be able to process queries involving large data sets efficiently such as by having physical table partitions. If the data is 10MB to 20MB, it probably won't matter on which platform we perform the SCV, for example doing deduplication and customer matching, but for large data (say greater than 1TB), it matters. You can analyze your situation by running analytical queries on your current platform. Extracting information from marketing data, registration data, order data, competition data, and subscription data and then updating the customer data including matching and deduplication for upsert (update and insert) is best performed on platforms specifically designed for large queries.

The fourth advantage of using a data warehouse for SCV is that the customer data in the data warehouse is already integrated from various source systems, so it enables us to combine customer attributes from different sources. If we have an ODS or a CDI hub, then we could do SCV there, subject to the earlier considerations. But in many cases where there is no ODS or CDI, the data warehouse can be the only integration point of customer data in the organization. So when we do an SCV in the data warehouse, we will work with complete customer data that has been integrated from various source systems.

Campaign Segmentation

A *campaign* is a communication sent to customers regularly or on an ad hoc basis via e-mail, post, RSS, or text messages and containing marketing promotions (cross-sale, up sale, and so on) or notifications. Weekly newsletters, new product tactical promotions, and price increase notifications are examples of campaigns. An order confirmation e-mail is an example of a communication sent to customers that is not a campaign. It is considered to be a transactional communication.

Before we move on, let me introduce some of the campaign terminology normally used in CRM. A *campaign* is a communication sent to customers. A *delivery channel* is the media used to send the campaign, such as post, e-mail, text message, or RSS. RSS is a web feed used to publish frequently updated content. Some delivery channels have several content formats. For example, in e-mail messages, there are two content formats: HTML format and text format.

Open rate and *click-through rate* are terms used in e-mail campaigns. Open rate is the number of e-mail messages that were opened by the customer divided by the number of messages sent. For example, if we sent 100,000 e-mail messages and 20,000 of them were opened, the open rate is 20 percent. The click-through rate, commonly abbreviated as CTR, is the number of customers who clicked the hyperlink embedded in the e-mail messages to go to the web site divided by the number of e-mail messages sent. For example, if we sent 100,000 e-mail messages and 4,000 of them were clicked, then the CTR was 4 percent.

The *delivery rate* is the number of e-mail messages that are delivered successfully divided by the number of e-mail messages sent. The *bounce rate* is the number of e-mail messages that are not delivered successfully to the intended recipient divided by the number of e-mail messages sent. For example, if we sent 100,000 e-mail messages and 98,000 were delivered successfully, then the delivery rate is 98 percent, and the bounce rate is 2 percent.

Now let's continue our discussion about campaigns. A campaign is a fundamental cornerstone of CRM activity. Put simply, the process of creating a CRM campaign is roughly as follows (bear in mind that this is different from company to company):

1. Based on the business need, we decide which customers we want to target (and quantify roughly how many), what message we want to deliver to them (just a brief paragraph describing the idea), the frequency of the campaign (for example, every week or one time only), the batch sizes (for example, in chunks of 150,000/day), the delivery channel (for example, 10 percent by RSS and 90 percent by HTML e-mail), and the expected results (for example, 15 percent open rate, 5 percent click-through rate, and $200,000 additional revenue/month). For example, we want to offer service Y to customers who purchased product X in the last six months.

2. Create a selection query that selects from a database a list of customers who satisfy certain criteria, such as customers who purchased product X in the last six months.

3. Compose the content of the campaign, one for each delivery channel and format. We check all the links in the content and test the campaign appearance/cosmetics on every major e-mail and RSS client to ensure that our customers will see the campaign as it was designed to be.

4. Set up the campaign in the campaign management system, paste the selection query, load the content file, add the control group, execute it, send it to testers, obtain final approval, execute it, and send it out to customers.

5. Monitor the delivery rate, bounce rate, open rate, click-through rate, and the revenue increase resulting from the campaign.

A campaign targets a list of customers. This list, as illustrated in step 2, is called a *segment*. The simplest form of a campaign is where we have only one segment. This is called an *unsegmented campaign*. It is rather strange that it is called *unsegmented* even though it has one segment, but that's the term used in CRM. A more complex campaign contains more than one segment. For example, we can divide the list based on where the customer lives; in other words, we send different offers for different areas. Or we can divide the list based on their preferred communication channel and format. We need to prepare separate content files for each campaign format, for example, one for HTML e-mail and one for text-only e-mail. When a campaign is segmented, each segment receives different campaign content, because the content is tailored to each segment. For example, we could have a campaign targeting two different segments: male and female, each with different content. It's not only the content that is different for each segment, but the actions could be different too, specifically the sending times, the number of send retries, the bounce treatments, and the further selections, to suit the segment we are targeting. For example, for segment 1 the best sending time is at lunchtime, and for segment 2 the best sending time is in the morning. The combination of content and actions that we apply to a particular segment is called *treatment*.

Whether the campaign is segmented (several lists of customers each receiving different campaign treatments) or unsegmented (one list of customers receiving one campaign treatment), we need to query the customer data to get lists of customers. This process is commonly known as the *list selection* process, and the SQL query is known as the *selection query*. Some tools do the segmentation first and then perform the selection query for each segment, and some tools combine the selection queries for different segments together in one query. To give you an idea, Listing 14-1 shows the simplest form of selection query for an unsegmented campaign.

Listing 14-1. *Example of a Selection Query*

```
select c1.email_address
from fact_subscription f
inner join dim_customer c1
  on f.customer_key = c1.customer_key
inner join dim_campaign c2
  on f.campaign_key = c2.campaign_key
where c2.campaign_name = 'Music Newsletter'
```

The selection query in Listing 14-1 retrieves the customer e-mail addresses for an e-mail campaign called Music Newsletter. There is no further selection on the query, which is why it is called an unsegmented campaign.

In my experience, there are four types of selection queries: permission, demographic data, customer activities, and campaign response:

Permission: Permission is basically the consent from a customer that we can send them this communication, such as a subscription to a newsletter on our web site. A permission selection query is basically a query selecting a list of customers from whom we have consent to send this communication. For any campaign we must always have a permission selection query. Listing 14-1 is an example of a selection query for permission.

Demographic data: Demographic data is a customer's personal attributes, such as age, gender, location, occupation, income, interest, and number of children. A demographic data selection query retrieves a list of customers based on these customer attributes, such as `where calculate_age(date_of_birth) between 20 and 30` or `where occupation = 'Student'`.

Customer behavior: Every business or organization conducts transactions or activities with their customers. Customer behaviors are the actions that the customers do or don't do within these activities or transactions. Each industry has different customer behavior. For the retail and e-commerce industry, it is browsing and purchasing behavior; for telecommunications and utilities, it is usage behavior; and for financial services it is account activities. Examples of customer behavior selection queries are a list of customers who made an order more than 12 months ago (known as *sleeping customers*) or customers who use their cell phone less than 10 times a month.

Campaign response: When a customer receives an e-mail campaign from us, the customer can have three responses: delete the e-mail (or do nothing), open the e-mail, or click a link on that e-mail. These three possible actions are called *campaign responses*. So, we can have a selection query producing a list of customers who have opened the previous three campaigns but have not made any purchase in the last three months and then target them specifically in the next campaign.

What is the benefit of using a data warehouse for campaign selection and segmentation? Well, it is easier and faster. Producing a list of customers who made an order more than 12 months ago is more easily done on a data warehouse than in an operational system. Consider a query to get a list of customers who have purchased certain product types in the last 12 months but did not purchase other product types, who have not been sent a campaign in the last three days, who have given permission for us to send them promotional campaigns, who live in certain cities, and whose customer status is active. This query runs faster (minutes rather than hours) in a dimensional data warehouse than in an OLTP system because the data model in an operational system is not specifically designed to support an analytical query like this. The main difference between an OLTP query and an analytical query is that an OLTP query retrieves a few records (in other words, where `order_id = X`), whereas an analytical query summarizes millions of records (such as the query I mentioned earlier). An OLTP system is primary designed to insert or update a particular record(s) with split-second performance. It is not designed to summarize millions of records. Hence, it could take hours to run analytical-type queries, not because of the hardware but because of the way the database is designed.

A regular campaign's segmentation queries may run once a week when it is operational. But when designing the campaign, the business user needs to run the segmentation queries many times to get the counts of intended recipients. This is a repetitive process, and if it takes hours to complete the counts, then it slows down the business process and decreases the user friendliness.

The other benefit is capacity. Campaign delivery and response data are large. A data warehouse can naturally cope with such demand using the Campaign Results fact table described in Figure 5-6 in Chapter 5. In that structure, various statuses are easily loaded into the fact table: sent, delivered, bounced, opened, clicked through, and so on. This campaign response data can then be used for the selection query on future campaigns, as described earlier.

Permission Management

We must send campaigns only to those customers from which we have consent. This consent is known as *permission*. Maintaining permissions is the most important thing in CRM operations because sending a campaign without a customer's permission means we are spamming. In some countries, the laws are very strict and include heavy penalties for spammers, including the Spam Bill in Australia, Penal Code Article 226-18 in France, and the CAN-SPAM Act in the United States.

There are four types of customer permission:

General permission: In this type of permission, the customer gives consent for us to send them any marketing-related communications. Sometimes the consent is extended to "affiliates" or "carefully selected partners" as well. This is usually done via a little check box when the customer registers, accompanied with very small print, or on a marketing preferences web page. This is generally known as *opt-in*. In CRM, it is common practice to do *double opt-in*. In other words, we send an e-mail to the customer's e-mail address, and the customer needs to click a link in that e-mail to confirm their consent. There are two major benefits of double opt-in:

- Customers can submit only their own e-mail address.

- The list contains only valid and tested e-mail addresses.

Specific permission: In this case, the customer allows us to send a specific type of communication, for example only transaction-related communications such as order confirmation e-mails, payment receipts, and e-tickets. Or they want to receive only e-mails related to products that they have purchased, such as a flight reminder, destination guide (for gifts), download link (for computer products), or product withdrawal notice. We cannot use specific permissions to send any other e-mails such as new products announcements. Specific permission also can be channel specific, such as "you can e-mail me, but you cannot call me."

Subscription: This type of permission is very specific. In this case, the customer subscribes to a specific campaign, such as subscribing to a weekly newsletter or music news (as in the case study Amadeus Entertainment). We can send them only the campaigns that the customer asked for in the format and delivery channel that the customer asked for. The permission cannot be used to send them anything else in any format.

Negative permission: Sometimes customers ask us not to send them anything. They don't want to receive any marketing material, news, announcements, product support, customer support, and transaction-related e-mails including order confirmation e-mails or payment receipts. For this kind of request where the customer revokes their consent, we could list them in a "banned e-mail addresses" table, and in every campaign we add the selection criteria like: `where e-mail_address not in (select e-mail_address from banned_e-mail_addresses)`. Alternatively, we could use `where not exist`. This table or list is also known as a *block list* or *black list*. Many CRM campaign management and e-mail delivery systems have this functionality; for example, we just need to configure them to point to the right table, and the system will filter it out when executing or sending campaigns.

Now that you know what permission is, what is the benefit of using a data warehouse for implementing permission? Permission is used in the selection query, and a dimensional data warehouse gives good performance when performing selection queries.

Subscription management is a transactional process and captured by the front-end applications, such as on the web site and customer service systems. General permission is also transactional in nature; that is, it is usually captured when customers register on the web site or when they become customers.

So, permission usually happens in the front-end applications, and it is used as a selection query when composing a list of customers for campaign recipients. Therefore, permission data needs to be transported from the front-end applications to the CRM data warehouse. This can be done via a daily ETL incremental feed, based on the created and last updated timestamps. The structure of the data warehouse to store the permission varies depending on which type of permission it is. For general permission, we can put it on the customer dimension, as follows: `alter table dim_customer add permission bit`. We then set the ETL to populate it with "True" or "False" based on the front-end permission data. Specific permission is also usually incorporated on the customer dimension as several True/False columns. Each column represents one specific permission. For example:

```
alter table dim_customer
add transaction_permission bit,
  promotion_permission bit,
  newsletter_permission bit
```

The implementation of subscriptions in the data warehouse is very different from the generic and specific permission. Subscriptions are usually implemented as a fact table, as shown in Figure 14-2, as we discussed in Chapter 5 when doing dimensional modeling.

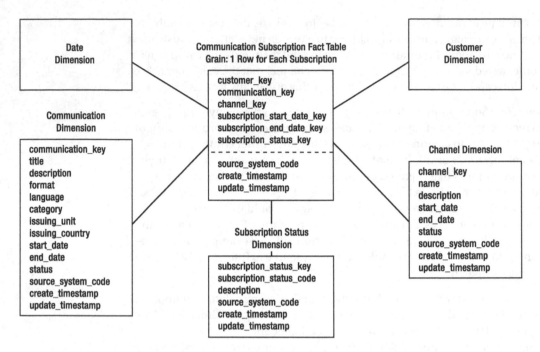

Figure 14-2. *Communication Subscriptions fact table*

The fact table in Figure 14-2 is called Communication Subscriptions (not just the Subscription fact table) because in the Amadeus Entertainment case study we have another kind of subscription: membership subscription, which is a kind of pay-monthly product where the customer can download *n* number of music and films.

The diagram in Figure 14-2 basically shows who subscribes to what and on which channel. Table 14-2 shows some sample data.

Table 14-2. *Sample Data for the Communication Subscriptions Fact Table*

customer_key	communication_key	channel_key	subscription_ start_date_key	subscription_ end_date_key	subscription_ status_key
1	1	1	241	0	1
2	2	1	219	0	1
3	1	2	178	298	2
3	2	2	169	0	1

Each subscription is implemented as a row in the fact table on Table 14-2, with a start date and an end date. We also have a status to indicate whether the subscription is still active. If the subscription is still active (status_key = 1), the subscription_end_date_key is 0 (unknown). If the subscription is not active (status_key = 2), the subscription_end_date_key is populated with the date the customer unsubscribed.

It is possible that the same customer subscribed to two different communications. In Table 14-2, customer 3 subscribed to communications 1 and 2. His subscription to communication 1 is not active, but communication 2 is still active.

The channel key column in the fact table shown in Table 14-2 indicates how the campaign will be delivered, such as by e-mail, text message, or RSS. The campaign format, however (text, HTML, and so on), is not in the fact table; but it is in the communication dimension instead, because the format is an attribute of a communication. A communication is something that we deliver to the subscribing customer on a regular or semiregular basis (many times, not one time only), such as a weekly newsletter or news alert. As you can see in Figure 14-2, a communication has a start date, end date, and status to indicate whether a communication is active. The category attribute groups common communications together and acts as a hierarchy, such as weekly or ad hoc tactical. A channel also has a start date, end date, and status to indicate whether it is active. In some implementations, particularly in multibrand and multinational organizations, we may want to add a brand and locale or country attribute in the communication dimension to indicate which company owns that communication.

Listing 14-2 shows the Data Definition Language (DDL) for Figure 14-2.

Listing 14-2. *DDL for Implementing Subscription in a Data Warehouse*

```
create table fact_communication_subscription
( customer_key                   int      not null
, communication_key              int      not null
, channel_key                    int      not null
, subscription_start_date_key    int      not null
, subscription_end_date_key      int      not null
, subscription_status_key        int      not null
, source_system_code             tinyint  not null
, create_timestamp               datetime not null
, update_timestamp               datetime not null
, constraint pk_fact_communication_subscription
  primary key clustered
  ( communication_key, customer_key, subscription_start_date_key )
)

create table dim_communication
( communication_key   int not null
, title               varchar(50)
, description         varchar(200)
, format              varchar(20)
, language            varchar(50)
, category            varchar(20)
, issuing_unit        varchar(30)
, issuing_country     char(3)
, start_date          datetime
, end_date            datetime
, status              varchar(10)
, source_system_code  tinyint    not null
, create_timestamp    datetime   not null
, update_timestamp    datetime   not null
, constraint pk_dim_communication
  primary key clustered (communication_key)
)
```

```
create table dim_subscription_status
( subscription_status_key    int not null
, subscription_status_code   char(2)
, description                varchar(50)
, source_system_code         tinyint
, create_timestamp           datetime
, update_timestamp           datetime
, constraint pk_dim_subscription_status
  primary key clustered (subscription_status_key)
)

create table dim_channel
( channel_key          int not null
, name                 varchar(20)
, description          varchar(50)
, start_date           smalldatetime
, end_date             smalldatetime
, status               varchar(10)
, source_system_code   tinyint   not null
, create_timestamp     datetime  not null
, update_timestamp     datetime  not null
, constraint pk_dim_channel
  primary key clustered (channel_key)
)
```

While we are on the permission management topic, it is relevant to talk about *opting out*, or revoking the permission. It is mandatory that the customer is able to unsubscribe or revoke their permission at any time from any campaign. If it is an e-mail campaign, we need to have a link on every campaign pointing to an unsubscribe page. This page will update the front-end database that will then be propagated to the data warehouse. As a result, the subscription will be deactivated, in other words, by updating the subscription end date and status. It is important that the propagation of unsubscription information to the CRM data warehouse is frequent, ideally intraday or at least once a day, so that we can make sure customers who have revoked their permissions do not get subsequent campaigns. If it is a general or specific permission, the ETL will update the corresponding permission column on the customer dimension from Y to N.

Delivery and Response Data

Campaign delivery data is about whether the campaign that we sent is delivered to the intended recipient. For example, if the campaign is delivered using an e-mail message, it may not get into the target mailbox because the mailbox is full. Campaign response data is about the reaction from the customer after receiving our campaign. For example, they may be interested in a particular offer in the e-mail and click it to purchase the product.

To understand campaign delivery and response data, let's go through the process of campaign delivery. Take the Amadeus Entertainment Music Weekly Newsletter, which has 100,000 recipients, as an example. After the campaign is created, it is executed and sent to the target recipients. Let's say that when the campaign was executed, there were 100,000 target recipients. Let's say 1,000 of these target recipients were filtered out because of the banned list table (refer to the earlier discussion of negative permissions), and 2,000 were filtered out because the recipient e-mail addresses have bounced four times. So, 97,000 actually went out: 90,000 by e-mail; 4,000 by post; 2,000 by RSS; and 1,000 by text message. Out of the 90,000 e-mail messages, say 86,000 reached the intended recipients, and 4,000 were undelivered (because the e-mail domain did not exist, because of an invalid mailbox name, because the mailbox was full, and so on). Out of the 86,000 e-mail messages that were delivered, 25,000 were opened/read, and 5,000 were clicked through; that is, the customers went to the web pages specified in the e-mail campaign. Out of these 5,000 customers, 500 made an order (purchased some products). Figure 14-3 illustrates the figures in this process.

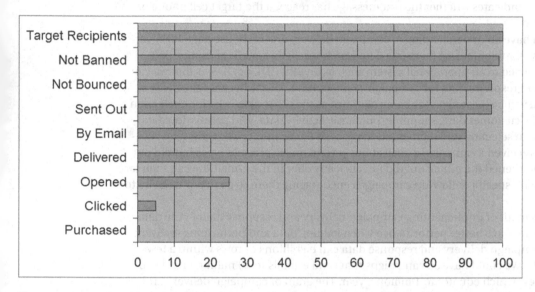

Figure 14-3. *Number of customers involved in each step of campaign delivery process*

The number of e-mail messages sent out, the number of messages delivered, the number of messages not delivered (bounced), and the number of e-mail messages not sent out (either because of banned list or bounce list) are called *campaign delivery data*, and the number of e-mail messages opened/read, the number of messages clicked by the customers, and the number of customers purchased some products are called *campaign response data*. Both campaign delivery data and campaign response data are important because they indicate the success or failure of the campaign; for example, if the open rate and click-through rate (CTR) are high, the campaign is successful.

The open and click-through rates vary from industry to industry. Amongst other things, they depend on whether we implement double opt-in (cleaner list), they depend on who the target audience is (business to business or business to consumer), and they depend on whether the segmentation is specific or general. If you still want a rough indicator, for business to consumer with double opt-in and specific segmentation, you can expect an open rate from 5 percent to 15 percent.

It would be useful to understand how campaign delivery and response data can be collected by the CRM system. In other words, how do we know that an e-mail has been opened or read? How do we know that the customer has clicked certain links in the e-mail? How do we detect which customer purchased which products and identify which campaign initiated the purchase? The techniques and methods of obtaining delivery and response data within the CRM systems vary greatly from application to application. If it is an e-mail campaign, the delivery status can be obtained from SMTP response codes, which is the number sent back by the target e-mail server, such as 250 for delivered, 530 for access denied, 552 for exceeding the mailbox limit, 521 for a domain that does not except e-mail, 421 for a domain that's not valid/available, and so on. Sometimes the interpretation of the response codes is not so straightforward; for example, code 250 can mean several things, because it actually means that the requested action is done OK, so the meaning depends on what the requested action was. For a text message, we need to use the appropriate protocol instead of SMTP, such as an SMS delivery report that indicates whether the text message has reached the target cell phone or cannot be delivered.

Now that you have an understanding of campaign delivery and response data, I'll cover the pros and cons of implementing them in a data warehouse. The benefit of using a data warehouse (as opposed to an operational system such as an ERP, CDI, or ODS) is that we can use the delivery and response data for campaign segmentation. This is because the delivery and response data will be located on the same platform as the other data used for a selection query (for example, customer data, shopping/purchase/activity data, and permission data) during the campaign selection and segmentation process. For example, we might select customers who have received a campaign e-mail about certain music product types but did not open the e-mail *or* opened the e-mail but did not click any offer in the e-mail. We can then target these groups with specific follow-up campaigns encouraging them to go to our web site to look at the products.

The second benefit of implementing campaign delivery and response data in the data warehouse is that we have better performance when loading data and performing analysis. The amount of campaign delivery and response data can be billions of rows within a few years. For example, we could have 35 campaigns that send e-mails to 20 million target subscribers every week, which equates to 1 billion a year. The grain of campaign delivery and response data is the number of target recipients. That means that for every message created by the campaign, we will have a row, whether the message is sent or not. Because of the volume, we can take advantage of a data warehouse platform, which handles a large volume of data better than operational systems. This is especially true when querying the campaign response data for customer analysis and purchase analysis, such as when analyzing customers who have clicked but not purchased or when performing demographic analysis against customers who have received certain types of campaigns in the last six months.

So, those are two benefits of implementing campaign delivery and response data in a dimensional data warehouse. But sometimes we are not able to do that if our CRM application is a packaged application. For example, the CRM application may not work with a dimensional data warehouse; it may work only with a highly normalized operational database. In this case, we could load the campaign delivery and response data from the normalized CRM database into a dimensional data warehouse for analysis.

Figure 14-4 shows the design of an implementation of CRM campaign delivery and response data in a data warehouse. It consists of a campaign delivery and response fact table with six dimensions.

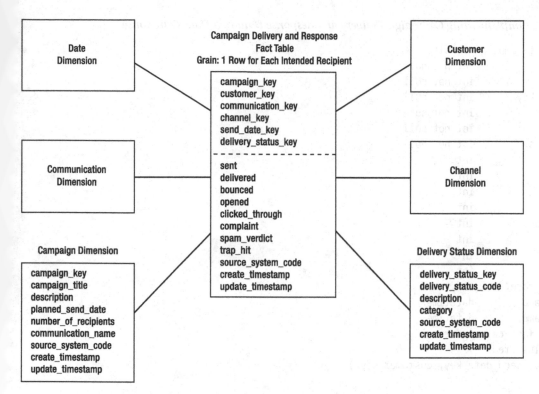

Figure 14-4. *Schema design for implementing campaign delivery and response data in a data warehouse*

Let's go through the schema in Figure 14-4. It has one fact table and six dimension tables: date, communication, campaign, customer, channel, and delivery status. The grain of the fact table is one row for each intended recipient in the campaign. For example, say we have 10 campaigns that were sent last week, each containing 20,000 customers. In this case, we have 200,000 rows in this fact table.

I discussed this schema in Chapter 5. But to refresh, let's go through each key column on the fact table. The campaign key identifies which campaign was sent, for example: Weekly France Music Newsletter 01/14/2008. The customer key identifies to which customer the campaign was sent. The communication key identifies the communication to which the campaign belongs. For example, the Weekly France Music Newsletter 01/14/2008 campaign is an instance of the Weekly France Music Newsletter communication. The channel key indicates how the campaign was sent, such as via e-mail. The send date indicates when the campaign was sent. The delivery status indicates whether the campaign was delivered successfully to the intended recipient.

Listing 14-3 shows the DDL of Figure 14-4.

Listing 14-3. *DDL for Implementing Campaign Delivery and Response Data in a Data Warehouse*

```
create table fact_campaign_result
( campaign_key            int not null
, customer_key            int not null
, communication_key       int not null
, channel_key             int not null
, send_date_key           int not null
, delivery_status_key     int not null
, sent                    int
, delivered               int
, bounced                 int
, opened                  int
, clicked_through         int
, complaint               int
, spam_verdict            int
, trap_hit                int
, source_system_code      tinyint
, create_timestamp        datetime
, update_timestamp        datetime
, constraint pk_fact_campaign_result
  primary key clustered
  ( campaign_key, send_date_key, customer_key )
)

create table dim_campaign
( campaign_key        int not null
, campaign_title      varchar(50) not null
, description         varchar(100)
, planned_send_date   smalldatetime
, number_of_recipients int
, communication_name  varchar(50)
, source_system_code  tinyint    not null
, create_timestamp    datetime   not null
, update_timestamp    datetime   not null
, constraint pk_dim_campaign
  primary key clustered (campaign_key)
)

create table dim_delivery_status
( delivery_status_key    int not null
, delivery_status_code   int not null
, description            varchar(50)
, category               varchar(20)
, source_system_code     tinyint   not null
, create_timestamp       datetime  not null
, update_timestamp       datetime  not null
, constraint pk_dim_delivery_status
  primary key clustered (delivery_status_key)
)
```

After we load campaign delivery and response data into the data warehouse, we can use it for various analyses, including calculating the campaign result statistics such as open rate, click-through rate, and purchase rate by any demographic attributes, by campaign type, and by product hierarchy. For example, we can compare the open, click-through, and purchase rates for different regions across all product categories. Or we can analyze them by occupation group, age group, and interest group. We can analyze how many customers clicked each link on the campaign we sent. We can compare the campaign response rates with the statistics from previous campaign sends, with the company-wide average and with the industry standards. Figure 14-5 shows the open rates across different regions by product category for a certain period.

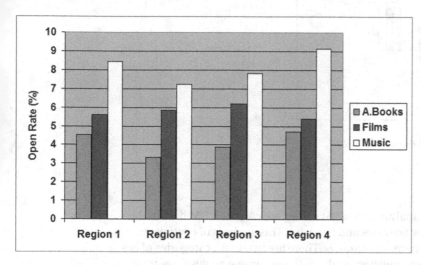

Figure 14-5. *Open rate across different regions by product category*

We can also use the campaign response data to analyze the effectiveness of certain product promotion campaigns by comparing the open rate and click-through rate across product types, as shown in Figure 14-6. The bubble size indicates the campaign size (the number of target recipients). The bigger the bubble, the bigger the campaign.

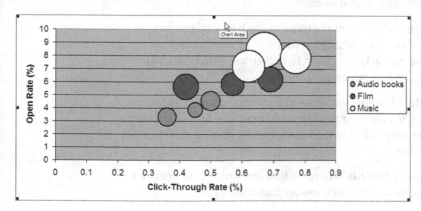

Figure 14-6. *Open rate, click-through rate, and campaign size across different product categories*

Campaign delivery data enables us to analyze the bounce rate across different e-mail domains and understand the reasons for the rate. The bounce rate is the number of e-mail messages not delivered divided by the number of e-mail messages sent. E-mail domains are the domain name of the customer e-mail address. For example, Figure 14-7 shows Amadeus Entertainment's average bounce rate for the top six e-mail domains in a particular week.

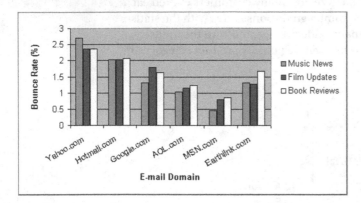

Figure 14-7. *Bounce rate across different e-mail domains*

Customer Analysis

In addition to the campaign response analysis discussed earlier, we can use CRM data in the data warehouse for analyzing customer activities and behavior. This analysis of customer activities and behavior is what we call *customer analysis*. There are two main categories of customer analysis: descriptive analysis and predictive analysis. In descriptive analysis, we try to understand or describe customer behavior and activities. In predictive analysis, we try to predict or forecast customer behavior and activities. The following are examples of descriptive analysis:

E-commerce industry: Purchase pattern by demographic, where we try to understand the purchase and browsing behavior of our customer group by demographic attributes, such as age, occupation, income, location, family, and interest.

Telecommunication industry: Usage analysis against products, such as analyzing a customer's cell phone usage to see whether the calling plan they are on now is the most appropriate one. We could then use the CRM campaign to encourage switching to the correct calling plan to increase customer service satisfaction.

Insurance industry: Risk pattern identification, where we calculate customer risk factors and insurance premiums according to customer activities. For example, for car insurance, the risk groups could be determined according to the base location, driving area, type of cars, vehicle usage, and traveling time.

Utility industry: Customer profitability analysis, where we find out which customers we are making money on and which ones we are losing money from and by how much.

As we can see, all these analyses describe, analyze, or explain the current situation about customer activities and behavior. Predictive analysis is different. It tries to predict or forecast customer activities and behavior. Examples of predictive analysis are as follows:

Utilities industry: Price sensitivity analysis, where we try to find out which customers would be likely to close their accounts when we do the annual price increase next month and what the financial implications are of losing them. This enables us to approach the customers to prevent the account closure from happening.

E-commerce industry: Sales forecasting, where we predict the quantity sold for each product type in the coming months and calculate the sale amount accordingly. We can then tailor the CRM campaigns accordingly to make the forecast inline with the sales targets.

Travel industry: Predicting which customers are likely to be interested in certain types of holiday, flight, or lifestyle product offers, based on the demographic data, previous booking data, and campaign response data. Another example is predicting which subscribers are likely to make a purchase when we send them promotional campaigns on certain product types.

Waste management: Forecasting which days are "heavy" days and which days are "light" days based on weight measurement data and customer business types, and arrange the pickup truck routing accordingly to increase fleet efficiency.

A CRM data warehouse contains customer data, permission data, campaign response data, customer activity data (purchase, shopping, subscription, gain, and loss), billing data, payments data, and marketing data (including promotions and campaigns). Because of its rich content, a CRM data warehouse is naturally helpful for customer analysis, be it descriptive or predictive. The methods to do customer analysis are similar to those of BI, such as reporting, analytics, and data mining. Descriptive customer analysis can be delivered using all of these three methods, while predictive customer analysis is usually delivered using data mining.

As an example of descriptive customer analysis, let's use SSAS to analyze film purchases by customer interests. For that, let's create a product sales cube, shown in Figure 14-8, using the same process we discussed in Chapter 12. This cube is similar to the one we created in Chapter 12. The only difference is that we have one more dimension here: customer.

We process this cube as we discussed in Chapter 12 and then browse it. Now let's set the cube browser to display the customer interest against the product type. For this, we put the Interest1 attribute from the customer dimension as the row field and the Product Type attribute from the product dimension as the column field. Put the Sales Value measure as the detail field, and filter the cube on product category = 'Films'. Figure 14-9 shows the result. I discussed how to do all this in Chapter 12, so you should be familiar with this.

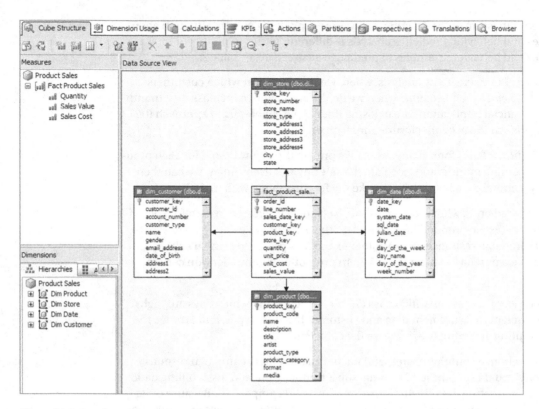

Figure 14-8. *Product sales cube with customer dimension*

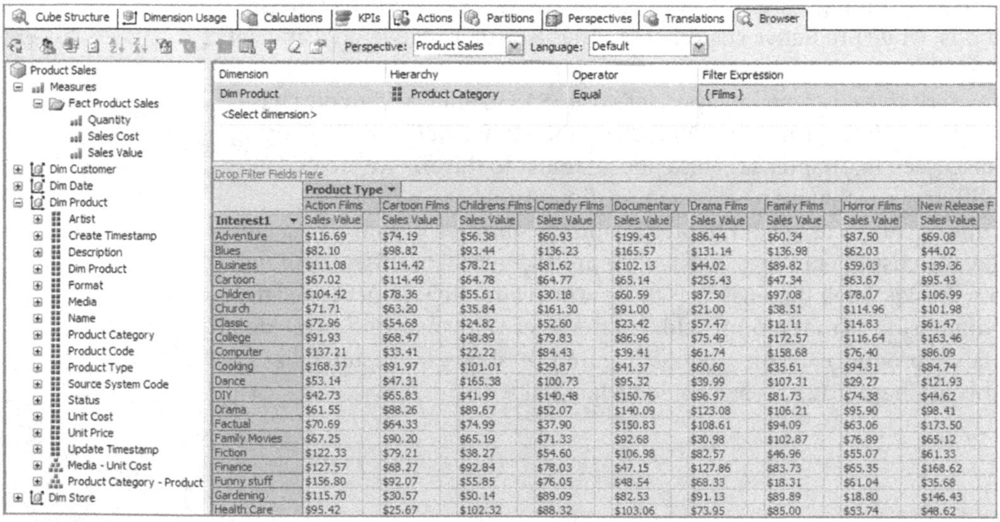

Figure 14-9. *Analyzing film purchases by customer interests*

In Figure 14-9 you can see that, for example, customers with a DIY interest purchased many more comedy films than those with a cooking interest. Customers with a cartoon interest purchased many more drama films than those with a church interest. We can also analyze the film purchases by other demographic factors such as age, gender, and income. For this we just need to swap the interest on the row field with other customer attributes.

This is an example of descriptive customer analysis. We did some predictive customer analysis in Chapter 13, when we predicted the purchase of music products using gender, interest, and occupation demographic factors using the Decision Trees mining model.

Customer Support

Most customer support activities are done on the operational systems, both the call center systems and ERPs. The customer service agents usually use these two types of systems to support and service the customers. Operational data stores are increasingly used for customer support too.

But sometimes a data warehouse is useful for customer support, especially utilizing data warehouse analytical nature and prediction capability. The following are examples of data warehouse usage for customer support.

Travel industry: Predeparture campaigns, where we send a campaign one week before the travel starts, to inform the customers about the weather forecast in the destination city, general information about the flight check-in time and security restriction, map of the area around the hotel, and destination information such as recommended restaurants. We can also use this opportunity to remind them to bring their passports if the destination is overseas and to ask whether they need a taxi to go to/from the airport, a car hire, attraction tickets, or a wireless Internet connection.

Telecommunication industry: To help individual customers get the right billing plan by analyzing all the calls made by the customer in the last three months (time, destination, duration, cost) and comparing it with all available plans to see whether there are any plans that have lower prices than the plan the customer currently has. The campaign can be set up to run once a month to advise all customers who have not been advised in the last six months (this would require campaign response data).

Utilities industry: To analyze individual customer's electricity and gas usage and advise the customers whether there is a better tariff plan in terms of costs, as well as giving them general energy-saving advice.

Financial industry: To analyze the overdraft and withdrawal activities for each customer (across all accounts) and advise them accordingly. For example, you could ask whether they want to increase their overdraft limit. The bank can calculate the limit they are prepared to give, based on the account activity information in the data warehouse.

E-commerce industry: A price alert, where you automatically advise the registered customer if certain products are now discounted below certain levels, for example, because new product lines will be replacing them soon. The campaign can run once a day matching the product prices and the customer interest and buying history and then advise the customers via e-mail, RSS, or text message.

Entertainment industry (like Amadeus Entertainment): Customized new title film/music announcements, where we advise the customers if his favorite artist or author has a new single, album, film, or book, as well as give information about the artist such as biography, web site, fans club, and coming shows.

The primary methods used to deliver this functionality are analytics and data mining. Some functionality would also require notification and subscription.

Personalization

Personalization is the customization of web sites, campaigns, offers, products, and services to a particular customer. For example, if John Smith browses the Amadeus Entertainment web site, the content he gets is different from the one Stella Sanchez gets. Customization is usually used on e-commerce web sites to make the products and offers more specific to particular customers.

Personalization is important because it increases the chances of the customers purchasing the products, which could increase sales revenue. The source data for personalization can be taken from shopping data (the pages that the customer looked at on previous visits), interest register (the interest text boxes/drop-down lists on the registration pages), or past purchases of similar customers (the similarity can be determined from demographic attributes). The source data can be analyzed using data mining models (decision trees, clustering, and other algorithms) to score a list of offers and products against individual customers. The output can then be wrapped as XML and fed to the personalized home pages on the web site. The output can also be displayed as "my store" or "my travel" or "My Amadeus," in other words, a page customized specifically to a particular customer, based on the personalization output.

The personalization output can also be fed into a personalized campaign that is then sent via e-mails to customers. Depending on the degree of personalization and the segmentation of the campaign (which could be a segment of one), the campaign can take days to execute or just a few hours (to just produce the raw XML files, not send out the e-mails).

The output of this analysis can also be stored in a dimensional mart, with time, customer, and product as the dimensions. The measure in the fact table itself is the likelihood score that the customer would be interested in those products. The data on this mart can then be used for recommendations, which are similar to personalized offer e-mails but are usually applied when the customers are still shopping on the web site. The recommendation can be as simple as "People who bought this item also bought ..." or can be as complex as analyzing the customer's demographics and then going to the likelihood mart to find the most likely product range.

The key to site content personalization and recommendation is identifying the customer, because we have to be able to tailor the site while the customer is still on it. Two approaches are commonly used for identification: logins and cookies. The best way to identify a customer is by self-authentication, in other words, asking the customer to log in. Although this may be inconvenient to customers (it's an additional step), it is a reliable and accurate method.

Cookies, on the other hand, are tiny files on the customer's computer that store a unique web site visitor ID to identify the customer the next time they visit the web site. This is more convenient to customers because they don't have to log in, but it is not as reliable as self-authentication. Some people delete their cookies or disable them, making the identification fail. The customers may even be using a public computer, which means the cookie could identify a different user.

Cookies on their own cannot identify customers. They simply act as a client-side mechanism for storing information. We still need to get a form of identification from the customer and then store this information as a cookie. Whether we use cookies or logins or both, we need to be able to identify the customer to be able to tailor the site content for personalization.

Customer Loyalty Scheme

In many organizations, especially commercial ones, a customer loyalty scheme is an important CRM activity. A customer loyalty scheme is a program to reward customers based on their contribution to the business. The contribution is measured in loyalty scores, usually calculated based on the revenue or profit generated by the customers. The main purpose of a loyalty scheme is usually to encourage customers to stay with us and eventually to increase company revenue or profit. A customer loyalty scheme can be implemented to all customers or just the top *n* customers based on the loyalty scores.

An example of a customer loyalty scheme is a frequent-flier program where customers collect air miles by flying with the airline or by using services from its partners. Customers can then use their air miles for booking a flight. A frequent-flier program could also have status tiers, where customers with more air miles get to higher tiers and can enjoy additional benefits such as executive airport lounge and priority check-in.

The calculated loyalty scores can then be stored as an attribute on the customer dimension. This makes it easier for the scores to be used in campaign segmentation for sending messages to customers as well as for analysis. In some loyalty scheme implementations, the scores are converted into *bands* (or classes). For example, 0.4 to 0.6 is band C, 0.6 to 0.8 is band B, and 0.8 to 1.0 is band A. The classes will then determine the rewards and benefits the customer gets, as well as drive the communication plan.

Customer loyalty schemes require some periodic reporting and analysis such as churn analysis and revenue analysis in order to measure the success of the program. *Churn analysis* basically analyzes how many new customers we are getting every period (week, month, and so on) and how many customers we are losing. *Revenue analysis* indicates how much additional revenue is generated by each customer band or class, compared to the control group. A control group contains customers who do not receive any rewards from the loyalty scheme. For example, if we have 100,000 customers in the program, we may want to allocate the top 25,000 as band A; the second 25,000 as band B; the third 25,000 as band C; and the bottom 25,000 as control group. Bands A, B, and C receive the good rewards (rewards for band A are higher than B, and B rewards are higher than C), but the control group gets nothing. After a few months, we compare their purchases. In theory, bands A, B, and C should produce more revenue than the control group.

New customers need to be added to the scheme periodically, and the loyalty scores need to be updated regularly across all customers. We also need to keep the permission for loyalty scheme up-to-date, including opt-ins, opt-outs, and unsubscriptions. Some customers may prefer not to be contacted including about the loyalty scheme, and we need to exclude them accordingly from the campaigns and notifications.

Summary

In this chapter, I discussed the implementation of a data warehouse for customer relationship management, including the following topics: permission, segmentation, response data, customer analysis, customer support, personalization, and loyalty scheme. We always need to keep the permissions up-to-date; that is arguably the most important thing in CRM, because otherwise we are spamming. Campaign delivery and response data are probably the next most important, because when our deliverability rate is low, the campaign does not reach the intended recipients, and the response data measures the campaign's success.

Customer analysis enables us to understand the current activities of our customers and forecast their behavior. There are two major types of customer analysis: descriptive and predictive. Personalization enables us to tailor our products and services, web sites, and offers according to a customer profile. The ability to identify the customer is the key to on-site personalization. In customer loyalty schemes, we calculate the loyalty scores to understand the customer value and analyze the improvements in terms of customer churn and revenue.

In the next chapter, I'll discuss the role of a data warehouse in customer data integration, search, and unstructured data.

■ ■ ■

CHAPTER 15

Other Data Warehouse Usage

In the previous two chapters, I discussed the implementation of data warehousing for business intelligence (BI) and customer relationship management (CRM). In this chapter, I will discuss data warehousing within the context of customer data integration (CDI) and unstructured data. I will also discuss the role of search in data warehousing.

Unlike BI and CRM, it would be incorrect to say "implementing data warehousing for CDI" because a data warehouse is a consumer of CDI. Data warehouses utilize the output or results of CDI. In most data warehousing systems these days, the customer dimension in the data warehouse is where customer data is integrated. But in the past few years, there has been a growing trend to integrate customer data in a normalized store outside the data warehouse, with the main argument being that the consumer of customer data is not just the data warehouse but probably other systems and applications as well.

Since 2005, CDI, unstructured data, and search have increasingly become more and more popular in data warehousing. Customer data integration (and master data management in general) offers high value to organizations by providing a single, valid, authoritative customer view for downstream applications such as data warehouses. The amount of unstructured data is probably five to ten times more than structured data; therefore, you can potentially gain more information from unstructured data than structured data. With the help of text analytics and digital image processing, you can extract useful information from unstructured data. Search as a user interface is useful in finding information in the data warehouse and presenting it to the end user.

These three elements (CDI, unstructured data, and search) could potentially fulfill the future of data warehousing because of the benefits they bring; hence, I'll discuss them in detail in this chapter.

Customer Data Integration

In this section, I will discuss what CDI is, what the benefits are, and how to implement it. In many organizations, customer data is scattered across different systems or applications. For example, in retail banking, the credit card division may be using a different system than the one used for savings accounts or loan management. The systems for life insurance and mortgages may also be different. Also, customer service or call centers may be using a different system. Because of this, the customer data is scattered across several systems. CDI is an ongoing process of retrieving, cleaning, storing, updating, and distributing customer data. This includes customer names, customer addresses, dates of birth, telephone numbers, e-mail addresses, occupations, communication preferences, interests, and subscriptions. Let's go through the five processes mentioned earlier:

- *Retrieving* means extracting the customer data from the source system.

- *Cleaning* means correcting incorrect data and removing duplicate records.

- *Storing* means putting the customer data in a central customer data store.

- *Updating* means modifying the customer data in the customer data store, according to the new values from the source system.

- *Distributing* means publishing the customer data so that other systems can use this customer data.

CDI enables you to have a cleaner, single, reliable version of customer data that the applications in the enterprise can use. This in turn can deliver business benefits such as the following:

- Increased customer satisfaction

- Better business analysis

- Reduced complexity of the processes that use customer data

CDI is implemented using a service-oriented architecture, as shown in Figure 15-1. In this figure, the customer data is in a central customer data store, with services built around the data store. No applications touch the customer data store directly. Instead, all applications must use the services to put the data in and to get the data out.

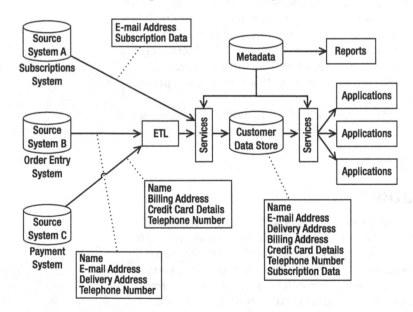

Figure 15-1. *Implementation of CDI*

In Figure 15-1, you can see that some source systems put the customer data into the customer data store by directly calling the services, like in source system A. But some source systems store the customer data only in their own databases, like in source systems B and C. For these source systems, you can build an ETL that retrieves and cleanses the customer data from the source system and calls the services to store the data into the customer data store.

The metadata database shown in Figure 15-1 contains the data definition, data structure metadata, and data integration rules. The data definition contains the meaning of each customer attribute in the customer data store. The data structure describes the database structure of the customer data store. It contains the data types and lengths of every column in every table in the customer data store, including the collation, constraints (such as null and unique), and whether the column is a primary key or a foreign key. It also contains the data hierarchy. The data integration rules contain the data mapping and transformations; for example, customer group code X in source system A is mapped to customer group code Y in the customer data store.

The customer data store is in normalized relational model. This model gives better performance over the dimensional model when used to retrieve, create, or update a single customer record or part of a customer record. Figure 15-2 shows an example of a customer data store schema.

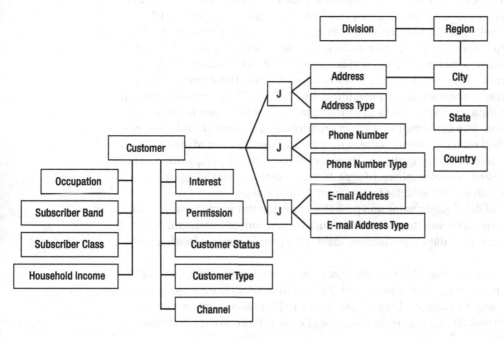

Figure 15-2. *An example of customer data store schema*

In Figure 15-2, the customer data store is designed so that a customer can have several types of addresses, telephone numbers, and e-mail addresses, such as for the home and office. This is implemented by using junction tables, marked as *J* in Figure 15-2.

In some cases in the customer data store, you'll need to store the historical values of customer attributes. This is required when some applications need to get the previous value, such as to explain an old transaction. You can do this by using a series of audit tables. Before changing the customer attributes, you store the original record with the old attribute values in an audit table, along with a timestamp when the change happened.

Unstructured Data

Generally, you can classify data into two big groups. The first group is essentially numbers, characters, and dates, such as 32, "John Smith," and 05/21/2008. You usually store this kind of data in a database. It can be a relational database, dimensional database or hierarchical database, or even a multidimensional database. This data is usually stored in tables, as rows and columns, where you can sort and query. This kind of data is called *structured data*.

The second group of data is not as discreet as the structured data. Instead, it is different kinds of multimedia, such as images, videos, web pages, presentations, telephone conversations, e-mails, documents, and music. This kind of data is called *unstructured data*. This data is usually stored in file servers, database servers, FTP servers, e-mail servers, content management systems (CMSs), and document management systems (DMSs).

The amount of unstructured data is a lot more than the structured data, but most of it is untouched by data warehousing. To give an illustration, say the sizes of all databases in three multinational groups of companies (9,000; 12,000; and 20,000 employees) are about 50TB, 30TB, and 5TB, respectively. The sizes of all documents, text files, presentation, working files, web pages, web site objects, video, audio, and e-mails in the file server, web server, FTP server, e-mail server, and database server are estimated to be about 200TB, 300TB, and 100TB, respectively, roughly from 4 to 20 times the size of the databases. These three groups are in different lines of business: e-commerce, manufacturing, and utilities. The e-commerce group has a 20TB group-wide data warehouse and a 5TB local data warehouse, which is the reason for the large database size. The manufacturing group produces a lot of artwork and multimedia designs (5MB to 50MB each set), which is the reason for the large amount of unstructured data, but almost each company in the group has its own systems (grown by acquisition). The utility group has centralized several mini/mainframe-based systems across the group and a 1TB data warehouse, which is the reason for the compact database size.

In the last 15 years of data warehousing and probably almost in the whole history of databases, we have been focusing on structured data. But since the amount of unstructured data is much larger than the structured data, it is understandable that people are now looking at the unstructured data.

So, how do you store unstructured data in the data warehouse? Traditionally, you store it as files in the file system and store the attributes and the links in the data warehouse. It is easier to understand this using an example. Let's say you have 1 million documents in various formats. Some are Microsoft Word documents, some are Microsoft PowerPoint presentations, some are PDFs, some are e-mail messages, some are text documents, and some are scanned invoices, signed contracts, and purchased orders. Each document has various attributes, such as the name or title of the document, the subject, an abstract or summary of the document, the type of the document, the version, the document number or ID, the classification, the date the document was created, the date the document was last edited/modified, the date the document was last printed, the size of the file, the number of characters, the words in the documents, the sentences and pages in the documents, the name of the author and author's company, the security settings (read-only, whether copying or printing is allowed, the password to edit the document, and so on), the fonts used in the document, the name and path to the related documents…and the list goes on.

You can store all these attributes in the data warehouse, that is, in relational tables. You then store the path to the files (or the URL of the web page) in a column in the same table so the application can get to the file to access it. You can also store these attributes and the links to the files/objects in dimensional format for analysis purposes. Or you can store the documents as binary objects or character large objects inside the database. The same method is applicable for storing different types of unstructured data such as video, audio, e-mails, and images. All kinds of unstructured data have their specific attributes by which they could be categorically and systematically stored. CMSs and DMSs can also often be used to store and manage unstructured data.

The previous methods have been on the market for many years and are considered "traditional" methods. There is a newer method for storing unstructured data in a data warehouse—well, it's not really a method to store documents in a data warehouse but more of a method to extract structured data from unstructured data and then store the extracted structured data in the data warehouse.

For documents, this method is known as *text analytics*. Text analytics is the process of transforming unstructured documents into structured, analyzable data by analyzing the linguistic structure of the text within the documents, parsing the text, extracting phrases, and identifying associations using techniques such as statistical analysis and categorization (combining phrases using predefined rules).

Let's go through the details of how text analytics works for documents. The first step is to convert the documents to text. Whether they are in Microsoft Word format, StarOffice format, scanned invoices, or PDF, the first step is to convert them all to text files. You may need to use optical character recognition (OCR) to convert them, such as in the case of scanned invoices or purchase orders. Once they are in text format, you can feed them all to text analytics software, which will parse the text files and extract the words and phrases from them.

The result is a list of words and phrases with their association scores reflecting the relations to other words or phrases. An association score is a decimal number ranging from 0 to 1 calculated for each phrase in relevance to another phrase. The higher the scores, the closer the relations. The association scores are important because they reflect how close two phrases are. You can use association scores to then group related entities and find relationships between entities. There are various factors affecting the scores, such as the relative "distance" to the other words, the words located in the same files, the synonyms or meaning of those words, and the number of occurrences. Within the text analytics application, various less meaningful prepositions such as (this is language specific) *an*, *on*, and *the* are weighted much less than more meaningful words such as *downtime*, *revenue*, and *Boston*. The same thing happens for past tenses, such as *sat* and *opened*; they are converted to the present tense. Similarly, for synonyms such as *big* and *large*, *gigantic*, and *huge*, they are also converted.

The text analytics application may also process the files in the context of a certain industry; for example, they could all be trading invoices, or they could be pharmaceutical patents, contracts, or candidate résumés/CVs. To understand the context, let's take the résumé example. The parser would recognize that words such as *SQL Server 2005*, *CRM*, and *Data Warehousing* are the candidate's skills, whereas *Oracle DBA*, *Data Architect*, and *Web Developer* are the candidate's past roles or titles. *Informatica*, *Teradata*, and *WebSphere* are the software that the candidate has used in the past. *Dallas*, *Los Angeles*, and *New York* are cities where the candidate lived or worked. *Citibank*, *The Home Depot*, and *T-Mobile* are company names where the candidate worked. The software can then use this understanding of the parsed text. The words are then processed using a data mining clustering algorithm to get the relationships. My point here is that a text analytics application that is developed specifically for the recruitment industry understands the context of the industry and is able to identify that certain phrases are skills, titles, software, cities, and company names, whereas a pharmaceutical text analytics application would be able to recognize the symptoms, research, diagnoses, chemical content, cure, and treatment phrases within hundreds of medicine patent files. The application understands the relationship between phrases, such as how skills are related to software and how symptoms are related to treatments. Because of this, when selecting a text analytics application, you need to ensure that it has the right "dictionary" for your industry. A text analytics application, which works well for pharmaceuticals, may not be good for processing claim documents within the insurance industry.

The scored lists describe which words have strong relations to other words. A pictorial representative of the result is probably easier to understand. Figure 15-3 shows the result of the résumé example.

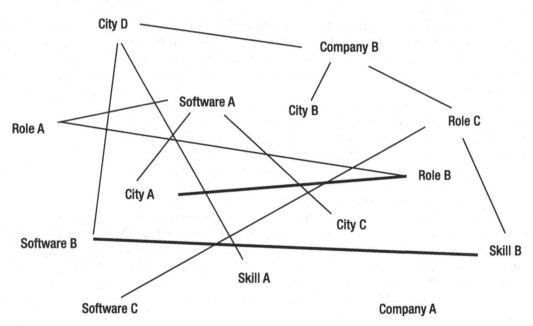

Figure 15-3. *Pictorial representation of the result of text analytics*

The line thickness reflects the strength of association between the phrases. For example, in Figure 15-3, city A is more related to role B than to software A, and software B is more closely associated to skill B than to city D. City C is related only to software A, and company A has no relation with any skill, software, or company. The other output of the analytics is grouping or classification according to the taxonomy of the phrases, that is, the list of cities, list of jobs, list of roles, list of software, and so on. It is often industry specific. In other words, text analytics or mining software that works well for car insurance claims may not have the vocabulary required to analyze food and beverage patents.

Once you have the lists and the association scores, you can store them in the data warehouse for further analysis. For example, you can ask questions such as, "What are the top five cities for software X?", and "Which software do you need to master if you want to be a good candidate for role C?", and "Which companies have the most of role A?"

The method you can apply for documents is also applicable for other types of unstructured data, such as images or audio. Of course, in this case, it is not text analytics but perhaps digital image processing or audio analysis, depending on the media type. For example, speech audio files could be parsed and categorized into questions, statements, and short comments based on the intonations, rhythms, and voice intensity (pattern recognition). Just like OCR, technology can convert scanned documents into text files, and speech audio files can also be converted into text files using voice recognition software. And from there, the same text analytics follow. A stream of outgoing e-mails can also be scanned, classified, and stored using text analytics. Common implementations of e-mail analysis are a junk mail filter and a customer service center's incoming e-mails (automatic categorization and routing).

One example of a scanned document application is invoices, which could be linked to a workflow system. Say there are 29 major suppliers in a company. Each supplier has a different invoice format. You could set up the software so it knows that for invoices from supplier A, the purchase order number is located in the upper-right corner of the document (in certain coordinates) in AAA99A format, the invoice amount is in the lower right, and the number is prefixed by a $, €, or £ symbol. The document archiving system then processes the documents from various suppliers; extracts the structured data such as the invoice number, purchase order number, supplier name, and order amount; and stores them all in a database, which could then be fed into the ERP system for invoice matching and payment processes and also be fed into a data warehouse for analysis purposes.

The metadata aspect of unstructured data conversion is also significant. All the attributes I mentioned can be stored, in addition to the output of the text analytics or mining. These attributes (subject/title, dates, author, and so on) are stored as metadata in the data warehouse. The metadata would then be retrieved by the client applications using a search facility (see the next section). Because of this, it is important to keep the metadata correct and up-to-date. You can do this by consistently updating the metadata every time you add or change the unstructured data. The metadata update should be an automated process that is executed every time you load or change the unstructured data.

Text analytics and unstructured data are particularly useful in the legal industry, the pharmaceutical industry, police departments, TV stations, political parties, national parliaments, and any other industries that deal with a lot of documents or images. They enable you to search a lot of information in a shorter period of time. The text analytics extract the terms and phrases from the unstructured data and categorizes them so the search engine doesn't have to read the unstructured data again. The search could be a lot quicker, probably less than 10 percent of the time required to browse the original unstructured data.

Another application is the e-mail store, which stores outgoing and incoming e-mails as unstructured data. The e-mails are then processed, and the resulting metadata, content lists, and association scores can be stored in a data warehouse. The users would be able to search the content and metadata later. The e-mail store application is particularly relevant for regulatory compliance (such as the Sarbanes-Oxley Act) and for CRM (such as customer queries and correspondence). Sarbanes-Oxley section 802 requires firms that audit or review an issuer's financial statements to retain relevant records including correspondence and communications sent or received in connection with the audit or review. Sometimes a court order requires the preservation of all e-mails containing information potentially relevant to a subject of litigation. If your e-mail system is set to delete e-mails more than n months old, you can use the e-mail store application to retain the relevant e-mails.

Search in Data Warehousing

When your data warehouse has grown to several terabytes and you have hundreds of stored reports, cubes, and many BI data models, it can help if you have a search facility that can assist the users in locating the right reports, cubes, and data models. A search facility is a tool that indexes data warehouse reports, analytics, or data models (both the metadata and the content) to enable the users to find information by typing the search criteria in a search text box. A search facility is capable of prioritizing the search results by relevance. Some vendors, such as SAS, search the business views and data structure in the metadata server in order to link the relevant information in the search results. Other vendors, such as Information Builder, search the structured data within corporate databases. Some vendors, such as Clarabridge, also search unstructured data along with the structured reports.

A typical search application consists of an indexer, retriever, and scoring routines. The indexer browses the folders for all of the file types (unstructured data files, and so on), then opens and crawls each file, and then stores the locations of those words in the repository. The indexer also collects the information about the reports, cubes, and data models and stores this information in the repository. It also stores previous searches and queries. The retriever accepts a value from the search text box, searches its repository and metadata, and displays the results to the end users. Before it is displayed to the end user, the scoring routine sorts the results according to a preset logic/algorithm. The scoring routine may also partition the result into more than one section to be displayed separately on the screen.

Within the search text box, you can type **sales** and it would list, say, nine sales reports, two BI models, and three Analysis Services cubes that are related to sales. Similarly, you can also search for things such as customers and subscriptions. The search would go through the report metadata (such as titles, columns, and so on), multidimensional metadata, data warehouse metadata, and BI data model metadata to find the relevant reports, cubes, and models. It could also search the content of the stored reports and previous searches. For example, there might be 12 variations of a product sales report for 2007 that are physically stored as snapshots in the report server database, all with different stores, customers, and product attributes. The search facility can find the relevant reports and highlight them for the BI users. Previous searches are what the users typed into the search box, which may speed things up a little bit.

Rather than trying to build our own data warehouse search facility in this book, I think it is better if I show how to implement one of the off-the-shelf search products from BI vendors. At the beginning of 2006, it was difficult to find search products in the market. But currently (the second half of 2007), almost every single BI vendor is working with Google to deliver a search product (some of them have already delivered, such as Cognos, SAS, Information Builder, and Clarabridge). BI or data warehouse search is quite a specialized area. A ranking algorithm to prioritize search results by their relevance, for example, is not straightforward to develop. And even if you manage to develop it, would it be better than the Google search algorithm? Indexing a pile of unstructured data, crawling structured databases, searching OLAP cubes, and correctly interpreting metadata are all challenging tasks within DW/BI search.

Searching the report's content, column titles, data values, and practically any text appearing on the report is better left to a search specialist company working with the BI vendors.

Three areas in data warehousing would benefit from a search facility. The first one is simplifying the user interface. In this application, search is used for querying structured data in the dimensional data store. I'm not talking only about long varchar data types but also about numeric, date, and short character data types. You can *supplement* the query interface with a search interface. A typical implementation is a simple text box where the data warehouse user can type anything. The application then searches the data warehouse for the relevant content. The following query is a typical data warehouse query to understand the sales amount per store:

```
select s.store, sum(f.sale_amount)
from fact_purchase f
join dim_date d on f.date_key = d.dim_key
join dim_store s on s.store_key = d.store_key
where d.month = 10
and d.year = 2007
and s.region = 'Midwest'
group by s.store
```

Rather than typing that query, the users can just type **October 2007 sales in Midwest** region. Or they can just type **Sales**; the search application will display the sales reports from all regions, and the user can then pick the Midwest region for October 2007. Yes, it is true that a BI application has made data warehouse querying and browsing very user friendly by providing an excellent user interface for data warehouse users. But search takes the user friendliness further. What can be easier than just typing whatever you want into a text box? You need to understand that the search facility does not replace the query function and BI tool function; instead, it just supplements them to make them more complete and easier to use.

The key here is that the search application needs to be aware that certain words are metadata while other words are data. For example, *subscription sales* and *subscription band* are facts/measures and dimensional attributes, so the search application can find them in the metadata. On the other hand, *Los Angeles* and *Classical Music* are data values, so the search application cannot find them in the metadata store; instead, they can be found in the data itself. The search results can be partitioned between the results found in the metadata area and the results that are found in the actual data. You need to bear in mind that in order for the search application to have this capability, the metadata behind the application must be excellent.

The second area to benefit from the search is the reports search, which I talked about earlier. The third area that benefits from the search is unstructured data such as documents, web pages, text files, images, videos, and audio files. In the previous section, I discussed how unstructured data can be processed by text analytics applications (or digital image processing for images) and provided a correlation diagram between related words or phrases. The source files can also be browsed and indexed by a search application, so it would be a lot easier to find information.

Summary

In this chapter and the previous two chapters, I discussed the implementation of a data warehouse for business intelligence and customer relationship management within the context of customer data integration, unstructured data, and search. There are other implementations of data warehouse for other industries such as for research/science/labs, geology, topology, earth sciences, astronomy, and particle physics.

Now that you have implemented a data warehouse for good uses, in the next two chapters of this book I will discuss the testing and administration aspects.

■ ■ ■

CHAPTER 16

Testing Your Data Warehouse

As with any other IT system, after you build the data warehouse with its ETL and applications, you need to test it thoroughly. You need to go through six types of testing. I'll introduce them here with a brief description, and in the rest of the chapter I will discuss them one by one:

ETL testing: In the ETL testing stage, you make sure that appropriate changes in the source system are captured properly and propagated correctly into the data warehouse. You also need to verify that the bulk load solution works as it was intended so it can do the initial data loading.

Functional testing: In the functional testing stage, you make sure all the business requirements are fulfilled.

Performance testing: In the performance testing stage, you verify that the data warehouse can handle the required load and volume.

Security testing: In the security testing stage, you make sure only the users who should be able to access the resources can actually access them.

User acceptance testing: In the user acceptance testing stage, the end users use the data warehouse system to verify the usability.

End-to-end testing: In the end-to-end testing stage, you let the system run for a few days to simulate production situations.

In this chapter, I will focus on the mechanism and procedure of how each type of test is conducted specifically within the data warehousing context. I will not discuss the general software testing methodology. The software testing methodology is the systematic arrangement and management of testing tasks to produce high-quality software. These testing tasks include creating a test plan, creating test cases, producing test data, performing unit testing, doing system tests and integration tests, doing system fixes, writing test results, conducting user acceptance tests, and writing test reports. The methodology explains how each task relates to each other in the project plan. The methodology specifies how to log errors, how to pass errors to the development team, how to get the fix back into the main release, how to judge how many passes of the test will be performed, how to log the test results, how to report the number of errors found and fixed to management, and so on and so forth. These are the items in the software testing methodology.

Instead, I will focus on the content of those tests specific to data warehousing. For example, when doing functionality testing, what part of the data warehouse do you need to verify? How does it differ from the functionality testing for an ERP system? How do you test the ETL?

How do you conduct a user acceptance test for a data warehouse? Do you test data quality? Those kinds of questions are the ones I will discuss in this chapter. So, let's discuss the six test areas one by one. In each area, I will discuss what the test is about, the purpose of doing the test, and how to perform the test.

Data Warehouse ETL Testing

ETL testing is important because ETL brings the data from the source systems into the data warehouse. If the ETL is incorrect, the data in the data warehouse will be incorrect. If the data in the warehouse is wrong, no matter how good the data model is and no matter how good the application is, you can't use the data warehouse. On the other hand, if the data is right but the data model is not perfect (it's missing some attributes here and there, for example) or the application is not right (it's not user-friendly enough, for example), then you can still use the data warehouse system. At least you can still query the data store directly by using a SQL query tool instead of the applications.

Essentially, a data warehouse system has three primary components: ETL, data stores, and applications. Of these three, ETL development takes the largest portion of data warehouse development effort. A general view in the data warehouse community is that ETL takes 60–80 percent of development effort, but in my experience ETL takes about 50 percent of the development effort, while data stores take 25 percent and front-end applications take 25 percent. The percentages vary depending on how complex your application is. The hardware and software platform is probably 10 to 25 percent of the combined three. Figure 16-1 shows this proportion. Because ETL is the largest portion, it requires a larger effort in testing than those of data stores, applications, and platform.

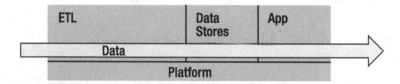

Figure 16-1. *Three major components of a data warehouse*

Figure 16-1 also shows that the ETL is the process that brings the data into the data stores, while applications deliver the data to the users. Users can also query the data warehouse directly without using applications.

The main objectives of ETL testing are the following:

- To make sure you get all the data you need, in other words, that you don't miss some data updates in the source systems.

- To make sure the data is correctly loaded into the data warehouse, that is, loaded in the right tables, on the right columns, in the right formats, at the right time.

- To make sure the incremental ETL is working according to the design, regardless of whether it is a batch architecture, a push architecture, or a service-oriented architecture.

- To make sure the bulk load script (if you have one) correctly loads the data into the data warehouse.

Now let's discuss the *how*. You start from the ETL architecture diagram and the ETL processes. You need to test that both the overall ETL process and the individual ETL tasks deliver the data correctly to the data stores. Say you have a daily batch consisting of 30 tasks, a weekly batch consisting of 3 tasks, and an hourly batch of 2 tasks. To test the ETL processes, you run the daily ETL workflow, making sure the tasks within the daily batch are executed in the correct order. Then you do the same thing with the hourly and weekly batches. You then check the data in the target, comparing it to the source system.

If you have any "push approach" or SOA-based ETL, you switch them on and make some transactions in the source systems, making sure the changes are captured and propagated properly into the data warehouse. You need to test whether there is any "data leakage" during the ETL run. Please refer to Chapter 7 for an explanation of what data leakage is.

One important feature to test is *recoverability*. Recoverability means that the ETL processes should be robust enough that in the event of failure the system can recover without data loss or damage. The ETL process needs to be built so that if the process is stopped at any point and rerun, there is no data loss. You test recoverability by listing the event types you want to be covered against, such as loss of electricity and disk failure. You then list the process types within the ETL system where the failures possibly occur, such as extraction process, DDS population process, and cube-building process. You then simulate the combination between each event type and each process type, followed by a rerun of the ETL processes. You then check that the process can continue as normal and there is no data loss.

For an SOA architecture doing trickle feed, you need to simulate message queue (MQ) failure or network failure where the messages sent by the source system don't reach the target system and need to be resent. You can simulate MQ failure by disabling the queue and the network failure by changing the IP address. If you build a notification or alert feature in the ETL, you need to test that the correct people are notified when certain events happen.

In some projects, you can use the incremental ETL architecture to do the initial bulk loading of the data warehouse. In other projects, you need to use a separate ETL architecture for bulk loading, because the incremental ETL is not designed to handle a big load, such as loading 200 million rows of historical transactions, for example. This is particularly true when you use real-time message-based ETL (SOA) for the incremental ETL that was designed to pick up, say, 10 to 100 rows every time. To determine whether the incremental ETL is capable of doing bulk initial data load, you need to test it. If the projected execution time is beyond what you can tolerate, you need to develop a separate ETL architecture for bulk loading. In either case, you need to verify that the bulk load script works, that is, that it loads the initial data completely and correctly into the target tables. It is essential to test that you don't miss any data around the cutoff date, because there is a potential gap between the bulk load cutoff date and the start date of the incremental load.

Functional Testing

Functional testing is about making sure that all business requirements are satisfied. Business requirements are data and capabilities that the users need from the data warehouse in order to perform their business tasks, such as the ability to analyze a particular customer activity by certain criteria, the ability to view certain data for a specific period, and the ability to drill down the data into a certain level to identify business problems.

Business requirements are identified at the beginning of a data warehousing project, which will then drive the design and development. Simply speaking, functional testing is just verifying that the data warehouse that you built satisfies all those requirements. In the case of the Amadeus Entertainment Group case study, you identified the business requirements in Chapter 4. The following are two of those requirements:

- The data warehouse should enable Amadeus Entertainment to analyze subscription sales (that's when a customer is subscribing to a package rather than to a product) over time by geographical area, by customer demographic, by stores and sales territory, and by product hierarchy. In addition, they also need to analyze by subscription duration and lead source (where the customers are coming from). They need to know the revenues, the costs, and the margins, which are evaluated every day for a period of one month in U.S. currency.

- At the store level, the ability to view the daily data in the last few weeks is important. The stores need to see the ups and downs of sales, costs, and profitability, and the stores need to be able to drill down to any particular day to understand the causes of low sales or low profitability problems, such as specific products, titles, media, or customers.

In functional testing, you test all these business requirements that you defined in the beginning of the project, as discussed in Chapter 4. For example, you analyze the cost of subscription sales for each month by stores and sales territory. You check that the data warehouse figures are correct. You do this by comparing it to the source systems. The figures on the data warehouse must match the figures from the source systems. Of course, it is not possible to check every single number. One testing technique is to verify the total, then drill down one level (verify all members), and finally drill down to the bottom level by picking n members. For example, in the case of the first requirement mentioned earlier, you need to get the total revenue, cost, and margin for a particular day and verify that these three figures are correct. Then you drill down one level. For geographical area, the highest level is country, so you check the total revenue, cost, and margin for each country for that particular day. Then you do the customer demographic, such as occupation or age group, that is, the total revenue, cost, and margin for each occupation or age group. Then you do other areas such as sales territory, product hierarchy, and subscription duration. Finally, after you finish testing the top level, you test the bottom level by selecting a few members. For example, for the product hierarchy, the bottom (base) level is the product code. You can pick a few product codes and check their revenue, cost, and margin for that particular day.

The product codes are not selected randomly but are based on the boundary values, such as the minimum and maximum values, for example product codes that are never purchased by the customers (minimum values) or product codes that are very active/popular (maximum values). You can also determine the boundary values based on product age, such as the newest product code and the oldest product code.

After checking the totals, you also need to verify the count of the dimension members at all levels. For example, if you have 12 product categories, 438 product types, and 25,034 products in the source systems, then the data warehouse needs to have the same numbers. In the case of the first requirement (subscription sales), the fact table type is a snapshot. If the fact table is incremental, like the Product Sales fact table in the Amadeus Entertainment case study, it is important to verify the total of the individual additive measures in the fact table within different time periods, such as a week, month, quarter, or year. For example, in the Product Sales fact table, you need to verify the total revenue, cost, and margin within various levels of time periods.

It is imperative that the tester understands how to verify the data warehouse figures. They do this by comparing the data warehouse figures to the source systems, either by querying the source system database or by running some reports on the source system applications. The testers need to know how to use the source systems to get the data warehouse figure that is being tested. In the earlier example, say that according to the data warehouse the total revenue for France on October 21, 2007, is $21,351.64. The tester needs to know how to use the source system to get the revenue for France for that day, including whether returns and cancellations are included, whether intercompany sales are excluded, and whether voucher codes are counted as face value or cost value. He needs to know what currency rate to use to convert from euros to U.S. dollars. To perform this test, you need somebody whose job involves calculating all this. It is likely that for different business areas you will need a different tester.

Functionality testing is not just about calculating the totals and comparing counts between the source system and the data warehouse. You also need to test things such as a slowly changing dimension, whether it is type 1, 2, or 3. You need to test the surrogate keys, including whether they link the fact tables and the dimensions properly. You need to test the referential integrity in the ODS. You need to test the date dimension, making sure that all the attributes are correct for all dates, such as for the fiscal week, fiscal year, week day indicator, last day of the month indicator, and week number. You need to check the dimension hierarchies, such as whether product code X belongs to product type Y. You need to test all customer attributes, such as whether all the demographic attributes of customer X are correctly integrated from two different source systems, according to the survivorship criteria. You need to verify all degenerate dimensions in all fact tables, such as order line number and purchase order ID. You need to test all control columns such as the loaded timestamp, source system code, and active flag. You need to test that all data quality filters work properly. And last but not least, you need to check the metadata, all seven types: data definition and mapping metadata, data structure metadata, source system metadata, ETL processes metadata, data quality metadata, audit metadata, and usage metadata. (I explained these types of metadata in Chapter 10.) During the testing, you need to verify that they are populated correctly.

Numerous business scenarios and business conditions need to be tested in functionality testing. First you identify a business event that you want to test (examples will follow). Then you prepare a test data in the test environment of the source system to simulate this event. You then run the ETL processes to bring the simulated data into the data warehouse and verify the data has been loaded into each data store correctly. This verification is done by comparing the data in the data warehouse to the source systems. Examples of the business events are when a branch closes and all its customers are reallocated to another branch, when you have a price increase, when you have a month-end or year-end process, and when a new fiscal calendar begins. There are also business events that are more day-to-day routine, such as interest rate changes, currency rate updates, supplier changes, stock audits, a new newsletter, returns and refunds, new calling plans, and customer re-sign-ups. These are real business events that would affect the data warehouse. Of course, different industries have different events; for example, a new calling plan is specific to the telecommunications industry, a customer re-sign-up is specific to finance and utilities, and a stock audit is specific to the retail or supply chain industry. You need to verify that the data in the data warehouse is still correct on all these occasions.

Test data is important in performing functionality testing. It takes a lot of effort to create the test data for a particular test condition. Unlike other application testing, in data warehouse functional testing you need to create the test data *in the source systems*, not in the data warehouse. You need to work with the source system DBA to create the test data. Sometimes it is rather difficult to simulate certain conditions in the source systems, and it is easier to use real events from production, such as a price increase. If the price increase percentages are different for each customer and they have been accumulated over a few years, it is difficult to create test data to simulate the increase. It may be easier to use the last annual price increase data from production and copy the data to the QA environment so you can search it to find the data you need for testing. Sometimes it is the reverse; that is, it is quite difficult to find a specific event in the production source system, and it is easier to create the event yourself, such as for a new product. You may find it difficult to find a certain product or customer with certain criteria that you need. In this case, it is easier to create the product or customer in the test environment.

Performance Testing

Performance testing verifies that all technical requirements related to the platform, capacity, latency, and response times are satisfied. In particular, you need to prove that the data warehouse system is capable of completing the data loading process in a particular amount of time. Performance testing is important because when developing the ETL processes, you use a small amount of data. You often focus on making sure the *functionality* of the ETL processes is correct. Now that it is developed, you need to run it in operational conditions in terms of work load, timing, amount of data loaded, and amount of data already existing in the target tables, hardware, indexes, partitions, number of users, type and amount of queries, cube-processing times, number of variables in data mining and predictive analysis, and so on. The data stores, the ETL, and the applications need to be tested in operational production conditions to ensure that they satisfy the performance requirements. For example, when developing the workflow to populate a fact table, you load hundreds of rows into a fact table that is nearly empty, and you run each workflow in isolation. In contrast, you know that when it is operational, the fact table would have hundreds of millions of rows and each load could be roughly millions rows, so many different workflows will run simultaneously. It is hardly surprising that a few months after the data warehouse is operational, this ETL workflow would run slowly in production, even though it ran smoothly on the development server. This is because the operational production conditions are different from the development conditions. The purpose of performance testing is to eliminate these types of risk.

There are two main areas to test the performance in a data warehouse. The first area is about the ETL, and the second one concerns the applications. In the ETL area, you need to verify that both the bulk load performance and the incremental load performance satisfy the required performance criteria. The bulk load is used to populate the data warehouse for the first time. The incremental load is used to populate the warehouse when it is operational. On the application side, the performance criteria are generally about the response times.

The purpose of doing performance testing is to satisfy the performance requirements. Some requirements are applicable to the whole data warehouse system (let's call these *general* performance requirements), while other requirements are applicable only to specific elements of the system (let's call these *specific* performance requirements). General performance requirements require the whole system to perform based on certain conditions, such as the availability of the data warehouse. Specific performance requirements require only those elements (such as certain ETL processes or certain tables in the data stores) to perform at certain levels. For example, the ETL process that extracts data from a particular source system needs to be completed within a certain time window. You need to ensure that both the ETL and the applications satisfy both the general and specific performance requirements.

So, what are the tasks you need to do to perform data warehouse performance testing? There are essentially three steps to carry out performance testing on the ETL processes: configure the test environment, run the bulk load processes, and run the incremental processes. Let's go through these three steps one by one:

1. First you need to configure the data warehouse test servers as per the production configuration. You create the data stores and set up the ETL processes; that is, you migrate the SSIS packages from development to test server. Then you need to connect the test server to the test version of the source system (sometimes known as QA) and set up all necessary connectivity and access. You load the test data into the QA environment. You run the whole ETL processes end to end using a small load to verify that the test environment has been configured properly.

2. You run the initial load ETL processes (be it T-SQL scripts or SSIS packages) to populate the warehouse and measure their performance, that is, when each task in the initial/bulk load ETL processes started and when each one completed. One way to measure the performance is by utilizing the ETL log and the timestamp column of the loaded table. Let me explain what I mean by the ETL log and the timestamp column. The ETL log is a table or file where the ETL system writes to. It is sometimes known as the audit table or file. In each ETL task or process, after each major step the ETL routine writes a row (if it is a table) or a line (if it is a file) in this ETL log, containing the essential statistics of the task, such as the data volume (number of records affected by the operation), the task name, and the current time. The timestamp column contains the time the row was loaded or modified.

   Both the ETL log and the timestamp columns are useful to measure the performance of the incremental ETL and bulk load because you can determine the duration of each ETL task. They are also useful for troubleshooting the root cause or finding the bottleneck of the performance problem as well as for doing fine-tuning in the data warehouse performance. You can do this by finding out the long-running/long-performing tasks, and then you try to make these tasks more efficient. Both take a little bit of time to implement (probably 30 minutes to an hour for each task) because you need to program each ETL task to write into the log, but they are extremely useful because they help identify slow-running tasks (I have seen a 50 percent increase in performance), so they are worth the effort.

Another way to measure the performance is using SQL Server Profiler. You set up SQL Server Profiler to log the time each SQL statement is executed. You can also utilize SSIS logging. SSIS logs runtime events as they are executed in SSIS. For this you need to enable logging on each task in all SSIS packages in the bulk load processes.

3. Then you run the ETL batches—whether it is daily, hourly, or weekly—in a particular sequence according to the prepared test scenario and measure their performance (speed). In incremental ETL, you can also use the same methods/instruments as the bulk load to measure the performance: ETL log, timestamp, SQL Server Profiler, and SSIS logging. For real-time ETL, you need to measure the time lag as well; that is, how many minutes after the transaction was made in the source system did the data arrive in the data warehouse?

The previous steps are about performance testing for ETL. For applications, to measure performance you can script the actions, or you can measure them manually. Scripting the actions means you use software to record the actions that a user does when using the applications. You then play the recording back to simulate many people using the system simultaneously while recording the system performance. Measuring them manually means you use the system interactively.

In application performance testing, you use the applications, whether they're reports, mining models cubes, or BI applications, using both normal scenarios and exception scenarios. Normal scenarios are steps that the users perform in regular daily activities. Exception scenarios are steps the users perform that result in errors.

As discussed in Chapter 6 when I talked about physical database design, you can do several things to improve application performance, such as indexing, partitioning tables, and creating summary tables. The one with the biggest results is creating summary tables (also known as *aggregates*), whether they are in the relational database (DDS) or in the cubes. This is because results have been calculated in advance, so all the application needs to do is to display them on the screen. But too many summary tables (or cube aggregates) could decrease the performance of the ETL, because populating them takes time. So, you need to be careful and strike a delicate balance between them. As I discussed in Chapter 6, summary tables needs to be at least 10 times smaller in terms of the number of rows, ideally 100 times smaller or more. Otherwise, there is no point in creating a summary table. Remember that a summary table needs to be updated every time the underlying fact table is updated. The ideal time to refresh the summary tables is immediately after the population of the underlying fact table. To be sure about the benefit, you need to measure both the time required to update the summary table and the improvement in application queries.

As discussed in Chapters 5–8, you need to think about the performance when you design the data warehouse, not tweak it when you finish building the data warehouse. You should start taking the performance into account when you design the architecture and again when you physically build the architecture (that is, server, network, SAN, and so on). Then you incorporate performance requirements when you design the data stores, both when you do the logical design (data modeling) as well as physical design (database creation). After that you design the ETL, also with performance considerations in mind. Then when you design the reports, cubes, mining models, and other types of applications, you need to design by keeping an eye on the performance factor. The whole thing should be designed for performance at every single step from the start of the project, not after the data warehouse system is built.

Security Testing

Security testing is about making sure that only the people and applications that are allowed to access the data warehouse can actually access it. In addition, you also need to test how people are accessing the data in the data warehouse, such as the tools used to access the data warehouse and the way the user supplies the security credentials.

As discussed in Chapter 4, these are the security requirements for the Amadeus Entertainment case study:

- All data warehouse users must be able to access the data warehouse front-end applications (report and OLAP) without logging in again. They just need to log in once to Windows on their PC or laptop.

- The data warehouse front-end applications must not be accessible from outside the company network.

- All front-end applications need to be web based, accessible from anywhere in the company network.

- All users should access the front-end applications from a central portal.

- Some users are allowed to access data from their own country only, but some users are allowed to access data from any country.

- Some "power users" are given access to the dimensional store to perform direct SQL queries.

- Certain sensitive data is viewable only by certain people. In other words, users must be authorized to access the data.

- "Who accessed what and when" must be auditable, meaning the user access activity needs to be recorded or logged.

A data warehouse consists of several data stores, and within each data store you have several data objects, such as tables, views, and stored procedures. The security requirements state which users should be able to access which objects. You verify these requirements by connecting to the data warehouse as those users and accessing those objects and by connecting as other users and trying to access the same objects.

You test the data warehouse security by accessing the data warehouse from the applications (such as reports and BI tools) and by issuing direct SQL queries to the data stores. If there is encrypted data such as credit card numbers, you should test accessing them as well. You also verify that the security audit table is populated properly and correctly, containing the username and the time they access the warehouse. You do this by comparing the actions you did on the applications and the security logs.

You need to test the security access from different network points according to the security requirements. Sometimes the requirement is that the data warehouse needs to be accessible from anywhere within the company network. Sometimes the requirement is to restrict the access to certain network segments only. And sometimes you need to enable external access (from outside the company), such as from the Internet. For this purpose, you need to work with the network engineer to identify all possible segments that need to have access to ensure your coverage. Once you've identified the network segments from which you need to test the connectivity, you need the network team to put your test clients into those segments. You can do this either by assigning a fixed IP to the client or by rerouting the client to the target segment. If the corporation consists of several legally separated entities (a situation such as this is common in large enterprises with a lot of acquisitions), you may need some firewall holes to be opened between the company's firewalls to allow the traffic between the entities. One way to test the connectivity is by asking the representative of the user population (for example, one from each region or office) to access the warehouse portal (from their computer) and access the applications from there.

User Acceptance Testing

The three tests mentioned earlier (functionality, performance, and security) are conducted by the data warehouse development project team. Once these three tests are completed, it is the end users' turn to test the data warehouse. This test is called the *user acceptance test* (UAT). This is where some key users use the data warehouse and its applications to find out whether it fulfills their needs. The users also test the user friendliness.

Before they start, you explain all the functionality of the data warehouse and its applications to the users. You walk them through the systems, explaining the components and the data flow architecture, to make sure they understand their way in, out, and around the system. You give the users with proper security access by creating user accounts in the applications for them. You populate the data warehouse with test data that satisfies the UAT scenarios, which can be from production or QA source systems. The test data may need to be tailored according to specific scenarios. You then ask the users to perform certain scenarios using the applications and ask them to record the results. You then let the users use the system to test the functionality, the user friendliness, and the appearance and have them write down their comments.

I want to point out here that UAT is done *after* you have conducted the ETL test, the functional test, the performance test, and the security test. This means that when users test the data warehouse and its applications, all the functionality written in the use cases is there, as per the functional specification.

The purpose of conducting a UAT is twofold. The primary purpose is to confirm that the system is capable of performing the tasks for which it was designed. The secondary purpose is to get user feedback, especially about user friendliness.

In the UAT, you confirm the system capability to perform the daily business tasks and fulfill the user needs. The test cases in the functionality testing are designed to cover all possibilities, based on the functional and nonfunctional specification that was derived from the business requirements. In a user acceptance test, ideally the test cases are designed to reflect day-to-day activities of different roles within the user base. It is not about how easy it is to administer the data warehouse,[1] but it's about how easy it is for the business users from each role to use the data warehouse and its applications to perform their tasks.

User friendliness of the same application is different from user to user because each has different responsibilities. For example, a particular user could be a regional manager who is not responsible for a particular store. Unlike a store manager, she does not need daily sales and cost reports. She doesn't need a breakdown by product type. She needs a regional

---

1. Unless you've created or deployed tools to accomplish this.

overview to see which branches are performing poorly and which ones are right on target. The same application could be more user friendly to a store manager than to a regional manager.

End-to-End Testing

At this stage, the data warehouse is almost ready to go to production. The ETL tasks have been verified in the ETL test. All the functionalities has been tested in the functionality test. The performance issues have been sorted out in the performance test. The security has been checked in the security test. The users have reviewed the data warehouse, and all their requests have been processed. Before deploying the data warehouse into production, there is just one more test to do: end-to-end testing where you verify the whole system from end to end.

To do end-to-end testing, you let the data warehouse ETL processes run for a few days to simulate operational conditions. The ETL batches are running automatically. A tester is querying the data warehouse every now and then and using some front-end applications. You check that there are no missing transactions, customers, or other data. You check that the data quality works fine. You check that the audit tables are populated. You check that the ODS tables are populated properly. You check that all the fact tables and dimension tables in the DDS are populated properly. You check that staging is correctly used and purged. You check the applications, reports, cubes, and mining models. It's like doing a final check of everything, but this time the ETL runs automatically, feeding the data into the data warehouse every now and then according to its schedule (daily, hourly, weekly, and so on).

Some people call this end-to-end testing *integration testing*. You can perform the end-to-end testing before the UAT. You can perform it after ETL and functionality testing.

When you do this test, you document everything: all the details regarding the configuration; all the details about the initial data; information about which code base you deployed, how to deploy them, and which cutoff date you loaded the data from; details of the security/functional account that you use to set up; and so on. You make note of anything and everything, because you need to repeat this deployment in production. The note is ideally in the form of a *deployment procedure*, which is a step-by-step list for deploying the data warehouse system to any environment.

After completing the end-to-end testing satisfactorily, you are now ready to migrate to production. So with that note, you approach the production system with care.

Migrating to Production

You are now ready to deploy the data warehouse to production. You will do the same thing as for end-to-end testing, except this time you are doing it in the production environment. You will execute the same scripts, copy the same executables/files, set the same configurations, load the same initial data, and activate the same ETL processes. You will do every single step in the deployment procedure that you created earlier.

But wait, before you do that, let's go through this "go live" checklist. This list is not specific to data warehouses. In fact, any system can use this "go live" checklist. This checklist covers the technical aspects of production deployment, such as environment, help desk, handover, user training, and documentation. It does not cover management aspects such as corporate communication, benefit realization, and project management.

1. *Prepare the production environment*: You make sure that the production environment is ready. This is necessary so the deployment of data stores and ETL process into production goes well.

   You may tend to just assume that the production environment is ready. You should not assume that. Instead, you need to check that the production SQL servers are built and configured properly and that all the application servers (report and analysis services) are configured correctly. All the things you went through in Chapter 6 need to happen to the production hardware, including disk carving/LUN masking, database configuration, storage allocation, and so on. The firewall between the network segment where the users are and the data warehouse SQL server needs to be opened. This may be a lengthy procedure, so allow plenty of time. If external access to the data warehouse applications is required, it may even take longer to open the firewall. Also, you need to check the licenses for all software used in production including SQL Server, Windows, BI applications, ETL software, and any e-mail clients.

2. *Coordinate with the help desk for first-line support*: Make sure that the help desk personnel can support the data warehouse and its applications. This is necessary to ensure that the data warehouse users will get proper support from the help desk.

   Just like what you did at UAT to the users, you need to go through the data warehouse with the help desk personnel. You explain all the functionality to them so that they know what the users are talking about when receiving call from the users. You set up user accounts with proper security for them to use. You agree with them who to contact for data problems, who to contact for access and security, who to contact for technical issues, and who to contact for business issues.

3. *Hand over the data warehouse system to the operation team*: You transfer the knowledge and responsibility from the development team (project team) to the operation team. This is necessary to ensure that when the project team is dissolved (after the project is closed), the users will get proper support for solving operational issues and enhancement requests.

   Just like what you did with help desk team, you go through the data warehouse with the operation team. You explain all the functionality to them, but in a more detailed level than the help desk. Ideally there should be a dedicated data warehouse administrator (DWA) within the support team who will support the data warehouse and all its applications. You explain everything to this DWA, including how the system works and the details of ETL tasks, DDS and ODS schemas, and practically anything he needs to know in order to be able to solve any problems that may arise. You give him all data warehouse design documents including architecture design, ETL design, schema design (ERD), cube design, report design, business requirements, functional requirements, and all testing documents. Ideally, the DWA joined the team at least three months in advance and is involved in the later phase of the development. The earlier the DWA is involved in the data warehouse development, the better. The DWA definitely needs to be involved in the end-to-end testing and in the production deployment. For a few weeks (say, two to three weeks), both the development/project team and the operation team support the data warehouse operation, and then after that, both parties sign the handover document to formally mark that the project has ended, the project team is dismissed, and the operation team is in charge to support the data warehouse.

4. *Train users and create documentation*: You train the end users and create a user manual. This is necessary to ensure that the users have proper knowledge to use the applications and query the data warehouse.

For the users to be able to use the data warehouse system properly, you need to explain all the functionality. You need to walk the users through the system. You explain what data is stored in the data warehouse and how the data is organized. You go through all the applications one by one—every single report, every single cube, every single mining model, and every single BI application. You put all this information in a nice and compact user guide and put it in the data warehouse portal so that all the users can read it.

5. *Liaise with the DBA*: You discuss the database administrative requirements with the DBA. This is necessary to ensure that the data warehouse databases will be supported properly by the DBA.

In some companies, the DWA is also the database administrator (DBA). But in some companies, they are two (or more) different people. You need to discuss the capacity planning and projected growth with the DBA, especially with regard to the disk space in the SAN. You also need to discuss the backup and test restore requirements with the DBA. In the case where the backup to tape is administered by a central person from a network department or data center, you arrange the backup to tape with them. The test restore needs to be performed regularly at least every six months. Also, discuss the disaster recovery (DR) plan with the data center people.

6. *Create the data warehouse portal*: This is necessary to ensure that the users have single access points to the data warehouse reports and applications, as well as the user guide and help desk numbers. Configure and set up the data warehouse portal correctly according to the structure that the users need. Don't forget to set the security arrangements as well.

Now that you have prepared everything, you are ready to deploy the data warehouse into production environment. When you migrate into production, there is no more testing.

Summary

In this chapter, I discussed testing the data warehouse: ETL testing, functional testing, performance testing, security testing, user acceptance testing, and finally end-to-end testing. I also discussed a short "go live" checklist that you need to follow when deploying the data warehouse to production.

You should not underestimate testing. It usually requires quite a significant amount of time. If you count, there are six types of data warehouse testing. Essentially, in testing you do anything necessary to verify that the data warehouse is working properly. A good data warehouse consists of hundreds if not thousands of data elements and application parts, and each of them needs to be verified. And you should always remember that testing involves fixing. You need to include the time required to fix the errors or accommodate the change requests.

In the next chapter, which is the last chapter of the book, I will discuss the operational aspects of a data warehouse—that is, how to administer a data warehouse as well as how to maintain it.

CHAPTER 17

∎∎∎

Data Warehouse Administration

The tasks of migrating a data warehouse to production fall into three categories according to the personnel involved, as displayed in Figure 17-1. First, the BI manager creates the user guide, and the development team writes the system documentation and the support manual. Second, the business intelligence manager (BIM) trains the business users, and the development team trains the data warehouse administrator (DWA) and support desk personnel. Finally, the DWA sets up the users, and the data warehouse goes into operation.

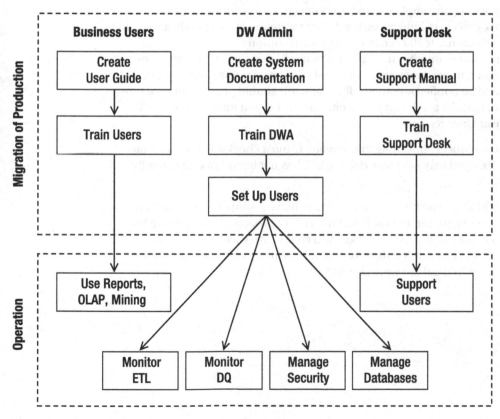

Figure 17-1. *Migration to production and operations*

This chapter is about the second half of the diagram in Figure 17-1: operation. In particular, I will discuss the DW administrator tasks, including monitoring ETL, monitoring data quality, managing security, and managing databases. I will also discuss system enhancements such as bringing a new piece of data into the warehouse and updating the applications.

Monitoring Data Warehouse ETL

One of the most important things in data warehouse administration is monitoring the ETL processes. The ETL processes feed the data warehouse with data. If the ETL is not running at all for that day, it's not that bad, because it means the data in the warehouse is old, that's all. But if the ETL is running halfway on that day, that's bad, because the data could be in an incomplete state. It's not necessarily wrong, but it's incomplete.

For example, say the ETL batch starts with extracting data from the source systems into the stage and then loading the data into the ODS. The ETL then loads the data from the ODS into the DDS, starting with the dimension tables first and then moving on to the fact tables. When loading the second fact table, the process stops halfway because of an error. Let's say out of 46 branches, data from 20 branches was loaded completely, the 21st branch was halfway done, and the remaining branches were not touched. The regional totals would be incorrect because the data was not complete. The data warehouse was not ready to be consumed by the users because it was halfway through the loading process. To avoid this situation (because you are risking serving incomplete or incorrect data to the end user), in some implementations you can block end users from accessing the data warehouse (so only the DWA can access it) until the data warehouse is 100 percent ready for consumption.

This is why it is important to monitor the ETL, checking whether the ETL process executes successfully. I cannot emphasize enough that this should be an automated process, and if any task fails, you should be notified automatically. Again, this should not be a manual process. This is so important that I'm going to repeat it one more time: you must automate ETL monitoring. Why? There are four reasons:

- First, if it is a manual process (meaning that somebody must check it before you know that the ETL ran OK), you may not know that the ETL has not been working correctly for a week!

- Second, you need to automate the ETL monitoring to make it simpler and quicker to do the monitoring. The ETL processes may have hundreds of tasks, and it could take hours to check them. To make it simpler and quicker, you could have exception-based reporting, meaning you get a report only if there is something wrong. This way, you need to check only a few tasks that did not work correctly.

- Third, you need to automate the ETL monitoring process because it could fail in the middle of the night (say at 1 a.m.), and nobody would notice anything until 9 a.m. when everybody comes to the office. Then it's too late to do anything to get the data warehouse ready for that day. If you notice earlier (say it got reported automatically to the on-duty operations team, which may be outsourced offshore because of the hours of operation), then they could check and fix it so the warehouse is available in the morning. This is especially important if the data warehouse is used for CRM rather than for BI, because the campaign must go out on a certain day of the week (maybe every day). If CRM campaigns don't run for that day, the revenue would be directly affected.

- Finally, you need to automate the ETL monitoring process because of consistency. In an automated process, the same queries and the same steps are executed every single time, so you can guarantee the consistency. Manual checks are more prone to error, and they are also tedious.

Ideally, the ETL batch should not fail because of bad data, but in practice this happens. Bad data should go to the data quality quarantine area and not be loaded into the data warehouse. Alternatively, it could be automatically corrected according to the business rules and loaded into the warehouse. Either way, the ETL should not fail because of bad data. Please refer to Chapter 9 for more information. If your ETL uses service-oriented architecture and the data validation is using XSD, when bad data fails the XSD validation, the ETL should not fail. If your ETL is batch-oriented, when your data firewall encounters bad data, the ETL batch should not stop with an error. It should continue working until the end of the batch.

You can do two things to monitor ETL processes:

- Notification

- Reconciliation

Notification means the system needs to let you know whether the ETL is working OK or failed. *Reconciliation* means you compare the source and target data to find out whether the data in the data warehouse is correct.

More specifically, notification is a process of monitoring the data warehouse ETL tasks and informing the operations personnel of the status of those tasks. There are two approaches generally used for notification: either the ETL tasks themselves internally log their statuses or an external monitoring system checks the ETL tasks periodically. The internal approach is usually cheaper to set up, and it gets more information about the status of ETL tasks (because it's done from the inside), but when a certain task hangs in memory, it would not be able to send the notification. The external approach is potentially more expensive (you need to get monitoring software such as GFI, Nagios, MOM 2005, or Microsoft SCOM 2007), and the information about the ETL task is more limited (because it's done from the outside); however, it is more reliable. In other words, you still get notification even if an ETL task crashes.

For the internal approach, you can set up e-mail and text message notification at the end of the ETL batch. In SSIS, you do this by adding a Send Mail task to the SSIS package, as shown in Figure 17-2.

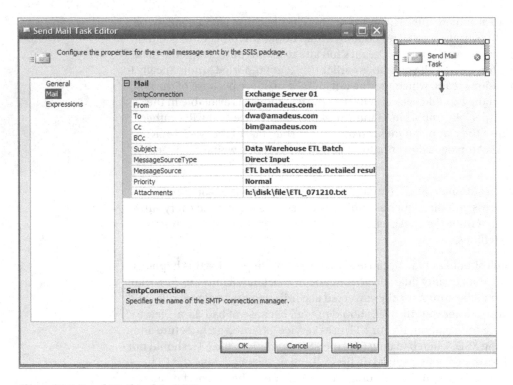

Figure 17-2. *Send Mail task in SSIS*

You could arrange the SSIS tasks in every package to write the execution results (whether it failed or succeeded) into an audit table, along with the timestamp when it happened. (Please refer to Chapter 10 where I discussed the ETL process metadata.) The Send Mail task at the end of the batch can then export this table as a text file or spreadsheet and attach it to the e-mail. You can also filter it to report only the processes that failed. Or you can also set it so that it sends you an e-mail (or a text message) only when a task fails. In other words, if everything works fine, you won't get any notification.

For the external approach, you install the monitoring system and specify the individual ETL tasks you want to monitor. You then configure the notification such as who to notify and how. This is usually part of a bigger monitoring system, not just covering data warehouse ETL tasks but also data warehouse databases and SQL Server health checks.

Reconciliation, as opposed to notification, means comparing the data in the source systems to the data in the data warehouse. *Comparing* means checking whether the summary values (such as the number of records or total values) and detail data (such as a particular fact table row) in the data warehouse are the same as in the source system. For the summary values, you can compare the counts for a particular period (such as for the previous week) or the total for all periods. Using a particular period means fewer records; hence, it's quicker, but the all-periods approach is obviously more thorough. You can combine both approaches; for example, every day you could check a certain period, and every week you could check all periods. An example for a particular period is this: if in the source system you have 723,094 product sales transactions for last week, in the data warehouse you should also have 723,094 transactions for last week. An example of the all-periods approach is comparing the total number of active customers.

The reconciliation process is a systematic comparison between the data in the data warehouse and the data in the source system. *Systematic comparison* means checking a series of predefined summary values and detail data periodically. You can do this using a program that launches SQL queries to both the source system and the data warehouse database to get the totals. The reconciliation process can send a report to the DWA that contains the total counts from both the source system and the data warehouse. The report can be filtered to report only the discrepancies; that is, if there are 100 summary values to check and three of them don't match, then the report contains only three items. If all of them match, it is better to still send a report saying that everything is OK. Otherwise, the DWA could wonder whether there is a problem with the report generation.

When comparing the detail data, the reconciliation process can select some samples to test some values, comparing between the source systems and the data warehouse. The sample can be selected carefully based on the business value. The other consideration of selecting the sample is the coverage; that is, you need to ensure that all dimensions and facts are covered. For example, you can check the measures on the last fact table row loaded into the warehouse to ensure that they match the values in the source systems. Similarly, you can pick up the last row updated in each dimension to compare them with the source systems.

You need to be careful when the ETL combines data from several different source systems using a certain formula. When reconciling this measure with the source system, you need to apply the same formula that was used to calculate the measure. If the formula is changed in the ETL, you also need to update the formula in the reconciliation process.

The reconciliation process needs to be executed regularly as an ongoing process to ensure that the quality of the data that you load into the data warehouse is good all the time.

Monitoring Data Quality

Now I'll quickly recap the data quality (DQ) processes discussed in Chapter 9. Bad data from the source system is picked up by one of the ETL tasks and will be loaded into the data warehouse. The data quality rule within the ETL workflow picks up the bad data and decides which action to take: reject the data (if it's outside the tolerance limits), allow the data into the warehouse (within the tolerance limits), or fix the data automatically (according to predefined rules and values). The failed data is stored in the DQ audit tables, along with additional audit information such as the time it happened, which rule was violated, and the correction status.

A series of DQ reports queries the DQ audit tables for the purpose of finding out when a DQ rule was violated, which/how many data rows are impacted, which/how many source/target tables were impacted, what action was taken, what the status is, and what the values of the source data were. These reports are sent out (usually by e-mail) to various users according to their functional groups. Different people are responsible for different data quality rules/areas. The reports can be web-based so that in the DQ e-mail you can just put the links (URLs) to the reports, rather than the whole reports.

The users review the data quality reports and take actions to correct the data in the source system. Every day (or every week, depending on the report frequency), these users read the DQ report associated with their area of responsibility, such as CRM, subscriber sales, product sales, supplier/purchasing, inventory, and so on. They check the data in the warehouse and ask the source system users to correct the bad data so that the next time the ETL runs, the data is correct.

Bear in mind that the solution is not always correcting the data. The solution can also be adjusting the data quality rule. This is because sometimes the DQ rule can be out-of-date, perhaps because the current condition is different from the condition when the rule was created. What was considered bad data years ago could be OK for today. For example, you could have a DQ rule that says if the number of customers who unsubscribed was not within 35 percent of the last three months' moving average, then raise this as a warning. It may be that the customer subscription behavior was so dynamically up and down that the business user responsible for the CRM DQ area decided to change the DQ rule to "within 65 percent of the last one month's average."

Although the business users are responsible for checking the violation of DQ rules within their own business areas, the BIM needs to monitor the overall trends, such as the following:

The number of DQ rules violation over time: This is to find out whether the number of data quality rules violations generally tends to decrease over time, as shown in Figure 17-3. The number of data quality rules violations generally reflects the quality of the data in the data warehouse because the rules are designed to capture bad data. It is also useful to find out whether there are any rules with an increasing number of occurrences, such as rule 7 in Figure 17-3. From week 11 to week 20, while the violations of other rules went down, the violation of rule 7 went up. You need to find out whether the bad data for rule 7 is corrected in the source system.

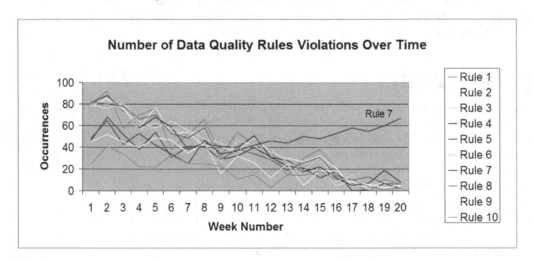

Figure 17-3. *Number of data quality rules violations over time*

The geographic dispersion of rule violations: This is to find out the number of rules violations per geographical unit, such as branches or stores, regions, and divisions, as shown in Figure 17-4. This chart is per rule; that is, each rule has its own chart.

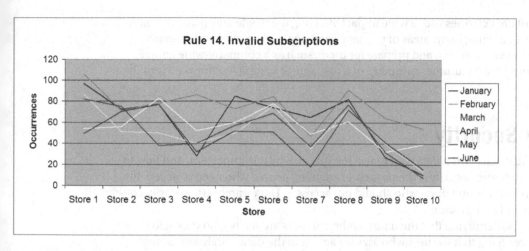

Figure 17-4. *Geographical dispersion of rule violations*

The other overall data quality analysis: To find other data quality analysis that you can do for your own particular situation, you can have a look at your DQ rules. If the DQ rule is about a dimension, then you can analyze the data by the attribute of that dimension. If the DQ rule is about a measure of a fact table, then you can analyze the data by any dimension of that fact table. For example, if the DQ rule is about the product dimension, then the DQ violation can be analyzed by product type and product category.

From data quality analysis, sometimes you'll find problems, such as the increasing number of rule violations shown in Figure 17-3. Common DQ problems are a high quantity of violations (either persistently high, steadily increasing, or spikes) and uneven distribution of violations (high only for a specific product type, store, or other item). The causes of the problems are different in each organization. A systematic approach to understanding the causes of these problems in your situation is to analyze the corresponding rows on the audit table to study each rule violation, look at the rule formula in the metadata database, and examine the source values in the source systems. This enables you to find the root of the problem. These are several common causes:

- There is no proper validation in the front-end application. In this case, you need to add or fix the validation in the front-end application.

- A one-off event was happening in the source system, such as a large data load. In this case, you need to do a manual one-off data correction in the source system by asking the source system DBA to execute a data change script.

- The DQ rule is out-of-date. In this case, you need to update, fix, or deactivate the rule.

- There's no specific rule covering a particular DQ area or issue. In this case, you need to create a new rule to cover that area.

The data quality trends need to be monitored continuously. It is possible that the number of violations for a particular rule could decrease and reach a steady plateau and then suddenly increase again. Sometimes the increase could happen across many rules. The possible causes of this kind of event are activities with a wide impact affecting the whole company or organization and therefore affecting many areas of the data warehouse. These events are usually known in advance, so you can plan and prepare for them, such as a company-wide annual price increase, a merger with another company, or a new source system feeding data into the data warehouse.

Managing Security

In this section, I will discuss what data warehouse security is, why it is important, and how to manage it. Data warehouse security is the process of enabling people who need to access the data warehouse and preventing those who should not access it. Data warehouse security covers authentication and authorization.

Authentication is identifying that the data warehouse users are really who they said they are. This includes verifying that the user who asks for access to the data warehouse should genuinely have access. You can do this by checking with the user's superior or the BIM. After verifying the user, you can create the user. You also need to remove leavers or movers from the list of data warehouse users. *Movers* are people who moved departments and are no longer doing their data warehouse roles. *Leavers* are people who left the company and don't need access to the data warehouse anymore.

Authorization is verifying that the user has access to a data warehouse object before allowing the user to access it. This includes giving or blocking access to the data stores, databases, reports, cubes, mining models, portals, and dashboards. This is done using security groups and security roles.

A security group is a collection of users with the same access rights. The purpose of creating security groups is to make the security administration simpler and to make the access rights consistent across the group. A security role is a functional position with the ability to do certain tasks. A user or a group can then be assigned to that role, making the user or group capable of doing the tasks that the role is capable of doing.

Other security tasks are checking security logs and applying security patches. The DWA needs to check Windows and the SQL Server security log, as well as the front-end application such as SSRS and BI applications. Applying SQL Server and Windows security patches to SQL Server installations and Windows servers used by the data warehouse is required to minimize the possibility of people exploiting known SQL Server and Windows vulnerabilities.

Managing data warehouse security is important because a data warehouse usually contains a lot of data from different source systems. It is used as a foundation to make important business decisions and to run applications such as CRM. If you don't protect this data, unauthorized people will be able to read the data. Or worse, they may be able to modify the data, resulting in inaccurate decisions being made or some problems in the CRM operations.

Now let's talk about the *how*—how to manage data warehouse security. Ideally, you need to put a process in place that covers capturing the security request, verifying the user, granting the necessary access, and removing inactive users. For example, new users need to fill in a form stating who they are, which department they're in, which part of the data warehouse they need to access, the purpose (short-term project, daily operation, regulatory audit, and so on), which environment (dev, QA, or production), and how they would like to access it (via SSRS, SSAS, BI application, or ODBC).

It is important to state for how long the user needs the access. For example, a member of a customer loyalty project may need access to the DDS via ODBC for three months to analyze the customer data. The request is then approved or authorized by either the manager of the requesting user or the BIM.

The DWA can then grant the access to the new user. If a security group for similar users already exists, the DWA adds the new user to the existing security group. If such a group doesn't exist, the DWA creates a new security group. Even if there is only one member to the security group, the DWA would still need to grant the access to a security group, not directly to the user account. This is necessary so that when people change positions, they don't carry the security access with them.

You need to be careful with leavers and movers. As I explained earlier, leavers are people who have left the company, and movers are people who have moved to other departments and have new roles. The problem here is that usually HR is aware of the leaver, but they don't inform the DWA. You need to set up a process where HR notifies the BIM or DWA when people leave their jobs.

The other thing you need to be careful about is a request for a short-term project. More often than not, after the project is finished, the access is still active. This provides a security threat and needs to be fixed urgently. To minimize the chances of this situation recurring, you need to establish a process where all accounts are made to expire after a certain period. On top of that, you need to set up a routine security audit to remove all inactive accounts.

Managing Databases

Data warehouse database management is the process of maintaining the databases used by the data warehouse. Maintaining a database means ensuring that enough disk space is always available, backups are performed regularly, indexes are maintained and optimized, and database statistics are up-to-date. In this section, I'll explain what databases are involved. In a SQL Server–based data warehouse system, you have the stage database, ODS or NDS database, DDS database(s), and Analysis Services databases (cubes). You may also have a metadata database, a data quality database, and archived databases.

Why is it important to maintain the databases in a data warehouse? Well, almost all data in the data warehouse is stored within the databases, and the data in the databases is used to support making business decisions.

The scope of data warehouse database management includes the following. I created this list based on my experience. There may be other activities that are specific to your situation.

Maintaining capacity: One of the most important aspects of managing a SQL Server database is to make sure there is always enough disk space. You don't want tomorrow's ETL load failing because there is not enough space. If you use SAN, you need to make sure the data warehouse has enough space allocation. As the data warehouse size grows, you also need to evaluate whether you need to increase the memory of the server, whether it is the SSIS server, the SSAS server, the SSRS server, or the database server.

Backing up databases: As with any databases, backups need to be scheduled, executed, and monitored. As I explained in Chapter 6, full recovery model is not required for the stage, NDS, and DDS databases. Simple recovery is more suitable for them. Full recovery model is suitable for an ODS database. A good time to back up the databases is after the daily ETL batch is run successfully. In many organizations, backing up to hard media is centralized across servers. If this is the case, you need to back up the databases to disk, ready for the centralized tape backup process to pull it to tapes. You also need to arrange off-site backups.

Testing database restore: It is important to restore the database backup regularly. A database backup is useful only when it is in good condition, and the best way to test that it is in good condition is to restore it. At the very least, you need to test restoring the stage, DDS, NDS, ODS, and Analysis Services databases every three to six months. These frequencies are from my own experience as well as from other DWAs' experience. For your own environment, you may want to use different frequencies. I have found that most people back up, but a disciplined, periodic test restore is something that is still rare.

Maintaining indexes: Depending on the fragmentation levels and the performance of the ETL loading the table, you need to defrag the index or re-create the index. From my experience, you need to consider maintaining the index when the fragmentation is greater than 15–25 percent. I recommend creating a SQL query for each fact table to benchmark the index performance. Once the response time of this query is less than the benchmark, then you need to reindex. In SQL Server 2005 and newer, re-creating indexes is an online operation; that is, users can still access the table being indexed. The exception for this is the clustered index. You can find out the fragmentation using the sys.dm_db_index_physical_stats dynamic management function. This function returns the size and fragmentation information for the data and indexes of the specified table or view. You also need to find out whether certain queries require additional indexes to be created. You can do this by comparing the response times of those queries against the benchmark.

Maintaining table partitions: This includes adding new partitions and removing the old ones (and archiving them) to maintain data warehouse performance, as discussed in Chapter 6. Also, as the fact tables become larger and larger, you may want to convert a fact table from a nonpartitioned table to a partitioned table to improve query performance. It is important to place the partition on the correct filegroup so that you need to back up only the latest partitions (provided that you arrange the partition scheme by date). Please refer to Chapter 6 about implementing table partitioning for data warehousing.

Changing the schema: Occasionally after the data warehouse is in production, you need to update the database schema. What I mean by schema is the database structure, table definition, triggers, views, and stored procedures. This is usually because of development/ enhancement requests (see the next section).

Changing the data: In contrast to the schema changes, sometimes you have a request to load data directly into the data warehouse. One possible cause is integration with another data warehouse or because you have a new source system.

Creating a DDS database: Part of the database maintenance is to create a new database. Sometimes you receive a request from a project team to create a DDS database for the purpose of thorough data analysis specifically for that project. This DDS is a subset of the main DDS containing a certain data mart and for a certain time period. For example, Amadeus Entertainment, for the purpose of issuing a new product range, requires the last six months of data of the product sales data mart.

Making Schema Changes

After the data warehouse goes live and operational, sometimes there are changes in the business processes that generate new data or change or reduce data. For example, installing a new human resources system adds a new data source for the employee dimension in the data warehouse. A new call center system generates a new data source for the customer dimension in the data warehouse. The new piece of data can also come from existing systems. It can be a new attribute, a new measure, a new dimension, or even a new data mart. This requires schema changes in the data warehouse.

Because the data warehouse is now operational, such requests should be regarded and treated as change requests. As with any IT systems, you need to establish a formal procedure to deal with data warehouse change requests. The business user needs to fill in a form describing the request and the reasons or justifications to support it. In the request, the business user needs to mention what data changes are required, where the data is coming from, what the format is, and what information it contains, as well as a sample of the real data. This is necessary so you can understand what schema changes are required to support this change. The requests are then analyzed and prioritized by the BIM and forwarded to the DWA for estimates, and so on, before they are approved for implementation.

As an illustration, please look at the example shown in Figure 17-5. The data warehouse is operational in production, and you have a change request from the business to bring in two new attributes from the source systems. One attribute is from the subscription sales area, and the other one is from the fulfillment operation.

The solid stripes indicate new columns or impacted columns in the databases. As you can see in Figure 17-5, the two attributes flow from the source system to the stage, then to the ODS, and then to the DDS. In my experience, this kind of quick diagram really helps the design, planning, and implementation. It also helps the testing. The diagram gives an overall view of the changes so you know which areas in the data warehouse are impacted. You may want to consider using the diagram in Figure 17-5 when you need to change the data warehouse schema. The diagram is also useful for understanding the overall data flow in your data warehouse, even when you don't have any schema changes.

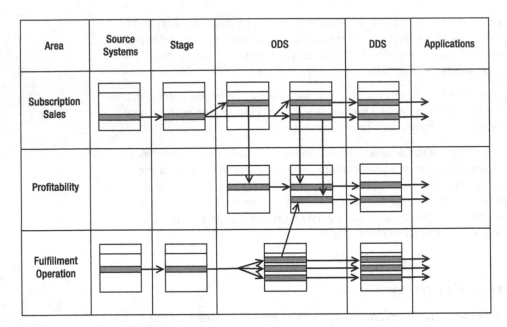

Figure 17-5. *Updating the data warehouse schema*

To create the diagram in Figure 17-5 for your own situation, you can start by drawing the six column headings. Then in the Area column, list your fact tables that are affected by this change. In each cell under Source Systems, Stage, ODS, and DDS, list the tables affected by the change, and mark the columns that will need to be updated or created. Connect those tables with arrows to show how the data flows between tables.

You should not underestimate the size or complexity of the work. It may sound simple when you first hear it: "Two new attributes…ah, that's easy; it's probably going to take me a week." If you count all the arrows in Figure 17-5, you'll see that 21 ETL tasks are involved. If you count all the solid stripes in the stage, ODS, and DDS databases, you'll see that 18 columns are impacted in 10 different tables. That's excluding the impact to modify the applications, such as report and OLAP cubes, which I will discuss in the next section.

Bringing a new piece of data into the data warehouse requires data modeling, schema changes, ETL modifications, new data quality rules, ETL testing, integration testing, and a lot of regression testing. It is not as simple as it looks. You need to define the business requirements and then translate this into a functional specification, as discussed in Chapter 4. Then you update the data model and create the schema change diagram as shown in Figure 17-5. Based on this diagram, you specify the changes required in ETL processes, along with the data quality rules updates. You then code the enhancements and test the changes. You run the system from end to end to ensure that the new data flows through the warehouse correctly. You then rerun the same system test that you did before the data warehouse went into production to make sure this change does not affect any existing functionality.

Updating Applications

After the data warehouse is in production, there will be requests from the users to enhance the applications, such as to add columns in a report, to add a new attribute in the cube, or to update a calculation in the BI application. If you look at Figure 17-5 earlier in the chapter, after the data has been modified, the applications need to be updated too.

Just like when you bring a new piece of data into the warehouse, you also need to have a process for updating the application. The procedure is similar to the one mentioned earlier. In other words, the business user needs to fill in a form describing the request and the reasons or justifications supporting it. In the request, the user needs to specify which area of the data warehouse application needs changing, what changes are required, a summary of the new functionality, and the screen/page mock-up if it requires user interface changes. If it is report changes, the request needs to mention what data changes are required, as well as any changes to the report layout. This is necessary so that you understand the impact of the change to the data warehouse applications. The requests are then analyzed and prioritized by the BIM by determining the change's impact to the business and the financial value generated by the request. The BIM then forwards the request to the DWA for estimates, and so on, before they are approved for implementation.

Once the change is approved for implementation, you then translate the business requirements to functional specifications, and at the same time you write a high-level test plan to verify the use cases in the functional specifications. You then determine the impact of the request to the data warehouse application. It helps to draw the impacts in a diagram like Figure 17-5 so you know exactly which page and applications are affected and how the data will be flowing across applications. You then specify the changes required in each page, cube, or report in the form of technical specification documents. You then code the changes required in each application and test the changes by running the application using test data specifically prepared for testing each change. You then run the data warehouse from end to end, including the ETL processes to make sure that the changes have no negative impact on all the other areas of the data warehouse. Once the technical test is completed, the updated application needs to be tested and verified by the business users before it is implemented in production.

A request to change the application does not necessarily require a schema change. The data may already be in the data warehouse but not be delivered to the application, such as adding a column in a report to display an existing dimension attribute.

Summary

In this chapter, I discussed data warehouse administration, including monitoring the ETL, administering databases, managing security, bringing new data, and updating applications. This is the end of the book. I hope this book has served its purpose—to provide you with a practical explanation of the essential topics in data warehousing that you need to understand in order to build your first data warehouse.

Throughout this book, I used Amadeus Entertainment as the case study. I discussed the architecture and methodology, gathered the requirements, designed the data model, created the physical databases, built the ETL, and developed the reports, cubes, and mining models for that project. I hope it has been a useful experience for you as your first project. Now it's time to go out there and implement all these concepts in real projects. I wish you great success in your data warehousing journey.

■■■

Normalization Rules

Normalization is the process of removing data redundancy by implementing normalization rules. There are five degrees of normal forms, from the first normal form through the fifth normal form, as described in this appendix.

First Normal Form

The following are the characteristics of first normal form (1NF):

- There must not be any repeating columns or groups of columns. An example of a repeating column is a customer table with Phone Number 1 and Phone Number 2 columns. Using "table (column, column)" notation, an example of a repeating group of columns is Order Table (Order ID, Order Date, Product ID, Price, Quantity, Product ID, Price, Quantity). Product ID, Price, and Quantity are the repeating group of columns.

- Each table must have a primary key (PK) that uniquely identifies each row. The PK can be a composite, that is, can consist of several columns, for example, Order Table (<u>Order ID</u>, Order Date, Customer ID, <u>Product ID</u>, Product Name, Price, Quantity). In this notation, the underlined columns are the PKs; in this case, Order ID and Product ID are a composite PK.

Second Normal Form

The following are the characteristics of second normal form (2NF):

- It must be in 1NF.

- When each value in column 1 is associated with a value in column 2, we say that column 2 is dependant on column 1, for example, Customer (Customer ID, Customer Name). Customer Name is dependant on Customer ID, noted as Customer ID ➤ Customer Name.

- In 2NF, all non-PK columns must be dependent on the entire PK, not just on part of it, for example, Order Table (<u>Order ID</u>, Order Date, <u>Product ID</u>, Price, Quantity). The underlined columns are a composite PK. Order Date is dependent on Order ID but not on Product ID. This violates 2NF.

- To make it 2NF, we need to break it into two tables: Order Header (<u>Order ID</u>, Order Date) and Order Item (<u>Order ID</u>, <u>Product ID</u>, Price, Quantity). Now all non-PK columns are dependent on the entire PK. In the Order Header table, Order Date is dependent on Order ID. In the Order Item table, Price and Quantity are dependent on Order ID and Product ID. Order ID in the Order Item table is a foreign key.

Third Normal Form

The following are the characteristics of third normal form (3NF):

- It must be in 2NF.

- If column 1 is dependent on column 2 and column 2 is dependent on column 3, we say that column 3 is transitively dependent on column 1. In 3NF, no column is transitively dependent on the PK, for example, Product (<u>Product ID</u>, Product Name, Category ID, Category Name). Category Name is dependant on Category ID, and Category ID is dependant on Product ID. Category Name is transitively dependent on the PK (Product ID). This violates 3NF.

- To make it 3NF, we need to break it into two tables: Product (Product ID, Product Name, Category ID) and Category (<u>Category ID</u>, Category Name). Now no column is transitively dependent on the PK. Category ID in the Product table is a foreign key.

Boyce-Codd Normal Form

Boyce-Codd Normal Form (BCNF) is between 3NF and 4NF. The following are the characteristics of BCNF:

- It must be in 3NF.

- In Customer ID ➤ Customer Name, we say that Customer ID is a determinant. In BCNF, every determinant must be a candidate PK. A candidate PK means capable of being a PK; that is, it uniquely identifies each row.

- BCNF is applicable to situations where you have two or more candidate composite PKs, such as with a cable TV service engineer visiting customers: Visit (<u>Date</u>, <u>Route ID</u>, Shift ID, <u>Customer ID</u>, Engineer ID, Vehicle ID). A visit to a customer can be identified using Date, Route ID, and Customer ID as the composite PK. Alternatively, the PK can be Shift ID and Customer ID. Shift ID is the determinant of Date and Route ID.

Higher Normal Forms

The following are the characteristics of other normal forms:

- A table is in fourth normal form (4NF) when it is in BCNF and there are no multivalued dependencies.

- A table is in fifth normal form (5NF) when it is in 4NF and there are no cyclic dependencies.

It is a good practice to apply 4NF or 5NF when it is applicable.

Note A sixth normal form (6NF) has been suggested, but it's not widely accepted or implemented yet.

Index

You Need the Companion eBook

Your purchase of this book entitles you to buy the companion PDF-version eBook for only $10. Take the weightless companion with you anywhere.

We believe this Apress title will prove so indispensable that you'll want to carry it with you everywhere, which is why we are offering the companion eBook (in PDF format) for $10 to customers who purchase this book now. Convenient and fully searchable, the PDF version of any content-rich, page-heavy Apress book makes a valuable addition to your programming library. You can easily find and copy code—or perform examples by quickly toggling between instructions and the application. Even simultaneously tackling a donut, diet soda, and complex code becomes simplified with hands-free eBooks!

Once you purchase your book, getting the $10 companion eBook is simple:

❶ Visit **www.apress.com/promo/tendollars/**.

❷ Complete a basic registration form to receive a randomly generated question about this title.

❸ Answer the question correctly in 60 seconds, and you will receive a promotional code to redeem for the $10.00 eBook.

Apress®
THE EXPERT'S VOICE™

eBookshop

2855 TELEGRAPH AVENUE | SUITE 600 | BERKELEY, CA 94705

Offer valid through 6/08.